Nana Göbel

The History of
Waldorf Education
Worldwide

Nana Göbel

The History of
Waldorf Education
Worldwide

1919 to 2019

1

The growth and development of
Waldorf education from the end of
World War I to the end of World War II

Waldorf Publications

Printed with support from the Waldorf Curriculum Fund

Published by:
Waldorf Publications at the
Research Institute for Waldorf Education
351 Fairview Avenue, Suite 625
Hudson, NY 12534

Title: *The History of Waldorf Education Worldwide*
Author: Nana Göbel
Translator: Jan Kees Saltet
Editor: Patrice Maynard
Proofreader: Judith Soleil
Layout: Ann Erwin
Cover photograph: Third grade of the Goethe School, Hamburg-Wandsbek, 1934
        Archive Helga Beeck

Contents

How Waldorf Education Came into Being:
Its Growth and Development until the End of World War II

Waldorf Education
1919 to 1945: School Portraits

Appendix

Foreword

IT IS HARD TO IMAGINE how, just after World War I, it was possible to found Waldorf education. Germany had lost the war; the country was going through a revolution and was more or less in a state of anarchy. These were the circumstances under which Rudolf Steiner and a circle of friends and coworkers were attempting to bring about a threefold social order, a movement aiming to rebuild the ailing countries of central Europe and make them flourish anew. This endeavor included the founding of a new educational system to reform not only K–12 schooling, but higher education as well. The new education was to be separate from the political sphere; it was to be steered, not by the government, but solely by what teachers and parents actually wanted for their children. Within that framework, the idea was that the government was there only to facilitate the process and set parameters, not to dictate the curriculum.

Rudolf Steiner saw early on that the movement to bring about a threefold social order would be short-lived, and indeed it was soon overwhelmed by the forces, both left- and right-wing, that wanted to cling to the old order. But the educational part of the movement survived. The result was a completely new educational model, which was put into practice by Emil Molt, an industrialist who wanted to found a school for the children of the workers in his factory. Emil Molt was driven by a strong social conscience; he saw the workers and their families as an extended family. He organized advanced courses in general education, held during the working day(!), and he was open to new ideas. His workers asked him if the children could not have the kind of education they were receiving. In order to bring this about, he turned to Rudolf Steiner and asked him if he could develop a completely new pedagogical system. Rudolf Steiner consented, and thus the first Waldorf school came into being in Central Europe during this time of great social and economic upheaval.

In this translation of the first volume of Nana Göbel's work, we can see how endlessly fruitful Rudolf Steiner's ideas were, as she chronicles how they were put into practice and what it took to do so. Nana Göbel is the CEO of the organization, *Freunde der Erziehungskunst* [Friends of the Art of Education], which has offices in Berlin and

Rudolf Steiner on May 6, 1908,
on his first visit to Oslo; with
Marta Steinsvik and her daughter, Kari.
Behind right, Marie Steiner von Sivers

Karlsruhe. In Waldorf circles it is common knowledge that no one is more familiar with the Waldorf movement worldwide. In her introduction, she modestly states that this is due to her work, but the reverse is true: It is due to her enormous effort, organizational talent, and tremendous memory that the Freunde, as the organization is commonly known, is what it is today. She has been instrumental in making it into an organization which helps to establish Waldorf schools throughout the world, build up kindergartens, and support institutions for special education.

Oddly enough, there was neither a comprehensive description of the first Waldorf School in Stuttgart, Germany until now, nor a chronicle of the development of the international Waldorf movement. Looking ahead to the centennial celebrations, Tomas Zdražil, professor at the Hochschule in Stuttgart, wrote a standard book about the first school. Nana Göbel has done the same for the worldwide movement. Reading through this book, we witness a phenomenal development, unparalleled in history. Ten years after the first school was established in Stuttgart in 1919, Waldorf schools had been started in Switzerland, the Netherlands, England, Norway, Hungary, and the United States of America, where the first school was founded in New York City in 1928. At present there are about 1200 schools in 60 countries. What brought this about?

The answer to this question lies in this book and its subsequent volumes. It is not for nothing that the German title of the book is *The Waldorf School and Its People*, for it is they who embody the program. It is a book about people.

Reading through the many facts and events, one thing stands out. The book contains hundreds of names and biographical sketches of people who not only wanted this education, but actually took the steps to make it a reality. The book preserves hundreds of biographies which are thus saved from oblivion and made available now to those who make this new education their business in the 21st century. As one reads, one gradually becomes aware of an enormous global network of people, all of them inspired by the groundbreaking insights Rudolf Steiner gave the early teachers and supporters of this education. These insights reveal what a child truly is and give unprecedented glimpses into human development. Apart from reading how these many individuals were inspired to devote themselves to Waldorf education, we see how they then linked up with others, often miraculously.

It is breathtaking for the reader to see how this art of education unfolds, thanks to people who recognize its potential. Thus, we can become aware that we are not dealing with an electronic World Wide Web here, but a network of people who are united in their experience of a true recognition of the insights Rudolf Steiner gave, and who subsequently develop an inexhaustible energy to put them into practice. We witness a worldwide web of intentions and convictions of what education has to be in our time.

In her preface, the author anticipates that the book will come across as a reference work. I can assure you, however, that the book reads like a novel. It is indeed a breathtaking saga, and never becomes dull. At no point does one have the feeling of, "Oh, here's yet another school," because the narrative is couched in biographical events, which make for gripping reading. What is more, the book allows us to become aware of the tireless efforts and unconditional dedication of these pioneers, which we can take to heart.

Above all, we must thank Nana Göbel for her enormous service to the Waldorf school movement, because this book allows us to "re-possess" our history, to use the words of Oliver Sacks, who reminds us that there is no identity without memory. And this is very valuable because, in the second hundred years of Waldorf education, much will depend on our identity within a changing world. To "re-collect" it, knowledge of our roots is indispensable. This book has done a great service in preserving that memory—a major accomplishment.

> – Christof Wiechert
> Former leader of the Pedagogical Section
> at the Goetheanum in Dornach, Switzerland

Preface

HAVING WORKED IN A supporting role of the worldwide Waldorf movement for over 40 years, I felt strongly that a history needed to be written to pay tribute to the many thousands of teachers, students, and parents who have been instrumental in creating the world's largest independent school movement. Packed as it is with collected data and research, the resulting text is by no means easy to read. It has turned out to be more of a reference work.

Of course I was only able to record stories known to me. It goes without saying that a complete account of the development of the Waldorf school movement would contain many more facets, since it has been shaped by many more people than I have been able to include. For that reason I'm asking forbearance on the part of those whose perspective I have been unable to represent or was unaware of. All those whose names are not mentioned, and they are many, are no less in my estimation than the ones I have named in the text. I would ask those not mentioned by name to please feel included, and in any case to feel my gratitude in our common striving to anchor a pedagogy in this world which recognizes truly human education. And to those who feel not rightly understood in their approach, I offer my apologies beforehand.

My work within the framework of the *Freunde der Erziehungskunst* [Friends of Waldorf Education] has formed the best preparation for this undertaking. Since 1973/74 I have been consciously a part of the Waldorf movement: in the beginning as a Waldorf student, then next to my University studies as a founder, and since 1978 as a board member, later also as managing director. I want to express my profound gratitude to the many teachers—in kindergarten, grade school, and high school—who have shared their schools' stories over the course of the last 40 years, always with incredible openness and through which I have received sometimes enthusiastic, sometimes sobering insights into the situations of their institutions.

AMONG MY GREAT TEACHERS were my father, Thomas Göbel; my high school mentor, Wolfgang Schad; the doyen of the German school movement, Ernst Weissert; and of course Jörgen Smit, the Pedagogical Section leader with whom I was privileged to work in the Youth Section for many years. I am profoundly grateful to these four men, who taught me not only to observe and understand the world, but also supported me in my intentions and impulses to take an active role in this world, full of miracles and unpredictable perspectives as it is.

I WISH YOU much joy in discovering the history of the Waldorf school movement.

– Nana Göbel

How Waldorf Education
Came into Being:
Its Growth and Development
until the End of World War II

The Years 1919 to 1925

THE END OF WORLD WAR I marked the end of the Empire of the Habsburgs, the dominance of the Prussians, and the rule of the German aristocracy. At the same time, it marked the end of a spiritual culture in central Europe exemplified by Johann Wolfgang Goethe, Friedrich Schiller, and Friedrich Wilhelm Hegel. The Industrial Age was no longer confined to the area around the River Ruhr in Germany and the Midlands in England but had spread to the whole of Europe. This development had gone hand in hand with the influence of machine power, especially as warfare had become more and more mechanized in the course of World War I. A new era had begun. Even though people at the time were not yet fully able to grasp consciously how fundamentally different this era was, people did feel they were facing a foreign and hostile world. The war had demanded a high toll, shedding the blood of thousands of young people who had entered the war singing, marching off with an inexplicable enthusiasm that proved to be short lived. The traditional 18th- and 19th-century Christian values, which had marked not only the German-speaking areas, began to dissolve. In this respect the First World War really does mark the beginning of a new era. There was a widespread feeling of rootlessness, and people slowly picked up the threads without a clear sense of how to carry on and give shape and meaning to their lives.

For some the new era heralded the start of years of euphoria, leading to the glorious 20s, and for others the revolutions leading to the various socialist experiments of the ensuing 70 years. With the loss of 19th-century values after the war, people were waiting in vain, however, for a new approach to education. Nobody questioned the Protestant Prussian traditions of the German state schools, and they stayed the way they had always been. Those who created the Weimar Republic did not have a modern vision that might have questioned the role the state played in determining the content and structure of education. Education based on freedom and self-determination on the part of those responsible is, sad to say, still a remote ideal today, and it actually seems even more remote than it was in 1919. In writing the constitution of the new Weimar Republic, people were primarily concerned about clarifying the relationship between school and various religious denominations. The SPD [Social Democratic Party], wanted to bring about a permanent separation of state and church in the creation of a national *Einheitsschule*, or *Gesamtschule* [a single secondary school system,

The Swabian entrepreneurs Berta and Emil Molt,
whose impulse gave birth to the first Waldorf School

or comprehensive school]. The centrist political parties could not seriously entertain such a concept. They were much more concerned about pushing for schools that were tied to the various religious denominations. A compromise was found, however, that strengthened the involvement of the parents. These were the circumstances which formed the legal and social conditions for educational institutions in Germany back in 1919.

The Swabian entrepreneur Emil Molt was keenly aware of the continuing social injustice after the war and was in close conversation with the workers in his factory as they came back from the war. Thus, he conceived the idea of founding a school. The social norms of the prewar years were bankrupt and, especially among the workers of the large factories, there was an atmosphere of openness for ideas about a new and more just society. It was against this background that Rudolf Steiner spoke in the halls of large factories around Stuttgart about possibilities for a new structuring of society in a way that would do justice to the human being. He spoke about a new order to meet political, economic, and cultural questions. Rudolf Steiner was invited again and again in the months after the war, in 1918/19, to speak to the workers of firms like Bosch and Daimler and to win followers for the new movement of social threefolding. This so-called *Dreigliederungsbewegung* was set in motion by a number of enthusiastic people but was not successful in the long run. Emil Molt was also involved with this movement, especially in its manifestation in Stuttgart, and put a lot of work into trying to implement it. Like many of his fellow entrepreneurs, Emil Molt had also been taking part in the activities of the Anthroposophical Society for a number of years and felt connected by destiny with this movement, as did his wife, Bertha Molt. Thus, it came about that Emil Molt spoke to Rudolf Steiner after a lecture to the workers of the Waldorf Astoria cigarette factory and a meeting of the factory's collaborative leadership council and told him about his impulse to found a new school for the children of the workers of his factory. It was obvious to him that he had to turn to Rudolf Steiner and ask him to design an anthroposophical pedagogy, but of course he did not know whether Steiner would respond in the affirmative to his request. Without hesitating, Rudolf Steiner said yes and pledged his willingness to work together with him. In 1921, in Oslo, Rudolf Steiner looked back on what he called the most important social question which arose at that time. He said: "When the catastrophes of the war ceased for the time being, there was a widespread longing in several parts of Central Europe that gave rise to the Free Waldorf School."[1]

As always when these two, Emil Molt and Rudolf Steiner, really wanted to do something, things moved quickly. As early as April 1919, two teachers were working with them on sketching out the first ideas together. They were E. A. Karl Stockmeyer, a teacher from Baden, and the language specialist Herbert Hahn from the Baltic region. E. A. Karl Stockmeyer was assigned the task of working out the initial school concept in order for it to be presented to the authorities. Already in May their plans were positively received by the ministry of culture of Württemberg. Right at this early stage they were promised approval by the authorities. One thing of decisive importance for Rudolf Steiner was the fact that the minister in charge of schools in Württemberg, Berthold Heymann, barely a year in office, did not stipulate that the future teachers would need to have passed the local teacher certifications. He only required they had to show their CVs and academic credentials. Without Berthold Heymann's generous understanding, the Waldorf School would not have come into being. For that reason, he definitely counts among the most important people who paved the way for this new pedagogy.

Early in June 1919, Emil Molt bought a beautiful property located on the Uhlandshöhe, a destination often chosen by Stuttgarters to go for a walk on Sundays and drink coffee in the restaurant on the Kanonenweg. He was able to purchase the building using the profits from the sale of cigarettes in the years 1917–1918. E. A. Karl Stockmeyer was sent out on a journey through the whole of Germany to find teachers. The Waldorf Astoria company took on the legal and economic responsibilities for the founding school and gave it its name. Thus, the outer perimeters were successfully laid for the new school, a school that was to serve the development of underprivileged children and promised to be a community school.

1 Rudolf Steiner: *Waldorf Education and Anthroposophy*. CW 304, 1997, p. 134.

The inner pedagogical preparation of the Waldorf School came about through a course given by Rudolf Steiner for an anthroposophical study of the human being, through which the teachers were given a tool to understand the development of children and adolescents. This course, which lasted 14 days, began the evening of August 20, 1919, with an introduction about the intention of the spirit of the pedagogical movement. What Steiner said that first evening was not written down and has come to us only through later recollections written by a few of the colleagues who were there. Rudolf Steiner brought the Waldorf impulse in connection with those beings of the spiritual world to which the teachers could turn in future—for their individual preparation of the lessons, for their collaboration with colleagues, and for their contribution to world development in general. This was the large, overarching vision Rudolf Steiner had as he depicted the meaning of the founding of this school that evening. He was certain that every individual teacher was able to plant the seed for future developments both individually and in collaboration with the colleagues in the community of teachers, when—and this he saw as an absolute prerequisite—the connection to the beings of the spiritual world was consciously sought.

The intentions for the new art of education were explained by Rudolf Steiner from August 21–September 5, 1919, in three sessions each day. In the morning he held a lecture about the human foundations of the education. These lectures were published under the name *Allgemeine Menschenkunde* [The Foundations of Human Experience].[2] During the second part of the morning, this first lecture was followed, after a short break, by a cycle of lectures about methodology and didactics.[3] In the afternoon, Rudolf Steiner gave practical exercises and answered questions for all those who had been asked to serve as future Waldorf teachers and had received an invitation to participate in this course.[4] Right from the start, anthroposophy and Waldorf pedagogy were closely linked with regard to the preparation and inner attitude of the teacher. These three lecture cycles by Rudolf Steiner still form the essential foundation of Waldorf pedagogy today. What Steiner describes in these lectures about the way human beings grow and develop and the implications for schooling children and adolescents was augmented by many further lectures and courses given by Rudolf Steiner and countless studies since then by Waldorf teachers. In this respect Waldorf pedagogy is in an ongoing process of development.

On September 7, 1919, the opening celebration for the new Waldorf School took place, and the actual teaching of the 256 students started on September 16. Having taken part in the opening courses given by Rudolf Steiner by no means gave the teachers the pedagogical and social competence needed to accomplish this task. As a result, the new pedagogy was shaped and developed as it was being put into practice. Rudolf Steiner helped in this process as much as he could until the year 1925. Whenever he was in Stuttgart, he took part in the teachers meetings, which sometimes went deep into the night, and was indefatigable in answering questions, ranging from general to concrete. In every meeting

2 Rudolf Steiner: *The Foundations of Human Experience*. CW 293.
3 Rudolf Steiner: *Practical Advice to Teachers*. CW 294.
4 Rudolf Steiner: *Discussions with Teachers*. CW 295.

Emil Molt bought the restaurant *Uhlandshöhe* at Kanonenweg in Stuttgart, remodeled it for the Waldorf School, and in September 1919 the lessons began.

with him the viewpoints for the practice of the pedagogy were expanded, often starting with examples of individual children. After Rudolf Steiner's death in 1925, the next steps of development had to be accomplished by the teachers out of their own capacities.

Right from the start, two impulses came together in the founding of the Waldorf schools, a pedagogical and a social impulse. On the one hand, the foundations for an education toward freedom had to be developed, on the other hand, the school had to truly serve the community. The school was open for children of all social and economic backgrounds. Children from the most diverse families and strata of society were to have the chance to learn together, grow up together, and build up a friendly understanding amongst themselves. In this endeavor, an important contribution was to be made in building up a society not split into different segments but held together by the glue that is formed when mutual understanding is built through sharing experiences and doing things together. This was not always easy because the Waldorf School in Stuttgart did not receive any public funds from the time of its founding until it was closed in 1938 and, instead, depended mostly on the private capital of Emil Molt and the Waldorf Astoria Company. It depended further on the contributions from many individuals and groups, both local and further afield, who supported the *Verein für ein Freies Schulwesen* [Association for Independent Schools] and only to a small extent on direct tuition and contributions from well-to-do parents. This was also the case during the Depression.

It has been postulated again and again that Waldorf pedagogy was part of the *Reformpädagogik*, a movement for educational reform in Germany, because it clearly shares a number of ideas with that movement. Thus, Waldorf pedagogy is often seen as one of the many attempts at school reform at the beginning of the 20th century.[5] A call for child-centered education was on everybody's lips at that time. In the form that Ellen Key chose, it even became a motto for the 20th century. Those who want to deny Waldorf education its originality use the argument that there were teachers there who taught first at other schools of the *Reformpädagogik*.[5] But those were not the founding teachers at all—a point often overlooked. It is true that Rudolf Steiner's orientation stemmed from the Austrian elementary school model, but that is a stale point somehow. There was little or no contact on Rudolf Steiner's part with the educational reform movements of his time. E. A. Karl Stockmeyer had his experiences in teaching in Baden in the background when he wrote down the initial ideas about the curriculum. It is often the case in history that certain ideas crop up in different places at the same time. The beginning of the 20th century bubbles over with new ideas, and they arise in the realm of pedagogy as well. And it goes without saying that Waldorf pedagogy is part of a larger movement toward renewal of education in this time and that it shares some basic ideas with the various attempts at school reform. But the most important, and at the same time most controversial basis is unique to Waldorf, namely that it is rooted in the anthroposophical view of the human being. And there is no doubt that the initiators of the first Waldorf School shared a longing for a fundamental renewal of education and wanted to do their bit to grow beyond common school practices such as rote learning and iron discipline.

Of equal importance to the direct pedagogical practice in the school for which Rudolf Steiner prepared the future teachers was the propagation of the larger aim of freedom in education for society in general. This did not result in dogmatically insisting on this principle because Rudolf Steiner was willing to make compromises when needed, which was actually quite unlike him. Such compromises had to be made for the Waldorf school on the Uhlandshöhe in Stuttgart both with regard to the school entrance age and the duration of the years of elementary schooling. Rudolf Steiner was fully conscious of the fact that the school movement would have to grow considerably in size in order to unfold the needed larger effect within society as a whole and to realize the aim of more freedom in education. For that reason, it was Rudolf Steiner's intention right from the beginning to found, not just one school, but hundreds of schools. Then as now, the point was that free human beings can only be educated in free schools.

---

5 Ehrenhard Skiera: Reformpädagogik und Schule in Europa. In: Theodor F. Klassen, Ehrenhard Skiera, Bernd Wächter (eds.): *Handbuch der reformpädagogischen und alternativen Schulen in Europa.* 1990, p. 15; Wilfried Gabriel, Peter Schneider: Die Waldorfschule und ihr internationales Umfeld. In: Hermann Röhrs, Volker Lenhart (eds.): *Reformpädagogik auf den Kontinenten.* 1994, p. 241ff.; Heiner Ullrich: Rudolf Steiner. In: Juan Carlos Tedesco (ed.): *Thinkers on Education,* Vol. 4, UNESCO 1997, p. 562f; see also Lothar Steinmann: Reformpädagogik und Waldorfschule. EK 10, 2001, p. 1115.

Rudolf Steiner in a photograph
from Otto Rietmann, 1917

For Rudolf Steiner, the word *free* in this context meant freedom from state intervention in education to begin with. In a positive sense, "free" meant that the innovative strength of each teacher to shape the lessons out of both psychological considerations and insights of what the subject demanded had to be safeguarded. *Free* also meant teachers being free and independent in basing their teaching on the particular students they had in front of them. For the individual teachers that meant the freedom to work without a prescribed and limiting curriculum as well. Freedom in education and the reduction of governmental oversight, for example to standards of hygiene or protective measures to prevent fire, were part of the concepts of the movement for social threefolding. Rudolf Steiner wanted to bring about a true change in society and open up real developmental opportunities for people by means of a completely different school structure. Freedom did not mean license for him, but rather a high degree of inner moral responsibility, something that can be seen in the way he described in his book, *The Philosophy of Freedom,* the inner path of development we need to tread in order to achieve freedom. In this respect, the ideal to found a school in which human dignity is valued was at the heart of the Waldorf school movement right from its inception.

During the 14 years after the founding of the first Waldorf School, there was relative freedom to build up the new school. Then the dark clouds of nationalism gathered, which pulled Germany down into a morass of abject barbarity such as the history of mankind had not seen before. In these first 14 years, enthusiasm for Rudolf Steiner's pedagogical impulse and anthroposophy grew in spite of the economic situation, which was downright catastrophic. Within this relatively short time, educators and parents embraced the ideas of the Waldorf school and founded

Ernst August Karl Stockmeyer,
the organizer of the First
Waldorf School

their own schools in many towns. The movement was not confined to Germany, but the idea caught fire in Holland, Switzerland, and England. During Steiner's lifetime six more Waldorf schools were founded. They were either started from scratch or existing schools were changed over, and this in spite of hyperinflation, devaluation of money, and general uncertainty in the whole of Germany. Rudolf Steiner was directly involved in founding a number of schools, chose the teachers in many cases, was in the know about other schools that were started, and also reacted skeptically in some cases. He sent colleagues to the schools and appointed founding teachers. He asked the experienced educator Max Kändler if he could build up the independent Goethe School in Hamburg-Wandsbek in 1922. This school was the third one founded in Germany; internationally it was the fourth.

For a long time, the story was spread in Waldorf circles that Rudolf Steiner had been opposed to starting the school in Cologne. This seems unlikely, because Rudolf Steiner suggested the founders of the school call it Neuwachtschule, and he also asked Konrad Müller-Fürer to go to Cologne as the founding teacher. It is certain, however, that E. A. Karl Stockmeyer was against the founding of this school. Be that as it may, the school belongs to the few attempts that failed. It was closed in 1925 after four years by order of the government of the Rhine province, and is therefore often not counted among the early pioneer schools.

The second Waldorf school, the Friedwart School, sprang up in Dornach, Switzerland, and grew out of the needs of the highly international group of parents who had settled in the vicinity of the Goetheanum, the center of the General Anthroposophical Society. Rudolf Steiner asked Marie Groddeck to be the founding teacher of this school and also suggested two other teachers for the founding of the Friedwart School. He even recruited the mathematician Ernst Blümel from his mathematical institute at the University of Vienna. Rudolf Steiner accompanied this school even more closely than the Waldorf School in Stuttgart, because it was housed in a former construction shed directly adjoining his own workshop. Whenever Rudolf Steiner was in Dornach, he visited the school, mostly before lunch, spoke with students, and gave various suggestions to the teachers. Much less is known about these suggestions than about those he gave in the Stuttgart Waldorf School, because nobody kept a running shorthand record, as did Karl Schubert in Stuttgart.

Rudolf Steiner accompanied every founding and tried to help, even when he had not been included right from the start. An example of this type of founding occurred in Essen, founded the same year as the school in Hamburg. At first Rudolf Steiner scolded Irene Burghardt and Margarethe Blass for not contacting him or the colleagues in Stuttgart beforehand. In spite of that he helped them later on when they were wringing their hands and turned to him because they had not been able to find appropriate teachers. Thereupon Rudolf Steiner sent René Maikowski to Essen and asked him to start teaching right away.

Likewise, Rudolf Steiner was directly involved in the founding of the school in The Hague in 1923, the seventh founding internationally, affirming one teacher, rigorously rejecting others. With warm interest he also accompanied the building up of Waldorf pedagogy in England, where he held essential pedagogical lectures in the years 1923 and 1924. He sent Violetta Plincke to England as well as Juliet Compton-Burnett, whom he had known in Dornach as a eurythmy student.

Rudolf Steiner visited the Stuttgart Waldorf School very regularly, and he also visited Cologne, Kings Langley, and The Hague. The schools in Hamburg-Wandsbek and Essen he did not visit. During his lifetime, seven schools came into being. After Stuttgart in 1919 came the Friedwart School in Dornach and the Neuwachtschule in Cologne, both in 1921, followed by the Goethe School in Hamburg-Wandsbek in 1922 and the Rudolf Steiner School Essen that same year. In 1922 the teachers of the Priory School in Kings Langley, England, began to work out of the principles of Waldorf education and transform their school into a Waldorf school, even though the British Waldorf movement did not appear to give wholehearted approval to these fledgling attempts for decades. The seventh of the schools founded during Steiner's lifetime, the Vrije School, came into being in The Hague, Holland, in 1923.

Thus, the Waldorf movement began in four countries: Germany, Switzerland, England, and Holland. All the schools had different names, from Friedwart School, Neuwartschule, and Goethe School to Vrije School, the last one of which was suggested by Rudolf Steiner for the school in The Hague. That way one did not build a unified chain of schools of course, with a patented name, but a differentiated, free school movement that took different forms in different places. What bound them together in a real way was not meant to be achieved through an outer stamp, but instead Rudolf Steiner wanted teachers to be in frequent contact with one another, exchanging ideas

E. A. Karl Stockmeyer (left) and Herbert Hahn (right) in front of the Waldorf School, 1922

and holding together in that way. What he deemed most important was that teachers would find their inspiration in the same spiritual sources. As long as he was alive, he was the arbiter. Conflicts, of which there were many, were discussed with him and it was his task to resolve them. His resolutions were accepted without question.

In meetings and discussions with the teachers, Rudolf Steiner always referred to his lectures about the nature of the human being, which he had given in August and September of 1919. It was expected that all teachers would read and study these lectures as a basis for their work. This, however, was not so easy, because only hand-typed versions or mimeographed copies were available, which Rudolf Steiner himself had not reviewed or proofread. These copies were in the possession of a few teachers and were guarded carefully and not passed on to just anybody. Every time someone became interested and wanted to read the lectures, Rudolf Steiner was asked and had to decide if the copies were to be made available. This way of working was somewhat restrictive and also promoted a kind of attitude. At a time when a certain small-mindedness reigned in the Anthroposophical Society around him as well, Rudolf Steiner himself acted generously. I'm not aware of any case in which he blocked passing these copies on to others. He regularly gave the teachers courage when they were in despair about poor discipline or poor results. Mostly, his encouragement was not something general in the vein of "They will learn by and by," but he specified: "They will lear when the right enthusiasm is there."

In social and economic questions, people also followed his advice in the early years of the Stuttgart Waldorf School, even though his competence in this realm was certainly not as advanced as in other areas. He counted on specific people. One such pillar was E. A. Karl Stockmeyer. Not only did Stockmeyer and his wife, Anna, live on school property, he also took care of the administration, led the teachers meetings, and saw to every little detail. He served the Waldorf ideal with all fibers of his being and put his whole life and work into its service without a trace of vanity, without expecting anything in return.

Another pillar was Caroline von Heydebrand, who took Steiner's indications on human development very seriously and internalized them. Diminutive of stature and squeaky of voice, she gained the respect of even the loudmouths among her students. Her attention was focused equally strongly on the larger idea and on the individual cases of her children. Of course, it did not escape her attention that some children were hungry at the beginning of the 1920s, so she always had something in reserve to pass out to the hungry children during the ten o'clock break. School doctor Eugen Kolisko was equally aware of this problem, which affected about a third of the students. Together with two mothers, he organized the school kitchen where these children could get a hot lunch. So, the business of the school was not confined to education proper, but it functioned as an educational institution for the whole human being, and that included taking care of physical health. Ilse Rolofs-Kändler in Hamburg did likewise when she noted the hunger of the children during the first months of school. She always cooked a soup for children to eat before going home after classes ended.

Of Rudolf Steiner's connections with various people involved with the endeavor, the most enigmatic was his relationship with Emil Leinhas. The latter's involvement was through his activities within the movement for Threefold Social Order and the corporation *Der Kommende Tag* [The New Day], which brought him in connection with the Waldorf School. Rudolf Steiner backed even the most abstruse decisions Emil Leinhas made. These included decisions that directly harmed Emil Molt and the Waldorf Astoria Company.[6] In spite of such disappointments, Emil Molt and his wife, Berta, faithfully continued supporting the Waldorf idea throughout. Despite setbacks, he firmly piloted the Waldorf School through all the dangerous waters of the ensuing years, an inner attitude that demands our respect all the more. Emil Molt was one of the most noble among the founders of the Waldorf School in Stuttgart.

In the other Waldorf schools, Rudolf Steiner did not get involved in the social and economic affairs but entrusted them to E. A. Karl Stockmeyer. The fact that he left it to him to take care of those affairs indicates that he saw the school in Stuttgart as a leader, providing a model for the others. This function can also be seen in the fact that Stuttgart teachers were charged with counseling and mentoring new school initiatives.

6 Further details of the relationship between the Waldorf School on the Uhlandshöhe and the Waldorf Astoria Company and to The Coming Day, Inc., as well as to the decisions of Emil Leinhas, can be found in the school portrait of the Waldorf School Stuttgart Uhlandshöhe.

Either E. A. Karl Stockmeyer or Herbert Hahn regularly corresponded with teachers of the other schools. Walter Johannes Stein, Hermann von Baravalle, and Caroline von Heydebrand lectured in many cities as well as at conferences organized together with Rudolf Steiner in Germany, Holland, and England. The special role the Stuttgart Waldorf School played was affirmed through a letter written on March 17, 1925, by Günther Wachsmuth at the behest of Rudolf Steiner, in which the Stuttgart teachers were asked to take on the leadership of all schools in Germany working out of the anthroposophical pedagogical impulse. It should be noted that Günther Wachsmuth only wrote about the German schools, not about schools in Switzerland, England, and Holland. This pedagogical leadership role applied to two areas: the application of anthroposophical pedagogy and the checking of the economic underpinnings.

The Years 1925 to 1933

AFTER RUDOLF STEINER's death on March 30, 1925, those who were responsible for the Waldorf schools had to regroup to begin again. Difficulties arose not so much in continuing the running of the schools, which proceeded with totally normal challenges. What presented difficulties were the different opinions, contrary assumptions, and potential conflicts that now rose to the surface, which had always been limited through Rudolf Steiner's mediation and kept in check through the self-control of the various individuals involved. With the pivotal person gone, his peacemaking and impulse of spiritual renewal were missing.

Within the General Anthroposophical Society, deep divisions arose likewise. The leadership of the society had been given over to the colleagues on its leadership council, although they were in no position to take over the leadership in collaboration. Deep rifts appeared in the days right after Rudolf Steiner's death. This inability largely rendered the anthroposophical efforts ineffective, which extended to their inability to adequately assess the nationalism arising from the abyss of the racial delusions of the National Socialists and to take a position against it with commensurate sharpness. Even though E. A. Karl Stockmeyer and some of his colleagues made attempts to keep the Stuttgart school neutral within these conflicts, he did not succeed, at least not to a sufficient enough degree. The various attitudes and loyalties of teachers toward individual members of the Leadership Council of the General Anthroposophical Society stayed in check for a few years, until now they surfaced to a degree that led to incisive decisions. In 1932 Hermann von Baravalle left the Stuttgart school and went to England. From there he began his lecture tours in the United States. During the Second World War, he became one of the strongest pioneers of many Waldorf schools founded in the US. Caroline von Heydebrand also left the Stuttgart school, for the above-mentioned reasons. But this was still to come.

Teaching continued in the schools founded thus far, with the exception of Cologne, due to the missing state license mentioned earlier. The pedagogical situation

The Stuttgart Waldorf School community in 1927

remained problematic at the Priory School in Kings Langley, due to low enrollment and colleagues leaving the school because they could not put up with the social situation and the coldness of winter in unheated classrooms.

By contrast, the New School in London saw a bundling of forces that attracted highly interesting and engaged teachers. The strong role which the school played in spreading Waldorf pedagogy in the English-speaking world was already thus founded in this early phase. Conferences were organized, often in collaboration with Stuttgart, and practicums by teachers from as far away as New Zealand were facilitated. The Hamburg school was built up further under the solid leadership of Max Kändler and, located so far in the north, remained unaffected by larger problems. Thanks to the ever-generous financial support offered by the building contractor couple Emilie and Hans Pohlmann, the Goethe School in Hamburg could occupy its own building in 1925, which included a large hall. The school grew and colleagues had to be found. This was no easy task, and still is not. The collaborative leadership model became too much for a group of newly appointed teachers of the Goethe School in Hamburg in the closing years of the 1920s. The stalwart strictness of the members of the founding association did not give newer members enough space and they complained about not

Ein Bild aus dem Handarbeitsunterricht in einer mittleren Klasse
und eines aus dem Buchbindeunterricht in einer der Oberklassen

being given enough say in the administration. No solution was found in the resulting tussle inside the College of Teachers. Consultations in Stuttgart led nowhere. As a result, four colleagues and the school doctor left the Goethe School in Hamburg-Wandsbek and founded the Waldorf School in Hamburg-Altona, which became the twenty-first school internationally.

Whereas the Hamburg school managed largely without supervisory visits from Stuttgart, the situation in Essen was very different. As early as March 20, 1925, the

Rudolf Steiner School Essen received a letter from E. A. Karl Stockmeyer, apprising the colleagues of the new situation that had come about following Günther Wachsmuth's letter of March 17, 1925. One could say that E. A. Karl Stockmeyer followed up promptly on the leadership role given to the Stuttgart Waldorf School, but one could also get the impression that this happened so quickly it did not give colleagues time to adapt to Stuttgart's leadership role. Very young new colleagues, such as Heinrich and Wilhelm Wollborn, Ella and Martin Rothe, had just joined the school at this time, followed a few years later by Wolfgang Rudolph as well as Maria Schröfel, all of whom became leading teachers well into the 1970s at the schools in Bochum, Hannover, Berlin, and others. But in the 1920s the school in Essen had no patronage of a well-to-do donor. Teachers had to live with meager salaries and were left to their own devices pedagogically—without any support. Trouble was soon brewing largely due to the leadership claims made by Margarethe Blass, which she based on a private conversation with Rudolf Steiner. When tensions rose, Stuttgart colleagues were apprised of the situation through many letters asking them for counsel and help. Emil Molt, Paul Baumann, and E.A. Karl Stockmeyer drove to Essen in 1930 and discovered a pretty desolate social and financial situation. Their suggestions for change only calmed the waves for a short time but were thwarted in the long run. Attempts made by Erich Gabert, who came for a full month in 1931 from Stuttgart to Essen, failed as they came up against resistance from Margarethe Blass. Further intervention attempts by colleagues from Stuttgart could not stop further escalation of the situation in Essen. At the end of the school year, 13 out of 20 teachers and half the students left the school.

One of the most persistent problems of the Waldorf school movement thus lay in the way the schools were led and in the complicated legacy of Rudolf Steiner's tasking the teachers with the governance of the schools in a republican manner. When the question was asked how to shape the governance of the school in Stuttgart, Rudolf Steiner had suggested a mostly republican model, in the manner of a teachers' republic. The school should not have a vertical leadership structure, in which a director decrees from the top down according to what he or she thinks is right. Rather, decisions should be made horizontally, arising out of a collaborative process of those concerned. Thus, a highly modern form of governance was to be established and carried by a group of people who shared a will to work together in shaping the institution.

However, Rudolf Steiner also voiced the conditions that would make this possible in a fruitful way: Only when there is an ongoing communal search to foster a spiritual bond will it be possible to bring about the necessary harmony or, in the words of Rudolf Steiner, *Einheitliches* [unity]. The harmony created by this ongoing endeavor will enable us to make the necessary decisions. This type of leadership did not pan out everywhere. It caused conflicts in many faculties and led to schisms, especially because not everybody involved was engaged in this endeavor to seek the common ground that unifies us. Notwithstanding all the difficulties facing teachers among each other and in the structural, administrative, economic, and strategic leadership of their schools, most colleagues did manage to put in a huge effort at the same time. They often taught more than 30 teaching hours per week and made do with low salaries. In spite of all, enthusiasm for the pedagogical ideas of the Waldorf schools was unbroken.

A further ongoing challenge of Waldorf schools, more or less from the outset, was the lack of teachers. A sufficient number of teachers were available only for the founding of the first Waldorf School; all subsequent initiatives were on a serious

Prospectus for the
Independent Waldorf
School, Stuttgart,
from August 1926

Die Freie Waldorfschule
ist die erste Pflegestätte der Pädagogik Rudolf Steiners.

Sie ist im Jahre 1919 als eine Stiftung Emil Molts von Dr. Rudolf Steiner begründet worden und wurde bis zu seinem Tode 1925 von ihm geleitet. Sie hat 50 von ihm berufene Lehrkräfte, Lehrer und Lehrerinnen, 28 Klassen und etwa 1000 Schüler (1919/20: 12 Lehrkräfte, 8 Klassen und 250 Schüler).

Die Waldorfschule nimmt *Knaben und Mädchen* vom Beginn der *Volksschulpflicht* an auf (also auch für die Grundschulklassen)* und führt sie bis zur *Hochschulreife* humanistischer und realistischer Richtung.

Der eigentliche *Lehrgang* umfaßt 12 Jahre, in denen nach den pädagogischen Grundsätzen Rudolf Steiners die Erziehung geführt wird; außerdem besteht eine *Vorbereitungsklasse für die Reifeprüfung*, in der diejenigen Absolventen der Waldorfschule, die das wünschen, auf eine außerordentliche Reifeprüfung vorbereitet werden. Ferner ist ein *Kindergarten* angegliedert, in den Kinder vom vollendeten dritten Jahr an aufgenommen werden, sowie eine *Fortbildungsklasse* für solche Knaben und Mädchen, die nach vollendeter Volksschulpflicht einen Beruf ergreifen mußten.

Keine Sonderung nach Begabung, nach Berufswahl oder nach Geschlechtern. *Knaben und Mädchen* sitzen in allen Klassen zusammen. — „Die Erziehung ist eine Arbeit an den Seelen in der Gemeinschaft, und die Seelen werden nicht in Gemeinschaft erzogen, wenn man sie von vornherein in männliche und weibliche trennt." (Rudolf Steiner.)

Die Waldorfschule ist *Tagesschule* und hat *kein Internat*.

*

Pädagogische Grundsätze. Die anthroposophische Geisteswissenschaft Rudolf Steiners weist den Weg zu wirklicher Menschenerkenntnis und lebendigem Kindesverständnis. Dadurch gibt sie dem Lehrer den Schlüssel zur wahren Führerschaft. Anthroposophie wird nicht gelehrt, aber in ihr findet der Lehrer die Grundlagen seiner erzieherischen Maßnahmen.

Der Lehrplan der Waldorfschule ist deshalb nach den leiblich-seelisch-geistigen Entwicklungsstufen des Kindes gegliedert, die sich

* Sie ist als private Volksschule im Sinne des Art. 147,3 R.V. anerkannt.

---

teacher search after the first school year. Inventive, capable, healthy teachers engaged with the anthroposophical worldview were and are always welcome.

In the three years after the death of Rudolf Steiner, 1925–1927, seven more schools were founded in seven countries, and an eighth was attempted. Waldorf pedagogy spread in Europe, as much between East and West as between North and South. The easternmost school at this time was the Waldorf school in Budapest, which was largely German speaking. The fledgling school in Lisbon was the southernmost

zeigen als Zahnwechsel (Beginn der Volksschulzeit) und physiologische Reife (Ende der Volksschulzeit) und in weniger auffälliger Weise um das 9. und das 12. Lebensjahr. Gesunde Erziehung muß ihre Maßnahmen nach diesen wirklichen Lebensabschnitten richten und nicht nach Gesichtspunkten äußerer Zweckmäßigkeit, die nur in der speziellen Fachbildung in Betracht kommen sollten. Deshalb wird z. B. Schreiben und Lesen in der Waldorfschule grundsätzlich nicht so schnell gefördert wie sonst heute. Das soziale Leben verlangt nicht, daß ein Kind mit sieben Jahren lesen und schreiben kann.

Die „wissenschaftlichen" Unterrichtsfächer (Deutsch und Literaturgeschichte, Geschichte, Kunstunterricht, Mathematik, Naturgeschichte, Physik, Chemie und Geographie) werden nicht nach einem Stundenplan gegeben. Statt dessen wird täglich morgens von 8 bis 10 Uhr, bisweilen bis 11 Uhr, ein bestimmtes dieser Gebiete durch mehrere Wochen hindurch unterrichtet, bis das dem Alter der Kinder entsprechende Ziel erreicht ist. So können die Schüler durch längere Zeit ihr Interesse einem einzigen Gebiete zuwenden.

Die übrigen Erziehungsgebiete: Sprachunterricht, Malen und Zeichnen, Handarbeit (auch für Knaben), Werkstatt-Unterricht (auch für Mädchen), Gartenbau, Eurhythmie, Turnen, Gesang, Technologie, Hilfe in Unglücksfällen, Stenographie, Feldmessen und technische Mechanik werden, soweit sie fortgesetzte Übung erfordern, nach 10 Uhr stundenplanmäßig gegeben.

Zwei moderne Sprachen, Englisch und Französisch lernen die Kinder vom ersten Schuljahr an.

Latein und Griechisch werden nicht von allen Schülern betrieben. Der Unterricht in diesen Sprachen beginnt im 5. Schuljahr und wird als einheitliches Fach gegeben. Von der 9. Klasse an ist Griechisch gegen Englisch wahlfrei.

Eurhythmie ist Pflichtfach durch alle Klassen hindurch.

Der ausführliche Lehrplan (zum Preise von M. 1.— erhältlich) gibt an, wie der Gang der Erziehung durch alle Klassen und mit Hilfe der verschiedenen Fächer den jungen Menschen schrittweise ins *moderne Leben* hineinführt, in dem er sich als freier Mensch den eigenen Weg suchen muß.

Religionsunterricht wird als Angelegenheit der Religionsgemeinschaften betrachtet und durch deren Vertrauenspersönlichkeiten erteilt. Neben dem evangelischen und katholischen Unterricht wird auf

initiative. The New School in London—continued after World War II as Michael Hall School in Forest Row—was the westernmost school, and the Rudolf Steiner school in Oslo, the northernmost founding. Added to these came the Rudolf Steiner school in Basel in 1926 and the Rudolf Steiner school in Zürich in 1927, as well as the Waldorf school in Hannover in 1926 (the fifth founding in Germany and the ninth internationally), and a beginning was made for a Waldorf school in Vienna in 1927. These foundings came either out of initiatives of parents or of teachers, rarely

Wunsch der beteiligten Eltern ein freier Religionsunterricht erteilt dessen Orientierung im Sinne der anthroposophischen Pädagogik gehalten ist, das heißt, es wird der christliche Religionsunterricht so gegeben, wie es den Idealen des anthroposophischen Denkens entspricht.

*

Das Schulgeld beträgt M. 35.— im Monat und umfaßt für die acht Volksschulklassen auch die Kosten für Hefte und Bücher.

Keinerlei staatliche oder sonstige öffentliche Unterstützungsgelder. Damit die Schule auch Kinder unbemittelter Eltern aufnehmen kann, hat sich der „*Verein für ein freies Schulwesen*" (Waldorfschulverein) *E. V. Stuttgart*, als Besitzer der Schule zur Aufgabe gemacht, Beiträge für den Schulbetrieb zu werben. Er hat heute etwa 150 Schulpaten und etwa 5600 außerordentliche Mitglieder, die einen Monatsbeitrag von M. 2.— bezahlen. Die Satzungen, die man gratis erhält, enthalten alles Nähere.

Wer die Waldorfschule unterstützen will, trete dem Schulverein als Mitglied bei. Er hat Ortsgruppen in den größeren Städten Deutschlands und Mitglieder in über 20 Ländern der Erde.

Die Mitglieder erhalten das sechsmal im Jahr mit 32 Seiten erscheinende Mitteilungsblatt „*Die Freie Waldorfschule*" gratis.

*

Man schreibt

in Angelegenheit *der Schule:*

An die Leitung der Freien Waldorfschule, Stuttgart, Kanonenweg 44.

in Angelegenheiten *des Schulvereins:*

An den Vorstand des Vereins für ein freies Schulwesen (Waldorfschulverein) E.V. Stuttgart, Kanonenweg 44.

*

Sprechstunden des Verwaltungsrates der Schule für Schüleraufnahmen Dienstag bis Freitag von 3 bis 4 Uhr nachmittags.

both together. This remained a characteristic trait of the way schools were founded throughout the century. It was either teachers or parents who took the initiative; they seldom or never founded a school together.

The way these new schools were founded also determined the nature of the ensuing challenges that schools faced, especially internally. With regard to the different way teachers looked upon their own schools, the two Rudolf Steiner schools in Basel and Zürich, very different in character but founded in short succession, are an interesting example. While Basel had the pedagogical task as its central aim and guaranteed the legal side by means of a school board, which employed the teachers, Zürich established itself as an independent entrepreneurial undertaking, under the overall control and direction of Curt Englert. The parents were responsible for tuition, but they themselves determined how much and contributed to a common pot. The teachers operated as independent entrepreneurs, each taking from this common pot to cover their needs. This contrast between Basel and Zürich, which went far beyond the way they were conceived, has continued for decades. It is no surprise, in fact, that among the freedom-loving Swiss, a form was pioneered here that freed itself completely from hierarchical structures with regard to the economic basis.

Many innovations in these years arose in the face of specific, concrete situations. Already in 1921, there were deliberations in Stuttgart about how to support older students who wanted to switch to a vocational training instead of aiming for college. The German authorities back then already gave their tacit approval to plans that aimed to build up vocational institutions of higher education, because students would not have to transfer. There was no official permission, however. Further vocational training was set up to enable continuing education and additional artistic activities for students who wanted to get training in home economics. Especially, Alexander Strakosch and Julia Charlotte Mellinger took care of organizing this education, which was carried on in the evenings. For reasons unclear to me from my research, it was discontinued in 1931. The impulse to provide vocational training within the framework of Waldorf pedagogy only reemerged at the end of the 1960s, in the Hibernia school in the Ruhr region and in Kassel in the 1970s.

Friedrich Wickenhauser gave the impulse for orchestral music to the Waldorf School in Stuttgart. This inspiring music teacher and conductor brought enthusiasm for a whole variety of instruments, which he put into the hands of his students. He was able to perform large symphonies with the students, which truly were peak experiences. The case could be made to call him the grandfather of the Waldorf Youth Philharmonia of Baden-Württemberg, which carries on the impulse for orchestral music in the southern German region. The fact that Waldorf schools throughout the century are connected in people's minds with solid musical work is just as much due to this teacher as it was later with Jürgen Schriefer in Bochum-Langendreer or Gustav Gundersen in Oslo.

One of the decisive pedagogical innovations brought by Rudolf Steiner is the polarity between sculptural and musical forces in the human being,[7] and he revealed how important they are for human development, opening up their usefulness in pedagogical work. They are forces that work in building up our bodies and that can be employed in lessons in various subjects, which is to say that they can be used to either

---

7 Rudolf Steiner expands on these two forces in his lecture cycle, *Balance in Teaching*. CW 302a, 1993. The theme was deepened further by Armin J. Husemann: *Der Musikalische Bau des Menschen. Entwurf einer Plastischen Menschenkunde*. 1993.

enhance or diminish those forces. A teacher ignorant of the working of the sculptural and musical forces risks working too strongly in one or the other direction, which plants the seeds for illnesses of various sorts. The faculties of the Waldorf schools that had been founded so far now began to explore how such forces manifest and to address them in their lesson preparation. The pedagogy that pays attention to these forces contributes to the health of children and youth. Educating in this way builds resilience and health for life.[8] Especially Eugen Kolisko also furthered a growing understanding about these forces among the first Waldorf teachers.[9] He was a very experienced school doctor and as such was invited again and again to the other, newly founded Waldorf schools, such as the Vrije School in The Hague, deepening the work of the teachers through his thoroughly penetrated contributions. During such visits he was also consulted about individual children and gave hygienic and medical suggestions. He was highly esteemed for those two things.

The year 1928 saw the expansion of the Waldorf movement to the North American continent. The first Waldorf school outside Europe was founded in New York City both by some members from anthroposophical circles as well as people interested in pedagogical renewal. Virginia Field Birdsall was the first teacher who worked with Irene Brown, a longstanding anthroposophist who provided the financial means and the driving force to get the school off the ground. Olin Wanamaker took on the responsibility for the board of the school and was its first president. His daughter attended the Waldorf School in Stuttgart, so he was already familiar with Waldorf pedagogy. That was the model school, where short trainings were given and practice teaching opportunities offered. The group of founders felt a close spiritual affinity with Stuttgart. Only years after its founding, Swiss and later German teachers who had emigrated from Nazi Germany came to New York, where they found spiritual kinship and a place to work.

The year 1928 saw three more founding attempts in Germany. The Rudolf Steiner school in Berlin began successfully, but the initiatives in Nürnberg and Bremen were not given permission from the state. Both of these blocked initiatives had well-trained teachers with certificates, and they had reasonably good relations with the local authorities. The refusals must have been politically motivated. Waldorf schools in Bremen and Nürnberg did come into being shortly after World War II, the one in Nürnberg in 1946, followed by Bremen in 1949. The Rudolf Steiner school in Berlin, by contrast, continued to develop and grew into a stable institution with many engaged teachers, who created a flourishing pedagogical operation. Similarly strong foundings took place in 1929 in Dresden and in Kassel and Breslau in 1930. In all these places teachers from Stuttgart held introductory lectures and seminars, and

8 Research into the way this works can be found in Tomas Zdražil: *Gesundheitsförderung und Waldorfpädagogik.* 2000.
9 Eugen Kolisko: *Vom Therapeutischen Charakter der Waldorfschule.* 2002; Eugen Kolisko: *Auf der Suche nach Neuen Wahrheiten.* Goetheanistische Studien. 1989.

Exhibition of the Waldorf School Stuttgart in the town hall in Berlin-Schöneberg on the occasion of a conference of the Central Institute for Education, June 1926

anthroposophical groups had been actively working over the course of many years. It became clear that those schools which could build on such a well-prepared foundation thrived and had much better conditions out of which to work. One initiative in 1929, in Dortmund, did not get off the ground, in part because it lacked the support of the local Anthroposophical Society. The initiatives started at the beginning of the 1930s in Darmstadt, Frankfurt am Main, and Meissen likewise did not get beyond the wishful stage. There also were attempts to apply Waldorf pedagogy within state schools in these years. Such a state school teacher was Lotte Riemann in Hamburg, who conducted her class in accordance with Rudolf Steiner's Waldorf principles to the extent that she was able. She belonged to a larger group of anthroposophical teachers working in state schools.[10]

The expansion outside of Germany began to stall, probably due in part to the worldwide economic crisis. A small Waldorf school arose in Bergen, Norway, in 1928, and preschools were founded in Prague and in Bratislava in 1930. The start of the Waldorf school in Bergen had been preceded by a few years of teaching to a handful of children since 1926. In Prague and Bratislava, the concept was to start with a small school after kindergarten work had been built up successfully. In cases where there were not enough children for a school or when the economic means were not present, as in Berlin in 1923, teaching started as homeschooling.

10 Obituary, N 42, October 21, 1934, p. 169.

Early Childhood Education

DURING A CONVERSATION conducted by Rudolf Steiner with the twelfth graders of the Waldorf School in Stuttgart on April 10, 1924, one girl stated her intention to become a kindergarten teacher. Thereupon he remarked: "What matters most is that the children love their teacher, and everything else follows from that."[11] With regard to preschool education, we have few other indications from Rudolf Steiner.

The Stuttgart Waldorf School only managed to organize a first Waldorf kindergarten a few weeks before the end of the school year 1926, supported by E. A. Karl Stockmeyer and Herbert Hahn. Earlier attempts failed because of a lack of space and also because Elisabeth von Grunelius, who had specifically been taken into the teachers' circle for this task, found no one in the collegium to help her carve out the necessary space. She left the school, exhausted at one point, but returned in 1926, bringing with her the necessary funds to build the kindergarten classroom. In this three-room classroom, the work of the kindergarten began with 25 children.

In her earlier meetings with Rudolf Steiner, Elisabeth von Grunelius spoke about preschool education and asked him how a kindergarten teacher could prepare for her pedagogical task. His answers flowed into her work. In an essay she wrote in 1932, she said: "I would like to look upon the kindergarten as a place where children would have a first opportunity to come together to play and experience joyful warmth and comradery. The task of an educator in such a place would be to organize a children's kingdom within the restlessness of our present-day civilization, in an atmosphere of freshness and wakeful understanding in which children could develop fully in accordance with their developmental stage of life." This remark was followed by an explanation of the essence of imitation. She added, "The child's path has to do with getting to know the world, to understand it, and make it her own. In doing so, the child takes part in profound moral forces, and all she experiences as beautiful, true, and good in her surroundings is what she wants to be able to do. This is the way the young child learns until approximately the time of the change of teeth. This learning mode is not intellectual. The child joins in all the processes around her, in all she does, touches, hears, and sees, learning from the gesture. By nature, the child in kindergarten is not receptive to coaxing, commands, or corrections from the adults around her. When one educates through imitation, the child has an example, which is a free stimulus for the development of her will. Educating through imitation demands of course self-education of the educator in every way, including artistically and spiritually. […] When one takes into account this principle of imitation, there is no definite pattern or fixed form that everybody has to follow, but imitation allows every child the freedom to imitate according to her inclinations and capacities, starting where she is and in her

---

11 Rudolf Grosse: *Erlebte Pädagogik*. 1998, p. 101.

Elisabeth Grunelius with her kindergarten class, Stuttgart, 1934

own time. She can choose to imitate what she sees at her own pace. She feels free and is genuinely so."[12]

The demand Elisabeth von Grunelius set for herself to be worthy of imitation was towering, as was her respect for the individual being of the child. She created a soul space in which the children entrusted to her could unfold. She allowed only a few people to visit her kindergarten, and among these was Klara Hattermann, who built up the early childhood movement anew, starting in Hannover. Klara Hattermann was gifted with such a firm will that Elisabeth von Grunelius could not deny her persistence. Klara simply stood by the entrance of the kindergarten every morning until finally she was granted special permission for a practicum visit.

Elisabeth von Grunelius led the kindergarten until the Waldorf School was closed by the Nazi regime in 1938. She emigrated to the United States and established the Waldorf kindergarten in Kimberton, Pennsylvania. After that she founded the kindergarten on the campus of Adelphi University in Garden City, New York, before returning to Europe in 1954.[13] Klara Hattermann founded a small kindergarten in Hannover in 1931 that was separate from the Waldorf school in that city. She was able to run it until 1941 in a two-room apartment she had rented. When this was no longer possible, she moved to Dresden and led a hidden, small kindergarten there for

12 Elisabeth von Grunelius: Das Kind im Kindergarten der Freien Waldorfschule. In: EK 4, October 1932, p. 173.
13 Helmut von Kügelgen: Elisabeth von Grunelius zum 90. Geburtstag. In: LR 30, 1985, p. 67; http:// biographien.kulturimpuls.org/detail.php?&id=1406 (last visited on December 14, 2017); Manfred Berger: *Frauen in der Geschichte des Kindergartens: Ein Handbuch.* 1995.

a while. After the Second World War, she continued her work. Not only was she able to inaugurate the kindergarten training in Hannover, but also the annual Whitsun conference in Hannover, started in 1951, which was highly important for the Waldorf early childhood movement for decades.

In the 1920s there was no teacher training for Waldorf schools yet, and the number of Waldorf kindergartens remained small. Those were very different times, of course, with very different circumstances, and the need for an early childhood education outside the home was becoming obvious. The first Waldorf kindergartens outside Germany began in Prague in 1928 and in Bratislava in 1930, in each case initiated by individual women and totally independent from Stuttgart or Dornach. In 1931 Gerda Langen began a kindergarten on the construction site of the Goetheanum in Dornach, but abandoned the effort a little later when she was asked to take a class at the Rudolf Steiner school in Basel in 1933. The eurythmist Gulle Brun started a Waldorf kindergarten in her home in Oslo-Smestad and found a few highly enthusiastic children and parents to join her.

Most Waldorf schools founded before 1932 did not have their own kindergartens. This changed in the ensuing years when some initiatives, for example the Waldorf School in Hampstead, London, and the Geert Groote School in Amsterdam, started off with pedagogical work for preschool children that then went on into elementary school. The spread of the Waldorf kindergarten movement was thus the result of individual initiative, following the pattern of the Waldorf school movement as a whole. It was not the result of a strategic directive from some central organization. In this respect the Waldorf school movement is one of the oldest grassroots movements.

The Years 1933 to 1945

From 1933 on the Waldorf movement expanded further and further across the world. A few teachers from the Waldorf School had moved to Switzerland and Austria or to England and the United States, driven either by the situation in Germany or the conflicts within the Anthroposophical Society. This expansion started in the areas not affected by National Socialism, especially in England and in the United States. Between 1934 and 1939, five Waldorf schools were founded in Great Britain, some of them by highly motivated and active women. Brenda Lewis in Ilkeston followed an impulse similar to that which had motivated Emil Molt; she wanted to have a school based on Waldorf pedagogy for the children of the workers of her parents' hosiery factory. Two teachers, Margaret Bennell and Cora Nokes, became acquainted with Waldorf pedagogy early in the 1930s and needed a few years to find a suitable location and to find and train the teachers necessary to open a school. They founded the Wynstones Steiner School in Gloucestershire.

In Edinburgh, the founding of the Waldorf school is credited to Pelham Moffat, PhD, who lectured and conducted seminars in education in collaboration with the eurythmist, Inez Arnold. After the Berlin Waldorf School had closed on its own initiative, she was out of work and ended up in Scotland after a stint in Sweden. She was able to share her practical experience and to practice eurythmy gestures with the participants, while Pelham Moffat had trained in Stuttgart and done practicums at the Stuttgart Waldorf School. The founding of the Edinburgh school succeeded even though the Second World War broke out shortly afterward. It continued to develop during the war, and for a time, they had to evacuate to the countryside, which was like paradise for the children.

The school in Hampstead, London, had sprung from a wider circle of anthroposophical work, with the original plan to have Erich Gabert start it and be the lead teacher. After the closing of the Stuttgart Waldorf School, he was out of work. But with the outbreak of the Second World War, he could no longer get a visa and had to return to Germany. The little school was then reorganized by a few women and functioned as a kind of family center for working with young children. London proved to be a rough place for this venture as well as for other initiatives, and the school had to close again in 1953.

Except for a few colleagues in the Elmfield school, no Jewish anthroposophists who had been forced to emigrate from Germany or Austria had taken part in these school foundings, in contrast to the situation in special-needs education institutions being established in England at this time, and especially in Scotland where Viennese doctors and curative education colleagues worked with Dr. Karl König to get this work off the ground. Whereas the colleagues from Pilgramshain in Silesia and from other special-education institutions continued their work in England, the founding impulses of the Waldorf school movement in England and Scotland stemmed almost exclusively from English or Scottish educators or socially engaged people. The initial impulse for the little Elmfield Steiner School was to be a school for the children of the coworkers of the curative education institution Sunfield Childrens' Home in Clent. These plans were soon expanded, and when Eileen Hutchins came on board as its first lead teacher, more children from the surrounding area came as well. Eileen Hutchins led the Elmfield Steiner School until 1984. Expansion of Waldorf pedagogy in England was therefore primarily homegrown and independent of those who managed to emigrate in time from central Europe, where human rights violations were increasing by the day.

Between 1938 and 1942 four more Waldorf schools came into being in the United States in addition to the one in New York City, all of them strongly influenced by Hermann von Baravalle. He gave courses about Waldorf pedagogy at numerous universities and presented many lectures about this educational impulse. In 1937 he was invited to come to the US to teach at the well-known progressive Edgewood School in Greenwich, Connecticut. His lessons as well as his enthusiastic lectures about Waldorf pedagogy were so convincing that the leaders of the Edgewood School decided to continue the school as a Waldorf school starting in 1938. This experiment lasted until 1942. It is just not so simple to practice Waldorf pedagogy when one does not do much with the inner foundations. This instance shows that Waldorf pedagogy cannot be established from the top down, not even in a progressive, reform-oriented school with receptive teachers. Waldorf pedagogy clearly works only when all colleagues are searching for the unifying factor and foster it. When that is not the case, as shown at the Edgewood School during the war, conflicts and struggles will emerge.

Beulah Emmett, who chaired the college of teachers at the Edgewood School, left the school in 1942 and founded the High Mowing School in Wilton, New Hampshire, another endeavor supported by Hermann von Baravalle. This Waldorf school is still functioning today as a high school with boarding facilities, presently united with the adjoining Pine Hill School.

In Vanceboro, Maine, on the Canadian border, there was a school attempt set in motion by Marion and Roger Hale as financiers and organizers, which lasted no more than two years. It turned out that the school was too remote, the population too skeptical, and the area not attractive enough for teachers. Even though it had been started with the best intentions, this rash attempt had to be broken off. The schools in the US that were started with thorough preparation had a much greater chance of survival than the ones that had funding but no other conditions to provide long-term stability.

As in Vanceboro, a couple with ties to industry stood behind the founding of the Kimberton Farms Waldorf School in Phoenixville, Pennsylvania. Alarik Myrin, a rich Swedish industrialist, who had earned his fortune in oil, and his wife, Mabel Pew, who came from an influential philanthropical family, planned to establish a Waldorf school on their farm west of Philadelphia. As Hermann von Baravalle was well known in the US as a Waldorf expert, he was the obvious choice for mentoring. He traveled there and plans were thoroughly discussed in many visits and conversations. Hermann von Baravalle happened to know that Elisabeth von Grunelius, from the Waldorf kindergarten in Stuttgart, as we know, had emigrated to the US. What a wonderful opportunity that could be! She was invited, started a Waldorf kindergarten on the Kimberton farm, and went on to become the head of the school. Virginia Field Birdsall was recruited to be the first class teacher; she had been one of the founders of the New York Rudolf Steiner School and was one of the most experienced Waldorf teachers in the country. Conversations between Hermann von Baravalle and Alarik Myrin continued, and Myrin's appreciation grew as he gained a deeper and deeper understanding of Waldorf pedagogy. Thus, he conceived the plan to found many more Waldorf schools in the US. Of course, he had to solve the problem of the lack of teachers. He welcomed the contact that Hermann von Baravalle arranged for him with Paul Dawson Eddy, director of Adelphi University, where von Baravalle was employed as a mathematics teacher. After promising conversations, these three gentlemen, different as they were, undertook the creation of a Waldorf teacher training program at Adelphi University in Garden City on Long Island. As life had come to a standstill in many parts of Europe, with cities bombed out and culture destroyed, and while the majority of people in eastern and central Europe were struggling for their survival, the Waldorf movement in the United States was unaffected and thrived. Schools were founded and a teacher training was initiated, providing the basis for one of the most sizable aspects of the Waldorf movement, which could then expand even further after the war.

During this time, the first Waldorf initiatives came into being in Asia and in Latin America. The Dutch people living in Bandoeng, which was then in the Dutch colony of Indonesia, felt the need to found a Waldorf school. As early as 1934 Waldorf classes were organized for the children of a handful of parents who were interested in anthroposophy, albeit limited exclusively to that colonial enclave. However, it was a seed.

In Buenos Aires, two women, Ingeborg Knäpper and Eli Lunde—one from Germany and one from Norway—founded a kindergarten in 1939, which was followed by a Waldorf school in 1941. These initiatives had no contact with the Spanish-speaking majority of the population to begin with but remained within the German-speaking minority. The parents of many of the children had been large landowners in the country for many years, involved in large-scale agricultural enterprises. The teachers, however, came directly from Europe, each with their own individual story of leaving the mother country or fleeing from Nazi Germany, as was the case for Ingeborg Knäpper and Herbert Schulte-Kersmecke. The little kindergarten initiative gradually grew, protected by families such as the Lahusens, and attracted other emigrants, whose destiny led them to Buenos Aires. It would be decades before Waldorf pedagogy landed in the broader majority of Argentinian society.

Even in 1933 new Waldorf schools were still coming into being in Germany and Holland. The last one opened in Germany before World War II was the so-called Selter School in Marburg. Not starting from scratch, Waldorf pedagogy was introduced into a school founded by the sisters Anna and Johanna Selter, a school that had been in existence since 1898, inspired by Dalton pedagogy. In Holland, the schools in Zeist and Amsterdam were started in 1933. Both schools were not discovered during the occupation of Holland by the National Socialists and continued to function despite highly burdensome outer circumstances. In Amsterdam this was mainly thanks to the name Geert Groote School, which does not hint as to its origins. The Vrije School in Zeist was so small that it too went undetected. The Vrije School in The Hague, however, was closed by the National Socialists on July 12, 1941, thus suffering the same fate as the Waldorf pedagogical institutions in Czechia, Poland, Austria, Hungary, and Norway.

All ten Waldorf schools in Germany folded in 1933, each in their own individual way. A few schools closed by their own decision when the compromises demanded by the National Socialists became too impossible to make. The Rudolf Steiner school in Berlin and the Waldorf School in Hamburg-Altona were the first to do so. Other schools were gradually brought to their knees, for example: When teachers in Hamburg-Wandsbek were conscripted, the school could not function without them. Some schools were finally closed down by order of the state authorities. Neither a

Caroline von Heydebrand, class teacher
at the First Waldorf School and
editor of the magazine,
Zur Pädagogik Rudolf Steiners

consistent stance or a uniform system was achieved by the *Bund der Waldorfschulen*, the overarching association of the Waldorf schools in Germany, which had already been founded by then. Rather each individual school had to make the decision on its own and accomplish it in its own individual way. How teachers of the German Waldorf schools stood individually with respect to the National Socialists in power is the subject of the chapter "Collaboration during the Time of National Socialism," which also portrays how that worked out in the individual schools.

From 1919 to 1945, a total number of 36 Waldorf schools were founded: eleven in Germany, three in Switzerland, three in Holland, seven in England, one in Hungary, three in Norway, five in the United States, one in Austria, one in Sweden, and one in Argentina. Of all these schools, 25, or two-thirds, remained open during the time of National Socialism in Germany and the Second World War: in Switzerland, the United States, and England. Of these, 18 Waldorf schools worked on without interruption, even though some of them had to evacuate to other locations.

Curriculum and Textbooks

Dr. Caroline von Heydebrand taught from day one as a class teacher at the Waldorf School in Stuttgart. She was busy as a bee. She taught, wrote, edited, held lectures, and traveled to new schools, congresses, and conferences, actively promoting the new pedagogical impulse in ceaseless activity. She followed up on several indications by Rudolf Steiner and developed materials that she needed for her work in the classroom. Other people could benefit from this material, she thought. After talking about shaping a reader for the first grades, she developed the very first Waldorf book, the reader *Der*

Das Wichtigste aus der Literatur der Waldorfschule:

DR. RUDOLF STEINER:

Die Erziehung des Kindes vom Gesichtspunkte der Geisteswissenschaft. 10.–19. Tsd. Philosophisch-Anthroposophischer Verlag, Dornach bei Basel 1921. 57 Seiten.   Preis brosch. M. 1.—

Der Lehrerkurs Dr. Rudolf Steiners im Goetheanum 1921. Wiedergabe der Vorträge Rudolf Steiners durch Albert Steffen und Walter Johannes Stein. Der Kommende Tag A.-G. Verlag, Stuttgart 1922. 137 Seiten.   Preis brosch. M. 3.—, geb. M. 4.—

In Ausführung der Dreigliederung des sozialen Organismus. Enthält u. a. auch eine Anzahl Aufsätze über Pädagogik. Der Kommende Tag A.-G. Verlag, Stuttgart 1920.
Preis brosch. M. 1.50, geb. M. 2.—

Die Methodik des Lehrens und die Lebensbedingungen des Erziehens. Philosophisch-Anthroposophischer Verlag, Dornach bei Basel, 1926. 73 Seiten.   Preis brosch. M. 2.—

Pädagogischer Kurs für Schweizer Lehrer. Berichtet von Albert Steffen, Verlag der Freien Waldorfschule, Stuttgart 1926. 45 Seiten.   Preis brosch. M. 1.—

DR. HERMANN v. BARAVALLE:

Geometrie in Bildern. Sechs Zeichnungen mit Erläuterungen in brauner Mappe. Im Selbstverlag des Verfassers, Stuttgart 1926.   Preis M. 5.—

PAUL BAUMANN:

Op. 1 Nr. 1	Kleine Sonate für Klavier und Violine (leicht)	Preis M. 1.50
Op. 2	Lieder der Freien Waldorfschule:	
	1./2. Heft: Kinderlieder mit Klavierbegleitung	„ „ 1.—
	3. Heft: Lieder mit Klavierbegleitung	„ „ 1.50
	4. Heft: Chöre	„ „ 1.50
Op. 3	Trio für 2 Violinen und Klavier (mittelschwer)	„ „ 4.50
Aus Op. 4	2 Lieder nach Texten von G. F. Daumer mit Klavierbegleitung	„ „ -.80
Aus Op. 5 und Op. 9	Zwei Klavierstücke	„ „ -.80
	Chorbuch, alte und neue Lieder für gemischten Chor	„ „ 1.80

DR. CAROLINE v. HEYDEBRAND:

Gegen Experimentalpsychologie und -Pädagogik. Stuttgart 1921. 30 Seiten. Preis brosch. M. -.50

Pädagogisch-Künstlerisches aus der Freien Waldorfschule. Stuttgart 1925. 45 Seiten und 17 ganzseitige Abbildungen auf Kunstdruckpapier.   Preis M. 2.50

Vom Lehrplan der Freien Waldorfschule. Sonderheft aus „Die Freie Waldorfschule", Mitteilungsblatt für die Mitglieder des Vereins für ein freies Schulwesen (Waldorfschulverein) E.V. Stuttgart 1925. 40 Seiten.   Preis M. 1.—

STUDIENRAT PAUL OLDENDORFF:

Pädagogik auf anthroposophischer Grundlage. Sonderabdruck aus „Pädagogisches Zentralblatt" 1924. Heft 8/9, 28 Seiten.   Preis M. -.50

Erziehungskunst. Sonderheft aus „Soziale Zukunft", Heft 5—7. Enthält Aufsätze von Rudolf Steiner, Albert Steffen u. a. 84 Seiten.   Preis M. 1.—

„Die Freie Waldorfschule". Mitteilungsblatt für die Mitglieder des Vereins für ein freies Schulwesen (Waldorfschulverein) E.V. Stuttgart. Jährlich 6 Hefte mit 32 Seiten zum Preise von M. 3.—, das einzelne Heft soweit noch vorrätig M. -.50

....

An anderen Zeitschriften, die über die Ziele der Freien Waldorfschule und die an ihr gehandhabte Pädagogik Aufsätze veröffentlicht haben, sind in erster Linie zu nennen:

Das Goetheanum. Internationale Wochenschrift für Anthroposophie und Dreigliederung. Redaktion Albert Steffen, Dornach (Schweiz).

Die Anthroposophie. Wochenschrift für freies Geistesleben, Stuttgart, Urbanstr. 31 A. Schriftleiter Dr. Kurt Piper.

„Die Drei". Monatsschrift für Anthroposophie, Dreigliederung und Goetheanismus. Herausgeber: Anthroposophische Gesellschaft in Deutschland. Schriftleitung Dr. Kurt Piper u. Dr. Erich Schwebsch, Stuttgart.

Weitere Aufsatzliteratur ist in vielen Zeitschriften des In- und Auslandes zerstreut.

....

Alles zu beziehen durch die

Freie Waldorfschule Stuttgart, Kanonenweg 44

Postscheckkonto Stuttgart Nr. 21 253 -:- Girokonto 4775 bei der Städt. Girokasse Stuttgart
Österreichische Postsparkassa Konto Nr. 72 079

Prospectus for the First Waldorf School, Stuttgart from
August 1926 with announcement of important literature

Sonne Licht [The Light of the Sun]. This was followed by a second book, a selection of texts which she worked on with Ernst Uehli, resulting in the biblical reader, *Und Gott sprach…* [And God Spoke…]. Both books were in active use in German Waldorf schools far into the 1960s and 1970s. I loved these books myself as a young child in school and spent much time reading them. Never afterward were there books that were used as widely by all Waldorf teachers. The number of books increased, but none were as widely and uniformly accepted. Whereas the first readers created common ground, something unifying, differentiation increased after that, which always brings the opportunity for openness and individualization, but inevitably goes hand-in-hand with a loss of unity.

Caroline von Heydebrand's work was also something to build on. Already in 1925, she published a first overview of the curriculum from grades 1 through 12 in a special edition of the magazine of the school association in Stuttgart.[14] Later she published a greatly expanded version of Rudolf Steiner's indications for the curriculum. For several decades, Caroline von Heydebrand's curriculum book was the go-to for all Waldorf teachers.

In the wake of the publishing of Steiner's pedagogical lectures, his explanations, indications, and suggestions became publicly accessible. Next, Dr. Erich Gabert published the notes from the faculty meetings Rudolf Steiner held with the first Waldorf School faculty, based on the shorthand reports of Dr. Karl Schubert. As a result, a wider base came into being for putting Rudolf Steiner's indications together. After years of preparation, E. A. Karl Stockmeyer edited Rudolf Steiner's curriculum indications, which he had collected and put together. In 1955 they appeared as 11 hectographs. This was followed in 1965 by a second and, in 1976, a third, improved edition of this source material, commissioned by the pedagogical research division of the *Bund der Freien Waldorfschulen*, the German Waldorf Schools Association. E. A. Karl Stockmeyer intended to stress on the one hand that there is no fixed curriculum for the Waldorf schools, and on the other hand that there are many indications, recommendations, and explanations from Rudolf Steiner, so that each individual teacher has a basis to get acquainted with a curriculum outline within which to individualize the curriculum for the children in her care.

In the course of the years, local pedagogical requirements necessitated school-specific curricula and the question arose if it would be necessary to create a basic collective survey. The Hague Circle took up this question in the early 1990s and charged Tobias Richter with the task of writing down the pedagogical task and aims of the Free Waldorf School on the basis of an existing work on which the Waldorf teachers in Austria had collaborated. Many colleagues, first among them Georg Kniebe from the Stuttgart Waldorf School on the Uhlandshöhe, worked on this

---

14 Caroline von Heydebrand: Vom Lehrplan der Freien Waldorfschule. In: MVfS, special issue of October 1925, p. 3ff.

foundational book together with Tobias Richter. Others involved were Bengt Ulin from the Kristoffer Skolan in Stockholm, Shirley Noakes of the Waldorf School in Edinburgh, and Dr. Heinz Zimmerman of the Rudolf Steiner school in Basel. The final version was revised by Dietrich Esterl and Christof Wiechert and published in 1995. Using this edition as a basis, but substantially expanded, Tobias Richter published the book, *Pädagogischer Auftrag und Unterrichtsziele–Vom Lehrplan der Freien Waldorfschule*.[15] This was often referred to as the Richter plan and was also translated into English. In the year 2000, Martyn Rawson created a précis of this book, with authorship attributed to Richter and Rawson, adding material relevant for the English-speaking world and publishing it under the title, *The Educational Task and Content of the Steiner Waldorf Curriculum*. This became a compendium used by many English and American teachers throughout the world. Whereas the German edition has been worked over and expanded numerous times, the last time in 2016, the English version is still in process. In America, however, many individualized curricula are being developed, adapted in accordance with local circumstances. In the meantime, there is a global trend to work in research groups on curriculum questions, with the intention to integrate material relevant in particular cultural contexts in a meaningful and age-appropriate way.

In his work, *5 Dimensionen* [5 Dimensions], Valentin Wember chose a completely different approach. The central question for him is not the what, when, or how, but the question of "why?" in the inner development of each individual teacher.

Establishing Free Christian Religion Lessons

ON THE EVENING of August 20, 1919, at the opening talk for the participants of the pedagogical course, Rudolf Steiner said concerning the teaching of religion: "We do not want to establish a school that promulgates a worldview here in the Waldorf School. The Waldorf school should not be a school promulgating a worldview, where children are stuffed with a lot of anthroposophical dogma. We do not want to teach anthroposophical dogmatism. Anthroposophy is not the content of our lessons, but we strive toward a practical application of anthroposophy. We want to turn the anthroposophical insights we have won into real-life practice in our lessons. [...] Religious education will be given within the religious denominations. We will only practice anthroposophy in the way we teach. So we will distribute the children among the religion teachers according to the denominations they adhere to."[16] As

---

15 The fourth completely revised edition of this book appeared in 2016.
16 Rudolf Steiner: *Faculty Meetings with Rudolf Steiner 1919–1924*. CW 300a, p. 63; Rudolf Steiner repeats this position during a question-and-answer session after the first lecture for new parents of the Stuttgart Waldorf School on August 31, 1919. See *Rudolf Steiner: The Spirit of the Waldorf School*. CW 297.

Herbert Hahn, one of the founding teachers of the Waldorf School and, until 1961, responsible for religious instruction

early as September 25, 1919, the topic came up in the faculty meeting of the Waldorf School in Stuttgart.[17] The question was how to organize religious instruction for four children with atheist parents and 56 from anthroposophical households. This group did not fit any of the denominations, and the way religious instruction was organized was not an option for them. Since they could not partake in either the Catholic or Protestant lessons, nor in the Jewish ones, an alternative needed to be devised. Rudolf Steiner was asked for a suitable suggestion. In response to these questions from parents, Rudolf Steiner designed free Christian religion lessons, because "pedagogical conscience" demanded that they be given some form of religious instruction.[18]

Rudolf Steiner asked two teachers to build up these free Christian religion lessons: the Baltic German, Herbert Hahn, and the German-American, Friedrich Oehlschlegel.[19] Herbert Hahn took grades 1–4 for these free religious lessons, Friedrich Oehlschlegel took grades 5–8. The students were grouped together in these age groups and each group was taught two periods a week.[20] In the teachers meeting of September 26, 1919, Rudolf Steiner gave indications about the themes that should be included. He recommended the lower classes work on basic questions of life, soul, consciousness, and nature in such a way that children can experience that "spirit reigns in nature." He recommended the upper grades talk about questions of destiny, the riddles it poses, and about the distinction between inherited traits and marks of individuality. A few years later the practice of combining grades was dropped and religious instruction was, with a few exceptions, taught in the grades, i.e., to children in groups of the same age. This change was made primarily for reasons of organization and size.

17 See also Report by Erich Gabert in Rudolf Steiner: *Faculty Meetings with Rudolf Steiner*. CW 300a, p. 35ff.
18 Rudolf Steiner: *The Kingdom of Childhood*. CW 311, p. 140.
19 Not much is known about Friedrich Oehlschlegel, and hardly anything is written down about him. In: *Soziale Zukunft*, which Roman Boos started publishing in 1919, there is a contribution by Friedrich Oehlschlegel in the issue of August 5, called Das Prügeln in der Erziehung [Punishment in Education]. In this article he argues against corporal punishment and the harm it can do. He writes in such a trenchant way and describes the soul trauma it causes so exactly, that one gets the impression he was a victim of it himself in his youth.
20 Herbert Hahn: Vom Entstehen des freien christlichen Religionsunterrichtes in der Waldorfschule und vom Einrichten der Sonntagshandlungen. In: *Zur religiösen Erziehung*. Published by the pedagogical research team of the Bund der Freien Waldorfschulen, the German Waldorf Schools Association, 2013, p. 51.

School friends Rudolf
Grosse and Walter Molt

Soon after these free religion lessons started, a few parents of attending students felt the need to have a conversation with the two teachers. A special parent evening was arranged, and the conversation took place on November 3, 1919, with the school's founder, Emil Molt, present. Toward the end of the parent evening, the teachers were asked to consider instituting a Sunday service and involve Rudolf Steiner for advice. Many weeks later, at Christmas time, Herbert Hahn and Friedrich Oehlschlegel had the opportunity to have a talk with Rudolf Steiner, which was recorded by Herbert Hahn. "Rudolf Steiner first listened in his usual patient and kind way, which made everybody open up. When the talk turned to including eurythmy in the Sunday service, he sat up and called out, 'Eurythmy!' in a tone of voice that stressed his astonishment. 'But that is a worldly art, is it not?' After a pause he added, 'If we want to consider eurythmy, I would have to give a special cultic form of eurythmy.' After a few more suggestions from our side, there was a longer pause. Suddenly Rudolf Steiner exclaimed, with the full weight of his whole being behind every word, 'In that case it will have to be a cultic ritual!' Then he explained in depth what it meant for him to participate in this undertaking. A few days later he gave the two teachers a sheet with the text of the Sunday service and the accompanying entrance meditation for those who conducted the service at the altar."[21] Participation in these Sunday services was strictly confined to students of the free religion lessons and their parents or guardians. All other people, including the anthroposophists who wanted to experience this service as well, were not allowed to attend. For Rudolf Steiner it was strictly a school event.[22]

Rudolf Grosse gave a detailed account about the religion lessons: "Our religion teacher was Dr. Herbert Hahn, and it still fills me with a feeling of great gratitude when I mention him. When we experienced him as a teacher, he was young in terms of his birth certificate, but that was not how it felt. He had a personality like no other teacher. He combined a remarkably cultivated form of expression with a warmth that was balm for the soul, a rare mixture that gave us a feeling of inner trust, even though he maintained a high degree of distance from the students. [...] Dr. Hahn was a highly refined and artistic storyteller in the religious lessons."[23]

Friedrich Oehlschlegel took a leave of absence early in 1920 and traveled to the United States in order to spread the basic ideas of social threefolding. He took the original texts for the religious services with him on this trip. His psychological

21 Johannes Tautz in Gisbert Husemann and Johannes Tautz (eds.): *Der Lehrerkreis um Rudolf Steiner*, 1979, p. 34.
22 Rudolf Steiner: *Faculty Meetings with Rudolf Steiner*. CW 300a, 1975, p. 137f.
23 Rudolf Grosse: *Erlebte Pädagogik. Schicksal und Geistesweg.* 1968/1998, p. 88.

instability increased to such a degree during his journey that he could neither go back to the Waldorf School on the Uhlandshöhe nor manage to gain a firm footing in the US. He must have burned the original text of the services given by Rudolf Steiner, and he disappeared without a trace. Because Friedrich Oehlschlegel had journeyed to the US, Herbert Hahn had to continue the new assignments on his own for the time being. The celebrations of the ritual began on February 1, 1920, when Herbert Hahn held the Sunday service for the first time in the *Säulensaal* [Pillar Hall] of the Waldorf School on the Uhlandshöhe. Whenever he was in residence in Stuttgart, Rudolf Steiner took part in these services.

Fritz Graf von Bothmer

In 1920 a Christmas service was added and in 1921 a youth service, both requested by students. The Christmas service for the children was celebrated for the first time on December 25, 1920, and the youth service on Palm Sunday of 1921.[24] When the religion teachers had a conversation with Rudolf Steiner on December 9, 1922, they told him about the request made by Johanna Wohlrab, a senior, for another service for the upper grades. This prompted the so-called Offering Service, the texts of which Rudolf Steiner gave to Herbert Hahn, Karl Schubert, and Maria Roeschl in March 1923. This ritual was held for the first time on Palm Sunday 1923 by the three teachers. A year later, Rudolf Steiner remarked that "what is being done in this ritual,"[25] in close connection with the religion lessons, served "to deepen religious feeling to a remarkably high degree." Rudolf Grosse, a fellow student of Johanna Wohlrab in this high school class, experienced these celebrations intensively. "These rituals meant a great deal to large parts of the student population. Only pressing circumstances would persuade us not to attend these Sunday services, and I have rarely experienced a more profound, celebrative mood in my life than in this ritual. I cannot even come close to expressing the inwardness that lived in the hearts of the students as we experienced this Christ impulse. A big impression was created because of the holy seriousness of the teachers celebrating the ritual and, by extension, the devotion with which Graf von Bothmer, for example, carried out the task of supervising the waiting students as if it were part of the very ritual.[26]

Rudolf Steiner wanted to make sure the free religion lessons were carried out in the same way as the Protestant or Catholic lessons. Therefore he stressed that Herbert Hahn and Friedrich Oehlschlegel and their successors, in their capacity as religion

24 Helmut von Kügelgen: *Das Religiöse Element*. In: LR 14, 1976, p. 58f.
25 Rudolf Steiner: *The Kingdom of Childhood*. CW 311, 1963, p. 142.
26 Rudolf Grosse: *Erlebte Pädagogik. Schicksal und Geistesweg*. 1968/1998, p. 88f.

teachers, should function for these lessons not as teachers of the Waldorf School and members of the faculty, but as employees of the Anthroposophical Society.[27]

At the request of Friedrich Rittelmeyer, Herbert Hahn described for the first time on January 2, 1938, that the religious element had not been part of the initial planning for the Waldorf School. According to Herbert Hahn, Rudolf Steiner thought "that the central place of the anthroposophical worldview in which Waldorf pedagogy was anchored would provide what otherwise would have to be met in separate religion lessons."[28] Many people interpreted this as meaning that separate religious lessons were not part of the original plan. In the course of ensuing decades, however, the opinion gained ground that the ethical and religious element inherent in the lessons complements the religion lessons.[29]

At the internal autumn conference of the German Waldorf Schools Association in 1951, a cautious beginning was made for a collaboration between those who were responsible for the free religious lessons in the schools in Stuttgart and The Hague, presided over by Herbert Hahn and Jan van Wettum. Mindful of both careful and conscientious use of Rudolf Steiner's original texts on the one hand, and open to local needs and circumstances on the other hand, the religion teachers of the Waldorf School in Stuttgart took responsibility for appointing, or rather recognizing, new teachers for this task. At the same autumn conference, Herbert Hahn was charged with contacting schools where free religious lessons were cultivated in other countries. The participants in this conversation had the intention to gradually build up a body that could be responsible for free religion education on the international level as well. To this group of people belonged, among others, Herbert Hahn, Erich Gabert, Magdalena Kiefel, Ilse Staedtke, and Heinz Müller. They were joined in later years by Wolfgang Rudolph as well as Johannes Tautz and Helmut von Kügelgen. Daan van Bemmelen and Wim Kuiper took on the responsibility for the Netherlands, and A. W. Mann for England. These people wanted to be guardians of the free religion education and the rituals for which Rudolf Steiner had been asked. More people were chosen to become part of this body only at the end of the 1960s: Gottwalt Hahn and Erich Weismann for Germany, Bengt Ulin for Scandinavia, and Eileen Hutchins for Great Britain. Among

27 Rudolf Steiner: *Konferenzen mit den Lehrern der Freien Waldorfschule.* GA 300c, 1975, p. 119f.; Günter Altehage: *Religion, Weltanschauung, Waldorfschule.* 2007, p. 31f.

28 Günter Altehage: *Religion, Weltanschauung, Waldorfschule.* 2007, p. 60, with reference to Herbert Hahn: Vom Entstehen des freien christlichen Religionsunterrichtes und vom Einrichten der Sonntagshandlungen. In: *Zur Religiösen Erziehung.* Edited by the pedagogical research team of the Bund der Freien Waldorfschulen, the German Waldorf Schools Association, 1997, p. 49.

29 Lecturing to approximately 1000 teachers coming from all over the world, Helmut von Kügelgen gave a wide-ranging and fundamental presentation about the free Christian religion lessons, including the esoteric dimensions of teacher preparation. These lectures took place during the international Waldorf teacher conference at Easter 1986, in Dornach, Switzerland, and a summary can be found in LR 32, 1986, pp. 8–21. He emphasized that there are basic conditions to be met to foster this element. It has to live strongly in the faculty, and people have to want it and be unanimous about it.

Emmy Smit and Daan van Bemmelen, 1926, founding teachers of the Vrije School in The Hague

their tasks were: giving permission to appoint additional religion teachers; handling the organization of the religion lessons in a school; mentoring religion teachers and counseling them in solving interpersonal issues; fostering established traditions such as maintaining connections with others in the field; and preparing conferences for religion teachers.[30]

In 1967 there was a first religion teacher conference at the Goetheanum, where this work has been carried forward on a regular basis ever since. As the Waldorf movement grew, the need arose to create an international body. In 1983 the members of this body were: Rudolf Bosse (Frankfurt), Brigitta Carlgren and Bengt Ulin (Stockholm), Otfried Dörfler (Basel), Tilde von Eiff, Helmut von Kügelgen, and Johannes Tautz (Stuttgart), Gertraud Flegler (Kassel), Leonora Gerretsen and Wim Kuiper (The Hague), Friedhold Hahn (Stuttgart), Karla Kiniger (Edinburgh), Heide Reisser (Vienna), Johannes Timm (Evinghausen), Rüdiger Voigt (Hannover), and Claartje Wijnbergh (Amsterdam). A further differentiation came in 1996, when responsibilities for individual countries were agreed on.

In 1995 religion teachers started to grapple with questions arising from the planned publication by the Rudolf Steiner *Nachlassverwaltung* [publications administration] of the texts that formed the basis of the services. This came about because, up to that time, texts had been passed on from person to person among the religion teachers. Accusations mounted that religion teachers were being overly secretive and, though some of these reproaches were justified, in religion teacher circles people were unanimous that research and thoughtful penetration of the texts and contents were in place. To further protect these lessons, people agreed to keep to three basic rules: These texts are not for individuals, but were given to school communities, which should guard them carefully; no one holding the services should

30 Helmut von Kügelgen: Aus der Religionslehrertagung. In: LR 1, 1970, p. 2ff.

appoint him- or herself, but should be asked to carry out this assignment, and the appointment should be confirmed by the general Anthroposophical Society; form and content of these services belong together, and the rituals should be continually penetrated consciously and separated from services held by priests.[31] According to the publication aims of the Rudolf Steiner *Nachlassverwaltung* [the board presiding over the publication of the works Rudolf Steiner left behind], the representatives of the body of religion teachers were clear that these lessons can continue only in the form originally intended, when colleagues keep to the three agreements indicated above.

The questions surrounding religion lessons became came more and more poignant at the end of the 20th and the beginning of the 21st centuries, at least in Europe. Observance of religious practices within established denominations declined to such a degree that a natural relationship to these lessons was no longer a given. Furthermore, new social realities demanded religion lessons that were accessible to children of highly diverse social backgrounds. Life in an increasingly liberal and diverse society, thrown back more and more on its own inner resources, likewise demanded a new form of inner religiosity, which comes out in the way we treat one another and respect each other as human beings. Günther Altehage and many religion teachers with him gave these precepts a lot of thought.[32]

Teacher Training for Waldorf Schools

Pedagogical Collaborative Tübingen-Jena-Zwätzen

THE NEW SCHOOL IDEAS developed after World War I to build up the Waldorf movement were well received by many, not only by educators but also by university students. One circle where Waldorf pedagogy was worked on intensively was the pedagogical collaborative of young students founded in 1921 in Tübingen, later called the Jena-Zwätzen Circle. Some of the young people asked Rudolf Steiner for a course but were not quite able to formulate their questions clearly enough. They described—inadequately by their own admission—what they wanted. They were occupied with questions of inner development as well as societal questions. All of them participated in the so-called Pedagogical Youth Course given by Rudolf Steiner and planned to become educators later. As early as the spring of 1923 they organized their own Waldorf teacher training in Tübingen. Herbert Hahn and Karl Schubert often came for "intimate conversation and courses, usually after holding a public lecture in Tübingen. Caroline von Heydebrand took a warm interest in the

---

31 Helmut von Kügelgen and Manfred Schmidt-Brabant: Zur Veröffentlichung der Handlungstexte und zur Erweiterung der Teilnehmerkreise an der Opferfeier. In: N October 29, 1995, p. 174.

32 Günter Altehage: Religionsvielfalt und Waldorfschulpädagogik. Zugleich ein Beitrag zum Selbstverständnis des Waldorflehrers. In: LR 69, 2000, pp. 5–25.

In front of the entrance of the new building of the Waldorf School on the Uhlandshöhe 1925

group as well."[33] Participants in this initiative were: Ernst Charrois, Wilhelm Dörfler (1899–1980), Karl Ege, Anne Fried-Politzer, Gerbert Grohmann, Friedrich Hiebel, Wolfgang Kelber, Elisabeth Klein, Fritz Kübler, Eduard Lehmann, Wilhelm Nicking, Karl Rittersbacher, Ella Rothe, Georg Moritz von Sachsen-Altenburg, Helle Schmidt, Minchen Sprang, Ilse Staedke, Hildegard Staedtke-Gerbert, Ernst Weissert, and Heinrich and Wilhelm Wollborn.[34] These students kept to a strict schedule each day. In the morning they studied basic anthroposophical works together, including, as a matter of course, Rudolf Steiner's eagerly anticipated articles as soon as they had appeared in the newsletter *Was in der Anthroposophischen Gesellschaft vorgeht* [What Is Happening in the Anthroposophical Society]. One could not be more up-to-date at that time. After that came courses in the different disciplines: Gerbert Grohmann practiced plant study with the participants; Wilhelm Dörfler gave an introduction to music theory; Friedrich Hiebel elucidated the mystery dramas of Rudolf Steiner;

33 Friedrich Hiebel: *Entscheidungszeit mit Rudolf Steiner*. 1986, p. 326.
34 Christiane Haid: *Auf der Suche nach dem Menschen. Die Anthroposophische Jugend- und Studentenarbeit in den Jahren 1920–1931*. 2001, p. 224, Anm. 93.

others taught eurythmy or English. So, this teacher training course was formed in such a way that the participants taught each other. In the evening the participating students walked in the hills surrounding Tübingen. Two companies from Heidenheim, Voith and Zöppritz, sponsored the endeavor. Anne Fried-Politzer (1903–1998) painted a totally different picture: "The work in this group absorbed most of our time. We shared in intense study, ecstatic highs, and personal dramas. Couples changed partners, careers were built up, and connections were formed, which in some cases would end in tragedies and death. We were surrounded by the craziness of the times we lived in, but we lived in illusions and ignored warning signals. I only had the sensation as if everything was permeated by the intoxicating and poisonous smell of rampant growth of flowers."[35] In the summer of 1924, many young people gathered in Tübingen in order to prepare to become teachers. The course started with about 35 people. Caroline von Heydebrand, Jürgen von Grone, and Karl Schubert from Stuttgart had been invited to give lectures. Friedrich Hiebel sketched the motive and aim of the course as follows: "A movement for educational renewal and instituting a free spiritual life sounds lofty, but the words remain hollow without deeds. We believe that genuine searching on the path to the spirit will lead to progressing from words to deeds."[36]

In early October 1924 this pedagogical working circle, as they called themselves, moved to Jena-Zwätzen, where some of the members lived, and that's how this circle got its name. Colonel Richard Seebohm[37] put a house on the Galgenberg in Zwätzen, a suburb of Jena, at the disposal of the students—into which 30 to 40 students were able to move—who wanted to continue and complete their self-organized free teacher training. Anne Fried once again described the situation in Jena with a clear feeling for nuances: "In the autumn the group moved into a large and dark house on the Galgenberg in Zwätzen near Jena. An elderly man who was close to the Waldorf school put it at their disposal. It was a curious house that had been built years ago as an educational institution but had never been occupied. It had many small, single rooms, a hall to gather in, a large kitchen, and an octagonal dining room with an octagonal table that had room for about 40 people, so it served our purpose well. The monthly stipend from home that some of us received was the capital we lived on. We wrestled with the study material, we were learning, discussing, suffered cold and hunger, and tried hard to keep personal problems to a minimum. The villagers at the bottom of the mountain frowned upon the fact that young men and women lived in one house

---

35 Anne Fried: *Farben des Lebens. Erinnerungen.* Leipzig 1991, p. 73.
36 Friedrich Hiebel: Aus der Tätigkeit des Pädagogischen Arbeitskreises in Tübingen. In: N 36, September 14, 1924, p. 144; Friedrich Hiebel: The Activities of the Educational Centre at Tübingen. In: AM September 14, 1924, p. 110ff.
37 Richard Seebohm was one of the early anthroposophist. He married Adelheid von Zastrow and they had three daughters. The youngest daughter, Adolphine, was introduced to Rudolf Steiner by her father when she was 16 years old. She became a nurse, emigrated to the Netherlands, and married L.F.C. Mees. Her three children were Rudolf Mees (a banker), Arnica Esterl-Mees (a storyteller) and Wijnand Mees (a eurythmist).

together without supervision. It was a point of honor for us to give no grounds for any rumors. We led an ascetic life, took turns cooking and doing chores in the house, and found our own way to spend our spare time."[38]

Friedrich Kübler (1901–1945) and Wilhelm Dörfler (1899–1980) were essentially responsible for the coordination of the training, which was based on the pedagogical lectures Rudolf Steiner gave at Easter 1924. Students who had gathered there—most of them were 20 or 21 years old—belonged to the youth movement and shared a strong social and socio-pedagogical interest. They wanted to try out a way to live and work together, to have these two aspects—living and working—not mutually exclusive. Friedrich Kübler, one of the founders and spokesmen of the working circle, taught a class at the Waldorf school in Hamburg, starting in 1929. Wilhelm Dörfler later took up tasks at the Goetheanum in Dornach that were not confined to education. Other members of the working circle in Jena were Friedrich Hiebel, Gerbert Grohmann, Ella Roothe, Ilse[39] and Hildegard Staedke, Helle Schmidt, as well as Willy Beck, a cofounder of the Waldorf school in Tübingen in 1949. Then there were the brothers Heinrich and Wilhelm Wollborn, who started to work after the war for the Rudolf Steiner school in Essen in the Ruhr region.

So almost all members had come along from Tübingen to Jena. Hildegard Staedtke, later Gerbert, had met anthroposophy as a 19-year-old, had heard lectures by Rudolf Steiner, and had been given the choice by her father to either be supported by him financially and do a *proper* study in Tübingen or Munich, or to go on studying in the anthroposophical group of students and live without a stipend and access to her parental home. She opted for anthroposophy.[40] In Jena, Gustav Spiegel found his way to the group. He studied German language and literature, became a civil servant, and later joined up again with colleagues from the pedagogical working circle. Ernst Weissert, who studied classical philology in Jena, likewise joined the group. It was clear to him from the start that the thinking behind the whole effort was to sow a seed for a free teacher training in close alliance with the Waldorf impulse.

In 1924, Ernst Weissert and Friedrich Hiebel came back to Jena, full of enthusiasm, from Rudolf Steiner's speech course in Dornach. Now they wanted to pass on what they had experienced to their friends. Ella Rothe reports how Ernst Weissert came across: "He was 19 years old, mobile, blond, and dressed in a black velour suit. Having just absorbed what was given in Dornach, he was bursting with enthusiasm and tried to work on speech formation with us, out of the nature of sound. […] The spark of enthusiasm did not quite catch."[41] Rudolf Steiner had assented to giving a second youth course in October 1924, for which all the inhabitants of the house

---

38 Anne Fried: *Farben des Lebens. Erinnerungen.* Leipzig, 1991, p. 75.
39 Ilse Staedtke studied in Jena and wrote a dissertation, "Schiller and Waldorf Pedagogy." When the Waldorf school in Kassel was founded, she took the first grade in 1930.
40 Ekkehard Randebrock: Hildegard Gerbert (December 27, 1903–April 13, 1983). In: LR 27, 1983, p. 71.
41 Ella Rothe: Der Student und junge Kollege. In: LR 23, 1981, p. 16.

in Jena-Zwätzen made careful preparations. Because of Rudolf Steiner's illness, this course was not to be.

The teacher training in Jena-Zwätzen was also supported by the Stuttgart teachers Caroline von Heydebrand, Herbert Hahn, and Karl Schubert. The working group organized a first holiday course at Easter and a second one in August 1925, in which 60 people participated. Every morning started with reading a lecture by Rudolf Steiner from the teacher course held in Dornach at Christmas 1921/22, followed by a thorough discussion—even though everybody had the impression as if one had just swum the first lap with the whole ocean of teacher training still lying ahead. Karl Ege and Ernst Lehrs from the Stuttgart Waldorf School were present. Frau Rabinowitsch gave an hour of eurythmy every day and two hours of speech formation.[42] The working circle sent out its own

Christoph Boy. Because of his balanced judgment, this esteemed colleague was entrusted with the directorship of the Waldorf School in 1933.

newsletter and reached an increasingly large audience. From April 8–11, 1926, they organized a conference with Wilhelm Dörfler, Gerbert Grohmann, Herbert Hahn, Heinrich Hardt, Caroline von Heydebrand, Fritz Kübler, Helle Schmidt, and Otto Wiemer. Caroline von Heydebrand reported about the aim of this conference: "The teachers of the Waldorf School are working together with the leading members of the Pedagogical Working Circle Jena-Zwätzen, in order to gradually realize ideals that Rudolf Steiner planted in their hearts with regard to teacher training. [...] We hope that we will succeed, in collaborative work within the pedagogical workshop Jena-Zwätzen and the Waldorf School in Stuttgart, in building up a teacher training, which can serve the art of education as Rudolf Steiner has given it to us."[43]

In 1927 the group closed shop in Jena and accepted the invitation of Maria Röschl to continue the work within the framework of the Youth Section at the Goetheanum. Thereupon Friedrich Kübler and Wilhelm Dörfler moved to Dornach.

Teacher Seminars in Stuttgart, at the Goetheanum in Dornach, and in Zürich, as Well as Other Trainings

IN 1925 THE RUDIMENTS of a pedagogical seminar appeared in Stuttgart, and soon after, a one-year course came into being. While this was going on, extensive practicums were arranged at the Waldorf school on the Uhlandshöhe, and this enabled many

42 Friedrich Kübler: Report of the Educational Vocation Course. In: AM October 25, 1925, p. 347ff.
43 Caroline von Heydebrand: Die Tagung der im Aufbau begriffenen Lehrerbildungsstätte Jena-Zwätzen. In: G 13, March 28, 1926, p. 104.

future colleagues to enter into the profession of Waldorf teaching. Hardly a day went by without somebody sitting in on one class or another and following what was going on in the lessons. Starting in May 1928, the teacher seminar in Stuttgart was built up more consistently and one-year courses introduced people to the pedagogy of Rudolf Steiner.[44]

E. A. Karl Stockmeyer and Erich Schwebsch were responsible for the following announcement: "The courses are planned to be in two stages. The first stage will begin with a year's course in human development and artistic training in sculpture, painting, music, eurythmy, gymnastics, and speech formation. Apart from that, the existing, 'advanced level' courses as given at the Goetheanum will offer further study in specific areas of life and knowledge. Workshops will further the anthroposophical basis of this pedagogy and its methods and didactic aims. We cannot guarantee practicums for participants in the independent Waldorf School. The second stage of the practical/pedagogical training in the classroom itself may come about for those participants who are invited to do so by the teachers of the independent Waldorf School."[45]

In contents, the teacher training of the first years bore the stamp of what teachers such as Hermann von Baravalle, Herbert Hahn, Eugen Kolisko, Alexander Strakosch, and Erich Schwebsch had achieved themselves. The rich spiritual productivity of these first Waldorf teachers worked strongly on the participants. Courses in methodology, for example, were given by Christoph Boy. Students who experienced this course were highly impressed by how intensively the interest of the teacher in the students was fostered. Caroline von Heydebrand read the lecture cycle *The Foundations of Human Experience* to them. These lectures were not worked on in workshops at the time.[46] It was a freely chosen pedagogical study, not tied to any degree or recognition, in other words, an additional training. This additional training was regularly arranged in the years that followed.

High school teachers were more or less left to their own devices; there were no systematic courses for them. Being versatile was sufficient in those days. Those who attended lessons could learn from the students what high school lessons looked like and why Rudolf Steiner had put so much emphasis on the boundless interest teachers should have in their students. René Maikowski described such a lesson. "When I attended a lesson by [Walter Johannes] Stein one day, he conducted a brilliant lesson, as so often, entered into all kinds of objections, but won each argument. As he went out at the end of the period, all students were still knocked flat. Suddenly one student came to the front in great agitation, pounded with both fists on to the podium, and cried:

44 Erich Gabert: *Lehrerbildung im Sinne der Pädagogik Rudolf Steiners. Das Lehrerseminar der Freien Waldorfschulen.* 1961, p. 31.
45 Announcement in ZPRSt 2–3, December–January 1927/28, p. 88; Wenzel M. Götte: *Erfahrungen mit Schulautonomie.* 2006, p. 356ff.
46 Ernst Michael Kranich: Gründungsversammlung des "Seminar für Waldorfpädagogik Stuttgart." In: LR 25, 1982, p. 33.

'I cannot stand this any longer!' When I asked him what was the matter, he said, 'He's got an answer for everything, we could just as well pack it in!'"[47] Hearing this truth, which came from the bottom of the student's heart, René Maikowski recognized one of the most common errors made in high school teaching.

For November 1, 1926, Curt Englert-Faye announced the start of a teacher training in Zürich. He stressed: "An attempt shall be made to work out of Rudolf Steiner's art of pedagogy on the basis of Swiss conditions."[48] The Rudolf Steiner school in Zürich organized regular workshops in education from then on.

The announcement of teacher training courses in Stuttgart, starting May 2, 1933, gave a detailed list of who would teach what subject[49] as follows:

Painting and sculpture, Mr. Strauss, Mr. Wolfhügel
Speech formation: Mrs. Karin Haupt
Singing, music theory and harmony for the lower school: Mrs. Wilke
Speech eurythmy: Mrs. Baumann
Tone eurythmy: Mrs. Vogel
Gymnastics: Count Bothmer
Handwork: Mrs. Hauck, Mrs. Rommel
The irrational in education: Mr. Bindel
History in the middle grades: Dr. Gabert
Botany: Mr. Ege
Anthroposophical basis of pedagogy and what that means in the classroom:
    Miss von Heydebrand, Miss Mellinger
Medical questions in education: Dr. Kolisko
The human being: Dr. Lehrs
Basic anthroposophical concepts: Dr. Röschl
Aesthetics: Dr. Schwebsch
Introduction to the philosophical work of Rudolf Steiner: Mr. Stockmeyer
How to look at art: Mr. Uehli

Anyone wanting to either explore Waldorf pedagogy or prepare more intensively to actually become a teacher tried to study for a while in Stuttgart. Important personalities in the Waldorf school movement in other countries were inspired by their stay at the Uhlandshöhe. One of the students of the teacher training center in Stuttgart who was there from 1933/34, Henry Barnes (1912–2008), built up the American Waldorf school movement after returning to the United States and left a lasting imprint on it in his lifetime.

47 Letter of René Maikowski dated May 2, 1989, to Johannes Tautz, Archiv C. Brosamer.
48 C. Englert-Faye: Memo. In: N 44, October 31, 1926, p. 182.
49 EK 1, April 1933, p. 333.

Students of the eleventh and twelfth grades of the New School in London before 1945 with their teachers Lucy Dennison (left) and Francis Edmunds (right)

In 1933 a Waldorf teacher training started in Holland as well, albeit with single courses to begin with. Two years later, in 1935, these courses took place regularly three days a week in Zeist, where Daan van Bemmelen, one of the founders of the Vrije School in The Hague, had moved with his family in 1934. Together with Bernard Lievegoed and Herbert Hahn, he trained new teachers. This tradition was retained in the second half of the 20th century as well. Teacher training for Dutch Waldorf teachers took place in Zeist into the 1990s. As the Waldorf teacher training in Stuttgart was kept up, the Waldorf movement also established itself more and more in Switzerland. It was carried by members of the educational working group in Dornach, also with regard to teacher training.

In teacher training the emphasis was on artistic work and individual shaping of the lessons, especially in elementary school: "Every beginning teacher will come face-to-face with feeling inadequate. This realization is a stimulus to acquire what one does not have, through painting, sculpture, doing eurythmy, making music, and practicing speech formation. New impulses for all the arts radiate out from the Goetheanum, where they are at home. Anyone coming to Dornach can practice them. […] In Dornach one can study various pedagogical lectures of Rudolf Steiner, but especially what lies at the root of this art of pedagogy down into the detail, namely anthroposophy itself. Every individual teacher must study anthroposophical and educational books and lectures by Rudolf Steiner, for anyone eager to do so will find that their content appeals to the spiritual activity one must muster to understand it. Therefore, it is not merely content that can be handed down. Anthroposophical pedagogy resists being transmitted by traditional methods. It cannot be compared to ordinary alternative educational reform efforts. [...] Thus understood, every individual therefore carries the responsibility for, and takes the risks of, his or her own self-education, which will come about through a course of study determined by individual circumstances. This goes against current tendencies. People would like to be led, guided, or even leashed, and yet they think they know better at the end than their teachers. So self-education starts right there." To help with training for the practical work in the classroom "conversations help, once or twice every week. [...] Specific instructions for the individual subjects (history, mathematics, geography, etc.) are not given. The necessary knowledge in different disciplines is left to the individual to be gained in any ordinary place where they are being taught in our civilization today."

At the end there is the following summary: "It would be desirable that those who decide to seek out a pedagogical training in this sense at the Goetheanum would have completed an ordinary course of study or degree in whatever form this is required locally, for only those who have met the ordinary requirements which our present-day civilization demands of educators would be qualified to recognize and value what anthroposophy has contributed to the field of education."[50]

When the teacher training in Stuttgart had to be stopped in 1938, it was still possible to do a teacher training in Switzerland, and the offerings were expanded in May 1943 by courses given at the Friedwart School at the Goetheanum. Marie Groddeck started an "artistic and many-sided teacher training" upon repeated requests from England especially, where the schools "have always suffered from a lack of trained teachers."[51] She wrote: "It is understandable that right there, in a country in the throes of the horrors of war, the realization would dawn that reconstruction after the war has to start immediately and directly with the human being, that is to say, with education."

Furthermore, in the autumn of 1936, teacher training courses were started in London, carried by the teachers of Michael Hall School, especially L. Francis Edmunds and Cecil Harwood, Arthur Sheen, Augustus William von Kaufmann, Jesse Darrell, Marjorie Watson, and Elizabeth Jacobs. From 1938 onward these courses were augmented by Friday lectures, held by people such as Caroline von Heydebrand, L. Francis Edmunds, Arthur Sheen, Cecil Harwood, and Karl Nunhofer in Rudolf Steiner House, Park Road, London.

---

50 J. de Jaager, C. Englert, Marie Steiner: Welche Möglichkeiten pädagogischer Ausbildung bestehen zur Zeit am Goetheanum? In: N 18, May 6, 1934, p. 73.
51 Marie Groddeck: Lehrerschulung am Goetheanum. In: N 20, May 16, 1943, p. 79.

Organizing a teacher training independent from state-required trainings is therefore a central concern in the process of building up the Waldorf school movement. Prompted by sheer necessity, also by strategic circumstances later, various forms of teacher training were organized at the nodal points of the Waldorf school movement, invariably just a few years after the schools had been founded. For right from the start people saw that ordinary state qualifications had to be supplemented by practicing the arts and working with the anthroposophical underpinnings. Stuttgart, Dornach, London, and Zeist were the first to develop into training centers for the movement as early as the 1920s and 1930s.

The Impulse to Found a World School Association

IN FOUNDING THE FIRST free Waldorf School in Stuttgart, Rudolf Steiner already pursued the intention to found a world school association, with the task to spread knowledge about Waldorf pedagogy throughout the world and build up a broad basis of support. In the conferences with the teachers that Rudolf Steiner attended, financing the school was a recurrent theme. On July 29, 1920, somebody asked about the economic foundations of the school. Thereupon Rudolf Steiner asked Emil Molt to elucidate the financial situation, as he was the one who was most familiar with it.[52] It so happened that Rudolf Steiner was giving a public lecture that evening, and therefore he was asked if he would agree to ask the audience to support the school. Caroline von Heydebrand and Herbert Hahn had already put together an appeal to be distributed amongst the members of the audience. Not only did Rudolf Steiner agree, but was highly pleased about the appeal they had written. He did add a few general remarks. When one wants to receive financial support from a larger circle, one should start at home, which is actually a basic principle of fundraising. To that end supporters in Stuttgart should be asked to support the Waldorf School Association locally and, with that, the Waldorf School in Stuttgart, whereas other people should be made enthusiastic about supporting the general idea of the Waldorf school, Waldorf pedagogy, and independent education in general—and that would require the founding of a world school association. "Therefore, we have to found a world school association, whose aim will not be confined to supporting the Waldorf School in Stuttgart, but the founding of schools working out of these principles."[53] These questions were discussed further that afternoon, without Rudolf Steiner present.

At the start of the meeting of July 31, 1920, there were hardly any questions. Rudolf Steiner used the opportunity to put the world school association on the agenda again. E. A. Karl Stockmeyer immediately came with the practical proposal to found the world school association straightaway and collect money that way. Following

---

52 Rudolf Steiner: *Faculty Meetings with Rudolf Steiner.* CW 300a, 1975, p. 182.
53 Ibid., p. 183f.

a lecture by Rudolf Steiner the evening before, a collection had been launched for the Waldorf School Association in Stuttgart—not for the larger endeavor. Rudolf Steiner wanted these two tasks, financing the Waldorf School in Stuttgart, on the one hand, and the furthering of Waldorf pedagogy and spreading the establishment of independent schools, on the other, to be distinct from one another, as represented in the teachers meeting of July 29, 1920. He did not want to ask for support for one thing one day and something else the next day. He was afraid, and rightly so, that such a course of action would weaken all endeavors and cause confusion. "We cannot heap attempt upon attempt. Because the planning of the World School Association has been crossed by yesterday's action."[54]

In the meeting of September 22, 1920, the theme came up again. Somebody mentioned that a German section of this World School Association could be founded now, whereupon one would have to first found the World School Association as such, before thinking of a German section. Referring to the earlier deliberations, Rudolf Steiner stressed that the reasons of July 1920 no longer applied. "We no longer have the momentum we could count on back then. Now we have to find a different approach to founding the World School Association."[55] Rudolf Steiner was astonishingly adept at making adjustments to the real-life situation with regard to his long-term planning. And as circumstances changed very fast, he changed his approach correspondingly—too fast for many of his coworkers. They had hardly digested the previous approach for the planned World School Association, and now everything had changed again.

Then on September 22, 1920, Rudolf Steiner considered it much more promising to found the World School Association not in Stuttgart or Dornach, but preferably in London, and since that was not possible, in The Hague. The Hague was now mentioned for the first time as a possible starting point for this international venture, conceived as spanning the whole world. For then it would have an international flair right from the start. In this meeting Rudolf Steiner tried to impress on the teachers, who thought very much in somewhat abstract terms, that it would be essential to find people who would be able to create the necessary mood in others, to fire them up and speak to unspoken questions living in people's hearts. The teachers, however, spoke only about propaganda.[56] At the end of this whole exchange, the decision was made to take up the theme again at the time of the higher education course planned for October and to try to co-opt the students who would be participating in that.

On the whole, the results of the discussions about the World School Association were a big disappointment. During the first higher education course, held October 12–16, 1920, at the Goetheanum, Rudolf Steiner decided to talk once again and in more depth about his intentions within the framework of an evening when the floor was open for questions. This time he was no longer concerned only about economical

54 Rudolf Steiner: *Faculty Meetings with Rudolf Steiner*. CW 300a, 1975, p. 202.
55 Ibid., p. 229.
56 Ibid., p. 231f.

questions, but—and that was new in October 1920!—about freeing the school from being dependent on the state. "When the Waldorf School was founded, I said: Great, the Waldorf School is great. But founding the Waldorf School is not enough, and we have to do more. This is just a tiny beginning, the beginning of a beginning. We will have truly founded the Waldorf school only when we have laid the basis for ten more such Waldorf schools in the next quarter year. Only then will the Waldorf School make a difference. In view of the present-day social situation in Europe, founding a single Waldorf school with 400, or 500, or 1000 children if you will, just will not cut it. Only when one Waldorf school spawns more, when they spring up everywhere, will they really make a difference, and then only when they are grounded in real, practical life. Raving about the ideas of the Waldorf school by itself is not enough, and people should fully realize that this should go hand-in-hand with advocating for independence from the state. Unless we insist, with all the strength we have, that the state leave this school its freedom and muster the courage to strive for the separation of school and state, the whole Waldorf school movement will be for the birds, because this movement makes sense only when it grows into a free spiritual life."[57]

The World School Association was to make as much money as possible within the shortest possible time to enable the founding of independent schools, the beginning stage of a free spiritual life. A few days later Rudolf Steiner specified that founding the World School Association should devolve to all those who had appeared in Dornach coming from outside Germany. "For it is necessary that we found school after school in all areas of the world from out of the pedagogical impulse that reigns in the Waldorf school. […] One day it will be possible to found this World School Association. It'll be a long time before this could be done from London, but it would be possible to do it from The Hague or a similar location[…]"[58] At that point Rudolf Steiner mentioned all the countries with representatives sitting in the hall at that moment, and he called on them to found a World School Association, to gather the material means to realize the culture he intended for all educational institutions both at the high school level and beyond—but only when a sufficient number of people would be convinced of its necessity.

On February 24, 1921, in Utrecht, on February 27, 1921, in The Hague, and on February 28, 1921, in Amsterdam, furthermore in Rotterdam and in Hilversum, Rudolf Steiner spoke extensively about the idea of a World School Association, hoping, of course, that such an impulse would be heard in the liberal-minded and open Netherlands. After a lecture in Utrecht, he answered a question from the audience as follows: "Well now, the overall aim here is to work toward a real freeing of the spiritual life, and with that the life in schools. To achieve that a form of a World School Association will be necessary. It should not be necessary anymore to ask the

---

57 Rudolf Steiner: *Soziale Ideen, Soziale Wirklichkeit, Soziale Praxis.* GA 337b, 1999, p. 248.
58 Rudolf Steiner: *The New Spirituality and the Christ-Experience of the 20th Century.* Lecture of October 17, 1920. CW 200, 1980, p. 29.

question whether Waldorf schools can be built up in many different countries. There will have to be a point when this becomes the obvious thing to do because a sufficient number of people are convinced[…]. A large movement would have to come into being, whereby, in fact, every individual who is aware of the needs of the time would become a member, so that the power of such a world league would prompt the founding of such schools everywhere. But something else will be needed when we are talking about such a World School Association—allow me to say this by the by, so to speak—namely that a certain form of idealism living among people has to die out. For example when somebody talks about the spiritual, anthroposophy, being something so lofty that it should not be debased by material things because it would contaminate anthroposophy if it were touched by base matter. This kind of idealism, which is so over-idealistic that the spiritual is dressed up with phrases of all kinds, extolling anthroposophy to such a degree that it gets lifted into some sort of cloud-cuckoo land and in the meantime keeps the checkbook closed, idealism of this sort does not go together with matters such as the founding of a World School Association. What is needed is a form of idealism that does not skimp when it comes to writing checks that support the ideals of mankind. Anthroposophically inspired spiritual science will have to penetrate into practical reality, that is to say not remain in the clouds but come down to the monetary level."[59]

Rudolf Steiner, who normally only pointed to areas of work that needed to be done in answer to a question to that effect, did not give up on this one when questions were asked concerning the World School Association, again in Holland. On February 27, 1921, in The Hague, Rudolf Steiner lifted the World School Association onto the level of another international organization, similar to the way this was done with the predecessor of the United Nations, the League of Nations. He said: "Basically people from all nations who have come to see that a free, emancipated spiritual life has to be at the basis of our educational system have to unite to form an international World School Association, which would do more to unify people in terms of real life forces than many another league founded today out of old principles of governance and out of old, abstract assumptions. Such a bond of nations, which would lie at the heart spiritually of a World School Association, would bring us a good deal further in bringing people from all over the globe together in a great, gigantic task […]. I am convinced that founding such a World School Association will be the most important task for the social development of humanity, as it would awaken a sense for real, concrete, free, spiritual life-wide circles."[60]

In Holland, Pieter de Haan and Josef van Leer picked up this idea. During the second anthroposophical *Hochschulkurs* [university course] in Dornach, Josef van Leer gave a kind of interim report about his activities at an evening of conversation on

---

59 Rudolf Steiner: *Erziehung zum Leben*. GA 297a, 1998, p. 41f.
60 Rudolf Steiner: *Waldorf Education and Anthroposophy 1*. CW 304, 1979, p. 56f.

April 8, 1921: "Highly esteemed listeners, a few weeks ago we talked about the World School Association for the first time in The Hague and in Amsterdam. Nothing will come of it, however, if we do not take immediate action. We did collect about 150 names the evening in The Hague, but names alone are not enough. Our friends in Holland are of good will but are too weak [...]. When you speak in England in this day and age about a free spiritual life, everybody will say: 'We do not need one, we have one.' Of course, this is not a real-life example, yet it is so. And as far as England's upper class is concerned, they can afford to educate their children the way they like, they do not need state-qualified teachers. When one wants to spread the word about a World School Association in England, one is dealing with quite different circumstances than in Germany, in Holland or in Switzerland. I believe Scandinavia, Holland, England— even when not neutral, but that does not matter—all those central European nations should unite. The Dutch were largely in favor, but those 25 well-known names will not help much. Dr. Steiner held about ten lectures in Holland, but even among the thousands of people who were there, there were maybe three voices for direct steps, and it will be difficult even to get those three to follow through.

"The question was asked, How do we spread the word? Every country will be a different story as far as practical steps are concerned. Our friends in Stuttgart know best what to do, because they are actively involved in the work. Therefore, I'd like to propose that the 25-plus people who are here, coming from our various countries— America, England, France, Switzerland, Italy—divide into different groups this very evening and decide how we will go about it! That's my proposal, that we do this right now [...]. Now I'd like to open the floor to ask if my proposal is the right starting point."[61]

Rudolf Steiner thanked Josef van Leer at the end of the evening, but reminded everybody that the work still needed to be done. However, Pieter de Haan and Josef van Leer's plans did not work out.

The idea of the World School Association was also picked up in Norway. Together with Christian Bugge, Fritz Brinck, and Christian Morgenstierne, Otto av Morgenstierne von Munthe (1884–1975) occupied himself intensively with Rudolf Steiner's ideas for social threefolding. He wrote about them, gave lectures, and planned the founding of a Rudolf Steiner school in Norway. In September 1921 he proposed to Rudolf Steiner to organize an international central office to work globally for the threefold social order and the impending organization of a World School Association in Dornach and offered to preside over this himself. The idea foundered this time as well. But he did succeed in gathering means to support the Goetheanum and organized traveling groups to Dornach.[62]

---

61 Rudolf Steiner: *Soziale Idee. Soziale Wirklichkeit. Soziale Praxis.* GA 337b, 1999, p. 252f.
62 Terje Christensen: Otto Christopher af Morgenstierne von Munthe. In: Bodo von Plato (ed.): *Anthroposophie im 20. Jahrhundert.* 2003, p. 544.

At the occasion of the laying of the foundation stone for the new school building of the school on the Uhlandshöhe on December 16, 1921, Rudolf Steiner spoke anew about the World School Association: "The school being founded here is seen as a model school for others. One thing is still missing, namely that the whole world comes to see that the founding of a model school like this is not enough, that such schools are needed everywhere, that hundreds and hundreds of people unite to form a World School Association in order to found these types of schools everywhere [...]. And until this impulse will be fulfilled in the world, the idea of the Waldorf school will not be able to fulfill its task."[63]

At the members meeting of the Association for Independent Schools the following year, on June 20, 1922, Rudolf Steiner came back to the idea of a World School Association and lamented that he had found people to be interested in the idea but that it had not yet been carried out, a "lamentable fiasco."[64] Attempts by Prof. Millicent Mackenzie after the lecture cycle Rudolf Steiner gave in August 1922 in Oxford, England, also did not lead to action. The initiative went no further than forming a founding committee. There were conversations in the leadership of the Anthroposophical Society in Dornach and among the faculty of the Waldorf School in Stuttgart right after the death of Rudolf Steiner in 1925, but these did not lead to any decisions.

Later in 1925 supporters in Holland, led by the General Secretary of the Dutch Anthroposophical Society, F. W. Zeylmans van Emmichoven, turned to the teachers of the Waldorf School in Stuttgart and to the board of the General Anthroposophical Society (*Allgemeine Anthroposophische Gesellschaft,* AAG) in Dornach in order to come to agreements about founding a World School Association.[65] Albert Steffen, however, one of the members of the Executive Council of the General Anthroposophical Society, declined to accept the leadership of the planned World School Association in a conversation of January 1, 1926, in Dornach. His fellow council member, Elizabeth Vreede, was then asked if she could become secretary, but refused likewise, pointing to Albert Steffen's decision. During this conversation, F. W. Zeylmans also mentioned the names of those from the Stuttgart Waldorf School he wanted to be involved in the venture, namely E. A. Karl Stockmeyer and Eugen Kolisko.

During a session with all board members in the days right after, however, they nominated Elizabeth Vreede to be a contact person between the AAG and the World School Association. In that position she took part in one session devoted to the topic and reported to Albert Steffen on January 12, 1926. But the venture was born under an unlucky star. On January 13, 1926, Elizabeth Vreede received a Dutch document that

---

63 Rudolf Steiner: *Rudolf Steiner in the Waldorf School.* CW 298, lecture of December 16, 1921. 1980, p. 119.
64 Ibid., Lecture of June 20, 1922, pp. 157–158.
65 Lilly Kolisko: *Eugen Kolisko. Ein Lebensbild.* 1961, p. 116ff. The events described here are taken from this account by Lilly Kolisko.

said a World School Association had been founded in Dornach on January 4, 1926, and that she herself had taken part in that as a representative (not as a contact person) of the Executive Council of the AAG. Now this was not in accordance with the report Elizabeth Vreede had given to Albert Steffen. She wanted to inform him about these latest developments, which could only too easily be misinterpreted. Albert Steffen had a visitor however, and for that reason he could not receive her and postponed the appointment. The Dutch documents also reached the Waldorf School in Stuttgart and caused quite a bit of commotion because a few people in Stuttgart were not exactly enthusiastic about founding the World School Association in Holland. It was reported that the World School Association had been founded in the presence of Elizabeth Vreede and had been sanctioned by the board of the AAG. Emil Leinhas threatened to resign from the board of the Association for Independent Schools if it were the case that the World School Association would be founded in the way it was reported.

Under much pressure, it was decided that the position of the Executive Council of the AAG should be clarified first before a decision could be made about further steps. It was a question whether the Waldorf School would join such a World School Association. So, a delegation consisting of Emil Molt, E. A. Karl Stockmeyer, and Herbert Hahn drove to Dornach on January 17, 1926, to meet with Albert Steffen. However, Steffen had not been informed yet by Elizabeth Vreede and declared the founding null and void. After the three delegated persons had returned to Stuttgart and had reported Albert Steffen's stance on January 19 to the faculty meeting of the Waldorf School, F. W. Zeylmans van Emmichoven was invited for a conversation. He traveled to Stuttgart and a conversation with him took place on January 22. This conversation achieved such a degree of consensus that they wanted to see the events of January 4 as a first step and wanted to plan further steps together. The plan was to talk with Albert Steffen to convince him to head the venture after all.

Before Albert Steffen could be contacted, he was privately informed—falsely, it was found out later—that the World School Association had been founded without his knowledge with the assent of Elizabeth Vreede, his colleague on the board. Still, as the chair of the Association for Independent Schools in Stuttgart, Albert Steffen was upset. Thereupon he directly addressed the members meeting on January 24, 1926, to make this alleged attack on his authority public and to make a counter move that can only be understood to mean that the interpersonal relationships among the board members had already been severely disturbed. For he announced the founding of a Rudolf Steiner Society to save the work of Rudolf Steiner. This was supposed to be a place that would foster the substance of anthroposophy inside the society, not within any one section in particular, an institution which would represent the work of Rudolf Steiner to the general public, which had not happened up until that point in time according to him. Marie Steiner was to take on the honorary protectorate of this society. The other board members knew nothing about it yet. Fred Poeppig (1900–1974), an eyewitness, commented on hearing Albert Steffen's initiative that the latter had soon lost faith, a few months after the death of Rudolf Steiner, in the "healthy further development of the Anthroposophical Society [...]," to the point where he could only see "the founding of a parallel society as the sole guarantee for the continued existence of the anthroposophical movement."[66]

On February 6, 1926, a meeting took place in Dornach attended by many members of the AAG. The activities surrounding the World School Association were on the agenda. Albert Steffen, Carl Unger, W. J. Stein, and F. W. Zeylmans van Emmichoven presented their viewpoints. From the contrasting accounts it became clear that the members were faced with a deep split within their society. The crisis that had been festering underground erupted due to these clashes surrounding the founding of a World School Association, and the plan foundered.[67]

There was a new attempt in 1929. Daniel N. Dunlop called people together for a conversation in London, a meeting that was also attended by younger colleagues from Germany, at least according to Ernst Weissert.[68] The upshot of this conversation is unclear at this point.

At the general meeting of the AAG on April 14, 1935, Daniel Dunlop, Willem Zeylmans van Emmichoven, Pieter de Haan, and Eugen Kolisko, among others, were expelled from the AAG.[69] As they constituted some of the most important people who stood for the impulse of the World School Association, the idea of the World School Association was discredited for decades.

All later plans and attempts failed as well; only in the 1970s did there arise a growing civic movement in society at large that allowed comparable organizations, such as Amnesty International and Greenpeace, to come into being. In the year 1973, the Dutch Waldorf movement celebrated its fiftieth anniversary with a large public conference about freedom in education. At this conference Rudolf Steiner's impulse to form a World School Association emerged again with a certain verve. In its wake Jan Beijer, Henriette van Dapperen, Hans Peter van Manen, Willem F. Veltman, and Paul Vink, a colorful mix of teachers, parents, and former students, mainly from The Hague, held a meeting on March 16, 1974, at the Vrije School in The Hague to discuss the question: "What steps can we take toward a World School Association?"[70] A number of Dutch supporters of the movement for the threefold social order, a few former students, parents, and teachers of the Dutch Waldorf schools, and the Dutch Anthroposophical Society attended. Also present were Bruno Gloor from Zürich

66 Lorenzo Ravagli: http://www.anthroweb.info/geschichte/geschichte-ag/alexanderlegende-und-spiritisten.html (retrieved December 15, 2017).

67 Emanuel Zeylmans: *Willem Zeylmans van Emmichoven. Ein Pionier der Anthroposophie.* 1979, p. 159.

68 Ernst Weissert: Von inneren Lebensgesetzen und -hoffnungen unserer Schulbewegung. In: *Forum International* Nr. 9, February/March 1976, p. 13. Except for this indication, this meeting has not been confirmed.

69 Thomas Meyer: *D.N. Dunlop. Ein Zeit- und Lebensbild [D.N. Dunlop. A Man of Our Time].* 1996, p. 317f.

70 Invitation for a meeting in The Hague on March 16, 1974, Archiv BFWS 8343; Protocol in Archiv NG.

and four representatives from Germany, among them Dr. Manfred Leist (German Federation of Waldorf Schools) and Andreas Büttner (former student). Especially Hans-Peter van Manen and Willem F. Veltman were very familiar with the concept because they had studied the idea of the World School Association for years in the context of the history of the Dutch Waldorf school movement. A further meeting resulted, which took place at the annual meeting of the German Federation of Waldorf Schools on May 4, 1974, in Pforzheim. Many announcements remained so many empty words. The threefold social order activists who were there could not capitalize on the possibilities and interest awakened there, and no further action was taken.

The only initiative that had arisen prior to these conversations among students and former students who had organized the first international Waldorf student conference at the Waldorf school in The Hague in 1975 was the publishing of a magazine called *Forum International* in Holland and Germany, which was dedicated to freedom in education. It should be noted that Ernst Weissert had written an article in *Forum International* in which he gave his opinion that the proclamation of a World School Association in the 1970s would remain a mere paper tiger,[71] arguing that, after the Second World War, the state monopoly had taken root everywhere to an alarming degree and registering that there was no longing for freedom in education.

For that reason the Federation of Waldorf Schools had decided to work practically for the worldwide Waldorf movement, doing so by promoting cooperation between teacher trainings and schools; by building up collaborative work among parents in Germany; and by founding the Hague Circle. Some of the members of the Waldorf student group described above—Andreas Büttner and Christa Geraets, Nana Göbel, Jean-Claude Lin, Andreas Maurer, and Paul Vink—started to build up the *Freunde der Erziehungskunst* [Friends of the Art of Education] in Germany in 1976, and a few years later the *Internationaal Hulpfonds* (International Financial Aid Fund) in Holland.

Both these organizations have worked since then with the impulse of the World School Association in a practical way and facilitated free education by providing financial help and support. People from Holland, Belgium, and Germany who were interested in the World School Association met in Krefeld in March 1977, in Stockholm on October 14, 1977, and April 7–9, 1978, once again in Hilversum.[72] The friendly conversations and the thoroughly prepared contributions by Hans-Peter van Manen and others aroused new enthusiasm but did not result in concrete further action.

---

71 Ernst Weissert: Von inneren Lebensgesetzen und -hoffnungen unserer Schulbewegung. In: *Forum International* Nr. 9, February/March 1976, p. 14.
72 Protocols, Communications and Reports in Archiv NG.

National and International Cooperation from 1919 to 1945

IN A LECTURE given on October 17, 1920, Rudolf Steiner noted: "Yes, it is fine that we have this one Waldorf School, but in and of itself it is nothing. It'll only become something when we would found ten more Waldorf schools in the quarter year, and more after that."[73] And at the members meeting of the Association for Independent Schools held June 17, 1921, Rudolf Steiner repeated that the founding of the Waldorf School on the Uhlandshöhe was only a beginning and that the mission of the Waldorf school would be fully realized only when more schools would be founded in rapid succession. "This model school is only a beginning in our time, because it is necessary to carry this spiritual impulse into education at large so that it can support the establishment of the threefold social order, which demands a truly free spiritual life with regard to education. This spiritual impulse can be achieved only when the Waldorf school idea becomes widespread."[74] It is clear that Rudolf Steiner was pursuing a vision of a large global school movement from the start, a movement that would spread further and further, in the context of a vision of self-determined education in contrast to education hemmed in by state regulations. He was not at all pleased by the fact that, by June 1921, no further Waldorf schools had been planned and did not mince his words about that at the first Annual General Meeting.

Arild Baron Rosenkrantz (1870–1964) organized a summer course in August 1921, held for English artists in Dornach, in which Millicent Mackenzie (1863–1942),[75] professor emerita of pedagogy at the University College of Cardiff, and her husband, John Stuart Mackenzie, professor emeritus of philosophy, took part. Impressed by this introduction to anthroposophical spiritual science, she organized a trip for English-speaking participants to a lecture cycle by Rudolf Steiner, which he held together with some colleagues from Stuttgart at Christmas 1921. Approximately 40 people answered her invitation and traveled with her and her husband from England to Dornach. Hundreds of people from a variety of European countries came and heard the so-called Christmas course for teachers, published under the title *Die gesunde Entwickelung des Menschenwesens. Eine Einführung in die anthroposophische Pädagogik und Didaktik* [Soul Economy and Waldorf Education].[76] Upon returning from Dornach, she initiated an educational conference in Stratford-upon-Avon, planned for April 1922, where Rudolf Steiner spoke. She founded and presided over the Educational Union, with the aim to spread Rudolf Steiner's pedagogical ideas in English and American education circles and in the public domain. She also organized

73 Rudolf Steiner: *The New Spirituality and the Christ-Experience of the 20th Century.* Lecture of October 17, 1920. CW 200, 1970, p. 28.
74 Rudolf Steiner: *Rudolf Steiner in the Waldorf School.* CW 298. Lecture, 1980, p. 95.
75 http://biographien.kulturimpuls.org/detail.php?&id=403 (site visited December 14, 2017); John Paull: Rudolf Steiner and the Oxford Conference: The Birth of Waldorf Education in Britain. EJES 3 (1) 2011, p. 54.
76 Rudolf Steiner: *Soul Economy.* CW 303, ⁴1987.

the summer course, "Spiritual Values in Education and Social Life," in Oxford, where Rudolf Steiner lectured (August 1922). At the close of the conference a resolution was published.[77] Next, she organized a public lecture by Rudolf Steiner held at Essex Hall in London on August 30, 1924. Through all her activities she became a leading personality in bringing the ideas of anthroposophical education to England, ideas that motivated the founders of English Waldorf schools.

Millicent Mackenzie, the first female professor in Great Britain, 1899. She organized Rudolf Steiner's 1922 educational lectures in Oxford.

Likewise, ideas about anthroposophical education were carried to middle-European countries and the East through the activities of Moritz Bartsch (1869–1944), rector in Breslau. Moritz Bartsch presided over the teacher society in Breslau and, as such, he was a spokesperson of a socially engaged group of teachers. Back in December 1908 he had become acquainted with Rudolf Steiner after a lecture in Breslau. This marked his entry into his own anthroposophical work which, from then on, he devoted himself to tirelessly. After the Stuttgart Waldorf School had been founded, he enthusiastically

---

77 The statement adopted by the Oxford Conference on Monday, August 28, 1922: The Oxford Conference Statement and Resolution:

1. At the close of this Conference on Spiritual Values in Education and Social Life we place on record our deep gratitude for all that we have received in the conference. The whole course of it has borne witness to the existence in our time of a widespread search and striving for the spiritual basis of human life. This striving has been expressed in the conference by men and women of widely different outlook and experience, and not least by those who, with firsthand knowledge of the appalling dangers from class and national conflict in our age, are actively working for political and economic understanding. The need for a practical cultivation of the spiritual life has thus been brought home to us the more insistently.

2. We are convinced that the mainspring of social life and health lies in the spiritual nature of man. Our complex and difficult civilization requires a fuller and freer inflow of the basic spiritual impulses. Such inflow can only take place through the individual human beings who are born into the world and unfold their faculties within it. Education in the widest sense of the word must open out the way. True education, therefore, whether of the child, the adolescent, or the adult, presupposes the deepest reverence and respect for the freedom of the human spirit in every individual.

3. The teachers in every age have in their hands the rising generation, who will accomplish, not what the older generations predetermine for them, but what springs from the fresh impulse of the evolving human spirit. They must be fully in touch with the world, autonomous in their profession, responsible to the conscience of humanity, working out of their own free spirit to pave the way for the unfolding spirit in their pupils.

4. Dr. Rudolf Steiner's lectures, for which we express our especial gratitude, have vividly brought home to us the human educational ideal. He has spoken to us of teachers who work freely and cooperatively, unfettered by external restrictions and regulations, evolving their educational method simply and solely from their perceptions of human nature. He has spoken to us of the kind of knowledge the teacher needs—a knowledge of man and of the world, not only scientific, but intimate, intuitive, artistic.

5. We therefore feel that the impulse should go out from this conference, to form a worldwide association for the foundation and support of schools in which the teachers will work freely and cooperatively on the basis that has been indicated. We propose that a provisional committee be formed to take the preliminary steps for giving effect to this resolution.

Participants in the conference "Spiritual Values in Education and Social Life" in Oxford, 1922

propagated the idea of the Waldorf school—also to the world at large. In 1925 he traveled through Germany, giving lectures in 35 towns, starting in Tübingen with a talk. "Present-Day Thoughts Concerning Education and the Independent Waldorf Schools. "[78] His lectures resonated strongly with the public, and this was not confined to people within the Waldorf school movement. The *Badische Volksschulzeitung*, a newspaper in Baden, southern Germany, wrote: "The fact that our Catholic standpoint does not endorse Steiner's teachings does not include a condemnation of the school. Much in the methodology seems promising for the world of today. We know that our modern school system, its academic achievements notwithstanding, has largely failed us. The Waldorf school is against one-sided intellectual education. Is there not a good reason that modern people possess so little feeling for authority, reverence, and piety? Criticism is justified, and we endorse the idea of this school, even though we reject any attendant philosophy."[79]

The *Hamburger Anzeiger*, a northern German paper in Hamburg, wrote: "The spiritual founder (of the Waldorf School) is the anthroposophist Rudolf Steiner. Whether one recognizes him as a philosopher or not, this school is a stroke of genius, based on a tremendous amount of work and comprehensive spirituality. At its heart is religiosity. It points the way to the future."[80] Rector Moritz Bartsch organized another lecture tour concentrating on education, held March 10–20, 1926, in Czechoslovakia, with major lectures in Brünn and Prague. Hans Eiselt, who led the German-speaking

---

78 Johannes Kiersch: Moritz Bartsch. In: Bodo von Plato (ed.): *Anthroposophie im 20. Jahrhundert.* 2003, p. 56.
79 Badische Volkszeitung: January 28, 1925, printed in: EK 2, June 1933, p. 360.
80 Hamburger Anzeiger: March 19, 1925, printed in: EK 2, June 1933, p. 360.

anthroposophical group in Prague at the time, reported that his words found a positive echo with people.[81] His many lectures also paved the way for the founding of the Waldorf school in Breslau. Therefore, we owe it to a few individuals that the ideas of Waldorf education spread among interested Europeans, and these people put a lot of effort into making these ideas public and accessible. We owe it to all the people who attended Rudolf Steiner's lectures in Stuttgart, called *Allgemeine Menschenkunde* [The Foundations of Human Experience], that the ideas of the Waldorf school were taken up in central Europe and were put into practice. It was they who went on to build up schools in Stuttgart, Hamburg, Essen, The Hague, and Cologne. Following the expressed wish of Rudolf Steiner, they attempted to connect both nationally and internationally. This was done especially by organizing conferences, but also by having an open-door policy in the school on the Uhlandshöhe. There was a steady stream of guests who wanted to personally get to know the new education, as was the case in January 1923 when 17 teachers from England visited lessons. In the same year the school received visitors from Japan, China, Persia, and India,[82] and the teachers had the impression that they were better able to understand the artistic and spiritual motivation behind the school than many a European visitor. Shortly before his death, when Rudolf Steiner could no longer travel and visit the Stuttgart Waldorf School, Günther Wachsmuth, at the time a member of the board of the AAG, wrote a letter on his behalf on March 17, 1925, that clearly formulated the special role the first Waldorf School was to play in the later building up of the Waldorf school movement. This is what it said:

> To the leadership council of the Waldorf School Stuttgart:
> On behest of Dr. Steiner, we would like to let you know that the faculty of the Waldorf School is authorized to take on a leadership role in Germany in guiding the schools that want to apply the anthroposophical pedagogical method. The responsibility thus given entails giving leadership both in matters of pedagogy and of finance by checking on economic viability. Schools that do not meet the requirements in these areas cannot be seen as representative of anthroposophical pedagogy.
> On behalf of the General Anthroposophical Society
> Dr. Günther Wachsmuth[83]

The teachers of the Waldorf School in Stuttgart, supported since 1920 by the Association for Independent Schools, took this assignment very seriously, feeling that they had been authorized by Rudolf Steiner, and from then on they had an even

---

81 Hans Eiselt: Vorträge von Rektor Bartsch in der Tschechoslowakei. In: N 22, May 30, 1926, p. 91f.
82 Alexander Strakosch: *Lebenswege mit Rudolf Steiner. Erinnerungen.* 1994, p. 427.
83 Letter of Dr. Günther Wachsmuth, dated March 17, 1925. Archiv LS 2.2.062.

2 2 62

Goetheanum,

Freie Hochschule für Geisteswissenschaft.

Sekretariat: Dornach b. Basel, Schweiz. Telephon: Dornach 133.
Haus Friedwart 1 Stock. ▬▬▬▬▬ den 17. März 1925

An den Verwaltungsrat der Freien Waldorfschule

S T U T T G A R T.
===========================

Im Auftrage Dr. Steiners möchten wir Ihnen mitteilen, dass in Zukunft die Waldorfschul-Lehrerschaft autorisiert ist, die Leitung über sämtliche in Deutschland befindlichen Schulen auszuüben, welche anthroposophische Pädagogik anwenden wollen.

Diese der Waldorflehrerschaft übertragene Verantwortung bringt es mit sich, dass diese Führung sich sowohl auf die Anwendung der anthroposophischen Pädagogik als auf eine Prüfung der wirtschaftlichen Grundlagen erstreckt.

Diejenigen Schulen, welche diesen Voraussetzungen nicht entsprochen, können nicht als Vertreter Anthroposophischer Pädagogik angesehen werden.

Für den Vorstand der Allgemeinen
Anthroposophischen Gesellschaft:

[signature]

Letter from Günther Wachsmuth of March 17, 1925, on behalf of Rudolf Steiner's regulating the leadership of the Waldorf school movement in Germany

greater sense of responsibility for any further steps. They therefore took part in the establishment of the other Waldorf schools in Germany as well as in other countries in some cases. They authorized the appointment of teachers, sent teachers to individual schools, and trained them in Stuttgart. They maintained a rich correspondence with all schools and initiatives. People such as E. A. Karl Stockmeyer, Herbert Hahn, Emil Molt, and Caroline von Heydebrand became important mentors with a great deal of moral authority. People sought their counsel in actual and potential conflicts of all kinds, and their advice was much requested.

In order to spread the Waldorf idea, conferences were held and local groups were founded by the Association for Independent Schools. Starting as early as 1923, a large public education conference was held every year in the springtime. Teachers from Stuttgart spoke there and talked shop about pedagogical challenges of all kinds. Shortly after the death of Rudolf Steiner an education conference was held in Stuttgart April 2–6, 1925, which was remarkably well attended. The conference was titled "Anthroposophical Study of the Human Being as a Basis for Education," and about 900 participants came. It was organized by the Executive Council of the General Anthroposophical Society together with the faculty of the Waldorf School in Stuttgart. Lectures were given by several teachers: Hermann von Baravalle, Count von Bothmer, Caroline von Heydebrand, Eugen Kolisko, Paul Oldendorf from Berlin, Karl Schubert, Walter Johannes Stein, and Rudolf Treichler. The Goetheanum was represented by Marie Steiner.[84] Directly after this conference, the organizers stayed in Stuttgart for two more days for extensive deliberations on how to guide the Waldorf school movement in a unified way after the death of Rudolf Steiner. They very much had in mind what Steiner had repeatedly said concerning the unifying element needed to give faculties a coherent direction. They were well aware of how utterly necessary this was and how Steiner had repeatedly pointed to the necessity of building this up out of one's own forces in order to create a strong alliance against the splintering and dividing tendencies that will naturally arise.

At this time the Goethe School in Hamburg-Wandsbek and the Rudolf Steiner school of Dr. Blass-Burghardt in Essen were regarded as schools working out of the Waldorf impulse. In these conversations in April, it was decided that these two schools would confer from then on with the Waldorf School in Stuttgart in all matters of appointing teachers and deciding financial questions.[85] In doing so, the Waldorf School in Stuttgart was to play the leading role in further developments in Germany; this was confirmed in accordance with the letter from Günther Wachsmuth. It was

84 Paul Oldendorf: Report on the Education Conference. AM November 8, 1925, p. 361ff. (Extended summaries detailing the contents of each individual lecture. It should be noted that these reports first appeared in the *Lehrer Journal fuer Ost und West Preussen* [*Teacher Journal for East and West Prussia*], Volume 56, Nr. 30/31) Continued in AM November 15, 1925, p. 371f, and January 22, 1925, p. 378ff.

85 E. A. Karl Stockmeyer in Mitteilungsblatt für die Mitglieder des Vereins für ein freies Schulwesen, Heft 8, March 1926, p. 24.

to be more than a leading role in fact, because the representatives of the two schools in Hamburg and Essen granted part of their autonomy for the sake of furthering the development of the movement as a whole.

The members meetings of the Association for Independent Schools were extremely important to bring about cohesion in the German Waldorf schools and to facilitate the exchange of information. A lot was written about these meetings in the newsletters so that local groups could follow how things developed as well. This was important because a large part of the contributions for the Stuttgart Waldorf School was raised in local groups. At the members meeting of the Association for Independent Schools on September 20, 1925, the news-sharing was not confined therefore to the Stuttgart school, but mention was made that the school in Essen had 200 students by now, the Goethe School in Hamburg-Wandsbek had about 100 students, and the school in Holland counted circa 100 students at that point. It was also reported that England had two smaller schools and that the Goetheanum in Switzerland had added a school for further education. Apart from that, the latest numbers of the Association for Independent Schools were presented, comprising about 60 local groups at the time, who were actively propagating Waldorf pedagogy. In March 1923, the Association for Independent Schools had 2898 members in Germany, and there were 660 members in 20 countries outside Germany. This number had grown to 4294 members in Germany by July 1925, and to 1152 outside of Germany. That meant that the number of members of the association had grown to 5446, not counting the donors and parents of the students—an enormous growth in a time that was not knitted together by modern media and in which every newsletter had to be sent by snail mail! Due to this huge enthusiasm and the willingness to contribute, the Stuttgart Waldorf School was able to cover its costs.

Interest in Waldorf school pedagogy was growing in Europe, mainly in the west, the north, and in central Europe. For central Europe, this was in large part due to the efforts of Rector Moritz Bartsch, who gave lectures on Waldorf pedagogy in 35 cities in 1925 alone. On February 26, 1925, for example, he was invited by Paul Besmöhn (1877–1964), member of the justice department and leader of the local group, to speak in Königsberg, and his lecture was described in great detail in the local teacher newsletter of East and West Prussia.[86] The majority of press comments was enthusiastic about the new light on the horizon in an ever gloomier pedagogical landscape. The successful conference of 1925 in Stuttgart was continued the next year, and from March 25–30, 1926, the fourth public education conferences, named "Der Weg des Kindes durch die Schule im Lichte der Pädagogik Rudolf Steiners" [The Child's Path through School in Light of Rudolf Steiner's Pedagogy], took place. Hermann von Baravalle, Paul Baumann, Christoph Boy, Clara L. Düberg, Herbert Hahn, Caroline von Heydebrand, Eugen Kolisko, Julie Lämmert, Ernst Lehrs, Bettina

86 Reprinted in A March 29, 1925, p. 50ff.

Mellinger, Friedel Nägerlin, Hans Rutz, Karl Schubert, Albert Steffen, Marie Steiner, and Ernst Uehli taught at this conference and it was attended by about 1000 people. Next to fulfilling their obligations in school, the faculty of the first Waldorf School was extremely active. Alone or together with others, they lectured at education conferences in various countries. In Holland, for example, a pedagogical conference for members took place on May 8 and 9, 1926, in which Daan van Bemmelen, J. van't Hof, Eugen Kolisko, Max Stibbe, Elizabeth Vreede, Günther Wachsmuth, and Ita Wegman played roles.

One conference was especially important to the Stuttgart teachers, namely the one that took place May 31–June 2, 1926. It was successfully hosted and co-organized in collaboration with the *Zentralinstitut für Erziehung und Unterricht* [Central Institute for Education] in Berlin, and its theme was "Die Freie Waldorfschule." It was organized by Dr. Paul Oldendorff and financed by the Zentralinstitut.[87] This was the first time a conference had been organized in cooperation with a public institution. Paul Oldendorff, a grammar school teacher from Berlin-Neukölln who had a special interest in Rudolf Eucken, would later become one of the most important pioneers of the Waldorf school in Berlin, founded at the end of the 1920s. The head of the *Zentralinstitut*, Privy Councillor Ludwig Pallat, gave the opening address. Other speakers were: Hermann von Baravalle, Moritz Bartsch from Breslau, Paul Baumann, Count Fritz von Bothmer, Herbert Hahn, Caroline von Heydebrand, Ella Kocherhanns, Eugen Kolisko, Margarethe Kugelmann (1895–1970), Paul Oldendorff, Natalie Turgenieff-Pozzo (1886–1942), Hans Rutz (1889–1973), Erich Schwebsch, Walter Johannes Stein, and Max Wolffhügel.[88] There were about 700 participants in the conference as a whole, and some events even drew up to 1000 people. On display was student work from the Stuttgart Waldorf School. Representatives of the Prussian ministry of culture and numerous public school teachers took part, and the mood was open and positive throughout, which gave rise to the hope that the ground had been tilled for a future opening of a Waldorf school in Berlin.

Caroline von Heydebrand was one of the most prolific lecturers. Soon after her return from Berlin to Stuttgart, she was off to London again, to attend a conference at the New School the weekend of June 19–21, 1926, in order to give lectures that were very happily received. Especially her lecture about the artistic base of teaching was experienced as a guiding light. She created this conference together with Violetta Plincke, eurythmists from London, and children of the New School, whose eurythmy

---

87 Günther Böhme: *Das Zentralinstitut für Erziehung und Unterricht und seine Leiter. Zur Pädagogik zwischen Kaiserreich und Nationalsozialismus.* Karlsruhe, 1971.

88 Report on the MV in Mitteilungsblatt für die Mitglieder des Vereins für ein freies Schulwesen, Jg. 1926/27 Nr. 3, October 1926, p. 14; Paul Oldendorff: Einige Vorbemerkungen zur Tagung der Freien Waldorfschule im Zentralinstitut für Erziehung und Unterricht in Berlin. In: N 18, 2. May 1926, p. 75f.; Paul Oldendorff: Die Tagung der Freien Waldorfschule im Zentralinstitut für Erziehung und Unterricht. In: N 25, 20. June 1926, p. 105f.; M. Bartsch: Die Freie Waldorfschule. In: G 25, 20. June 1926, p. 199f.

demonstrations contributed to the success of the conference.[89] This conference was more or less a coming-out, in which the daily practice of this form of education was introduced to the public in England, which so far had only made the acquaintance with the background thinking by several lectures given by Rudolf Steiner. In Lillehammer, a pedagogical course with Curt Englert-Faye was held for Norwegian and Swedish teachers in August 1926.[90]

So, there was a lively international series of conferences going on, resulting in a lot of travel for the Stuttgart teachers, which was more of a to do back then. The next international conference in 1926 was held in The Hague, Holland, October 28–November 5. It was announced as "Rudolf Steiner's Answers to the Demands of the Time." The conference was carried by the leadership of the Dutch Anthroposophical Society together with the faculty of the Vrije School in The Hague. The usual teachers held lectures: Hermann von Baravalle, Paul Baumann, Margarethe Blass, Daniel Nicol Dunlop, Cecil Harwood, Caroline von Heydebrand, Jan van 't Hoff, Eugen Kolisko, Ernst Lehrs, Siegfried Pickert, Walter Rummel (1884–1953), Hans Rutz, Erich Schwebsch, Walter Johannes Stein, Max Stibbe, Max Wolffhügel, Gerlind Zaiser (1899–1972), and Willem Zeylmans van Emmichoven. An exhibition featuring schoolwork from Stuttgart and The Hague was organized to introduce the public to actual student work done in Waldorf schools. The newspaper *De Telegraaf* reported extensively on October 31. The afternoon of November 3, Count Fritz von Bothmer, with children of the Waldorf School in Stuttgart, presented a public performance of the gymnastic lessons he had developed [now known as Bothmer Gymnastics] in the *Koninklijke Schouwburg*, the theater in The Hague. It is said that Daniel Dunlop shared his idea of an anthroposophical world conference with a small circle of people.

During the members meeting of the Association for Independent Schools, held in 1926, E. A. Karl Stockmeyer reported that the propaganda for the idea of the Waldorf School had fallen short in the past couple of years due to the economic woes and that preparatory steps were therefore to be made to come to a more comprehensive organization (World School Association). No details were mentioned yet.[91]

After a short Christmas break, many colleagues at the Waldorf School on the Uhlandshöhe took off again right away. At the invitation of the teacher society in Silesia, a conference with the theme "Rudolf Steiner's Educational Impulse" took place from January 3–6, 1927, in the trade union hall in Breslau. Hermann von Baravalle, Herbert Hahn, Elisabeth Hensel (1887–1954), Caroline von Heydebrand, Eugen Kolisko, Karl Schubert, Erich Schwebsch, Walter Johannes Stein, E. A. Karl Stockmeyer, Alexander Strakosch, Ernst Uehli, and Max Wolffhügel traveled there.

89 Notes on the Education Conference held at the New School, London. In: N 28, July 11, 1926, p. 117f.
90 Letter of C. Englert-Faye dated August 28, 1926, to E. A. Karl Stockmeyer. Archiv LS 3.18.09.
91 Mitteilungsblatt für die Mitglieder des Vereins für ein freies Schulwesen, Jg. 1926/27, Nr. 3, October 1926, p. 14.

With this conference a big step toward founding a Waldorf school in Breslau was taken and the public was very interested.

The next big education conference was held in Stuttgart as in previous years, April 8–13, 1927. At this conference E. A. Karl Stockmeyer presented the *Gesellschaft für die Pädagogik Rudolf Steiners* [Society for Rudolf Steiner Education]. This was intended to be a kind of central society that would be a hub to knit the German sister schools together organizationally. It was in line with Stockmeyer's intentions to build up a World School Association that this German society would in turn form part of a worldwide organization serving Rudolf Steiner's pedagogical impulse. E. A. Karl Stockmeyer—in accordance with Günther Wachsmuth's letter of March 17, 1925, and the ensuing conversation with his colleagues in April 1925—was firmly convinced that the mother school in Stuttgart should be a model for newly founded schools. He wanted to create a unified school movement, not niche schools that would be short-lived.[92] E. A. Karl Stockmeyer made the following remarks concerning this point: "The task of the Waldorf School Association became harder and harder to carry out. Therefore we set out in the autumn of 1925 to work anew on a plan of Rudolf Steiner's, namely the plan to found a World School Association, which he had intended to start up as early as 1920. It was intended to bring about possibilities to found free schools everywhere. This association would not be limited to promoting schools working out of the impulse of Steiner's pedagogy, or Steiner inspired schools, but to promoting independent schools in general.

"For a variety of reasons, this World School Association did not get off the ground in 1920 or thereafter. We wanted to take up this plan in a different form now, this time as a society with the aim to propagate Steiner's pedagogy specifically. We hoped that such an institution would unify an otherwise quite differentiated movement, and that this unity would both lend the movement strength and open up new avenues for financial support. In our initial attempts, it soon became clear that we could only make progress once associations were founded in each separate country. Two such associations were founded by 1926, one in England and one in the United States. Preparations were also made in Germany to found such an association which led to the founding of the Society for Rudolf Steiner Education in Germany in the spring of 1926."[93]

E. A. Karl Stockmeyer also made clear how individual tasks and societies would be profiled and coordinated, saying at the end: "The Society for Rudolf Steiner

92 E. A. Karl Stockmeyer: Waldorfschule?–Schulbewegung? In: N 52, December 25, 1927, p. 206; E. A. Karl Stockmeyer: An die Mitglieder des Vereins für ein freies Schulwesen. In: Mitteilungsblatt für die Mitglieder des Vereins für ein freies Schulwesen Heft 6, April 1927, p. 27ff.; E. A. Karl Stockmeyer: Über die Aufgaben der Schulbewegung. In: ZPRSt 1, October 1927, p. 8; Norbert Deuchert: Die Anfänge einer internationalen Schulbewegung. BhB Advent 1985, p. 88.
93 E. A. Karl Stockmeyer: Über die Aufgaben der Schulbewegung. In: ZPRSt 1, October 1927, p. 6ff.

Education in Germany will collaborate closely with associations in other countries, including all manner of special school societies that have the same aim. It sees the totality of these associations with all the schools they represent as the carrier of the global movement for Rudolf Steiner's education."

So, it was very clear that the Waldorf education movement had been conceived as a world movement and was to be organized accordingly. When is a unified approach meaningful, fruitful, and productive, and when is it hindering and laming? This remained an essential question of the Waldorf school movement throughout the century. Autonomy of individual schools and commonality go together; they even depend on one another. If applied in the wrong place, however, the two aspects can hinder one another. It has not always been possible to find the right balance.

In 1928 five schools with their school associations had become members of the Society for Rudolf Steiner Education: Stuttgart, Hamburg, Essen, Hannover, and Berlin, as well as the two school associations in Nürnberg and Breslau, where schools were to be founded as well. No long-term results were reached internationally. The two newly founded schools in Switzerland replied to E. A. Karl Stockmeyer with a memo, titled "Waldorf School? School Movement? An Answer to Mr. E. A. Karl Stockmeyer, February 17, 1928."

In this memo they rejected the plan for a second school building in Stuttgart, saying that the larger school movement had a more urgent need for the money. More importantly, however, they opposed the idea of a model school, saying, "One can only copy or reject the model, a free relationship is impossible!" Werner Witzemann had formulated this opinion January 21, 1928; it was echoed both in Holland and in Norway. Signe Roll from Oslo wrote a letter to Erich Gabert, dated February 24,[94] stressing that Rudolf Steiner's pedagogical ideas were an archetype of human education that could be realized differently depending on people, place, teachers, and children. So, she stressed the aspect of autonomy of individual schools, which several teachers, particularly those outside of Germany, urgently wished to bring about as a contribution to featuring individual schools.

Hermann von Baravalle, Caroline von Heydebrand, and Karl Schubert traveled to England once again July 22–24, 1927, in order to give lectures at the Kings Langley Education Conference.[95] These lectures were held in the large barn of the school and were meant to support the hesitant growth of the Priory School in Kings Langley. Lectures were well attended and the discussions afterward were stimulating. Many listeners had never heard anything about Waldorf pedagogy and were especially impressed by Karl Schubert's lively accounts of his work with learning-disabled children. The teachers thus supported not only the large public conferences but also smaller local events like these. This involved a great deal of travel and public

---

94 Archiv LS 3.16.013.
95 M. Mackenzie: The Kings Langley Education Conference. In: N 37, September 11, 1927, p. 147.

appearances, a stupendous workload that especially the three lecturers who had come to Kings Langley took upon themselves.

Conferences featuring Rudolf Steiner's pedagogy were held in Essen (May 13–15, 1928), in Hamburg (May 30–June 4, 1928), and in Hannover (October 3–5, 1925). The conference in Hamburg was the sixth largest Waldorf school educational conference held someplace other than in Stuttgart for the first time. Among the lecturers was Dr. Margarethe Blass of the school in Essen, who gave a talk about "The Moral Effect of Rudolf Steiner's Pedagogy."[96] Just as the above-mentioned polemics between E.A. Karl Stockmeyer and the Swiss, especially Curt Englert-Faye, were at their height, *Menschenschule* published a critique written by several Swiss participants in the educational conference in Hamburg of 1928. It said: "In contrast to earlier conferences, where only representatives of the Independent Waldorf School spoke, this time there were also speakers from the host school in Wandsbek and the Rudolf Steiner school in Essen. Allowing this little bit of an expansion marked a notable relaxation in the heretofore strictly closed uniformity, which was beneficial. In spite of this beginning differentiation where different personal nuances could be voiced, there still was a pretty stiff, almost clique-like uniformity in ethos, style, and habits of all speakers, which was not all that edifying. After all, the generally uniform way of putting things and the recognizable jargon of every individual speaker betrayed a certain dependence on the 'mother and model school' in Stuttgart, as if an absolute and infallible dogma of the 'anthroposophical norm in education' had been realized there, to be copied and conformed to."[97]

Curt Englert-Faye formulated his opinions even more sharply in an exchange of letters with E.A. Karl Stockmeyer in 1927 and 1928. On September 12, 1928, he let him know: "I do have to say, however, whenever I'm faced with this one thing that comes up whenever there are differences of opinion, that I need to register a patent tendency toward Catholicism within the so-called school movement that is a matter of exclusive cliquishness based on emotional abstractions. It has gotten so far, now that these elements have become the norm within the school movement, that every moral right and every spiritual authority of the Waldorf School (Uhlandshöhe) comes down to continuing to dispense goods they have been entrusted with, handing them on to third parties, even though these third parties have access to the same sources out of which things came to the Waldorf School before. […] This right of dispensation, however, is nothing more than a comedy, which nobody can take seriously anymore."[98] This was specifically in reference to the accessibility of the lectures Rudolf Steiner gave in 1919 and the professional meditations that Rudolf Steiner had entrusted to the Waldorf teachers. In the 1920s and 30s there were no printed versions of these texts as

96 Margarethe Blass: Die moralische Wirkung der Pädagogik Rudolf Steiners. In: ZPRSt 1, April 1929, p. 9ff.
97 Curt Englert-Faye: Msch 12, 1928, p. 393.
98 Note written by Curt Englert-Faye dated September 12, 1928, to E.A. Karl Stockmeyer, Archiv LS 3.18.42.

there are today. Those who wanted to read them had to ask the faculty of the Stuttgart school. The usual procedure was to write a letter to E. A. Karl Stockmeyer or to Herbert Hahn, sometimes other colleagues, with the request to receive these texts. When such a request came during Rudolf Steiner's lifetime, the faculty in Stuttgart would ask Rudolf Steiner for his permission. Of course, that was a simple way to avoid making a personal decision. After Rudolf Steiner's death, many letters were written to Dornach and to the board of the Anthroposophical Society, especially Marie Steiner and Albert Steffen, to ask for permission to publish the texts. This procedure was experienced by many as a form of tutelage, to which people did not want to subject themselves. Also, there was a dilemma. On the one hand, the Stuttgart teachers felt a responsibility toward Rudolf Steiner because he had charged them with the responsibility. On the other hand, they did not want to exercise the function of controlling others. So, here we have a dilemma of freedom, which inevitably will arise and is unavoidable.

In the meantime, the Association for Independent Schools in Stuttgart was expanded further because the school was primarily dependent on financial support from its members. In 1928 the association was represented in 11 countries, each with somebody who carried the main responsibility and a local group leader.[99]

> Argentina (Buenos Aires): Franz Schneider
> Austria: Othmar von Noeth (Graz), Paula Köhler (Innsbruck), Josef Pippich
>   (Klagenfurt), Hans Kienesberger (Gmunden), Otto Paul Tiefbrunner
>   (Linz), Dr. Viktor Lawatschek and Karl Behensky (Salzburg), Helmuth
>   Alscher-Bassenheim (Vienna)
> Czechoslovakia (Prague): Dr. Hans Eiselt
> Denmark (Copenhagen): Johannes Hohlenberg
> England (London): Nina Beverly
> Finland: Ida Moberg (Helsingfors), Lisa Wegelius (Wasa)
> France (Strasbourg): Elisabeth Weissbach
> Holland (Rotterdam): Lena Struik
> Independent State of Danzig (Zoppot): Lili Leidreiter
> Sweden (Stockholm): Rut Nilsson
> United States (Chicago): Ida Bilz

The seventh large education conference was held in Stuttgart again March 21–26, 1929, on the theme "Was hat Anthroposophie in der Erziehung dem Sozialen Leben zu gaben? [What Can Anthroposophy in Education Contribute to Social Life?]." In contrast to previous conferences, this one was meant as an internal conference for practicing Waldorf teachers. As in previous years, experienced teachers held the lectures: Hermann von Baravalle, Paul Baumann, Karl Ege, Caroline von

---

99 Aus der Schulbewegung. In: ZPRSt 2, July 1928, p. 90.

Heydebrand, Robert Killian, Eugen Kolisko, Walter Johannes Stein, Alexander Strakosch, Martin Tittmann, and Ernst Uehli. The teachers of the Waldorf school in Zürich decided not to come and felt misunderstood by the Germans. This stance must have been caused by the uniform attitude of the Stuttgart teachers, who were actually not quite as unified internally as it seemed from the outside. In any case, the stance the Swiss teachers took remained a constant challenge: to seek the unity behind the Waldorf impulse not in outer appearances of sameness, but in the common spiritual source. Mutual tolerance was not easily established between the two groups; it was quite a learning process in how to get along.

In order to further Waldorf pedagogy not only in German circles and spread the word more in the world at large, Caroline von Heydebrand traveled to Helsingör in August 1929, just as she had to Berlin in 1926, in order to attend the fifth Congress of the World Society for Educational Renewal held in Schloss Kronborg. There were presentations on Dalton-plan pedagogy and Montessori, for example. Well-known educators from 43 countries attended the Congress. Caroline von Heydebrand reported: "I was torn between boundless admiration for the intellectual handstands in some of the presentations on the one hand, especially the ones from the field of psychological analysis, and a deep horror concerning human development across the globe on the other." A little later she writes: "Again and again one finds oneself thinking: How human are the people who want to be educators and how inhuman are the methods that they contrive!"[100]

Starting in 1929 there were also pedagogical summer courses in Norway with Hermann von Baravalle and Annamarie Groh (1891–1976). These conferences, organized by the Rudolf Steiner school in Oslo, strengthened the collaboration between northern European Waldorf teachers and offered the opportunity to interested outsiders to learn more about Waldorf pedagogy. The conference for educators was continued July 5–26, 1931, at the community college of Vonheim in Follebu with Edith Maria Granström (1884–1956) and Annemarie Groh. About 40 Norwegians and some Swedes took part. Directly after that, July 27–August 11, 1931, a pedagogical course initiated by Anna Wager-Gunnarsson (1873–1957) and Lisa Svanberg took place in the Swedish town of Viggbyholm, again attended by a number of Norwegian teachers. Curt Englert held twenty lectures, Signe Roll, six. The lectures and the discussions afterward were so engaging that people often did not hear the bell for lunch. There was eurythmy and painting in the afternoon.[101] In July 1932 the fourth of these Norwegian summer courses was organized.

The public conferences on education organized by the independent Waldorf school in Stuttgart continued. The eighth conference took place April 12–16, titled "Cultural Questions of the Present and Rudolf Steiner's Pedagogy." All teachers,

100 Caroline von Heydebrand: Nachklänge. In: ZPRSt 6, February 1930, p. 317f.
101 Ingeborg Sjögren: Aus Schweden. In: N 46, November 15, 1931, p. 182f.

be they German, Swiss, Dutch, English, or Norwegian, faithfully and tenaciously took on the task of representing Waldorf pedagogy to the outside world. And this in difficult times, when the economic circumstances were catastrophic and traveling was strenuous. It took a great deal of selflessness, and teachers often sacrificed family life and health for the great cause of a school where children can grow into healthy and self-reliant people. Sacrifices were made to make this all possible and, instead of an Easter holiday, another conference was organized.

The Central Institute for Education in Berlin planned a conference about new school initiatives, especially the movement for educational reform, to be held in 1930. The Waldorf School on the Uhlandshöhe was invited to take part in the preparation but declined. It is an open question as to why; it is not clear whether it was due to the incredible workload, the fact that the Stuttgart conference took place more or less at the same time, that teachers were overtaxed and had to concentrate on pressing questions within the school itself, or that it was due to people not perceiving or being interested in the political and educational situation in society at large. Instead of the Stuttgart teachers, Curt Englert-Faye, together with Dr. Wolfgang Rudolph from the school in Essen, went to Berlin, where the conference took place April 10–12, 1930.

Two years later the Stuttgart teachers took part again in full force. For Whitsun 1932, the Central Institute in Berlin, led by Prof. Ludwig Pallat, sent out an invitation to take in yet another conference at the Waldorf school in Berlin. The conference "… ran splendidly. It had been originally planned to last three days, but was prolonged two days because the eurythmy offerings and the gymnastic demonstrations had to be repeated two times. In answer to the wish of many of the participants, discussion sessions were organized for the afternoons. Pedagogical publications from Berlin reported enthusiastically about this singular conference. The general *German Teachers Journal* wrote on June 1: "Even the large halls of the new town hall Schöneberg, the Bürgersaal, and the Brandenburghalle, where a great variety of student work was exhibited that showcased what the Waldorf school is about, could hardly handle the number of visitors. About 1000 people came every single day." The article closes with the announcement that plans were afoot "to showcase the pedagogical work of Waldorf teachers, which had recently been highly acclaimed in Württemberg, and to create a constant field of activity with lectures and courses in Berlin in the future."[102]

There was a great wish to spread the new insights and action opportunities offered by anthroposophy and to reach as many people as possible as long as the political situation still allowed it. Thus, the idea of an international youth conference was born, to be organized as a summer camp, the Kamp de Stakenberg. Hans Grelinger pursued the idea to organize a meeting place where younger people could get to know anthroposophy and could meet the older anthroposophists. The general secretary of

---

102 Report by Ernst Uehli in EK Heft 2, June 1933, p. 362f.

the Dutch Anthroposophical Society, Frederik Willem Zeylmans van Emmichoven, supported him, and the Dutch Society shouldered the planning. After a full year of preparation by Hans Grelinger, this rich event took place in August 1930. One way the news was spread was by sending around pamphlets written in German, Dutch, and English. It was a festive event where many liberal and open-minded people with international backgrounds met. The campground was prepared to accommodate 400 participants but had to be expanded to harbor far over 1000 young people who came from all European countries. A few people came from as far away as China, India, and Africa. The many youngsters who came found something that formed a counterbalance to the fanatical spirit of that time, something that inspired them and affected people far and wide, which in turn had its effect on the expansion of the Waldorf movement internationally.

In order to bring about cooperation among the German Waldorf schools, which founded an association a few years later, it was important that conversations could take place—without pressure from National Socialism— before the actual founding occurred. There were several common challenges the schools needed to discuss. There was a meeting in Hannover November 8–9, 1930, where the Prussian schools could talk about problems they all faced.[103] When the question was discussed whether any money should be requested from the government, the teachers from Berlin rejected any such proposals because they wanted to avoid any state interference with the pedagogical work. Emil Molt also rejected any form of state control.

The ninth official education conference—a Stuttgart staple of these early years—took place March 27–30, 1931, and was named "Erziehung im Zeitalter der Technik" [Education in the Technical Era]. It was followed by the tenth public education conference on the theme of "Goethes Metamorphosengedanke in seiner Bedeutung für die Erziehung" [Goethe's Idea of Metamorphosis and Its Significance for Education], held in 1932. This was the last public conference organized by the Waldorf School Association in Stuttgart.

In 1933 the teachers of the Stuttgart Waldorf School still organized a series of public lectures June 13–July 15,[104] but after that no more public lectures were announced. The lectures held in 1933 were announced in *Erziehungskunst* [The Art of Education] in such a way that one notices how one had to kowtow to those in power already this early. In other announcements, one can notice the reference to German idealism and how much they built on that: "From the moment the Waldorf School was founded by Rudolf Steiner, the teachers were inspired by the creative impulses of German idealism. This has been a steady inner orientation that has informed every single educational measure, serving as a counterweight to the present

---

103 Wenzel M. Götte: *Erfahrungen mit Schulautonomie*. 2006, p. 288f. and report in Archiv LS 3.4.099.
104 EK 2, June 1933, p. 383f.

intellectual and materialistic attitude that has exercised such a pernicious influence on German education in the last decades. Working in this vein, the teachers would like to continue to contribute actively to the nationwide effort to shape the German educational system and elevate our citizens, in that all our striving and experience serve to further the impulses of German idealism."[105] Specific mention should be made of a number of activities that created cohesion in working together with parents who supported Waldorf education. There were monthly assemblies, school concerts, festivals in summer and autumn, and, especially, performances of the Christmas plays from Oberufer. Ernst Weissert later remembered that a mother experienced these festivals in the Waldorf School as "light in the darkness."[106]

Pedagogical Working Group/ Pedagogical Section at the Goetheanum

WITH THE FOUNDING OF THE General Anthroposophical Society at the end of 1923 and the beginning of 1924, Rudolf Steiner also inaugurated the *Freie Hochschule für Geisteswissenschaft* [Free School for Spiritual Science] with its separate sections. Rudolf Steiner himself led the Pedagogical Section. Its task was not to guide individual schools or kindergartens, but to direct and coordinate further pedagogical research and to lead the continuing development of Waldorf pedagogy. Marie Steiner reports on what happened during Rudolf Steiner's illness, when he was no longer able to lead the affairs of the Pedagogical Section. She writes: "Dr. Steiner had been in charge of the Pedagogical Section and, during the last phase of his illness, he indicated that the faculty of the Waldorf School had to supervise the affairs of the Section while he was incapacitated."[107]

After the death of Rudolf Steiner the leadership was transferred to the Executive Council of the General Anthroposophical Society. From that point onward there were different—at times conflicting—interpretations of how to carry on the work of the Pedagogical Section. A few teachers from the first Waldorf School, appointed by Rudolf Steiner, considered themselves the guardians of the pedagogical impulse of the Waldorf school and viewed the [Stuttgart] faculty as the section, a viewpoint the board at the Goetheanum rejected.[108] Other teachers of schools founded by 1925 saw the need to create a center of the Waldorf movement in Dornach. In 1927, Curt Englert-Faye organized open pedagogical discussions at the large conferences at the Goetheanum; these were actually quite well received.

---

105 EK 2, June 1933, p. 383f.
106 Ernst Weissert: Von den Motiven und Lebensphasen der Schulbewegung. In: EK 8/9, 1969, p. 318.
107 Marie Steiner in: *Pädagogische Arbeitsgruppe am Goetheanum*. Msch 5, 1947, p. 15.
108 Ibid.

During the large conferences in the years after that, he extended invitations for internal discussions, but these were only sparsely attended. Questions and requests for pedagogical deepening, however, continued to be addressed to Marie Steiner. Therefore Marie Steiner asked Albert Steffen, the head of the Executive Council of the General Anthroposophical Society, whether he could imagine leading the Pedagogical Section himself, but he declined. When asked if he could entrust the leadership to Marie Steiner, Isabella de Jaager (1892–1979), and Curt Englert, he agreed and gave them his blessing.[109] Thereupon the Pedagogical Working Group at the Goetheanum was founded in 1931.[110]

The first activity this group organized was a conference right after the large Michael conference. It took place October 7–13, 1931. It had the title "Geistes-schulung und Menschenbildung" [Spiritual Training and Education] and was carried by Swiss teachers.[111] The speakers were Willi Aeppli (Basel), Hermann von Baravalle (Stuttgart), Roman Boos (Basel), Curt Englert-Faye (Zürich), Friedrich Eymann (Bern), Isabella Niederhäuser de Jaager (Dornach), Max Leist (Bern), Marguerite Lobeck-Kürsteiner (Zürich), Karl Rittersbacher (Basel), Marie Steiner (Dornach), Alexander Strakosch (Stuttgart), Ernst Uehli (Stuttgart), Johannes Waeger (Zürich) and Hans W. Zbinden (Zürich). There were, however, many teachers who were against such a collaboration for various reasons, and they did not take part in the Dornach conferences organized by this working group.

Interestingly enough, the Michael Conference of September 28–October 5, 1932, was billed as the first international pedagogical conference by the leadership at the Goetheanum. In his introduction, Albert Steffen made no mention of the previous conference and made it seem as if this conference at the Goetheanum marked a new beginning for international cooperation. Speakers at this conference were Paula Dieterich (Hamburg), Elisabeth Klein (Dresden), Marie Kruse (Berlin), Erich Schwebsch (Stuttgart), Julius Solti (Hamburg), Albert Steffen (Dornach) and Max Wolffhügel (Stuttgart). Ernst Weissert, at that time teaching at the Rudolf Steiner school in Berlin, was present at this international conference and experienced it as a high point in the next phase in school development after Rudolf Steiner's death.[112]

Whereas the activities of the teachers of the Waldorf School in Stuttgart had been the face of the school movement and were also seen as such by the general public,

109 Curt Englert, together with Hans Werner Zbinden and Paul Jenny, his classmates from the humanistic grammar school in Basel, founded the Waldorfschule in Zürich, which started in the spring of 1927. Andreas Dollfuss and Oddvar Granly: Curt Englert-Faye. In: Bodo von Plato (ed.): *Anthroposophie im 20. Jahrhundert.* 2003, p. 175f.
110 Reported in N 35, August 30, 1931, p. 140.
111 H.R. Niederhäuser in a letter to Ernst Weissert dated December 14, 1965, Archiv BFWS 8239.
112 Ernst Weissert: Dr. Paula Dieterich. In: LR 8, 1973, p. 68; Ernst Weissert: Von den Motiven und Lebensphasen der Schulbewegung. In: EK 8/9, 1969, p. 315. Ernst Weissert: Aus der Arbeit des Bundes der Freien Waldorfschulen. Die Schulbewegung 33 Jahre nach dem Wiederbeginn. BhB 1978, p. 12.

now the pedagogical activity emanating, in the widest sense, from the Goetheanum gained prominence, especially because of the Pedagogical Working Group and Curt Englert-Faye. Publications such as the magazine, *Menschenschule* [Human School] (edited by Curt Englert-Faye), seemed to be more in tune with the times than the bimonthly *Zur Pädagogik Rudolf Steiners* [Rudolf Steiner's Pedagogy], later named *Erziehungskunst* [Art of Education], even though the contributions in the latter were more thorough both in content and methodological underpinnings.

These conferences at Michaelmas were followed by a workshop July 20–August 3, 1933, which was organized by the Pedagogical Working Group and led by Johannes Waeger and Hans Werner Zbinden. Another one followed in the year after that, July 16–August 9, 1943, led by Curt Englert-Faye, Hans Jenny, Karl Rittersbacher, Alexander Strakosch, and, again, Johannes Waeger.

Working Together During the Time of National Socialism

AFTER THE National Socialists came to power in Germany in January 1933 and established their grip on the country, within the next five months[113] by such means as the institution of the Civil Service Law and through *Gleichschaltung* [measures to impose conformity and establish totalitarian control], darkness rapidly descended over Germany.[114] Now the Waldorf schools had to figure out how to deal with the new rulership, and nobody knew yet how far they would actually go. Elisabeth Klein of the Waldorf school in Dresden suggested early on that a uniform information policy toward the authorities should be adopted. To that end she proposed founding a central union of Waldorf schools[115] and, expecting impending centralization of education, she was for seeking contact with the National Socialist officials in charge in Berlin, as had previously been done by seeking contact with the state governments.[116]

Reactions to the proposal were mixed. Herbert Schiele of the Rudolf Steiner school in Berlin was highly skeptical, while Dr. Günther Beindorff, board member of the Waldorf School in Hannover, was in agreement. He approached René Maikowski of the Waldorf School in Hannover. It was possible to get a foot in the door in the ministry of culture because René Maikowski's brother, Hans Eberhard Maikowski, *Sturmbannführer* [Assault Unit Leader] and SA [storm trooper] officer, was murdered

---

113 Volker Ulrich wrote an article to show how quickly a power takeover can happen, even though everybody believes that a despot can be held in check. He uses the example of National Socialism and refers to Donald Trump. In: *Die Zeit*, January 26, 2017, p. 17.

114 Uwe Werner: *Anthroposophen in der Zeit des Nationalsozialismus (1933–1945)*. 1999, p. 101; Wenzel M. Götte: *Erfahrungen mit Schulautonomie*. 2006, p. 278.

115 Ibid., p. 98f.

116 Letter by Elisabeth Klein, dated March 31, 1933, addressed to the faculty of the Waldorf School in Stuttgart, Archiv LS 3.6.052.

on January 30, 1933, probably by his fellow officers, and was celebrated as a martyr and national hero.[117]

Representatives of the Waldorf schools met on May 10, 1933, in Berlin and held the legendary "couch conversation" in the apartment of Anni Heuser and Inez Arnold, both teachers in Berlin.[118] Christoph Boy (Stuttgart), René Maikowski (Hannover), and Ernst Weissert (Berlin) took part and formed the *Reichsverband* [National Union] of the Waldorf schools,[119] renamed *Bund der Waldorfschulen* [German Federation of Waldorf Schools] in June of the same year because the *Reichsverband* for private schools refused to accept another *Reichsverband* as a member. This union was set up in an attempt to be able to negotiate politically and to have a way to represent the interests of the Waldorf schools under the National Socialist regime. Christoph Boy's balanced judgment was widely recognized outside the Stuttgart Waldorf School.

René Maikowski

He and René Maikowski of the Waldorf School Hannover were the ones who were to advocate for the German Waldorf schools. The stronger the attacks from the outside, the more intense the inner life of the schools became, also with respect to the collaboration between school boards and faculties.[120] In the beginning, however, there were fundamental differences in people's willingness to compromise and meet the requirements of the Nazi regime. In the years to come, very different scenarios resulted in different schools.

As a first step to guarantee the continued existence of the schools, it had been decided in the conversations of May 10 to request corporate membership for the Waldorf schools in the National Socialist Teachers Union (NSLB).[121] Christoph Boy, in his capacity as head of the Stuttgart Waldorf School, was given the task to pursue this. This step was supported by many faculties, as shown, for example, in a letter of June 1933 written by Herbert Schiele of the Berlin Rudolf Steiner School. He wrote to Christoph Boy in Stuttgart, requesting that the Waldorf schools solidify their position as quickly as possible in order to prevent provocations or repressive measures.

---

117 Uwe Werner: *Anthroposophen in der Zeit des Nationalsozialismus (1933–1945)*. 1999, p. 100; Heinrich-Wilhelm Wörmann: *Widerstand in Charlottenburg*. 1991, p. 40f.; Hans Eberhard Maikowski attended the Waldorf School in Stuttgart for some time. He did not achieve much as a student and his reports were so poor that Herbert Hahn recommended he not show his reports at all in job interviews, but to assert that he had changed his ways when he applied. Archiv LS 3.3.128.

118 Manfred Leist: *Entwicklungen einer Schulgemeinschaft. Die Waldorfschulen in Deutschland*. 1998, p. 18.

119 Uwe Werner: *Anthroposophen in der Zeit des Nationalsozialismus (1933–1945)*. 1999, p. 101 and note 251.

120 Ernst Weissert: Von den Motiven und Lebensphasen der Schulbewegung. In: EK 8/9, 1969, p. 318.

121 Christoph Boy informed the other Waldorf schools on May 16, 1933, about the request for corporate membership, Archiv LS 4.2.015.

One of the suggestions he made was that individual teachers should try to become members of the NSLB, but only when it was really necessary. Christoph Boy then exchanged letters with the NSLB coordinator, Gottfried Schiele, who thought that should not present any problems. But a week later Gottfried Schiele barred Waldorf teachers from becoming members, his reason being that the principles of the two organizations were totally incompatible.[122] In spite of all these efforts to arrive at a common stance, schools disagreed right from the start in their positions toward the National Socialist regime. Paul Baumann argued with the minister of culture and head of the NSLB, Hans Schemm (1891–1935), which prompted him to write an article in the monthly *Nationalsozialistische Erziehung* [National Socialist Education]. He wrote, "Many tenets of the National Socialists, put into grand language now by Führer Adolf Hitler and his cohorts, have lived in the schools for more than a decade, often swimming against the stream of public opinion...." Waldorf teachers in Berlin were critical of this contribution.[123] So, we can see two ways of dealing with the situation at that point in time. On the one hand, attempts were made to try to get the regime to recognize Waldorf schools, and on the other hand, people clearly distanced themselves from the National Socialist government. Both positions were articulated by individuals as well as faculties and also within the movement as a whole, and there were clashes on all three levels.

The ensuing years demonstrated how far the two different courses of action could be pushed. At the behest of the faculty of the Stuttgart Waldorf School, Ernst Uehli wrote a memorandum for the independent Waldorf School in Stuttgart to formulate the pedagogical aims of the Waldorf school anew. In his preface he says: "The faculty of the independent Waldorf School wants to offer data that can serve as a basis for people to form an opinion about the spiritual and economic basis of the school, as well as articulate its social aspirations and place within German cultural life."[124] Ernst Uehli gave an elaborate description of the first 14 years of the school and a picture of how this idea unfolded culturally, socially, pedagogically, and economically. He explained the thinking behind a school having to function free from state intervention, to be coeducational and open to all strata of society. He also painted a picture of the national and international dimensions of the Waldorf movement. Of course this memorandum, printed in the magazine *Erziehungskunst*, was meant to be a declaration of where the faculty stood vis-à-vis the National Socialist regime. The memorandum ended by pointing out that the Waldorf school is not a school to advocate a worldview, that religion was taught according to the denominations of the parents, and that the education fosters healthy and artistic development overall.[125] Since the National

122 Wenzel M. Götte: *Erfahrungen mit Schulautonomie.* 2006, pp. 416 and 455.
123 Uwe Werner: *Anthroposophen in der Zeit des Nationalsozialismus (1933–1945).* 1999, p. 104; Wenzel M. Götte: *Erfahrungen mit Schulautonomie.* 2006, p. 426.
124 Ernst Uehli: Denkschrift der Freien Waldorfschule in Stuttgart. In: EK 2, June 1933, p. 345ff.
125 Ibid.

Socialist regime placed great value on conformity within the educational system, the teachers probably felt the necessity to sharply define the Waldorf school's position in that respect and to make it public.

If the continued existence of Waldorf schools had been considered hopeless in 1933, this memorandum surely would not have been printed. In the first months of 1933, only very few people could foresee which direction this regime would take.[126] The same edition of the magazine *Erziehungskunst* also contained an address by Erich Gabert, which he probably held during a national holiday because national holidays, such as May 1, became obligatory as a result of the conformity measures imposed by the regime.[127] Erich Gabert spoke to the students about the inner nature of the German people and quoted page after page from Johann Gottlieb Fichte, summarized as follows: "He spoke about three things. To be German means to have character, to be German means that every individual has to make a personal decision, and to be German does not mean being something that one is of one's own accord, but something one can only become by inner effort." Then he quoted Rudolf Steiner, and his address culminated in the tradition of Johann Wolfgang Goethe, Friedrich Schiller, and Johann Gottlieb Fichte with the following words: "German is not something one is; one has to work to become German!"[128]

In this manner, that is to say by stressing inner change, which develops a new virtue whereby head and heart come close together, the faculty of the Stuttgart school attempted to remain faithful to the impulse of Waldorf education. Thus, they continued to work and at the same time give expression to—without ever saying so directly—their abhorrence of a crass nationalist interpretation of what it means to be German. There was frequent mention of what it means to be German, or rather become German, in the hope—a naïve hope, it soon turned out—to give to Caesar what is Caesar's.

On July 3, 1933, Herbert Schiele (Berlin), Paul Baumann (Stuttgart) and Carl-Erdmann von Metzradt (Stuttgart) met in Berlin with Hans Schwemm, who had founded the NSLB, in order to pursue further the idea of membership in the teachers union. Herbert Schiele announced the conclusion they reached, namely that Hans Schwemm definitely wanted to include the Waldorf schools in the National Union.[129] Inclusion of the eight Waldorf schools in the national union of independent (private)

---

126 Volker Ullrich: "Ruhig abwarten! [Wait patiently.]" [He wrote:] "This position will bring him to his senses, his cabinet will reign him in. A dictatorship? Unthinkable." How journalists, politicians, writers and diplomats commented on Hitler's nomination to Chancellor of the Reich. In: *Die Zeit*, January 26, 2017, p. 17.

127 Order to celebrate May 1. See for example letter of April 28, 1933, by Erich Schwebsch to Albert Steffen, Archiv LS 2.2.368.

128 Erich Gabert: Lecture at the occasion of a national holiday in the Waldorf School. In: EK 2, June 1933, p. 372ff.

129 Uwe Werner: *Anthroposophen in der Zeit des Nationalsozialismus (1933–1945)*. 1999, p. 104.

educational institutions, a subsection of the NSLB, was confirmed on August 23, 1933.[130] After the winter of 1933/34, Hans Schwemm withdrew his support.

In the first phase of the negotiations with the National Socialist authorities early in 1934, the Waldorf schools received protection from Hess's office, granted by three civil servants, Philipp Bouhler, Alfred Leitgen, and Ernst Schulte-Strathaus.[131] In April 1934, with the appointment of Bernhard Rust, who was called to fill the post of minister of science, education, and civic schooling, the situation deteriorated. He had now become one of the leaders of the Reich and occupied a rank similar to those of Alfred Rosenberg and Rudolf Hess. In May 1934, Bernhard Rust received a memo concerning the Waldorf schools, which Ernst Schulte-Strathaus, coworker of Rudolf Hess since April 1934, had written to Hitler's deputy. In it, Ernst Schulte-Strathaus argued that the aims of the Waldorf schools were basically in accord with those of National Socialism and that the Waldorf school experiences should therefore be made use of. This was an argument used as a strategy to secure the survival of the Waldorf schools.[132] It gave the schools a little reprieve, because Bernhard Rust was willing to wait until an independent position had been worked up, a delay he actually communicated to the individual state ministers.

Also in May 1934, *Reichsleiter* Philipp Bouhler, one of the three supporters on the staff of Rudolf Hess whom Elisabeth Klein had contacted, asked Education Minister Bernhard Rust to take up a unified position with regard to the case of the Waldorf schools. Philipp Bouhler declared himself in favor of the Waldorf schools, telling Elisabeth Klein that there were no objections from the side of the NSDAP [*Nationalsozialistische Deutsche Arbeiterpartei,* Nationalist Socialist German Worker's Party, the Nazi party] to the Waldorf schools' continuing. This was very important for the Waldorf school in Dresden, as it was housed in buildings rented from the National Socialist Teachers Union.[133]

So, the supportive measures carried out by the above-mentioned three civil servants on the staff of Rudolf Hess worked out positively in the short run. After Philipp Bouhler had declared his position, Education Minister Bernhard Rust approached Minister of Culture Christian Mergenthaler requesting that the enrollment ban threatening the Stuttgart Waldorf School be lifted.[134]

Neither the negotiations nor the cooperation between German Waldorf schools particularly restricted the schools' functioning at this time, but there was

130 Letter of the National Union of Independent Educational Institutions to the Waldorf School Association, dated August 23, 1933, Archiv LS 4.6.013.
131 Uwe Werner: *Anthroposophen in der Zeit des Nationalsozialismus (1933–1945).* 1999, p. 114, note 299.
132 Ibid., p. 113.
133 Ibid.
134 Norbert Deuchert: Zur Geschichte der Waldorfschule 1933–1940. BhB Advent 1984, p. 72; Norbert Deuchert: Der Kampf um die Waldorfschule im Nationalsozialismus. In: Flensburger Hefte Sonderheft 8, 1991, p. 116.

another conflict that was becoming gradually more acute and had a laming effect. As mentioned before, conflicts had broken out after the death of Rudolf Steiner in the leadership of the Anthroposophical Society, conflicts that had smoldered for a number of years and had gradually affected relationships among Waldorf teachers in Germany. Individual teachers, including those in the Waldorf School in Stuttgart, sided with factions in the Executive Council of the General Anthroposophical Society. The majority of the Stuttgart faculty felt connected to the so-called Goetheanum leadership, whereas others felt a solidarity with the circle around Ita Wegman. This led to a deep crisis in the German Federation of Waldorf Schools and mistrust toward the faculty of the Stuttgart Waldorf School and, for the time being, the school lost its strong coordinating position.[135] It is clear this also stood in the way of developing a unified political strategy. During the meeting of representatives of the Federation of May 6, 1934, René Maikowski of the Waldorf School in Hannover was asked to work alongside first chairman Christoph Boy, who had fallen ill. He continued his tireless work for the preservation of the Waldorf schools.

He visited Ernst Schulte-Strathaus personally in Munich, and through him gained access to Rudolf Hess.[136] The latter had been briefed first by Ernst Schulte-Strathaus, whereupon he appointed a committee to get better acquainted with anthroposophy, biodynamic agriculture, and Waldorf pedagogy. In addition, René Maikowski was in contact with leading personalities of the National Socialist government, such as *Sturmbannführer* [Senior Assault Unit Leader] Otto Ohlendorf of the SD [*Sicherheitsdienst*, the intelligence agency of the SS and the Nazi Party], Lothar Eickhoff of the ministry of the interior, and also with leading educator, Alfred Bäumler, in the office of Rosenberg, who dealt with the assessment of philosophical questions in the NSDAP.[137] Alfred Bäumler, who was also leader of the *Hochschule für Politik* [Academy for Affairs of State] and taught at the University of Berlin, was charged in the end with drawing up an official assessment of the Waldorf schools.

In 1934/35 communication channels between the Waldorf School on the Uhlandshöhe and the sister schools broke off, demonstrated by the fact that no more letters went back and forth and no more information was exchanged. It got quieter and quieter in the individual schools as they had to draw more and more on their own resources. By contrast, Dornach was strongly promoting international understanding during this time, as shown by a journey to the United States undertaken by Günther Wachsmuth, Ehrenfried Pfeiffer, and Hermann von Baravalle October 12–December 12, 1934. The three of them traveled mostly independently apart from meeting for a few communal events, for example in Chicago. Each of the three travelers held 50 (!) lectures as they traveled from one coast to the other. Günther Wachsmuth lectured

135 Uwe Werner: *Anthroposophen in der Zeit des Nationalsozialismus (1933–1945)*. 1999, p. 115ff.
136 René Maikowski: *Schicksalswege auf der Suche nach dem lebendigen Geist*. 1980, p. 145.
137 Norbert Deuchert: Zur Geschichte der Waldorfschule 1933–1940. BhB Advent 1984, p. 72.

about general anthroposophy; Ehrenfried Pfeiffer explained how these foundations worked out in biology, agriculture, and medicine; whereas Hermann von Baravalle, in his capacity as educator, mathematician and physics professor, lectured about the anthroposophical understanding of child development.[138] This journey was a milestone in the development of the anthroposophical movement in North America.[139]

On March 2, 1935, René Maikowski of the German Federation of Waldorf Schools sent an official 20-page document to Rudolf Hess, as had been agreed upon with Ernst Schulte-Strathaus. It gave an overview of the program of the Waldorf school and the need to keep the elementary school grades together.[140] In this document, the Waldorf school approach for the elementary school was contrasted with the much more abstract education offered by state schools. The inner vitality of the students was safeguarded, the document explained: "The slumbering creative forces within the child, the root of national identity and vitality, are essentially destroyed by present-day intellectual methods. The living, artistic methodology of the Waldorf school, going from doing to understanding, from the heart to comprehension, strengthens and preserves these forces."[141] The document also explains how Waldorf schools fostered community building.

All these efforts had no effect in the long run, as Bernhard Rust had made up his mind long ago. This became obvious in March 1936 when he wrote to the educational authorities of the different German states: "I request that measures are taken that no more students are accepted into the Waldorf schools, respectively Rudolf Steiner schools (based on the anthroposophical worldview)."[142] Right around that same time, the faculties of the Waldorf schools were ordered to swear allegiance to Adolf Hitler. Both ordinances led some schools to decide to close as such, for example in Hamburg-Altona and in Berlin. Other teachers attempted to get their schools recognized as experimental schools, for example in Hannover and Dresden.

As teachers in Germany carried on a tough fight to preserve what remained of the independent and denominational schools and the restrictions imposed by the National Socialist regime became more and more oppressive, the work could continue unhampered in other countries. The *Vereniging voor Vrije Opvoedkunst*, the Dutch federation of Waldorf schools, extended an invitation to attend a seminar titled "Education and Health" held in Amsterdam April 24–26, 1936. Also, in 1936,

---

138 Described by Henry B. Monges: Die Dornacher Gäste in Amerika. In: N 2, January 13, 1935, p. 6f.; Günther Wachsmuth: Erfahrungen einer Amerikareise I. In: N 3, January 20, 1935, p. 10; Günther Wachsmuth: Erfahrungen einer Amerikareise II. In: N 4/5, January 27, 1935, p. 13ff.; Ehrenfried Pfeiffer: Zwischen zwei Ozeanen. In: N 9, March 3, 1935, p. 33f.

139 Henry Barnes: *Into the Heart's Land*. 2005, p. 200ff.

140 Archiv LS 4.3.020, BArch, Ella 0751-35, pp. 243–262.

141 BArch Ella 0751-35, p. 246.

142 Uwe Werner: *Anthroposophen in der Zeit des Nationalsozialismus (1933–1945)*. 1999, p. 136 and note 370.

pedagogical Easter courses were started in the new hall of the New School in London, with the collaboration of former Stuttgart teachers Caroline von Heydebrand and Eugen Kolisko, as well as Max Stibbe from Holland. The last Easter course in this cycle took place in 1939, as the political reality in Europe made such conferences impossible for the time being. Waldorf education activities in Switzerland continued to flourish, almost untouched by what was happening elsewhere in Europe.

In April 1936 René Maikowski made a new attempt to secure the continued existence of Waldorf schools. He fought tirelessly for the future of the Waldorf school movement in National Socialist Germany, and above all for the students who had been entrusted to him. He also did not give up after his colleagues changed their minds. Afterward, he got flak for this, of course. This uncovers the deep split within the Waldorf movement in these years, which was only lightly covered up. There was no real trust that could form the basis of cooperation, and neither was there a real common stance to defend the interests of the Waldorf school movement. René Maikowski was later accused of going too far in snuggling up to the system, for example in the way he wrote to the Gestapo on November 18, 1935. There he protested the house searches in the Waldorf school in Dresden, and once again gave a detailed account of Steiner's explanations of the way the physical/bodily nature intertwines with the soul/spiritual nature of the human being and how this forms the basis of Waldorf pedagogy. This account actually shows more of an inner unwillingness to compromise, coupled with a conviction that Waldorf education makes sense for the students even under the National Socialist regime.[143]

In my own encounters with René Maikowski in the 1970s I recognized him as somebody who certainly did not "cozy up." My impression was more that he was an enthusiastic proponent of Waldorf education and at the same time retained his enthusiasm for Germany in its ideal sense, to such a degree that he tried to use the contradictions within the National Socialist system, thereby making more concessions than seems appropriate in hindsight. But, of course, we are judging from the safe distance of our time without having to face the necessity to take action the way he had to. His brother had suffered as a child because of the deprivations of World War I, with its widespread hunger and the collapse of many of the old values. Thus, his brother did not have the support as a child, which he then compensated for by joining the National Socialist *Schlägertrupps* [attack squadrons]. One also has to take into account how differently people adapted to the 12 years of unjust Nazi rulership, and that individuals either gradually changed their minds or radically shifted their allegiance. In any case, René Maikowski made a further attempt by proposing to Rudolf Hess that the Waldorf schools change into experimental schools in the context of the shifting educational landscape at the time.

143 BArch Ella 2836-35, pp. 274–285.

In front of the administrative building of the Waldorf School, Stuttgart, 1937

This idea of changing status into an experimental school helped later generations keep their schools alive, as was the case in the Ukraine and Romania. In this case however, subjecting oneself to the National Socialist system was obviously untenable. That is why the teachers of the Waldorf schools in Hamburg-Altona and Berlin decided to close of their own account. Supported by his colleagues in the Stuttgart Waldorf School, Count von Bothmer was highly skeptical about René Maikowski's idea, whereupon René Maikowski modified the plan. In the months that followed, the schools in Stuttgart, Kassel, and Breslau likewise came to the conclusion that they had to close their schools.

René Maikowski kept pursuing the aim of Waldorf schools becoming recognized as experimental schools, and he was supported in this endeavor by Elisabeth Klein.[144] We now know that this hopeful course of action completely underestimated the

144 Uwe Werner: *Anthroposophen in der Zeit des Nationalsozialismus (1933–1945)*. 1999, pp. 138, 208; Norbert Deuchert: *Zur Geschichte der Waldorfschule 1933–1940*. BhB Advent 1984, p. 78.

intentions of those in command. As early as March 3, 1936, Reinhard Heydrich, head of the secret police, pointed out to the ministry of the interior that the teachers of the Waldorf schools had to be replaced by tried-and-true National Socialists.[145] In the meantime, ministers of the interior and of education likewise wanted to close the schools.

Lola Jaerschky (1902–1991), a eurythmy teacher at the school in Berlin who stepped down from her position because she was half Jewish, looks back on the conflicted and split situation of these years and paints the following picture: "It was hard for those involved to make the right decisions. There were many long meetings after every new order from the authorities. Did we have to comply? What would happen if we refused? Could we absorb another blow, compensate for what was being asked of us? Teachers could no longer avoid becoming members of the National Socialist teacher union. Together with the older students, teachers had to take part in rallies and march along. We were obliged to hoist the flag at the beginning and the end of the school year with the whole school in attendance. We had to listen to speeches transmitted on the radio and partake in ordained festivals. We had to hide our opinions and become adept at finding obfuscating replies. It was painful, but we put up with this because there was no other way and we had to survive. Thus, we became complicit for the greater good. It was possible to suppress a feeling of guilt, but many people consciously took on this burden and used the feeling of guilt as a sting, painful but awakening. It all depended on how one did the inevitable. One could be either shy or brazen about it or use humor to put up with it.

"One could use ordinary words and symbols differently or substitute a hidden meaning of one's own. But it was also possible to expose the grand deception and recognize evil, the father of all error, as a mighty adversary. When the 'Heil Hitler' greeting was introduced, before and after every lesson—mind you, every lesson, including eurythmy and religion—we raised our arms with a thought of impending doom. […] In 1938, teachers were required to swear 'the oath of absolute faithfulness,' signed and sealed on paper. Every individual had to swear to the head of state. The faculty of the school in Berlin felt that one could not combine this pledge with being a Waldorf teacher. To pledge allegiance to a power that one recognized as evil was incompatible with the vocation of being a teacher at the Rudolf Steiner school. So, the faculty itself closed the school. It was as painful as the death of a living being, but the hope of a new start remained, a 'resurrection,' even though it was unclear if a turn of events would ever come."[146]

In September 1936 the Waldorf schools of Stuttgart and Hamburg-Altona took the initiative to call together a meeting of representatives of the Waldorf schools, which took place in Kassel. Once again there was a clash of opinions between those who

145 BArch Ella 0602-36, pp. 295–296.
146 Lola Jaerschky: Aus der Zeit des Nationalsozialismus. In: EK 5, 1980, p. 290f.

favored cooperation with the National Socialist authorities by trying to go for the status of experimental schools and those who did not. At this meeting, a new committee of five people was chosen to take on the leadership of the German Federation of Waldorf Schools: Count Bothmer and Ernst Uehli from Stuttgart, Martin Schmidt from Kassel, together with René Maikowski and Elisabeth Klein. With this, the latter got her first official appointment to the German Federation of Waldorf Schools. But they could not come to an agreement. Count Bothmer and Ernst Uehli were against the plan from this meeting onward, but three Waldorf schools worked toward achieving the status of experimental schools.

Ernst Uehli formulated a resolution, to which all those present could agree: "We can try to keep the Waldorf schools in Germany going as long as the schools do not endanger the vitality of the central idea. When too many compromises are made and school organisms are crippled inwardly and outwardly to such a degree that the vitality of the idea is endangered by their continued existence, then we will have to close."[147] This resolution was a last attempt to give a semblance of unity, masking the actual controversies under the surface. Even during the meeting in Kassel, schools that were willing to apply for the status of being experimental agreed to go ahead individually and fill out the applications. Such a crass exclusion—especially of the representatives of the Stuttgart Waldorf School—did not remain without consequences. At the next session of the newly elected leadership group in October 1936 in Berlin, a final decision was made at last to reject the idea of experimental schools.

René Maikowski, however, had kept on pursuing his idea in the meantime, without informing Count Bothmer and Ernst Uehli.[148] In November 1936, René Maikowski took a next step—taken, of course, without consulting the others and without their consent. On behalf of his school in Hannover, he wrote to the ministry of education that the aims of the Stuttgart Waldorf School were not identical with those of the German Federation of Waldorf Schools and stressed once again the special value of Waldorf education for the German school system.

To Count Bothmer, René Maikowski justified this step by saying that his school had also been hit by repressive measures. All hopes to be able to come to a unified stance toward the Nazi regime had now been dashed. In the meantime, people criticized each other openly. Anni Heuser of the Rudolf Steiner school in Berlin criticized Elisabeth Klein of the Waldorf School in Dresden publicly from then on, reproaching her for harming the Waldorf schools with her stance.[149] So the Waldorf schools in Hannover, Dresden, Hamburg-Wandsbek, and Kassel all applied for the

---

147 Norbert Deuchert: Der Kampf um die Waldorfschule im Nationalsozialismus. In: Flensburger Hefte, Special Issue 8, 1991, p. 121.

148 Uwe Werner: *Anthroposophen in der Zeit des Nationalsozialismus (1933–1945)*. 1999, p. 210f.; Norbert Deuchert: Der Kampf um die Waldorfschule im Nationalsozialismus. In: Flensburger Hefte, Special Issue 8, 1991, p. 122f.

149 Archiv LS 4.3.252 and 4.3.254; Karen Priestman: *Illusion of Coexistence*. 2009, p. 109.

status of official experimental schools. The schools in Stuttgart, Hamburg-Altona, and Berlin refused to apply despite urgent requests from Elisabeth Klein and René Maikowski, each with different degrees of vehemence.[150] This clearly cemented the split in the Waldorf school movement.

On November 10, 1936, the request of the Waldorf school in Hannover to be accepted as an experimental school was rejected, and René Maikowski heard that only the Waldorf schools in Dresden and Hamburg-Wandsbek would get permission.[151] This was deeply disappointing for him, since he had been working all these months for the survival of his school. Thereupon, René Maikowski protested officially to Hermann Göring against the suppression of the Waldorf schools, signing his letter as head of the German Federation of Waldorf Schools. Elisabeth Klein delivered the letter.

After they received a copy, Ernst Uehli and Count Bothmer protested and stepped down resolutely from the leadership of the German Federation of Waldorf Schools, followed later by Martin Schmidt. The Waldorf schools in Berlin and Hamburg-Altona sided with the two Stuttgart teachers. The faculty of the Stuttgart school brought this conflicted situation to an end and informed René Maikowski: "We refuse to be officially represented further by you and Mrs. Klein."[152]

Speaking for the faculty of the Rudolf Steiner school in Berlin, Anni Heuser announced to René Maikowski that her school would leave the Federation, not for financial reasons, but for internal ones.[153] So, the end of 1936 also marked the end of collaboration within the framework of the Federation. This was not confined only to Germany. There was no longer collaboration of Waldorf schools either internationally or across different regions. Within the individual states, faculties were in touch, but it was no longer possible to organize conferences and meetings, with the exception of Switzerland, which had remained neutral.

Schools in Germany that had not yet closed now made their decisions without consulting other schools. The situation only got more complicated. In February 1937, the minister of education, Bernhard Rust, announced new permit quotas for experimental schools and tried to limit their number to a minimum. In the meantime, it became harder and harder to disregard the seriousness of the threats. Those who saw what was coming and people who had become victimized emigrated or went into exile. Those who waited longer barely had a chance to get out at all.

More and more émigrés found their way to the Waldorf school in The Hague, the English Waldorf schools, and the United States, and planted the seeds of Waldorf

150 Karen Priestman: *Illusion of Coexistence*. 2009, p. 108.
151 Uwe Werner: *Anthroposophen in der Zeit des Nationalsozialismus (1933–1945)*. 1999, p. 211; Karen Priestman: *Illusion of Coexistence*. 2009, p. 135.
152 Archiv LS 4.3.304; Uwe Werner, *Anthroposophen in der Zeit des Nationalsozialismus (1933–1945)*. 1999, p. 211.
153 Karen Priestman: *Illusion of Coexistence*. 2009, p. 170f.

pedagogy in tough times. It was partly from these seeds that the later growth came in North America and certainly in South America. Initial fine threads were spun in Asia and Africa.

In spite of these increasingly tense and restricting circumstances, teachers of the Waldorf School in Stuttgart invited representatives of all Waldorf schools to Stuttgart on the occasion of Rudolf Steiner's 76th birthday. Except for Hannover and Dresden, there were representatives from all schools. One more time an attempt was made to work together. René Maikowski and Emil Kühn, who in the meantime had become the successor of the late Emil Molt in heading the Stuttgart school association, were nominated to be heads on equal footing of the German Federation of Waldorf Schools.[154] This was probably the last large comprehensive get-together before the outbreak of the war.

The Waldorf School of Hamburg-Altona closed April 6, 1936; the Waldorf school of Hannover on July 9, 1937; and the Rudolf Steiner School of Berlin on August 26, 1937; the only further thing they could do was to prepare their students for the transition into state schools. The Waldorf schools of Stuttgart, Kassel, Breslau, and Hamburg prepared for closure, each in their own way, and in the meantime, Elisabeth Klein fought on.

Ministry of the interior representative Lothar Eickhoff visited the Rudolf Steiner School of Dresden in November 1937, at the behest of Rudolf Hess and with the knowledge of Minister Bernhard Rust. Lothar Eickhoff was accompanied by Alfred Leitgen of Hess's staff, Alfred Bäumler from the office of Rosenberg, and Otto Ohlendorf of the Security Office. Alfred Bäumler wrote up a report after this visit that was, according to all experts, the most serious commentary on Waldorf pedagogy written by a National Socialist educator.[155]

Here are two quotes from his extensive evaluation, which show on the one hand that his observations were relatively unbiased, but that he had to recommend on the other hand to retain the ordinance to cease accepting students into the Waldorf schools. "Whereas our worldview focuses on the racial forces forming the human being in history, Rudolf Steiner's worldview is dominated by the vision of the overarching human spirit throughout the course of history. [...] Therefore the educational theory of Steiner has no place for a notion of tribal community. [...] Community, the way Rudolf Steiner conceives of it, means a spiritual community." So these and other observations made by Alfred Bäumler demonstrated how incompatible

---

154 Norbert Deuchert: Der Kampf um die Waldorfschule im Nationalsozialismus. In: Flensburger Hefte, Sonderheft 8, 1991, p. 127.

155 Uwe Werner: *Anthroposophen in der Zeit des Nationalsozialismus (1933–1945)*. 1999, p. 220; Detlef Hardorp: Die deutsche Waldorfschulbewegung in der Zeit des Nationalsozialismus. Rassebegriffe im Denken Rudolf Steiners. In: Inge Hansen-Schaberg (ed.): *Waldorfpädagogik*. Reformpädagogische Schulkonzepte Band 6, 2012, p. 139f.; Karen Priestman: *Illusion of Coexistence*. 2009, p. 199. (The full report of A. Bäumler is published in the appendix.).

Waldorf pedagogy was with National Socialist conceptions and, therefore, should not be carried on under this regime.

Alfred Bäumler also recognized the following: "As far as the methodology is concerned, we have to recognize that Steiner's curriculum constitutes the first thoroughly planned nonintellectual educational system. This curriculum really breaks with the principle of mere schooling of the head and influencing the will through the intellect. This system does not merely practice physical, musical, and artistic education as an add-on, but starts from a new premise altogether. The curriculum and pedagogical practice are conceived not in a scientific but in an artistic spirit and carried out correspondingly."[156]

Alfred Bäumler was impressed as a teacher and recommended at the end of his evaluation to adopt some of the methods into what state schools tried to do. Achim Leschinsky was one of the first to do research into Waldorf schools during the time of National Socialism and confirmed that "possibilities to preserve Waldorf schools lay primarily in the inner fragility of National Socialism."[157]

Even though the option of experimental schools was discussed anew during the months that followed, giving rise to renewed dreams about the continuing existence of just a few Waldorf schools, the die had long been cast among those in power, especially Bernhard Rust, whose sole reason for not acting more drastically was his consideration for Rudolf Hess.[158] In February 1938, when he was certain that Hess was in agreement, Rust concluded the case.[159] The Waldorf School in Stuttgart was closed April 1, 1938.

The official policy was and remained contradictory, as shown by the fact that Waldorf schools in Dresden and Hamburg-Wandsbek were allowed to remain open, and by Education Minister Bernhard Rust's cancellation on April 14, 1938, of the ordinance halting enrollment, and his dangling the possibility of state experimental schools. This decision was communicated to the state government in Hamburg, but not to the Waldorf School. Therefore, no timely measures could be taken to counteract the shrinking and eventual closing of the Stuttgart Waldorf School.

Even though this was going on and some schools were clearly closed, René Maikowski wrote once again to Bernhard Rust and to *Ministerialdirektor* [head of the cabinet] Thies on October 25, 1938. In a four-page document he requested that the Waldorf schools in Dresden, Hamburg-Wandsbek, and Hannover be allowed

---

156 Karen Priestman: *Illusion of Coexistence*. 2009. A. Bäumler's valuation is published in full in the appendix.

157 Letter by Achim Leschinsky of August 8, 1983, to René Maikowski, Archiv C. Brosamer.

158 René Maikowski made a renewed at attempt in a document addressed to Minister Rust, dated March 25, 1938, to put the option of being an experimental school on the table for Hamburg and Dresden. In this document, he wanted a guarantee that teaching in blocks, artistic methodology, special-education class and free choice of teachers would be maintained at all cost. See BArch Ella 804-33, pp. 269–272.

159 Uwe Werner: *Anthroposophen in der Zeit des Nationalsozialismus (1933–1945)*. 1999, p. 223.

to function as experimental schools recognized by the government. He demanded freedom in choice of teachers; continued implementation of the Waldorf curriculum, as well as teaching in blocks; continuation of artistic subjects, eurythmy above all, as well as practical subjects; special education carried on in the special-help classroom; continuation of the practice of coeducation; the principle of the class teacher; and the work in faculty meetings—all this to guarantee a unified school system comprising 12 grades. The content of this document makes no compromises, nor does René Maikowski show any willingness to compromise with the regime. He did demand that a decision be made soon.[160] The Waldorf school in Dresden survived until the end of June 1941.

Pedagogical Working Group at the Goetheanum during the Time of the Nazi Regime and up to the End of World War II

FROM 1936 ON, the Waldorf schools in Germany were mainly trying to survive. The regular contacts with Waldorf schools in other countries had come to a standstill and were virtually nonexistent. During that period of time, activities of the Pedagogical Working Group at the Goetheanum continued independently and seemed completely

---

160 Letter of October 25–27, 1938, BArch EIIa 2586-38 / 62-68.
161 Public pedagogical conferences were held on the following dates: July 20–August 2, 1936, with Hermann von Baravalle, Gerhard von dem Borne, Oswald Dubach, Friedrich Häusler, Hans Jenny, Wilhelm Lewerenz, Wilfried Overhage, Arnold Wadler, Johannes Waeger; July 19–August 5, 1937, with Karl von Baltz, Hermann von Baravalle, Walter Dettwyler, Hans Jenny, Marie Savitch, Ernst Uehli, Johannes Waeger, Hans Werner Zbinden; October 4–9, 1937, with Hans Jenny, Günther Schubert, Arnold Wadler, Johannes Waeger; April 3–9, 1938, with Curt Englert-Faye, Johannes Waeger, Hans Werner Zbinden; August 7–13, 1939, with Friedrich Eymann, Hans Rudolf Niederhäuser; August 4–10, 1940, with Friedrich Eymann, Marie Groddeck, Hans Rudolf Niederhäuser, Max Schenk, Jakob Streit, Johannes Waeger, Hans Werner Zbinden, on the theme: "Anthropologie als gemeinsame Grundlage der Pädagogik und Medizin" [Anthropology as the Common Basis for Education and Medicine]; April 11–17, 1943, with Marie Groddeck, Louise van Blommestein, Max Leist, Günther Schubert, Charles von Steiger, Jakob Streit, Georg Unger, Johannes Waeger; April 11–15, 1944, with Friedrich Eymann, Elisabeth Fischer-Roy, Marie Groddeck, H. Kessler, Max Leist, Hans Rudolf Niederhäuser, Marianne Ruof, Marie Savitch, M. Schaffner, Günther Schubert, Johannes Waeger, Ernst Weidmann on the theme: "Spracherziehung vor den Forderungen der Gegenwart" [Modern Speech Education]; July 16–22, 1944, with Karl Bäschlin, Ernst Bühler, Friedrich Eymann, H. Huber, Max Leist, Hans Rudolf Niederhäuser, Günther Schubert, Johannes Waeger, Hans Werner Zbinden on the theme: "Lebendiger Geographie-Unterricht bildet Weltinteresse und Liebe zum Nebenmenschen" [Living Geography Lessons Create an Interest in the World and Love for Others]; April 9–15, 1945, with R. Ammacher-Tschabold, Ernst Bühler, Friedrich Eymann, Marie Groddeck, Werner Jaggi, Max Leist, Lilli Lüscher, Emilie Naef, Hans Rudolf Niederhäuser, Johannes Waeger; July 16–22, 1945, with Friedrich Eymann, Werner Jaggi, Heinrich Kern, Rudolf Kutzli, Robert Pfister, Max Schenk, Johannes Waeger, Hans Werner Zbinden on the theme: "Der Goetheanismus, ein Impuls zu einem lebendigen Naturkundeunterricht" [Goetheanism: an Impulse for Living Physics Lessons].

Pedagogical workshops were held on the following dates: March 30–April 5, 1937, with Curt Englert-Faye, Hans Jenny, Marie Savitch, Max Schenk; April 11–19, 1939, with Curt Englert-Faye, Friedrich Eymann, Hermann Klug, Günther Wachsmuth, Johannes Waeger; March 31–April 6, 1940, with Friedrich Eymann, Alma Mlosch, Hans Rudolf Niederhäuser, Jakob Streit, Johannes Waeger; April

untouched by what was happening in Germany. Both public pedagogical conferences and longer workshops were organized regularly in Dornach, Switzerland.[161]

Regular coworkers were: Hermann von Baravalle, who had left the Stuttgart school and had gone to live in Dornach in the meantime; Curt Englert-Faye from Zürich; Friedrich Eymann, who fought for Waldorf school pedagogy in state schools in the canton of Bern; Hans Jenny, also from Zürich; Wilhelm Lewerenz, cello player and music teacher; and Hans Rudolf Niederhäuser, Johannes Waeger, and Hans-Werner Zbinden, all three members of the Rudolf Steiner school in Zürich.

Due to problems starting in 1938, referred to as a "pedagogical crisis," the Pedagogical Working Group at the Goetheanum, led by Isabelle de Jaager, Johannes Waeger, and Hans Jenny, stopped functioning temporarily in the years 1938–1939. Soon thereafter, in 1939, it was announced publicly that their work would resume.[162] The Executive Council of the General Anthroposophical Society affirmed the working group on May 7, 1939, announcing that "the Pedagogical Working Group at the Goetheanum is officially recognized as an institution that is anchored in the section. Those entrusted with the leadership have the confidence of the executive council, necessary to carry out their task."[163] In 1939 Marie Steiner, Curt Englert-Faye, Isabelle de Jaager, Johannes Waeger, and Hans Jenny were the leaders of the Pedagogical Working Group at the Goetheanum. From August 7–13, 1940, they organized a public pedagogical conference with the title: "Von Fichte zu Rudolf Steiner" [From Fichte to Rudolf Steiner]. The introduction says: "The path from Fichte to Rudolf Steiner clearly reveals the foundations of morality and social life. This path can show us the place of education within the social context." This series was continued in April 1942 with the theme "Handarbeit, Handwerk und Kinderspiel" [Handwork, Crafts, and Play].

When the Berlin Waldorf school closed its doors in 1938, Curt Englert-Faye asked the experienced teacher Anni Heuser to move to Dornach and build up a solid,

15–20, 1941, with Marie Groddeck, Walter Heim, Alma Mlosch, Johannes Waeger; October 12–19, 1941, with Marie Groddeck, Emilie Naef, Marie Savitch, Jakob Streit, Assja Turgenieff, Johannes Waeger on the theme: "Über die Metamorphose der leiblichen und seelischen Kräfte im Kindesalter" [Metamorphosis of Forces Underlying Body and Soul in Childhood]; April 7–12, 1942, with Marie Groddeck, Hilde Langen, Alma Mlosch, E. Roy, M. Schaffner, Max Schenk, Jakob Streit, Assja Turgenieff, Johannes Waeger, Emma Weideli, Hans Werner Zbinden, on the theme: "Über Handarbeit, Handwerk, Kinderspiel" [Handwork, Crafts, and Play]; August 3–9, 1942, reduced program due to military service and sickness of carrying participants; October 12–16, 1942, with Hans Rudolf Niederhäuser; January 10–16, 1943, with Assja Turgenieff; August 2–8, 1943, with Marie Groddeck, Alma Mlosch, Charles von Steiger, Johannes Waeger, Hans Werner Zbinden; January 10–16, 1944, with Hans Rudolf Niederhäuser, Assja Turgenieff; January 9–14, 1945, with R. Ammacher-Tschabold, Elisabeth Fischer-Roy, Marie Groddeck.

162 Report in N 6, 5.2.1939, p. 24. Account of the Pedagogical Working Group and Exposé by N. Grossheinz-Lavalle; Events organized by the Pädagogischen Arbeitsgruppe am Goetheanum, Dornach, Msch 5, 1939, p. 187.

163 Report in N 19, May 7, 1939, p. 75.

ongoing teacher training. This plan failed, because the outbreak of World War II kept Anni Heuser in Rome and Curt Englert-Faye in Norway. More to the point: Marie Savitch, the very strict leader of the stage group at the Goetheanum at that time, would not allow Anni Heuser's friend and colleague, Elena Zuccoli, to go because of a scheduled eurythmy performance, so the two had to stay a week longer in Dornach before traveling to Rome. And this week was decisive, because when they did go to Rome, war had broken out and they could not return anymore. They remained in Rome for the entire duration of the war and, after some initial hurdles, they were able to do solid groundwork there for anthroposophy, Waldorf pedagogy, and eurythmy. The planned teacher training in Dornach was started a few years later by Willi Aeppli of the Rudolf Steiner school in Basel.

In 1940, the Pedagogical Working Group at the Goetheanum started publishing a collection of materials for the schools. The first books to be published were *Griechische Heldensagen* [Greek Myths] by Hans Rudolf Niederhäuser and *Naturfabeln* [Nature Stories] by Jakob Streit. The books were meant to be readers for the children, thus unwittingly carrying on an impulse given earlier by Caroline von Heydebrand.

On May 6, 1943, the teacher training started, housed by the Friedwart School at the Goetheanum in Dornach and directed by Marie Groddeck.[164] Requests to form such a training had come especially from England, where there was a shortage of anthroposophically trained teachers. The whole executive council at the Goetheanum was in accord with establishing this training.

The Pedagogical Working Group at the Goetheanum continued holding regular events and announced them as workshops or practice weeks. Contributions focused often on lectures about Rudolf Steiner's indications and on artistic exercises. The circle of people who gave the lectures was drawn primarily from teachers from the Rudolf Steiner schools in Basel and Zürich. The number of participants was manageable. Hans Rudolf Niederhäuser indicated that the most important task of the Pedagogical Working Group at the Goetheanum was fostering contact among all Rudolf Steiner school teachers, artistic practice, and an exchange of ideas. Conferences and practice weeks aimed at training teachers. Themes of the meetings arose from questions and challenges flagged by individual participants.[165] At times, the themes were put in the context of the events of the world war raging all around, even though this was relatively rare. Thus the theme of the public pedagogical conference at the Goetheanum of July 1944 was "Lebendiger Geographie-Unterricht bildet Weltinteresse und Liebe zum Nebenmenschen" [Living Geography Teaching Fosters an Interest in the World and Love for One's Fellow Human Beings],[166] which can be interpreted as a reference to

164 Marie Groddeck: Lehrerschulung am Goetheanum. In: N 20, May 16, 1943, p. 79.
165 Hans Rudolf Niederhäuser: Über die pädagogische Arbeit am Goetheanum. In: N 20, May 14, 1944, p. 79.
166 Program of the conference in: Msch 6, 1944, p. 192; Review by E. Naef in: Msch 9, 1944, p. 286f.

what was happening in the surrounding countries, even though seen from the safe distance of Switzerland, which was neutral and not affected.

On October 20, 1944, a festival was organized at the Goetheanum to commemorate the 25th birthday of the founding of the art of education inaugurated by Rudolf Steiner. War and destruction were all around. Therefore at least in this place there should be a commemoration of the founding of Waldorf pedagogy.[167] In these years there were frequent misunderstandings between those responsible for the Pedagogical Working Group under the protection of Marie Steiner and two members of the executive council, Günther Wachsmuth and Albert Steffen. The situation can only be explained as a spillover of the much sharper conflicts they had about other questions. Sometimes these misunderstandings and mutual accusations were discussed publicly.[168] This certainly did not help the strengthening of the pedagogical impulse.

Next to the work at the Goetheanum there was the *Freie Pädagogische Vereinigung* [Free Pedagogical Society] in Switzerland, doing work of a different nature, whichever way one wants to look at it. It always positioned itself independently from the Goetheanum and had the intention to work toward integrating Waldorf pedagogical impulses into the ordinary school system. On March 11, 1945, the Society organized a pedagogical conference in Bern with Max Leist and Marie Steiner, as well as a performance of the speech chorus led by Marie Steiner.[169] On May 6, 1945, the Free Pedagogical Society held its regular general meeting in Bern, led by Max Widmer.[170] After the death of Marie Steiner in 1948, the Pedagogical Working Group at the Goetheanum could no longer be continued.

167 Festival, N 42, October 15, 1944, p. 168.
168 Albert Steffen: Zur Urteilsbildung der Mitglieder. In: N 42, October 19, 1947, p. 168.
169 Announcement in Gegenwart Nr. 10, Jan. 1945, p. 427f.
170 Announcement in Gegenwart Nr. 1, April 1941, p. 40.

Waldorf Education
from 1919 to 1945:
School Portraits

Founding and Impulse of the
First Waldorf School in Stuttgart

ON NOVEMBER 9, 1918, Emil Molt (1876–1936) was in Zürich for business. While there, he heard about the revolution that had broken out in Germany and the abdication of the monarchy, which entailed the collapse of the world of the emperor and the rulers. The news that the Republic had been proclaimed spread very fast. Even though he had planned to drive back to Stuttgart after that, he decided right there to make a detour. He took the train to Basel and went to visit Rudolf Steiner, whom he had esteemed very highly for years. He wanted to ask him what he thought about this new situation. Thus he found himself in the wooden double dome of the first Goetheanum that evening, sitting and listening to the first lecture Rudolf Steiner gave in a cycle called "Entwicklungsgeschichtliche Unterlagen zur Bildung eines sozialen Urteils." [Developmental Foundations for the Formation of a Social Judgment][171]

About a week later, Emil Molt was speaking with one of the supervisors in the Waldorf Astoria cigarette factory, of which he was the director. In this conversation he realized the magnitude of the tragedy of workers not having access to higher education due to financial circumstances.[172] This sparked something in him, and the idea for the Waldorf school was born. This is how he described this meeting and what went on in him after that.

"As I made the rounds through the factory, the supervisor told me about a newly appointed works-council member (Ludwig Speidel), whose little son had been recommended to go to a secondary school by his teacher, who saw his potential. I saw the joy and engagement of the supervisor and the pride of the father who operated the machine. I had a long conversation with him because I had not seen him after he had returned from the battlefield. I could experience the effect on a worker when his child receives the education the father himself was not destined to receive. The child would be able to get ahead, which one day would give him the chance to rise to higher positions and not always be harnessed to a machine, in contrast to the father.

---

171 Rudolf Steiner: *Entwicklungsgeschichtliche Unterlagen zur Bildung eines sozialen Urteils*. GA 185a.

172 Sophia Christine Murphy: *The Multifaceted Life of Emil Molt*. 2012, p. 137. Sophia Christine Murphy is the granddaughter of Emil Molt. For the biography of her grandfather, she used his diaries, which had survived the war and had been kept safe by her godfather, Walter Rau. She started working on this biography in the United States and finished it in Ireland, her husband's home country.

Waldorf Astoria cigarette box

"But I also experienced how the joy was dampened by the fact that the means for the education were not there, because the happy father simply was not in a position to pay for tuition and school books. That's when I experienced the whole tragedy of the working class—to be barred by lack of money from partaking in education the way those who could afford it could do, and I imagined what it could mean for social progress if many entrepreneurs could see the same thing. This conversation, even though it may not have been particularly significant for Mr. Speidel, sparked the thought in me of founding a school, even though the thought was not concrete in any way yet. But in my memory this conversation lives on as the hour in which the idea of the founding of the Waldorf school was born. That was in the middle of November 1918."[173]

Ludwig Speidel was not the only one who pointed out the educational needs of the children to Emil Molt in November 1918. At the time, Lina Gronbach worked in his household. He had employed her when it was no longer possible for her and her three children to work in the Waldorf Astoria factory, where she had always taken the children when she worked there. At home, he always gave her the Waldorf newsletter and asked for her comments. But she was a single mother who had to educate her children on her own, and she would fall asleep reading this newsletter at night. Therefore she could not give him the desired answer. One day she plucked up her courage and told him that she herself would always remain a factory worker, but that her children needed a better future. That was another hint for Emil. And in September 1919, she enrolled her three children at the Uhlandshöhe School.[174]

Emil Molt, director and co-owner of the Waldorf Astoria cigarette factory in Stuttgart, promised his workers after the outbreak of World War I that he would keep their positions for them after they came back from the war and that he would employ them again. Emil Molt distinguished himself in many virtues typical for entrepreneurship in Swabia at the time. Among these virtues were faithfulness as well as the validity of a promise once given. After the war had ended in 1918, he stood by his promise and had to employ a large number of workers. He had only enough work for the half day, but he employed them all.

---

173 Emil Molt: *Dr. Rudolf Steiner und die Waldorfschule.* DD 5, 1925, p. 365f.
174 Interview with Eva Gronbach, March 27, 2018, in Frankfurt. Eva Gronbach also recounted how her great-grandmother, in filling out the rubric Family Status, wrote down that she was a widow because it was not proper at the time to register children simply as a single mother.

Emil, Berta, and Walter Molt with friends in front of their house

That was one of the reasons why he was like a father to many workers and always remained so even after the later dramatic events in the factory. He saw that many had returned from the war inwardly traumatized, demoralized, and lost. This made him decide to offer them further education during the half days when he had no work for them. He hired Dr. Herbert Hahn (1890–1970), who originally came from the Baltic region, and asked him to shape the course offerings and coordinate their implementation.[175]

At the end of January 1919, Emil Molt met with Rudolf Steiner again in Dornach, together with Roman Boos (1889–1952) and Hans Kühn (1899–1969). Several initiatives sprang from their conversations on January 27 in Dornach, among them the *Aufruf an das deutsche Volk und an die Kulturwelt* [Proclamation to the German People and the Civilized World], designed to counter the program of the American President, Woodrow Wilson; a nucleus for the threefold social order movement; and the suggestion to found independent schools "in order to teach people what they need."[176] A fourth initiative was the publication of the memoirs of Helmuth Graf von Moltke, in order to counteract the assertion that Germany bore the sole blame for the outbreak of World War I.

In April 1919, Stuttgart experienced the storm of revolution, which had been expected already in November 1918 and had taken place in Munich. The establishment of a soviet republic was being prepared. Called by the radical left Spartacists and

---

175 Sophia Christine Murphy: *The Multifaceted Life of Emil Molt*. 2012, p. 134; Herbert Hahn: *Der Weg, der mich führte*. 1969, p. 636.
176 Johannes Tautz: Schulgründung im Revolutionsjahr 1919. EK 8–9, 1969, p. 309ff.

The Waldorf Astoria cigarette factory at Hackstrasse 9-13 in Stuttgart

independents, a general strike began April 1, but soon collapsed mid-April. The state of emergency was lifted again. On April 11, Emil Molt called E. A. Karl Stockmeyer, asking him to help build up a school for the children of the workers and employees of the Waldorf Astoria cigarette factory and offering him the leadership of the planned school.[177] It was to be directed as part of the factory and be carried by it financially. On April 22, Rudolf Steiner was in Stuttgart again and gave a public lecture in the Stadtgartensaal.[178] The Threefold Association was founded that same evening, and a work committee was appointed, consisting of Emil Molt, Prof. Wilhelm von Blume, Dr. Carl Unger, Hans Kühn, Emil Leinhas, Max Benzinger, and Theodor Binder.[179]

Emil Molt had been orphaned and uprooted when he was 13 years old. At age 14, his relatives put him in the lyceum of Prof. Weizsäcker in Calw, a school for difficult boys.[180] Once there, he managed to find his bearings after the bitter loss of his parents. He engaged in school work and developed his own intentions for life. After his final exam, he stayed in Calw and was employed as an apprentice in the Georgii firm. Under the strict tutelage of Emil Georgii, he learned the basics of business management, and it was also in Calw that he met Berta Heldmaier. She was the

---

177 E. A. Karl Stockmeyer: Die Entfaltung der Idee der Waldorfschule im Sommer 1919. EK 8–9, 1989, p. 655; E. A. Karl Stockmeyer: *Die Entfaltung der Idee der Waldorfschule im Sommer 1919–zum 7. September 1949.* LR 56, 1996, pp. 3–18.
178 Rudolf Steiner: *Neugestaltung des sozialen Organismus.* Lecture of April 22, 1919, in GA 330, 1983, p. 13ff.
179 Christoph Lindenberg: *Rudolf Steiner. Eine Chronik.* 1988, p. 405.
180 Today called Hermann-Hesse-Gymnasium Calw: http://hhg-calw.de/geschichte (site visited February 3, 2017).

love of his life; throughout their faithful partnership, she mediated for him and was his constant inspiration. They both knew from the moment they first met that they wanted to go through life together. Under the societal mores of that time, however, it was very complicated to meet alone before being married.

So it took some ingenuity to find ways to see each other and speak with one another on occasion. It was only after Emil Molt came back from a job with the firm of Hamburg and Co. in Patras, Greece, which began when he was twenty years old, that he asked the Heldmaier family for their permission to marry Berta. After the wedding, the couple

Emil Molt completed his vocational training in the trading house of Emil Georgii (fifth house from the right).

went to live in Stuttgart, where Emil occupied a position in Georgii's son's newly founded firm, Georgii & Harr, Inc. Working for this firm, he gained the knowledge that enabled him later to become chief shareholder and business manager of a newly founded factory, the Waldorf Astoria cigarette factory.

As part of the ongoing education program that Herbert Hahn organized, Rudolf Steiner held his first lecture for the workers of the Waldorf Astoria cigarette factory on April 23, 1919. Directly after this lecture, Steiner participated in a session of the factory counsel at which Emil Molt spoke about his intention to found a school.[181] In this very session Emil Molt asked Rudolf Steiner whether he would take on the leadership of the new school. Rudolf Steiner promised Emil Molt to help him found this school for the children of the factory workers. "How great was our joy when he said yes!"[182] This moment was designated by Emil Molt as the birth moment of the actual founding of the Waldorf School, not only the idea. And he worked tirelessly for the school in the coming months and years.

The day after, on April 24, the first committee meeting of the Threefold Association took place. The conversation turned to schools and the necessity to free schools from state tutelage. When asked for specifics, Rudolf Steiner answered, "First and foremost, I would never found anthroposophical schools. Anthroposophists have to transform methods and organization, but never teach anthroposophy. Spiritual freedom is the first thing we have to understand. The thing to avoid most is teaching a worldview." In answer to another question, Rudolf Steiner added: "There is an

181 Sophia Christine Murphy: *The Multifaceted Life of Emil Molt.* 2012, p. 143.
182 Emil Molt: *Dr. Rudolf Steiner und die Waldorfschule.* DD 5, 1925, p. 367.

additional pedagogical factor here: If we were to educate children up to their 14th year according to a cookie-cutter model and would then release them into present-day competitive society, we would turn all children into nervous weaklings. But when there is freedom in the school, truth will reign instead of mendacity, and that will make up for it. For education it's much less important what religion the child is being taught than that one meets children with a truthful heart."[183]

Rudolf Steiner, 1923

On April 25, 1919,[184] Rudolf Steiner held a lecture for the workers of the Daimler automobile factory in Untertürkheim, after which a memorable conversation took place later that evening in the blue hall of the building of the Anthroposophical Society, Landhausstrasse 70, after ten o'clock at night.[185] Rudolf Steiner, Herbert Hahn, E. A. Karl Stockmeyer, and Emil Molt were there.

Looking back, Emil Molt called this conversation the first teachers meeting, which was about basic questions on how to shape an independent school. E. A. Karl Stockmeyer, who was a state school employee in Baden teaching mathematics and natural science, had, of course, been asked to join this conversation since Emil Molt had tapped him on the shoulder earlier.[186] During this evening conversation, Rudolf Steiner sketched a curriculum and a daily schedule[187] for the first time, referring to

183 E. A. Karl Stockmeyer: Die Entfaltung der Idee der Waldorfschule im Sommer 1919. EK 8–9, 1989, p. 657.

184 Emil Molt: *Dr. Rudolf Steiner und die Waldorfschule*. DD 5, 1925, p. 361: "The first lecture for workers took place in the Waldorf Astoria factory on April 25, 1919. I cannot think of this day without a feeling of the highest happiness, because a pure enthusiasm gripped all of us when we heard this gospel of the social question from him. In connection with this, a session of the factory counsel, which I was part of, took place, during which we asked Dr. Steiner officially to take on the leadership of the school. We were overjoyed when he said yes! We could only feel it as a historical inauguration, which only future generations would know how to value rightly. When we told him we had 100,000 marks at our disposition, he smiled and said in his customary good-natured way, 'A modest start, but it's a beginning at least.'"

185 Herbert Hahn: *Der Weg, der mich führte*. 1969, p. 656; E. A. Karl Stockmeyer: Von den ersten Schritten zur Waldorfschule. In: *Rudolf Steiner in der Waldorfschule*. Edited by Caroline von Heydebrand. 1927, p. 35. E. A. Karl Stockmeyer: Aufzeichnung über die Unterredung mit Dr. Steiner am Freitag, den 25. April abends 10 Uhr. [Notes about the conversation with Dr. Steiner on Friday, April 25, ten o'clock at night]. Archiv LS 10.10.12.

186 Christoph Lindenberg: *Rudolf Steiner. Eine Biographie 1915–1925*. 1997, p. 667.

187 Herbert Hahn: Von Tagen und von Stunden, die zum Werden der Waldorfschule führten. ZPRSt III, September 3–4, 1929, p. 127; Herbert Hahn: *Der Weg, der mich führte*. 1969, pp. 658–665; Sophia Christine Murphy: *The Multifaceted Life of Emil Molt*. 2012, p. 144; Emil Molt: *Entwurf meiner Lebensbeschreibung*. 1972, p. 204.

E.A. Karl Stockmeyer

the former Austrian elementary school plan. At this point in time, Rudolf Steiner was thinking of a school going up to eleventh grade and imagined that the upper two grades could be tied in with university. These two years should serve general education—comparable to an American college—after which professional studies would follow. According to the notes of E.A. Karl Stockmeyer, the teaching aims for the schools were formulated as follows by Rudolf Steiner: "In German, teaching should go up to business correspondence; in history, after a general course, national history should be studied; the same for geography, first a general course, then the national geography. There should be world languages, especially English, mathematics and physics with special emphasis on mechanics; natural history; drawing; painting, above all; singing; and gymnastics. […] Dr. Steiner stressed that Latin is merely a remnant of convent schools—Greek, however would be more valuable. He said that grammar schools produce educational mummies and would definitely disappear in the future. Mechanics is much more important than Latin."[188]

In this conversation Rudolf Steiner suggested hiring Herbert Hahn and E.A. Karl Stockmeyer as teachers for the 100 or 120 Waldorf Astoria children and to teach them in two parallel classes. Rudolf Steiner ended the conversation with a remark about the nature of testing. "The nature of testing has to change in such a way that state exams are dropped and that the doctor qualification remains as the real academic examination. However, passing such a test should not give people a special privilege. In life there is free competition."[189] After this conversation, Emil Molt charged E.A. Karl Stockmeyer with working out a plan for the new school, detailed enough that it could be presented to the State ministry of culture.[190]

Because Emil Molt had waited in vain for the ministry to give him a state building for the school, he was looking for a suitable building, and a happy coincidence helped him. On May 1, 1919, the workers of the Waldorf Astoria celebrated the day in Café-Restaurant Uhlandshöhe and were happy to invite Emil Molt for the festival and the dance afterward. The very next day he said, "That would be the ideal spot for our school!"[191]

---

188 E.A. Karl Stockmeyer: Aufzeichnung über die Unterredung mit Dr. Steiner am Freitag, den 25. April abends 10 Uhr. Archiv LS 10.10.12.
189 Ibid.
190 Ibid., pp. 654–667.
191 Sophia Christine Murphy: *The Multifaceted Life of Emil Molt*. 2012, p. 146.

On Tuesday, May 13, 1919, at 10:00 a.m., a conversation took place with the minister of culture for Württemberg, Berthold Heymann (1870–1939), and school superintendent Dr. Friedrich Reinöhl. Berthold Heymann occupied the position of minister of culture only November 9, 1918–October 31, 1919, and served in no ministerial post after that. But he is the one who had his hand on the tiller. It is he who had to make the official decision to give the Waldorf School permission to operate and, without him, the school would not have been able to start on the scale it did.

In the course of this conversation between Rudolf Steiner, Emil Molt, E. A. Karl Stockmeyer, the minister, and the superintendent, the prospect

Berthold Heymann, the Württemberg minister of culture

was raised that they would get permission from the authorities and, what was highly important, that they would be allowed to employ people who had an academic degree without the stipulation of taking the teacher diploma. The ministry was inclined to apply criteria of academic training and life experience in giving permission.[192] In order to make granting permission possible, Berthold Heymann cited a Württemberg law from the year 1836 that permitted private schools to employ teachers without an official state diploma. E. A. Karl Stockmeyer reported in a handwritten manuscript dated December 3, 1938,[193] that this attitude of Minister Heymann's, that he was not demanding state testing of teachers, was the decisive factor for Rudolf Steiner to go ahead and found the school. The minister also approved the request for coeducation of girls and boys, but not the shift to starting school at age seven, which was prescribed by law to be a half year later. School inspection, according to the minister, should confine itself to hygiene and to what the state prescribed in that respect, so that at least the requirements of the state school would be met.

Ten years later Dr. Reinöhl reported, "I still remember the power of conviction and the passion with which the gentlemen stood for the idea of the new school. The old saying came to mind: 'If it's good it'll survive, if it's bad, it'll go under.' You can

192 In this conversation Rudolf Steiner said, according to Emil Molt, with reference to class size, that it was the same to him whether there were 25 or 125 children in one class. What would be lost in terms of individual attention would be gained by the students working together. Only the first four weeks would be difficult until one had organized the work. See also E. A. Karl Stockmeyer: Skizzenhafte Aufzeichnung über die Audienz beim Kultminister Heymann am Dienstag, den 13. Mai 10 Uhr. Archiv LS 10.10.13.

193 E. A. Karl Stockmeyer: Von der Gründung und ersten Entwicklung der Freien Waldorfschule in Stuttgart im Jahr 1919. Archiv LS 10.10.04.

also turn this around. The work has proved itself and has grown into a gigantic tree spreading its branches far beyond this town and state. So it must have value and caliber."[194] How quickly were these basic tenets for an independent school abandoned in the ensuing decades!

E. A. Karl Stockmeyer was still teaching in Mannheim then and could come to Stuttgart for only a few days at a time. When he was in Stuttgart again on May 25, he spoke with Rudolf Steiner about the future teachers and suggested a few persons who could be considered. Of those, only Herbert Hahn really became a teacher. In this conversation they also exchanged more ideas about curriculum possibilities.[195] A few days later, on June 1, they continued their conversation, and Rudolf Steiner suggested Dr. Caroline von Heydebrand and Dr. Rudolf Treichler as possible teachers as well as Michael Bauer, on whose collaboration he was very keen. In the same conversation of June 1, Rudolf Steiner asked E. A. Karl Stockmeyer to travel through the different German states like a theater director collecting an ensemble and talk to teachers who were involved in the movement.[196] "We cannot use people who would just lean on us; we need people who have earned their spurs out there in the world."[197] As soon as enough teachers would come together, Rudolf Steiner wanted to hold a course and then decide who should really participate in the school.[198]

From her brother, Caroline von Heydebrand had heard the first rumors about the founding of a school in Stuttgart and had therefore written a letter dated June 2, 1919, to E. A. Karl Stockmeyer in which she offered her services. The letter ended with the sentence, "I have always cherished the wish to organize a little school on an anthroposophical basis."[199] Financed by Emil Molt, E. A. Karl Stockmeyer started his tour on June 26, after Rudolf Steiner had drawn his attention to Leonie von Mirbach in Halle and Friedrich Oehlschlegel in Marburg. Leonie von Mirbach was born in Alexandria, Egypt, had spent most of her childhood in Riga, and then attended the lyceum in Tübingen. She had moved from Tübingen to Munich to study philosophy and biology. There she got to know anthroposophy and then went to Marburg and Halle.

E. A. Karl Stockmeyer's journey carried him from Munich and Nürnberg to Halle, Leipzig, Dresden, Breslau, and from there on to Berlin, Hamburg, Hannover, and, on the return journey, to Bochum, Elberfeld, and Hagen. In Munich, E. A. Karl

---

194 Dr. Friedrich Reinöhl: Ansprache zur 10-Jahresfeier. ZPRSt, Februar 1930, p. 328f.
195 E. A. Karl Stockmeyer: Die Entfaltung der Idee der Waldorfschule im Sommer 1919–zum 7. September 1949. LR 56, 1996, p. 10f.
196 Johannes Tautz: E. A. Karl Stockmeyer. In: Gisbert Husemann and Johannes Tautz (eds.): *Der Lehrerkreis um Rudolf Steiner*. 1979,² p. 48.
197 Rudolf Steiner 1919, unidentified source.
198 E. A. Karl Stockmeyer: Die Entfaltung der Idee der Waldorfschule im Sommer 1919. EK 8–9, 1989, p. 664.
199 Margrit Jünemann: *Caroline von Heydebrand. Pionierin der Waldorfpädagogik*. 2003, p. 36.

Johannes Geyer, class teacher at the Waldorf School in Stuttgart from 1919 to 1933

Stockmeyer met Hertha Koegel and Dr. Rudolf Treichler, as well as Michael Bauer, who felt too old to join, however. In Nürnberg he got to know Andreas Körner; in Halle/Saale he met Leonie von Mirbach and Elfriede Herrmann; in Breslau, Moritz Bartsch and Gertrud Ehmling; in Berlin, Rudolf Meyer; and in Hamburg, Johannes Geyer. On July 14 he returned to Stuttgart.[200] Earlier, on July 12, he had sent Emil Molt a letter containing a list of 19 names, four of which turned up in the end on the list of the group of founding teachers.[201]

On May 30 Emil Molt was offered the piece of land with the Restaurant Uhlandshöhe, situated on what was then the Kanonenweg. Molt wrote: "It was as if the place was made for our purposes, which Steiner confirmed when we looked at it together, but the selling price was really beyond my means." A few days later Emil Molt bought the idyllic 29-plus acres on the southern slope of Stuttgart for the sum of 450,000 RM,[202] paid for out of his own resources, even though he had reserved only 100,000 RM from his factory's net profit of 1918 for this purpose. That was a sum Rudolf Steiner had considered modest but a good start when Emil Molt mentioned it during the conversation of April 23.

During the war years 1916–1917, Emil Molt foresaw that it would become very difficult to continue to produce cigarettes in Germany because the reserves of tobacco would dwindle and be difficult to replenish. He possessed more than others anyway because he had bought large amounts in September 1914 in Dresden. For these reasons he took the initiative to found another Waldorf Astoria branch in Switzerland.[203] Through the Swiss venture he bought more tobacco, for which he earned credit from neutral Swiss banks. In addition, Emil Molt had stockpiles in Xanthi and Smyrna (Izmir). The governmental agency controlling the tobacco industry had pressed him to put part of his stored tobacco at the disposal of other firms. He saved the stockpiles in Turkey by promising to earmark the 200,000 kg of tobacco in Izmir for that purpose and booked that amount off the inventory list of his firm so that the amount met

200 E. A. Karl Stockmeyer: Die Entfaltung der Idee der Waldorfschule im Sommer 1919–zum 7. September 1949. LR 56, 1996, p. 16.

201 Letter from E. A. Karl Stockmeyer to Emil Molt, dated July 12, 1919. Archiv LS 10.10.17.

202 Dietrich Esterl: *Die erste Waldorfschule*. 2006, p. 58ff.; Dietrich Esterl: *Emil Molt 1876–1936. Tun, was gefordert ist.* 2012, p. 95ff.

203 Sophia Christine Murphy: *The Multifaceted Life of Emil Molt.* 2012, p. 119; Dietrich Esterl: *Emil Molt 1876–1936. Tun, was gefordert ist.* 2012, p. 43; Emil Molt: *Entwurf meiner Lebensbeschreibung.* 1972, p. 144.

the quota allowed by the governmental agency (*Zitag*) overseeing this. That is why Waldorf Astoria, Inc., had sufficient resources for a long time and was able to make additional profit which partly came from sales abroad and that remained in Zürich, where the Swiss branch was located. Large amounts of the money from these profits enabled Molt to buy the property on the Uhlandshöhe.

On June 1, Rudolf Steiner first sketched out the ideas for teaching in blocks, which would be worked out further in the coming weeks and months and which became one of the fundamental methodological elements of Waldorf pedagogy: "If we are serious about our mandate to make education healthy, it will be necessary to make sure that growing human beings can stay with one thing for as long as concentrated occupation with one thing is needed at their stage of development."[204]

In the application for approval of the Waldorf School, which was sent in on July 2, 1919, Emil Molt wrote that he wanted to found "a private school for the employees and workers of our factory."[205] A few days later, on July 18, Emil Molt received preliminary permission from minister of the interior, Johannes von Hieber (1862–1951),[206] who succeeded Berthold Heymann in 1920 as minister of culture and who became president of the state of Württemberg in 1924.[207]

On July 15, E. A. Karl Stockmeyer had a conversation with Rudolf Steiner in which a list of incoming faculty was drawn up for the first time, based on all the conversations E. A. Karl Stockmeyer had had on his tour. At this time the two of them agreed on Paul Baumann, the Rev. Johannes Geyer, Herbert Hahn, Hertha Koegel, Rudolf Meyer, Leonie von Mirbach, Friedrich Oehlschlegel, and, of course, E. A. Karl Stockmeyer himself.

Emil Molt describes in his memoirs how he picked up Rudolf and Marie Steiner in Dornach on August 19, 1919, in his firm's large automobile. He had never seen Rudolf Steiner as joyful and content as on this journey through the Valley of the Elz, via Haslach into the Kinzig Valley and then to Freudenstadt via Zwieselberg, Emil Molt's favorite stretch.[208] They arrived on time for the evening, when the people invited for the teachers course were welcomed cordially. On August 20, the future teachers gathered in order to partake in the preparatory course the morning after, the course that was to form the foundation stone for the new education. Twenty-four people participated: Paul Baumann, Elisabeth Dollfuss (who would become Elisabeth Baumann after her marriage a few weeks later), Johannes Geyer, Herbert

204 Rudolf Steiner: *Geisteswissenschaftliche Behandlung sozialer und pädagogischer Fragen*. GA 192, 1964, p. 127ff.
205 Norbert Deuchert: *Waldorfschule und Staat 1919–1938*. BhB Advent 1986, p. 75.
206 Facsimile in Dietrich Esterl: *Die erste Waldorfschule Stuttgart-Uhlandshöhe 1919 bis 2004. Daten–Dokumente–Bilder*. 2006, p. 53.
207 For an account of the objections of the Social Democrats and the counter arguments, see: Albert Schmelzer: *Die Dreigliederungsbewegung 1919*. 1991, p. 234f.
208 Emil Molt: *Entwurf meiner Lebensbeschreibung*. 1972, p. 206.

The Zur Uhlandshöhe restaurant, a popular Sunday destination.
Emil Molt acquired it in 1919 for the Waldorf School.

Hahn, Elfriede Herrmann, Caroline von Heydebrand, Luise Kieser (as a guest from Heilbronn), Hertha Koegel, Andreas Körner (as a guest from Nürnberg), Hannah Lang, Rudolf Meyer, Leonie von Mirbach, Berta and Emil Molt, Dr. Ludwig Noll, Friedrich Oehlschlegel, Walter Johannes Stein (as a guest from Vienna), Marie Steiner, E. A. Karl Stockmeyer, Alexander Strakosch (as a guest), Rudolf Treichler, Mieta Waller-Pyle, Karl Emil Wolfer (as a guest), and Hermann Heisler. To these listeners, some of whom helped to shape the venture and became teachers, Rudolf Steiner voiced the following intentions for the Waldorf School:

"To achieve a renewal of modern spiritual life, the Waldorf School must be a true cultural deed. We must reckon with change in everything; the ultimate foundation of the whole social movement is in the spiritual realm, and the question of education is one of the burning spiritual questions of modern times. We must take advantage of the possibilities presented by the Waldorf School to reform and revolutionize the educational system.

"The success of this cultural deed is in your hands. Thus, you have much responsibility in working to create an example. So much depends upon the success of this deed. The Waldorf School will be living proof of the effectiveness of the anthroposophical orientation toward life. It will be a unified school in the sense that it considers how to teach only in the way demanded by the human being, by the totality of the human essence. We must put everything at the service of achieving this goal. [...] Therefore we will organize the school not bureaucratically, but collegially, and will administer it in a republican way. In a true teachers' republic, we will not have the comfort of receiving directions from the Board of Education. Rather, we must bring to our work what gives each of us the possibility and the full responsibility for what we have to do. Each one of us must be completely responsible. […] We can achieve that sense of unity through this course if we work with all diligence. […]

"We must be conscious of the great tasks before us. We dare not be simply educators; we must be people of culture in the highest sense of the word. We must have a living interest in everything happening today, otherwise we will be bad teachers for this school. We dare not have enthusiasm only for our special tasks. We can only be good teachers when we have a living interest in everything happening in the world. Through that interest in the world we must obtain the enthusiasm that we need for the school and for our tasks. Flexibility of spirit and devotion to our tasks are necessary."[209]

The planned courses took place August 21–September 5. Starting in the morning at 9:00 was the lecture cycle "Allgemeine Menschenkunde" [General Anthropology, 14 lectures] and, after a 15-minute break, a second lecture cycle at 11:00, "Methodisch-Didaktisches" [Methodology and Didactic, also 14 lectures]. In the afternoon from 3:00 to 6:00 were "Seminarbesprechungen und Lehrplanvorträge" [Seminar Meetings and Curriculum Lectures] with extensive contributions [by Steiner].[210]

Johannes Tautz, a longtime teacher at the Waldorf School on the Uhlandshöhe who knew a wealth of stories from the time when the school was founded, repeatedly pointed out the importance of this world-historical cultural deed and made sure that the different levels of meaning would not be lost on the teachers of his time. He explained that the founding on the earthly plane was complemented by a founding from out of the spirit, and this happened in three phases. "To begin with, the course given in August 1919, *The Foundations of Human Experience*, in which Rudolf Steiner laid the foundations for the new pedagogical work. This involves something important, namely that the teachers have to figure out how to individually establish the connection with the spiritual powers at whose behest and in whose mandate every individual teacher will work.[211] Then the world of the third hierarchy is pointed out, the world of those beings, whose support the pedagogical work needs. As a third step, the pathways are shown to these beings, who can be approached every evening for their helping support. Thus teachers can practice accessing this source, which Rudolf Steiner opened up at the founding of the school. One can only go on this path by one's own decision. In principle, it is a matter of 'self-calling.' The results will be seen by all the others."[212]

---

209 Rudolf Steiner: Opening Address, August 20, 1919. In: *The Foundations of Human Experience*. CW 293.
210 Rudolf Steiner: *The Foundations of Human Experience*. CW 293; *Practical Advice to Teachers*. CW294; *Discussions with Teachers*. CW 295.
211 Recalled later by Caroline von Heydebrand, Herbert Hahn, and Walter Johannes Stein, but not taken down by the stenographer.
212 Johannes Tautz in an article, Die Gründung und Führung der ersten Waldorfschule, made available for the participants in the International Conference in 1988. Archiv BFWS.

The First School Year

ON SEPTEMBER 7, 1919, the school was opened with a festive celebration in the large auditorium of the municipal park, with over 1000 people attending. At the beginning and at the end of the celebration there was music by Johann Sebastian Bach. Emil Molt greeted the assembled guests and gave a picture of the founding motives, after which he addressed the expectant children and the teachers:

"[...] Ladies and gentlemen, dear children! The idea to found the Waldorf School did not spring from a personal whim, but from the perception of a real need in our present time. That's how the thought came to me. I simply felt it was necessary to create the first so-called comprehensive school and really answer a social need, so that in the future not only the sons and daughters of the well-to-do, but also the children of simple workers will be able to acquire the kind of education that is necessary today in order to rise to a higher level of culture.

"[...] In this sense it is highly satisfying for me that it was possible to give life to this school. But what is needed today is not just an institution; it needs to be filled with a new spirit. And in order that such a spirit will fill this institution, we are beholden to anthroposophically oriented spiritual science, and for that reason I have to express my profound gratitude here to the one who has given us this spiritual science, our beloved Dr. Rudolf Steiner. But I also express my gratitude to the authorities for giving us permission to create this institution, so that today we are fortunate enough to be able to carry out our intentions and make them a reality. [...]"[213]

After that Rudolf Steiner gave the opening speech for this festive occasion. A significant part will be quoted here because of its fundamental importance.

"For me, ladies and gentlemen, it has been a sacred obligation to take up what lay in our friend Herr Molt's intentions in founding the Waldorf School, and to do so in a way that enabled the school to be fashioned out of what we believe to have won from spiritual science in our present time. This school is really intended to be integrated into what the evolution of humanity requires of us at present and in the near future. Actually, in the end, everything that flows into the educational system from such requirements constitutes a threefold sacred obligation.

"Of what use would be all of the human community's feeling, understanding, and working if these could not condense into the sacred responsibility taken on by teachers in their specific social communities when they embark on the ultimate community service with children, with human beings who are growing up and developing? In the end, everything we are capable of knowing about human beings and about the world only really becomes fruitful when we can convey it in a living

---

213 Emil Molt's speech is printed in a different translation in *Rudolf Steiner in the Waldorf School*. CW 298, 1996, p. 11ff.

Program for the opening of the Waldorf School on September 7, 1919

way to those who will fashion society when we ourselves can no longer contribute our physical work.

"Everything we can accomplish artistically achieves its highest good only when we let it flow into the greatest of all art forms, the art in which we are given, not a dead medium such as sound or color, but living human beings, incomplete and imperfect, whom we are to transform to some extent, through art and education, into accomplished human beings.

"And is it not ultimately a very holy and religious obligation to cultivate and educate the divine spiritual element that manifests anew in every human being who was born? Is this educational service not a religious service in the highest sense of the word? Is it not so that all the holiest stirrings of humanity, which we dedicate to religious feeling, must come together in our service at the altar when we attempt to cultivate the divine spiritual aspect of the human being whose potentials are revealed in the growing child?

Science that comes alive!

Art that comes alive!

Religion that comes alive!

In the end that is what education is.

"[…] Into [the] intellectual attitude of humanity must come the conviction that spirit is alive in all natural existence, and that we are capable of recognizing this spirit. This is why, in the course that preceded this Waldorf venture, in the course intended for teachers, we attempted to found an anthropology or science of education that will develop into an art of education and a study of humanity that will once again raise from the dead what is alive in the human being. The dead—and this is the secret of our dying, contemporary culture—is what makes people knowing, what gives them insight when they take it up as natural law. However, it also weakens the feeling that is the source of teachers' inspiration and enthusiasm, and it weakens the will. It does not grant human beings a harmonious place within society as a whole.

"We are looking for a science that is not mere science, that is itself life and feeling. When such a science streams into the human soul as knowledge, it will immediately develop the power to be active as love and to stream forth as effective, working will, as work that has been steeped in soul warmth, and especially as work that applies to the living, to the growing human being. We need a new scientific attitude. Above all we need a new spirit for the entire art of education. [...] The conviction that the call resounding from humanity's evolution demands a new spirit for our present age, and that we must carry this spirit into the school system first and foremost, is what underlies the efforts of this Waldorf School, which is intended to be a model along these lines."[214]

This address was followed by recitation, singing, and a small eurythmy performance by a few students of the future combined seventh/eighth grade, Fritz Koegel[215] and Walter Molt among them. Humorous poems by Christian Morgenstern, such as *Der Lattenzaun* [The Picket Fence] and *Das ästhetische Wiesel* [The Artistic Weasel], were also on the program. The future students moved very ceremoniously in their eurythmy smocks (which the students called a "special bag") and could hardly suppress their laughter because, in Walter Molt's pocket, sewn especially on to his smock, a little mouse was hopping along.[216]

After that, E. A. Karl Stockmeyer addressed the teachers, and Mr. Saria addressed the workers of the Waldorf Astoria, Inc.[217] Following this, they all went up to the

---

214 Rudolf Steiner: *Rudolf Steiner in the Waldorf School*. CW 298, 1996, p. 14ff [with one small adaptation by the translator of this book].

215 Fritz Koegel passed his final exam at the Waldorf School on the Uhlandshöhe in 1928, after which he studied at the Technical College in Stuttgart. As a young engineer he constructed fighter jets with the Messerschmidt company. When the Nazi regime took over, he changed jobs and worked for the research department at the research Institute for automobiles in Stuttgart. In 1938 he married Lotte Kraus. While he was an American prisoner of war, he received a letter from her in which she wrote: "The teacher seminar has started up again. I have registered you." On his return he decided to become a Waldorf teacher and, together with Dr. Erich Gabert and Dr. Emil Kühn, he built up the Waldorf School Stuttgart-Kräherwald, starting in October 1948. Ernst Weissert asked him to join the Executive Council of the German Federation of Waldorf Schools. See: Manfred Leist: Fritz Koegel 75 Jahre. LR 26, 1983, p. 87; Sylvia Bardt and Gottfried Lesch: Fritz Koegel (December 21, 1907–May 13, 1997). LR 61, 1997, p. 83ff.

216 Sophia Christine Murphy: *The Multifaceted Life of Emil Molt*. 2012, p. 152.

217 Facsimile of the invitation in: Dietrich Esterl: *Die erste Waldorfschule Stuttgart-Uhlandshöhe 1919 bis 2004. Daten–Dokumente–Bilder*. 2006, p. 69; Christoph Lindenberg: *Rudolf Steiner. Eine Biographie. 1915–1925*. Volume 2, 1997, p. 674.

Uhlandshöhe, where the grades were assigned and the teachers introduced. In the evening, Berta and Emil Molt invited the teachers together with Marie and Rudolf Steiner to go to the Stuttgart Opera House to see *The Magic Flute*.

The day after that, on September 8, 1919, at ten o'clock in the morning, the very first faculty meeting was held. They discussed the beginning of school, the teachers were assigned their classes, and the daily schedule was determined. Methodological firsts were laid down: teaching in age groups, coeducation, teaching different levels within one class, no selection by means of grading or doubling classes. There was no precedent for any of these.[218] There were other indications Rudolf Steiner gave this day that did not become part of Waldorf traditions: in grades one through five there was to be both English and French every day. Singing, music, and eurythmy were to be taught in the afternoon, whereby gymnasts were to watch eurythmy and eurythmists were to watch gymnastics.

A week later, costly and time-consuming renovations to the café, carried out by a friend of Emil Molt's, architect Emil Weippert, were far enough along that school could start in this space. Anna and E.A. Karl Stockmeyer moved into the janitor's apartment under the roof. On Tuesday, September 16, 256 excited children appeared on the school grounds.[219] Of them, 191 were Waldorf Astoria children, i.e., their parents or family worked in the Waldorf Astoria cigarette factory. Before the lessons given by the 12 teachers in their eight classrooms began, Emil Molt gave a talk. After that the children went to the classrooms with the teachers. The grades were led by the following teachers:

First grade: Leonie von Mirbach (1890–1973)
Second grade: Rev. Johannes Geyer (1882–1964)
Third grade: Hannah Lang (1892–1968)
Fourth grade: Hertha Koegel (1881–1923)
Fifth grade: Dr. Caroline von Heydebrand (1886–1938),[220]
    the biggest class with 47 pupils!
Sixth grade: Friedrich Oehlschlegel (1891–?)
Seventh and eighth grades: E.A. Karl Stockmeyer and Dr. Rudolf Treichler
    (1883–1972), who alternated blocks.

Herbert Hahn, Dr. Walter Johannes Stein (1891–1957), Paul Baumann (1887–1964), and Elisabeth Baumann-Dollfuss worked as subject teachers. In addition, the faculty included Rudolf Steiner as the director, Marie Steiner guiding the eurythmy

218 Dietrich Esterl: *Emil Molt 1876–1936. Tun, was gefordert ist.* 2012, p. 108.
219 Erich Gabert: *Rudolf Steiner: Konferenzen mit den Lehrern der Freien Waldorfschule.* AG 300/1, 1975, p. 43. In Dietrich Esterl: *Die erste Waldorfschule Stuttgart-Uhlandshöhe 1919 bis 2004. Daten–Dokumente–Bilder.* 2006, September 18, 1919, is given as the first day of school. In Dietrich Esterl: *Emil Molt 1876–1936. Tun, was gefordert ist.* 2012, p. 107, September 14, 1919. In Emil Molt: *Entwurf meiner Lebensbeschreibung.* 1979, p. 208, it says eight days after September 7.
220 Wilhelm von Heydebrand: Aus Aufzeichnungen für die Familienchronik. LR 33, 1987, p. 6of.

Dagmar Tillis, class teacher 1923–1936, and Helene Rommel, handwork teacher 1919–1959 at the Waldorf School in Stuttgart

department, Emil Molt as "protector" and Berta Molt (1876–1939) as school mother and later handwork teacher. In the course of the first year, Rudolf Treichler had to give more and more foreign language periods, and so Walter Johannes Stein took his place and led the class together with E. A. Karl Stockmeyer until graduation. From that point on, grades seven and eight each had only one class teacher. At the end of October 1919, handwork was added as a subject, which was taught for a long time by Helene Rommel (1887–1973)[221] and Berta Molt together. Helene Rommel taught handwork for 33 years at the school, from 1919 until 1959. The first school year was splendid, and everything had a special verve and enthusiasm.

So, the first 12 Waldorf teachers had not had much time to prepare for their new task, only for 14 days in fact, and they barely knew each other. From one day to the next, they were now supposed to work together as a college, consult together, make decisions together. This happened in weekly faculty meetings, as was suggested by E. A. Karl Stockmeyer in the meeting with Rudolf Steiner of September 25, 1919. When he made this suggestion, Rudolf Steiner answered, "That would be a very good thing. Something to look forward to with joy. Such meetings should be held in a truly republican way."[222]

Ever since that time Waldorf schools hold faculty meetings on Thursday afternoons and evenings, during which essential (sometimes also nonessential) questions are considered. This also shows that Rudolf Steiner and Emil Molt had no ready-made school concept, but that the pedagogical and organizational forms of the Waldorf school developed slowly, changed and are changing, then as now, with each new person entering. Dr. Karl Schubert (1889–1949) joined the faculty in 1920 and kept a stenographic record of faculty meetings held with Rudolf Steiner. Thanks to these stenographic records, which are the basis for the printed edition of the teachers meetings with Rudolf Steiner, and especially thanks to the painstaking work of Erich Gabert, we now have three volumes of these *Konferenzen* available to us in print.[223]

221 Helene Rommel's youngest brother, Gerhard (see LR 24, 1984, p. 82), came into contact with Waldorf education through her. He changed from studying agriculture to eurythmy and became a eurythmist and pianist. From 1927 he worked as a eurythmy accompanist at the Stuttgart school. After the war he joined the faculty of the Waldorf school in Ulm, where he stayed until his retirement. One of Helene's older brothers was the well-known general nicknamed Desert Fox.

222 Rudolf Steiner: *Conferences with the Teachers of the Free Waldorf School in Stuttgart, 1919–1924, Vol. 1.* CW 300a, 1975, p. 83.

223 Rudolf Steiner: *Faculty Meetings with Teachers, Vols. 1–3,* edited by Erich Gabert, Hans Rudolf Niederhäuser, and Anton Rodi. CW 300a-b, GA 300c, Dornach 1975. Before that, *Faculty Meetings with*

Rudolf Steiner had the final say in appointing the teachers. He pulled in spiritually productive, artistically active people who could take initiative. Only a small number of them had a teaching diploma, and therefore they all had to present a written curriculum vitae to the Stuttgart authorities, the agreed-upon prerequisite for official permission for the school. Dr. Rudolf Treichler, Dr. Walter Johannes Stein, and E. A. Karl Stockmeyer were prepared extremely well academically. For example, in his university studies in Heidelberg, E. A. Karl Stockmeyer had striven for a truly universal education; he studied mathematics, physics chemistry, geology, botany, philosophy, astronomy, comparative anatomy, and architecture. Walter Johannes Stein, who had grown up in Vienna and had gone to school with Eugen Kolisko, had studied mathematics, physics, and philosophy and had received a PhD in theory of knowledge. Rudolf Steiner asked him—in an approach he took with many teachers—not to teach subjects he was familiar with, but history and literature. Most of the teachers had been versed in anthroposophy for a long time, but this was different in the case of Hannah Lang. When she applied, Rudolf Steiner invited her with the words, "Join us. Then we have at least one person from Swabia among us."[224]

These first teachers[225] later became the most important advisors to newly founding schools and gave lectures about the new pedagogy in the whole country. The pioneers Herbert Hahn and E. A. Karl Stockmeyer occupied an important position, since they left an essential mark in the preparatory stage. E. A. Karl Stockmeyer built up the school administration and organized the school. He was a totally self-reliant, inwardly independent human being who could admire other people's achievements. That's how he fostered cohesion among the faculty of teachers.

Among the students of the first hour was Fritz Koegel (1907–1997). He was 12 years old in 1919 and went to the sixth-grade class of Friedrich Oehlschlegel. His mother, the painter Hertha Koegel, lived alone with her children in Munich after her divorce, and there she had heard about anthroposophy and Waldorf pedagogy. She was introduced to E. A. Karl Stockmeyer by Rudolf Treichler during his tour through Germany as a theater director, and that's how she got invited to help shape the new Waldorf School. She was only granted a year there before she became seriously ill and died soon thereafter. After the death of their mother, Fritz Koegel and his sister were adopted by the DelMonte family, which was part of the inner circle of anthroposophists in Stuttgart.

Teachers, edited by Erich Gabert and Hans Rudolf Niederhäuser. Manuscript print in eight volumes. 3rd Edition, Stuttgart, 1962. In preparation for the 100th anniversary of the founding of the School, Christof Wiechert, in cooperation with the Rudolf Steiner *Nachlassverwaltung*, is preparing a detailed, revised, and supplemented new edition of the conferences.

224 Gisbert Husemann and Johannes Tautz (eds.): *Der Lehrerkreis um Rudolf Steiner in der ersten Waldorfschule.* 1979, p. 19.

225 One can find in-depth biographies of the first Waldorf teachers in: Gisbert Husemann und Johannes Tautz (eds.): *Der Lehrerkreis um Rudolf Steiner in der ersten Waldorfschule.* 1979.

In the same class as Fritz Koegel was Friedrich Kipp (1908–1997), the son of the mayor of Höfingen. On the first day of school these boys received a Swabian *Butterbrezel* [pretzel], just like all the other students. For when the teachers asked Rudolf Steiner what would be a good thing to give the children for this first day of school, he recommended these Swabian *Butterbrezel*, "so that they will not forget the day." Friedrich Kipp remembered it well later. In high school, because he was bored and caused some mischief, he received an assignment to organize the natural science collection, which was a pedagogical find. Before school started in the morning he could be busy doing birdsong tours, so sometimes he was tired during main lesson. Later in life, he became one of the preeminent Goethean scientists.[226]

In the faculty meetings the daily challenges of the new task were discussed, and the subjects under consideration were both the children—in the course of the year, they talked extensively about over a hundred children—and the lesson content, for example, mathematics, geography, or history. Rudolf Steiner became an advocate for the children, for the pedagogy he wanted begins with the child! Looking back on the first school year at the beginning of the meeting of June 23, 1920, Rudolf Steiner said: "As I already said, we have generally made great progress. In the first year it was apparent that you struggled with the subject matter, but you made progress in all areas. What is important though, is what kind of progress you made and that in the coming years we work more with those ideas that are consistent with and related to the Waldorf school. I believe that progress lies in what the students have learned, as well as what the teachers have slowly discovered about how to treat the students. Everything has progressed, even the pranksters. The pranksters have become strong pranksters, but that does not hurt anything. That is simply a side effect. Many have even become better behaved, more cultivated, more intellectual."

Then Rudolf Steiner slowly came to the point he really wanted to make and went on to say, "In my opinion, we must put more value upon psychology in the future. We must work with psychology. You should not understand that as abstractly or theoretically as it may appear. That might look as though we want to analyze the children. When we become accustomed to understanding the children psychologically, we will slowly find a relationship to them that results purely from our activity. That understanding of the children will not remain as a mere recognition but will become another relationship if you really try to understand them. [...] I do not so much mean that the children must achieve this or that, but that you ask yourselves what the children can achieve in accordance with their psychological makeup. Always work

226 Wolfgang Schad: Friedrich Alexander Kipp (March 17, 1908–June 30, 1997). N December 14, 1997, pp. 248–250 with references to the most familiar works of Friedrich Kipp, especially *Die Evolution des Menschen im Hinblick auf seine lange Jugendzeit*. Stuttgart, 1980. Friedrich Kipp was also a gifted ornithologist, recognized far and wide. As a child I was able to admire his rich collection of bird skins which he left to the Natural History Museum in Stuttgart.

from the standpoint of the children. […] Each child is interesting."[227]

Walter Molt (1906–1974) was a student in grade seven/eight, the highest grade at the time. Because he was their only child, the Molts took in a boy in 1918 who was educated alongside Walter—his name was Felix Goll (1909–1977). The son of a Swabian painter of the Hölzel school, he had lost his mother early in life. After the mother's death, he and his siblings were distributed among friends. In the Molt family, Felix Goll grew up under the eyes of Rudolf Steiner, so to speak, because he often visited the Molts.

Walter Molt, only son of Berta and Emil Molt, and, of course, a Waldorf student

Felix Goll was in the first class of Caroline von Heydebrand, "a gentle lady for a strong young man, who at a later date jumped out of the window of the classroom in anger." After finishing school he became a woodworker in the furniture factory Behr, after which he switched to the art academy in Munich, and subsequently the craft-teacher seminar in Hildesheim. After many more stations of life, including the loss of his right hand in the war, he became a class teacher of grade three at the Stuttgart school in October 1945.[228]

Gerhard Ott (1908–1991) had been put in the fourth grade of Hertha Koegel, but "he didn't do well"[229] there and, on the advice of Rudolf Steiner, was placed a grade higher with Hermann von Baravalle. He chose Hermann von Baravalle and Dr. Eugen Kolisko as his role models, and they paved the way for his later work with Goethean natural science. As a child, Gerhard Ott already knew that he wanted to become a Waldorf teacher one day, a dream he realized in Stuttgart, then Hannover, then as a groundbreaking pioneer in Dresden, and again in Hannover upon his return to Germany after having fled.[230]

At the opening of the school, Rolf Gutbrod (1910–1999) was placed in the same grade. Hertha Koegel, however, soon became ill and had to give up the class after just one year. Rudolf Steiner invited Alexander Strakosch (1879–1958), the learned engineer who worked for the Austrian railroads where he was head of the signal department, to the Waldorf School. Alexander Strakosch was just the right teacher for Rolf Gutbrod,[231] and he became his lifelong role model. Rolf Gutbrod later became a university professor; architect of the *Liederhalle* in Stuttgart and the German

227 Rudolf Steiner: *Faculty Meetings with Rudolf Steiner*. CW 300a, 1998, p. 104ff. There are similar remarks in later meetings, for example on October 15, 1922, and on March 27, 1924, in CW300b.
228 Ernst Weissert: Felix Goll (February 6, 1909–November 23, 1977). LR 16, 1977, p. 73f.
229 Rudolf Steiner: *Faculty Meetings with Rudolf Steiner*. CW 300a, 1975, p. 196.
230 Lotte Hopp: Gerhard Ott (October 29, 1906–December 11, 1991). LR 48, 1993, p. 67f.
231 Michael Tittmann: Rolf Gutbrod (September 13, 1910–January 5, 1999). LR 66, 1999, p. 75.

Hermann von Baravalle, senior teacher of mathematics and physics at the Stuttgart Waldorf School, 1920–1937

pavilion at the world exhibition in Montréal in 1967; and a cofounder of the Kräherwald Waldorf School.

On November 3, 1919, the first monthly assembly took place. At that time, schools in Württemberg had one day a month off, and that day usually fell on the first Monday of the month. Rudolf Steiner suggested taking the Thursday for that and having everyone use the time to show each other what had been achieved, take stock, and collect their thoughts. This way he changed a school tradition of Württemberg into a community event and the monthly assembly came into being.[232] For Christmas 1919, a Christmas play was performed for the first time. The teachers put on a piece called "The Lazy King," written by music teacher Paul Baumann, in the domed building of the Goldener Hirsch on the Schlossplatz in downtown Stuttgart, at the occasion of which Rudolf Steiner put elaborate makeup on some of the players.[233]

Looking back on the founding of the first Waldorf School in Stuttgart ten years after the event, Emil Molt wrote: "The original idea that led to the founding of this school was first and foremost inspired by social considerations. The thinking was to give the children of the workers and employees the same education and training as children of middle-class parents.

"It was clear at the time that the social gap could be closed only when education no longer depended on money alone, and that our whole cultural, economic, and political progress could be possible only when all children, regardless of social status of the parents, could take part in the same education in our time."[234] For his own son, Walter G. Molt, who, due to the activities of his parents, was left far too much to the "care of soulful ladies," the school didn't prove to be exactly what he needed. Of course everybody had the expectations that Walter, being the son of the founder, would behave like a model child. That must have been too serious for him. After some time he left the school in order to learn a profession in England and in Italy.[235]

On March 8, 1920, the definitive word came from the state that the school had official permission to function, granted by Dr. Friedrich Reinöhl, the Protestant Württemberg school superintendent, with only one caveat: that there could be "new ordinances regarding private schools"[236] at some future time.

232 Rudolf Steiner: *Faculty Meetings with Rudolf Steiner*. CW 300a, 1975, p. 112.
233 Rudolf Treichler, Sr: *Wege und Umwege zu Rudolf Steiner*. Printed Manuscript 1974, p. 77.
234 Emil Molt: ZPRSt, Heft ¾, September 1929, p. 106.
235 Christine Murphy: Walter G. Molt (May 5, 1906–May 4, 1976) p. 72.
236 Norbert Deuchert: Waldorfschule und Staat 1919–1938. BhB Advent 1986, p. 76.

In April the so-called *Hilfsklasse* [extra-help class] was established, led by Karl Schubert,[237] who founded a whole new pedagogical field in doing so. Individual children with special needs from grades one through six came into this class. His activity was interrupted for a short time when he had to fill in for a teacher who had become ill, but he resumed the work in September 1921, and he carried on regularly until the school's closing in 1938. His work is the foundation of all later efforts in Waldorf schools to help children with learning difficulties or special needs.

Karl Schubert, teacher for children with special needs and creator of special education, 1920–1949

In the course of the very first school year Elisabeth von Grunelius (1895–1989) was called to join the founding faculty in the spring of 1920, with the request to build up kindergarten work. She had completed the training at the Comenius kindergarten seminar in Bonn and after that at the Pestalozzi-Fröbel Haus in Berlin. She had been interested in anthroposophy since she was 14 years old because of a woman who had worked in her parents' house, Julia Charlotte Mellinger. She had helped with the building of the Goetheanum in Dornach for some years and had met with Rudolf Steiner once or twice. He thought of her when they were looking for a kindergarten teacher.[238] The beginning of the school year had been shifted to the autumn in Württemberg that year, so Rudolf Steiner asked Elisabeth von Grunelius to make a start by working with a group of children from Easter until the autumn. She managed to play with 33 children[239] for a few months, but then there was no more room in the school and no more strength in her for the kindergarten,[240] because every year space had to be made for an upper grade. This way the much-needed founding of the kindergarten was postponed again and again, and Elisabeth von Grunelius left Stuttgart. It took a few years for her to regroup and return to Stuttgart.

On June 17, 1925, Herbert Hahn wrote to her to confirm that the faculty would accept her offer to found a kindergarten on the Uhlandshöhe.[241] Working in Barmen at that time, she had written to the faculty with that offer on May 24, 1925. Shortly after Whitsun the decision was made by the School Association to build up a kindergarten. They thanked Elisabeth von Grunelius for offering to construct the kindergarten building using her own means. From a distance she took care of answering

237 Erich Gabert in Rudolf Steiner: *Faculty Meetings with Rudolf Steiner*. CW 300a, 1975, p. 45.
238 Helmut von Kügelgen: Die erste Waldorfkindergärtnerin. EK 12, 1989, p. 1098.
239 Erich Gabert in Rudolf Steiner: *Faculty Meetings with Rudolf Steiner*. CW 300a, 1975, p. 46.
240 Elisabeth von Grunelius in a letter to E. A. Karl Stockmeyer, September 29, 1922. Archiv LS 325.02.
241 Herbert Hahn wrote this on June 17, 1925, to Elisabeth von Grunelius. Archiv LS 325.10.

Bettina Mellinger, class teacher of the Waldorf School in Stuttgart, 1922–1952

the necessary questions, while E. A. Karl Stockmeyer took care of managing the practical aspects in Stuttgart. She was attentive to every single detail. The question of the fine grit of sand for the sandbox was worth a special postcard to Stockmeyer, who did his best to fulfill all her directions. It took until Easter 1926 before the first Waldorf kindergarten began in a wooden shed-like building on the school grounds under the direction of Elisabeth von Grunelius.[242]

On June 7, 1920, Rudolf Steiner traveled to Stuttgart once again and stayed there for an unusually long time because of complications in The Coming Day venture. He also used this opportunity to visit lessons and was in the hall when the students shared the results of their work at a monthly assembly on June 10. When the students were finished with their performances, Rudolf Steiner gave a talk to the students, as was his custom whenever he was present at a monthly assembly. Three aspects will be highlighted here.

Rudolf Steiner once again summarized what should be fostered in the Waldorf school: "Love for each other, love for our teachers, love for God who speaks to us from everything."[243] He sketched in simple pictures how light and warmth work variously on nature and the human being. Whereas sunlight calls forth plant growth and takes care that plants can grow out of the ground, the human being needs light in order to grow, that is to say, to learn. "The soul finds its sun and people from whom it can learn something."[244] Then, toward the end of the talk, Rudolf Steiner once more placed the spiritual ground of the Waldorf school before the teachers and students there, emphasizing how he wanted the school to be understood and grounded. "There is a spirit that is always meant to reign here, the spirit that your teachers bring to this place. Out of the spirit of the cosmos they learn to bring this spirit here to you. In this way they are taking the words of St. Paul to heart. The spirit of Christ reigns throughout our school; whether we are doing arithmetic, reading, writing, or whatever we do, we do it with the attitude that the Christ awakened in us: 'I am with you always, even unto the end of the world.' This is the spirit that is meant to reign here, and it will reign through what your teachers bring to you with love, patience, and forbearance. May it also reign through what lives in your souls."[245]

242 Helmut von Kügelgen: Elisabeth von Grunelius zum 90. Geburtstag. LR 30, 1985, p. 66f.
243 Rudolf Steiner: *Rudolf Steiner in the Waldorf School.* CW 298, 1996, p. 35.
244 Ibid., p. 36.
245 Ibid., p. 37.

The next evening Rudolf Steiner was present at a parent evening. He used these days in Stuttgart for an intensive exchange with the teachers. Thus he participated in faculty meetings on June 9, 12, and 14, 1920. Meetings ordinarily took place only once a week, but because Rudolf Steiner was there and because of the many accumulated questions, they held these three days in a row. One of the few consultations about kindergarten pedagogy took place on June 12.

Apart from that, the first school year drew to a close, and therefore they talked on June 14 about student reports and what they should look like. These consultations are an example of the way questions and problems that emerged were solved in the moment. There were no ready-made concepts or models to be implemented. Consensus was soon reached about written reports, in which students were characterized both with regard to their strengths and weaknesses in learning. Rudolf Steiner asked only that teachers harmonize among themselves a bit and not write things that were overly contradictory. In this context Rudolf Steiner spoke up sharply and railed against students repeating a year (being held back): "It would not be good to cultivate the principle of repeating classes."[246]

On May 19, 1920, the *Verein Freie Waldorfschule* [Independent Waldorf School Association] was baptized as the legal body representing the school. It had seven founding members, with Rudolf Steiner as president and Emil Molt as deputy president. Up to this point in time, the school had functioned legally and economically as a part of the Waldorf Astoria cigarette factory, and in his function as business manager of the factory, Emil Molt appointed and paid the teachers. Many teachers soon experienced this situation as too limiting and patriarchal, and this caused a groundswell of protest directed against Emil Molt. In founding the school's own legal carrier, the teachers welcomed a different form for the hiring procedure that they hoped to find.

This, however, was only one side of the coin, and the other side soon became apparent. Even though the school was on its way to functioning independently as a legal entity, it now also had to take solving chronic financial problems in hand. This was another agenda item for the faculty meeting held with Rudolf Steiner on July 24, 1920. In this meeting it became crystal clear that new rooms had to be built or found, and new teachers had to be appointed—but there was no money. Rudolf Steiner played with the ideas of possible sources and cheered the teachers up with a report on the development of shaving cream and hair lotion in Dornach, the sale of which could potentially finance a gymnasium and a eurythmy hall in the long run. In addition, he made the suggestion to found a World School Association, with which one could build international financial support for the Stuttgart school and others.

---

246 Rudolf Steiner: *Faculty Meetings with Rudolf Steiner*. CW 300a, 1975, p. 148f. [translation modified].

ON THE BASIS of article 146 of the constitution of the Weimar Republic, a law for the state of Württemberg was passed (in tandem with a federal law), intended to establish an education in the Weimar Republic that would break down the deep class divisions of the 19th century and create a basis for more equality among all strata of society. As a result, the Waldorf School would no longer be allowed to accept children into grades one through four, just like all the other private schools in Württemberg. On August 5, 1920, they were given until spring 1924 to dismantle the first four grades.[247] After that point in time a new class could be started only on request. Of course, this ordinance was disastrous for the whole idea of the Waldorf school, which was conceived as a coherent continuum of kindergarten through grade twelve; therefore everything should be done to ensure maintenance of the principle of starting school for children in grade one.

On September 28, 1920, Emil Molt and Rudolf Steiner sent a request to the school authorities of Württemberg that they not apply this ordinance to the Waldorf School. They argued that the Waldorf School accepted children regardless of the financial circumstances of parents, so no class separation would take place. As a result, establishing a new first grade in 1921 was permitted, but the dismantling of the first four grades was postponed until 1925, and the number of elementary school students was limited to 240.[248] However, there turned out to be no strong communal political will for this intended social reform through education. It got abandoned in the initial phase, and by-and-by the school boards in the various German states each created their own ordinances.[249]

The Second and Third Years of the School

ON SEPTEMBER 20, 1920, the second school year started with 420 children in 11 grades and 19 teachers. Robert Killian (1891–1960), and the newly arrived Maria Uhland, later Uhland-Hahn (1893–1978), took the first two grades. Rudolf Steiner valued the pedagogical work of Maria Uhland highly and pointed out several times that very good pedagogical conversations took place in her lessons. She kept on teaching at the school until 1931.

In addition, Hedwig Hauck (1873–1949) moved from Berlin to Stuttgart and began teaching at the school in the second year. In Berlin she had taught painting at the Drawing and Painting School of the Society for Women Artists, as well as drawing at the Technical University. She became a handwork teacher without having had anything to do with this subject before. When she mentioned to Rudolf Steiner that she had not been trained to teach handwork, he replied, "But we want to have

---

247 Wenzel M. Götte: *Erfahrungen mit Schulautonomie.* 2006, p. 202, note 564.
248 Norbert Deuchert: Waldorfschule und Staat 1919–1938. BhB Advent 1986, p. 80.
249 Ibid., p. 78.

you, you will learn it by and by."[250] Thus she learned together with the children, developed the curriculum for handwork, and stayed at the school until 1938. In the same school year the sister of Caroline von Heydebrand came to Stuttgart with her son Ernst, and she took care of them in a house in which other teachers lived as well.[251]

In order to deepen the study of the human being and give the teachers further viewpoints for their work, Rudolf Steiner gave four lectures at the beginning of the school year, which were published under the name "Meditativ erarbeitete Menschenkunde" [Balance in Teaching].[252] But the situation at the beginning of the school year was not at all relaxed and straightforward.

Robert Killian, class teacher at the Stuttgart Waldorf School, 1920 to 1960

During the summer holidays, E.A. Karl Stockmeyer had traveled to Dornach with a memorandum and had communicated to Rudolf Steiner that the faculty wished to have a new constitution and had questions about the role of Emil Molt. The only problem was that nobody had talked with Emil Molt beforehand. Therefore he didn't know anything about a written complaint. He might have had a sense that there was grumbling going on, but no more than that. Therefore the tensions in the relationship of the teachers with Emil Molt, and especially with the Waldorf Astoria company, surfaced in the very first faculty meetings of the new year with Rudolf Steiner.

The leading teachers did not want to be employees of the Waldorf Astoria cigarette factory anymore; they wanted to sail under their own flag. That was a risky proposition, because the economic existence of the school still rested—except for a few donations—on the efforts of Emil Molt and the tuition payments of the Waldorf Astoria, Inc. In the meeting of September 21, 1920, Rudolf Steiner backed Emil Molt fully, but he stood behind the college of teachers as well, with the words: "In a certain way, we have now come to the core of the problem. The faculty is prepared to go with Mr. Molt and all the things resulting from the historical relationship, but it does not want to have anything to do with the Waldorf Astoria Company. […] We need only to see Mr. Molt for himself and not in connection with the company. If we move on to this healthy ground, we will understand one another better."[253] Now it was a matter of finding the necessary financial and administrative expertise in order to set the School Association, founded back in May, on a firmer footing. But the necessary skills were not there.

250 Hedwig Hauck: Autobiographische Skizze. MPK Ostern 1950, pp. 35–42.
251 Ernst von Heydebrand later taught mathematics and physics in the high school of the Waldorf school in Heidenheim. See Emil Munk: Dr. Ernst von Heydebrand. LR 39, 1990, p. 105.
252 Rudolf Steiner: *Balance in Teaching*. CW 302a.
253 Rudolf Steiner: *Faculty Meetings with Rudolf Steiner*. CW 300a, 1998, p. 166.

Class 6a of the Stuttgart Waldorf School with their teacher, Caroline von Heydebrand, 1920

On December 21, the teachers performed a play for the students again in the downstairs Säulensaal, as it was known [Column Hall]. This time it was the Shepherds Play from Oberpfalz. Ernst Uehli played Joseph; Elisabeth Baumann, Mary; Paul Baumann and Rudolf Treichler, the shepherds.[254] Even though a different play was chosen in the years after that, the tradition was established that has been carried on in Waldorf schools in areas with a Christian culture to this very day, a tradition to present a nativity play as a gift to the students shortly before Christmas, a real living experience for them to enjoy.

In order to guarantee depth and quality in the art history classes in the upper school, Rudolf Steiner insisted on recruiting Dr. Erich Schwebsch (1889–1953) to join the school. This succeeded, and Erich Schwebsch started teaching after Easter in 1921. Countless students experienced the great historical sweep of cultures through his highly erudite, scintillating presentations. Erich Schwebsch taught until the school closed in 1938 and immediately after the war again from 1945 onward. At the suggestion of Max Wolffhügel, Fritz Graf von Bothmer (1883–1941) was asked to join and teach gymnastics around the same time.

Max Wolffhügel had made his acquaintance at lectures given by Rudolf Steiner in the *Prinzensälen* [Prince Hall] of Café Luitpold in Munich and later met up with him again when he was a lieutenant of the Royal Bavarian Lifeguards in World War I. Due to a snowstorm, his maneuvers were canceled, which gave him the chance to be introduced to Rudolf Steiner. In spite of advice to the contrary, he went and learned what his future profession was to be. He thought about it for a few weeks,

---

254 Rudolf Treichler, Sr: *Wege und Umwege zu Rudolf Steiner.* 1974, p. 77.

then asked Rudolf Steiner in a second conversation how he should prepare for this task. The answer: "With joy!"[255] Count Fritz von Bothmer developed his own art of movement, which to this day is the basis of gymnastics teaching in many Waldorf schools and became known as Bothmer gymnastics.

In faculty meetings before the summer holidays, the need for more space had been anticipated but nothing had been done about it due to lack of funds. Emil Molt now facilitated the purchase of the piece of land east of the school grounds through The Coming Day, for the price of 500,000 marks. This is the piece of land where the eurythmy school and Rudolf Steiner House are today.[256] Unfazed by the grumbling against him, unfazed by the memorandum and the teachers' demands for reducing his power, Emil Molt simply took care of the needed expansion of the grounds and prepared the ground for the further growth of the school.

Erich Schwebsch, senior teacher of literature and art history, 1921–1953

Just like any other school, the Waldorf school was subject to state inspection, as had been known from the initial conversations with the ministry of culture. The first appointment for an inspection was on June 11 and 12, to be done by the top state inspector Wössner.[257] But he didn't come, and on June 22 the inspection was postponed until the beginning of the new school year, followed by the next appointment for an inspection February 13–21.[258]

In anticipation of the third school year, Rudolf Steiner held a lecture cycle from June 12–19, 1921, eight lectures known as the Supplementary Course and published as *Menschenerkenntnis und Unterrichtsgestaltung*.[259] Unlike *The Foundations of Human Experience*, in which he had essentially talked about the development of the human being between the ages of seven and fourteen, Rudolf Steiner began lecturing about adolescence. Of course the teachers were hoping for more to come. At the time this course was given, the first members meeting of the Waldorf School Association, founded in 1920 and which had grown to over 1400 members in Germany and abroad, was held. The tasks, challenges, and achievements of this association and the

Fritz Graf von Bothmer, first sports teacher at the Stuttgart Waldorf School, 1922–1938, who developed the unique exercises named after him, Bothmer gymnastics

255 Max Wolffhügel: Graf Bothmer. MPK Easter 1950, p. 30.
256 Emil Molt: *Entwurf meiner Lebensbeschreibung*. 1972, p. 205.
257 Letter by school inspector Eisele of June 1, 1921, to the Waldorf School. Archiv LS 4.1.043.
258 Letter by school inspector Eisele of December 7, 1921, to E. A. Karl Stockmeyer. Archiv LS 4.1.065 and 4.1.066.
259 Rudolf Steiner: *Waldorf Education for Adolescents*. Eight lectures given from April 12–19, 1921. CW 302.

The second grade in the Stuttgart Waldorf School with their teacher, Leonie von Mirbach

interests reaching beyond the confines of the Uhlandshöhe school are discussed in the chapter "National and International Cooperation from 1919 to 1945."

The school kept growing and growing. The third year of school began with 540 students, 15 grades, and 30 teachers. At the all-school meeting on June 18, 1921, for the beginning of the third school year, Rudolf Steiner gave a heartwarming talk to the students, in which he used the word *tüchtig* in many senses of the word. *Tüchtig*, a German word meaning "thoroughly industrious, hard-working, and able to cope with all hindrances" was applied by Steiner here to mean "to learn to think and work" in the sense of working hard to live up to your potential, in the eyes of other people as well as of God and the spiritual world. And Rudolf Steiner began his talk with something he often repeated to the students: "You will actually learn most when you really love your teachers."[260]

This is, in a nutshell, the most important maxim for Waldorf teachers—or any other teachers for that matter—that education is relationship and that development can only happen in relationship.

In this year, Berthold Faig (1910–1980), born in Jerusalem, became a student at the school. After graduating from the school and completing his agricultural training in Worpswede, among other places, he returned to the school to teach gardening in 1937 and continued this assignment from 1946 onward. From then until 1973, he was the main force in landscaping the school grounds and the garden in the former quarry behind the school.[261]

260 Rudolf Steiner: *Rudolf Steiner in the Waldorf School*. CW 298, p. 103.
261 Klaus Matzke: Berthold Faig. LR 22, 1981, p. 82ff.

In August 1921, the first issue of the magazine *Die Freie Waldorfschule* [The Independent Waldorf School] came out, which was published at irregular intervals until April 1927. Then it was replaced by the bimonthly, *Zur Pädagogik Rudolf Steiners* [Rudolf Steiner's Pedagogy]. In 1932, this magazine was named *Erziehungskunst* [The Art of Education]. Caroline von Heydebrand became editor in 1927, assisted by Friedrich Hiebel from 1932–1934, when Erich Schwebsch took over the position of assistant editor. The magazine appeared until February 1937 and then again after the time of National Socialism and World War II.

Within the confines of the Waldorf School building the lessons of the fledgling eurythmy school also took place. It was wonderful for the eurythmy students—some of them still high school age—to meet the schoolchildren during the breaks and hear what they had to say. Else Klink (1907–1994) was accepted into the sixth grade in 1921. Her class teacher was Hermann von Baravalle, and she stood out on the playground because of her thick braids. Alice Fels (1884–1974), who led the eurythmy school, taught eurythmy in her class. In the very first eurythmy class students became so wild that the teacher could only save herself under the grand piano. Rods, shoes, everything was flying through the air,[262] and Else Klink must also have been involved to some extent. A few years after this wild start, she studied eurythmy with Alice Fels, and in 1935 she took over the leadership of the Stuttgart Eurythmy School at the request of Marie Steiner. During the war, the eurythmy school went into hiding. Afterward, Else Klink managed to build it up again, and she led it until 1991. She brought the Eurythmeum to the public eye and made it into a recognized cultural factor in Stuttgart.[263]

In the early years of the Waldorf School, plans were carried out more quickly and innovatively, if not more radically, than in the years after that. Because older students had been attending right from the start, there were—even in this early phase—students who graduated and went on to a vocational training. They had therefore only been able to partake in one or two years of general schooling and art. For them the vocational school offerings proved very dry. Therefore, further education classes were started on November 11, 1921, targeting these particular students as well as students who had completed elementary school at age 14 and were also attending vocational school. This effort was meant as complementary to vocational schooling and was carried through on Tuesdays and Fridays in the afternoon by Alexander Strakosch who taught courses called Art of Living and History through Art, and by Herbert Hahn, who taught literature. The year after that, eurythmy lessons were added.[264]

262 Elena Zuccoli: *Eine Autobiographie.* 1999, p. 57.
263 Magdalene Siegloch: Else Klink (October 23, 1907–October 23, 1994). In: Bodo von Plato (ed.): *Anthroposophie im 20. Jahrhundert.* 2003, p. 374ff.
264 Announcement of October 1921. Archiv LS 3.26.002 and October 1922. Archiv LS 3.26.003.

AT ROUGHLY THE SAME TIME that the Waldorf school was being created, efforts to develop new forms in business had continued as well. Emil Molt, together with other entrepreneurs, worked hard to put associative forms into practice, based on Steiner's ideas for the Threefold Social Order. In the course of these efforts, which still await thorough reappraisal, the businesses of Carl Unger and José del Monte, as well as many other undertakings were combined into a new corporation with the programmatic title *Der Kommende Tag* [The Coming Day].[265] Because of the combined number of businesses in The Coming Day, there were many more workers' children now, all possible candidates for the Waldorf School. As a result, Rudolf Steiner considered it a necessary to also found a Waldorf school for these children[266]—but his call went unanswered. The teachers had more than enough to do to keep their own school going. In the conversations about the further building up of the corporation, the idea arose to merge the Waldorf Astoria, Inc., with The Coming Day, Inc. To bring that about, conversations were held in March 1921 with several shareholders. When both Max Marx and Richard and Emil Abraham from Hamburg, the leading shareholders of Waldorf Astoria, Inc., had given their consent in principle, negotiations were held about the merger and details were settled. From then on, the Waldorf Astoria cigarette factory was dependent on the well-being of The Coming Day.

Prompted by mistakes made in the governing body of The Coming Day, Rudolf Steiner appointed Emil Leinhas (1878–1967) as CEO of The Coming Day during the general meeting of September 22, 1921, without having spoken a word about it to Emil Molt beforehand—an affront. But Emil Molt's all-enduring faithfulness to Rudolf Steiner stood the test as he drove Rudolf Steiner back to Dornach that very afternoon. He just kept his mouth shut, gritting his teeth. However, the relationship between Emil Molt and Emil Leinhas had been very tense even before this because Emil Leinhas did not want to be bound to promises Emil Molt had made earlier in his function as director of Waldorf Astoria, Inc.

It was part of Emil Molt's character and his management style to keep his word. And now Emil Leinhas was the de facto chief executive officer, and in that position Emil Molt was his subordinate. Therefore Emil Molt was dependent on his decisions. Now that he was in charge of The Coming Day, Emil Leinhas decided he should participate in some meetings with the Waldorf School, which used to be Emil Molt's prerogative. In addition, the reserve capital that Waldorf Astoria, Inc., had built up allowed him, in his position as sole chief executive, to make expenditures he knew would please Rudolf Steiner. Thus he financed the International Laboratories, from which Weleda sprang, as well as the building of a clinic—decisions that went very much against the entrepreneurial instincts of Emil Molt. Capital reserves dwindled.

---

265 Dietrich Esterl: *Emil Molt. 1876–1936. Tun, was gefordert ist.* 2012, p. 135ff.
266 Rudolf Steiner: *Faculty Meetings with Rudolf Steiner.* CW 300a, 1975, p. 254.

Postwar inflation was on the increase. At this economically tense juncture, Emil Leinhas conceived the notion that *The Waldorf Newsletter* should be dropped, citing cost-saving measures as the reason; but the real reason was that he did not like the newsletter.

Emil Leinhas, Managing Director of The Coming Day, Inc.

The Waldorf Newsletter had been instituted by Emil Molt for his workers in the factory. He had devoted much care in building up this internal communication and education organ, and he was passionate about it. Therefore Emil Leinhas's measure to drop it was a strong vote of no-confidence, or even a condemnation of Emil Molt. Those were catastrophic days. At the same time, the decision was made at the general meeting of The Coming Day on December 15, 1921, to issue 34 million marks' worth of new ordinary shares and one million marks' worth of preference shares. Rudolf Steiner did not intervene either, so on this December day Emil Molt came to realize how much power he had lost because of his idealism and the probably over-rash transfer of ownership. He no longer had the power to act within his own company, and he also could not prevent Emil Leinhas from spending more money even though he should have been saving. Unable to sleep, Emil Molt paced the cold streets until early in the morning.[267]

The next morning, December 16, 1921, there was a foundation stone celebration. The occasion was the dedication of the first building designated specifically for Waldorf school use, at which Rudolf Steiner was present. With the help of the Dutch entrepreneur Joseph E. van Leer (1880–1934), a building fund had been built up during the previous months, collecting donations of up to 400,000 marks from Germany, Holland, Austria, Italy, and Poland, a fund that was to guarantee paying off the mortgage for the schoolhouse, which amounted to about 4.6 million marks.[268] In his oration, Rudolf Steiner emphasized with warm words that the Waldorf School could only exist because Emil Molt had the right idea at a crucial time in history and because he was willing to put his fortune at the disposal of the school. The fact that Berta Molt contributed just as much has only become known to posterity. Rudolf Steiner wrote the following words for the foundation stone of the first Waldorf School:

267 Sophia Christine Murphy: *The Multifaceted Life of Emil Molt*. 2012, p. 180ff.
268 Dietrich Esterl: *Die erste Waldorfschule Stuttgart-Uhlandshöhe 1919 bis 2004. Daten–Dokumente–Bilder*. 2006, p. 78.

May there reign here spirit strength in love;
May there work here spirit light in goodness;
Born from certainty of heart,
And from steadfastness of soul,
So that we may bring to young human beings
Bodily strength for work,
Inwardness of soul and clarity of spirit.
May this place be consecrated to such a task;
May young minds and hearts here find
Servers of the light, endowed with strength,
Who will guard and cherish them.

Those who here lay the stone as a sign
Will think in their hearts of the spirit
That should reign in this place,
So that the foundation may be firm
Upon which there shall live and weave and work:
Wisdom that bestows freedom,
Strengthening spirit-power,
All-revealing spirit-life.
This we wish to affirm in the name of Christ,
With pure intent and with good will. *

At Christmas time in 1921 the teachers performed the Oberufer Christmas plays for the first time,[269] which has become a well-established tradition in many Waldorf schools, as indicated above. In the year after that it turned out that there were problems with the performance rights. In connection with this, Rudolf Steiner made it only too clear that, had he been asked beforehand, he would have revised the texts in many places.[270] But that never happened.

At the end of January 1922, it became clear that the problems in the The Coming Day could not be solved. During a meeting in Dornach therefore, held by Emil Leinhas for the business management, it was decided in the presence of Rudolf Steiner to sell Waldorf Astoria, Inc., to create more liquidity. Emil Molt was only informed by Emil Leinhas a week after these shattering decisions in Dornach had been made. Emil Molt was deeply hurt and deeply upset, understandably so. His wife Berta as well as the von Moltkes and others helped him to come to accept the deal in

---

* Translation by E.M. Hutchins

269 Rudolf Steiner became acquainted with these plays through his professor, Karl Julius Schroer, in Vienna. They have been handed down as Christmas plays from the region of present-day Bratislava.

270 Rudolf Steiner: *Faculty Meetings with Rudolf Steiner.* CW 300/2, 1975, p. 193.

a conversation held in Breslau on January 30. Just think what burdens this man had to bear, the disappointments and errors he had to suffer!

For the sake of saving The Coming Day, he finally consented to approve the sale under the condition that both the tuition for workers' children would continue to be paid and that the pensions promised to his workers would be honored. Emil Molt took it upon himself to use his old connections and found a bankers' consortium that would have financed the sale of Waldorf Astoria, Inc. But Emil Leinhas wanted to go it alone and, without consulting Emil Molt, he went ahead and sold the cigarette company to a discount bank in Mannheim on March 23, 1922.[271] This bank did not keep the company long and sold it to speculators in November of the very same year. As soon as Emil Molt read this in the paper, he drove to Mannheim, only to find out that the news was correct and that the majority of shares had been sold to Kiazim Emin, a tobacco importer. This man was now Emil Molt's new boss, thanks to the business failure of the consortium and the rashness of Emil Leinhas.

HAVING BEEN POSTPONED multiple times, the first official inspection of the Waldorf School took place February 13–21, 1922, carried out by School Inspector Eisele.[272] He concluded that the unusual mixture of teachers with their varying prerequisites definitely had the best intentions, but that a firm curriculum and reliable teaching goals were lacking. In Caroline von Heydebrand's class there was nothing to be criticized. The students' behavior was exemplary that day, so much so that she asked the class afterward what was the matter. They answered, "but Miss von Heydebrand, we would never want to disgrace you!"[273] Visiting the eighth grade, Inspector Eisele noticed how blatantly students were copying from each other and concluded that the necessary discipline was lacking in the class.

In any case, he got the impression that there was too much dilettantism in many respects. Even though he saw the idealism of the teachers, he also noticed their shortcomings in many subjects. So the outcome was not as positive as the teachers, convinced of their good work, had hoped. This was transmitted to Rudolf Steiner and he was there at the next faculty meeting on October 15, 1922. He said, "The school inspector's report was somewhat depressing for me. From what you told me earlier, I had thought he was ill willed. But the report is full of good will. I must admit that I found everything he wrote necessary. For example, you are not paying enough attention so the students are always copying from one another. The things contained in the report are true, and that is so bitter."[274] And the volley of criticism went on from there.

271 Sophia Christine Murphy: *The Multifaceted Life of Emil Molt.* 2012, p. 200.

272 Dietrich Esterl: *Die erste Waldorfschule 1919–2004.* 2006, p. 116f.

273 Bettina Mellinger: Caroline von Heydebrand. In: Medizinisch-Pädagogische Konferenz, Jg. 3, Nr. 1, Easter 1950, p. 22, and based on Gisbert Husemann and Johannes Tautz (eds.): *Der Lehrerkreis um Rudolf Steiner in der ersten Waldorfschule.* 1979, p. 30.

274 Rudolf Steiner: *Faculty Meetings with Rudolf Steiner.* CW 300b, 1998, p. 400.

WITH THE PROPERTY TRANSFER of the Waldorf Astoria to The Coming Day, some pieces of land on the Uhlandshöhe (the parcels bordering Emil Molt's property on the north and the south) came under the ownership of The Coming Day. In May 1922, Emil Molt sold his own parcel to The Coming Day and informed the Waldorf Schools Association by letter on May 24, 1922, that he put the sum of money resulting from this transaction at the disposal of the association, a contribution amounting to 1,020,000 marks altogether. Emil Molt added another 300,000 marks earmarked for the future kindergarten.[275] Emil Leinhas attempted to call the assessments of the parcels into question with a counter-report and created the impression in the minds of E.A. Karl Stockmeyer and his Waldorf School colleagues that Emil Molt's main concern was the sale.

He didn't mention Emil Molt's donation of the proceeds from the sale to the school association. The process of this donation was shrouded through various complications and instigated misunderstandings. The facts are hard to verify and obviously have to do with Emil Leinhas's desire for recognition. Emil Leinhas, who had thus far only squandered other people's work, made it seem as if he was the new boss or at least the new benefactor of the school. Emil Molt bore the allegations and remained silent. E.A. Karl Stockmeyer did reveal the relevant facts, thus setting the record straight, when the Waldorf School Association was dissolved on March 25, 1940.[276]

Teaching continued in the school as it had before, but not to everybody's satisfaction. This came out clearly in the teachers meeting of October 15, 1922, where essential shortcomings were aired. Rudolf Steiner criticized the upper school teachers for being out of touch with the students. There was too much lecturing and not enough attention to skill building, i.e., the way of teaching had too much of an academic style and there was not enough real schooling going on. Instead of mobilizing the students from within and creating a sense of responsibility, lessons were geared toward sensationalism and entertaining students.[277] A year later, Rudolf Steiner became even sharper and told the teachers that they should not put themselves on a pedestal but should put more effort into the lessons. He said the students "do not know enough"[278] and therefore the Waldorf school idea ought to be carried out much more thoroughly and perfectly.

275 Dietrich Esterl: *Emil Molt 1876–1936. Tun, was gefordert ist.* 2012, p. 171ff., and facsimile of the letter of Emil Molt, p. 172.
276 E.A. Karl Stockmeyer: Skizzen aus der Aufbauzeit des Waldorfschulvereins in: *Mitteilungen an die Mitglieder des Waldorfschulvereins.* May 1940, p. 18.
277 Rudolf Steiner: *Faculty Meetings with Rudolf Steiner.* CW 300b, p. 406.
278 Ibid., CW 300b and GA 300c, p. 45.

The Fourth and Fifth School Years

On June 20, 1922, the fourth school year started in Stuttgart with 640 pupils in 19 grades with 37 teachers. As in every year so far, they met in the gym, where the whole student body gathered, and every single class was welcomed. Some students came from far away and were called *Pensionäre*, that is to say, students staying with host families. Many teacher families lived in narrow circumstances and were able to augment their incomes that way. One of these students was Rudolf Grosse (1905–1994), the future head of the Pedagogical Section at the Goetheanum. He said goodbye to the grammar school he was at in Zürich—without informing his mother—and initiated his entry into grade 10. In 1921, he had heard a lecture by Rudolf Steiner in Zürich, where he came from, that moved him very much.

As he was listening to the lecture, he discovered that his German and history teacher, Dr. Jacques Hugentobler, was also in the audience. This teacher had suggested he look into the Waldorf School, and this meant a lot to him. He came to the Waldorf School on May 1, 1922, and his experiences there were life changing, especially the Parsifal lessons of Walter Johannes Stein, which Rudolf Steiner visited and contributed to.[279] Emil Molt got to know him when he did a holiday practicum at the Waldorf Astoria and invited him to come live in his house because of his narrow economic circumstances, which gave him more opportunities to meet Rudolf Steiner. Rudolf Grosse became the first Waldorf student who declared that he wanted to become a Waldorf teacher when his class met with Rudolf Steiner at the end of twelfth grade. For his further studies he followed up on suggestions given by Rudolf Steiner, and he was given the task to educate a boy from Bern, Switzerland.

For his work with the boy, Rudolf Steiner gave him the following advice: "It is all-important that he comes to love you, which in turn will give him the moral strength to find himself." In 1922 Siegfried Pütz also joined the high school and was able to attend the Waldorf School for the rest of his high school career, until 1924. Later in life he wrote that the basis for all that he accomplished was laid in these years.[280] Siegfried Pütz[281] first boarded with the family of Karl Schubert, which was highly inspiring for him, and subsequently stayed with Caroline von Heydebrand in the Libanonstrasse in a house where Count Fritz von Bothmer and Robert Killian lived as well. The house was full of music, there were house concerts, many people visited and there was much conversation. Thus, he became better acquainted with the teachers.

---

279 Johannes Tautz: Zum 80. Geburtstag von Rudolf Grosse. LR 30, 1985, p. 69.
280 Kurt Herold Lampe: Siegfried Pütz. LR 19, 1979, p. 107ff.
281 Siegfried Pütz became a sculptor and art teacher. He worked from 1950 at the Waldorf school in Ottersberg. In 1967 he started the *Freie Kunst-Studienstätte für das soziale Wirken der Kunst* [Independent Center to Study the Social Contribution of Art in Society].

Students on a 3½-day trip with Hermann von Baravalle into the Murg Valley to visit the Kraftwerkes and Heidenheim to explain the technological lessons, July 1923

On September 4, 1922, the School Association was renamed *Verein für ein freies Schulwesen* [Association for Independent Schools] and the circle of ordinary members with voting rights expanded to include all coworkers and the parents. People who wanted to enable a child to attend the school could now also become members and sponsor a student. In addition, the Association for Independent Schools was to play a guiding role for newly founded schools. Of course, the school and the association also needed people to take up the daily management tasks. For that reason, Emil Molt appointed a coworker for that task, Margarete Sczeppainz from Strassburg. It was she who kept the books from then on until the school closed in 1938, and she did so in such a thorough and accurate way that many people were slightly intimidated by her strictness. She became a "Rock of Gibraltar" for the managers and boards that came and went.[282] In 1945 she returned to the school.

As the value of the mark decreased, which led to hyperinflation in December 1922, individuals and institutions had more and more trouble coping, a situation that lasted until the end of 1923. The school experienced great financial difficulties due to inflation and the economic crisis.[283] The school was able to keep going thanks to donations from benefactors outside of Germany (Switzerland, Holland, England, Sweden, and Norway). But there was not enough money to complete the urgently

282 Ernst Weissert: Margarete Sczeppainz. LR 19, 1979, p. 114.
283 Dietrich Esterl: *Die erste Waldorfschule Stuttgart-Uhlandshöhe 1919 bis 2004. Daten–Dokumente–Bilder.* 2006, p. 80.

needed building. The third floor would have remained unfinished were it not for Friedrich Widmer (1889–1966), a teacher in Zofingen, Switzerland, and later founding teacher of the Waldorf school in Basel. It was he and a few colleagues who took the initiative to take out a loan of Fr.10,000, and this amount was paid to the Waldorf School on December 1, 1922. Thanks to this financial assistance from Switzerland, the new school building could be completed. At Christmas time in 1923 many entrepreneurs came together in Dornach, and a guarantee committee[284] was formed by six entrepreneurs, Emil Molt among them, that was able to cover the monthly deficit of the Waldorf School with an amount of 3000 goldmarks.[285]

Because of animosity, tensions below the surface, and partisanship in the faculty, there were extensive debates in the faculty meetings of January 23 and 31, 1923, about management and governance of the school. It was fundamentally clear to Rudolf Steiner that the well-being of the Waldorf School depended on the inner harmony of

---

284 Dietrich Esterl: *Emil Molt 1876–1936. Tun, was gefordert ist.* 2012, p. 178.
285 The monthly school budget for the school year 1922/23 was about 500,000 marks, of which 110,000 marks was contributed by the 2200 members of the Association for Independent Schools.

One of the first grade classes of the Stuttgart Waldorf School in the 1923/24 school year with their teacher Dagmar Tilliss

the faculty and that clique-building had to be strictly banned.[286] After long debate in both meetings, the faculty changed the governance structure of the school on January 31, 1923, and installed an executive council of three faculty-appointed members: Paul Baumann, Herbert Hahn and Erich Schwebsch.[287] With this management structure in place the work could at least proceed.

At the monthly assembly of March 1, 1923, the first one after the Goetheanum in Dornach had burned to the ground, Rudolf Steiner was highly enthusiastic about the eurythmy performance and the student contributions. Afterward, Rudolf Steiner addressed the assembly. With great warmth of heart, he strongly emphasized three things for the children to work on. He stressed the importance of diligence, attentiveness, and love for the teachers.[288] In a variety of ways he spoke about these three virtues in terms of a golden vessel that each individual can shape within in order to master the challenges of life.

A few weeks after Easter—for in the meantime the opening of the school year had been gradually shifted to come after Easter—the fifth year of the Waldorf school opened with a celebration. At that point in time, there were 687 students in 21 grades at the school and 39 teachers. It was April 24, 1923, and on this occasion Rudolf Steiner spoke with special earnestness to the students about Christ as the great benefactor of humanity, telling them how the faculty were seeking to understand him,

286 Rudolf Steiner: *Faculty Meetings with Rudolf Steiner*. CW 300b, 1975, p. 238.
287 Ibid., p. 244ff.
288 Rudolf Steiner: *Rudolf Steiner in the Waldorf School*. CW 298, 1980, p. 165.

and how he inspired the teachers. He reminded the teachers that they wanted to work out of his spirit.[289]

Caroline von Heydebrand was very happy that day to take a first grade for the first time, because in 1919 she had taken a fifth grade. The welcoming in of the new children was celebrated in the great eurythmy room of the school. There was a long table in front of the hall, in front of which Rudolf Steiner stood with the two teachers who were to take the parallel classes. Caroline von Heydebrand stood to the right and to the left Dagmar Tilliss. Seated in a half circle in front of them were the parents with their children, waiting for their child to be called up. Each child came up when called, was greeted by Rudolf Steiner, and handed over to his or her teacher with the words: "This is your teacher."[290]

At the members meeting the next day, April 25, 1923, teachers were appointed as voting members to the Council of the Association for Independent Schools. In addition, it was decided that the official director of the school—which in this case was E. A. Karl Stockmeyer—should be a member of the association.

The faculty welcomed Hanns Strauss (1883–1946) as a new colleague. Together with his wife, Marie Strauss (1883–1977),[291] he had spent quite some time at the Goetheanum, where they helped with the carvings during the building of the first Goetheanum. They belonged to the avant-garde of Munich artists; Hans Strauss studied painting at the Munich Art Academy and Marie Strauss designed textile prints and rugs in the *Deutsche Werkstätten* [German workshops]. They formed friendships in Munich that continued in Stuttgart, and to this circle of friends belonged Count Fritz von Bothmer, Anna and Max Wolffhügel, Alexander Strakosch and his wife, as well as Ernst Uehli. Hans Strauss threw himself completely into the new task and only came home to sleep. This time of hyperinflation impacted the households of the teachers: They had to adopt a Spartan lifestyle, which demanded a lot of ingenuity to make ends meet, especially on the part of the wives of teachers.

In most families, guests were welcome. Often, they were hungry high school students without family in Stuttgart, or the host students with whom homework had to be done, just as with one's own children. Marie Strauss, Marianne Tittmann, Felicia Schwebsch, Anna Stockmeyer, Anna Wolffhügel, and other teachers' wives carried a lot. Quietly and without fuss, they contributed—too often without any recognition— an immense amount to the success of this first Waldorf school. Olga Leinhas-Svardström (1883–1980) was another new member of the faculty. She was one of the four Svardström sisters, known as the "Swedish Nightingales" who had toured Europe in the early 1900s, giving concerts everywhere. In 1909 she had married Emil Leinhas. After her divorce in 1923, Rudolf Steiner suggested to her that she come to

---

289 Rudolf Steiner: *Rudolf Steiner in the Waldorf School*. CW 298, 1980, p. 168ff.
290 Margrit Jünemann: *Caroline von Heydebrand*. 2003, p. 48.
291 Michaela Strauss: Marie Strauss (June 28, 1883–April 6, 1977). LR 15, 1977, p. 92f.

the Waldorf school, not as a singer, but as a handwork teacher next to Berta Molt. In order to also teach in the upper grades, in 1924 Rudolf Steiner suggested that they learn bookbinding.

The two handwork teachers Berta Molt and Olga Leinhas first learned this craft in the cardboard factory of José del Monte and then at the State Academy of Fine Arts in Stuttgart, thus preparing themselves to introduce this subject at the school.[292] Because of the assignment Rudolf Steiner had given them, the two women became very close through their work together, which was also palpable in the shared tasks they had in the Sunday service for the children. Their friendship was astonishing, given that the relationship between Emil Leinhas and Emil Molt was very tense and not easy to understand.

Bettina Mellinger (1885–1953)[293] was also new to the faculty this school year and took a class. She was a very welcome addition since she had the necessary teacher certificate for Württemberg. It turned out that she was an essential complement to the faculty for completely different reasons. She organized meals for the children of the Waldorf Astoria workers especially, and she also arranged trips for these children to Welzheimer Wald, a forested region in northeast Württemberg, and holidays on the North Sea and in Tirol, Austria.

The 17-year-old Alexandre Leroi (1906–1968) had become acquainted with Rudolf Steiner through friends of his mother. After attending a lecture, probably on March 25, 1923,[294] he asked Steiner if he could attend the Waldorf School. Permission was given and Alexandre Leroi joined the tenth grade. After a year or two, he and his school friends, Karl Nunhöfer (1904–1988) and Alexis von Vivenot, conceived of a plan to start a Waldorf newsletter, to be distributed to all former students. Alexandre Leroi carried this newsletter even during his medical studies. It came out regularly until 1938.[295]

At Christmas 1923, all three *Christmas Plays from Oberufer* were performed for the first time in the newly built gymnasium, which doubled as an auditorium. What had started as a performance of a play written by Paul Baumann in 1920 now took on a form that could be carried on. The music, composed by Leopold van der Pals for the three Christmas plays, became an integral part of the tradition.

A large-scale pedagogical Easter conference was held in Stuttgart April 7–13, 1924, which had the theme "The Place of Education at Home and in Society at Large." The executive council in Dornach and the Waldorf School faculty organized it

292 Berthold Faig: Olga Leinhas-Svardström (September 25, 1883–September 19, 1980). LR 22, 1981, p. 76ff.
293 Magda Maier: http://biographien.kulturimpuls.org/detail.php?&id=460 (site visited March 16, 2017).
294 May Vera Leroi and Willem F. Veltman: *Alexandre Leroi. Ein Menschenschicksal im Umbruch der Zeiten.* 1998, p. 35, note 13.
295 Ibid., p. 38.

together and many teachers of the Waldorf School—W. J. Stein, E. Schwebsch, H. von Baravalle, K. Schubert, M. Röschl, M. Wolffhügel, C. von Heydebrand, E. Kolisko, P. Baumann—gave lectures and workshops.

On the evening of April 8, Rudolf Steiner held the first lecture in a cycle that was woven into the conference, called "Die Methodik des Lehrens und die Lebensbedingungen des Erziehens" [The Methodology of Teaching and the Living Conditions of Education].[296] About 1700 people came to hear it in the Gustav Siegle house in downtown Stuttgart.[297] Ernst Weissert was 19 years old when he attended, and decided then and there to become a teacher. After World War II he was one of the core personalities involved in the rebuilding of the German Waldorf school movement, and he carefully and unwaveringly worked toward working together internationally. Rudolf Steiner's lecture cycle continued over the next few days every morning at nine. In retrospect, E. A. Karl Stockmeyer said, "In these lectures we were given a basic outline of a truly contemporary teacher training."[298] At the end of the fifth lecture, Rudolf Steiner closed with a verse that seems to encapsulate what humanity needs for the 20th and 21st centuries.

To bind the soul to matter
means to grind the soul to dust.

To find oneself in spirit
means to unite human beings.

To behold oneself in humanity
means to build worlds.[299]

This school year also saw the first specially arranged final exam at the end of twelfth grade. From 1924 onward, the school had a regular final exam, the *Abitur*. Valdo Bossi, one of the twelfth graders, conceived the idea that the whole class should ask for a conversation with Rudolf Steiner. This request was fulfilled and thus it was that Rudolf Steiner had a conversation with the 17 students of this first graduating class on April 10, in which they talked about their plans for the future. Among the students were Walter Molt, Rudolf Grosse, Karl Nunhöfer, Ulrich Schickler, Adalbert von Keyserlingk (a group known as the pentagram), Karin Ruths-Hoffmann and others. During the conversation, Rudolf Grosse stated his firm wish to become a Waldorf teacher, upon which Rudolf Steiner recommended he should first attend

296 Rudolf Steiner: *The Essentials of Education*. CW 308, Anthroposophic Press, 1997.
297 Christoph Lindenberg: *Rudolf Steiner—Eine Chronik*. 1988, p. 571. Published at the time in the *Neue Preussische Lehrerzeitung* Nr. 22, May 31, 1924, and in the *Pfälzische Lehrerzeitung* Nr. 10, May 15, 1924.
298 E. A. Karl Stockmeyer: MVfS, March 8, 1926, p. 23.
299 Rudolf Steiner: *The Essentials of Education*. CW 308, Anthroposophic Press, 1997, p. 82.

lectures on philosophy and literature and do practice teaching in grades one through four. He was given Caroline von Heydebrand as a mentor.[300] On April 29, Rudolf Steiner spoke with the twelfth grade of the coming year and recommended first instituting a preparatory class before doing the final exams, so that the twelfth grade curriculum would not be compromised by test preparation.

The Sixth and Last School Year with Rudolf Steiner

ON APRIL 30, 1924, the opening assembly was held for the sixth school year, with 784 students in 23 grades and 47 teachers. Because of the large number of applications for the fifth grades, the two fourth grades had been split into three for the fifth grade. Just like every other school year, Rudolf Steiner gave a talk at the opening assembly in 1924. It was his custom to ask the students each year whether they loved their teachers. So, the students expected the same question this year as well. Now this time the students had plotted amongst themselves that they would reply with a loud "no," come what may. Rudolf Steiner started off by saying to the new first graders that they would now have to learn to sit still for quite some time and that they would have to learn to love their teachers, and then went on to say, "Now that you've been away from school for quite some time, I would like to ask you whether you have forgotten your love for your teachers during the holidays?"[301] Unwittingly, they all roared, "NO." Whether Steiner had gotten wind of their plan beforehand is not known.

Shortly before the beginning of the school year, Dr. Erich Gabert (1890–1968) had received a telegram from Rudolf Steiner, asking him to start teaching in Stuttgart straightaway. The newly created fifth grade, 5c, needed a class teacher. He was one of the last teachers personally invited by Rudolf Steiner. Erich Gabert became a pillar for the first Waldorf School, teaching from then on until the school was closed and when it reopened after the war.

He made major contributions to the development of the Waldorf school movement. What he wrote about history teaching was of fundamental importance and so was his editing of the faculty meetings with Rudolf Steiner.[302] In addition, he left his mark on many generations of teachers in the German Waldorf school movement because of his work in the teacher seminar in Stuttgart.

---

300 Johannes Tautz: Zum 80. Geburtstag von Rudolf Grosse. LR 30, 1985, p. 70. Rudolf Steiner asked Rudolf Grosse in September 1 to come to Dornach because he had a curative education assignment for him, which he accepted. He was 19 years old at the time, and after that he became a teacher at the newly-founded Waldorf school in Basel for 21 years. He remained in that school until 1956, after which he was asked to become a member of the Executive Committee of the General Anthroposophical Society in Dornach.

301 Rudolf Steiner: *Rudolf Steiner in the Waldorf School.* CW 298, 1980, p. 204.

302 Rudolf Steiner: *Faculty Meetings with Rudolf Steiner.* CW 300b, 1975, p. 21.

Dr. Eugen Kolisko, the school physician, in the doctor's office of the school, circa 1930

Dr. Caroline von Heydebrand was born in Breslau, had grown up with nine brothers, and studied German language and literature. In the faculty meeting of March 30, 1923, Rudolf Steiner said about her, "There's no for or against when Dr. von Heydebrand is concerned. Everybody will be happy when she takes the first grade." In her classroom, she set up a cupboard that contained honey, Ovomaltine, baked goods, and little gifts.[303] During the ten o'clock break she kept back hungry children from poor workers' families and fed them.[304] Even though she was not outwardly imposing, the delicate, round little woman had great authority and exerted a strong influence on both her children and colleagues.

Auguste Unger, Dr. Carl Unger's wife, had also taken note of the plight of the children, and so had Mrs. Böhm, the wife of Director Böhm. The two women took the bull by the horns and organized a little school kitchen, collected contributions, and cooked, all the while having an open ear for the children. The school doctor, Dr. Eugen Kolisko, and Bettina Mellinger were equally aware of the consequences of undernourishment and malnutrition. They always rolled up their sleeves to lend a hand and support the mothers. Dr. Kolisko wrote a report in the association newsletter on

303 Friederun Henkel-von Dechend: Erinnerungen einer Schülerin. LR 33, 1987, p. 63.
304 In the faculty meeting of February 14, 1923, the school doctor reported that 180 out of 650 students were seriously undernourished. See Rudolf Steiner: *Faculty Meetings with Rudolf Steiner*. CW 300b, 1975, p. 285.

the school's effort to feed undernourished children.[305] The food was financed through a Dutch fund, brokered by Mrs. Stibbe. Food was donated by other countries as well. England, Czechoslovakia, and Switzerland all chipped in. Ambassador Olsen organized a food transport all the way from Oslo, which supplied the kitchen for two whole months.

In June 1924, the fourth regular members meeting of the Association for Independent Schools took place.[306] After an address by Rudolf Steiner, E.A. Karl Stockmeyer gave a detailed report about the past school year, which was the first year it had a full K–12 program. The members present were informed—once again—of the dire financial situation. The school had grown tremendously, there was no state support, and the cost per student per month was around 35 marks. Few parents were actually in a position to pay this amount. In the meantime, the number of members of the association had grown to 3400 in Germany and over 900 in 20 other countries, ranging from South America, South West Africa, and Australia, to as far away as China and Java, in addition to a few European countries. The member contributions amounted to about 14,000 marks per month, there was the opportunity to sponsor students, and these sources combined helped to keep the school afloat.[307] Yet it was not enough to cover the monthly deficits. Therefore E.A. Karl Stockmeyer used every opportunity to find more members and sponsors. He fairly regularly reported to English members and asked them to find additional sponsors.[308]

On July 14, Marie and Rudolf Steiner traveled to Stuttgart to attend a few very important meetings the next day. At ten o'clock in the morning of July 15, a conversation was started with the anthroposophical shareholders of The Coming Day, Inc., to apprise them of the dire liquidity situation they were in. That they were in a precarious position was explained by the fact that the Waldorf School, the therapeutic clinic in Stuttgart, the research institute and the publishing house were sapping the rest, and therefore their solvency could no longer be guaranteed by the businesses in the conglomerate. Capital invested in these four institutions had a share value of 35,000 out of a total of 109,000 shares. In order to resolve this dire situation, the proposal was to liquidate the publishing house, dissolve the research institute, and to ask the Waldorf School and the clinic to go it alone.

---

305 Dr. E. Kolisko: Kinderspeisung in der Waldorfschule. MVfS Heft 4/5, July 1924, p. 64, and issue number 1, June 1926, p. 31.

306 Caroline von Heydebrand gave a detailed report about the talk Rudolf Steiner gave at this members meeting. MVfS issue 4/5, July 1924, p. 3ff.

307 The number of students at the beginning of the school year of 1923/24 was 687. Waldorf-Astoria, Inc., paid tuition for 172 children, parents of 140 children could afford it themselves, and 153 children were covered by sponsors paying alone or in groups. See also E.A. Karl Stockmeyer: Finanzbericht für die 4. MV. MVfS issue 4/5, July 1924, p. 14; Wenzel M. Götte: *Erfahrungen mit Schulautonomie*. 2006, p. 237.

308 The Waldorf School Union. AM May 10, 1924, p. 134f.

In view of the pressing need, shareholders were implored to consider donating their shares in order to keep especially the Waldorf School alive. The appeal was heard, 23,100 shares were donated and with that the survival of the Waldorf School was assured.[309] The lease agreement between the Association for Independent Schools and The Coming Day, however, was not signed until September. In spite of this, the agreement was approved at the fourth general meeting of The Coming Day that same afternoon, and the governing council relieved of liability. During the ensuing months the businesses still in the corporation were sold or given back to their original owners. Emil Leinhas had failed completely.

The Waldorf School had thus been fortunate enough to be saved thanks to the generosity of the anthroposophical shareholders. After this had been accomplished at the general meeting, the day continued with a faculty meeting, which began at 8:30 p.m. Serious conversations followed. Rudolf Steiner spoke especially about the moral attitude of the teachers toward the pupils as being the absolute prerequisite for the "continued existence of the Waldorf School." Furthermore, he used the words, "if the Waldorf School were to continue," after which he went on to say "So,... this lack of contact with the children, that is something we have to tackle. It weighs heavily on me. I have noticed this through other symptoms as well. We have a long way to go before teachers will have gained deep enough insight into the psychological constitution of individual schoolchildren [...]."

Rudolf Steiner noted the following: A certain distance between teachers and students, not enough affinity for establishing contact with the students, and too much of an academic tone. "You are giving lectures"—especially in the upper grades.[310] We can trust that the teachers of this first Waldorf School were bending over backward, that they were trying to relate to the students and actually were close to them to a certain extent.

Taking this into account, these admonitions by Rudolf Steiner should not be taken at their surface value. So, he ended this meeting with a review of some of the basic maxims for being a teacher. "What is needed above all is enthusiasm and interest. You cannot teach enthusiasm. [...] We need enthusiasm. What we do not need is aloof superiority and clever reflection. We must demand of ourselves, as a matter of principle, to not be tired."[311]

September 3, 1925, was the last time Rudolf Steiner visited the Waldorf School in Stuttgart. The first order of the day was signing the leasing contract between The Coming Day and the Independent Association for Waldorf Schools. After that, Rudolf Steiner had a conversation with the former students of the twelfth grade, who reported

---

309 Christoph Lindenberg: *Rudolf Steiner–Eine Chronik.* 1988, p. 590.
310 All these quotes are taken from Rudolf Steiner: *Faculty Meetings with Rudolf Steiner.* CW 300b, translated here from GA 300c, 1975, p. 187.
311 Ibid., p. 190.

on their first professional experiences. In the evening there was a short meeting with the teachers, in which he announced, "I want to give lectures in September or in the first half of October about the moral side of education." It was as if he had a premonition of what clearly proved to be the greatest challenge for schools in decades to come.

From his sickbed Rudolf Steiner was still able to ask the mathematician Ernst Bindel (1890–1974) to join the faculty as a new teacher. Ernst Bindel was a man who brought form to the school. He was a tireless worker with a highly developed pedagogical imagination. Until a ripe old age he published many works, which were not limited to his own field of expertise. He taught at the Stuttgart school from age 35–74, and for many generations of students he managed to bring to life how mathematical thinking grows and develops. "His lessons were never boring, and his creative productivity was always full of vitality. He had an abundance of humorous ideas and he was fiery, intense, and economical at the same time."[312]

Two weeks before his death, Rudolf Steiner wrote to the teachers of the Waldorf School. I would like to specifically highlight two aspects from this handwritten letter.[313] Rudolf Steiner reminded teachers of what had been achieved by common effort and asked them to pause and gather strength from their achievements in order to support each other in the future.

> *…What we have brought about together,*
> *May it give strength to the teachers,*
> *May it draw us together through mutual counsel…*

These lines are often understood as an endorsement of school leadership through internal counsel, i.e., the handing over of the leadership from Rudolf Steiner to the college of teachers. Now to the second aspect. The good spirits standing guard over the school will be able to be active and work through the deeds of the teachers as divine spiritual power only when the faculty is faithfully mindful of the fruitfulness of anthroposophy. Thus Rudolf Steiner laid the leadership of the Waldorf school entirely in the hands of the faculty and gave the essential conditions under which this can succeed.

A few days later, when Dr. Steiner's illness had progressed even further, a letter arrived signed by Dr. Günther Wachsmuth. It read as follows: "On behest of Dr. Steiner, we would like to let you know that the faculty of the Waldorf School is authorized to take on a leadership role in Germany in guiding the schools that want to apply the anthroposophical pedagogical method. The responsibility thus given entails giving leadership in matters of both pedagogy and finance by checking on economic

---

312 Ellen Schalk: Zum 100. Geburtstag von Ernst Bindel. LR 40, 1990, p. 91.
313 Zur Vertiefung der Waldorfpädagogik. Dornach 2000, p. 89f.

viability. Schools that do not meet the requirements in these areas cannot be seen as representative of anthroposophical pedagogy."[314]

The teachers of the Stuttgart Waldorf School saw this letter as a mandate for them to guide and oversee the building up of the Waldorf school movement, an obligation that was carried out practically by E. A. Karl Stockmeyer especially. Extended exchanges of letters with new school initiatives demonstrate the way E. A. Karl Stockmeyer carried out this sponsorship. After World War II this mandate was transferred to the *Bund der Freien Waldorfschulen* [German Waldorf Schools Association] and maintained throughout the century, albeit interpreted in various ways, depending on temperament and individual circumstances.

Rudolf Steiner died on March 30, 1925. Emil and Berta Molt drove to Dornach together with many of the teachers in order to be present for the ceremonies. Back in Stuttgart a solemn assembly to commemorate the founder was also held with the children of the school. A new era began for the teachers, for now there was no longer an arbitrator to maintain order, no central authority accepted by all. Now it became a matter of practicing collaborative leadership, as Rudolf Steiner had anticipated in his letter.

Developments from 1925 to 1933

THE LIQUIDATION OF The Coming Day, Inc., was carried out in the first months of 1925. Emil Leinhas, still its sole director, was of the opinion that the world had not developed an understanding for the thinking behind this foundation, and that the corporation could therefore not grow as strongly as it should. He didn not recognize his own part in this, or, more specifically, his management strategy. After the final collapse only the Waldorf School remained, and Emil Leinhas changed the name from The Coming Day, Inc., to *Uhlandshöhe AG für Grundstücksverwaltung* [Uhlandshöhe, Inc., for Property Management]. He stayed on as the economic director.

On September 20, 1925, the fifth regular members meeting of the Association for Independent Schools was held in Stuttgart. Before the start of the meeting, Walter Johannes Stein gave a lecture with the title "Anthroposophy as the Basis of Waldorf Education," in which he explored the interesting question of how one can work on the capacity to perceive development and acquire an eye for growth processes. Emil Molt opened the meeting and gave a memorial tribute to Rudolf Steiner's work for the Waldorf school. He reminded people that Rudolf Steiner had called the first lecture cycle for teachers a festive celebration in the course of world development, and expressed his deep gratitude for everything that parents, friends, teachers, and students

---

314 Written by Dr. G. Wachsmuth on behalf of the Executive Council of the General Anthroposophical Society on March 17, 1925, addressed to the Leadership Council of the Independent Waldorf School in Stuttgart. Archiv LS 2.2.062.

Christoph Boy, a class teacher from 1920 to 1934 at the Stuttgart Waldorf School, joined the Leadership Council in 1925.

had been granted in learning from him. Against this background, Emil Molt called on everybody to embrace what had been given and to do everything in their power to enable Waldorf education to spread.

The first item on the agenda was choosing a new chair after the death of Rudolf Steiner. In order to guarantee continuity and work closely together with Dornach, Albert Steffen, head of the General Anthroposophical Society, was asked to also become chairman of the school association. The motion passed unanimously. Emil Molt continued on as vice president until 1936. Due to health reasons, Paul Baumann stepped down from the leadership council at this meeting, having occupied this function since 1923. Christoph Boy (1887–1934) took his place.

Rudolf Steiner had invited Christoph Boy back in 1921 to come teach at the school, and he gained the respect of a fifth grade that had gotten out of hand and, with that, the respect of the faculty of teachers. Christoph Boy was recognized by his colleagues as a faithful, unsentimental person with an unfailing sense of duty. He staunchly stood by his personal moral principles, and his strength showed also in his ability to bear up under adversity. "He was rock solid, he could affirm others, and his roots were deep"[315] said Herbert Hahn. He was totally reliable and on occasion his directness was felt as bluntness. A friend once said of him, "Sometimes it seemed as if his angel stood behind him with arms crossed." The children loved this teacher and kept coming back to him for advice long after they had left his class. In describing this taciturn man, Berta and Emil Molt put it this way, "Our dear friend said relatively little. When he spoke, he usually hit the nail on the head and his words always carried weight. He was able to take initiative at the right time. Deeply religious by nature, it was far from him to let his head hang. The opposite was true. He hid his religiosity deep inside and one only saw it come out in the form of gentleness and inwardness. He never used the name of God in vain."[316]

The members meeting continued with a report by E. A. Karl Stockmeyer. In the school year 1924/25 the school had grown to 24 grades (including an extra-help class) with a total of 864 students, who were taught by 47 full-time teachers.[317] Thirty of these children came from abroad, 139 came from out of town and lived with Stuttgart families, and 28.3 percent of the children had not been in any other school but attended the Waldorf school from the beginning.

315 Herbert Hahn: Begegnungen und Eindrücke. MPK, Nr. 1, Ostern 1950, p. 13.
316 Emil and Berta Molt: Christoph Boy†. N 42, 21.10.1934, p. 168.
317 This includes all students coming and going. The school year began with 784 students and ended with 758 students. See report by E.A. Karl Stockmeyer: MVfS Heft 8, March 1926, p. 22.

Emil Leinhas came next and reported on the financial situation.[318] The cost per student per month was 38 marks on average, an amount covered by tuition (60 percent), contributions from members of the Waldorf School Association (16 percent), and donations (16 percent). That left a deficit of 8 percent. At the beginning of the school year, the tuition was still 25 marks per student per month; raised to 30 marks in the course of the year, it was still not enough. This situation prompted some people to actively lobby for an education league (the World School Association) to involve wider circles and cover the deficit. In 1926 an initiative of this kind was taken up in Holland, but in the emerging conflicts within the Anthroposophical Society, the effort floundered miserably.[319]

Württemberg schools were inspected every three years back then, and the second official school inspection of the Waldorf School was carried out from October 19–November 13, 1925. This inspection was important since it would be decided at this time whether the Waldorf School would be allowed to keep grades one through four going or whether the authorities would apply the law that private schools should dismantle these grades.[320] The inspection was carried out by inspector Dr. Friedrich Hartlieb, who wrote afterward: "Whoever becomes acquainted with the Waldorf School will not fail to notice that it is led by a unique faculty of teachers. From the first moment on, the relationships between the teachers seemed exemplary to me. They serve each other with love. There is a lot of give-and-take and sharing of strengths amongst them. Petty quarrels, jealousy and rivalry are beneath them. The whole of this faculty's professional work is animated by a unifying spirit, something high and holy, to a degree I have never found in any other educational institution."[321]

318 Expenditures 1924/25: General administrative costs: 46,538,21 marks; wages and fees 289,705,56 marks; traveling costs etc. 14,995,77 marks; teaching aids 6,368,49 marks; lesson materials 4,543,81 marks; library 7,119,48; school garden 1,712,99 marks; miscellaneous 1,033,59 marks; inventory depreciation 2,945,17 marks. Total: 374,863,07 marks. Income: tuition 207,755,06 marks, members contributions 57,838,91 marks, one-time donations 75,996,59 marks, miscellaneous items 405,93 marks. Total income: 341,996,49 marks. Deficit therefore: 32,866,58 marks.

319 Sophia Christine Murphy: *The Multifaceted Life of Emil Molt.* 2012, p. 240f.

320 N 2, 10.01.1926, p. 5. In accordance with the revision of the elementary school law of 1920, private schools were given until 1924 to phase out grades 1–4. On November 30, 1921, this period was extended by one year for the Waldorf School, i.e., until the spring of 1925. On February 26, 1926, the Waldorf School was granted a reprieve and could function as an integrated elementary school with grades 1–8. This was the result of an amendment to the private school ordinance, which was put into place at the end of 1925. See also note 153.

321 N 2, January 10, 1926, p. 5ff.; 4, January 24, 1926, p. 13f.; 5, January 31, 1926, p. 17ff. and 6, February 7, 1926, p. 21ff, which has copious quotes from the revision report by Dr. Friedrich Hartlieb. Shortly thereafter, Dr. Hartlieb published an essay, "Die Freie Waldorfschule am Stuttgart," in an extra contribution to the teacher Journal of Württemberg Nr. 9 of October 8, 1926, which was a highly positive endorsement, complete with examples to clarify the pedagogical impulse. In 1930 he published this article at the same time he gave his tribute at the occasion of the Ten-Year Jubilee. This was accompanied by another essay, which had appeared on October 16, 1929, in the *Stuttgarter Neues Tagblatt*, reissued as a brochure by the publishers of the teacher journal of Württemberg.

Thus, he sang the teachers' praises, for which the whole faculty was grateful, and so were the association members when, in their next meeting, they were apprised of what he had written. The report was certainly also an expression of his deep appreciation of the pedagogical impulse and after this introduction, the report continued with a nuanced evaluation of the achievements of individual grades: "Five grades received the mark 'very good' for their educational accomplishments, 12 grades the mark 'good,' two grades the mark 'satisfactory.' As far as the outcome was concerned, three grades could be given the mark 'very good,' ten grades the mark 'good,' and six grades the mark 'satisfactory.' It might be interesting to note that a grade six in which the children had been there from the beginning, and a grade 7/8, in which the children had attended the Waldorf School for six years, scored very good overall scores, and these very classes had been given all manner of recommendations when they were inspected before by my predecessor in February 1922. This all goes to show that the accomplishments of the Waldorf School should not be judged by the accomplishments of the lower and middle grades, but by the achievements of the upper classes, and that the faculty of the Waldorf School has grown more and more into carrying out what they set themselves to do. They are true to their general mission and it shows in individual instances."[322]

Such a balanced evaluation was what schools that were founded later would have wished to get from inspectors. Instead, inspections often stipulated adaptations in the curriculum and made all manner of demands, especially in grades one through four. Interestingly, state inspector Friedrich Hartlieb felt such a personal connection to the Waldorf School that he organized a conference for the regional school inspectors at the Stuttgart Waldorf School on May 21, 1926, during which he gave participants a personal tour. His reports had positive consequences for the school.[323]

On February 26, 1926, the school received a written notification from the ministry of culture in Württemberg, that said, "Due to the fact that the educational authorities have a particular interest in the continued existence of the Waldorf School for pedagogical reasons, this school can be recognized as a private school going from grades one through eight, on the basis of article 147, State Ordinance section 2, reserving the right of recall at any time, so long as the mandatory conditions of article 147 section 1 of the State Ordinance are fulfilled."[324] After all conditions had been fulfilled in May 1926, all limitations on the number of pupils in the elementary school grades were lifted by special permission of the Protestant state school inspector. This was a big success for the school, for it meant that the legal recognition as a *Gesamtschule* [comprehensive school] was secured for the time being.

322 Nachrichtenblatt 4, 1926; in the Nachrichtenblatt 1926, Nr. 2–6, more extensive extracts from the report were published. A shorter version is printed in Norbert Deuchert: Waldorfschule und Staat 1919–1938. BhB Advent 1986, p. 88.
323 MVfS, Nr. 3, October 1926, p. 12.
324 Ibid., p. 11.

In the school year 1925/26 a third parallel class was established for the last time, bringing the total number of grades to 26, with 51 full-time teachers and a class to prepare for the final exam, which had 18 students in it. One of these was Alfred Schmid (1911–1988),[325] who later became a teacher at the school. In the same year, Erica Smith (1900–1994) joined the faculty, and her English lessons made quite an impression on students, among them Else Klink, the longtime visionary leader of the Stuttgart eurythmy school. Erica Smith was born in Rawalpindi. She was the daughter of a British officer and moved with her mother to the Isle of Man after the early death of her father. There a decisive meeting with the Raab family took place, which brought her into contact with anthroposophy and Waldorf pedagogy.

The meeting came just in time for her to hear Rudolf Steiner's lectures in Torquay in the summer of 1924. She was introduced to him, and during the ensuing conversation Rudolf Steiner invited her to come teach at the Waldorf School in Stuttgart, charging Hermann von Baravalle with the task of accompanying her there. On September 3, Rudolf Steiner made sure she could partake in the last meeting he held with the Stuttgart faculty. Erica Smith and Hermann von Baravalle married in April 1925, and in 1939 the two of them moved to the United States.[326]

A few weeks before the end of the school year in 1926 the first Waldorf kindergarten was founded by Elisabeth von Grunelius (1895–1989). She was supported in this effort by Herbert Hahn, and she herself had raised the funds for the building of the kindergarten. The work began in a three-room wooden building with 25 children. Elisabeth von Grunelius had been part of the faculty from the beginning, charged with taking on the founding of the kindergarten. In meetings with Rudolf Steiner she had already started talking about the education of the preschooler, and she had asked him how a kindergarten teacher should prepare for her pedagogical task. His suggestions found their way through her into the Waldorf early-childhood teacher training. In an essay of 1932, she wrote: "I would like to look upon the kindergarten as a place where children would have a first opportunity to come together to play and experience joyful warmth and comradery. The task of an educator in such a place would have to be to organize a children's kingdom within the restlessness of our present-day civilization, in an atmosphere of freshness and wakeful understanding in which children could develop fully in accordance with their developmental stage of life."

This remark was followed by an explanation of the essence of imitation. She added, "The child's path has to do with getting to know the world, to understand it and make it her own. In doing so, the child partakes of profound moral forces, and all she experiences as beautiful, true, and good in her surroundings is what she wants

---

325 Magda Maier and Klaus Charisius: Alfred Schmid. LR 36, 1988, p. 110f. Alfred Schmid began to teach as early as 1935, just after he graduated. He became a gifted chemistry and geography teacher at the school—his excursions to the Alps were famous—during the first decades after World War II.
326 Rex Raab: Erica von Baravalle (December 18, 1900–December 18, 1996). LR 53, 1995, p. 97ff.

to be able to do. This is the way the little child learns until approximately the time of the change of teeth. This learning mode is not intellectual. The child joins in all the processes around her, in all she does, touches, hears, and sees, learning from the gesture. By nature, the child in kindergarten is not receptive to coaxing, commands, or corrections of the adults around her. When one educates through imitation, the child has an example, which is a free stimulus for the development of her will. Educating through imitation demands of course self-education of the educator in every way, including artistically and spiritually. […] When one takes into account this principle of imitation, there is no definite pattern or fixed form everybody would have to follow, but imitation allows every child the freedom to imitate according to her inclinations and capacities, starting where she is and in her own time. She can choose to imitate what she sees at her own pace. She feels free and is genuinely so."[327]

The demands she put upon herself to be worthy of imitation were sky high, and her respect for the individuality of each child was commensurate. She created a soul space in which the children entrusted to her care could blossom. Only few people were allowed to do a practicum in her kindergarten, one of whom was Klara Hattermann (1909–2003), who rebuilt the Waldorf preschool movement after the war using Hannover as a basis.

Klara Hattermann simply posted herself by the door of the kindergarten every morning and kept this up until she got special permission to do a practicum. Next to Klara Hattermann, Elisabeth von Grunelius also trained Ellen Leroi to become a Waldorf kindergarten teacher. Together with Maya Krückenberg, Ellen Leroi built up a kindergarten in the center of Stuttgart, which she headed until she had to flee the National Socialists. Elisabeth von Grunelius led the kindergarten until the school was closed in 1938.[328] After that she moved to the United States and began there by building up the kindergarten in Kimberton, Pennsylvania, and afterward the kindergarten on the campus of Adelphi University in Garden City, New York. She returned to Europe in 1954.[329] Klara Hattermann had carried on her work and not only established the kindergarten seminar in Hannover, but also the Whitsun conferences there, the first of which was held in 1951. These conferences were highly important for the kindergarten movement and continued for decades.

For the running of the Waldorf School, the donations collected through the Association for Independent Schools were vital. E.A. Karl Stockmeyer fostered the connection with the local branch groups and sent out newsletters on a regular basis, in which he reported on the developments in Stuttgart, called on people to engage

327 Elisabeth von Grunelius: Das Kind im Kindergarten der Freien Waldorfschule. EK 4, Oktober 1932, p. 173.
328 May Vera Leroi and Willem F. Veltman: Alexandre Leroi. *Ein Menschenschicksal im Umbruch der Zeiten.* 1998, p. 40.
329 Helmut von Kügelgen: Elisabeth von Grunelius zum 90. Geburtstag. LR 30, 1985, p. 67; http:// biographien.kulturimpuls.org/detail.php?&id=1406 (site visited May 15, 2017).

more in the study of Waldorf pedagogy, and asked for donations. He was well aware that the aim to attract as many non-anthroposophical members as possible was not easy to attain. In the newsletter of May 1926 he put it as follows: "Rudolf Steiner's pedagogy can never be separated from anthroposophy. Yet this education has to be represented in such a way that people who know nothing about anthroposophy and have no inclination to occupy themselves with it can also see its value for the future of our culture. On the other hand, the origin of this education, which lies in anthroposophical spiritual science after all, should never be denied."[330]

At the sixth members meeting of July 22, 1926, Emil Molt addressed the members of the association, some of whom had come from far away to attend. After welcoming them, he pointed to the portentous first seven years of the school. By way of introduction, he pointed to the contrast between pedagogical success, visible in increased enrollment, and economic misfortune. "The spiritual and economic side do not go hand-in-hand here."[331] E. A. Karl Stockmeyer gave a review of the work that had been accomplished. A total number of 986 children (including children leaving and coming in midyear) attended the school in the year of reporting, 1925/26, and the number of foreign students living with host families in Stuttgart continued to grow: 156 students came from other locations in Germany, 37 from abroad.

It was after 11:00 p.m. that Emil Leinhas started his financial report, talking about the spells of big financial worries in the spring of 1926, which had only been relieved by large donations of a few American friends. It was probably due to the general economic malaise that fewer host families were able to pay tuition, which accounted for about half of the monthly deficits. The meeting was adjourned around midnight.

School resumed on September 7, 1926. Starting this year, the number of parallel classes was limited to two, because the faculty decided in the course of the 1927 school year that the school could not expand to more than two parallel grades. Any other parallel grades created so far would therefore have to be phased out. As a result, there were two gigantic ninth grades this school year, which created "many a headache" for the faculty.[332]

Sophie Porzelt (1897–1975) joined the faculty of the school in 1927 and taught English for six years, after which she took over a class.[333] She had a disarmingly gracious personality,[334] as Magda Maier put it, and she came to play a strong role in the decision-making process, at times quietly, at times in a more pronounced way. Her contributions and clear judgments were frequently decisive in internal decision-

330 E. A. Karl Stockmeyer: An die Leiter der Ortsgruppen des Waldorfschulvereins. Mai 1926. Archiv LS 5.9.02.
331 Members meeting report. MVfS Nr. 3, Oktober 1926, p. 7.
332 E. A. Karl Stockmeyer writing to Curt Englert-Faye, March 5, 1928. Archiv LS 3.18.42.
333 Dietrich Esterl: Die erste Waldorfschule Stuttgart–Uhlandshöhe 1919–2004. Daten–Dokumente–Bilder. 2006, p. 74; Magda Maier: Sophie Porzelt (February 5, 1897–December 12, 1975). LR 12, 1976, p. 92.
334 Ibid.

making within the Waldorf school movement. After the school closed, Sophie Porzelt first worked in Maine, close to the border between the United States and Canada. During the war, however, she worked as a teacher at Schloss Spezgart, a branch of the Landerziehungsheim Salem, a private boarding school near Lake Constance in southern Germany.

After the war she immediately came back to the school in Stuttgart and took on a class. Together with Erich Schwebsch and Erich Gabert she formed the core of the faculty and played an even stronger role than before. Another teacher who started in 1927/28 was Erika Zoeppritz (1900–1991). She was the daughter of a well-to-do factory owner and as a child she had the privilege of having private teachers and later attended painting school and art academy in Dresden and Munich. In 1926 she first did a practicum at the school and was trained to become a craft teacher. She stayed on until the school was closed and taught everything from spinning to building model airplanes.[335]

On February 17, 1927, the town council of Stuttgart decided to support the School Association with a building subsidy of 40,000 marks and a building loan of 80,000 marks, later augmented with 25,000 marks, to build an addition to the main building.[336] It is remarkable that this subsidy was passed unanimously in the town meeting, that is to say, all parties were in favor. Since this concerned a building subsidy only, they added: "The Waldorf School receives no state support nor any support from the town of Stuttgart. [...] This cannot be otherwise, since we are dealing with a school that is built up in such a way that it remains free in all respects."[337]

At the large education conference of Easter 1926, the question was asked how nationalism was being dealt with in the school. In answer to that, Erich Schwebsch wrote an article in the school newsletter. He wrote: "The Waldorf School basically avoids anything that promotes particular sympathies or agendas in any way, shape or form. We do this because we are of the opinion that any sectarian bias diminishes us as human beings, even limits us and makes us less able to grow to our full potential. Therefore, there is neither a nationalist nor pacifist nor globalizing orientation in the way we conduct our lessons, but only a sense of responsibility toward the developing human being. [...]. We are seeking to foster an understanding of the world at this moment in time, and are always looking to build foundational capacities to become truly human."[338]

---

335 Georg Kniebe: Erika Zoeppritz (November 7, 1900–August 12, 1992). LR 46, 1992, p. 71.
336 E.A. Karl Stockmeyer: Über die Aufgaben der Schulbewegung. ZPRSt 1, Oktober 1927, p. 7; Ernst Uehli: Denkschrift. EK Juni 1933, p. 351. It was an interest-free loan for a total of 105,000 marks. Afterward, however, the school was notified that interest had to be paid from April 1, 1935, onward, which amounted to a hefty yearly sum of 5,000 RM; see report of the 14th general meeting.
337 E.A. Karl Stockmeyer: Über die Aufgaben der Schulbewegung. ZPRSt 1, Oktober 1927, p. 4.
338 Erich Schwebsch: Wie wird in der Waldorfschule der nationale Gedanke behandelt? MVfS Heft 6, April 1927, p. 25.

The fifth education conference of the Waldorf School took place in Stuttgart April 8–13, 1927. Curt Englert-Faye participated in it and deemed it worthy of an extensive report, supplying comments on all the lecturers.[339] Later he engaged in polemics with E.A. Karl Stockmeyer; this time he targeted Erich Schwebsch. "Many listeners would have wished for more humanity and truth in the ethos and pathos of his talk. True enthusiasm needs no words and will, in occasions of this kind, find commensurate simplicity of expression." Walter Johannes Stein, Karl Schubert, and Alexander Strakosch were more to his liking. In their professional area, they were in sync with what the times demanded, he thought. Walter Johannes Stein gave a historical overview, exploring the different qualities of "truthful" and "right" over time. Karl Schubert spoke "with great warmth of heart" about anthroposophical curative education, and Curt Englert put him in the same league with Pestalozzi. E.A. Karl Stockmeyer and above all Alexander Strakosch gave an overview of the way technology and physics, next to traditional and industrial manual work, are featured not only in physics lessons, but can be integrated in the curriculum from kindergarten up to high school.

Alexander Strakosch, technology teacher at the Stuttgart Waldorf School from 1920–1934 and cofounder of an advanced level vocational education

Shortly before the end of the school year, on July 15, 1927, the next general meeting was held with the usual reports. After the holidays, from October 1927 onward, the newsletter of the school, an internal publication up to then, was changed into a public magazine called *Zur Pädagogik Rudolf Steiners*. Caroline von Heydebrand was chief editor; she solicited many articles and was one of the most active contributors herself. In 1927 she also published a book of memories, called *Rudolf Steiner in der Waldorfschule,* in which she collected contributions that empathetically depict highly inspiring and deeply felt examples of Rudolf Steiner's work with the children of different grades. The profound goodness of Rudolf Steiner's working with the children lived on longest in Karl Schubert, and his testimony forms part of the book. From 1932 onward, the magazine *Zur Pädagogik Rudolf Steiners* was renamed *Erziehungskunst–Zweimonatsschrift. Zur Pädagogik Rudolf Steiners* was also the name of the society founded by the association and chaired by E.A. Karl Stockmeyer, a society intended by Stockmeyer as a basis for a community-wide school movement.[340]

There were attempts in 1927 to start a second Waldorf school in Stuttgart, but this was efficiently and effectively blocked by E.A. Karl Stockmeyer and others. This is

339 The article in Msch 5, 1927, pp. 173–180, has no name under it, but style clearly points to Curt Englert.
340 E.A. Karl Stockmeyer: Über die Aufgaben der Schulbewegung. ZPRSt 1, October 1927, p. 8; Norbert Deuchert: Die Anfänge der internationalen Schulbewegung. BhB Advent 1985, p. 88.

Julia Charlotte Mellinger, who together with Alexander Strakosch, built the vocational continuing education program

mentioned in a letter from E. A. Karl Stockmeyer to Curt Englert.[341] There was not much further talk about this initiative at that time because the economic competition was too overwhelming. But in the school year 1929/30 new attempts by parents emerged to found a second Waldorf school, because many children could no longer be accepted into the Uhlandshöhe school. According to Stockmeyer, however, the interest was not serious enough to take on economic responsibility for a second school.[342]

Inner and outer activities continued. Many new students came and were accepted in all grades. Among them was Hans Rebmann (1912–1999), who had a strong interest in technology, studied mathematics and physics, and worked for Telefunken in Berlin, after which he returned as an upper-school teacher to *his* school.[343]

On March 18, 1926, Alexander Strakosch and E. A. Karl Stockmeyer wrote to the Württemberg department for vocational schools asking that the *Fortbildungsschule* [school for further vocational training], established in 1921, be officially recognized.[344] The plan was to develop it into an official vocational school, intended to enable students to have more general education along with their vocational training. The request was not granted at first, upon which they sent in more arguments to justify the undertaking, including lesson plans. Thereupon the education minister lifted the requirement to attend a separate vocational school.[345]

After the Easter holidays in 1927, the continued vocational training school started up, headed by Dr. Julia Charlotte Mellinger (1880–1951). Within this training the possibility was also given to complete a training in home economics, preparing students to practice this subject in children's homes and hospitals.[346] Along with cooking and household classes, the subjects were: chemistry, physics, nutrition, introduction to psychology, first aid, economics, business, and materials science. The number of periods was the same as in ordinary vocational schools, eight to ten per week. Artistic subjects were painting and eurythmy. The students attended one morning or afternoon a week, depending on time off given by their employers, as well as evenings from 6:00 to 8:00 p.m. This *Fortbildungsschule* ran until September 1931.

341 Archiv LS 3.18.27.
342 E. A. Karl Stockmeyer: Bericht über das Schuljahr 1929–1930. Berichte an die Mitglieder des Vereins für ein freies Schulwesen (Waldorfschulverein) e. V. Stuttgart, Nr. 7, November 1930, p. 2.
343 Elisabeth von Kügelgen: Hans Rebmann (June 17, 1912–October 22, 1999). LR 68, 2000, p. 90ff.
344 Archiv LS 3.26.004.
345 Written by Stuttgart's school superintendent. Nr. 426 March 17, 1927. Archiv LS 3.26.013.
346 Announcement of the continued vocational training. ZPRSt 6, February 1929, p. 296.

Friedrich Wickenhauser, music teacher at the Stuttgart Waldorf School from 1928–1964

Julia Charlotte Mellinger was a political economist who had been familiar with anthroposophy for a long time.[347] She also led the *Waldorf-Spielzeug & Verlags GmbH* [Waldorf Toys and Publishing House, LLC], which published the magazine *Zur Pädagogik Rudolf Steiners* as well as the books written by Caroline von Heydebrand and other Waldorf teachers. The publishing house had to be given up in 1941 after the Waldorf School was closed and sales dropped. When it was refounded, it was called *Mellinger Verlag* after her.

In 1928 Friedrich Wickenhauser (1902–1977) became a member of the faculty. He was a versatile and energetic young teacher who was full of joy and had a sense of humor. He had grown up in Linz where he studied to be a teacher and a musician. He was an organ student of the important church musician Johann Nepomuk David. When he was at a conference in Dornach, he became acquainted with music teacher Paul Baumann. This then led to his appointment as music teacher at the Stuttgart Waldorf School, where he effortlessly inspired a love of music in the students. A multi-instrumentalist, he was able to give lessons to students on a variety of instruments from French horn to bass, and built up an orchestra at the Waldorf School. By soliciting donations for instruments, he succeeded in building up a full symphony orchestra. He would suggest a particular instrument to students who did not seem to have an affinity for a particular instrument and often succeeded in awakening a love for that instrument. Some of his students went on to become professional musicians.

He was a multifaceted teacher, who performed music ranging from Bruckner symphonies to fiery Gypsy music. They also did carnival concerts with a Viennese ladies' ensemble, announced as "Fräulein Fingersauser" [Dexterous Dames]. At

347 Jan Pohl: Julia Charlotte Mellinger. In: Bodo von Plato (ed.): *Anthroposophie im 20. Jahrhundert.* 2003, p. 512.

the farewell assembly at the occasion of the school closing on March 30, 1938, he performed the second movement of Beethoven's Fifth Symphony with the students, which made a clear statement. After the war he was back immediately and taught until 1964. Music truly flourished during his time at the school.[348]

That same year, 1928, Herbert Hensel entered the first grade. When he was in high school, he gave a brilliant performance as Caesar in the 11b class play directed by Erich Schwebsch. In 1945 he completed his PhD and later was appointed physiology professor at the University of Marburg.

November 3–4, 1928, the eighth regular members meeting of the Association for Independent Schools was held. The financial situation continued to be tight, so Emil Molt suggested forming an economic advisory committee for the association. This committee consisted of "a number of highly reputable manufacturers from the higher echelons of Württemberg economic life."[349] From this meeting onward, information about the financial situation of the Waldorf School was sent out at irregular intervals by means of a newsletter to the members of the Association for Independent Schools. It remained a precarious venture economically, and in addition there was an undeniable decline in association membership.

In the spring of 1929 representatives of the Reemtsma company, which had grown to be the majority shareholder in the Waldorf Astoria, Inc., informed Emil Molt that the Stuttgart manufactory would have to be closed because it was no longer profitable and that the workers were to be let go and the machines destroyed. On March 7, 1929, he was told his own position would be terminated at the end of the year.[350]

Tough negotiations followed, and Emil Molt succeeded in getting Philipp Reemtsma to agree to take over the tuition payments of the workers' children for ten years (4000 RM per month). In November 1935 the Reemtsma company attempted to go back on this agreement, but Emil Molt fervently pleaded with them and succeeded once again in securing further tuition payments, which continued until the school closed in 1938.[351] On May 4, 1929, Emil Molt invited all his coworkers of the Waldorf Astoria, Inc., and their families to a meeting in the Waldorf School, which was followed on May 24 by an official goodbye party for the firm, which was held in the Wulle beer brewery to accommodate the large number of people invited.

In his extensive address, Emil Molt expressed gratitude for the work they had accomplished together and called to mind that they had not only shared a place to work, but had a destiny together in creating a positive example of economic, interpersonal

348 Friedhold Hahn: Friedrich Wickenhauser. LR 15, 1977, p. 88ff.
349 Report to the members of the Association for Independent Schools, Nr. 3, February 1929.
350 Sophia Christine Murphy: *The Multifaceted Life of Emil Molt.* 2012, p. 256. It came out later that Reemtsma had other motives as well, because Emil Molt had steered the firm back into a healthier economic course after the destructive actions of Emil Leinhas.
351 Dietrich Esterl: *Emil Molt 1876–1936. Tun, was gefordert ist.* 2012, p. 186.

cooperation in a time of great turmoil in society. They had formed a counterimage to mega-capitalist trends, where people are set up against each other.[352] On June 14, 1929, a general parent meeting was called, in which E. A. Karl Stockmeyer, standing in for Emil Molt, gave an explanation of how the closing of the Waldorf Astoria, Inc., had come about.[353] E. A. Karl Stockmeyer was also firmly convinced that the existence of the Waldorf School was only justified when the children of workers would be able to attend the school. And after the Waldorf Astoria, Inc., had closed, he saw considerable problems as to how to enable workers children to find their way in to the school. Life confirmed his view.

At the occasion of the ten-year anniversary of the Waldorf School a special issue of the magazine *Zur Pädagogik Rudolf Steiners* was published, in which the Waldorf teachers not only hearkened to the founding impulses but also contributed treatises about the teaching of science, eurythmy, and handwork. More or less at the same time a special issue of *Anthroposophie* (No. 44) came out, featuring contributions by teachers. Eugen Kolisko wrote the introduction, Caroline von Heydebrand contributed "The Pedagogical Message of Anthroposophy," and Alexander Strakosch wrote an article about the ten-year celebration of the work of the Waldorf School in Stuttgart.

But the pinnacle of the commemoration was a big celebration on the evening of October 16, 1929, with over 2000 people filling the Liederhalle to overflowing. The opening address was given by Emil Molt, followed by choir music and speech choruses by the students. Herbert Hahn gave an extensive talk entitled "The Face of the Waldorf School," which gave a picture of the cosmopolitan nature of the school, its global reach as well as its roots in German cultural tradition. Stuttgart's mayor, Dr. Ludwig, saluted the assembly, and then it was the Protestant school superintendent Dr. Friedrich Reinöhl's turn to speak on behalf of the board of education.

He had been favorably inclined toward the Waldorf School right from the start, and had especially valued the warm interpersonal contact between teachers and students, an aspect he had characterized and singled out for praise in his written report. He said, "When we judge a person or thing, do not we take into account how this person or thing affects us? In dealing with this person or thing, we sense whether we gain or lose inwardly, whether we grow tall or shrink and shrivel, whether our horizons are expanded or contracted. When I look at it this way, I can honestly say that it gives me great joy that my professional activities have given me the opportunity to form a personal relationship with the independent Waldorf School, its teachers, and its work. I wish from the bottom of my heart that the independent Waldorf School may continue to grow, blossom, and thrive."[354]

352 Sophia Christine Murphy: *The Multifaceted Life of Emil Molt*. 2012, p. 259.
353 Printed in LR 32, 1986, p. 74ff.
354 Friedrich Hartlieb: Ansprache. ZPRSt 6, Februar 1930, p. 328ff.

After that, parents and representatives from other Waldorf schools, for example Max Stibbe from The Hague, spoke to the assembly. At the end, after Erich Schwebsch had thanked all those present, there was music to close the evening. There was a remarkable amount of appreciation, praise, and attention by the media, more than there had ever been up to then. Every major newspaper published articles about the Waldorf School and its pedagogy. In connection with the jubilee, superintendent Dr. Friedrich Hartlieb wrote an article about the life of the independent Waldorf School in the *Stuttgarter Neues Tageblatt* of October 16, 1929. Eugen Kolisko commented afterward. "This article fully recognizes the spirit of the Waldorf School and Rudolf Steiner's pedagogical impulse. We can feel seen and understood in our efforts."

And there was more to come. Two parents of the Waldorf School, Paul and Gertrud Fundinger, brought out a commemorative booklet published by Ernst Suhrkamp Buch- and Kunstverlag Stuttgart, which was a compilation of contributions from parents, without exception gracious, heartwarming, and grateful. A few parents and friends of the school—and this was a wonderful side effect of the festive jubilee—collected donations at this time earmarked for social initiatives the school had sponsored. They collected 10,229 marks, which went to the school kitchen, medical care, and the establishment of a space for all those children who could not go home during the day because their parents had to work.[355]

In spite of this, financial worries continued. In 1929/30, the council of the Association for Independent Schools consisted of Albert Steffen, Emil Molt, E. A. Karl Stockmeyer, Robert Killian, Emil Leinhas, and Ernst Bindel, as well as the chair of the executive council of the school. In November 1928, an advisory council had been appointed within the association, which had a number of reputable regional businessmen in it by now. They were: director Hermann Binder; director Heino Brinkmann; Dr. von Grunelius, manufacturer; Rudolf Haaga (manufacturer in a circular knitting-machine factory); Consul Hans Holz; Hans Kleemann (manufacturer of construction equipment); Dr. Gustav Kilpper; Walter C. Knoll (furniture factory manufacturer); Dr. Emil Kühn, manufacturer; Julius Mailänder, manufacturer; Hans Raether, manufacturer; Eugen Schmid (representative of machine works Carl Unger); Josef Tiefenthal, manufacturer; Dr. Hans Voith, mechanical engineering manufacturer; and Otto Wagner.

The financial worries were discussed with them and they were asked to help with additional fundraising. We can get a sense of the magnitude of the worries from an appeal that E. A. Karl Stockmeyer wrote to the members of the Association for Independent Schools.

"In turning to you once again with this urgent appeal, we are fully aware that this is a tough test of your love and willingness to sacrifice. And we know very well that a range of different emotions come up for you when our letters reach you. But we

---

355 Bericht über die Jubiläumsspende. ZPRSt 4, Oktober 1930, p. 184.

have no choice! We must maintain our school. And we are convinced you also want it to survive. We really do have cause for worry. Almost all sources of income have been dwindling. The local groups have kept their support up relatively well, even though member support has declined considerably after reaching a high point in 1926/27. [...] We can only express our deepest gratitude for the gifts people have made, the countless sacrifices hidden behind these numbers. From everything we know about the work of the local groups, we know how much faithfulness and love for the Waldorf School exists there. When we've viewed the slow decline of the contributions since the year 1926/27, we know that many people are simply maxed out due to the fact that many of us have been totally absorbed by the current economic struggles, but also because our whole anthroposophical movement is facing a crisis. Unless this crisis is conquered, we will make no progress in the Waldorf School either."[356]

The latter point was very important. It was a fact that the bitter trench warfare within the Anthroposophical Society after the death of Rudolf Steiner was weakening the whole movement both inwardly and outwardly. Just as E. A. Karl Stockmeyer predicted, the stagnation was only overcome after reconciliation within the Anthroposophical Society had come about, and only then did the Waldorf School movement start to grow again.

The financial worries of parents, friends, and teachers of the Waldorf School were within bounds compared to the collapse of the New York stock market of October 24, 1929. The world economic crisis affected the whole of life—and different people found different ways of coping. Emil Molt, in his pragmatic way, talked with his wife Berta about the large garden behind the house, wondering whether it would be put to better use now by growing vegetables for the children and teachers rather than beautiful flowers. Thereupon Berta Molt employed gardener Hauck to take care of the land, with an additional small pedagogical task of watching over Werner, the six-year-old son of Marie Kübler, a cook. And then there were others who had a less pragmatic approach and were more given to lamenting the situation.

After a short intermezzo at the Rudolf Steiner school in Essen, Dr. Friedrich Hiebel (1903–1989) came to the Stuttgart school in 1930 and first taught Greek and Latin before taking a class.[357]

Herbert Hahn (1890–1970) had been representing the Stuttgart school in the task of fostering contact with schools abroad since 1931. In those days—perhaps later as well—it was socially unacceptable for a colleague to start a relationship with another. These circumstances forced Herbert Hahn and Maria Uhland to leave Stuttgart and from 1931 until 1938 they worked at the Vrije School in The Hague. They married in 1943. Maria Uhland-Hahn returned to Stuttgart after the war and, after a short detour in Tübingen, she taught at the Uhlandshöhe school until 1961.

356 E. A. Karl Stockmeyer: An die Leiter unserer Ortsgruppen. November 1930. Archiv LS 5.9.54.
357 Johannes Tautz: Friedrich Hiebel. LR 39, 1990, p. 109f.

Walter Johannes Stein, senior teacher of German and history at the Stuttgart Waldorf School from 1919–1932

In 1931, the schools in Stuttgart and Hamburg were each looking for a eurythmy teacher. Hedwig Diestel and Elise Charlotte Schulz both applied and were accepted, Hedwig Diestel in Hamburg and Elise Charlotte Schulz in Stuttgart. Elise Charlotte Schulz (1905–1992) had grown up in Gottesberg in Silesia, studied in Breslau, and did the eurythmy training in Dornach, completing her studies at age 26. Count Fritz von Bothmer testified later that she had stood her ground in the classroom and had achieved "many an artistic result" with the students. She and Berta Seyler got through the war thanks to the fact that she had done a massage therapist training, so that she could keep her head above water as a masseuse. When the school reopened, she returned immediately and kept teaching eurythmy at the school and the teacher seminar in Stuttgart up to the age of 80.[358]

In 1932 Walter Johannes Stein (1891–1957) left the Waldorf School because of the conflicts in the Anthroposophical Society after Rudolf Steiner's death. He took a position that placed him in the minority, which became untenable socially within the Stuttgart school. People agitated against him behind his back, he felt, and he was not willing to accept censure in carrying out his work.[359] Therefore he emigrated to England and became a coworker with Daniel Nicol Dunlop, working for the World Power Conference, which the latter had founded.

In September 1932 Carl-Erdmann von Metzradt (1892–1977) was appointed as a new teacher. For a period of time he had grown up in the house of Helmuth von Moltke because he and his sisters did not get along with their stepfather. After some years in England and South Africa he returned to Germany in 1929, and he harbored a plan to found a children's home modeled after Pestalozzi in Schloss Hohenfels at Lake Constance. The stock market crash caused him to abandon this idea, and for a few years he taught at the Salem private school. From there he was summoned to the Waldorf School in Stuttgart. Christoph Boy soon involved him in the negotiations with the regime. In the last conversation he had with the leader of the National Socialist Teachers Association (NSLB), Hans Schemm, in the spring of 1934, the latter urged him to leave Germany if he continued to refuse to take the oath and swear allegiance to Hitler Germany. He stuck to his decision not to swear the oath of allegiance to Hitler and to do everything in his power to prevent the increasing grip of the National Socialists. For that reason, he only taught at the Waldorf school for two

---

358 Ernst-Michael Kranich: Elise Schulz zum 80. Geburtstag. LR 31, 1985, p. 66; Georg Kniebe: Elise Charlotte Schulz (December 10, 1905–November 13, 1992). LR 47, 1993, p. 100f.
359 Johannes Tautz: *W.J. Stein. Eine Biographie.* 1989, p. 107.

years, after which he emigrated to England. His best friend and godfather, Herzog von Württemberg (1896–1964),[360] who equally staunchly opposed National Socialism, assisted him in this effort. Pater Odo von Württemberg had to emigrate as well, and together with Sir Wyndham Deedes (1883–1956) he helped von Metzradt to survive financially during the first years in the foreign country. He began to give courses in England and later he built up a small private school in Ireland.

Of course, the children of Waldorf teachers went to school on the Uhlandshöhe. In 1931, Gottwalt Michael Hahn, the youngest of four sons of Emily Hasselbach-Hahn and Herbert Hahn (a first marriage), was born, and his teachers were Hans Rutz and after that Karl Ege. The assembly held at the occasion of the closing of the school in 1938 affected him deeply, and he decided to work for the movement later in life. In 1932, Isolde Bindel entered the school. She was the daughter of math teacher Ernst Bindel. Markus Kühn (1925–1979), son of Dr. Emil Kühn, who was a manufacturer in the furniture firm Behr and worked in the Threefold Social Order movement, was also enrolled. Many of the students of these first Waldorf School years later took leading positions in socially and ecologically responsible endeavors. Markus Kühn became business director of the Hiberniaschule in Wanne-Eickel, and, shortly before his premature death, of the Alanus Hochschule in Alfter near Bonn. Isolde Bindel, later his wife, became a eurythmist and taught at the Rudolf Steiner school in Bochum-Langendreer.

The Years Leading up to the Closing of the School in 1938

THE NATIONAL SOCIALISTS came to power at the beginning of January 1933, and this affected the life of the school immediately. The Württemberg ministry of culture straightaway issued an edict that all schools were obliged to celebrate the national Day of Labor on May 1, 1933. All teachers and students were obliged to take part. Fortunately, the Waldorf School playground did not have a radio installation, so the demand that all should listen to the proclamation from Berlin could not be obeyed. There was no way around the obligatory singing of the German anthem and one verse of the Horst Wessel song. Hermann von Baravalle was able to provide the necessary balance in his speech to the children.[361]

The teachers of the Uhlandshöhe school, notably Hermann von Baravalle, Fritz Graf von Bothmer, Karl Ege, Erich Gabert, Caroline von Heydebrand, Eugen Kolisko, Erich Schwebsch, E. A. Karl Stockmeyer, Ernst Uehli, Elly Wilke, and Max Wolffhügel, held a public series of lectures from June 13 until June 15, titled "Overcoming Intellectualism and Materialism in Education." This series was announced as follows in *Erziehungskunst*: "At the present moment, all those working

---

360 Deborah von Metzradt wrote this on December 18, 2016. Archiv NG.
361 Erich Schwebsch in a letter to Albert Steffen, dated April 28, 1933. Archiv LS 2.2.368.

in education, no matter where or in what position, will feel a calling to work together in order to contribute to building up a new education out of the German spirit. Ever since the founding by Rudolf Steiner, the teachers of the Waldorf School have attempted to work out of the creative forces of German idealism. This has been carried out with inner conviction and informs the minutest details of the lessons, with the sole aim of going beyond the intellectualism and materialism that have had such a pernicious influence on the German school system during the last decades. To fulfill this aim, we want to do our part and contribute actively to the general attempts to form the German educational system and educate German citizens. In the announced series of lectures, we therefore want to show the ways we have worked so far to bring this about and offer this contribution in the hopes that others might find inspiration in their struggle to shape new ways for education in Germany."[362]

Paul Baumann engaged in polemics with the Bavarian minister of culture and head of the NSLB, Hans Schemm, who thereupon requested he write an article in the monthly *Nationalsozialistische Erziehung* [National Socialist Education]. In the June 1933 issue he wrote "Many tenets of the National Socialists, put into grand language now by Führer Adolf Hitler and his cohorts, have lived in the schools for more than a decade, often running counter to public opinion" […]. Many Waldorf teachers took issue with this article, and sharp criticism was raised, especially in Berlin.[363]

In December 1933, Caroline von Heydebrand wrote an article about the relationship between the Waldorf School and the Anthroposophical Society. She clarified the relationship as follows: "The Waldorf School was conceived as a 'cultural necessity for our time' and was established as a truly public institution. It wants to take its place within Germany and contribute through its pedagogical measures to the unhampered unfolding of the truly German spirit, in the way it was understood by J.G. Fichte and J.W. Goethe. Waldorf education takes its cue from true human development, and with that as a basis it wants to prepare resilient and responsible human beings for their role in society in their country. The Waldorf School was not founded by the Anthroposophical Society and is not an organ of that. The teachers of the Waldorf School are spiritually linked to the Anthroposophical Society in such a way that they see their work as a part of the totality of anthroposophical striving. The teachers have a feeling of gratitude toward the spiritual, artistic, and scientific challenges their freely chosen striving requires, and in so doing they can receive various impulses from the work of the School for Spiritual Science at the Goetheanum in Dornach. This was founded in 1923 by Rudolf Steiner.

"Through the work in various sections informed by Goethe's spiritual striving in research methods according to Rudolf Steiner's interpretation, anthroposophy is

---

362 EK issue 2, June 1933, p. 383f.
363 Uwe Werner: *Anthroposophen in der Zeit des Nationalsozialismus (1933–1945)*. 1999, p. 104; Wenzel M. Götte: *Erfahrungen mit Schulautonomie*. 2006, p. 426.

turned into practice in a variety of spheres of life. The results can only be experienced as emanating from the German spirit. Leading personalities and active members of the General Anthroposophical Society strive to foster German spiritual life and do so in full clarity and with a high degree of purpose. The teachers of the Waldorf School work in complete accordance with these aspirations."[364]

On November 20 and 21 there was an inspection by the ministry of culture. It was carried out by Chief Inspector Frommann together with a few others after the school had requested financial support from the city of Stuttgart.[365] The chief inspector had come to the conclusion that the Waldorf School formed a foreign body within the National Socialist school system, and that it therefore no longer had the right to exist. Young citizens were to be removed from this atmosphere permeated by Jewish occultism.[366]

In the course of conversations with this inspector several demands were made, such as the dismissal of Jewish teachers and the appointment of a director, so as to be in compliance with the leader principle. As a result of this, Paul Baumann was appointed school director on January 25, 1934, after the Christmas holidays, with Christoph Boy as his deputy.[367] Among the members of the faculty, Christoph Boy enjoyed nearly unanimous trust.[368]

The regular inspection of the school was done at three-year intervals and was carried out February 1–10, 1934, by Chief Inspector A. Bauser, who had taken the place of the deceased *Oberschulrat,* Friedrich Hartlieb. Except for a few critical remarks, he had a generally positive impression.[369] The prime minister and minister of culture of Württemberg, Christian Mergenthaler (1884–1980), disregarded this report and based his stance on what Inspector Frommann had concluded. He continued to carry out a vehement campaign against private schools, especially denominational ones, as well as the Stuttgart Waldorf School. He had been a member of the National Socialist party since 1922 and swallowed its dogmas hook line and sinker, which explains his adamant fight against members of the Protestant state church and anthroposophists. On February 10, 1934, Christian Mergenthaler signed the following decree: "The ministry of culture has issued an order on February 10, 1934 (number 2339), that no students are allowed to be accepted into the first grade of elementary school, because the educational practices of the Waldorf School are not in line with basic tenets of National Socialism. Furthermore, it cannot be expected that the teachers, who are

364 Caroline von Heydebrand: Waldorfschule und Anthroposophische Gesellschaft. EK 5, Dezember 1933, p. 500.
365 Wenzel M. Götte: *Erfahrungen mit Schulautonomie.* 2006, p. 525.
366 Uwe Werner: *Anthroposophen in der Zeit des Nationalsozialismus (1933–1945).* 1999, p. 107.
367 Paul Baumann wrote this on January 25, 1934. Archiv LS 4.2.235.
368 Caroline von Heydebrand: Christoph Boy. In: MPK Nr. 1, Easter 1950, p. 9.
369 Uwe Werner: *Anthroposophen in der Zeit des Nationalsozialismus (1933–1945).* 1999, p. 107.

undeniably devoted to their anthroposophical ideal of education in their work, could be convinced to subscribe to these tenets."[370] This was the first step in the gradual stifling of the Stuttgart Waldorf School.

A number of parents of the Stuttgart Waldorf School had subscribed to National Socialist ideology. Among these was Leo Tölke, an employee in the publishing house of the Waldorf School, who somehow managed to combine membership in the Anthroposophical Society with the National Socialists. In January 1934 he wrote a report about the Waldorf School in Stuttgart to the upper division of the SD [security service] in southwestern Germany, followed by a nine-page document in March 1934 in which he expressed the opinion that one only needed to replace a few teachers in order to steer the school into a fully National Socialist direction.[371] Another such parent was Eugen Link, a member of the NSDAP [Nazi party] and an air force officer. Together with his wife Margarete Link he was a member of the parent council.[372] Another parent, Hermann Mahle, an industrialist and member of the NSDAP, had been asked to join the council of the school association by Leo Tölke, and people wanted to have his advice on how they were to set about negotiating with the authorities. In the session of April 20, 1934, Hermann Mahle proposed to radically replace all council members with Nazi party members who supported the Waldorf School.[373] Hermann Mahle had been asked to join the council at a time when Emil Molt was convalescing in Italy for an extended period of time.[374] The council of the association was therefore rudderless, which proved to be disastrous.

The National Socialist group of parents, supported by Hermann Mahle, organized NS parent meetings[375] and invited Nazi representatives in an attempt to convince even the board to make the school a National Socialist institution, which led to open conflicts with the faculty. Else Moll, a convinced National Socialist teacher, was let go at the end of 1934.[376] In the spring of 1934, Alexander Strakosch (1879–1958), Ernst Lehrs (1894–1979), Friedrich Hiebel (1903–1989), and Karl Schubert (1889–1949) had to leave the school because the National Socialist Aryan paragraph was now being enforced. The dismissal of these colleagues was accepted without much resistance, except by Christoph Boy, in the vain hope that the school might survive.

From then on Karl Schubert taught the children of his extra-help class, a group of close to 40 children at the time, in a private residence. He and the children in his care survived the time of National Socialism in Stuttgart unharmed, even though Karl

---

370 Uwe Werner: *Anthroposophen in der Zeit des Nationalsozialismus (1933–1945)*. 1999, p. 107ff.
371 Ibid., p. 118.
372 Wenzel M. Götte: *Erfahrungen mit Schulautonomie*. 2006, p. 509.
373 Ibid., p. 510.
374 Ibid.
375 For example on March 16, 1936, under "Ausschluss der Lehrer," see Wenzel M. Götte: *Erfahrungen mit Schulautonomie*. 2006, p. 512.
376 Ansgar Martin: *Waldorfschulen 1933–1945: Eine Chronik*. 2015, p. 8.

Schubert was at least half Jewish. This was quite miraculous. Eugen Kolisko (1893–1939) was let go and left the school for two reasons, probably. For one thing, he didn't want to subject himself to the restrictions and compromises demanded by the National Socialist educational authorities for the teaching of biology and anthropology in the high school, specifically the demands regarding heredity and race. What also played in was the fact that he and W. J. Stein were in the minority with regard to the conflicts within the Anthroposophical Society. After a brief time in the Black Forest, he and his wife Lili emigrated to England in 1936. Dr. Gisbert Husemann (1907–1997), a new member of the faculty, took over his responsibilities as a natural sciences teacher in the high school and as the school doctor.

After he had been forced to leave the school, engineer Alexander Strakosch, who had been responsible for the teaching of technology for many years, developed plans for differentiated offerings in the high school of the Stuttgart Waldorf School. Thus, he made plans for building up a practical stream, opening up the possibility for students to specialize in various directions, such as business management, technology, and home economics, which had already been established in the work of the vocational school.

A condensed version of faculty discussions about contemporary issues was published in the magazine *Erziehungskunst* under the title "Steiner Education and the Demands of the Present Time." In the introduction, it says: "Those who experienced the collapse of the year 1919 and felt an urgent responsibility to do something were clear that only a renewal from out of the depths of the German people would be able to free us from the spiritual, social, and economical needs of the time. Materialistic thinking had weakened the will. Young people had to be given the opportunity to create a better future. They should not have to be educated in these old thought patterns."[377]

After a few remarks about the continued relevance of Rudolf Steiner's indications, the article went on to say: "Outer circumstance have developed to such a point that young graduates have a harder and harder time following something like a true calling or finding any fruitful path in life. This is caused by the dire economy on the one hand, and by the present-day uncertainty concerning the training requirements for various professions on the other." The article goes on to stress the necessity of a thorough general education for children ages 15–18, independent from professional training aims.

At the 13th members meeting on June 3, 1934, it was announced that Albert Steffen would be stepping back as the head of the school association, prompted by a memorandum from the school directed to the National Socialist regime postulating a more distant stance of the school vis-à-vis the Anthroposophical Society. Emil Molt was elected chairman.[378] At this occasion Emil Molt stressed his allegiance to the

---

377 EK 6, Februar 1934, p. 537f.
378 Dietrich Esterl: *Emil Molt. 1876–1936. Tun, was gefordert ist.* 2012, p. 211ff.

Goetheanum in Dornach, which he and the remaining teachers saw as the center of the spiritual movement of which the Waldorf School forms a part.

Emil Molt's health had been less stable for a number of years now and he spent Christmas in Brissago at the Lago Maggiore in Switzerland together with his wife Berta, his son Walter, and his daughter-in-law, Edith. Between Christmas and New Year's Day they were visited by Flossie von Sonklar and Emil Leinhas. The visit was not altogether unexpected, for Emil Leinhas had continued on as treasurer of the school association and director of the *Uhlandshöhe AG für Grundstücksverwaltung* [Corporation for Property Management], and he came to inquire whether Emil Molt could continue to support the corporation with a generous check for paying the school's rent, as he had done every year. In the meantime, Emil Molt had retired and lived on his pension and a few savings and therefore could not be as generous as he had been in years past. In spite of that, he signed a check. In the course of the day, Karl Ege showed up as well, so the day ended with laughter, because Karl was a master teller of jokes, in this case about Stuttgart, anthroposophy, and the Nazis.[379]

In 1935 Caroline von Heydebrand (1886–1938) left the school because the rifts within the faculty had become unbridgeable, and because her forces were depleted after the death of Christoph Boy in 1934. She first emigrated to Holland and then England, where she tried to assist in building up Waldorf education.

Georg Hartmann (1909–1988), who had grown up in Göppingen as the son of the mayor, took over Caroline von Heydebrand's class. At the suggestion of his friend Karl Schlemmer he had been educated at the Bauhaus in Dessau, where he had exciting exchanges of ideas with artists like Paul Klee, Wassily Kandinsky, and Oskar Schlemmer.[380] He was well prepared, for he had attended the teacher seminar from December 1932 onward and had already substituted now and then. During this time he was lucky enough to be able to live with Emil and Berta Molt,[381] something that had been arranged by his father, who was on intimate terms with Emil Molt and Herman Hesse.

Conflicts and rifts within the faculty resulting from the deep controversies within the Anthroposophical Society took so much out of everybody that there was no energy left to seriously tackle National Socialist ideology. "No strength was left, and no more resources were at our disposal."[382] A tragic course of events indeed.

In March 1935, Eugen and Margarete Link visited Emil Molt in Brissago, where he and Berta Molt stayed for another period of convalescence. After this visit his

379 Sophia Christine Murphy: *The Multifaceted Life of Emil Molt.* 2012, p. 293.
380 Antonie Sorg: Georg Hartmann. LR 37, 1989, p. 108; Friedrich Behrmann: Georg Hartmann (March 21, 1909–October 31, 1988) N 8.1.1989, p. 7.
381 Michael Toepell: Georg Hartmann. In: Bodo von Plato (ed.): *Anthroposophie im 20. Jahrhundert.* 2003, p. 273.
382 Wenzel M. Götte: *Erfahrungen mit Schulautonomie.* 2006, p. 509.

health took a turn for the worse. The Links made an attempt to convince him of their idea of a National Socialist Waldorf School, and later on in Stuttgart, they made it seem, in his absence, as if he backed them during the ensuing conflicts. After a session on February 18, 1935, the school council made a written request that there would be no review of the affairs of the Waldorf School at the general members meeting of the Anthroposophical Society in Dornach, as had been customary.[383] This demand was cosigned by the teacher representative on the council.

Hermann Mahle called a meeting for National Socialist parents on March 16, 1935, which took place in the faculty room of the school without any teachers present.[384] The notes of the meeting say that in matters of school leadership the parent council should always be involved; that in teachers meetings there should be no more mention of the Anthroposophical Society; that the faculty should do what was demanded by the school leadership; that foreign teachers should consider themselves guests; and that a member of the parent council should be present at every faculty meeting. Now the differences between the faculty and the parents became more pointed. When Emil Molt heard about this in Brissago, where he stayed in touch by telephone and through letters, he wrote to Ernst Bindel, E. A. Karl Stockmeyer, and Robert Killian: "[...] I do not quite understand that you, as members of the faculty, no longer respect the principle of self-governance of the faculty and allowed it to be put in jeopardy. Please help us safeguard the inner freedom of the faculty of teachers for now and in perpetuity. This is a test for us to show what we stand for."[385]

On March 20, 1935, Paul Baumann stepped back as leader of the school because he no longer saw a valid basis for continuing to serve in this position. At last the faculty was so alarmed that a letter was sent to the council of the Association for Independent Schools on March 21, claiming its right to be autonomous. "By this intervention in the decision-making process of the faculty of teachers, certain people on the council of the Association for Independent Schools have now demonstrated they would be willing to undermine the true autonomy of the Waldorf School. [...] The faculty of teachers, however, is serious about its autonomy. [...] The faculty of teachers wants to preserve its sovereignty in the spiritual leadership of the school under all circumstances."[386]

On March 30, 1935, the tenth anniversary of the death of Rudolf Steiner, Fritz Graf von Bothmer, in his capacity as director, as required by the state, Hermann von Baravalle, Erich Gabert, and Erich Schwebsch were chosen to be the leadership group. All four teachers were opposed to National Socialism. Teachers and members of the association council now had an adversarial relationship. In order to strengthen the

---

383 Archiv LS 50.2.514.
384 Wenzel M. Götte: *Erfahrungen mit Schulautonomie*. 2006, p. 512f.
385 Dietrich Esterl: *Emil Molt 1876–1936. Tun, was gefordert ist*. 2012, p. 219ff.; Archiv LS 50.2.513.
386 Wenzel M. Götte: *Erfahrungen mit Schulautonomie*. 2006, p. 512f.

Fritz Graf von Bothmer during his time as head of the Stuttgart Waldorf School

counterbalance in the Association for Independent Schools, the teachers and Emil Molt teamed up and tried to do anything in their power to counter the danger of inner erosion. But this was not sufficient. Emil Molt and the faculty also needed the support of the members of the association. Representatives of 60 local groups convened for a meeting on July 14, 1935. The leading personalities gathered before the members meeting in the teachers' room to take counsel amongst themselves. The head of the local group in Ulm noted later: "Compared to the same gathering the spring before, a radical change in the inner attitudes of those present had taken place." In the reports of this 14th general meeting on July 14, 1935, they also had to look again at the deteriorating economic situation. There were several causes for the increasing financial difficulties, all of them connected to the change in political circumstances. The ban on new students led to a loss of income. The interest on the building loan, suddenly imposed on April 1, 1935, increased expenses, as did the tax on tuition income, which had to be paid starting January 1, 1935.

Emil Molt and Count Fritz von Bothmer wrote a report dated July 1935, the introduction to which closed with the following words: "Our deepest wish is to serve the German people and German spiritual life with an art of education that we have recognized as truly innovative and eminently promising for the future. A deep sense of responsibility toward our people obliges us to keep the spiritual basis of this pedagogy pure. If we were to deny it, we would not only become untrue, but we would harm and destroy the school itself."[387]

This attitude became the guiding principle for the remainder of the Nazi dictatorship. Pressured by the National Socialists to appoint a director, the teachers had asked Count Fritz von Bothmer to take on this function. This turned out to be not a simple assignment, for in order to guarantee the further existence of the school he somehow had to manage to keep the conversation going between two different worlds. The task was made easier because he found an excellent physical education colleague to assist him; his name was Peter Prömm. Originally from Siebenbürgen, Peter Prömm had trained as a teacher in Hermannstadt and was doing a eurythmy training with Elsa Klink at the same time.[388] During the 14th general meeting, he openly stated, probably in deference to the National Socialist parents who were there,

387 Bericht an die Mitglieder des Waldorfschulvereins Nr. 14, July 1935, p. 5.
388 Jochem Nietzold: Dr. Peter Prömm. LR 36, 1988, p. 112f.

that he supported Waldorf students who wanted to join the Hitler Youth, whether that was seen as a compromise or not. "I would welcome any students who decide to join."[389] In order to guarantee the continued existence of the school and to fill in the financial holes, it was decided at this members meeting to ask for an additional contribution of 10 RM per member.

Dr. Peter Prömm, gym teacher from 1934 and school doctor from 1949 at the Stuttgart Waldorf School until 1969

Christian Mergenthaler, the prime minister of the National Socialist government of the state of Württemberg, was an early opponent of anthroposophy and the Waldorf schools. He also opposed all private and denominational schools. He agitated from the inside by means of the National Socialist group within the parent body of the school, which had been colluding with the ministry of culture since 1934, and exerted pressure from the outside by means of several actions, such as the February 12, 1934, ban on accepting new children in the early elementary school. Other measures he took included levying income tax on the school tuition payments and charging interest on the building loan the city of Stuttgart had earlier granted interest free. Norbert Deuchert expressed the opinion[390] that Christian Mergenthaler wanted to attack the whole German Waldorf school movement by slowly stifling the Stuttgart Waldorf School.

It is interesting to note that the National Socialist parents, consisting of 53 party members and 22 members of other National Socialist group,[391] didn't want to lose Waldorf education for their children. They even claimed that the reinstating of the early grades in 1935 was due to their influence,[392] which had the bitter corollary that National Socialist parents were now appointed to the council of the Association for Independent Schools—and that the word "independent" was henceforward dropped from the name of the association. However, the Waldorf School was allowed to have a first grade again in the spring of 1935 because on January 10, 1935, Minister of Culture Christian Mergenthaler had so instructed his elementary school department in writing.[393] Both Count Fritz von Bothmer and the Nazi parents informed the

389 Fritz Graf von Bothmer: Bericht des Leiters der Schule. Berichte an die Mitglieder des Waldorfschulvereins Nr. 14, July 1935, p. 8.

390 Norbert Deuchert: Waldorfschule und Staat. 1919 bis 1938. BhB Advent 1986, p. 85.

391 Numbers taken from: Bericht an die Mitglieder des Waldorfschulvereins Nr. 13, August 1934.

392 Norbert Deuchert: Waldorfschule und Staat. 1919 bis 1938. BhB Advent 1986, p. 85.

393 Mergenthaler wrote this on January 10, 1935. BArch Ella 0465-35. In it he points out that a general ban on accepting students in the first grades of private elementary schools would not be possible because it was in conflict with paragraph 2, section 2 of the elementary school law, as laid down on February 26, 1927.

city school inspector, so that he was kept fully abreast of the internal disputes and arguments regarding ordinances affecting the school's direction.

He notified the National ministry in Berlin as well.[394] In October 1935, the council of the school association finally took a stance in their battle with the Nazi parents by siding with the faculty, and notified the parents of this. Parents like Leo Tölke and former teacher Else Moll were asked to cease their activities. Despite all this, Hermann Mahle remained faithful to the school and asked that the decisions of the council would be based on prior assent of the faculty.[395]

On January 28, 1936, Dr. Friedrich Reinöhl signed a letter from the school department, forbidding religious instruction by teachers sponsored by the Anthroposophical Society.[396] This was just one of the blows the minister of culture aimed at the school in order to undermine it. More skirmishing was ahead. On February 2, 1936, a further attempt was undertaken to turn the school into a National Socialist institution. Eugen and Margarete Link, in a missive titled "Maintaining Rudolf Steiner's Pedagogy," directed to Emil Molt, made the next move. They suggested that the leadership of the school be handed over to Margarete Link; Emil Molt was to be asked to step back; Hermann Mahle was to be asked to take over the chairmanship of the school association council; and the connection with the Association for Independent Schools should be dissolved by decree.

A parent meeting was held shortly after, during which Leo Tölke presented these suggestions again. On behalf of the faculty of teachers, Count Fritz von Bothmer rejected them and expressed complete confidence in Emil Molt.[397] The faculty of teachers stated its position in writing, especially with regard to the points raised by the National Socialist parents. It rejected all of their proposals in a very clear and unambiguous statement. It spelled out that only an experienced Waldorf teacher can lead the school and that the school needs freedom in determining the curriculum, the hiring of teachers, the accepting of students as well as the preservation of its status as a "comprehensive school." In addition, they emphasized that the school was well taken care of as a member of the German Federation of Waldorf Schools[398] and would not part ways with this federation. At the same time, the National Socialist parents and Emil Leinhas in the council asked Hermann von Baravalle to sever ties with the Goetheanum so as not to give National Socialist authorities any cause for retaliations. Hermann von Baravalle put up a vehement defense and made a counter proposal, which was that a fund for jobless Waldorf teachers should be instituted in

---

394 Written June 13, 1935. BArch Ella 1459-35.
395 Wenzel M. Götte: *Erfahrungen mit Schulautonomie.* 2006, p. 514f.
396 Uwe Werner: *Anthroposophen in der Zeit des Nationalsozialismus (1933–1945).* 1999, p. 128; Archiv LS 5.1.040.
397 Wenzel M. Götte: *Erfahrungen mit Schulautonomie.* 2006, p. 516f.
398 Uwe Werner: *Anthroposophen in der Zeit des Nationalsozialismus (1933–1945).* 1999, p. 135; Archiv LS 4.5.017.

Switzerland.[399] Individuals such as Emil Molt were harassed by insinuating that they were Jewish. Molt's telephone, for example, was tapped, and the Gestapo searched his house.[400]

In February 1936, Emil Molt finished his autobiography, which contains no information about the years between 1920 and 1935, with the following words: "At the moment of writing, February 1936, the worries for the preservation of the school are bigger than ever, but I cannot imagine that responsible people can be so blind as to abolish this institution, which is a cultural factor known throughout the world and expresses so much of the essence of German spiritual life."[401]

Within the framework of a campaign against private schools, a decree was issued on March 12, 1936, by Education Minister Rust, addressed to the educational authorities of the states, in which he says, "I request that you issue decrees that no more new students will be accepted into the Waldorf schools, i.e., the Rudolf Steiner schools built on the anthroposophical worldview."[402] This ban on taking in new students was relayed to the Stuttgart Waldorf School by the regional school bureau on April 1, 1936,[403] and the Württemberg minister of culture confirmed it on March 27, 1936, stating that the school needed to be in compliance with this decree.[404] Christian Mergenthaler used this written order as an occasion to once again request an order from the minister of the Reich that early elementary grades be dissolved. The minister answered on June 4, 1936, with a very brief missive to refrain from any further measures against the Waldorf School in Stuttgart.[405] So it was clear there was no unified policy at this time. The German Federation of Waldorf Schools reacted by sending a request to Rudolf Hess, asking him to allow the Waldorf schools to exist as experimental schools.

Eugen and Margarete Link as well as Leo Tölke had been approaching several parents, which led them to request a parent evening to clarify matters; it was held the evening of May 23. Parents of former students and members of the school association had also been invited to the meeting. Count Fritz von Bothmer, in his capacity as leader of the school, gave a talk that clearly still held up the hope that the first four elementary grades would be allowed to function and that the school could continue.

In a report on this meeting we read, "It turned out that the parents are united with the teachers in that they share an uncompromising will to give the children the benefit of an undiluted Rudolf Steiner education in the truest way the teachers can

399 Dietrich Esterl: *Emil Molt 1876–1936. Tun, was gefordert ist.* 2012, p. 224.
400 Sophia Christine Murphy: *The Multifaceted Life of Emil Molt.* 2012, p. 297.
401 Emil Molt: *Entwurf meiner Lebensbeschreibung.* 1972, p. 210.
402 Uwe Werner: *Anthroposophen in der Zeit des Nationalsozialismus (1933–1945).* 1999, p. 136.
403 Ibid., p. 138.
404 Mergenthaler in a letter of March 27, 1936, to the minister. BArch Ella 0829-36/339.
405 Minister of the Reich in a letter of June 4, 1936, to the minister of culture in Stuttgart. BArch Ella 829 M/342.

realize this art. It is their conviction there is no better education to answer the tasks of the present time."[406] Emil Leinhas and Ernst Bindel were able to present a balanced closing of the year. The representatives of the National Socialist parents, Eugen and Margarete Link, as well as Hermann Mahle, stepped back from the council of the school association. They probably realized by now that they had no part in the true inner life of the school.

On June 16, 1936, Emil Molt died. He had been a true father for the School: upright, straightforward, and unshakable. Ironically, Emil Leinhas, who for decades had had a tense relationship with him, was the one who wrote a friendly and even loving tribute to him, which was addressed to the members of the Association for Independent Schools.[407] Emil Kühn was chosen as his successor on the school association council. In the notes of the meeting of October 6, 1936, it says, "He wants to carry on the business in such a way that the furthering of the financial aims and the ideals of the school association purely serve the pedagogy." Emil Kühn did carry on the business until the closing of the school, including the dismantling of the school association.

In April 1937, the Stuttgart Waldorf School was officially put under the supervision of the department for secondary schools in Württemberg. That meant that Christian Mergenthaler had sole jurisdiction from then on. In May 1937, Chief School Superintendent Frommann once again submitted a devastating report on the Stuttgart Waldorf School, stating it harbored "a faculty totally opposed to National Socialism," combining Jewish individualism with subversive tendencies. "Parents of the students and friends of the Waldorf school [...] were and are gradually welded by the faculty into a body that uniformly rejects National Socialism completely. It provides a safe haven for many hidden opponents of the movement."[408] For that reason both the school and the association were to be viewed as a political danger.[409]

Further steps were taken to make life hard for the Waldorf schools. Education Minister Rust issued a decree on August 6, 1937, in which the school association was no longer recognized as a nonprofit organization and had to pay a yearly tax of 10,000 marks. One more little burden to deal with.... On October 12, 1937, the mayor of Stuttgart wrote to the prime minister and to Minister of Culture Mergenthaler, urging the imminent closing of the school because it was unbearable for the city that "more than 500 children are educated in a spirit that is worlds apart from National Socialism" and because he could well use the building to house a state school.[410] This

---

406 V.H.: Report on the parent evening. Bericht über den Elternabend. Berichte an die Mitglieder des Waldorfschulvereins Nr. 15, July 1936, p. 12.

407 Emil Leinhas: Emil Molt. Berichte an die Mitglieder des Waldorfschulvereins Nr. 15, July 1936, p. 1f.

408 Facsimile of the report from Frommann of May 29, 1937, in Norbert Deuchert: Zur Geschichte der Waldorfschule 1933–1940. BhB, Advent 1984, p. 75f.

409 Norbert Deuchert: Waldorfschule und Staat 1919 bis 1938. BhB Advent 1986, p. 87. Quotes from Bundesarchiv Koblenz, Bestand NS 15, 303–305 (B 1/58, 178).

410 BArch E 3227-37/189; Uwe Werner: Anthroposophen in der Zeit des Nationalsozialismus (1933–1945). 1999, p. 237 and note 155.

demand was wholeheartedly supported by the minister of culture. On October 25, 1937, Christian Mergenthaler wrote to the national education minister: "I once again request that there be an official decree to close the Stuttgart Waldorf School at the end of this current school year. As I have repeatedly reported, this school is not equipped to educate German children in a National Socialist sense."[411] Anticipating the imminent closing of the school and knowing that part of the large faculty of teachers would no longer have a means of income, an association was founded in October 1937 called the "Teacher Fund to Assist Former Faculty of the Stuttgart Waldorf School," which was to receive 84,000 RM from the school's reserves.[412]

In the meantime, attempts from certain quarters to close the school continued alongside negotiations to keep the school going, which later proved to be in vain. On December 8, 1938, Alfred Bäumler's assessment of the Waldorf schools had been completed and sent to the staff of the deputy of the Führer [Hitler]. This document closed with the following remarks: "In its present state, the curriculum of the Waldorf schools cannot remain in operation. Therefore the ordained ban on further enrollment must be upheld. [...]. In deference to the great advantages of Waldorf pedagogy one could consider building up experimental state schools that use the Waldorf curriculum in a modified form."[413]

The experimental school idea did not provide a chance to survive in the long run, however. It didn't work for the Waldorf School in Stuttgart, which became less and less willing to compromise any longer. The logical consequence of this was that the Waldorf School on the Uhlandshöhe was closed by Minister of Culture Christian Mergenthaler on March 11, 1938, by withdrawing its permission to operate.[414] The ordinance was to go into effect on March 31, 1938.

In 1934, Karl Schubert had been stripped of his teaching credentials, as had other teachers of Jewish origin. Because of his military service in World War I however, Karl Schubert had been granted special permission to continue the special-education class.[415] Therefore this class had some sort of external status. This so-called *Hilfsklasse* [extra-help class] was overlooked when the school was closed, so Karl Schubert could continue to carry it up to the end of the war.

In Ilkley, Rudolf Steiner once said about Karl Schubert: "Any child who enters this extra-help class will soon develop an extraordinary love for Dr. Schubert, who is so eminently suitable for this task because of his capacity for love. [...] These qualities, building the art of pedagogy through aptitude, capacity for love, dedication, and

---

411 BArch Ella 3227-37/188.
412 Uwe Werner: *Anthroposophen in der Zeit des Nationalsozialismus (1933–1945)*. 1999, p. 238.
413 Ibid., p. 221.
414 Dietrich Esterl: *Emil Molt 1876–1936. Tun, was gefordert ist*. 2012, p. 239; Archiv LS 8.11.012 (copy from Bundesarchiv Koblenz).
415 Uwe Werner: *Anthroposophen in der Zeit des Nationalsozialismus (1933–1945)*. 1999, p. 105 and note 265. Written order from the federal department of elementary schools directed to the regional school board in Stuttgart, dated April 14, 1934; Archiv LS 4.2.323.

Martha Haebler, class teacher from 1923–1960, in conversation with Martin Tittmann, class teacher from 1923–1956

sacrifice, are of the utmost importance. [...]"[416] Sad to say, when the school was reestablished again after World War II, it no longer harbored Karl Schubert's highly important impulse, despite its future potential.

The closing meeting of the Waldorf School in Stuttgart took place on on March 30, 1938, the last day of school before the Easter holidays. At nine o'clock in the morning, all grades gathered outside on the school grounds, in order to lower the obligatory flag. After that everybody—pupils and teachers, guests, friends and parents—went into the hall, which was full to overflowing. Every class was addressed separately by their teacher.[417]

"In all addresses the unshakable certainty resounded that something spiritual that is alive may be put in the grave outwardly, but must rise up again one day." Afterward, notes were written about 19 of the addresses. Apart from that, the whole event was documented minutely by an American woman who was present.[418]

Martin Tittmann gave the picture of fruits and seeds to the third graders and ended with the words: "Dear children, what you have received here in the Waldorf school were precious fruits from a wonderful tree. But today we hand you a kernel for you to plant in your heart; plant it in the best soil of your heart, guard the seed, and cherish the little plant. If you do that, a tree will grow that will bear such precious fruit that it'll make you healthy in body, strong in soul, and wholesome in spirit." Erich Gabert spoke to the tenth graders and gave them a picture from the Parzifal legend, concluding his contribution to the students as follows: "This is an experience people in our time have to go through. What is given to us will break apart after some time and will have to be forged anew."

Erich Schwebsch began his address to all students, teachers, and staff with these words: "At this Easter time, the Waldorf School has now entered a veritable period. Spurned, reviled, judged, scourged, and crucified, we put it into the grave today with pure hearts. But the important thing, both for us now and for the future, is the way in which we put it into the grave, not as something ruined or ill in itself, but—and let us carry this in our hearts—as a miracle of blossoming, vibrant life."

Count Fritz von Bothmer gave the closing address. In it he said among other things: "Try to fathom, dear children, that a man like Dr. Emil Molt built a home for

---

416 Rudolf Steiner: *A Modern Art of Education*. CW 307, lecture 12.
417 Four of the addresses at the occasion of the closing of the Waldorf School in Stuttgart in March 1938 have been published in LR 20, 1979, p. 1ff.
418 With thanks to Patrice Maynard for supplying the English text. Archiv NG.

a spiritual leader like Rudolf Steiner to create this work. Emil Molt was a rich man and a great merchant. He could have stacked up worldly honors, but he gave his riches to this school and opened a way into the future for you and all young people. His faithful life's companion stood by his side, our dear school mother, who cannot be amongst us because she is tied to her house by a severe illness. [...] Emil Molt died on June 16, 1936. At that time, dark clouds already threatened the school, which have now released this lightning flash.

"But the moment this cloud threatened to turn into a sea of sorrow and suffering, a ray of light broke through and in the shine of the rainbow we can hear a jubilant song: 'The Waldorf school lives and will live.' We have all experienced the spiritual power of the school in these weeks, and there is nothing that can rob us of this conviction." He closed with the words: "Now it is my task to announce that the Waldorf School is closed by decree of the Württemberg government. We want to seal our school in the innermost depths of our hearts and preserve it for the future, by the power of love."

That same evening a memorial celebration was held at the occasion of the death day of Rudolf Steiner, and on the evening of March 31, 1931, there was a closing celebration. Erich Schwebsch, Emil Kühn, Fritz Graf von Bothmer, E. A. Karl Stockmeyer, Erich Gabert, Sophie Porzelt, Martha Haebler, Konrad Sandkühler, and Karl Ege were sitting in the front row, and behind them were Bettina Mellinger, Caroline von Heydebrand, Ernst Blümel, and many others.

In the presence of friends from Holland, England, and the United States, a picture was given of the vitality of the Waldorf School, and gratitude was expressed once again to the founders Emil Molt and Rudolf Steiner. Tender words were spoken to remember the love that had lived in this school. People also expressed the certainty that the seed would germinate again, and the idea of the Waldorf school would find its resurrection. Count Fritz von Bothmer closed the evening's gathering by speaking the words of the foundation stone of the Waldorf School.

In August 1938 the school grounds of the Waldorf School in Stuttgart had to be sold to the real estate office of the city of Stuttgart at the urging of the National Socialist government. The city used the building first for the Uhlandschule,[419] a state school, and later for an army training school. Part of the proceeds of the sale, an amount equal to the investments Elisabeth von Grunelius had made for the kindergarten, was paid to her to enable her to take her next step in life.[420] After the war, in 1945, the city leased the property to the Waldorf School Association. It was not until 2004 that the school property could be reacquired, following negotiations to renew the lease.[421]

---

419 Permission for the bill of sale copied in Dietrich Esterl: *Emil Molt 1876–1936. Tun, was gefordert ist.* 2012, p. 240.

420 Memo by Emil Kühn dated October 14, 1938, regarding payment of 15,700 RM. Archiv LS 3.25.037.

421 Dietrich Esterl: *Emil Molt 1876–1936. Tun, was gefordert ist.* 2012, p. 107.

1920: Class 1a at the Stuttgart Waldorf School

1920: Class 1b at the Stuttgart Waldorf School
with their teacher, Christoph Boy

1920: Class 3 at the Stuttgart Waldorf School
with their teacher, Johannes Geyer

1920: Class 4 at the Stuttgart Waldorf School
with their teacher, Robert Killian

1920: Class 5 at the Stuttgart Waldorf School with their teachers,
Alexander Strakosch (l) and Elisabeth Baumann (r)

1920: Class 7 at the Stuttgart Waldorf School with their teachers,
Rudolf Treichler (l), Eugen Kolisko (c), and Karl Schubert (r)

1920: Class 8 at the Stuttgart Waldorf School with their teachers
Walter Johannes Stein (l), Edith Röhrle-Ritter (c) and E.A. Karl Stockmeyer (r)

1920: Class 9 at the Stuttgart Waldorf School with their teachers
(middle row, from left to right: Walter Johannes Stein, E.A. Karl Stockmeyer,
Edith Röhrle-Ritter, Max Wolffhügel, and Rudolf Treichler

1921: Class 1a at the Stuttgart Waldorf School
with their teacher, Clara Düberg

1921: Class 3a at the Stuttgart Waldorf School
with their teacher, Julie Lämmert

1921: Class 3b at the Stuttgart Waldorf School with their teachers,
Elisabeth von Grunelius (l and Erich Schwebsch (r)

1921: Class 4a at the Stuttgart Waldorf School with their teachers,
Carl Albert Friedenreich (l) and Paul Baumann (r)

1921: Class 5b at the Stuttgart Waldorf School with their teachers,
(left to right) Rudolf Treichler, Wilhelm Ruhtenberg and Paul Baumann

1921: Class 7a at the Stuttgart Waldorf School
with their teacher, Caroline von Heydebrand

1921: Class 7b at the Stuttgart Waldorf School
with their teacher, Hermann von Baravalle

1921: Class 8 at the Stuttgart Waldorf School
with their teacher, E.A. Karl Stockmeyer

At the members meeting of the Association for Independent Schools on July 16, 1939, the decision was made to lend financial support to the schools in Dresden and Hamburg-Wandsbek and to move the headquarters of the association to Berlin, in order to prevent it from being closed. The same was decided for the "Teacher Fund to Assist Former Faculty of the Stuttgart Waldorf School," but the opposite happened, because, right before the registration in the Berlin registry, a police examination was carried out.

The Stuttgart Gestapo spoke out against the registration of the fund. The security office argued: "Registering the fund is undesirable because there is a real danger that the association managing this fund could grow again into an underground organization of the forbidden Anthroposophical Society."[422] As the various security offices were in the process of discussing this, the legal advisor for the Waldorf School Association, attorney Frings, made an appeal to the SD [security service] headquarters in Berlin on January 20, 1939, requesting that the Stuttgart Gestapo's claim against registering the fund be lifted. At first, he was put off, and it took until March before he received a verbal reply that the claim of the Gestapo could not be reversed and that the available funds should be funneled to the National Socialist Teacher Union. Attorney Frings and Emil Kühn reacted swiftly, took out the available money and divided it among the needy teachers' families or returned it to the donors.

The Waldorf School Association's request for entry into the register received similar treatment. Alfred Bäumler (1887–1968), leader of the science department in the Rosenberg office,[423] was asked by the police in Berlin to investigate the registration request. On January 13, 1940, he wrote: "We have grounds for suspicion that such an association, founded by former anthroposophists, will carry on the line of the Anthroposophical Society in one form or another. Notwithstanding the merits of the practical efforts made by Waldorf schools, permission for entry into the register of associations is to be denied based on philosophical and political grounds."[424]

On Easter Sunday, March 25, 1940, the termination meeting of the Association for Independent Schools was held. In May 1940, the members received the last edition of the members newsletter containing these words by Karl Ege: "The closing of the school and the termination of the Waldorf School Association is certainly an unspeakably painful blow. However, in the same way that carrying burdens and conquering obstacles in personal life offer the possibility of strengthening the soul and cleansing our humanity, we may also view this stroke of destiny in that light. All of us

---

422 Uwe Werner: *Anthroposophen in der Zeit des Nationalsozialismus (1933–1945)*. 1999, p. 239 and note 161.
423 Hitler charged Alfred Rosenberg with the supervision of the whole of the philosophical and ideological schooling of the NSDAP. The department's designation was such a mouthful that it was shortened to Supervision Department or Rosenberg Office.
424 Uwe Werner: *Anthroposophen in der Zeit des Nationalsozialismus (1933–1945)*. 1999, p. 240 and note 163.

who are affected have the chance to metamorphose this blow of fate into something positive when it enables us to gain a clearer view of what needs to be done and probe the deeper impulses that move us, lending them more depth and firmness in the process.

"Please join us now in directing our attention much more consciously and intensively to the great demands of our time and in penetrating the underlying thoughts that led to the founding of the school back in 1919. Let us try to understand what is happening in our time and learn to read the needs of today and the demands of the future. Let us do so with unshakable positivity and the quiet certainty that the course of time itself will necessitate the reemergence of what is now denied and spurned. And when we are once again called to help and work together, may we be ready and able when the moment comes."[425]

The task of liquidating the association fell to Dr. Emil Kühn, and the office at Schellbergstrasse 20 was closed on June 30, 1940. The foundation stone of the school on the Uhlandshöhe remained intact during the war and withstood the firebombing of 1943. Today it lies in its original place.

425 Karl Ege: Ausblick. MVfS May 1940, p. 11f.

1921: The Friedwart School in Dornach

A FEW PARENTS, first among them the painter Hermann Linde,[426] had asked Rudolf Steiner as early as 1920 to found a Waldorf school in Dornach. This came about on January 1, 1921, with the establishment of a continuing education school, which was later called the Friedwart School, a school for children of various ages from various countries and backgrounds. The first teachers were Marie Groddeck, the mathematician; Dr. Ernst Blümel from 1921 until 1927; and Hilde Boos-Hamburger. It was housed in a wooden building next to Rudolf Steiner's workshop, which also housed the canteen for the workers and the gardeners' workshop. Marie Groddeck (1891–1958)[427] took up this teaching assignment at the wish of Rudolf Steiner, as did Ernst Blümel and Hilde Boos-Hamburger.

Hilde Boos-Hamburger had first come to Dornach on September 20, 1920, only for the opening of the first Goetheanum. She had completed her studies in modern languages in Berlin already and decided to stay in Dornach in order to complement her studies by doing eurythmy and speech formation. However, instead of studying these subjects, she soon found herself in a responsible position in this school, assigned by Rudolf Steiner with teaching history, literature, and language. Teaching language was a major challenge because students came from ten different countries, ranging from Norway and Sweden to Italy, from France to Russia, the United States, and Australia. A number of the children did not speak a single word of German. "With the help of Grimm's Law, which pictured the sound shifts with a triangle, comparative linguistics was practiced in a living way, so that students got to experience the genius of language and achieved a thorough knowledge of foreign languages without recourse to translation. Even grammar was derived from sound in a masterful way."[428]

She cultivated good relationships with the students, who tended to turn to her rather than other teachers to seek advice about their personal lives. Hildegard Boos-Hamburger (1887–1969)[429] taught painting for a while at the school, until she had to step back for family reasons. Louise van Blommestein (1882–1965) succeeded her in her capacity as art teacher. At the suggestion of Mr. and Mrs. Linde,[430] Rudolf Steiner approached Dr. Ernst Blümel (1884–1952), who left his position as an assistant at the mathematical institute of the University of Vienna in order to follow this call and take on the leadership of the continuing education school in Dornach. Ernst Blümel

426 Ernst Blümel: Rudolf Steiner und die Fortbildungsschule am Goetheanum. G 3.10.1926, p. 318ff; Marie Groddeck: Die Fortbildungsschule am Goetheanum. N 35, August 28, 1927, p. 138.
427 Martina Maria Sam: Marie Groddeck. In Bodo von Plato (ed.): Anthroposophie im 20. Jahrhundert. 2003, p. 239.
428 Brenda Binnie: Der Impuls der Friedwartschule. EK 6, 1968, p. 211.
429 Roy Wilkinson and Jan Pohl: Hildegard Boos-Hamburger. In Bodo von Plato (ed.): Anthroposophie im 20. Jahrhundert. 2003, p. 106.
430 E. Brenda Biermann-Binnie, Agnes Linde, Anna Cerri: Erinnerungen an Rudolf Steiner und die Fortbildungsschule am Goetheanum (1921–1928). 1982, p. 8.

had taken part in the natural science courses given by Rudolf Steiner, and had made an impression on people in the autumn of 1920 at the occasion of the opening of the first Goetheanum, where he gave three lectures titled "Central Questions of Modern Mathematics."[431]

From right: Hilde Boos-Hamburger, Ernst Blümel, Marie Groddeck

After one year they found out that the canton of Solothurn had a law against running an independent elementary school, because elementary school students were only allowed to attend official state schools. Therefore the Friedwart School could only teach older students from the second year onward, and they had to let go of the younger children.

Only students ages 14 years and up could attend the school. Since the school was close to Rudolf Steiner's atelier, he often visited, usually between 12:00 and 1:00 p.m.[432] At these occasions he would give suggestions for the painting lessons as well as important indications for Ernst Blümel's geometry lessons. Next to that he laid down the schedule, for example, determining that there should be five to six periods of eurythmy every week and two periods of Greek gymnastics. Painting, modeling, and artistic handwork were given eight periods a week at the end of the morning. Natural sciences and languages were taught in blocks, two and a quarter hours per day, followed by one hour of another academic subject. Ernst Blümel reports on one of Rudolf Steiner's visits during a block on the human being, and how he taught both teacher and students as follows:

"You have heard here about the threefold nature of the human being, how we have a nerve-sense system, a rhythmical system, and a metabolic system. Now I would like to draw your attention to another threefoldness in the human being, namely a threefoldness within the glandular system of the human being. First we have the liver. It takes care of maintaining order in the metabolic system itself, so that materials are stocked in the liver when too much nutrition is taken in, so that they can be drawn upon when needed. This is well known.

"Then we have the spleen—what is its task? Look, for example Jov here (one of the students) may have the habit of eating a good size slice of bread with butter at ten o'clock. One day she forgets to bring one. Now you know how when food is digested the lymph is built up, which then enters the blood. Now without the special arrangement that is there, lymph would go into the blood at ten o'clock one day, but not on another day. Such an irregularity would not be tolerated by the circulating blood, which works in such a regular way. Our hearts would become ill if it were like that. So, you see, the spleen is there to prevent that. It takes care that lymph enters the

431 Renatus Ziegler: http://biographien.kulturimpuls.org/detail.php?&id=76 (site visited June 18, 2017).
432 Rudolf Grosse: *Erlebte Pädagogik*. Fourth edition 1998, p. 134.

Early classes of the Friedwart School were held in the wooden hut next to the carpentry shed at the Goetheanum.

blood as regularly as possible. It regulates the rhythmical system of the human being.

"And then there is the thyroid gland. What does it do? Well, when we are digesting food, and also when we are tired, a number of toxic substances accumulate in the lower part of our system, and these toxins strive upward into our head. If the thyroid gland would not be there, these toxins would penetrate the head and do much harm to it and affect our thinking as well. The thyroid gland is there to prevent this by only allowing substances into the head that the head can use. So the thyroid gland is a guardian, a regulator for the nerve-sense system of the human being."[433] This was the way, almost as an aside, Rudolf Steiner outlined important foundational facts to understanding the bodily functions of the human being. Ernst Blümel felt very grateful for this presentation.

After the death of Rudolf Steiner, the Friedwart School was placed in the care of Marie Steiner, at the request of the parents. She especially promoted and enlivened the arts in the school.

Because of her initiative the school got its own home after seven years, Haus Friedwart. The school was housed there as a boarding school from February 1928 onward, led by Marie Groddeck after the former head, Ernst Blümel, had transferred to the Stuttgart Waldorf School. There were also a number of students who transferred to the Stuttgart Waldorf School in order to do their final exams there. Among these students were Harald Friedeberg, Georg Köhler, and Julian Wedgwood in 1925. There was a regular exchanges of letters about such student transfers between the Friedwart School and the Stuttgart Waldorf School. Tuition was 600 Swiss francs per year, and since this amount did not increase and classes never had more than 14 students, the school regularly ran at a deficit. The deficit was picked up by the Goetheanum, and this became more of a burden when currency lost its value and the Swiss franc became expensive.[434]

During the first 15 years of the Friedwart School, students from 23 countries were educated there, among them Brenda Binnie from England and Fröken Lunde from Norway. These two students had joined the faculty by 1936. During WWII, the school was temporarily housed in Chalet Balmeli in Sachseln in central Switzerland.[435] After the death of Marie Steiner, Marie Groddeck and her students had to leave Haus Friedwart at Christmas 1950, which led to much unpleasantness and left a lot

433 Ernst Blümel: Rudolf Steiner und die Fortbildungs-Schule am Goetheanum. G 3.10.1926, p. 319.
434 Friedwartschule am Goetheanum. Brochure, undated.
435 Herbert Heinz Schöffler: *Das Wirken Rudolf Steiners 1917–1925*. 1964, p. 364.

Students of the Friedwart School in Dornach
From top left: Georg Köhler, Harald Friedeberg, Paul Baumgartner, Brenda Binnie, Lea van der Pals, Margaret Eckinger, Marie Groddeck, Felizitas Stückgold, Signe Neovius, Luise van Blommestein, Agnes Linde, Hildegard von Steiger, Madeleine Hotz

of bitterness in its wake. Marie Groddeck continued the school in Obere Holle in Arlesheim. Under her leadership, the Friedwart School continued to function until 1956.[436] Marie Groddeck died in 1958.

1921: The Waldorf School in Cologne

The founding of the Waldorf School in Cologne sprung from the wish of Gertrud and Wilhelm Rudolf Goyert (1887–1954), who wanted a school for their own children.[437] Wilhelm Rudolf Goyert was a cosmopolitan art dealer who counted many public figures among his friends. He had met anthroposophy through the painter Hans Wildermann.[438] With this art gallery he built up his own company at Drususgasse 5/7 in a building that contained exhibition spaces, a library, and lecture halls as well as his private residence. He wanted to put this multipurpose house at the disposal of anthroposophical work. Rudolf Steiner gave the house the name *Neuwachthaus*.

In April 1921 Gertrud Goyert contacted E.A. Karl Stockmeyer, the business manager of the Stuttgart Waldorf School, and told him about the idea of founding a school in Cologne. E.A. Karl Stockmeyer was of the opinion that they first had to contact the local authorities, and Rudolf Steiner as well. After all, he was the one who should personally lead the school, as he was doing in Stuttgart. Things turned out differently. At Easter 1921, Konrad Müller-Fürer took the first grade of the Neuwachtschule, a class of 12 children, to be housed in spaces renovated specifically for that purpose in *Kunsthaus Goyert* [Art Gallery Goyert].

Konrad Müller-Fürer didn't really feel prepared for this work and was planning to take up his artistic work again afterward, in line with his training. He had first

436 Heinz Zimmermann and Robert Thomas: *Die Rudolf Steinerschulen in der Schweiz*. 2007, p. 12.
437 Mitteilungen aus der anthroposophischen Arbeit in Deutschland Nr. 29, 1954.
438 Andreas Goyert: Wilhelm Rudolf Goyert. In Bodo von Plato (ed.): *Anthroposophie im 20. Jahrhundert*. 2003, p. 234.

heard Rudolf Steiner lecturing back in 1906 in Berlin and had met him a few times. Upon returning from World War I, he very much wanted to work at the first Waldorf School as an art teacher. In order to realize this wish, he approached Rudolf Steiner and traveled to Stuttgart to meet with him. But Steiner told him that no position was open for him at the time, and that he should take the first grade in the fledgling school in Cologne instead.

This is how Konrad Müller-Fürer himself describes what happened: "When I called the Stuttgart Waldorf School, Dr. Steiner himself came to the telephone and said, "I've heard about your intention. But we are not yet at that point here. It'll take us a year. Would you be willing to take a first grade in a new school for the time being? Do come up and let's talk about it. The woman who is founding the school is also here." "But this is a totally new idea to me!" was my first reaction. His answer: "You want to work artistically, don't you?—how is that different from working with little children?—and then after a year you can come here."

Konrad Müller-Fürer decided to take on this task and started teaching the first grade; Rudolf Steiner also visited one of his lessons. At that occasion he also visited a eurythmy lesson of Alice Fels (1884–1974), who was in Cologne for a short time before she built up the eurythmy school in Stuttgart. In a talk with Rudolf Steiner a few months later, Konrad Müller-Fürer expressed his doubts about the quality of his lessons, to which Rudolf Steiner replied: "Still, it was very good. You only have to keep on building it up."[439] As there was no teacher to take his class, Konrad Müller-Fürer stayed in Cologne until his class had completed fourth grade at Easter 1925.[440] These accounts contradict the opinion that the school in Cologne was founded against Rudolf Steiner's advice.[441]

On April 3, 1922, official approval was given for the school to operate as an experimental pedagogical institution—a year after it had been founded. The local authorities first intended to give definite approval only once certain provisions had been met, especially with regard to the teacher exams, but they ended up not extending the permit at all. Even Rudolf Steiner seems to have been of the opinion that such stipulations from the authorities were unacceptable. After permission had been refused locally, the school went around the local state school department in Cologne—a maneuver that didn't help the relationship—by applying for permission in Berlin. The Federal ministry in Berlin requested a report about the Stuttgart Waldorf School before granting its approval.[442]

Gertrud Goyert initiated the founding of an association to carry the school venture, called Freie Neuwachtschule, which was incorporated July 15, 1922, a year

---

439 Letter written by K. Müller-Fürer in LR 7, 1973, p. 54.
440 Hildegard Müller-Fürer: Bericht über die erste Waldorfschule in Köln 1921–1925. LR 4, 1971, p. 36.
441 Ernst Weissert: Von den Motiven und Lebensphasen der Schulbewegung. EK issue 8/9, 1969, p. 316.
442 Wenzel M. Götte: *Erfahrungen mit Schulautonomie.* 2006, p. 298 referring to Fritz Karsen: *Deutsche Versuchsschulen der Gegenwart und ihre Probleme.* Leipzig 1923, pp. 89–100.

after the little school had started.[443] The school slowly grew, and therefore they started to look for a new location. Soon thereafter they moved into the old house of a painter, located on a narrow street called Auf dem Hunnenrücken 22.[444] The street had buildings on one side that faced a high wall, behind which was the bishop's palace. Next to Konrad Müller-Fürer, Helmut Hessenbruch (1901–1974),[445] Dr. Walter Birkigt (1896–1969),[446] and Franz Tabuschat (1893–1927) taught in the school. The last two were sent from Stuttgart with the consent of Rudolf Steiner.[447] Then there were Mr. Ebersold and Johanna Doflein (1877–1967). The latter was recommended by Rudolf Steiner, but her colleagues did not approve of her. Antonia Förster (later Ebersold; †1977) taught eurythmy and took the place of Alice Fels. Gottfried Husemann gave religion lessons for the Christian Community. When the number of students grew to 75 there was hardly room anymore in the narrow building.

As the teachers were paid at very irregular intervals, Hellmut Blume (1891–1971) jumped in to help. He was a former colleague of Emil Molt who had recently moved to Cologne. Blume enlisted the help of Max Hummel, and together they worked on establishing a more stable situation. In addition, Hellmut Blume succeeded in engaging hitherto skeptical members of the Anthroposophical Society, first among them Karl Künstler (1874–1971). Together with the parents and friends of the school they organized a series of workdays on Saturdays to renovate and expand the classrooms.

During the period of time when inflation was skyrocketing, Max Hummel, the engineer who was responsible for the school's finances, would come once or twice a week with a heavy attaché case full of paper money and empty it onto the meeting room table. Then Konrad Müller-Fürer was always the one to pass the banknotes around. When all the money had been divided among them, everybody ran off so they could still buy something with the money, which decreased in value by the hour.[448]

The teachers had a hard time getting along. There were clashes between different personalities, and the sharp positions Helmut Hessenbruch tended to take up didn't help either.

443 Next to Gertrud and Wilhelm Rudolf Goyert, founding members included Paul Kretzschmar (1882–1964); Konrad Müller-Fürer; Wilhelm Salewski (1889–1950), who was a priest at the Christian Community in Düsseldorf at that time; Walter Bastanier (1872–1955), a banker in Düsseldorf; and Max Benirschke (1880–1961), an architect who also lived in Düsseldorf.

444 The name of the painter was Stöcker and he was the father of Hedda Hummel, who was sometimes the stenographer of lectures given by Rudolf Steiner. There was a rumor that she was in fact the half-sister of Konrad Adenauer, born from an extramarital liaison of Johann Konrad Adenauer.

445 http://biographien.kulturimpuls.org/detail.php?&id=348 (site visited June 18, 2017).

446 Heinz Herbert Schöffler (ed.): Das Wirken Rudolf Steiners. 1917–1925. Volume IV, 1964, p. 346f.; Mario Zadow in: http://biographien.kulturimpuls.org/detail.php?&id=73 (site visited June 18, 2017).

447 Letter written by Hellmut Blume on March 9, 1963, to the German Federation of Waldorf Schools. Archiv BFWS 25733.

448 Hildegard Müller-Fürer: Bericht über die erste Waldorfschule in Köln 1921–1925. LR 4, 1971, p. 37.

Hildegard Müller-Fürer remembers several factors that led to the closing of the school. First of all, there were two high-ranking personalities involved: the Archbishop of Cologne, who had to witness the school in action on a daily basis from across the street, and then his friend, the mayor of Cologne, Konrad Adenauer. Both of them were in positions of authority when the regional counsel of Cologne found the students' skills lacking in a report after an inspection. This led to the closing of the school in 1925.

The Archbishop of Cologne clearly took sides in the discussion about new school legislation on how to interpret the constitution of the Weimar Republic. The constitution was seen as interfering with the inalienable rights of the Catholic Church. All parents who dared to send their children to normal state schools instead of Catholic schools were accused of being apostates or disobeying the church.[449]

In such a climate it is no wonder that the chances for a Waldorf school venture to succeed in Cologne were limited. The governing authorities of the Rhine province wrote on February 26, 1925, that the school had to close because of "insufficient student achievements, a curriculum that was completely divergent from what was generally taught in elementary school, and because of failure to comply with the condition stipulated when permission was first given, which was that science had to be taught by certified teachers."[450]

Another way to look at it would be that we are dealing with a premature birth here with little chance of survival. After the closure of the Cologne Waldorf School, the School Association of the Neuwachtschule was transformed into a local branch of the Association for Independent Schools.[451]

A second attempt to found a Waldorf school in Cologne did not get further than the founding of an association on April 4, 1930, also because the Stuttgart colleagues clearly advised against it.[452] Not until the founding in 1980 did the venture take off. With great support from the local community, the school then developed into a full-fledged Waldorf school with about 460 students today.

449 Stefan Leber: *Weltanschauung, Ideologie und Schulwesen.* 1989, p. 57.
450 Von Heinsberg, from the Department for Churches and Schools, in a letter dated February 26, 1925, to the leadership of the Neuwachtschule. Archiv LS 3.20.034; Wenzel M. Götte: *Erfahrungen mit Schulautonomie.* 2006, p. 298, note 789.
451 In a letter from E. A. Karl Stockmeyer to Margarethe Blass on March 20, 1925. Archiv LS 3.3.04.
452 Wenzel M. Götte: *Erfahrungen mit Schulautonomie.* 2006, p. 300.

1922: The Goethe School in Hamburg-Wandsbek

School Founding and First Teachers

THE GOETHE SCHOOL in Hamburg-Wandsbek was founded May 22, 1922, with intensive support from Hans and Emilie Pohlmann, who owned a construction company. They put their villa at the disposal of the undertaking and guaranteed the teacher salaries for the first three years. Hans Mathias Pohlmann (1880–1947)[453] was determined to build up a Waldorf school in Hamburg and asked Rudolf Steiner to help him in the search for a reliable founding teacher. Rudolf Steiner was happy to oblige. Here is a little prelude to introduce the man he ended up proposing.

Dr. Max Kändler (1871–1936) had come to Stuttgart in 1919/22 to hear pedagogical lectures. Rudolf Steiner had known him for about 20 years. Max Kändler was a school inspector in Greiz in the district of Vogtland [a district in Thuringia, central Germany] and he supervised schools in a large area. He had met anthroposophy through Michael Bauer, who had invited him to hear lectures by Rudolf Steiner in Nuremberg. It was at one of those that Rudolf Steiner had asked him, "How did you like my lecture?" to which Max Kändler, to his own surprise, replied, "I would like to become a member."[454]

Max Kändler organized evenings in Greiz to read lecture cycles, which led to the unfolding of a rich cultural life. Thus he became a go-to person for many young teachers, supplying them with reading material even during World War I. In 1918, he was the only one of local prominence in Greiz who was not apprehended. Faced with the question whether he wanted to move to Hamburg, Max Kändler asked for one night to think about it before he said yes to it, even though it was not easy for him at age 50 to give up a secure position. The educational authorities in Greiz promised him that he could come back anytime if he wanted.

Wandsbek, which at the time lay just outside Hamburg, belonged to Prussia in 1922. That was the reason that Max Kändler had to apply in Berlin to get permission for the school to operate, and approval was constantly being postponed by the authorities. Thereupon Max Kändler sent a telegram to the Prussian education department in Berlin just before Easter 1922. It read: "Since no news to the contrary has reached me, I assume that permission has been given; we will start May 22, 1922."[455] After teaching had begun, written permission actually did come in the mail: It had been worth the risk. Rudolf Steiner determined that Max Kändler's 18-year-old daughter, Ilse Kändler, (1903–1981) should teach the eurythmy lessons. She had studied

---

453 Jan Pohl: http://biographien.kulturimpuls.org/detail.php?&id=1064 (site visited June 25, 2017).
454 Ilse Rolof: Von der Entstehung der Goethe-Schule in Hamburg-Wandsbek. LR 5, 1972, p. 66.
455 Ibid., p. 67.

eurythmy with Lory Maier-Smits at Steiner's own recommendation. When she tried to convince him that she needed better preparation for this task, he countered, "We have no time for that now!" In addition, she was to take on handwork and painting, to which English teaching was added in the end as well. The motto was that enthusiasm would have to be there to make up for the lack of experience.[456] Max Kändler received the following verse for the school from Rudolf Steiner:

Out of the seriousness of the times
Must be born
The courage to act.
Give your teaching,
What the Spirit gives you,
And you will liberate humankind
From the nightmare
Of materialism,
Burdening us all.

The Pohlmanns' villa at Juthornstrasse 4a was provisionally readied for occupation before the father moved in with his daughter and son, Thomas Kändler. Everything in the house was so hastily put together to start off with that they thought Mrs. Kändler should not be subjected to dealing with a situation like that. Therefore she was asked to stay with relatives in Thuringia for a while, until circumstances in Hamburg were more favorable for a move.

There were seven children in the first grade. They had to be picked up at the tram station and brought back at the end of the day. Ilse Kändler cleaned the classrooms herself,[457] and many a time soup was prepared for children who were hungry because they very often had to (and wanted to) stay after school.

The whole endeavor was undertaken without support from the Anthroposophical Society in Hamburg, which even warned parents against putting their children in the new school. When the second grade was started, Rudolf Steiner sent Heinz Müller from Jena to Hamburg. He had just finished his teacher's exam and gave up the follow-up higher education he had planned, because he was called to work at the new Goethe School in Hamburg. "It cannot be a fringe school. Make sure there's always an expansive, cosmopolitan attitude ruling everything in the school!"[458] That was the motto he was given for the road ahead. Once again there was resistance from the Anthroposophical Society and only a few children were registered. In spite of

456 Ilse Rolofs: Von der Entstehung der Goethe-Schule in Hamburg-Wandsbek. LR 5, 1972, p. 68.
457 Lasse Wennerschou: Vom Werden der Heileurythmie. Aus den Lebensläufen von Ilse Rolofs und Trude Thetter. Undated.
458 Heinz Müller: *Spuren auf dem Weg.* 1983, p. 80.

The school began at the villa of Hans Pohlmann, Jüthornstrasse 4a, on April 22, 1922.

Hans Pohlmann

that, a bustling life soon developed in the villa because Thomas Kändler, who had become a priest in the Christian Community in the meantime, also celebrated the children's service there and gave lectures. They sat on borrowed chairs, school desks were stacked in the garden. Heinz Müller painted such a colorful picture of the scene in his memoirs that it merits quoting in full.

"Dr. Kändler was a truly impressive character. His hair was slightly wavy with strands of gray, his eyes rested on one with thoughtfulness and benevolence. One immediately felt one could trust him. He extended his hand in a very friendly way, and I was surprised at how tender and articulated it was, as was his whole figure. He called his wife to come up, introduced me to her, and in no time we were all sitting together at the family table. 'Now I'd first like to start by telling you how it came about that I sent you the telegram,' he started off. 'At the delegates' meeting, where you were also present—I remember vividly seeing you there in your colorful outfit—Dr. Steiner told me he would give me a name at Easter of someone who could come to our school.' Hearing nothing further, he had taken the train to Stuttgart to ask Rudolf Steiner in person, and he had said, 'Why don't you write'—he looked in his notebook here—'to Heinz Müller, Jena, Lutherstrasse 2.' Dr. Kändler had thanked him, but asked hesitatingly whom he should ask instead in case Mr. Müller would not be able to come. After all, it was pretty late in the year, and the new school year would start soon. Rudolf Steiner replied as if he had not heard the implication of that question, 'You only need to write to Heinz Müller, Jena, Lutherstrasse 2.' 'Yes, Herr Doktor, I understood what you said, but to whom should I turn when he's unable to come?'—'Well, just go ahead and start by writing to him!'

"So Dr. Kändler had no choice but to approach me, and he said he believed that Rudolf Steiner knew what he was doing when he insisted on sending him to

Ilse Kändler

Dr. Max Kändler

me, because he knew I would say yes. Of course I had said yes, because I had said as much to Dr. Steiner, telling him I would go wherever he would send me. At that point the question came up for me, 'How did it come about that there is a school here, and where is it?'—'You're in it!' 'Here in this house?' I said. 'Yes, downstairs are three rooms, we can go down afterward and look at them straight away!'

"Since it turned out I knew nothing about the founding of the school, the conversation first turned to that topic. I learned that building engineer Hans Pohlmann, strongly influenced by his wife Emilie Pohlmann, had promised Rudolf Steiner he would put a building for two or three grades at the school's disposal. In addition he had guaranteed to pay the salaries for four teachers for the next three years. Furthermore, he had pledged to build a new school building, planned to house eight elementary school grades and a hall for singing and eurythmy.

"The school grounds should be large enough to enable expansion of the school up to grade 13. At this point in the conversation, however, we first went downstairs to see the school rooms. In one room Dr. Kändler had his class, which numbered over 20 children by then. In this room he taught main lesson and French as well, 'as best he could,' he added. He also enjoyed teaching free Christian religion lessons and music. From that room we went into a larger room, separated from the classroom by a sliding door. In it were a piano and a harmonium for teaching music and eurythmy, and Dr. Kändler also held the Sunday service there for those children who took part in it.

"I was told that the newly founded Christian Community also held its first religious services here, for as long as the community was still small. For that purpose Herr Pohlmann had had an altar built and thus this eurythmy and singing room could quickly be turned into a cultic space with the help of some colorful fabric, an altar cloth, a candelabra with seven arms, and the picture of Christ by Leonardo da Vinci. After it had been transformed that way, the children could then listen devotedly to the teacher holding the service, and the community members had a space to listen to the words of their priest.

"Then when it came time to make room for the lessons again, things that would only stand in the way could be stored in a shed in the garden. So everything was improvised, but very beautiful as well! The last thing they showed me was my future classroom. It was small, but I would start off with only eight children to begin with. At this point Ilse Kändler told her story. She had been trained in eurythmy by Lory Maier-Smits and had been sent to Hamburg together with her father to build up the school.

"Her objection that she would still want to do a training at the school for arts and crafts was turned down, because Dr. Steiner had told her there was no time for that now. Therefore she now taught eurythmy and beginning English. When they had mentioned that there was no handwork teacher, Rudolf Steiner had said she could also give handwork lessons, for she had wanted to do a training in spinning and weaving after all. So that was how it had gone for her.

"Dr. Kändler then asked me when I could start. This time I did not want to be so rushed, and requested eight days to get ready, if time allowed, and then I asked about lodging. Dr. Kändler kindly offered that I could live with him first to give me time to look for a room of my own. 'But now,' he said, 'I would still like you to meet the founder of our school. We will visit Herr Pohlmann; he now lives in a new house close to his factory in the eastern part of Wandsbek.'

"So we went on our way, through the beautiful woods of Wandsbek, until we came to the desolate industrial zone, where really stinky factories had been built. One of them, not distinguished in any way, was situated pretty deep down on a few ponds, and that was Hans Pohlmann's factory. He was a structural engineer, and manufactured insulating hollow bricks to be used as building components that preserved heat to an extraordinary degree. Several scientific research institutes had given him great testimonials, which had garnered him a large amount of contracts. First brought together by the common task of building up the school, the two gentlemen, Pohlmann and Kändler, had soon become fast friends. When we arrived, they first exchanged heartfelt greetings, then I was introduced, Mrs. Pohlmann joined us as well, and we soon found ourselves on a tour of the factory building.

"Herr Pohlmann pointed to the machines and installations, rubbed his hands gleefully, and said something like, 'so what you're seeing here is actually the milk cow which I hope will enable me to provide for you and a few other teachers and put our school on a firmer footing by and by. Now let's also go and see the garden.' Mrs. Pohlmann, who had more or less stayed in the background during the conversation, now voiced the wish to take us to the hall, which was the regular meeting place of one of the Anthroposophical Society's branches in Hamburg, led by Hans Pohlmann and Max Kändler. Wonderful, colorful light came through the stained-glass windows which portrayed scenes from the life of Jesus of Nazareth, Elias, St. John, etc.

"There were pictures on the wall with bright and clear colors and energetic forms. There were also lofty wooden sculptures with generously large surfaces. That's where I first heard the name of the painter Roberto Sobeczko. He was one of the young people who helped with the first performances of the mystery dramas in Munich and he had also helped with the carvings of the first Goetheanum. He taught art and sculpture at our independent Goethe school from 1926 until the time the school had to close.

"So it still took a while before I would get to know him personally. In the meantime, Herr Pohlmann had changed and was playing with his children outside on the lawn. A few other children had joined them, among them the children of the shop manager and from other families who lived there, all of whom would one day become

'Goethe students.' But then time was up, the workers poured out of the factory, and I had to get ready to return to Jena."[459]

THE THIRD TEACHER who came was Otto Altemüller (1900–1964), who joined right after he had completed his study of history and philosophy in Munich and Münster. He was also sent by Rudolf Steiner. Ilse Kändler later reported, "Our enthusiasm had to make up for all the mistakes we also made, of course. There were many things we had to figure out by ourselves, for in the beginning we only received a little bit of help from the Stuttgart Waldorf School, until Rudolf Steiner insisted that all his pedagogical indications and courses were put at our disposal, so that he did not have to repeat everything. The school now began to grow considerably, in contrast to our salaries. We simply divided what came in, which wasn't much."[460]

So during Rudolf Steiner's lifetime, the selection of the first teachers of the school in Hamburg was in his hands, exactly as it was in Stuttgart. After his death, the Stuttgart colleagues were consulted about which teachers were to be appointed. This even went so far that many a teacher first had to go to Stuttgart and introduce him or herself and get approved before a contract could be signed. The Stuttgart influence sometimes went too far for Max Kändler, which led him to complain that the people in Stuttgart tended to see their role as one of leadership with obligatory subordination.[461]

The school flourished, and therefore in March 1924, Hans Pohlmann obtained a site of around 5000 square meters situated at Bleicherstrasse 59. As early as 1925, the new school building was built by his company. There was space for ten grades together with the necessary spaces for special subjects and an auditorium that could hold 400 people. In 1928, 1929, and 1930 additional buildings were added with more classrooms, a gymnasium, classrooms for special subjects, and a school kitchen.

During the years of economic hardship, his firm suffered like everybody else, but Hans Pohlmann was always there for the school, no matter how many worries he had. During that period the school was plagued by many economic worries, of course.

During this time the arrangement was still in force that the local Hamburg group of the Association for Independent Schools of Stuttgart paid its membership dues to the Stuttgart school. This was an uncomfortable arrangement for the teachers in Hamburg, and therefore Max Kändler wrestled with E. A. Karl Stockmeyer to get him to agree that the Hamburg school was allowed to solicit donations in their area of operation and keep them. At the end of this wrestling match, which was tenacious but carried out with consistent friendliness, the Stuttgart school granted Hamburg this

459 Heinz Müller: *Spuren auf dem Weg.* 1983, p. 73ff.
460 Ilse Rolofs: Von der Entstehung der Goethe-Schule in Hamburg-Wandsbek. LR 5, 1972, p. 69.
461 Wenzel M. Götte: *Erfahrungen mit Schulautonomie.* 2006, p. 295.

The main building for the Goethe School in Hamburg-Wandsbek at Bleicherstrasse 59, built at the initiative of Hans Pohlmann

small concession.[462] In autumn 1925, Dr. Paula Dieterich (1892–1974) became part of the faculty and took a class. She originally came from Ratingen in the Rhine district and had just finished her PhD about Christian Morgenstern in Cologne. A few years before, she had come into contact with anthroposophy through her neighbors and had been able to hear lectures by Dr. Steiner in Cologne.[463] In 1928, Martha Somann (†1995) joined the faculty. The year after that she moved to Stuttgart and taught English there, but moved back to Hamburg after the war. In 1929, Dr. Friedrich Kübler (1901–1945) came, who was one of the founders of the pedagogical working group in Jena-Zwätzen, and started to work with high ideals. He married Helle Schmidt, who also formed part of the pedagogical working group, and they started a family. He was conscripted in 1943 and sent to the Balkan peninsula. He never returned from the war in Yugoslavia and was given up as missing in action.

It was a sober life, there was hardly money for the teachers, and people had to improvise. In spite of these extremely modest circumstances, the school counted 430 students in 1930 and 17 teachers. They were: Otto Altemüller, Dr. Franz Brumberg, Dr. Paula Dieterich, Gertrud Jasper, Dr. Max Kändler, Lucie Kralemann, Henni Lembcke, Dr. Merz, Beatrice Müller, Heinz Müller, Ilse Kändler-Priess, Olga Schwandt, Roberto Sobeczko, Dietrich Steinmann, Dr. Hans Theberat, and Senta Uebelacker. Two school doctors worked alongside the teachers, Dr. Victor Thylmann (1893–1951) and Dr. Julius Solti (1899–1983). The school secretary was H. Priess,

462 Wenzel M. Götte: *Erfahrungen mit Schulautonomie.* 2006, p. 295.
463 Rolf Speckner: Paula Dieterich. In: Bodo von Plato (ed.): *Anthroposophie im 20. Jahrhundert.* 2003, p. 148.

and the janitor was M. Stange. By that time, Otto Altemüller had become teacher of the so-called *Hilfsklasse* [extra-help class], in which he took care of students of all age groups. Like Karl Schubert in Stuttgart, he worked magic through his great love for these children and awakened the best in them. His mere presence on the playground during recess was enough to nip conflicts in the bud.

Conflicts about Self-Government

IN 1931, tensions that had been simmering for quite some time within the faculty led to a surprising exodus of four teachers who left the school with a number of their students. The discord was sparked by the fact that the constitution of the School Association had assigned decision power solely to a group of nine persons, the so-called Founder Group. The composition of the Founder Group was only determined by the fact that members were there at the beginning, not by a process of voting. New members were appointed by the members of the Founder Group and could not be elected by the members of the School Association.

This way of doing things had been recommended to Max Kändler by Rudolf Steiner in order to prevent straying from the school idea in a system whereby special interest groups could intervene when the right to vote was open to anybody. That, however, was totally different from the idea of giving everybody an equal right to vote, which had become the established procedure during the Weimar Republic, a procedure that especially the majority of younger colleagues was convinced was fair.

There were too many conversations, grueling meetings, and journeys to Stuttgart.[464] In the end, Paula Dieterich (1892–1974) together with Dr. Franz Brumberg (1896–1973), Gertrud Jasper (1900–1995), Henni Lemcke,[465] and the school doctor, Dr. Julius Solt, founded the Waldorf School on the Flottbeker Chaussee 101 in Hamburg-Altona,[466] which was destined to thrive socially and have healthy cooperation among the teachers.

The school in Altona began at Easter 1931 with five grades, 90 children and the aforementioned five teachers. When the school closed at Easter 1938, it had 360 students in ten grades. After the war, Paula Dieterich devoted herself primarily to building up of the Anthroposophical Society in Germany, and she became one of the most important figures in the anthroposophical movement because of her public lectures, her indispensable role as a member of the advisory council of the Waldorf schools in Hamburg, and her widespread engagement in Hamburg.

---

464 A very elaborate portrayal of the conflict is to be found in: Wenzel M. Götte: *Erfahrungen mit Schulautonomie.* 2006, pp. 322–332.

465 Henni Lemcke was a public school teacher in Hamburg before she became a class teacher at the Stuttgart Waldorf School in the school year 1927/28. See the report on the eighth regular members meeting, November 3 and 4, 1928.

466 Ernst Weissert: Dr. Paula Dieterich (February 19, 1892–January 5, 1974). LR 8, 1973, p. 68.

New teachers had to be found, and one of them was Dr. Hermann Schüler (1903–1978), who was born in Tsingtau (now called Quingdao) and taught mathematics and physics. He was reserved and somewhat distant toward other people. Due to his love of facts and the exactness of his presentations he was highly respected by the students. After the war, he returned to teach in his school. Hedwig Diestel (1901–1991) came to teach eurythmy. She had successfully completed her training with Isabella de Jaager in Dornach. "I can still see her today, the youthful, vivacious young woman who soon won our hearts with her even features and her friendly eyes. Even though we loved her, we were up to all manner of things in her lessons. She would energetically call us to task, but without ever losing the humorous expression in the corners of her eyes. That was exactly what made her so lovable."[467] In 1934 Arthur Fuchs (1907–1975), who had just completed his elementary school teacher training in Vienna and had studied at the Goetheanum, came to the school and took a first grade, which he led until the closing of the school.[468]

Under the National Socialist Regime

As COULD BE EXPECTED, the school in Wandsbek was not unaffected by the measures taken by the National Socialist regime when they came to power. In May 1933 the leader of the local National Socialist Teachers Union, A. Schümann, demanded that one teacher be appointed head of the Goethe School.

On May 27, 1933, A. Schümann pointed out to Christoph Boy of the Stuttgart school that membership in the National Socialist Teachers Union might not be sufficient to fulfill the demands of *Gleichschaltung* [a series of measures imposed to enforce conformity].[469] In 1936 private schools were no longer allowed to accept children into first grades. Civil servants had to reenroll their children in state schools, a measure that hit Waldorf schools hard. Reports written by the National Socialist school inspection officials, above all the one written by Wandsbek school inspector Scheer, who visited the school for several days in October and November of 1933, mentioned mostly satisfactory student accomplishments.[470]

It turned out that this interested school inspector was a Freemason and he was soon put back into service in elementary schools.[471] On January 5 and 6, 1937, there

467 Sieglinde Heilmann: Hedwig Diestel (December 23, 1901–April 19, 1991). LR 47, 1993, p. 88. Hedwig Diestel could no longer teach after she lost her hearing, after being trapped during the bombing of Freiburg in 1944.
468 Obituary of Arthur Fuchs. LR 11, 1975, p. 84.
469 Karen Priestman: *The Illusion of Coexistence.* 2009, p. 94; Archiv LS 4.2.025.
470 Report on his school visits: http://schulewandsbek.createweb.de/Chronik/Scheer_33.htm (site visited January 20, 2017)
471 Frithjof Altemüller: *Erinnerungen an meinen Vater Otto Altemüller.* 2013, p. 44.

One of the classes at the Goethe School, September 1934

was another inspection by Inspector Viernow,[472] who accompanied federal school Inspector Thies from the central Prussian ministry of education. In his judgment, there was a pleasant, trusting relationship between teachers and students, but the teaching methods left a lot to be desired and mastering certain areas of knowledge was not valued, for example, of early Germanic history. Then the shortcomings were listed: there was no picture of Hitler in the classroom; there was glorification of universal humanity; there was no Nazi combat song, and no emphasis on building German character traits. So the school inspector criticized the fact that German character traits were not stressed in this education, and that instead of heroic discipline one could see big boys knitting socks or doing cross stitch. His overall conclusion was that the education was far too weak and feminine. School inspector Viernow summarized it like this, "On the whole, the undersigned comes away with the impression that the Goethe School in Wandsbek has remained untouched by the National Socialist spirit." In order to be able to go on teaching their pupils, the teachers of the Goethe school, unlike many other colleagues in the Waldorf movement, obeyed the demand to swear allegiance to Hitler.

About 100 students from Altona, where the school was closed in 1936 by the teachers themselves, were thus enabled to continue their education at the Wandsbek school, provided that the school inspection authorities approved the necessary parental application. A few children were refused, in cases where they had not passed the elementary school selection procedure. At the request of Rudolf Hess, the Waldorf schools in Dresden and Wandsbek were exempted by the ministry of education from the general closing order for private schools and Waldorf schools. This was done on

472 BArch Ella 929/133; http://schulewandsbek.createweb.de/Chronik/Viernow.htm (site visited January 20, 2017).

The classes of Dr. Meyer-Fröbe, 1937

the grounds that positive results of Waldorf pedagogy should be secured for the benefit of state school pedagogy by allowing continued existence of two or three experimental schools, one of which was the Goethe School.

Both this measure and the enrollment ban of April 14, 1938, were not communicated straightaway to the Goethe School by the school inspector, and when it finally was relayed through the central education ministry on April 5, 1939, it was clearly done in a half-hearted way,[473] because the interference by Rudolf Hess caused incomprehension and resentment on the part of the school authorities in Hamburg. But it was totally impossible to countermand a measure taken by Rudolf Hess because of his trust relationship with Hitler.

Since Rudolf Hess had stepped in like that, Elisabeth Klein and Max Kübler hoped that he would support their schools in the long run. The local authorities in Hamburg were actually completely against changing the status of the Goethe School into an experimental state school, among other reasons because teachers were members of the Anthroposophical Society, and not one of them was a member of the NSDAP.[474] Apart from that the authorities wanted to use the school buildings for a vocational and trade school,[475] for which, in typical National Socialist state fashion, extensive discussions around protocols for disowning private school buildings took place in interministerial consultations involving arguments on the basis of Prussian laws stemming from 1922 and 1874.[476] So German thoroughness prevailed in procedures such as these as well.

473 Uwe Werner: *Anthroposophen in der Zeit des Nationalsozialismus (1933–1945)*. 1999, p. 228f.
474 Letter dated March 17, 1938, from the district president to the minister of education. BArch Ella 0748-38/45.
475 Letter dated April 23, 1938, from the Governor in Hamburg to the minister of education. BArch Ella 1095-38/41.
476 Note in a decree of the education minister, which was not to be published, dated March 31, 1938. BArch 4901–3285/3–42 f.

Members of the College of Teachers at the Goethe School, 1938: (left to right)
Adolf Rolofs, Dietrich Steinmann, Roberto Sobeczko, Martha Somann, Dr. Barg, Heinz Müller, Mr. Uebelacker, Hedwig Diestel, Senta Uebelacker, Dr. Fritz Kübler
(according to Hannelore Vierl, 2017)

In March 1940, the teachers wrote to the members of the School Association, "As you all know, the leadership of the Goethe School received a letter from the state education department on September 29, 1939. Under the heading 'School Closure,' the letter informed us that the Reich Governor has decided that all private general-education schools have to close their doors on September 30, 1939. The school leadership informed us on October 7, 1939, that the decree of September 29,1939, had become obsolete and was therefore emphatically revoked. However, the school was in effect closed, because all teachers were called up for emergency service in the Central Department of Nutrition. For that reason, the leadership of the school wanted to facilitate the transfer of children who are required to attend school into public schools, which then took place on October 13, 1939. Because the above-mentioned emergency service ends November 24, we have done everything in our power to bring clarity to the situation and bring about a definitive decision concerning the school's fate, now that the ministry has started a renewed review of their position toward us. So far we have not succeeded. [...]. We stop our work in the knowledge that we have done everything in our power to preserve the school and what it stands for, for the sake of your children. [...]"[477]

The invasion of Poland gave Reichsführer of the SS, Heinrich Himmler, the excuse he needed to interfere. Citing a lack of personnel due to the war, he ordered the Gestapo in Hamburg to conscript all teachers of the Goethe School and employ them to help with the distribution of food stamps or to work in other areas. So in effect the school was neither forbidden nor closed. Its functioning was effectually

477 Letter from the Goethe School Wandsbek, Inc., to the members of the Association of the Freie Goetheschule, dated March 1940. Gez. Dr. Kübler als Schulleiter, H. Pohlmann als Vorsitzender des Vereins. Archiv LS 3.1.233; Uwe Werner: *Anthroposophen in der Zeit des Nationalsozialismus (1933–1945)*. 1999, p. 229.

strangled by taking away the teachers, which forced them to dissolve the school. The students were distributed among state schools.

Hans and Emilie Pohlmann still looked out for the faculty after the school closing in 1939. Several teachers were recruited for punitive service and many teachers were in dire financial straits.

Otto Altemüller had been declared unfit for work because as a child he had contracted meningitis which had caused severe scoliosis. In spite of his delicate health, he now took care of the learning disabled children of his extra-

Heinz Müller, 1938

help class by visiting the children at home, which was forbidden, of course. On May 18, 1940, there was a last get-together of teachers, parents, and students, which gave them a chance to have a festive closing ceremony, during which Heinz Müller gave a courageous farewell speech.

He began by commemorating colleagues who had died, and then went on to say, "We started this work in ominous times. This place was dedicated to work springing from spirit power, born out of love, in spirit light and goodness. In the beginning there were rough storms that threatened to spoil the tender seed more than once. This was followed by a blossoming, which was radiant like summer, promising rich fruit. Then, much too soon, after a last hopeful glimmer, came an autumnal blight and withering. When Michaelmas day came around, the summer was definitely over. With winter's frost and coldness, every hope for the tender plant died off. However, we are left with a seed. There are only a few grains, sad to say, where there should have been many thousands! These seeds are resting in us. They also rest in our children. May they one day germinate, grow, and work as creative wisdom, strengthening spirit power, revealing spirit life. […]"[478] So the official end of the activity of the Goethe School was Easter 1940, and the teachers made this decision on their own. The teachers who took this decision in 1940 were: Otto Altemüller, Hedwig Diestel, Karl Froebe, Dr. Barg, Arthur Fuchs, Lucie Kralemann, Elisabeth Kübler, Dr. Friedrich Kübler, Dr. Hildegard Meyer, Heinz Müller, Ilse Priess-Kändler, Adolf Rolofs, Hans-Eberhard Schiller, Dr. Hermann Schüler, Olga Schwandt, Roberto Sobeczko, Martha Somann, Dietrich Steinmann, and Senta Uebelacker. Hans Pohlmann had no choice but to sell the property to the city, because he could no longer keep the school grounds and the buildings without any prospect of reopening. Many teachers now carried on Waldorf teaching in private home visits, which was a considerable risk.[479]

478 Bulletin of the Rudolf Steiner School Hamburg-Wandsbek. May 1972.
479 http://schulewandsbek.createweb.de (site visited January 20, 2017).

Rebuilding after 1945 and Further Developments

EMILIE AND HANS POHLMANN were always full of hope about starting anew after the war. In 1946, they were able to support the project to rebuild the Hamburg-Wandsbek Rudolf Steiner school. The first financial step was taken by charging admission for the Christmas plays, and the amount that was taken in was matched by Hans Pohlmann. Thus the basis was laid to begin repairs on the heavily damaged school building. The Pohlmanns also helped by supplying building materials and by putting their trained workers at the disposal of the rebuilding of the school building, 80 percent of which had been destroyed by the war.[480] May 8, 1946, was a glorious day for them, for they were able to be present at the reopening of the school. They started off with 270 students and nine grades. Boards on bricks served as school benches, chairs of all kinds were brought in. Spirits ran high. There was an all pervasive hunger for culture and spirit after the time of oppression. Parents wanted a school in which children would be educated to "become good human beings." Hans Pohlmann died one day before the end of the first postwar school year.

Since the Hamburg authorities had not legally outlawed and dissolved the school in 1939, the School Association still existed formally. Therefore the association of the nine founding members could immediately begin work again on April 11, 1946. Carl Friedrich Steub, Heinz Müller, Dr. Fritz Rascher, Alfred Sleumer, Martha Somann, and Emilie Pohlmann stepped down. The remaining members were augmented by Dr. Johannes Hemleben, J. Schürer, Franz Westermann, Johannes Hendrik van Grootheest, Dr. Paula Dieterich, and Dr. Annemarie Pönitz.[481] It is a remarkable feat, and a humorous turn of destiny as well, that Paula Dieterich now worked together again with her former colleagues of the Wandsbek school from the time before the split that led to the Altona school initiative.

The Goethe School was renamed Rudolf Steiner School. Next to the persecution of war crimes, the secret intelligence service of the English occupation had, among other things, the task to support any democratic efforts in the British occupation zone, or initiate new ones. Of course they knew about Waldorf schools and anthroposophy. They had the impression that successful work had been achieved before the closing. Then there were previous school reports by civil servants who found fault with the lack of sympathy for National Socialism on the part of both teachers and students. So these things were now positive testimonial.

Therefore no obstacles were put in the way of reopening the Waldorf school. In spite of all the things that had to be improvised, the number of students grew so fast that they soon had to teach in two shifts. One group was taught from eight until one

---

480 Ernst Wüst: Emilie Pohlmann (June 22, 1884–April 16, 1972). LR 5, 1972, p. 56.
481 http://schulewandsbek.createweb.de/Chronik/ab1946/Neubeginn1946.htm (site visited January 20, 2017).

in the afternoon, the other group from one until six, alternating every two weeks. There was regular distribution of food in the school by the English and care packets from America during the holidays, which each time were oases in the desert of general hunger that lasted a long time. In 1948 the school already numbered 800 students, the first final exam took place in March 1951, and in the autumn of 1951 there were 25 grades with 1036 students.

The building inspector justly frowned upon the overuse of the ruins. Therefore the search started for a piece of real estate for a second school in the western part of the city. The Rudolf Steiner School Association acquired Villa Ephraim at Elbchaussee 366, which was for sale. The piece of land it was on seemed big enough for future expansion. High school students got to work with cleaning up and light demolition work. The spacious villa was transformed section by section, and could be used for lessons from 1952 onward by students who moved there from Wandsbek. Yet the much-needed relief for Wandsbek was not yet in sight. In the meantime, the city began with the renovation of the main building.

The main building was not ready for use yet, and therefore buildings in the wider vicinity were provisionally renovated for teaching. For many lessons, it was necessary to carry chairs back and forth. The ground plan was changed; for example, the entry at the Bleicherstrasse (Kattunbleiche) was rerouted to the Wandsbeker Allee. Instead of the former plaster they now used a type of yellow bricks.

The inauguration of the newly built main building was celebrated on September 15, 1956. Immediately afterward, the construction of a 12-grade wing was started along the Wandsbeker Allee. On June 19, 1958, there was no longer a lack of space and the school was now as spacious as it had been before the war. Beginning in the 1970s, lively changes began to take place within the school. In the meantime, the school in Nienstedten had grown so big that it became a separate school.

Since there were two Waldorf schools in Hamburg now, the names Rudolf Steiner School Hamburg-Wandsbek and Rudolf Steiner School Hamburg-Nienstedten were chosen.

The school's constitution was changed and the Founder Group, the nine-member body with the sole right to vote, was abandoned. The members meeting was given the constitutional right to make decisions and appoint board members. At irregular intervals, parallel classes were instituted in order to deal with the overwhelming number of applicants. There were heated discussions about the number of parents and teacher representatives on the board, until it became clear that if teachers did not manage to bring across the idea of the school to the parents, there was even less of a chance for them to accomplish things than when the teachers on the board were in the majority. Therefore it was determined to have four parent representatives on the board and three teacher representatives. In 1974 a school was founded in Hamburg-Bergstedt, about 12 km northwest of Wandsbek, but this brought no noticeable relief in terms of the number of students. As a result, four pavilion structures were erected on the other side of the Wandsbeker Allee to be used for kindergartens, subject-lesson spaces, and eight grades. In the end, several schoolrooms were rented in the school on the Bandwirker Strasse. As an alternative to the narrow quarters of the teachers' room, the first floor of Andersen's bakery was used more and more frequently. Teachers could be reached by telephone there, which was necessary because it was hard to survey and patrol what was happening on the school grounds.

Without having a specific project in mind, the School Association decided at this time to start saving up for building projects, which could either take shape in the form of an expansion of the existing school or a new building. The city offered several school buildings that were becoming available, the last of which was the Weissenhof school. The school grounds offered just enough room for the needed expansion, even though the playground space was a little on the small side. Construction began as the summer holidays started in 1983. The new building was ready for occupancy on January 8, 1985.

1922: The Rudolf Steiner School in Essen

Two Women Founders of the School Take the First Steps

IRENE WOLLBORN (1893–1980), whose maiden name was Burghardt, had been prevented from teaching in public schools because of her bad eyesight. During World War I she began teaching girls after they had finished elementary school, and this she managed to do quite successfully. After the war she found her way to the Anthroposophical Society after a colleague had introduced her, and there she met Dr. Margarethe Blass (1887–1971). The latter had studied mathematics in Heidelberg and had been the first woman in Germany to earn a PhD in mathematics. She had written a thesis titled "Concerning a Problem of Integrating Differential Functions with Two Independent Variables," after which she had worked a few more years as an assistant. After a few years she gave up the idea of an academic career for family reasons, because her father had become a widower and had asked her to return to Essen in 1921 in order to help him in the household.

In late September 1920, which was still during her time in Heidelberg, a friend had taken her along to Dornach to attend the so-called first *Hochschulkurs* [academic course] at the Goetheanum. This course lasted three weeks and was aimed primarily at university students, but many teachers took part as well, including several teachers from the Stuttgart Waldorf School.

In this course Rudolf Steiner spoke about boundaries to knowledge and how to surmount them through a modern path of schooling. Attending these lectures and experiencing the mood of her fellow students became a life-changing experience for Margarethe Blass, because she suddenly came to the realization that her future mission lay in the anthroposophical movement. After she had moved to Essen, she linked up with a group of anthroposophists there and that is how it came about that she met

Irene Burghardt at a study group. One evening, Irene gave her such a vivid picture of her work that Margarethe Blass asked if she could take part in the education of the young girls. Irene Burghardt was very happy to take her up on this offer because Margarethe Blass's support would enable her to guarantee a good education in natural science and mathematics for her pupils. A little time after that a few parents approached the two women and asked them to also teach their children in elementary school. These questions were the seed that led to the Waldorf school in Essen, because it prompted the two women to turn to the local school inspector in order to inquire if they could get official permission to start an elementary school. They met a school

Margarethe Blass, one of the founders of the Rudolf Steiner School in Essen

inspector with an astonishingly open mind. But he wanted to go further than this brief impression gained through a short conversation and some documentation, and he decided to visit the two women and get to know them as teachers.

After he had observed their work with the girls, he made the recommendation that they should start doing elementary school teaching. The two women faced considerable challenges. Up to then, they had taught in Irene Burghardt's parental home, but would that be enough in the long run? Who would be able to finance this school? And would a Waldorf school in Essen really be in the cards? It was totally clear to the two women that they did not want to build up any old school, but a Waldorf school.

So at Easter 1922 Margarethe Blass drove to Dornach in order to consult with Rudolf Steiner. Upon her return, she reported to Irene Burghardt and told her about her conversation with Rudolf Steiner, who had warned her that it would be very difficult to start such a work in Essen. He had said, however, that if the two women wanted to undertake this venture, they should study the pedagogical courses he had given to the teachers of the Waldorf School before it was founded. He also invited the two women to partake in his next pedagogical course.

In spite of these warnings, they went ahead with their preparations. On November 2, 1922, the Waldorf school in Essen started with 15 children ages 6–9, as well as with the older students of Irene Burghardt. With growing numbers of children, they had to find another location, because the 30 children did not actually fit any more in the parental home of Irene Burghardt, no matter how willing they were to make do in cramped quarters. In the old town, close to the town hall, there was a youth hostel, which the two teachers fixed up and decked out with beautiful colors so that it could harbor the children.

Irene Burghardt-Wollborn, one of the founders, as a retiree of the Rudolf Steiner School in Bochum Langendree

There was one snag, however, which was that they still did not have an official permit. At that point resistance came from an unexpected corner. The teachers of those children who had switched schools lodged a complaint with the educational authorities and wanted to have the children back in their state schools. The parents, however, especially workers and employees in the Krupp factory, put up with police protocols and penalties and stuck to their wish to send their children to the new Rudolf Steiner school. They took the initiative and turned to the political parties in Essen to make sure that the request for permission was discussed in the town meeting.

As this was going on, Margarethe Blass decided to turn directly to the Prussian ministry of culture, and to that end she requested a conversation with the Prussian minister for science, Dr. Otto Boelitz (1876–1951). Before the conversation had even taken place, the town council discussed the request for permission. The initiative of the parents had apparently made an impression, because it was decided to approach the Prussian minister of culture directly. Since the occupation of the Rhineland and the Ruhr area after World War I, it was in his jurisdiction to give permission. The conversation was arranged for August, and Dr. Otto Boelitz, who was an international educational expert himself, decided to send somebody to the Waldorf School in Stuttgart to get a reference. If this reference was positive, approval would be given to the school in Essen.

Life in the occupation zones of the Ruhr area was anything but easy at this time. The two women had traveled to Stuttgart using English passes in order to partake in courses for speech formation and eurythmy. On the return journey they were astonished to find that their passes had been declared invalid by the French occupational troops; and since the passes had not been recognized as valid, they could not return to Essen. Irene Burghardt found some people with the necessary know-how who could help her and they were able to find a loophole. She managed to get back a little later than planned for the beginning of school, and her children cheered her loudly on her return.

Wilhelmine Deus joined the faculty at this point, as well as Dr. Erika Mundt (1887–1962), who taught a few periods. When the new school year began at Easter 1924, the school had grown to 120 children in five grades. So they were facing the pressing question of where to find additional teachers. This has been a question for the Waldorf school movement from the beginning, because, then as now, there are more children than trained teachers. Faced with this situation, the two women decided to go to Stuttgart and Dornach during the Easter holidays to attend Rudolf Steiner's lectures, hoping that he would be able to help.[482] And this actually worked out, even though Rudolf Steiner was of the opinion that it would not be easy to find somebody who would take on the task and move to Essen. Nevertheless, René Maikowski (1900–1992) turned up at Whitsun 1924, after Rudolf Steiner had asked him shortly before to go and help with the work in Essen.

When René Maikowski mentioned this request from Steiner in a conversation with Walter Johannes Stein, Stein thought this was a mistake, because Rudolf Steiner had recently said in a faculty meeting in Stuttgart: "We will not worry about them, they are doing their own thing." This made René Maikowski uncertain, so he went to Rudolf Steiner again in order to clear this up once and for all. Rudolf Steiner's answer was, "Yes indeed, that's what I said, the people there had made a start and called it a Waldorf school, without contacting us. But the two women have come to me in the meantime to report on the state of affairs and ask for help. They had not dared to ask us earlier, because they had not come all that far. However, they are trying very hard and we should help them."[483] René Maikowski also asked Rudolf Steiner at this occasion when he should start. That was on a Friday. Rudolf Steiner replied he could easily begin on Monday, and which class it would be he would find out when he had the children in front of him.

So René Maikowski came to Essen at Whitsun 1924, and he took the upper level, which was a combined grade 8/9. At this point the children already had been distributed among different spaces in the surrounding state schools because the capacity of the youth hostel had long since been exhausted. On June 6, 1924, Irene Burghardt and Margarethe Blass wrote a letter to the Stuttgart faculty to ask for Rudolf Steiner's lectures on the foundations of human experience so that their faculty could study them.[484] Because Rudolf Steiner had given permission, E. A. Karl Stockmeyer said yes. In other cases he was less forthcoming. So the pedagogical preparation was from hand to mouth so to speak. In any case, the art of education was new for all teachers and had to be acquired as they were teaching.

During the third pedagogical course given in Torquay, England, held in August 1924, Margarethe Blass had another conversation with Rudolf Steiner. According to her account, Rudolf Steiner had told her that the school would need leadership and that he himself was not able to take that upon himself. This led her to think that she had the right, and above all the duty, to practically lead the school by herself. This opinion or interpretation would cause considerable problems down the road.

The relationship of the school in Essen to the Waldorf School in Stuttgart changed after the death of Rudolf Steiner due to the March 17, 1925, letter signed by Dr. Günther Wachsmuth that charged the Stuttgart faculty with the leadership of all

---

482 Irene Wollborn: Vom Werden und Schicksal der ersten Rudolf Steiner Schule in Essen. LR 5, 1972, pp. 70–76.
483 René Maikowsk:, *Schicksalswege auf der Suche nach dem lebendigen Geist.* 1980, p. 115.
484 Letter written by I. Burghardt and M. Blass to E. A. Karl Stockmeyer, dated June 6, 1924. Archiv LS 3.3.01.

The ninth grade of the Rudolf Steiner School in Essen with their teacher, René Maikowski, in front of their school building, April 1925

German Waldorf schools. Three days after that, E. A. Karl Stockmeyer wrote a letter to Essen to apprise the teachers there of this new situation. It now became necessary to write progress reports on a regular basis, and to get the go-ahead from the Stuttgart faculty in the hiring of new teachers.

After Easter 1925, Heinrich Wollborn (1904–1987),[485] who was 21 years old at the time, took the next first grade. E. A. Karl Stockmeyer sent him to Essen, instructing Margarethe Blass that she would be the one to mentor him.[486] His economic background was precarious, and he hoped to remedy this by becoming a teacher. He studied Waldorf pedagogy in Tübingen with the Pedagogical Working Group, and now that he had to follow the call from Essen, he renounced the chance to teach in a state school. In Essen he met his future first wife, the eurythmist Cläre Rother from Berlin. Like the other teachers, he earned 180 marks per month, when the money was available.

In August of 1925, Irene Burghardt and Margarethe Blass participated in the summer course in Stuttgart, because they were looking for more teachers and were hoping to find enthusiastic young colleagues there. They found the musician Hermann Vetter (1889–1970)[487] from Ravensburg and hired him. They also wanted to hire

485 Rüdiger Voigt: Heinrich Wollborn. LR 34, 1987, p. 88ff.; Conrad Schachenmann: Heinrich Wollborn (April 22, 1904–March 18, 1987). N 16.8.1987, p. 256ff.
486 Letter written by E. A. Karl Stockmeyer, dated April 14, 1925. Archiv LS 3.3.05.
487 In the spring of 1930, Hermann Vetter and his wife Henny Vetter voluntarily stepped back from the faculty of the Rudolf Steiner School in Essen. Archiv LS 3.3.198 and 199.

The tenth grade class of the Rudolf Steiner School in Essen, 1926

Ernst Weissert to teach gymnastics, but he felt he was a little young at 20 years. In this and the following years Ella Rothe, born Loth (1903–1982), Elisabeth Friedrich, Wilhelm Wollborn (1903–1989), Friedrich Tschirley, and Martin Rothe joined the faculty, all of whom were endorsed by the Stuttgart faculty.[488] Alexander Strakosch became a new, part-time colleague as well.

They all had to teach under extremely modest economic conditions. Teaching 30 periods a week was the norm, and at times teachers had to teach main lesson in two grades, first from 8:00 to 10:00 a.m. in one class and then from 12 noon to 2:00 p.m. in another class, with subject classes in between. In addition, there were meetings, conversations with parents, and lectures to be held in Essen, Bochum, and Dortmund. Friedrich Tschirley did not manage to win the hearts of the students. After a few months it was made clear to him that he had to leave the school. Dr. Wolfgang Rudolph (1900–1966), who was a teacher at a technical college in Neuhaus-Igelshieb (Franken), was asked by the faculties of both Stuttgart and Essen to take on a sixth grade. He thereupon worked hard to pass an exam to qualify him for teaching at the elementary school level, but even though he tried to do it as quickly as possible, it took longer than planned. To help out in this situation, Alexander Strakosch of the Stuttgart Waldorf School jumped into the breach and temporarily took over the bereft sixth grade.

488 Letter written by Herbert Hahn, dated July 1, 1925. Archiv LS 3.3.14.

The College of Teachers of the Rudolf Steiner School in Essen, 1926:
Front row: Ella Rothe, Margarethe Blass, unidentified eurythmist, Wilhelmine Deuss, René Maikowski;
Back row: Heinrich Wollborn, Irene Burghardt, Martin Rothe

The Private Waldorf School in Essen Becomes the Rudolf Steiner School in 1926

IN THE SCHOOL YEAR 1926/27 the number of students had grown to more than 200 and the name of the school was changed from Einheitliche Volks- und höhere Schule Dr. Blass-Burghardt [Comprehensive Elementary and Upper School Dr. Blass-Burghardt] to Rudolf Steiner School. This name change was celebrated on July 8, 1926, in the sold-out opera house of Essen with a festive performance by the students of the eight grades which the school had grown to by then. Bright occasions such as this one were followed by dark times. There never was enough money, and Heinrich Wollborn, who was responsible for the finances, frequently had to send letters to E. A. Karl Stockmeyer to ask for more financial support from the Association for Independent Schools. These requests became more and more urgent,[489] and in September 1926 it was even necessary to ask for a monthly sum of 1500 marks to make ends meet. Even though the Stuttgart Waldorf School suffered considerable financial problems, it was able to meet these requests. In November 1926, Heinrich Wollborn once again sent a telegram to Stuttgart with the urgent request to send money straightaway. Even though only 50 percent of the salaries could be paid in Stuttgart as well, E. A. Karl Stockmeyer sent 1500 marks.

On October 24, 1926, the *Essener Rudolf Steiner Schulverein* [Association of the Rudolf Steiner School in Essen] was founded, which was to create a transparent legal basis for the school. Council members were Margarethe Blass, Irene Burghardt, Wolfgang Rudolph, Friedrich Schuster, and Hans Mothes, MD.

Since there now was a Steiner School Association in the Ruhr area, they had to solve the question of how to form relationships with the local groups of the Stuttgart

489 Telegram sent January 3, 1926. Archiv LS 3.3.62.

Teachers and students at the Rudolf Steiner School in Essen, 1926

Association for Independent Schools. A meeting was held on November 17, 1926, where it was decided by the leaders of the local groups in Essen, Bochum, Dortmund, Elberfeld, Barmen, Düsseldorf, and Cologne to have only one local group per town in the future and that they would officially become local groups of the School Association in Essen. They were of the opinion that this was also in accordance with the wishes of the Stuttgart Association for Independent Schools because for the long term it would be necessary to have a unified collaboration across the region among the associations. The members would remain members in both associations, in Stuttgart as well as in Essen.

The contributions from the above-named seven local associations were sent to the Rudolf Steiner school in Essen from that point onward. So, these contributions no longer went to Stuttgart, and for that reason E. A. Karl Stockmeyer announced that the additional amounts that Stuttgart had sent almost every month to the school in Essen would have to be diminished as a result. In spite of that, the financial problems of both schools remained critical and the times grew darker. Not only did the school have to move to a shabby, rickety, 100-year-old school building situated in a remote industrial quarter of Essen,[490] but the school was not able to properly pay salaries or bills either. A heap of debts kept mounting and letters kept being sent to Stuttgart, begging and clamoring for support. Erich Schwebsch and E. A. Karl Stockmeyer answered them patiently, and in 1927 they kept supporting the school financially on a regular basis.

490 Heinrich Wollborn: Aus der Arbeit der Rudolf Steiner Schule in Essen. ZPRSt 2-3, December 1927/ January 1928, p. 84ff.

BECAUSE OF RAPID GROWTH, incoming colleagues did not have enough time to get to know the spirit of the Waldorf school in Essen or become acclimatized, and this accounts for some of the problems that resulted. Anton Schmid and Maria Schröfel (1896–1978) now joined the school. The latter was a professional fashion designer, educated at the Stuttgart Art Academy. She came in 1926 to teach handwork and remained until 1929. She met Lili Groh in Essen and the two became fast friends, a friendship that lasted their whole lives. After a number of internal conflicts in the school, Maria Schröfel left Essen in 1929, worked for a while in Dornach and Basel, and finally accepted a position at the Rudolf Steiner school in Berlin. In 1929 Ella and Martin Rothe left the school for similar reasons. Their departure was shrouded by peculiar circumstances and they left against their will.[491] Dr. Friedrich Hiebel (1903–1989) came to the school in Essen in order to take a second grade. The year before he had finished his PhD in Vienna and was now able to fulfill his long-cherished wish to work at a Waldorf School. It was his first position as a teacher. A year later he switched to Stuttgart.

The conflicts within the faculty, which soon involved parents as well, could not be resolved internally. In the meantime, the school had grown to 600 students in 12 grades. The basic reason for the conflict was Margarethe Blass's stance described above. After speaking with Rudolf Steiner in Torquay in 1924, she was of the opinion that he had charged her to take on sole leadership. Many colleagues could not agree to that, and neither could they see justification of this empowerment, for that matter. What resulted was a split between colleagues who worked faithfully alongside Margarethe Blass (Irene Burghardt, Wilhelmine Deus, Elisabeth Friedrich, Wolfgang Rudolph, Helene Schievelbusch, A. Schmid, engineer, Therese Stoffel, Henny Vetter, Hermann Vetter, Heinrich Wollborn, Wilhelm Wollborn) and colleagues who were striving for self-administration (Ella Loth-Rothe, René Maikowski, Martin Rothe, and Maria Schröfel).

The split escalated because there were increasing conflicts and confrontations between Margarethe Blass and Maria Spira,[492] who was rooted in the anthroposophical youth movement and worked for a short time at the school. We leave aside here the question of whether these conflicts were justified or not. Maria Spira was too independent for Margarethe Blass, so much so that she orchestrated her dismissal.[493] Both parties left us accounts of the struggle.[494] Margarethe Blass also could not put up

---

491 Ella Rothe: Zum 50. Todesjahr. Martin Rothe (July 12, 1902–September 4, 1929). Printed manuscript 1978, p. 6. Archiv CB.

492 After she left, she married Wilhelm Rath, so after that her name was Maria Rath.

493 Letter written by Ella Rothe to René Maikowski, dated December 18, 1980. Archiv CB.

494 Archiv LS 3.3.150 and 3.3.154.

with the fact that Ella Rothe stood up for Maria Spira. She forbade her to teach after she had married Martin Rothe and did not pay the so-called spousal benefit to Martin Rothe.[495] Thereupon the couple left the school in 1929, as indicated above. He died shortly afterward.

Wilhelm Wollborn

In order to strengthen the economic basis of the school in Essen, colleagues in Stuttgart, especially Erich Schwebsch, had suggested for quite some time to organize a public conference in Essen. This idea was accepted, but not without hesitation. People then warmed to the idea and showed more willingness once there had been conversations with representatives of the local branch of the Central Institute for Education in Essen. The internal tensions notwithstanding, the teachers in Essen were able to organize a conference together with Stuttgart colleagues, which was held on May 14 and 15, 1928. The local branch of the Central Institute for Education sponsored the public conference; the theme was "Rudolf Steiner's Pedagogy and Its Importance for the Ruhr Area." Student work was showcased, and the lectures were written up afterward and published in the May 1928 issue of the magazine *Zur Pädagogik Rudolf Steiners* [On the Pedagogy of Rudolf Steiner].

In spite of the desperate financial situation and the continued dependence of the Rudolf Steiner school in Essen on financial support from Stuttgart, plans for a new school building were made in 1929, and the design drawings were published in the local newspaper, the *Allgemeine Zeitung* of Essen. The town offered a piece of land in Essen-Rellinghausen as a leasehold. Thereupon people in Essen asked the Association for Independent Schools in Stuttgart to take out a mortgage with which to enable the school in Essen to build a much-needed new building. They made this request with complete disregard of the financial situation and the means that were at the disposal of the Stuttgart Association. A crisis of confidence resulted, which neither visits by Paul Baumann and Erich Schwebsch, and after that by Emil Molt, Paul Baumann, and E. A. Karl Stockmeyer in the summer of 1930, were able to deflate.

The three colleagues from Stuttgart had traveled there at the express wish of the school in Essen. They looked into the economic situation, which led them to recommend that experienced parents should help deal with the finances because it was highly necessary. Parents that met the criteria were actually found and on July 12, 1930, they were asked to join the council of the association that was responsible for the school. A short time afterward, however, Margarethe Blass announced that

495 Letter written by Ella Rothe to René Maikowski, dated January 21, 1981. Archiv CB.

she was not able to work with this council, and one after the other, members stepped back again.

The efforts to help had failed.[496] Letters with more advice followed. A group of parents now declared themselves willing to take care of the desperate economic situation, but only under the condition that Margarethe Blass would not only step back from the school leadership but also give up her teaching position.

The developments in Essen were followed closely by the other schools, because there was a real worry that open scandals could endanger the situation of the school movement as a whole, which was precarious enough given the political tensions of the day.

Concerned colleagues in Stuttgart offered Margarethe Blass a position in Stuttgart for one year, and also offered to send one of the Stuttgart colleagues to Essen to replace her. She refused. Erich Gabert of the Waldorf School in Stuttgart was asked to come as an intermediary. The faculty in Essen agreed to this in June 1931, and Erich Gabert went to Essen for about a month. There he found a completely divided faculty and a deep crisis of confidence among the parents. According to Erich Gabert, there was far too much resistance on the part of Margarethe Blass, and he was not able to bring peace. Early in the summer of 1931, 13 colleagues out of 20 announced that they would leave the school by the end of the school year.[497] There were heated parent meetings, attended by almost 500 parents.

Not until then did the parents see how deeply divided the faculty actually was and they also witnessed the tenacity with which Margarethe Blass wanted to cling to her role. An overwhelming majority turned against her, which she had not expected.[498] On July 8, 1931, the 13 teachers wrote a letter to the parents asking them not to withdraw their children, in the interest of the children themselves.[499] In spite of that, about half of the students left the school. René Maikowski wanted to leave the school in 1929, and one night, after the college meeting, he made his decision. The next morning in school, one boy suddenly stood up in the middle of the lesson and said, "Herr Maikowski, last night I dreamt that you would leave the school. If you do that, I will cry so much that my tears will flood the whole school."

The whole class implored him to stay. René Maikowski was deeply moved by the voices of the children and promised them he would stay until the end of grade 8, which he did—without participating in the college meetings.[500] After the 13 teachers had left, Margarethe Blass, Irene Burghardt and Wilhelm Wollborn formed a

496 Erich Gabert: Bericht über die Lage an der Essener Rudolf Steiner Schule. Archiv NG; made available by Johannes Gabert.
497 Report by Erich Gabert, dated June 17, 1931. Archiv LS 3.3.336.
498 Report by Erich Gabert, dated June 29, 1931. Archiv LS 3.3.338.
499 Letter of July 8, 1931. Archiv LS 3.3.345.
500 René Maikowski: Schicksalswege auf der Suche nach dem lebendigen Geist. 1980, p. 134.

provisional leadership council of the school in Essen that would have the task to guide the school, now basically decimated, into the future. Heinrich Wollborn, Wilhelm's brother, belonged to the 13 teachers who were departing. After brief interludes in Stuttgart and the Black Forest, he went to teach at the Waldorf school in Breslau, where he stayed until he was conscripted into the army in 1940.

On July 17, 1931, Erich Schwebsch, Christoph Boy, and Paul Baumann sent the following notice to the Rudolf Steiner school in Essen: "The faculty of the Waldorf School can no longer assist you pedagogically or give further counsel, and hereby severs any further ties with the school in Essen led by Dr. Blass."[501] The council members of the School Association notified the parents on July 31, 1931, that they had officially resigned in a meeting held July 28, 1931.

Plans for a Second Waldorf School in the Ruhr Area

IN THE SAME MEETING the decision was made to found a Waldorf School Association for the Ruhr area, with the aim to find a different location in that region to build up an independent Waldorf school. All parents who were interested in an independent Waldorf school were invited to lend their support.[502] One of the 13 teachers who had left was Alwine Kiersch. She was asked to keep on teaching a few children and on November 2, 1931, she began teaching in the house of Frau A. Nelessen on the Moltkestrasse 36 in Essen. On March 14, 1932, Alwine Kiersch wrote to the faculty of the Stuttgart Waldorf School that her work would have the approval of the school inspector.[503] This work was to be the seed of a second Waldorf school, a real Waldorf school this time, it was claimed. After a while more children joined, and a second teacher came, Dr. Carl Brestowsky. He began lecturing far beyond Essen in order to spread the Waldorf school idea in the Ruhr area.

On January 29, 1933, a school association was founded to form a new legal entity. Alwine Kiersch and Carl Brestowsky were the teachers who represented the school on the council, Reinhart Boerner from Wanne-Eickel was chair, Frau A. Nelessen deputy chair, and K. Wirtz from Essen was the secretary, with W. Woehl as his deputy. M. Lüthje, Mr. Brown, and Margarete Boerner were also involved with the work.[504] However, the two teachers, Alwine Kiersch and Carl Brestowsky, were unable to work together, and the school did not materialize. For that reason, the chair of the new school association, Reinhart Boerner from Wanne-Eickel, stepped back as early as August 1933.

501 Letter of July 17, 1931. Archiv LS 3.3.364.
502 Document dated July 31, 1931. Archiv LS 3.3.373.
503 Document written by Alwine Kiersch dated March 14, 1932. Archiv LS 3.3.393.
504 Letter to the administration of the independent Waldorf School in Stuttgart. Archiv LS 3.2.301.

AFTER THE 13 COLLEAGUES left, Wilhelm Harrer, Werner Loose, Wilhelm Rüter, Dr. Paul Wissmann, and Elli Ney came as new teachers to the Rudolf Steiner school in Essen, as well as Irmentraut Salzmann, who taught eurythmy for a short time.[505] In 1933 the Jewish students were obliged to leave, and the children of civil servants and members of the NSDAP followed suit. The children who stayed in the school were from working-class families and the remaining number was around 400 children in ten grades. The economic situation became worse, and at the end of the school year 1935/36 circumstances were so dire that the faculty saw no way to keep the school going and decided to close it. Margarethe Blass told Count von Bothmer in a letter of March 28, 1936, that the school had been closed on March 26, 1936.[506] Margarethe Blass had thus lost both the school and her fortune. Alone and without work after the school had closed, she lived under meager circumstances in her parental home until she was invited to come live in Düsseldorf by a relative. The latter was head of a women's employment agency of the NSDAP in Düsseldorf and found work for her which did not oblige her to become a member of the NSDAP.

During the war she was working for Germans living in Hungary, Romania, and Yugoslavia, doing social work and giving lectures, and after the war she worked in the Protestant home for girls in Düsseldorf-Ratingen.[507] Irene Burghardt was evacuated during the war and lived in Bützow, a little village in Mecklenburg. She told many people about Rudolf Steiner and anthroposophy, amongst others Jürgen Schriefer, Hildegard Schultz, Kurt Kehrwieder, and Wolfgang Joerges. This group later fled the German Democratic Republic and together with Irene Burghardt-Wollborn and her husband Wilhelm Wollborn built up the Rudolf Steiner School Bochum-Langendreer in 1958, which was the first Waldorf school in the Ruhr area after World War II.[508]

Margarethe Blass died in 1971. The Rudolf Steiner School in Essen was founded later, in 1972, and at the time it was called *Freie Waldorfschule in Essen*. This founding took place in the beginning years of the second wave of Waldorf school foundings after the war. Already at that time, teachers and parents of the founding group were part of the *Ring freier Gemeinschaften aus anthroposophischer Initiative* [Circle of Free Communities Working out of the Anthroposophical Initiatives], where anthroposophically oriented institutions and persons worked together. These included

---

505 Marianne Garff: Irmentraut Salzmann. LR 4, 1971, p. 44.
506 Facsimile in Helga Lauten (ed.): *Die erste Essener Waldorfschule 1922–1936.* 2008, p. 108; Wenzel M. Götte: *Erfahrungen mit Schulautonomie.* 2006, p. 318, thinks the school was closed on March 26, 1936, by the Nazi authorities, quoting the letter written by Dr. M. Blass on March 28, 1936. The letter, however, does not mention that. Therefore I assume the closing was decided by the teachers themselves.
507 Diether Lauenstein: Ein Mensch und eine Schule in gleicher Tragik. LR 4, 1971, p. 40.
508 Ernst Weissert: Irene Wollborn (March 13, 1893–April 16, 1980). LR 21, 1980, p. 88f.

the Christian Community, a kindergarten, a home for the elderly, and several medical doctors. Right from the start they planned to found schools for children with special challenges. Today the school comprises three branches, one ordinary school and two schools for children with learning difficulties.

1922: The Priory School in Kings Langley, Hertfordshire

MARGARET FRANCES CROSS (1866–1962), head of the Priory School, and Hannah Clark (1845–1934), founder of the school, were both receptive to new educational methods. Margaret Frances Cross had led the school, also called Coombe Hill School, since 1909/10, and Hannah Clark had led a small boarding school before and was well known as a pioneer of coeducation in boarding schools. The school, a small boarding school about 20 miles north of London, was housed in an old building that was formally a Dominican priory, founded by King Edward I in 1308. It was coeducational, which was pretty unusual at the time; the food was vegetarian, and pupils and teachers shared the responsibility of doing the household chores.

Margaret Cross especially was interested in new pedagogical developments and therefore also in the educational method of Maria Montessori. She often attended conferences on the theme. It was at such a conference that she got to know the first British woman who was a professor of education, Millicent Mackenzie (1863–1942). The latter invited her, together with a few other British teachers, to come to Dornach in order to hear lectures by Rudolf Steiner. The plan was realized in December 1921, and thus they had the opportunity to hear the pedagogical course Rudolf Steiner gave for teachers[509] December 23, 1921–January 7, 1922, which was translated by George Adams-Kaufmann.

In April 1922 Margaret Cross traveled to Stratford-upon-Avon to once again hear a lecture by Rudolf Steiner. During this trip, Rudolf Steiner was also able to visit Kings Langley on April 16, 1922.

He described his impressions as follows: "The children of this boarding school, about 40 to 50 in number, have to do basically everything; in fact, there are no maidservants. The children have to get up early and do all the chores in the house. [...] They take care of the garden. The vegetables they eat they have first grown, harvested, and cooked themselves before they actually reach the table. This way the child gets a broad education for life and learns a great deal."[510] In 1922 Margaret Cross and Hannah Clark decided to turn their school into a Waldorf school.

Rudolf Steiner himself indicated that there would be quite a few obstacles to overcome. This turned out to be true, for in spite of the pedagogical innovations

---

509 Rudolf Steiner: *Soul Economy: Body, Soul, and Spirit and Waldorf Education*. CW 303.
510 Report dated April 30, 1922. Archiv LS 3.12.01.

Violetta Plincke, a teacher for a short time at the Waldorf School in Stuttgart, moved to England especially to teach at Kings Langley.

and the openness to new educational methods, the head of school had a staunch, old-fashioned style that caused many teachers to leave after a short time. The only exception was Hilda Burton, who had been working faithfully at the school since 1915 and stayed by Margaret Cross's side until the end.

In 1923 Violetta Plincke[511] came to the Priory School. She was the daughter of a wealthy English merchant who had married a woman from the Baltic region of Germany. She had grown up in St. Petersburg, spoke three languages, and had heard about Rudolf Steiner while still in Russia and Finland. She studied philosophy in Freiburg im Breisgau, and during that time she began to practice spiritual science and studied Rudolf Steiner's basic works. After finishing her university studies, she moved to Berlin to go deeper into anthroposophy. When she asked Rudolf Steiner how to best serve anthroposophy, he suggested she take a first grade at the Stuttgart Waldorf School, which she did in the school year 1921/22. It proved to be rough going, however.

In 1923 she moved to England and tried to help the two women introduce Waldorf education in Kings Langley. This proved to be difficult. She wrote to Rudolf Steiner that the soil needed radical plowing there.[512] After leaving the Priory School, she stayed in England, traveling widely and giving lectures.

The teachers of the Stuttgart Waldorf School helped the Kings Langley school in its fledgling phase by allowing, for example, Elfriede Glaser, C. Bartlett, and Hilda Burton to do extended practicums in Stuttgart. In spite of all these efforts, however, the situation in Kings Langley did not become more attractive. By 1928, the number of students had decreased to 22, which was partly due to the fact that the cold winters and the unsatisfactory living circumstances were hard to put up with.

Two German teachers, Maria Ilse and Inez Arnold, also left the school in 1928. Maria Ilse,[513] who had been part of the pedagogical working group in Jena-Zwätzen and had done a short training at the teacher seminar in Stuttgart, stuck it out for two and a half years nevertheless. Because the situation was so problematic, the Stuttgart school was willing to send Hermann and Erica von Baravalle for a limited time to Kings Langley to figure out whether and how the Priory School could be saved.[514] This offer was happily accepted, but in the end it proved impossible for the two teachers to travel to England.

511 Rudolf Steiner: *Faculty Meetings with Rudolf Steiner*. CW 300, 2. GA 300c, Dornach 1975, p. 94; Martin Sandkühler. In: Bodo von Plato (ed.): *Anthroposophie im 20. Jahrhundert*. 2003, p. 602f.
512 Magda Maier in Gisbert Husemann and Johannes Tautz (eds.): *Der Lehrerkreis um Rudolf Steiner*. 1979, p. 258.
513 Sieglinde Heilmann: Maria Ilse (April 15, 1901–May 8, 1981). LR 24, 1982, p. 66.
514 Letter dated September 21, 1928. Archiv LS 3.12.10.

Margaret MacMillan supported the school by publishing positive reports in the newspapers and bringing the school into the public eye. There were a few new applications, and by September 1928 the number of children attending had risen to 26. The two teachers who had left the school attended the world congress organized by Daniel N. Dunlop, where they told people about the less rosy aspects, which contributed to the further decline of the reputation of the Priory School in English circles. People outside the school were generally of the opinion that the school could only be saved if Margaret Cross would leave, because all efforts to move her to change her ways had remained without success. The school's tarnished reputation—justified or not—caused a mood of resignation among the remaining teachers.[515]

In 1928, during the conference to celebrate the opening of the new Goetheanum building in Dornach, the situation at the Priory School was discussed at great length. Members of the Executive Council of the Anthroposophical Society and teachers from Stuttgart as well as the New School (later called Michael Hall School) in London took part in the deliberations. Even though the outcome was that colleagues of the London school were urged to give assistance, the answer relayed by Cecil Harwood was that they declined to do so. All problems were put on the table in this discussion, but people were not able to come up with positive steps forward.

In the meantime, new teachers were appointed in Kings Langley with an eye to revamp the school. Among those was William Harrer (1905–1978), an engineer from Germany who did not want to be a bystander as National Socialism gained ground, and therefore preferred to emigrate. He stayed at the school for a short time until he traveled on to New York. In 1939 Margaret Cross asked the eurythmist Juliet Compton-Burnett (1893–1984)[516] to come to the Priory School and teach eurythmy. Juliet Compton-Burnett soon found teaching to her liking and also built up a small kindergarten, which became a combined grade 1/2 in 1941.

In order to keep the new impulse in Kings Langley alive, she asked her sister Vera Compton-Burnett (1891–1985) to come to Kings Langley as well and take the next first grade. Rudolf Steiner had charged the two sisters to bring eurythmy to England. Faithful to the call, Vera and Juliet Compton-Burnett had returned to England in the middle of the 1920s and had been teaching eurythmy in the first eurythmy school in London, The Goetheanum School of Eurythmy. They knew Rudolf and Marie Steiner and had been trained since 1922 in Stuttgart by Alice Fels, and by Lucy Neuscheller and Annemarie Donath in Dornach.

After a final performance of a solo in Dornach, sometime in 1924, Marie Steiner remarked to Vera that she still had a ways to go. Rudolf Steiner, however, did not give weight to this remark and emphasized that it would be necessary for England that

---

515 This is what M. Cross wrote to Dr. von Baravalle on July 29, 1928.

516 Heather Thomas: Juliet Compton-Burnett (†April 5, 1984). LR 28, 1984, p. 84; Vera and Juliet Compton-Burnett, as well as the well-known author Ivy Compton-Burnett, were daughters of the homeopathic physician, Dr. James Compton-Burnett (1840–1901).

she went back. It was said that he had told Vera Compton-Burnett at the end of her first year of training, "You will do very well and will come back to us here again and again."[517] So she went back to England.

Both sisters were teaching eurythmy in Kings Langley as well as being class teachers. Grade after grade was built up and it seemed as if the school was thriving with a strong faculty. Margaret Cross, however, could not embrace this way of working together.

In 1947 the new faculty was able to acquire a neighboring piece of land, and they moved into the house next to the Priory. A few children stayed with Margaret Cross and her old colleagues. The school kept going with a few children until 1955. Margaret Cross died in 1962.

The New School in Kings Langley

In 1949 the foundation stone for the New School was laid on the neighboring piece of land, the location of the Rudolf Steiner School Kings Langley. The school grew apace, and the number of children increased rapidly. Juliet Compton-Burnett took one class through from grades one through eight and, after that, two more that she took over halfway because their teachers left the school. Judith Brown, one of her former students, had vivid memories of Miss Vera and Miss Juli as being the most impressive moral authorities of the school.[518] Juliet Compton-Burnett also taught music. She remained with the school until she was very old and dealing with failing eyesight. At age 88 she worked three full days per week, practicing speech and verbal expression with the children. Her younger colleagues were very impressed by her wisdom and her courage for the truth, and she thus became a shining example to them. In the course of time the school expanded onto the piece of land of the old Priory School, which was integrated into the institution.

1923: The Vrije School in The Hague

RUDOLF STEINER was also actively involved with the founding of the school in The Hague, and, in contrast to the Hamburg school for example, visited this school more than once. The initiative to found this school came from a group of predominantly young people, among them Daniel Johan (Daan) van Bemmelen (1899–1982), Emmy Smit (1896–1986), Hélène Drooglever-Fortuyn (1874–1959), Elisabeth Mulder-Seelig (1893–1968), as well as Max Stibbe (1898–1973) and his fiancée, Paula Hoorweg (1898–1993).

---

517 Martina M. Sam: *Eurythmie. Entstehungsgeschichte und Porträts ihrer Pioniere.* 2014, p. 258.
518 Nat Brown: Vera Sabine Compton-Burnett (September 23, 1981–May 23, 1985). N 27.4.1986, p. 71f.

All of them took part in a course that Rudolf Steiner held in the grammar school located on the Laan van Meerdervoort in The Hague April 7–12, 1922.[519] A few teachers of the Stuttgart Waldorf School lectured as well. Daan van Bemmelen and Max Stibbe, who knew each other because they had both attended the same high school in The Hague, checked the entry tickets, Emmy Smit's ticket among them. So the future founders had all come together at that time, without knowing it or realizing what it would imply. Deeply impressed after a lecture, Emmy Smit approached the Dutch Anthroposophical Society after the course, and asked where a Waldorf school could be found in Holland, only to hear that such a school did not exist yet in the Netherlands. But her question did prompt a discussion that very evening about the possibility of founding a school. The conversation took place on Palm Sunday, April 9, 1922. Pieter de Haan (1891–1968) was there, who had organized the lecture tour of Rudolf Steiner and Emil Molt that had taken them to seven Dutch towns in the winter of 1920/21.[520] Other participants were his wife, Günther Schubert, Daan van Bemmelen, Max Stibbe, Hélène Drooglever-Fortuyn, Henk and Erna van Deventer, Cornelis Los, Madeleine van Deventer, Elisabeth Vreede, and Willem Zeylmans van Emmichoven. Herbert Hahn, Dr. Karl Heyer, Caroline von Heydebrand, Walter J. Stein, Hermann von Baravalle, Ernst Uehli, Carl Unger, Wilhelm Pelikan, Friedrich Husemann, and Eugen Kolisko from Stuttgart also took part.

During this very lecture tour in the winter of 1921/22, Rudolf Steiner spoke extensively in the Amsterdam Concertgebouw about the newly developed Waldorf pedagogy and on what it was founded, a lecture that was followed by a presentation by Emil Molt about the Waldorf School in Stuttgart. Daan van Bemmelen and his mother heard Rudolf Steiner and Emil Molt speak at that occasion. It was actually only the second lecture by Rudolf Steiner he attended, and it connected him directly with one of the themes of his life, the building up of an independent Waldorf school. A deep feeling of familiarity grew in him, and therefore it is no wonder that he participated in the meeting of April 9, 1922. "You will not need to worry about finding children and parents, Mrs. Fortuyn will take care of that," Eugen Kolisko said in the course of the conversation.[521] The meeting went until midnight. And, sure enough, Hélène Drooglever-Fortuyn, wife of the city council member and later mayor of Rotterdam, followed up. She initially thought that she would be able to start with enthusiastic teachers, but among members of the Anthroposophical Society who had positions in state schools she did not find a single one who would take up the challenge with her, as she had hoped. They did not want to give up the security of their employment status

519 Christoph Lindenberg: *Rudolf Steiner, Eine Chronik*. 1988. p. 483f.
520 The lecture tour took place from February 18–March 4, 1922. Rudolf Steiner gave lectures in Amsterdam, Hilversum, Utrecht, The Hague, Delft, Rotterdam, and Hengelo.
521 Helene Fortuyn in a letter to her sister Sanne Bruinier. Quoted in Frans Lutters: *Daniel Johan van Bemmelen*. 2012, p. 70. Emanuel Zeylmans writes that this remark stems from Herbert Hahn, in *Willem Zeylmans van Emmichoven. Ein Pionier der Anthroposophie*. 1979, p. 107.

as state school teachers in exchange for a position in an unsubsidized, experimental little school.

Emmy Smit and Daan van Bemmelen, however, planned to become Waldorf teachers. In order to prepare for that they began to study privately in order to get a teacher diploma. They wanted to found the school immediately after they had done their exams, and of course wanted to teach in it. Both of them took part in the so-called youth course, which Rudolf Steiner gave in October 1922, during which they received far-reaching and strong inner pictures for their future work.

Around the same time, Elisabeth Mulder, newly widowed, was preparing to emigrate to the United States with her two children in order to take a position as a private teacher there. She met Daan van Bemmelen when they were both doing a practicum at the Stuttgart Waldorf School and in their conversations they naturally came to talk about their future plans. Elisabeth Mulder's children urgently needed a school, so when her American employers went back on the arrangement she suggested they start the Waldorf school in The Hague. Daan van Bemmelen wanted to go ahead straight away, Emmy Smit preferred to prepare more thoroughly for the undertaking.

Thereupon they decided to ask Rudolf Steiner for advice. In July 1923, Emmy Smit and Daan van Bemmelen met Rudolf Steiner in Stuttgart. They told him of their plan and asked whether he thought it plausible. The answer they received was, "Yes, if you have the will." He had to repeat the words a few times before they sank in. Only when Daan van Bemmelen confirmed that they did have the will to found the school, Rudolf Steiner added, "It is not just a matter of will, but also of resolving to carry through to the end what you have set your eyes on. To not retreat when difficulties arise."[522]

Hélène Drooglever-Fortuyn was asked by telegram to make all the preparations, and even though she was less than enthusiastic about their unreasonable demand, she did organize everything that was needed, assisted by Max Stibbe.

After the summer holidays, the Vrije School in The Hague was founded on September 9, 1923. It was located in the private home of the Nieuwkerken family on the Columbusstraat in The Hague. The first grade had six children and was taught by Emmy Smit, the fourth grade had two children, taught by Daan van Bemmelen, and the seventh grade had two children, taught by Elisabeth Mulder. Daan van Bemmelen and Emmy Smit had been certified as elementary school teachers in the meantime, and Elisabeth Mulder had her upper school certification.

Max Stibbe, a lawyer, was slated to take on teaching English, which he did from November 1923 onward, after he had successfully passed his teacher's exam as well.

---

522 D.J. van Bemmelen: Het ontstaan en de wording van de Vrije School. VOK Oct. 1948, pp. 2–8. In this article, written at the occasion of the 25-year anniversary of the school, Daan van Bemmelen looks back and reports extensively on the birth of the Waldorf school in The Hague and the people involved. All later accounts are likely to be based on this article. See also Frans Lutters: *Daniel Johan van Bemmelen. Wiedergeboren am Beginn des lichten Zeitalters.* 2012, p. 113.

Dann van Bemmelen with his class in The Hague, 1925

Paula Hoorweg taught eurythmy. To interface with the authorities, the school needed a director, and Mrs. Witbols-Feugen was asked to take on this task. Rudolf Steiner visited the new school on November 17 and 19, 1923, and named it *Vrije School*, a name that holds a mandate Waldorf schools in Holland carry to this day. During the two days he visited, Rudolf Steiner visited lessons.

Daan van Bemmelen reported later about very important pedagogical indications he gave on how to handle what we would now call a hyperactive boy, as well as indications for a heavily traumatized child, who had been officially labeled a "retarded child" on acceptance into the school.[523] Rudolf Steiner also gave an account of a drawing lesson during his second visit, when he had come alone to the little school on the Columbusstraat. The children were able to understand Rudolf Steiner's slowly spoken instructions in German very well. He began by showing them how light and dark interact on a cup, a sponge, and a cloth. Thus he developed drawing in this fourth grade out of exact observation of light and shadow, and created a picture of a tree on the blackboard as well.[524]

During the pedagogical summer course of July 1924 in Oosterbeek near Arnhem,[525] a conversation took place between Rudolf Steiner, the small faculty of the Vrije School, the Executive Council of the Anthroposophical Society in Holland, and the Executive Council of the General Anthroposophical Society in Dornach. In this conversation Rudolf Steiner made decisions about the future collaboration between the Anthroposophical Society and the Vrije School, and determined how future

---

523 Daan van Bemmelen: Autobiographische Skizze, printed in Frans Lutters: *Daniel Johan van Bemmelen. Wiedergeboren am Beginn des lichten Zeitalters.* 2012, p. 129ff.

524 D.J. van Bemmelen: Rudolf Steiner, "De Vrije School." Msch 10, 1950, p. 301; Frans Lutters: *Daniel Johan van Bemmelen. Wiedergeboren am Beginn des lichten Zeitalters.* 2012, p. 136f.

525 Rudolf Steiner: *Human Values in Education.* CW 310.

communication should take place. He asked the Dornach council member Elisabeth Vreede to function as a liaison between the school and the General Anthroposophical Society. During the summer course many personnel questions of the school were also talked about with Rudolf Steiner.

Rudolf Steiner accepted Jan van Wettum (1900–1989) as a new teacher. He rejected Pierre Dekkers (†1963), saying he should become a good engineer rather than a bad teacher, and he requested that Elisabeth Mulder leave the school because of ongoing illness. In addition, he made sure that an older colleague joined the young faculty in order to represent the school to the outside world, and suggested the musician Henri Zagwijn (1878–1954) for this position.[526] All indications Rudolf Steiner gave were carried out. His authority was absolute and unquestioned.

In 1925, the school had grown to about 47 children and by the third school year the number had risen to 90. In the meantime, Jan van 't Hoff had completed his training in Stuttgart and came to the school in The Hague together with his wife Friedel van 't Hoff-Nägelin. Jan van Wettum and his wife Tootje de Boer (†1987) finally gave in to Daan van Bemmelen's persistent recruitment efforts and joined the school in 1927. Jan van Wettum took on the task of teaching math in the upper grades.[527] Just like his second wife, Cathrien Enuma, he taught at the Waldorf school in The Hague until 1967. Cathrien Enuma-van Wettum took five classes through from grades one through eight, after which she still accompanied the building up of the Vrije School in Middelburg in Zeeland together with her husband. Daan van Bemmelen and Jan van Wettum (as well as Max Stibbe), had grown up together in Batavia (present-day Jakarta) in Indonesia, so they knew each other because they had spent their youth together there.

During the school year 1925/26, the leadership of the school transitioned to the faculty, which formed an internal council consisting of Emmy van Bemmelen-Smit, Daan J. van Bemmelen, Jan van 't Hoff, and Max Stibbe, who were to represent the school. In 1927 Konrad Müller-Fürer, who had taught at the Waldorf school in Cologne in its initial phase, moved to The Hague and taught handwork at the Vrije School until 1939. In the meantime the school was governed by an association called *De Vrije School*, over which Hélène Drooglever-Fortuyn presided. This association was financed out of parental contributions, because they did not want to enter into a dependency relationship with the official authorities, which would have happened if they had accepted state support. Freedom was so important to them that they made do without state money, and by the same token there was no contact with the official authorities in the initial years.

---

526 Daan van Bemmelen: Autobiographische Skizzen, printed in Frans Lutters: *Daniel Johan van Bemmelen. Wiedergeboren am Beginn des lichten Zeitalters.* 2012, p. 171f.

527 Hans-Peter van Manen: Jan van Wettum. In: Bodo von Plato (ed.): *Anthroposophie im 20. Jahrhundert.* 2003, p. 915ff.

The assembled students and teachers of the Vrije School in The Hague, 1926

Shortly after the beginning of the school year 1927/28, Daan van Bemmelen asked the Stuttgart school to send a "person of ripe humanity"[528] to the Vrije School for some time, someone in whom the spirit of Rudolf Steiner was alive. This request was made because there were many young and inexperienced teachers who were inwardly tired, and it was granted. Dr. Karl Schubert came and helped the young faculty of The Hague school with their chronic internal difficulties. Max Stibbe wrote words of thanks after the visit: "A teacher of the Waldorf School is like a messenger of the spirit of Rudolf Steiner for us. Few of our teachers have known Dr. Steiner, and it is all the more beneficial to be helped in our work by people who worked together with Dr. Steiner for a long time. Because this work together with Dr. Schubert was so beautiful and fruitful, we would like to go on to speak about our next plans, without wanting to be immodest."[529] The next persons to be invited were one of the religion teachers and Christoph Boy.

528 Letter written by D.J. van Bemmelen to the Stuttgart Waldorf School, dated November 30, 1927. Archiv LS 3.12.13.
529 Letter by Max Stibbe dated February 22, 1928. Archiv LS 3.12.16.

Jan van Wettum reports that Frits H. Julius (1902–1970) studied biology at the University of Utrecht. As a student, he got to know two people who became friends for life: Frans Copijn and Tini Hissink, his future wife. His acquaintance with anthroposophy also stems from that time. When the chemistry teacher of the Vrije School in The Hague became ill in 1925, Frits Julius was asked to step in for her. A young man with blond hair and a sanguine temperament, he had an outspoken talent for using pictorial speech. A colleague introduced him to the natural scientific works of Johann Wolfgang Goethe edited by Rudolf Steiner, and these turned out to be the basis of a lifelong preoccupation. With a mixture of coaxing and support from his wife, he completed his studies in 1927 and became a teacher at the school in The Hague in 1928. Van Wettum writes: "He had a combination of two opposite talents that he was able to bring into harmony. On the one hand his thinking was pictorial and synthesizing; on the other hand he was open and sanguine. In this way he was able to find large-scale, harmonious correspondences in all phenomena of the material world, plants, animals, and human beings."[530]

The school grew, and after an interim stay at the Kranenburgweg they moved into three partially connected townhouses on the Speykstraat. The students could barely put up with the steep staircases, narrow corridors, and small rooms. Thus the wish arose for a proper school building, leading to deliberations on how to bring that about. As these conversations were going on, the town directed their attention to a building site on the Waalsdorperweg. One morning at breakfast, town council member Drooglever-Fortuyn told his wife that the building could be erected there. The faculty and board opted for designs by Frits Gerretsen and Chris Wegerif. The building was made possible by a highly generous single donation by Susanne Bouricius (1872–1934), together with many other individual donations. Susanne Bouricius owned many plantations in Indonesia, among them sugar plantations. She was equally magnanimous in her support of the building up of anthroposophical medicine and the anthroposophical clinic in The Hague, as well as the starting up of the Christian Community. She also made sure that people in the circles in which she moved gained an appreciation of all these efforts.

The 1928/29 school year started off with 229 students and 24 teachers. The inauguration of the new school building was celebrated on September 10, 1929, with many speeches, including addresses by representatives of the city of The Hague and the minister of education, and the event was crowned by a student performance of Joseph Haydn's *The Creation*. In the meantime, the number of students had grown to 250 in 12 grades, who could now occupy the newly built school building at Waalsdorperweg 12. The inauguration was embedded in a conference held September 8–15, to which several Stuttgart colleagues had come, among them Herbert Hahn, Karl Schubert, Hermann von Baravalle, and Walter Johannes Stein. Representatives

530 Jan van Wettum: Ein Brief zum Hingang von Frits Julius. LR 2, 1970, p. 46.

from other Waldorf schools included Margarethe Blass from Essen, Conrad Englert from Switzerland, and Cecil Harwood from England.

The financial situation of the school deteriorated due to the world economic crisis. The school had to economize, which inevitably entails salary cuts: 20 percent in 1931, and 16 percent in 1933. A few mothers in the school got to work and were able to build up a fund that could finance children whose parents were no longer able to afford tuition. Mrs. J.L. Donker-van Hengel devised the *Helpaktie*, for example, by buying wholesale and selling at retail price to parents. The small profits made that way—measured in cents—were donated to the school.

In 1931, Herbert Hahn came to teach in the school at the urgent request of its teachers,[531] and the Stuttgart school was happy to grant him a leave of absence because his colleagues found it hard to deal with his affair with Maria Uhland. The two of them remained in The Hague until 1938.[532] With the coming to power of the National Socialists in 1933, the neighboring countries were affected as well. In order to continue to exist, the school had to anchor itself more than before in its own cultural tradition. The school problems were aggravated by the conflicts within the General Anthroposophical Society, which culminated in the exclusion of Willem Zeylmans van Emmichoven (1893–1961), the head of the Dutch Anthroposophical Society, effective in 1935.

From 1927 until 1931 a publication appeared in Holland called *Ostara–Tijdschrift voor de Pedagogie van Rudolf Steiner* [Ostara–Magazine of Rudolf Steiner's Pedagogy], which was renamed *Vrije Opvoedkunst* [Free Art of Education] in 1930. It ceased to be printed in the year 1932, but publication of the magazine resumed in February 1933. It contained articles of fundamental importance by Daan J. van Bemmelen, Frits H. Julius, Henriette Janssen van Raay (1899–1992), Max Stibbe, and the publisher, Arnold C. Henny (1906–1994). Arnold Henny published this magazine for more than 40 years, making sure that the content was of a high level and contributing articles himself. The content also featured studies about Dutch history and the Dutch national spirit, studies that underlined the Dutch tradition of freedom of thought and tolerance as distinguished from more German tendencies.

Geert Groote (1340–1384) was signaled as a forerunner of anthroposophical spiritual science. Caroline von Heydebrand's book on the curriculum was edited and adapted to Dutch circumstances. Nobody imagined back in 1933 that National Socialism, unmasked early on by people like Arnold Henny, would ever be able to gain a foothold in Holland and threaten the country.

531 Letter from Jan van Wettum to Dr. Schwebsch, dated July 4, 1931. Archiv LS 3.12.045.
532 Herbert Hahn and Maria Uhland were living mainly in Zeist during the war, but traveled back and forth to The Hague. During the Occupation, Herbert Hahn took on translation assignments for the National Socialists who occupied Holland and at one occasion appeared in the Vrije School in uniform, which he was obliged to wear as a translator. I heard this story from both Wim Veltman and Christof Wiechert. This became a basis for rumor that he was a collaborator with the National Socialists. However, contrary to these rumors, my interviews with contemporaries have no evidence that this was the case.

The school building of the Vrije School, 1927

WHEN THE SCHOOL YEAR STARTED on September 1, 1936, the school had 292 students. In 1937, Wim Kuiper (1911–1992) became a class teacher at the school in The Hague. Much later, especially after the 1970s, he played a very important role for the Dutch schools in international collaboration. Arnold C. Henny, born in Batavia like Daan van Bemmelen and Max Stibbe, had a degree in law, but he also completed a two-year teacher training in Stuttgart and joined the school in 1939. At the same time he occupied a post in the press service of the government, connected officially to the foreign ministry. He was able to do full justice to both jobs.[533] Because he was at home in both of these worlds, he was highly esteemed by many generations of students. How he managed on top of that to also be the chief editor of the magazine, *Vrije Opvoedkunst,* for over 40 years is hard to fathom.[534]

After the summer holidays of 1939, the school building at the Waalsdorperweg was appropriated by the Dutch military. The school had to move into private quarters. For a while, lessons had to be given in the homes of several families, until the military moved out again. By way of goodbye, Dutch soldiers were invited to participate in a festive evening organized by banker Emile Ernest Menten (1882–1970). In the course of the evening they were also alerted to the opportunity of taking several courses held in the school. The school reoccupied its own building again and functioned there as well as it was able to.

After the Germans occupied Holland in May 1940, the school in The Hague was able to keep operating in its own buildings for the time being, despite having to provide quarters and endure searches of the archives and the library. But, sad to

533 Rinke Visser: *Zwaarte van Stofgoud en licht in diamant.* 2014, p. 49.
534 Rudolf Mees: A.C. Henny. http://biographien.kulturimpuls.org/detail.php?&id=346 (site visited January 21, 2017).

say, "for the time being" did not last. Just over half a year later, the school building was occupied by the German military after main lesson on December 14, 1940. The German military demanded that the school building had to be vacated in two hours. Once again, teaching had to be continued in private quarters. The German occupation forces wanted to be in control of everything, including school finances, and therefore other ways to manage the money had to be found at short notice. From one day to the next, tuition had to be paid into the private accounts of Frits Julius and Gerrit A. Gerretsen (1889–1960). The latter had been treasurer and financial head of the school since the founding of the School Association in 1923.[535] Because of this trick, at least the finances were beyond the reach of the occupational forces. The magazine, *Vrije Opvoedkunst,* ceased publication in March 1941, and its address list was hidden.

On July 12, 1941, the Vrije School in The Hague was closed following a Gestapo action against societies promoting secret doctrines and so-called occult sciences within the Reich. Societies of this nature were forbidden and their goods confiscated.

The library, lovingly built up by Max Stibbe, had already landed in the heating furnaces bit by bit. At an assembly right after the closing of the school, Frits Julius addressed the children and teachers who had gathered and said: "Outwardly the powers that are inimical to the spirit can seem to triumph, but the spirit is indestructible. It will grow in strength, and one day will surface again and be victorious."[536]

During the war, the estate Hagheweyde in Warmond became the center for all school affairs. It was owned by the family of Ernestine and Emile Menten, great supporters of the school in The Hague and partners of the investment bank, Heldring & Pierson. It also became the home of Paula and Arnold C. Henny with their four children. Emile Menten himself was imprisoned by the National Socialists, accused of assisting in spying, and he spent 16 months in jail.[537] Somebody stood up for him, and to that we owe that he was not taken to a concentration camp but released.[538] Jaant Loos (1915–1993) and Tootje de Boer taught about 25 children in a small room above the orangerie of the estate. School assemblies were celebrated there, and it also housed performances of the Christmas plays. The school inspector turned a blind eye.

After Holland was liberated on May 5, 1945, people immediately set to work to build the school back up again. It opened on September 2, 1945, with seven classes. From 1946 onward they were able to occupy their own building again after the military had finally cleared out.

535 Hans Peter van Manen: Gerrit A. Gerretsen. In: Bodo von Plato (ed.): *Anthroposophie im 20. Jahrhundert.* 2003, p. 214.
536 F.H. Julius: Vernietiging en opbouw van de Vrije School. VOK 1, October 1946, p. 38.
537 Olof van Joolen: De bankier van het verzet. *De Telegraaf,* November 23, 2016.
538 SS-Head Company Leader, Heinrich Kurt Otto Haubrock. claimed during interrogations to have saved E. E. Menten. See: http://www.weggum.com/E.E._MENTEN.html (site visited January 21, 2017).

1925: The New School in London–
Continued as Michael Hall School in Forest Row

WALDORF EDUCATION became known in larger circles in England when extensive press coverage was given to the conference "On Spiritual Values in Education and Social Life," held in Oxford in 1922. Prof. Millicent Mackenzie of the University of Wales, Cardiff, had organized the conference. She was the first female professor in England and was widely known in academic circles. President of the conference was H.A.L. Fisher, the minister of education, and even though he didn't put in an appearance, he wrote a multipage opening address that was read out loud. Twelve people held lectures on a variety of topics. In his opening words, Prof. J. Findlay of the University of Manchester introduced Rudolf Steiner, the main speaker and only guest from abroad, who would give a lecture each day. He characterized him as a great teacher and Goethe scholar who would not be influenced by the quiet, traditional atmosphere of Oxford, but would be sure to challenge everybody with rigorous thinking, mindful of long-term, overarching themes. Prof. Findlay emphasized that the basic assumption underlying the conference was the belief in the possibility of personal spiritual development, even though the link between a teacher's own development and their pedagogical activity in the classroom was not customarily made conscious.

In the course of this conference in Oxford, Rudolf Steiner gave 12 lectures, which were translated by George Adams-Kaufmann in a masterly fashion.[539] At the end of the conference, a worldwide organization to foster the founding of schools was inaugurated, as had been mentioned during the conference. In the two years after that Rudolf Steiner traveled to England to give two more lecture cycles on education, usually accompanied by a few Waldorf teachers. In 1923, at the invitation of Margaret MacMillan (1860–1931) and the Educational Union for the Realization of Spiritual Values in Education, Rudolf Steiner gave lectures in Kings Hall in Ilkley, Yorkshire;[540] in 1924, he gave seven education lectures in Torquay.[541] With these three lecture cycles he laid the foundation for the development of Waldorf education in the British Isles.

It is highly likely that his visit to Margaret MacMillan's kindergartens in Deptford, London, influenced the way he looked at early childhood education. Rudolf Steiner was deeply impressed by the artistic way she worked socially with neglected little children in this kindergarten.

---

539 John Paull: Rudolf Steiner and the Oxford Conference: The Birth of Waldorf Education in Britain. EJES 3 (1), 2011, p. 58; Christoph Lindenberg, *Rudolf Steiner. Eine Biographie. 1915–1925.* 1997, p. 689.

540 Rudolf Steiner: *A Modern Art of Education.* Lectures given in Ilkley, Yorkshire, August 6–17, 1923. CW 307. The lectures attracted international attention; even a few Russians came to attend them. The evening performances were shaped by students of the Stuttgart Waldorf School.

541 Rudolf Steiner: *The Kingdom of Childhood.* CW 311, 1979.

Erica von Baravalle tells a nice story from this summer visit, which greatly influenced her later work as a teacher. At one of the afternoon lectures, Rudolf Steiner announced that he had an important message before starting the education lecture. Everyone prepared to note down what he had to say, but he occupied himself with scratching the paper cover from the chalk. Then he stood there with the scraps of paper in his hand, at which point a participant suggested he put the paper scraps in the corner for the time being, and someone would clean them up afterward. But Rudolf Steiner made

Margaret MacMillan

a point of having someone fetch a wastepaper basket into which he then threw the scraps. The moral of the story was, in Steiner's original words: "What I wanted to say is this: No matter how much pedagogical knowledge you amass, if you throw the chalk wrapper on the floor in a corner and not in the wastepaper basket, your pedagogical knowledge will be to no avail."[542]

At the conference in Ilkley, four women who were enthusiastic about the new educational ideals decided to put them into practice. They asked for a conversation with Rudolf Steiner during which George Adams-Kaufmann was kind enough to interpret. After they had presented their plan, Rudolf Steiner said yes, according to the story. Having said that, however, he pointed out to the women that it was not enough for their school to be an attempt, but that it had to be a success story. It would actually have to be a modern, well-established school, so as not to do considerable harm to the reputation of this new form of education. In addition, Rudolf Steiner recommended they start with at least 100 children. For that reason they would have to carefully prepare the necessary steps and would especially have to find the right spot. For a location, Rudolf Steiner was against either a charming country estate or the East End of London, where the organizer of the Ilkley course of 1923, Margaret MacMillan, was working with the destitute. It should be mentioned as an aside that he valued her work highly. "It's a great experience to hear this woman talk about the social aspects of working with children of the poor."[543] He thought it was important to find a place for the school that would give access to children from all strata of society with the most diverse backgrounds. Accessibility was obviously of prime importance to him.

The decision was made. Interested parents were invited to come on the afternoon of November 22, 1924, to learn about the intentions of the new school initiative. As the schoolhouse had not been renovated or prepared, people were invited to come

542 Rex Raab: Erica von Baravalle (December 18, 1900–December 8, 1994). LR 53, 1995, p. 99.
543 Christoph Lindenberg: *Rudolf Steiner. Eine Biographie 1915–1925*. 1997, p. 692.

The students of the New School in London, circa 1926

to Brixton Hill.[544] Then, on December 20, 1924, things were to a point where the members of the Anthroposophical Society could be invited for tea.[545]

On January 20, 1925—at that time the school year began in the middle of January after the Christmas holidays—the New School, the first English Waldorf school (not counting the attempt of the Priory School) was founded in South London by Dorothy Martin (1900–1971), later Dorothy Darrell; Helen Fox (1892–1972); Effie Grace Wilson (1877–1960); and Daphne Olivier, later Daphne Harwood (1889–1950).[546] Rudolf Steiner wanted to make sure there was a man in this circle of four women, and so Daphne Olivier invited her friend and future husband, Cecil Harwood (1898–1975)[547] to join, for lack of a more qualified candidate. Cecil Harwood, in turn, was a friend of Owen Barfield (1898–1997). As schoolboys, they had sat next to each other in the first row and had been friends ever since. Owen Barfield was a barrister and a well-known literary figure in England. He later became an important anthroposophist whose studies on the history of consciousness have influenced many people in England and America.

So Cecil Harwood formed a connection to some well-known personalities and thus to educated English cultural circles. He attracted important people to the faculty,

544 The New School. AM 2.11.1924, p. 168; AM 9.11.1924, p. 176 and AM 16.11.1924, p. 184.
545 The New School. AM 30.11.1924, p. 200; AM 7.12.1924, p. 208.
546 Short biographies of the four founders are in: *Joy Mansfield: A Good School.* 2014, p. 102ff.
547 Rudi Lissau in Bodo von Plato (ed.): *Anthroposophie im 20. Jahrhundert.* 2003, p. 276ff.

and was to play an important role in years to come, not only for the school but also for the Anthroposophical Society in England, of which he was general secretary from 1937–1974. Cecil Harwood met Rudolf Steiner in Torquay in 1924 when he gave lectures on education there and signaled his willingness to partake in the founding of the school.

Thanks to generous gifts from Miss Stuttaford, Christopher Gill and Edward Melland, the beginning stage could be financed. The school started up in a beautiful big house on the Leigham Court Road in Streatham, which they were able to acquire with the funds available. It was situated in a quiet residential area with villas and big gardens. The ballroom of the Victorian house became the eurythmy room, the room with the billiard table became a small cafeteria. The women founders still had the opportunity to consult with Rudolf Steiner during the summer course in Torquay, where he made suggestions for the grade assignments and gave them courage. The big question, of course, was which children would come. Advertisements were placed, introductory evenings were held—all of which found little resonance. Instead of the hundred children Rudolf Steiner had demanded, there were seven. And thus the five teachers could get to work.

Soon after classes began, Arthur Renwick Sheen (1901–1959) found his way to the school and joined the four women. A clever, quick, cheerful, and warmhearted mathematician, he had applied for the position of natural science teacher. Soon he became indispensable both in his roles as a teacher and a treasurer. For the next decades he was one of the pillars of the school. During all stages the school went through, from Streatham to Forest Row, he and his wife Dorothy led a boarding house for those children who needed it.[548] He combined so many virtues that one can only stand back in amazement. Cecil Harwood gives an account of his abundant gifts in his compellingly poetic obituary.[549]

At the start of the new school year in autumn 1926, the number of children had grown to 100. Among them were some children with learning difficulties and handicaps, which added to the widespread prejudices about the background of the institution. The school was notorious as a "German school." Another factor that called forth mistrust was the fact that it was coeducational; boys and girls taught together was not done in private schools at that time.

In 1926, William von Kaufmann (1900–1986)[550] accepted a position as German teacher. With his love of beauty he soon took on teaching art classes and handwork lessons and he played an important role in building up the school. After consulting with Herbert Hahn, he initiated the free religion lessons at Michael Hall School. He

---

548 Martin Sandkühler: http://biographien.kulturimpuls.org/detail.php?&id=1458 (site visited February 12, 2017).

549 Printed in A. Renwick Sheen: *Geometry and the Imagination. The Imaginative Treatment of Geometry in Waldorf Education.* 2002.

550 Martina Mann in Bodo von Plato (ed.): *Anthroposophie im 20. Jahrhundert.* 2003, p. 494ff.

was a carrying force of this school for over five decades. On his father's side, he came from an old family in Hannover named Kaufmann. A younger half-brother of George Adams-Kaufmann, he was multilingual, having grown up in Poland, England, and Germany.[551]

After a three-month practicum at the Stuttgart Waldorf School, Jesse Darrell (1906–1991) came to the New School at the beginning of 1929. He had grown up with five siblings in a suburb of Liverpool and was the son of the boxing trainer. His brilliant achievements in school gained him a scholarship to go to Cambridge. According to his biographer, he was blessed with a kind sense of humor; he led five classes from grades one through eight (!), and was an unshakable pillar for the school. "There is often a wonderful mix of spontaneous laughter and curious attentiveness in his classroom." Obviously, he was a born teacher.[552]

The teachers regularly organized conferences and courses on Waldorf pedagogy to which they invited guest speakers from the Stuttgart school. So, for example, from June 11–14, 1926, they put on an education conference titled "The Art of Education," with Caroline von Heydebrand as a lecturer. Later, she was to take on a short, important task in English teacher training. Teachers of the Priory School also took part in this conference, and both the children of the New School and students of the London School of Eurythmy performed eurythmy exercises. Visitors from as far away as New Zealand were welcomed. These were the first signs of the important role the British Waldorf school movement played for the English-speaking world.

Another task was taken on at the New School early on, prophetically as it were, because groups for mothers and little children only became the norm in the 1980s. Every Thursday, starting June 9, 1927, mothers got together with their children and studied early childhood education together.[553]

IN THE COURSE of the years, the teachers became more accredited professionally. The school grew, and quarters became cramped. In 1929, the school had 101 students and eight teachers; in the year after that 136 students and 12 teachers. Early in the 1930s, the neighboring house, Leigham Court Road 41, was acquired, so that they finally had sufficient room and a big school garden. To everybody's relief, the two

<hr />

551 In a letter to Ernst Weissert dated July 13, 1965, Archiv BFWS 8211, he tells about his wife Liselotte Ehlen, who had been a student in the first Waldorf School in Stuttgart. In 1929, after her final exam, she studied gymnastics for several months with Count von Bothmer, and after that she also studied eurythmy. He reports: "So that's how it came about that Count von Bothmer was a witness when we got married, who stood next to her when Friedrich Rittelmeyer married us with thunderous words— the other witness, by the way, was Wolffhügel. So you see, we needed good angels." Their son, Christopher Mann (who married Martina Voith, thereafter called Martina Mann), and their daughter, Roswitha Spence (married to Michael Spence), also became pioneers of anthroposophy both in the United States and in England.

552 Hermann Koepke: Jesse Darrell (April 30, 1906–October 6, 1991). N 13.9.1992, p. 221.

553 The New School. AM 22.5.1927, p. 168.

The College of Teachers of the New School, 1926

old women who had lived there up to then, and had been mightily annoyed by the school, had moved out. Also, the school garden was connected to the garden of St. Elizabeth House, Leigham Court Road 98, where Helen Fox ran a boarding house for the younger children. She was able to house 18 children and served vegetarian food for those who wanted it.[554]

In 1931 Cecil Harwood started editing the magazine, *Child and Man*, which became the magazine that linked the British Waldorf movement together for many decades. The magazine also published some of Harwood's high-caliber literary translations of foreign poets.

When Effie Grace Wilson left the school in 1932 to help found the Michael House School in Ilkeston, Francis Edmunds (1902–1989)[555] came to the school as a new class teacher. Born in Vilnius, he had lived in Russia, Beirut, and Geneva. "It seemed as if a fireball had entered our school!" his wife Elizabeth remarked. He set everything around him in motion. He founded a choir, an orchestra, put on plays, took his students on excursions.[556] A renewing impulse went out from him and he taught at Michael Hall School until 1960. In 1962 he founded Emerson College, which harbored the British teacher training center.

554 Brochure in Archiv RSHL o. Nr.
555 Georg Locher, son-in-law to Fracis Edmunds: Francis Edmunds. In: Bodo von Plato (ed.): *Anthroposophie im 20. Jahrhundert.* 2003, p. 166ff.
556 John Meeks: Zum 85. Geburtstag am 30. März 1987 von Francis Edmunds. N 22.3.1987, p. 49.

Francis Edmunds was an outstanding personality and achieved many things. During the 1950s and 60s he did perhaps more than most for the spread of Waldorf education in the English-speaking world, especially North America. He was a sympathetic listener and was warmhearted and unprejudiced in meeting other people. While being open and interested, his thoughts were crystal clear at the same time. It was a joy to work with him and it was a delight to hear him speak.

The teachers of the school wanted to work together with others and would come every year to Stuttgart for an exchange. There were also colleagues in Stuttgart who came to help them for longer periods of time, for example Elly Wilke (1897–1961), who came in 1932 and introduced eurythmy in the school. Erich Schwebsch traveled to England in 1932 and lent support as a teacher and a coach.

Henry Barnes (1912–2008)[557] took a class at the New School soon after he had completed his training at the Stuttgart teacher seminar and done a practicum at the Sonnenhof, a curative education institution in Arlesheim in Switzerland. Through a stroke of destiny, he had been introduced to anthroposophy and Waldorf education after he had finished his studies at Harvard, and had immediately left for Europe in order to study Waldorf pedagogy in Stuttgart. Already back then he always dressed in a fine suit and wore impeccable clothes. He impressed people with his tall frame, and was a true representative of East Coast, American aristocracy, but his outer appearance did not show how unconventional he actually was. Shortly before the outbreak of the Second World War he went back to the United States with his wife, Christie MacKaye, where he took a class at the Rudolf Steiner school in New York. He became the most important pillar of the Waldorf school movement in the United States during World War II and for at least five decades after that.

In 1935 a dream came true. Between the two houses on Leigham Court Road a hall was built where—at last—they could have monthly assemblies and student performances. The hall was inaugurated on November 23, 1935, and was named Michael Hall. This marked the beginning of a new phase that found expression in a new name. The evening of the festive opening, Jesse Darrell held a lecture titled "Education in Modern Life," and from then on the New School, no longer new, became Michael Hall School. The new hall opened up new opportunities. In April 1936 and 1937, as well as in the two years after that, pedagogical Easter courses were held at the school where the speakers attempted to clearly place cultural developments of the time in the context of the stages of child development and the challenges they present. Caroline von Heydebrand, who had left the Stuttgart Waldorf School in the meantime and spent extensive periods of time in England, held a series of lectures during the Easter conference in 1936. In 1937, Eugen Kolisko and Max Stibbe held

557 Anne Riegel-Koetzsch and Ronald Koetzsch: "A Memorial Tribute. Henry Barnes" (December 8, 1912–September 18, 2008). *Renewal* 17.2, Autumn 2008, p. 5f.; John M. Barnes (ed.): *Henry Barnes— A Constellation of Human Destinies.* 2008, p. 20f.

guest lectures focusing on questions of individuality in relation to trends of the time, which they profiled sharply. These trends showed themselves in education infiltrated by increasingly shameless propaganda to arouse racial consciousness and promote efficiency in education. This theme was further worked out in 1939, also with the aim to counterbalance these tendencies.

In the introductory text for the Easter conference it said: "Can the conditions of the world, the rancor, fear, distrust, the rush to armaments, the growth of dictatorships, the steady suppression of individual liberty of thought and action, assure us of a true social future for mankind? What can we make of the recent clamor of racial animosity, the blood-creed, the attacks on Christianity and on all spiritual life?

"What can we give to our children to prepare them against the gathering storm of which we had a warning last autumn, and which threatens to break sooner or later with fearful destructiveness upon us all? Many have come to feel, through their own earnest thought and bitter experience, that unless some new impulses can enter mankind today, some new experiences of soul, a regeneration of the human spirit, leading to a complete re-valuation of life, there can be no hope and no future for human culture."[558]

In 1939, 250 children were being taught in the school. With the dark clouds of approaching war on the horizon, the big question became where to continue the school. They considered the school that had been founded at Wynstones in the meantime, but the building was much too small to house all the students. Through Arthur Sheen's efforts a new possibility was found and the faculty opted for it. During the Second World War, the school was evacuated to Minehead by the Sea in Somerset. From September 1, 1939, the school was to be continued using the building of the County Secondary School—with 130 children who had been divided among several families. However, the county school had already been occupied by another school that had likewise had to evacuate, so the plan did not work out. Luckily, the Baptist Community offered its hall for a while until an old, somewhat dilapidated house belonging to a rich Belgian baroness was fixed up and transformed into a new school building. This turned out to be a wonderful opportunity for all to pull together to make it work, whereby the students—so people remembered—learned more than in the school benches.

William von Kaufmann renovated an old stable and turned it into an assembly hall, the Stable Theater, in which student assemblies and eurythmy performances could be held. The neglected garden invited many an exploration, and the forbidding place became a welcome home for both students and teachers. And after a while, trucks came to bring school furniture, tables, and books from Streatham.

In order to spare his children trouble, William von Kaufmann took on a new name at the start of the war by simply leaving out half of his name so that he was

---

558 Announcement for a conference. Archiv RSHL o. Nr.

called William Mann from then on. His brother took his mother's name and became George Adams.

The school remained in Minehead by the Sea for seven years. By 1945 five children's homes had come into being to house children whose parents were unable to move to Minehead. That way Michael Hall became a boarding school.

It had been decided back in 1942 to not return to Streatham after the war but to look for a place with more potential for development. After a few failed attempts to find a place after the war, the school acquired Kidbrooke Park with the grounds around it for 40,000£, and the school moved to Forest Row in Sussex, where it still resides today. Depending on how one looks at the Steiner School in Kings Langley, either it or Michael Hall is the longest continuously operating Waldorf school to date. (Kings Langley officially closed March 29, 2019.)

1926: The Waldorf School in Hannover

Mathilde Hoyer Introduces Waldorf Teaching

MATHILDE HOYER (1890–1958)[559] started her career as a state school teacher and was employed by the City of Hannover. She was working in the *Bürgerschule* [city school] on Friesenstrasse 26, when she was introduced to the work of Rudolf Steiner and Waldorf education. She was so enthusiastic about the new form of education that she absolutely wanted to practice it herself. When she started with a new first grade at Easter 1926, she did everything she could to win the trust of the parents of her incoming first graders and of the local school inspector, Senator Gustav Porger. After she had had many conversations with the parents and had worked intensively with them, Senator Porger gave his permission, because he knew her well from her work up to that point and had faith in her. With official consent, Mathilde Hoyer started to work on the basis of Waldorf pedagogy, which implied coeducation. It was only natural that she did not want the Waldorf impulse to remain limited to her own class, so she looked for a colleague who was equally motivated, and succeeded in finding one for the next first grade.

At Easter 1927, Karl Rittersbacher (1900–1991) came as the new teacher and taught in the Kirchwender Strasse. Having successfully passed the second-level teacher exam in Tübingen and Jena, he was doing further studies in pedagogy and psychology, but left in order to be able to support the work in the new school in Hannover.[560] The school had grown to 83 students by then. A high point in the young

559 Bruno Sandkühler: http://biographien.kulturimpuls.org/detail.php?&id=1171 (site visited October 28, 2016).
560 Hans Georg Krauch: Karl Rittersbacher. http://biographien.kulturimpuls.org/detail.php?&id=573 (site visited October 28, 2016).

school's development was a Waldorf School Day at the end of January 1927, featuring two lectures by Caroline von Heydebrand, an exhibit of work done by pupils of the Stuttgart school, and presentations by the children of the Hannover school. The authorities in Hannover were amazed how strong people's interest in the new pedagogy was.[561]

Mathilde Hoyer, founding teacher at the Hannover Waldorf School

The third class teacher who joined them was Dr. Wolfgang Schuchhardt (1903–1993), who had studied German literature and art history. He came at Easter 1928 and stayed for a few years at the small school.[562] After he had been on the job only a few weeks, his class of 42 students was visited by Eugen Kolisko, the school doctor from the Stuttgart school, who strongly supported the young teacher in his efforts to get to know the children on a deeper level. "Thus these visits by Dr. Kolisko became high points for us teachers, because they enabled us to study the finer points of human development; we were impressed above all by his warmhearted enthusiasm for Steiner's contribution to a deeper understanding of the human being, which fired us again and again."[563]

In the meantime, the grades had found a home on the top floor of the *Künstlerhaus* [artist's house] of the city of Hannover, located on the Sophienstrasse. After a temporary withdrawal of the permit to practice Waldorf education,[564] the parents' faith in Mathilde Hoyer's method had grown so strong that they founded an association and worked to build up independently supported education.

By Easter 1927, this *Vereinigung zur Einführung der Waldorfschulpädagogik in Hannover* [Association to Support the Introduction of Waldorf Education in Hannover] had managed to convince the Prussian ministry of culture that they should approve an independently led school.[565]

Dr. Günther Beindorff (1890–1952), a member of the family who owned the Pelikan pen works in Hannover, was chosen as president. When the number of applicants necessitated instituting parallel classes, Günther Beindorff helped the school obtain a building on the Kaiserallee, not far from the Hindenburgstrasse. When they outgrew this building, the association was able to acquire the Garven Villa property on the Jägerstrasse. As demand grew, several new class teachers came to the school as well.

561 Karl Rittersbacher: Von den Anfängen. EK 9, 1977, p. 439.
562 http://biographien.kulturimpuls.org/detail.php?&id=650 (site visited October 28, 2016).
563 Wolfgang Schuchhardt: Die ersten Jahre. EK 9, 1977, p. 440.
564 Document dated 4/17/1926. Archiv LS 3.4.005.
565 Wenzel M. Götte: *Erfahrungen mit Schulautonomie*. 2006, p. 283, references a letter dated September 5, 1927. Archiv LS 3.4.033.

Werner Lamerdin with high school students of the Waldorf School Hannover in the 1930s

Maria Ilse (1901–1981) joined the school early in 1929 and remained until it had to close; then after 1945 she taught again until about 1965. One of the most influential pedagogical personalities of the Waldorf School in Hannover was Robert Zimmer (1896–1973), who also began to teach in 1929, taking a first grade. He is still known in the German Waldorf school movement to this day because of the collection of report verses he wrote, which were highly poetic and always profound. Students and colleagues venerated him, and he was depicted as "someone who radiated goodness, was attentive to everybody's needs, and had the devotion of a Franciscan monk."[566] Robert Zimmer was at the school for roughly the same time as Maria Ilse.

Other teachers who joined the faculty were: Heinz Lange, Dr. Hildegard Staedtke (later Gerbert), Werner Lamerdin, Karl August Faust, Gerhard Ott, René Maikowski (called *die Flamme* [The Flame] by the students), and Margarete Bartels. Karl Gerbert taught music. Hilde Jessel (later Sommer) took on eurythmy and was succeeded by Gretel Lamerdin. Bertha Bilfinger (later von Kries) taught handwork and Ludwig Gräbner[567] crafts. When the school in Budapest closed, Gretel and Werner Lamerdin followed the call to come to Hannover and were able to serve the school as experienced educators until it had to close. Dr. Manfred von Kries (1899–1984), MD, was the school physician. He had met anthroposophical medicine early on in life and was

566 Friedhelm Dörmann: http://biographien.kulturimpuls.org/detail.php?&id=804 (site visited October 28, 2016).
567 Maria Ilse: Schulgründung in Hannover. LR 6, 1972, p. 61f.

one of the pioneers who organized the so-called *Jungmedizinerkurs* [Course for Young Doctors] given by Rudolf Steiner. René Maikowski (1900–1992), whose father came from the Russian Empire and whose mother stemmed from a Huguenot family from French Switzerland, had grown up in Berlin; the family spoke French at home. Early in life he had met anthroposophy and the movement for social threefolding. He was a member of the circle that initiated the so-called *Jugendkurs* [Youth Course] given by Rudolf Steiner.[568] After teaching at the Rudolf Steiner school in Essen and serving a short stint in Lisbon, he came to Hannover.

Hildegard Staedtke-Gerbert (1903–1983) took the first grade in 1930 and, as she described later, was educated by the children to become a teacher. "I was facing a completely new task. It filled me with enthusiasm, but I had to learn through many a painful experience. It was the children who taught me to be an educator; I learned to judge from their reactions what had worked in my lessons and what had not.

"We young teachers had not been thoroughly trained in pedagogical methods and were seldom helped by experienced teachers. However, when one studied Rudolf Steiner's courses and allowed the events of the day to reverberate on the way home, one could perceive the voice of pedagogical conscience within, which replaces consultants and inspectors in a school that is based on freedom."[569]

Heinz Lange (1902–1982) joined the faculty in 1930, after he had attended the teacher seminar in Stuttgart and done a practicum with Christoph Boy. He taught Greek and Latin. One of his former students remembers that the girls never forgot to greet him with a polite curtsy when he was on duty supervising the hallways and stairwells.[570] In the years before the school's closure, the regime made the Nazi salute compulsory, and when they greeted him that way he replied by drawing a sign in the air with a silver pencil holder, making an upward S-curve. They knew what he meant. In 1930 Ludwig Gräbner (1901–1989) began to build up craft teaching, starting with furnishing the rooms in which the crafts were taught.[571]

568 Rudolf Steiner: *Rudolf Steiner Speaks to the Younger Generation*. CW 217.
569 Dr. Hildegard Gerbert-Staedtke: An der Freien Waldorfschule Hannover 1930–1937. EK 9, 1977, p. 441. In: Hildegard Gerbert, *"Heb auf, was Gott Dir vor die Türe legt": Erinnerungen*. Arlesheim 1973, p. 21, she looks back on her life and puts it this way: "That way I taught 30 children in my first class, wrestling every day to understand their individuality and trying to shape the lessons in a creative and imaginative way. The children taught me how to become a teacher. At the end of the first year, I had the feeling that I was surrounded by wood shavings. The intellectuality of my university studies had made me quite wooden, and that's what the children had been chipping away at. The process had not always been painless."
570 Gisela Römhild-Baldszun: Heinz Lange (June 9, 1902–September 7, 1982) LR 25, 1982, p. 90f.
571 Theodora Neumann: Ludwig Gräbner. LR 38, 1989, p. 122f. Starting in 1948, Ludwig Gräbner helped build up the Waldorf school in Heidenheim, which Heinz Lange, his former colleague from Hannover, had started.

Painful Learning Experiences with Self-Governance.
Start of Early Childhood Education.

IN 1930, Erich Gabert had to travel to Hannover because the faculty was no longer able to cope with an escalating conflict with one of the teachers. This conflict threatened to tear the school apart, which prompted the Hannover teachers to write a letter to Stuttgart to ask for help.[572] The Stuttgart teachers often had to take on tasks of this nature and understood it to be part of the duty they had been charged with in the letter written by Günther Wachsmuth on March 17, 1925.

In 1931, Klara Hattermann founded a small kindergarten in Hannover. Since the school had its hands full with its own problems, the kindergarten was built up as an independent institution. Klara Hattermann rented a two-room apartment and furnished one of the two rooms as a kindergarten. About 20 children came there every day. She led this home kindergarten until it had to be closed in 1941,[573] after which she—like many colleagues—moved to Dresden to run a small kindergarten that operated in partial hiding.

The Waldorf School in Hannover during the Time of National Socialism

WHEN THE SPECTER of National Socialism had grown to such proportions that it could not be disregarded anymore, the school tried to figure out how threatening the situation was likely to become for them. Günther Beindorff, in his function as head of the School Association, wrote to a friend in the ministry of culture on March 23, 1933, to get his take on the situation.[574] At this early date it was not quite clear how things would turn out, and therefore Counselor Dr. Helmut Bojunga answered him that he did not think the situation was dangerous, and advised Günther Beindorff to wait and see "if they want to get at the school."[575] A few months later the situation had grown decidedly more ominous.

René Maikowski's brother, Hans-Eberhard Maikowski (1908–1933), a graduate of the Stuttgart Waldorf School and an SA [storm trooper] officer, was touted as a Nazi hero and martyr of National Socialism after he was shot by a sniper[576] from his own ranks on January 30, 1933, during a torch parade at the occasion of Hitler's instatement. René Maikowski and others used his reputation many times to get a foot in the door when negotiating with National Socialist officers. René Maikowski

---

572 Wenzel M. Götte: *Erfahrungen mit Schulautonomie.* 2006, p. 287.
573 Susan Howard: "The First Waldorf Kindergarten. The Beginnings of Our Waldorf Early Childhood Movement." *Gateways* 49, 2005, p. 23.
574 Archiv LS 4.2.004.
575 Wenzel M. Götte: *Erfahrungen mit Schulautonomie.* 2006, p. 428; Uwe Werner: *Anthroposophen in der Zeit des Nationalsozialismus (1933–1945).* 1999, p. 99, note 237.
576 René Maikowski: *Schicksalswege auf der Suche nach dem lebendigen Geist.* 1980, p. 141; Heinrich-Wilhelm Wörmann: *Widerstand in Charlottenburg.* Berlin 1991, p. 40f.

himself had studied in the French-speaking part of Switzerland, where his mother was from, and, repelled by the demonic side of German authoritarianism, he had in fact wanted to stay there. After meeting Rudolf Steiner and anthroposophy he changed his mind.[577]

On July 4, 1933, the Waldorf school in Hannover was officially notified by Bernhard Rust, Prussian minister for science, art and education, that the school had three weeks to make changes and adopt the aim of "national political education." Failure to do so would lead to withdrawal of his permission for the continued operation of the school. This constituted the earliest move against a Waldorf school by the regime.[578]

The school, however, didn't reply and let the three-week ultimatum go by. Nothing happened. On September 26, 1933, Mathilde Hoyer and René Maikowski sent a 12-page organizational plan for the Hannover Waldorf School to the authorities.[579] In the last section of this text they outlined their position vis-à-vis National Socialism, a position that later led to allegations against René Maikowski of collusion with National Socialism. Mathilde Hoyer and René Maikowski did indeed express themselves vaguely, mainly in an effort to protect their school. They wrote: "[….] The faculty's position has a basis similar to that of the National Socialist state. The foundational spirit that has guided the Waldorf school ever since its inception has always rejected Marxism—or any of its manifestations. Waldorf education aims to conquer the materialist world conception through a spirit-penetrated approach to the curriculum and a fundamentally religious attitude[…]."[580]

In his recorded memories about the building up of the Waldorf school in Hannover, René Maikowski wrote: "Our task as teachers now was to keep working with the children, to protect them as much as possible from the negative influences of the party and Hitler Youth, and thereby provide a counterbalance. We often went hiking with our students, organized courses during the holidays, went on bicycle trips for several weeks, took the train to Denmark, the Alps, even as far as Austria. Especially Miss Maria Ilse and Gretel and Werner Lamerdin put in a huge amount of work to make this possible."[581] The fact that they opened their doors to the children after hours clearly shows the extent to which they were looking out for the needs of their students.

Early in 1934, René Maikowski wrote numerous letters to leading figures in the National Socialist ranks, such as the *Reichsminister* [Secretary of State], hoping to bolster the position of Waldorf schools in general.

---

577 Biographical note of René Maikowski. Archiv CB.
578 Uwe Werner: *Anthroposophen in der Zeit des Nationalsozialismus (1933–1945)*. 1999, p. 103 including note 256.
579 Document sent by the Hannover Waldorf school (R. Maikowski and M. Hoyer), dated September 26, 1933, to the Supervisory Bureau for Private Schools in Hannover. Archiv LS 4.2.177.
580 Uwe Werner: *Anthroposophen in der Zeit des Nationalsozialismus (1933–1945)*. 1999, p. 106.
581 René Maikowski: *Persönliche Erinnerungen an den Aufbau und die Geschichte der Freien Waldorfschule in Hannover*. Archiv CB.

Among these was an extensive letter of February 15, 1934, which he addressed directly to *Reichskanzler* Adolf Hitler. He started by saying that the Württemberg minister of culture, Christian Mergenthaler, did not want to dissolve the schools because of insufficient results, but because the teachers professed the anthroposophical worldview, "which is supposed to be contrary to the National Socialist spirit." He went on to ask for an evaluation by a newly appointed committee. This would clear up the misunderstanding, because "the life work of Rudolf Steiner, founder of the Waldorf school, sprung from the deepest foundation and innermost core of the German spirit." A little further down he says: "I am of the opinion that the work of these schools, which have been struggling quietly for years to achieve positive results that counterbalance the prevailing materialism of this time, is important for the spiritual rebuilding of Germany, especially today."[582]

At that time, many people who were interested in anthroposophy felt rooted in the stream of central European cultural life personified by Johann Wolfgang Goethe, Friedrich Schiller, and Novalis, a stream they wanted to continue at all cost.[583] They found themselves to be in inner opposition to communist convictions. In line with J.W. Goethe, they understood this cultural Germany not as a national idea but as a universally human lodestar. It remains an open question for me whether the hope that the National Socialists would accommodate the Waldorf schools was based on a naïve underestimation of National Socialism or not. Whether René Maikowski wanted to contribute to a spiritually understood mission of German culture in the sense described above, or whether his argument was a subterfuge that didn't reflect his innermost convictions: these remain open questions for me as well. In any case, the letter was sent on to the office of Rudolf Hess and from there to Minister of Culture Schemm, and nothing came of it. René Maikowski, together with Elisabeth Klein and Christoph Boy, went on to become some of the most active negotiators working on behalf of the German Waldorf school movement, whereby René Maikowski sometimes took a different stance from the teachers in Stuttgart.

It should also be mentioned that the majority of parents and teachers who were critical of the Nazi regime did not think this regime would last long; they simply hoped to get through this time with the least amount of damage. Teachers and parents at the schools worked intensively at fostering warm human relationships and truthful conduct, and avoided empty phraseology. They organized games and craft clubs in the afternoons, teachers went on class excursions and holiday outings in order to save children and youngsters from the party and their organizations, and, as they put it, to

---

582 Appeal written by R. Maikowski to the Reichskanzler [Chancellor of the Reich], dated February 15, 1934. Archiv LS 4.2.248.

583 J.W. Goethe/Friedrich Schiller, in the *Xenien*: "Zur Nation euch zu bilden, ihr hoffet es, Deutsche, vergebens; bildet, ihr könnt es, dafür freier zu Menschen euch aus." [In vain, German people, you hope to build up a nation for yourselves; instead, you are able to build up yourselves and become truly human.]

save them for different, more humanistic values. A close feeling of camaraderie arose among students, teachers, and parents, and the situation also brought about a heartfelt willingness to help one another.

At the same time, government official and school inspector Blume did all he could to try to effect a retraction of the Hannover school's permission to operate. To that end he wrote a letter to Minister Bernhard Rust on December 30, 1935, in which he used the argument that the school's philosophy was too much akin to that of the Anthroposophical Society, which was no longer legal by that time. In addition, Blume cited the results of his evaluation, painting a picture of an educational philosophy that was completely incompatible and unsuccessful.[584] So, as far as the authorities were concerned, the teachers had the wind against them. And, as some people had surmised, further steps to break down the Waldorf schools were soon to follow.

One of the steps that hit hard was Bernhard Rust's edict forbidding Waldorf schools to accept any more incoming students. He sent this to the educational authorities of all German states on March 12, 1936. Thus, the head of the government in Hannover was informed, but the Waldorf school was not. In contrast to their colleagues in Hamburg and Stuttgart, who by then had started closing procedures of their own accord and were not willing to swear the oath of allegiance to Hitler, René Maikowski opted for official recognition as an experimental school.[585]

The four Waldorf schools in Dresden, Hamburg, Hannover, and Kassel all attempted to gain official status as state-supported experimental schools. The German Federation of Waldorf Schools had actually agreed to a common policy, which the schools of Hannover, Dresden, and Hamburg did not stick to. On October 17, 1936, the Waldorf school in Hannover handed in a new request for official recognition,[586] a unilateral act that spoiled the trust relationship within the Waldorf movement. The Stuttgart teachers decided they no longer wanted to be represented by René Maikowski (Hannover) and Elisabeth Klein (Dresden).

In the wake of this new request came more school inspections. Dr. Erna Sturm, school inspector for the Hannover region and manager of NS women's affairs, wrote reports of her findings in a main-lesson book on race, a subject that Waldorf schools were now obliged to introduce. She found no mention of Judaism or the importance of cultivating racial awareness, nor was there any mention of official racial emergency measures. However, she did find a sentence in the main-lesson book that typified the school's philosophy for her: "Physical and psychological characteristics are hereditary, but what is most essentially human, the spirit, is solely our own possession."[587] Her

---

584 BArch Ella 0024-36.

585 Uwe Werner: *Anthroposophen in der Zeit des Nationalsozialismus (1933–1945)*. 1999, p. 208ff, which details the various positions people took with regard to the project of becoming "experimental schools," especially the position taken by the teachers in Stuttgart, who were highly critical.

586 Ibid., p. 210.

587 Bundesarchiv B 1/58 173 in Norbert Deuchert: Zur Geschichte der Waldorfschule 1933–1940. BhB. Autumn 1984, p. 78f.

overall judgment of the Waldorf school in Hannover was this: "The children are educated to become pan-Europeans, or world-republicans, and are prepared for global government."[588] The petition was unsuccessful. The official reply from the side of the Hannover authorities was: "As things now stand, continued existence of the Waldorf school in Hannover can not be counted on."[589]

Midway through 1936, the faculty of the Waldorf school in Hannover decided it was no longer tenable to keep the school going and that their only option was to prepare their students for transitioning to state schools. On July 9, 1936, René Maikowski wrote the following letter to the federal minister for science, education, and national identity building:

"…The Free Waldorf School of Hannover cannot continue to operate next year under the present-day circumstances while at the same time remaining faithful to the pedagogical demands of its curriculum. We find ourselves faced with the necessity to prepare our students for a transition to state institutions, during which time we have to introduce work principles that run counter to the demands of healthy education in the sense of Rudolf Steiner's pedagogy. The faculty of the Free Waldorf School of Hannover sees it as its duty not to burden the name and work of Rudolf Steiner with the compromises that would be required of us. The school has therefore decided, as of today, to drop the name Free Waldorf School, since the name holds an implicit obligation we can no longer honor. Instead, we will continue our work under the name Transitional Course of the Former Waldorf School of Hannover until its closure.

588 Bundesarchiv B 1/58 169 in Norbert Deuchert: Zur Geschichte der Waldorfschule 1933–1940. BhB Herbst 1984, p. 78f.
589 Uwe Werner: *Anthroposophen in der Zeit des Nationalsozialismus (1933–1945)*. 1999, p. 210 with reference to Archiv LS 4.3.283.

In conclusion, we state that the sole responsibility for the destruction of this German cultural treasure lies with the powers in office."[590]

This plan was put into practice and the remaining students were prepared for their transition to state schools. After all this, René Maikowski undertook yet another futile attempt to acquire a permit as an experimental school in Hannover, early in 1939. The attempt failed. When war broke out in autumn 1939, the school building was appropriated in the very first weeks, and the school's inventory was sold. The remaining four grades were split into two groups and were housed in the music school in the Lavesstrasse. This was facilitated by Ms. von Marcard and the lessons were continued by Mathilde Hoyer and Maria Ilse until Easter 1940.[591]

The School Is Built up Again after World War II

WHEN PEOPLE RETURNED to the destroyed city at the end of the war, Hans Reipert (1895–1981)[592] played a pivotal role in getting the school back on its feet. An uncompromising opponent of the Nazi regime, he had worked in Budapest between 1931 and 1933 and had then returned to his profession as an engineer and been employed as such up to the time he was conscripted. After 1945, Hans Reipert did everything in his power to get permission from the British occupational forces to reopen the school. René Maikowski was the one who negotiated with the school authorities and found himself dealing with the same head of school who had accepted the students into his school after the Waldorf school's closure before the war. His experiences with the Waldorf students had been so positive that he gave his assent right away.[593]

The group in charge of resurrecting the school succeeded in obtaining a former youth hostel situated on a lake called Maschsee. One by one, parents, teachers, and students found their way to the heavily damaged building and furnished it as well as they could.

The school reopened on October 2, 1945, and was thus the first school in Lower Saxony to do so. They began with eight grades. Heinrich Wollborn, who had taught in Essen and Breslau before the war, took the first grade. Some of the students lived in the building until 1948. At that point the boarding school moved out to Benefeld, and a new school was born there.

590 BArch Ella 2608-37/179; Uwe Werner: *Anthroposophen in der Zeit des Nationalsozialismus (1933–1945)*. 1999, p. 213 and note 79.
591 Friedrich Grasdorf was one of the students who attended this class until Easter 1940; he received his fifth grade report on March 20, 1940. Archiv CB.
592 Rüdiger Voigt: Hans Reipert (March 27, 1895–August 14, 1981). LR 24, 1982, p. 75.
593 René Maikowski: *Auf der Suche nach dem lebendigen Geist*. 1980, p. 160.

1926: The Rudolf Steiner School in Basel

THE PEDAGOGICAL IMPULSE connected with the founding of the Stuttgart Waldorf School was taken up in the Basel region early on. At the invitation of the head of the education department in Basel, Dr. Fritz Hauser (1884–1941), Rudolf Steiner held a lecture entitled "Geisteswissenschaft und Pädagogik" [Spiritual Science and Pedagogy] on November 27, 1919.[594] This lecture was received very well, whereupon about 70 interested members of the audience asked for a full pedagogical course, which Rudolf Steiner held for teachers in Basel from March 20 until May 11, 1924, including 14 lectures in all. Both this course and the ensuing lecture series Rudolf Steiner gave December 23–January 7, 1922, at the Goetheanum in Dornach, mainly for teachers in Switzerland,[595] kindled the impulse in a number of teachers to build up such a school in Basel as well. By way of preparation, a two-pronged approach was planned: To gather a number of teachers for whom Rudolf Steiner would then give a specific course, and to found a Swiss Association for Independent Education. An announcement went out on February 10, 1922,[596] inviting people to become members of this new association and making a first public announcement of the intention to establish a free educational institution.

In 1923, the *Goetheanum-Schulverein für Erziehungs- und Unterrichtsfragen auf Grund Echter Menschenerkenntnis* [Goetheanum School Association for Questions of Education Based on True Knowledge of the Human Being] was founded, and Rudolf Steiner became chair in June 1924. Other members were: Albert Steffen (1884–1963), who was a poet and head of the General Anthroposophical Society; Ernst Blümel (1884–1952), a mathematician who worked at the Friedwart School; Willy Storrer (1895–1930), a journalist; Arnold Ith (1890–1979), a transportation director in Zürich; Willy Stokar (1893–1953), a journalist in Schaffhausen; and Rudolf Geering-Christ (1871–1958), a publisher.

On November 15, 1923, the chair of the education department, State Councillor Dr. Fritz Hauser, wrote to the executive council of the School Association, at Bäumleingasse 11 in Basel, that the local government of the canton of Basel-Stadt had given initial permission for the founding of an independent private school on

---

594 Rudolf Steiner: *The Spirit of the Waldorf School*. CW 297, 1998, p. 157ff.

595 Rudolf Steiner gave three cycles of educational lectures for Swiss teachers in Basel and Dornach. The first cycle, April 20–May 11, 1920, was given at the invitation of the education department of Basel-Stadt (CW 301); the second one was the Christmas course for teachers, December 23, 1921–January 7, 1922 (CW 303); and a third course was held at Easter 1923, lecture cycles *Die pädagogische Praxis vom Gesichtspunkt geisteswissenschaftlicher Menschenerkenntnis* [The Child's Changing Consciousness as the Basis of Pedagogical Practice] (CW 306). In addition, Emma Ramser organized a lecture cycle in Bern at Easter 1924, published as *Anthroposophische Pädagogik und ihre Voraussetzungen* [The Roots of Education] (CW 309). Of course Rudolf Steiner also gave other pedagogical lectures in Switzerland, in Zürich, Olten, Aarau.

596 Appeal of February 10, 1922, in Archiv LS 3.11.03.6.

November 13, 1923, pending more detailed information regarding the location and faculty.[597] As early as December 1923, Albert Steffen, Friedrich Widmer (1889–1966), and Ernst Blümel wrote a letter to the members on behalf of the above-mentioned School Association. In that letter, they asked members to pledge regular donations to the coming school in Basel (in addition to their contribution to the Stuttgart school) and to enroll their children. On April 28, 1924, Rudolf Steiner, together with Albert Steffen, Ernst Blümel, and Friedrich Widmer, made a proposal to the director of the education department of Basel that met with approval. State Councillor Dr. Hauser had a positive view of the plans and invited Rudolf Steiner to give a talk about education to the entire state council; he approved a school that had a great deal of freedom to shape its own curriculum and to appoint teachers of its own choosing. Both of these freedoms have remained in place for the entire 20th century. The Basel Waldorf School started on April 26, 1926, with 30 children in three grades, in a building at Lindenhofstrasse 9. The first teachers were Emma Ramser and Friedrich and Maria Widmer. Emma Ramser (1885–1964) had grown up on a farm in Bern. She had to work hard to convince her parents to let her study at the teacher seminar in the canton of Bern. She did some teaching in England and after returning to Basel she met Rudolf Steiner and immediately became part of the initiative to found the school. In June 1925, she turned to E. A. Karl Stockmeyer to ask if she could do a practicum at the Stuttgart Waldorf School in order to prepare for her future task as a teacher in Basel. Herbert Hahn welcomed her warmly to Stuttgart.

In her capacity as the first founding teacher, she had also been asked to draw up a budget, which she faithfully sent to Stuttgart.[598] She felt obliged to state up front that the means at her disposal would not even begin to cover the costs. She wrote, "You will no doubt see from the figures that the budget looks far from promising. In spite of that, I'm determined to start next spring. [...] When there is a shortfall for the class teachers, we may expect that our nearest relatives will at least provide us with the bare minimum to keep us afloat. [...]"[599] Armed with this resolve and the willingness to sacrifice, which she so firmly stresses in this letter, she resolutely headed for the agreed-upon founding date in spite of warnings from Stuttgart.

Next to teaching, she was in charge of the school's finances until her dying day. Many a colleague, looking back on her life, considered the Basel Rudolf Steiner school her life's work. "She was a significant human being [...] When you asked her for advice, you could experience the all-encompassing clarity and objectivity of her thinking, her kind willingness to help, coupled with a quiet, noble capacity to hold back, which never allowed her to put personal matters in the foreground."[600]

597 Facsimile of this letter in: Robert Thomas, Heinz Zimmermann: *Rudolf Steiner Schulen in der Schweiz.* 2007, p. 109.
598 Archiv LS 3.8.006 and 3.8.007.
599 Emma Ramser in a letter to Herbert Hahn, dated September 15, 1925. Archiv LS 3.8.009.
600 Emma Ramser †Msch 4/5, 1965, p. 151.

Friedrich Widmer

Friedrich Widmer (1889–1966) studied arts and crafts in Basel and continued his studies at the art academy in Munich at the recommendation of his friend Karl Ballmer. He only discovered his bent for education when he was substituting as a teacher during World War I. He prepared the founding of the school in Basel and left his stamp on the school up to his death. Rudolf Grosse described him as follows: "He was a born individual who didn't do anything that didn't really spring from his own initiative. Therefore people around him had to adapt to him more than the other way around, which he was less inclined to."[601]

Marie Herzog (1891–1956) met Friedrich Widmer when she was a class teacher working at the regional school in Zofingen, where he had been teaching drawing since 1918. They married and, together with Emma Ramser, became pioneering teachers of the new Rudolf Steiner school in Basel.[602] Friedrich Widmer took the first grade, but he became ill in the course of the school year and was not able to teach the class for a few months. Emma Ramser found the solution to this problem when she met Rudolf Grosse (1905–1994) at the Goetheanum. She immediately asked him if he could take the class until July. He started teaching the next day. Having taken the initiative to apply to become a student at the Waldorf School in Stuttgart, where he was a student for a few years, he brought in some experience.

In being tasked by Rudolf Steiner to take care of Richard Grob (1912–1992),[603] whom he assisted in the Friedwart School, he received—as he puts it[604]—his own unconventional and short teacher training. So, in 1926 he started teaching at the school in Basel. He was 21 years old at the time. When Friedrich Widmer had recovered and continued the class himself, Rudolf Grosse was offered a position to teach English and gymnastics. He accepted, but did not have enough teaching periods to make ends meet. Therefore he had to earn a living for himself and his family in another way and found a task in curative education. Together with his wife, Lucia (1900–1981), he took care of ten boys who were diagnosed with mental and physical handicaps or developmental challenges. In 1928 he took a class at the Rudolf Steiner

601 Rudolf Grosse: *Erlebte Pädagogik*. Fourth edition 1998, p. 406.
602 Christoph Widmer: http://biographien.kulturimpuls.org/detail.php?&id=1449 (site visited October 28, 2016)
603 Richard Grob later studied natural sciences, became a high school teacher living in Bern, where he first became a town council member and later a member of the regional council of the canton of Bern. See Jakob Streit, Christiane Haid: http://biographien.kulturimpuls.org/detail.php?&id=243. His daughter Stephanie moved to Israel, married Gilad Allon, and built up the first Waldorf kindergarten in Israel and later the early childhood training center. His grandson, Eliah Allon, is a teacher at the Zomer Waldorf school in Ramat Gan, Israel, and a member of the Israeli Waldorf Forum.
604 Rudolf Grosse: *Erlebte Pädagogik*. Fourth edition 1998, p. 138f.

school in Basel and taught there until he was called to serve on the Executive Council of the General Anthroposophical Society in 1956. Willi Aeppli (1894–1972), a regional school teacher,[605] took the new first grade in 1927 and taught them all the way until eighth grade. He was valued by colleagues and students because of the selfless way he was able to listen and empathize. Besides, he had earned a lasting reputation as editor of the works of Ignaz P.V. Troxler.

Emma Ramser

In 1929 Rosa Raetz, later Ringel (1898–1994), joined the school. She had solid professional experience when she arrived and took five classes through from grades one through eight(!). She collaborated closely with founder teacher, Emma Ramser, as well as with her friend and upper school teacher, Dr. Clara Bosshardt (1894–1967), and also with Willi Aeppli. Clara Bosshardt taught for 35 years at the Basel school. In 1931, Gerda Langen (1903–1973)[606] started a kindergarten at the building site of the Goetheanum, where she was discovered working with the little children by teachers from Basel. They asked her to switch her pedagogical activities to the Basel school in 1933. She took a class from grades one through eight four times. So the school was lucky to have many experienced teachers who stayed with the school. Other teachers were Werner Witzemann (1895–1951), historian and linguist, and Ella Kocherhanns (1902–1975), eurythmist. Handwork was taught by Marie Raetz (1896–1979), the sister of Rosa Raetz.

Just like the school in Zürich and many others, the Basel school resisted their Stuttgart colleagues, and E.A. Karl Stockmeyer had to bear the brunt of it. It all started with an article he wrote in which he politely and clearly complained that more and more financial contributions went to other, younger Waldorf schools and no longer to Stuttgart. This started a debate around questions such as: Should the Stuttgart Waldorf School be viewed as a master school and be financed accordingly, or should it be seen as one-of-a-kind and not a model school, just like any other Waldorf school? Out of respect for the work of the Stuttgart colleagues, it was argued, it could happen that schools would also forfeit the freedom to build up their own unique identity on the basis of anthroposophical pedagogy.[607]

At the beginning of the new school year in April 1931, the school had eight grades with 123 children and moved into its own school building, a stately villa situated at Engegasse 9.[608] In 1933, the Basel school formed a ninth grade for the first time, which would have a special feature: People from various walks of life were invited to

605 Erhard Fucke: http://biographien.kulturimpuls.org/detail.php?&id=17 (site visited on October 23, 2016).
606 Gerda Langen: http://biographien.kulturimpuls.org/detail.php?&id=807 (site visited October 28, 2016).
607 Werner Witzemann, on behalf of the Basel faculty in a letter of January 21, 1928, to E.A. Karl
       Stockmeyer. Archiv LS 3.8.015.
608 As Rudolf Grosse wrote May 7, 1931. Archiv LS 3.8.038.

Pupils and teachers in front of and in the school building at Engelgasse 9, used from 1931 to 1967 for the Rudolf Steiner school in Basel

give courses about their work experience in order to give the students a firsthand look at the various professions out there in the world. Even though this was quite a different concept from the continuing education school model Stuttgart was pursuing, it was also the first attempt within the development of the Waldorf movement to give career orientation to the students. Friedrich Häusler (1890–1976), an engineer, joined the faculty for a short time as a new colleague after he had worked in Venice. In 1936 the school already counted 180 students and the number of applicants grew so strongly that not all children could be accepted due to lack of space.[609]

In 1943, a neighboring property could be purchased to give the school the necessary room to expand. The announcement came out with the following remark: "We can be grateful to destiny that we are allowed to work freely and can build up the school while being surrounded by the events of the war."[610] During the war years the teachers frequently gave public pedagogical lectures.

The titles of these lectures, given by Rudolf Grosse, Willi Aeppli, or Hans Erhard Lauer (1899–1779), do not reveal any influence of the events of the time. They were kept general and introductory.[611] On Saturday, April 22, 1944, a festival at the occasion of the opening of the new school building was held. Albert Steffen gave a speech, students performed, and former students gave a concert.[612] It is not known to me whether there was talk during this festival about the collapse of the civilized world around neutral Switzerland.

In 1947, the 21-year existence of the school was celebrated with a large school celebration held in the casino in Gundelding. There were eurythmy performances,

609 Heinz Zimmermann: Rudolf Steiner Schule Basel. In: *50 Jahre Pädagogik Rudolf Steiners.* Anniversary Issue 1969, p. 38.
610 N 14 April 4, 1943. p. 56.
611 Rudolf Steiner Schule Basel. N 5, January 30, 1944, p. 20; N 4, 28. January 1945, p. 16.
612 N 17 of April 23, 1944, p. 68.

orchestra contributions and recitations from the various grades. The next evening the official birthday celebration took place in the Hans Huber auditorium. Willi Aeppli welcomed those present and expressed thanks on behalf of the faculty to those who had made the founding possible. Rudolf Grosse spoke about Waldorf education, and there were artistic contributions by stage artists from the nearby Goetheanum. The *Nationale Zeitung* [national newspaper] called it a "solid festival."[613]

Hans Erhard Lauer taught German and history in the high school of the Basel school from 1939 until 1952, and he also led the high school choir. Even though he originally came from Germany, he had attended the humanistic grammar school in Basel and had met Rudolf Steiner when he was 17 years old. He worked in Vienna for a long time, among other things helping to prepare the West–East Congress in 1922. After the National Socialists occupied Austria, he returned to Switzerland.

The Rudolf Steiner school in Basel has functioned without interruption until this very day, which makes it the longest continuously operating Waldorf school in central Europe.

1926: Waldorf Education in Lisbon

ONE DAY Dr. Ita Wegman asked René Maikowski, who had just landed in Essen, whether he was interested in helping to found a Waldorf initiative in Lisbon. This request was unexpected, of course, but he took it seriously. After thorough consideration, he said yes to this Portuguese excursion and asked the two women who led the school in Essen to give him a two-year leave of absence. A deciding factor for him was certainly that he wanted to do Alexandre Leroi (1906–1968) and his mother a favor. Alexandre had recently completed his final exam at the Stuttgart Waldorf School[614] in spring 1926, and he and his mother harbored a wish to build up a Waldorf school in Portugal which they had discussed with Walter Johannes Stein.

There were not too many teachers to choose from, sad to say, and there definitely had to be somebody who could speak, if not Portuguese, then at least French. Walter Johannes Stein involved his friend René Maikowski, whose mother tongue was French, after all. The two men, by the way, were both told by Rudolf Steiner that they should research the Crusades, the Knights Templar, and related themes, so because of that they knew each other well. The Executive Council of the General Anthroposophical Society was asked for permission, and the council confirmed that Maikowski was

613 Das Wiegenfest der Rudolf Steiner Schule. N 11, 16. March 1947, p. 42.
614 Alexandre Leroi attended the Stuttgart Waldorf School from Easter 1923 onward, by his own choice. Before that he was at the Odenwaldschule and the Bergschule in Hochwaldhausen, Hessen, where he shared a room with Klaus Mann. See: Konrad Sandkühler: Alexander Leroi † EK 7/8, 1968, p. 277ff.; Peter Dudek: *"Wir wollen Krieger sein im Heere des Lichts"–Reformpädagogische Landerziehungsheime im hessischen Hochwaldhausen 1912–1927.* 2013, p. 209.

authorized to speak about anthroposophy in Portugal and to start a pedagogical movement there. René Maikowski was also very much pleased about the salary they offered. On April 1, 1926, he and his wife and their eight-month-old son boarded a ship in Hamburg and sailed along the Atlantic coast for a week until they reached Lisbon, accompanied by Alexandre Leroi.

The latter introduced the young Maikowski family to Lisbon society and through him they made the acquaintance of Dr. Carlos Alfredo dos Santos (1889–1965), a physician who was very enthusiastic about anthroposophy and Waldorf education and organized an official reception hosted by the dean of the medical faculty.

Work began with 18 children[615] in two grades, in a little house on the property of relatives of the Lerois, probably of the renowned and well-connected families Abecassis and Bensaude. At that time, the rich upper class of Lisbon had a definite interest in pedagogical innovations such as the one that was being tried out with this small group of children. René Maikowski observed that the children were intellectually very gifted and were able to take in content quickly, but that it was difficult for them to gain a certain depth.

The lifestyle of these families did not make matters any easier. To give an example: Three children couldn't be enrolled because they could not get to school by nine. The reason? Their hot chocolate was not brought to their rooms and served to them until 9:30 and there were only three chauffeurs available for the seven cars that were needed. The archbishop took a closer look at what was happening and was of the opinion that it was best to ignore the school for as long as it was so small. After one year the attempt in Lisbon was abandoned because no Portuguese people could be found who wanted to commit to this work. René Maikowski returned from Lisbon in the summer of 1927.[616]

1926: The Waldorf School on the Little Schwabenberg, Budapest

THE DRIVING FORCE behind the founding of the Waldorf school on the little Schwabenberg in Budapest was Maria von Nagy (1894–1982), PhD.[617] Her maiden name was Maria Göllner. After completing her studies in history, geography, and philosophy, she married Emil von Nagy (1871–1956), a progressive lawyer who later became minister of justice of Hungary. Twice a widower, he was the father of seven children. During World War I he acquired a woodland lot in a former quarry in the

---

615 The sixth regular members meeting of the Association for Independent Schools in Stuttgart. MVfS Nr. 3, 1926/27, p. 13.

616 René Maikowski: *Schicksalswege auf der Suche nach dem lebendigen Geist.* 1980, p. 123ff.; Norbert Deuchert: Die Anfänge einer internationalen Schulbewegung. BhB Advent 1985, p. 79.

617 Maria Göllner received her doctorate in 1918 with the subject: "The geographic foundations of ancient intellectual culture."

Buda Mountains, Kissvábhegy, high above the city, where he had a 14-room villa built with a landscaped park around it. The first time Maria von Nagy heard about anthroposophy and Waldorf education was in March 1921, when she visited an old friend in Dresden. On their way to the opera, the two women had probably started discussing the latest edition of *Das Reich*, a philosophical–anthroposophical weekly, which contained an article discussing all the pros and cons of anthroposophy and Rudolf Steiner. Their conversation could clearly be heard by all around them, and once inside the opera house, they were overheard by somebody sitting next to them who knew more about the subject. His name was Hans Reichert, and apart from liberally sharing his insights, he went a step further and met them again later, bringing Rudolf Steiner's *Philosophy of Freedom* along. After that first contact in Budapest, Hans Reichert (†1957) sent many more books to Maria von Nagy.

Maria von Nagy

She had been reading philosophy since she was a child and had occupied herself with the question of reincarnation, which prepared the ground for Steiner's approach, which became more and more meaningful to her as the years went by. In 1924, she met Rudolf Steiner personally and heard a whole series of his last lectures in Dornach. In her conversations with him, she proposed translating his works into Hungarian. When the question came up who could edit her translations, Rudolf Steiner thought he could do that himself, because he had learned Hungarian as a child.[618]

These meetings gave her the idea that she could open a German private school with a boarding school facility in the villa of her husband, since the children had grown up and moved out in the meantime. She acquired the necessary permits for the venture from Kuno von Klebelsberg (1875–1932), minister for religious affairs and education, who was a friend of hers and was open to pedagogical reform ideas.

One large room of the villa was refurnished as a classroom, another was turned into a dormitory. There is no record of what Emil von Nagy thought about her actions. In any case, the little educational institution opened on September 8, 1925, with a group of 20 14-year-old girls, mainly from the German-speaking upper class. A few weeks later, Maria von Nagy turned to the Executive Council of the General Anthroposophical Society and the board of the Stuttgart Waldorf School Association with a somewhat vehement letter,[619] requesting that the association take over her institute at short notice (by January 15), and that they should send a pedagogical leader because she lacked the necessary strength and health for this venture. A third

618 István Vámosi Nagy: *A kissvábhegyi Waldorf-iskola 1926–1933*. Manuscript printed in 1989. (Archiv Maria Scheily).
619 Proposal by Maria von Nagy. Archiv LS 3.10.05.

Street scene in Budapest, 1937

of the proceeds could be paid to the institution, a third to the Stuttgart Waldorf School Association, and a third to herself for her efforts to pave the way. On November 21, 1925, she wrote to her friend Marta von Stefanovic[620] that she definitely should convince E.A. Karl Stockmeyer, who was planning lectures in Vienna, to travel on from there to Budapest in order to discuss the next steps. At that point, E.A. Karl Stockmeyer did not have a clue about the tasks she had in mind for him, let alone about the next steps the association was asked to shoulder in taking on her school. The letter never reached E.A. Karl Stockmeyer and therefore the visit did not take place.

In the meantime, Maria von Nagy sent her own six-year-old son, István von Nagy (1919–1992), to the Stuttgart Waldorf School, where he joined the class of Rudolf Treichler. She must have changed her mind by then, for she started looking for a teacher herself. She found a woman from Vienna, Hannah Steiner (1895–1984), whose dearest wish was to teach in a Waldorf school. Interestingly enough, E.A. Karl Stockmeyer wrote a letter to Maria von Nagy in May 1926,[621] telling her that the faculty of the Stuttgart school recommended Hannah Steiner as a future teacher.

Hannah Steiner gave up her position as director of the Jewish community college in Vienna[622] in order to become a Waldorf teacher, and moved to Budapest. When she came on the scene, plans changed. From the autumn of 1926 onward, the Waldorf school was to be built up next to the boarding school, starting with grades one and two, to be led by Hannah Steiner. With that in place, von Nagy's son István was able to return to Budapest. Maria von Nagy obtained permission to open a Waldorf school in Budapest from her friend, Albert Steffen. Moreover, she received strong support from the only other anthroposophist in Budapest, Dr. Gustav Löllbach (†1952), and she also secured official permission from the authorities.

The school started on September 15, 1926, with 20 students in over three grades. Lessons were held in German, and the other languages taught were Hungarian, French, and English.[623] The authorities limited themselves to checking on the Hungarian classes in school inspections, which gave the three starting teachers considerable latitude. The first three teachers were Hannah Steiner, Gretel Poch (eurythmy) and Werner Lamerdin. Werner Lamerdin (1901–1943) came from a Huguenot family and had first worked at the Stuttgart Waldorf School. He brought along his sister,

620 Letter written by Maria von Nagy, November 21, 1925. Archiv LS 3.10.02.
621 E.A. Karl Stockmeyer, letter dated May 7, 1926, to Dr. Maria von Nagy. Archiv LS 3.10.11.
622 According to a letter sent by Hannah Krämer-Steiner on April 14, 1969, to René Maikowski. Archiv CB.
623 Reports by Hannah Steiner of April 5, 1927. Archiv LS 3.10.14.

who looked after the children in the boarding school for the time being. Gretel Poch (1904–1991) had spent part of her childhood in Stuttgart, where her father worked in the packing firm of José del Monte. Her father had been introduced to anthroposophy by del Monte, and had become a member of the Anthroposophical Society back in 1910. His three daughters had been introduced to Rudolf Steiner at the time, but later they still had ample opportunity to hear Rudolf Steiner and to meet him. Gretel Poch studied eurythmy, and took part in the tone eurythmy course given in Dornach in 1924, even though she had not yet reached the required age of 21.

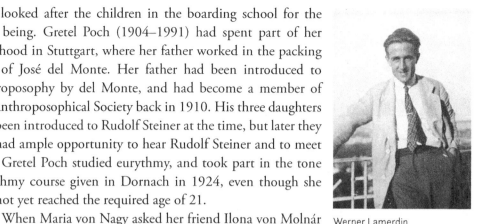

Werner Lamerdin

When Maria von Nagy asked her friend Ilona von Molnár (1891–1945), later Ilona von Baltz, to help her in her search for a eurythmist, she suggested Gretel Poch, who was happy to take up the challenge. When Gretel Poch first arrived, Hannah Steiner was not at all impressed by this new colleague and would have liked to send her back straight away because she was talking over the heads of the girls. Maria von Nagy, however, wanted to give her some time to adjust—and so she stayed. She learned from her future husband, Werner Lamerdin, how to approach the children, and thus grew into the profession. She felt very good up there on the little Schwabenberg, with a view of the Danube and Margaret Island, and, as she recounted later, loved her work.[624]

Maria von Nagy maintained good contacts with the anthroposophists in Dornach and Stuttgart. She kept in close touch and kept inviting them over to Hungary. After her father's death, he left her a considerable fortune, which allowed her to build a second building on the property, which was to become the actual school building. Herbert Hahn came to the foundation stone ceremony for the new building in 1927. A school association was founded on September 8, 1927, and on November 13, 1929, Albert Steffen, who was staying in Budapest at the invitation of the P.E.N. Club, came for the opening of the school building on the other side of the park. In addition to the teachers mentioned, Dr. Carl Brestowsky (1896–1974), who had been trained in Stuttgart, took the next first grade in 1927.

Carl Brestowsky[625] came originally from Siebenbürgen, studied at the Technical High School in Budapest, and went on to study German, history of culture, and Sanskrit in Vienna and Tübingen in the early 1920s. Meanwhile, he prepared for being a Waldorf teacher by traveling from Tübingen to Stuttgart, cycling through the nature preserve of Schönbuch in order to hear lectures by Rudolf Steiner whenever he could. In 1924, Steiner gave him permission to acquire the as yet unpublished education lectures of August 1919, which at the time was equal to being accepted into

624 Gretel Lamerdin Tells about Her Life. LR 29, 1984, p. 61f.
625 Edith Brestowsky: Lebensdaten von Dr. Carl Brestowsky. LR 10, 1974, p. 66ff.

The Waldorf School on the Little Schwabenberg

the community of Waldorf teachers. He did a practicum at the Waldorf School in Stuttgart from September 1926–July 1927, which effectively concluded his Waldorf teacher training. That very summer he moved to Budapest and took a class until June 1931.[626] The next class teacher for the first grade of 1928 was Ms. Weiss-Zoller from Zürich, but she was let go a year later.

Another teacher who came in September 1928 was Helene Hinderer (1900–1998), who had been trained in speech formation in Dornach. She soon began to give her own recitation evenings in the city and places further east. She stayed in Hungary until 1933 and then moved to Wuppertal via Dornach. Living in Hungary had become too difficult for her.[627] The year thereafter, in September 1929, Tibor Michnik came to the school, the first Hungarian Waldorf teacher to be trained in Stuttgart. He was living with the question of how to adapt the curriculum indications to Hungarian cultural circumstances and considered ways to do main lessons in the native tongue of the children. To help with that question, the Stuttgart faculty was asked for advice.[628] However, before the Stuttgart mentors had even had a chance to reply, the conflict among the members of the faculty had become untenable, and Tibor Michnik left after a short, disappointing period of time.[629] For the school year 1929/30 the faculty

626 Michael Schad: Student Memories of a Highly Respected Teacher. LR 11, 1975, p. 92f.; after the war, Dr. Carl Brestowsky became one of the most influential people in the founding and building up of the Waldorf School in Wuppertal between 1946 and 1962.
627 Eva Heep: Helene Hinderer (August 31, 1920–February 24, 1998) LR 63, 1998, p. 89f.
628 Letter of March 23, 1929, written by Werner Lamerdin. Archiv LS 3.10.32.
629 Letter of October 29, 1929, written by Tibor Michnik to Dr. Herbert Hahn. Archiv LS 3.10.35; Norbert Deuchert: Die Anfänge einer internationalen Schulbewegung. BhB Advent 1985, p. 80.

House of the Nagy famiy on the Little Schwabenberg in Budapest

consisted of Erika Meyer (grade 1), Minna Schuster from Siebenbürgen (grade 2), Dr. Carl Brestowsky (grade 3), Werner Lamerdin (grade 4), Erzsebet Hock from Budapest (grade 5), Sári Hadnagy from Budapest (grade 6), Klara Binét, János Potondy, Adél Homola, Gretel Poch (eurythmy), Edith Schieb (handwork), who married Carl Brestowsky while still in Hungary, Lenke Andor (Hungarian) and Elvira Papkovách (piano).[630]

The educators who worked in the boarding school were Hildegard Obstner, Willi Schulz, Eugen Huhne, Edith Schieb, Käthe Eisenmenger (who also took on the kindergarten and played the violin beautifully), Else Hummel, Marianne Kollendorfer, (who married Willi Schulz while still in Hungary), Lisi Lederer, and Maria Waldbauer, who supervised the boys in the boarding school, which she did very strictly. István von Nagy, who lived in the boarding house, recounts all these things and also that she was a master storyteller, using living pictures beautifully. The directors of the school were Josefine Kenessey, György Jankovich, and a third person whose name István von Nagy purposely did not mention.

As the school was being established, Maria von Nagy worked hard to take care of the finances and brought about that the German ministry of foreign affairs made funds available as well as the association for Germans living abroad. In spite of her efforts, money remained tight and the school was only able to manage financially because the teachers made sacrifices.

630 Letter of November 22, 1929, by Werner Lamerdin to the faculty of the Stuttgart Waldorf School. Archiv LS 3.10.41.

Hans Reipert, who was both an engineer and a eurythmist, taught at the school from 1931 until 1933. He was born in Eberfeld, and was happy and excited to live in Hungary with his wife, Irmgard. He was an uncompromising opponent of the Hitler regime and after 1933 he returned to being an engineer until he was conscripted. Immediately after the end of the war he spearheaded the efforts to gain official permission for the Waldorf school in Hannover to start up again, and together with others he was responsible for its reopening on October 2, 1945, the first school in lower Saxony able to do so.

Werner Lamerdin lived on as the most important, multitalented, and radiant teacher in the hearts of the students. He was practical, active in the arts and in music, and was able to meet students' questions and concerns directly. He built bridges among the circle of teachers and formed the innermost center of the school. Problems arose because, even though students were soon able to speak German well, their Hungarian left a lot to be desired. This fact did not escape notice and the parents began to lodge complaints.

At the beginning of the year 1933 Maria von Nagy had an accident and was no longer able to take care of the school because of a concussion; it took her months to recuperate. After the National Socialists came to power, the German teachers were no longer permitted to work. With Maria von Nagy on her sickbed and unable to do anything, the German teachers had to return home.

The third catastrophe to hit the school in this year was the unnamed director (his name was withheld on purpose), who lost school funds by betting on the horse races. Even though he confessed and began to pay his debts in small amounts, he died after a few years. Then, in the summer of 1933, the school buildings were put at the disposal of poor children and then the fourth catastrophe happened, an outbreak of scarlet fever. After all these disasters, the school on the little Schwabenberg had to close its doors. The School Association continued to exist and served as a mantle organization for anthroposophical work.[631]

During the war, the buildings of the von Nagy family and the school were heavily damaged. Before this destruction, Mr. and Mrs. von Nagy were able to give shelter to people like Sándor Török, the pianist Mihály Bächer, and others, who all survived the war and the Nazi regime. The parcel was declared public domain after the war and carved up. Maria von Nagy-Göllner emigrated in 1946 with both of her sons from her marriage with Emil. Her husband was not able to get an exit visa, and had to stay behind. She moved to Switzerland, where she became active socially and gave lectures. She also lectured in Australia, where one of her sons had settled, as well as in New Zealand. She died in Switzerland in 1982. Emil von Nagy survived two years of imprisonment by the communist regime, but died in solitude in Budapest in 1956.

631 Many of these details are from an interview with Maria Scheily on January 19, 2017, in Budapest.

1926: The Rudolf Steiner School in Oslo

EARLY IN THE 20TH CENTURY a few Norwegians had taken notice of Rudolf Steiner's efforts to actively spread spiritual science in central Europe, and between 1908 and 1923 they had invited him eight times to give lectures in Norway. On November 23 and 24, 1921, he was invited by the pedagogical association to give two lectures about education,[632] to be held in the prestigious Nobel Institute in Oslo, or Kristiania as it was called until 1924. The lectures were well attended, and a few people saw the tremendous potential. Conversations about starting a new school started in the Vidar group of the Anthroposophical Society in Oslo, spearheaded by the architect, Christian av Morgenstierne von Munthe (1880–1967). The general secretary of the Anthroposophical Society in Norway, Karl Ingerø (1889–1972) was also involved. When attending a few meetings in Dornach, he talked with Rudolf Steiner about the school they were planning, and Steiner pointed out that it would be a sensible thing to send the future teachers to Stuttgart or Dornach to study.[633].

Among those attending Rudolf Steiner's lectures in 1921, other people also conceived the idea of starting a Waldorf school in Norway. A number of women especially were moved to pick up the idea, among them Caroline Bokken Lasson (1871–1970), a singer, actress, and cabaret player, who became the first Waldorf teacher of French and music in Norway;[634] Signe Roll-Wikberg (1894–1979); and Nanna Thorne. Signe Roll, one of the important pioneers of Waldorf education in Norway, first did a curative gymnastics training before studying anatomy and physiology, physics, Latin and philosophy in Oslo and Basel. By 1919, she had acquired a broad education and also added education to the list of subjects mentioned above. She took part in Rudolf Steiner's education courses held in Basel, in Oxford in 1922, and in Arnhem in 1924. In addition, she did practicums at the Waldorf School in Stuttgart early in 1925 and the Vrije School in The Hague in the spring of 1926.[635] During the preparatory period in Oslo in 1924, she also had conversations with Curt Englert (1899–1945) from Switzerland, who had moved to Norway in the meantime and had married Elisabeth Faye (†1996).

Thus he had made the acquaintance of the Smit family, particularly with his brother-in-law, Christian Smit (1886–1960), who was a lawyer, anthroposophist, and later founder of the Christian Community. Christian Smit, Signe Roll, and the others who prepared the school founding cherished the hope to win Curt Englert-Faye as a steady coworker in the new school. In fact, the little group had assumed this right

---

632 Rudolf Steiner: *Waldorf Education and Anthroposophy 1.* CW 304.

633 Terje Christensen: Et fundament blir lagt. Perioden 1926–1945. In: Erik Marstrander (ed.): *Menneske først!* 1996, p. 50.

634 Terje Christensen: http://biographien.kulturimpuls.org/detail.php?&id=1120 (site visited October 11, 2016).

635 Ibid.

Curt Englert-Faye   Eva and Einar Lunde from Lillehammer

from the start. He moved to Norway in 1921 and lived there until 1926, working as an educator, and he had become quite well known in anthroposophical circles. But at the last moment he changed his mind and took up another task, following a call to come to Zürich, in order to work together with a few friends in founding, supporting, and building up a Rudolf Steiner school.

So a little group began to cast about and look for different ways to realize their wish to found the first Nordic Rudolf Steiner school. An important role in all this was played by the Scandinavian summer conference on education held by Eva and Einar Lunde (1875–1951) in Lillehammer in 1926. Einar Lunde was also interested in founding a Waldorf school and had sent a few of his ten children to the Friedwart School in Dornach, where a few other Norwegian children had been sent as well.[636]

His assignment in Zürich notwithstanding, Curt Englert-Faye was the leading personality of this summer conference, together with the Danish painter and well-known writer Johannes Hohlenberg (1881–1960).[637] The two of them each gave eight lectures, Curt Englert about education and Johannes Hohlenberg about Goethe's *Faust*. Signe Roll was one of the many enthusiastic people in attendance who were to play a role in the future, and it was there that she must have made a definite decision to found a Rudolf Steiner school. Since Curt Englert had in a way dropped out at the last moment by moving to Zürich, it was Signe Roll who took on the sole responsibility for the new founding.

On September 1, 1926, the new Rudolf Steiner school started at Oscargate 10,[638] with Signe Roll at the helm, teaching 12 students distributed among a first and a

636 Terje Christensen: Einar Lunde. In: Bodo von Plato (ed.): *Anthroposophie im 20. Jahrhundert*. 2003, p. 480.
637 Terje Christensen: Johannes Hohlenberg. In: Bodo von Plato (ed.): *Anthroposophie im 20. Jahrhundert*. 2003, p. 317.
638 Oscarsgate 10 was the home of the Anthroposophical Society in Norway at the time.

third grade. In order to help with the work, Signe Roll invited Herbert Hahn to Norway for a number of lectures in October and November 1926.[639] Herbert Hahn was a polyglot and loved such assignments, using his stay as a basis for his studies on the character of European peoples and their countries.

For the school year 1927/28, the 54 students in six grades moved into a former private school at Josefinesgate 34. Signe Roll had inherited[640] this house and put it at the disposal of the growing school, so that it now had a considerable property to call its own.

The schoolhouse of the Rudolf Steiner school at Josefine's Gate 34, Oslo, 1927–1936

Among the teachers were Marie Mathilde (Mimi) Geelmuyden (*1892),[641] Sigrid Kjelstrup, Karl Døbelin (1898–1976), Ragnhild Ingerø, Gunnhild Blekastad, and Paul Smit, engineer. It looked like positive growth, there was enthusiasm, there were teachers. Due to what we would now call philosophical differences, however, two members of the school board, Sophus Garman Clausen (1889–1967), a merchant/businessman who had financially supported the initial steps of the school, and Christian Smit, a Christian Community priest, both took their children out of the school, altogether ten of them, in early January 1929. As a consequence, five more children left. This was quite a loss for the school of course, and gave rise to many discussions.

Christian Smit (a lawyer as well a public official in Bergen and Hordaland at the beginning of the century) and Lily Faye, the sister of Elisabeth Englert-Faye, had seven sons together: Didrik (*1915), Jörgen (*1916), Christian (*1918), Arne (*1920), Bard (*1922), Paul (*1924), and Johannes (*1930).[642] Together with Sophus Garman Clausen, who had sent his son (also called Sophus) to the Friedwart School in Dornach,[643] Christian Smit wanted to found a new, independent school. Together with all the children of the Smit and Clausen families, Lektor Horne, a recent addition to the faculty, had also left. All this had happened because of the influence of a clairvoyant woman, Mrs. Wandberg—those who had left wanted to found a new school for the children together with her. A shock for all concerned.

639 Herbert Hahn in a letter to Signe Roll dated November 10, 1926. Archiv LS 3.16.09.

640 Terje Christensen: Et fundament blir lagt. Perioden 1926–1945. In: Erik Marstrander (ed.): *Menneske først!* 1996, p. 58f.

641 Mimi Geelmuyden was the daughter of Helga and Hans Christian Geelmuyden. Helga Geelmuyden was one of the most outstanding pioneers of anthroposophy in Scandinavia. See Terje Christensen: Helga Geelmuyden (1871–1951). In: Bodo von Plato (ed.): *Anthroposophie im 20. Jahrhundert.* 2003, p. 205ff.

642 Cordelia Böttcher: Christian Smit. In: Bodo von Plato (ed.): *Anthroposophie im 20. Jahrhundert.* 2003, p. 763.

643 Oddvar Granly: http://biographien.kulturimpuls.org/detail.php?&id=1128 (site visited October 11, 2016).

Seven grades remained in the Rudolf Steiner school, 64 students and nine teachers in all. They now had to deal with the aftermath of the shock somehow and replace the board members of the School Association. Two committed new members were found, Karl Ingerø (1889–1972), engineer, and Dr. Håkon Håkonsen (1881–1933), who joined on January 10, 1929.

Olina Røberg joined as a new teacher, but she had no training. Therefore, she was to complete an extensive practicum in the Stuttgart school in the first half of 1930, and completed a short teacher training that way.[644]

By 1932 it seemed as if they had come through, and the school had grown to 102 students by then. The new school did not work out because of the lack of pedagogical experience, and the children who had been pulled out were sent back to their former school.[645] The conflicts in the faculty now flared up again. Only 82 children were left in the school year of 1933/34. An attempt was made to get the equivalent of the ordinary cost per child in state schools from the government, but that did not work out. Salaries were reduced to a minimum.

In her effort to anchor Waldorf education in Norwegian culture, Signe Roll took a completely undogmatic approach. This is how she described this approach: "Only if we allow our work to be inspired by developing a wakeful eye and a true sense for the individual child will we be able to work with the practical indications in such a way that they do not become dogmas."[646]

To this day, highly talented teachers and people who are true masters share a similar motive.

Signe Roll stopped working as a teacher in the school in 1934, when she started her own family. Her remaining colleagues began to have trouble communicating, which affected the school considerably. People still hoped that Curt Englert-Faye would be able to save the situation, so they appealed to him and he did come in the autumn of 1935. He taught some classes, gave some lectures to teachers and parents, but did not want to take on a position of leadership.

The school was closed in June 1936 because the inner stability had been lost and the institution could not be brought to blossom again. Furthermore, it had gained a reputation of being a school for children with learning difficulties. Apart from that, financial problems became unsolvable. The faculty fell apart. Vult Simon and Gulle Brun, however, kept on working with their students and carried on a little Waldorf school at their private residence on Makrelbekken. (see also: 1932: Oslo-Smestad)

The collapse of the collaboration in the mid 1930s notwithstanding, Englert students in Bergen and Oslo were spiritually productive teachers. They found forgotten

---

644 Signe Roll in a letter dated February 28, 1939, to the faculty in Stuttgart. Archiv LS 3.16.19.
645 Nils Gustav Hertzberg: Über die anthroposophische Schulbewegung in Norwegen. Msch 9, 1947, p. 276.
646 Letter dated February 24, 1929, written by Signe Roll to Dr. Erich Gabert. Archiv LS 3.16.13.

treasures from Norway's cultural tradition in fairytales and songs. They connected with traditions that lived in Norwegian community colleges, where the living word was cherished. They wrote plays, poems, and stories; they composed music, put on plays and operas with the children, and were representatives of Waldorf education in an open and inclusive spirit. Some of them regularly contributed newspaper articles about art and culture and gained considerable recognition as writers. They always championed a spiritual worldview and could be sharply critical about materialistic tendencies and decadent trends. Until around 1970, anthroposophists thus were a considerable factor in the cultural life of Norway—admired but also sometimes intimidating.

1927: The Rudolf Steiner School in Zürich

WITHOUT FANFARE, the Rudolf Steiner school in Zürich opened on Monday, May 2, 1927, at Kinkelstrasse 36.[647] There were 12 children, distributed over grades 1, 2, 3, and 5, taught by Curt Englert and his Norwegian wife Elisabeth Faye. The couple had come back to Switzerland from Norway at the request of Walter Wyssling (1891–1926)[648] and his wife Rosa Wyssling (née Bitterli), who had spearheaded a parent initiative.

Walter Wyssling had completed his civil engineering studies in Zürich in 1915, specializing in the construction of power plants. He was employed at the building site of the water-power plant Chancy-Pougny on the river Rhône, close to Geneva, when he had a conversation with his boss Ernest Etienne (1876–1968).[649] In the course of this conversation, which took place in 1920, the latter told him about Rudolf Steiner, which led Wyssling to an in-depth study of anthroposophy.

But his engagement with spiritual science was not confined to study. He helped with the financing of the recently founded Stuttgart Waldorf School. Rosa Wyssling and Mrs. Etienne took part in the Christmas course given by Rudolf Steiner for teachers in Dornach in 1923, which deepened both their knowledge and their connections. They soon were part of a group of people in Switzerland who were working to spread Waldorf education. Thus they came into contact with the initiators of the Basel Waldorf school, Emma Ramser among them. Walter Wyssling met her in March 1924, when he was studying in Dornach for two weeks. After they had moved to Zürich in 1925, Walter and Rosa Wyssling wanted to make it possible for their four sons to have an education built on the principles of Waldorf pedagogy.

647 C. Englert to E.A. Karl Stockmeyer in a letter dated May 7, 1927. Archiv LS 3.18.18.
648 Andreas Dollfuss: Walter Wyssling. In: Bodo von Plato (ed.): *Anthroposophie im 20. Jahrhundert.* 2003, p. 945. Rosa Wyssling: Walter Wyssling. November 3, 1891–January 27, 1926. Msch 4/6, 1941, p. 128ff.
649 Wolfgang G. Vögele: Ernest Etienne. In: Bodo von Plato (ed.): *Anthroposophie im 20. Jahrhundert.* 2003, p. 183.

Walter Wyssling

"I would be happy when, in solving the question of the schooling of our own children, which occupies us very much, we would be able to contribute to a solution for the question of schools in Switzerland as a whole. Once a good beginning has been made somewhere, it will set an example that will not remain without followers. Human progress will depend very much on whether the children of today will be able to receive an education that takes spiritual realities into account,"[650] he writes in a letter of February 20, 1925. When their oldest son was ready to enter school, the parents considered sending him to the Stuttgart Waldorf School, but soon realized that moving a seven-year-old boy so far away from home would be detrimental to his health and well-being. In spite of that, they sent him anyway. It made the need to start a school—or at least Waldorf inspired homeschooling—all the more pressing in Zürich.

Through Dr. Alfred Usteri they heard that Dr. Elisabeth Vreede had mentioned Curt Englert in Norway, and they wrote him a letter on February 20, 1925.[651] In April 1925, they went to the education conference in Stuttgart, which was totally given over to commemorating Rudolf Steiner's death. While there, Walter Wyssling called all Swiss participants together to talk about founding a school in Switzerland. Even though he had not received an answer yet, Walter Wyssling told those gathered that he was certain Curt Englert would build up the school in Zürich. A few days later a letter did arrive with his answer, which was basically affirmative.[652] At the end of July 1925, Walter and Rosa Wyssling had a meeting with Curt and Elisabeth Englert-Faye, where they definitely committed to founding a Swiss school.

Curt Englert-Faye (1899–1945) had been a student at the humanistic grammar school in Basel, where he had befriended Hans Werner Zbinden (1899–1977) and Paul Jenny (1898–1971). This was during the time that the first Goetheanum was built, where his father was the principal engineer. After high school, he studied philology and history and completed his grammar school teacher's exam at the age of 22.[653] He was only 16 years old when Rudolf Steiner gave him permission to attend his lectures, and he could not stop telling his classmates about what he heard there—themes that moved him more than any other subject. This piqued their interest, so they came along

650 Rosa Wyssling: Walter Wyssling, November 3, 1891–January 27, 1926. Msch 4/6 1941, p. 131.
651 Hans W. Zbinden: Von der Entstehung der Rudolf Steiner Schule in Zürich. In: Lehrerkollegium der Rudolf Steiner Schule Zürich (ed.): *Zur Menschenbildung. Aus der Arbeit der Rudolf Steiner Schule in Zürich 1927–1977*. 1977, p. 28f.
652 Ibid., p. 31. The full letter by Curt Englert can be found there as well.
653 Andreas Dollfuss and Oddvar Granly: Curt Englert-Faye. In: Bodo von Plato (ed.): *Anthroposophie im 20. Jahrhundert*. 2003, p. 175f.

to Dornach now and then and also met Rudolf Steiner. What they gained from these visits changed their lives.

Curt Englert-Faye, 1930

While he was on a study trip to Italy, Curt Englert met a Norwegian friend. During their conversations it turned out that his friend was on the lookout for a private teacher for his siblings. Curt Englert did not deliberate long, said yes to tutoring them, and went to live in Norway, where he stayed from 1921 to 1926.[654] Now he had returned in order to help the Wysslings make their dream a reality.

In building up the Rudolf Steiner school in Zürich, his two classmates played an important role. Hans Werner Zbinden, MD, became the school doctor, remaining in that position until his death in 1976, and Dr. Paul Jenny, a lawyer, became chair of the School Association. Walter Wyssling died unexpectedly in January 1926 after a short, serious illness.[655] This might have meant the end of the founding impulse. The three school friends from Basel, however, did not question the validity of the initiative and carried on the work with even greater commitment. At Walter Wyssling's deathbed, Hans Werner Zbinden and Paul Jenny vowed to carry on this school initiative. They continued to spread the founding ideals and formulated the incorporation statutes of an association to further support the endeavor.

This association, named *Freie Schulvereinigung in Memoriam Walter Wyssling* [Independent School Association in Memory of Walter Wyssling], was founded in May 1926. At that time it only counted 20 members, and in and of itself was obviously not yet able to guarantee a sufficient financial base for the school. After initial conversations were held and a request was sent in, the association was approved by the educational authorities of the canton of Zürich. On February 24, 1927, the school received a preliminary permit pending oral clarification of a few points.[656] This official permit was granted by *Regierungsrat* [government councillor] Dr. Heinrich Mousson (1866–1944). In the very same year of the founding, the little school moved to Plattenstrasse 39, where it is housed until this day.

As he had done with Paul Jenny and Hans Werner Zbinden earlier on, Curt Englert looked up other school friends to get help. So he traveled to Winterthur, for example, to visit Hans Reinhart and discuss a problem that caused him quite a

---

654 Andreas Dollfuss and Oddvar Granly: Curt Englert-Faye (March 30, 1899–December 1, 1945). LR 76, 2002, p. 78.

655 Conrad Englert-Faye: Walter Wyssling. AM February 14, 1926, p. 45f.

656 There is a facsimile of this letter in Robert Thomas and Heinz Zimmermann: *Rudolf Steiner Schulen in der Schweiz*. 2007, p. 111.

Dr. Paul Jenny (left) and
Dr. H. W. Zbinden (right), 1937

headache. On the basis of mutual trust, and without any tangible collateral, Hans Reinhart promised to secure a loan for the building on the Plattenstrasse. That was the only condition still needed to be met before they could acquire the new school building. The school furniture came from a liquidation sale of the private school inventory of the two ladies Guignard and, with that, the initial preparations were concluded.

In May 1927, the first school year started with 12 children. On April 30, 1928, for the second school year, 35 children were enrolled in five grades with four teachers. Teachers who joined in the years after that were Johannnes Waeger (1902–1977),[657] the highly gifted artist Max Schenk (1898–1963), Marguerite Lobeck (1893–1986), and Gottlieb Heinrich Kessler (1898–1985), a class teacher.[658] The school did not have to look for teachers; they stepped up to the plate or were brought along. Looking back to the founding years, Curt Englert placed great value on the fact that the school never had to worry about teachers. In a lecture to parents of the school in 1936, he said, "I hope that people can see these things and can also grasp the fact that a school like ours is an organism involving people's destinies. As such it is objectively linked in with the whole!"[659]

The executive council of the association and the teachers on the faculty of the Rudolf Steiner school in Zürich, with Curt Englert in the lead, conceived of themselves as active opponents of "catholicizing, popish, monopolizing tendencies,"[660] which, in their perception, were at work in Stuttgart. They saw themselves as being vilified as "nationalists" because "people did not understand that it goes without saying that one has to work out of the full cultural life of a whole people. It was necessary to really form ideas about what Swiss history has contributed toward an understanding of the human being, or about fairytales, or mythical things."[661]

For the founders of the Rudolf Steiner school in Zürich it was very important to guarantee independence and autonomy in all areas. Therefore they did not want to accept any money with strings attached, only donations in the real sense of the

---

657 Andreas Dollfuss: http://biographien.kulturimpuls.org/detail.php?&id=956 (site visited June 18, 2016).

658 G.H. Kessler remained at the school for 19 years, after which he moved to England in order to help at Kings Langley. After that he lived in Edinburgh and in Kassel. After his retirement he helped the Christian Morgenstern Schule in Wuppertal. See: Waltraut Kessler-Offermann: Gottlieb Heinrich Kessler (May 18, 1898–September 11, 1985). N 5.10.1986, p. 161f.

659 Hans W. Zbinden: Von der Entstehung der Rudolf Steiner Schule in Zürich. In: Lehrerkollegium der Rudolf Steiner Schule Zürich (eds.): *Zur Menschenbildung. Aus der Arbeit der Rudolf Steiner Schule in Zürich 1927–1977.* 1977, p. 49.

660 Ibid., p. 47.

661 Ibid.

word. That way every teacher should be able to work out of independent insight and be free to decide. In order to guarantee this attitude in perpetuity, the teachers were not employed by the institution but were independent contractors. The faculty maintained the freedom to choose new members themselves, without any interference of the association. And the association only acted as a trustee where money and school property were concerned. Teacher salaries were arrived at by a process whereby teachers determined their own needs and were in conversation with an appointed colleague and the treasurer of the association to arrive at an amount which would enable them to do their work. The faculty and the council of the association knew only the total sum of the teacher salaries; details were known only to the two persons mentioned, one colleague and the treasurer of the association. The tuition parents paid was conceived of as a free, unconditional donation, not as payment for a service rendered. Such free donations of course did not give parents the right to have input, because "education can neither be bought nor sold."

As early as the beginning of 1927,[662] Curt Englert-Faye began publishing the pedagogical magazine, *Die Menschenschule* [Human Schooling], which he designed to be a mouthpiece for a specific, homegrown version of anthroposophical pedagogical views, born out of the Swiss confederacy. From a present-day standpoint, one can, of course, misinterpret such a formulation as a nationalistic delusion, but at the time he may have meant it as a pedagogical practice calling on one's individual resources and appealing to each teacher's willingness to change, taking a stance independent from the Stuttgart school. In any case, Curt Englert's relationship to the teachers in Stuttgart remained tense, but between him and E. A. Karl Stockmeyer a trusting and open correspondence was maintained, brutally honest at times. In almost every other letter to Stockmeyer, Englert wrote: "Please do not be angry with me that I put these things bluntly. After all, that remains the best way to understand one another." This correspondence also included the sometimes pretty sharp conflicts about donation money, because E. A. Karl Stockmeyer wanted to win Swiss donors for the Stuttgart school, whereas Curt Englert was of the opinion that enough donations could flow from Germany and that no appeal needed to be made to people in Switzerland. It goes without saying that he was of the opinion that Swiss donors were needed to sustain the two Swiss schools in Basel and Zürich. Apart from that, the discussion was about questions on how to shape an international school movement. With regard to this question, Curt Englert was direct: "If I'm allowed to express my personal opinion

---

662 In a letter to E. A. Karl Stockmeyer dated October 21, 1926, Curt Englert announced the publication of his own magazine in Switzerland, "which from now on will feature extensive pedagogical courses, in consultation with Frau Dr. Steiner." Archiv LS 3.18.11. This was disconcerting, and therefore Stockmeyer inquired on October 28, 1926, if he meant printing Dr. Steiner's educational lectures which had been entrusted to Englert. Archiv LS 3.18.12. On October 30, 1926, Englert replied that his words could not be misinterpreted, because Frau Dr. Steiner was entrusted with the publication of Dr. Steiner's works. Archiv LS 3.18.13.

in this matter, I would like to urgently request, in the interest of a truly flourishing school movement, that you keep our circumstances completely separate from your German problems and that you limit yourself to building up the foundations of the German school movement in the best way that you see fit." And he went on to insist once again that the Stuttgart school had only been mandated, in the famous letter of March 17, 1925, to play a leading role for the German movement, not for Waldorf schools in other countries.[663]

The school grew slowly. In the year 1930/31, there were 54 students in six grades,[664] with five teachers; in the year after that, 70 students with six main-lesson teachers. The committee in charge of supervising private schools wrote: "The Rudolf Steiner School, which breaks new ground, has made a step forward this year [1931/32]. The emphasis is primarily on building character and warmth of heart, not on content. It should be mentioned that the parents are constantly reminded of the unique position of the school. There is a strong bond between parents and school [...]."

For one thing, examinations were given in their own classrooms and by their own teachers. The testing went well; children responded quickly and naturally to the questions that were asked.[665]

Hans Rudolf Niederhäuser (1914–1983) took a first grade in 1935. He was 21 years old at the time and took this class from grades one through nine. Before that, he had done a state training and was planning to join Albert Schweitzer in Lambarene to work there as a foreign aid worker. After hearing a lecture by Curt Englert-Faye, however, he switched course completely and decided to stay in Switzerland to work as a Waldorf teacher. Hans Rudolf Niederhäuser taught for a total of 30 years at the Zürich Rudolf Steiner School.[666] Curt Englert left the school in 1937 and moved back to Norway, where he had been offered the position as general secretary of the Norwegian Anthroposophical Society.

After his departure, it became all the more obvious that the school had teachers of truly remarkable caliber in Johannes Waeger, Marguerite Lobeck, and Max Schenk. For decades, Marguerite Lobeck was a truly outstanding eurythmy teacher who was highly gifted poetically, writing plays that were performed in the summer. Johannes Waeger taught at the school for over 30 years, and was famous for his remarkable presentations as a teacher of philosophy and literature, for his inspired reflections on history, as well as for his piano playing. Max Schenk, a sculptor, worked on public relations locally but also gained wide recognition far beyond the city of Zürich.

---

663 Curt Englert-Faye to E. A. Karl Stockmeyer, March 2, 1928. Archiv LS 3.18.41.
664 Report on the year 1930, given by the board of the Independent School Association in Memory of Walter Wyssling to the general members meeting, p. 5.
665 See note 663.
666 Andreas Dollfuss: Hans Rudolf Niederhäuser. In: Bodo von Plato (ed.): *Anthroposophie im 20. Jahrhundert*. 2003, p. 561f.

With the start of World War II, during which Switzerland also had to mobilize, the question arose about the continued existence of the school. Would this place, which fostered true humanity in the growing child, be able to survive financially? An appeal was made to parents, friends and beneficiaries, asking them if they would be willing to continue to support the school.[667] Against this background, a meeting was held on October 16, 1939, hosted by the School Association in Memory of Walter Wyssling, focusing on ways to continue to support the School in the coming years.

The school grew slowly. In 1941 there were 160 students in nine grades, with 16 teachers, and the School Association counted 263 members. The financial picture had never been this bleak. The school could no longer be supported by parental contributions alone. The continued existence of the school was made possible by the generous donation of one particular sponsor, who contributed a large portion of the total income of 79,270.99 francs.[668] Despite wartime circumstances, three contiguous residences could be acquired and turned into school buildings during the years that followed. Moreover, in 1948 the school was able to build a new auditorium and a gym on the same premises, which continue to be used to this very day.

1927 (1929): The Rudolf Steiner School in Vienna

Two Grades Start in 1927

Toward the end of the 1920s, two Waldorf-based grades were opened at Buchfeldgasse 4, located in the eighth district of Vienna. At the time, people in Vienna were adjusting to a new political reality. In the early years of the First Republic, which had replaced the Habsburg monarchy, disillusionment had set in. Society was becoming more and more polarized, and people were highly upset by the obvious use of force on the part of the police. Austria had shrunk to the German speaking parts and was no longer the vivacious state of many nationalities it used to be. It had become a country in search of a new identity. Right-wing nationalistic forces were on the increase, which were diametrically opposed to the way Waldorf education appeals to universal humanity.

One of the driving forces behind the future school was Dr. Gusti Bretter (1896–1946), a sensitive, highly educated young woman (it is assumed she had majored in economics).[669] On September 15, 1927, she had already started a teaching initiative

---

667 Appeal in Msch 10, 1939, p. 366ff.

668 Report from the Board of the Independent School Association in Memory of Walter Wyssling about the school year 1940/41, addressed to the members meeting of June 21, 1941. It was given by the president, Dr. jur. Paul Jenny, Msch 4/6, 1941, p. 218ff.

669 At first she was in touch with Ita Wegman, a physician and executive council member of the General Anthroposophical Society; later it is said that she consulted a woman with clairvoyant capacities who lived on the Chiemsee.

Ferdinand Wantschura

on her own with elementary school classes in the English language school at Gumpendorferstrasse 105. The venture operated separately from the School Association, which had been founded at the same time. In addition, Dr. Bretter also organized pedagogical eurythmy courses, working with a second teacher, the eurythmist Berta Elbogen (1901–1932),[670] who was reputed to be a highly vivacious person.

It seems as if it was an idea whose time had come: several different people were beginning to work with Waldorf education and take initiative, but it took a while for these initiatives to find one another. Hannah Krämer-Steiner (1895–1984) had been carrying an impulse to found a Waldorf school in Austria for a long time. She had received permission from Rudolf Steiner to study his pedagogical lectures, probably starting in 1922. In addition, she had been working intensively with the anthroposophical youth movement. Because she had been asked by Maria von Nagy to become a teacher at the newly founded Waldorf School in Budapest, she did not partake in the early efforts to found a school in Vienna.

On April 2, 1927, about 50 people gathered in the house of the Dutch lumber merchant Jan van Leer (1880–1934) and agreed to found a Rudolf Steiner School Association in Vienna. Next to Jan van Leer and Gusti Bretter, the anthroposophical physician Ferdinand Wantschura, Alfred Zeiszig, Adolf Rawitz, and Cornelis Johannes Apel (1882–1962) were part of the preparatory group.[671] In order to spread the word and find interested people, the Rudolf Steiner School Association organized lectures by Hermann von Baravalle in the hall of the *Architektenverein* [architect association].

These efforts to reach a wider public came to a halt in the second school year, because all funds of the newly founded association were needed to pay for the deficit in the new elementary school initiative.

Two other kindergarten initiatives started in Vienna at the same time in 1927, one in the seventh district, a group led by Ilse Bode (1906–1988), and another playgroup in the third district, led by Hanny Leicht.[672] In 1928, Gusti Bretter's class moved to Habsburgergasse 3, into two combined, spacious apartments on the third floor of a large house that was primarily used for office space. So the location was—and is still—right in the center of Vienna, at the point where the narrow Habsburgergasse

670 Ernst Zawischa: Erinnerungen an die erste Rudolf Steiner-Schule in Wien. LR 7, 1973, p. 55ff and N 26.10.1969, p. 174.

671 Report to the Leadership Council of the Stuttgart Waldorf School, dated April 5, 1927. Archiv LS 3.22.001.

672 Mid-September report, 1927, Archiv LS 3.22.008, and announcement, Archiv LS 3.22.012.

merges into the wide Graben running from the Kohlmarkt to the Stefansplatz. The Rudolf Steiner School Association was incorporated on April 17, 1927, and Ferdinand Wantschura (1887–1966), an anthroposophical physician who also had a position as a city-appointed physician for the poor, was chosen to be the chairman. He somehow managed to steer the association through times of crisis, devaluation, and general poverty. As early as 1929, Gusti Bretter retired from the association and the leadership of her small private elementary school. As the brown specter spread, she emigrated to Sweden, worked as a journalist and archivist, and became involved in education again when the first Swedish Waldorf school was founded in 1946. Two people with connections

Hannah Krämer-Steiner

to Marie Steiner, Helmuth Alscher-Bassenheim (1904–1983) and Othmar Helf from Brunn am Gebirge, stepped in to take the abandoned grades further. In a letter dated May 5, 1929, the two of them reported to the faculty of the Stuttgart Waldorf School that they would carry on the work together with Berta Elbogen, Dr. Friedrich Hiebel, and Dr. Marianne Klein, starting in the autumn of 1929. They stated their intent to build it up as a faculty-run Rudolf Steiner school. They also gave assurance that they were backed by both the Anthroposophical Society of Austria and the Rudolf Steiner School Association of Vienna.[673]

1929: The Initial Years of the Rudolf Steiner School in Vienna

THE RUDOLF STEINER SCHOOL Association wanted to attract experienced teachers. To that end, they invited Hannah Krämer-Steiner to come to Vienna, asking her to become head of the school for the school year 1929/30. The day before the start of school, she was informed by the School Association that they had to withdraw her appointment on the grounds that she was Jewish. This was a profound shock. Friends invited her to stay in Pressburg (present-day Bratislava)[674] where she was able to recover.

It wasn't always easy for Ferdinand Wantschura to deal with the tensions and uncertainties that faced the young faculty. He therefore turned to Hans Baumann for help in 1930, with the request that the Stuttgart Waldorf School would mentor the small Viennese school and send an experienced teacher with sufficient authority to also represent the school outwardly.[675] Friedrich Hiebel and Marianne Klein had left

673 Letter of May 5, 1929. Archiv LS 3.22.013.
674 Andreas Worel: Hannah Krämer-Steiner (October 29, 1895–March 20, 1984). N 28.10.1984, p. 182.
675 Letter by Ferdinand Wantschura to H. Baumann, dated July 17, 1930. Archiv LS 3.22.019.

The third and fourth grades of the Vienna Rudolf Steiner School with their teachers, Helmut Alscher (left) and Hermine Schmidt (right), May 1931

the school by now, and Ferdinand Wantschura was afraid that other teachers might follow suit. In 1929, Friedrich Hiebel began teaching in Essen and soon thereafter moved to Stuttgart. Therefore Ferdinand Wantschura wanted to do everything in his power to support the good efforts of Helmuth Alscher.

Unfortunately, more than 33 children had not reenrolled, and the remaining faculty did not inspire enough confidence to attract more children. The Stuttgart school readily understood the situation, but was unable to come up with an immediate solution to the questions and problems since they could not immediately free up a colleague to come to the rescue. So Ferdinand Wantschura kept having the problem that the teachers were too conventional in their methods of teaching and were hardly able to convince more parents to come, despite efforts made in parent evenings or through public outreach. A rift resulted between teachers and the board of the association, which deepened and resulted in Ferdinand Wantschura and three other members stepping back in September 1930. Six new people were appointed to the board, and in the autumn of 1931 they succeeded in engaging Karl Ege of the Stuttgart Waldorf School to come to Vienna for a few weeks to provide additional training for the teachers.

Like all private schools at the time, the school had to meet a number of conditions. They were obliged to notify the authorities of any changes, every teacher had to be approved by the ministry of education, and they had to fight to keep their coeducation permit every single year. In 1932/33, when the fifth grade was about to start, they had to obtain approval to found a private *Hauptschule* [secondary school for fifth grade and up under the Austrian system], because the Austrian school system only provided room for elementary schools going through fourth grade. Approval was granted. Before being granted official recognition, students were obliged at the end of every school year to pass an examination demonstrating that they had mastered the materials prescribed for regular schools at their level. In June 1933, the private elementary school of the Rudolf Steiner School Association was provisionally granted official recognition for two years. The *Hauptschule* was officially recognized in March 1934.[676]

This obliged teachers to show test results and curriculum content every single year. Eurythmy and foreign languages, for example, simply did not appear in the elementary school curriculum documentation. So there was one curriculum for the city school inspector and another one to which the school actually adhered. The curriculum as reported to the city was followed only once a year, when the school inspector came—and the children were exemplary in the way they played right along with the changes.

In 1932, Bronja Hüttner-Zahlingen (1912–2000) came to join the small faculty. She had gone to grammar school and had been a classmate of Rudi Lissau (1911–2004) and Hans Schauder (1911–2001). In that way she met anthroposophy and the people who were to play an important part in her life. At age 20, she began to build up the Waldorf kindergarten work. She was forced to emigrate for 11 years to England, where she taught ancient languages at Michael Hall School and helped in the kindergarten. In 1955 she returned to Vienna and became the most prominent Waldorf kindergarten teacher in Austria.[677]

Ernst Zawischa (1904–1987) came to the Vienna school in 1933, after he had been a coworker for three years at Schloss Pilgrimshain, a home for children in need of special care in Silesia. His cousin Hans Michael Rascher and his wife Ilse, Dr. Karl König, and Albrecht Strohschein worked in the same home. Ernst Zawischa was immediately put in charge of the new first grade after he had done a three- or four-day practicum at the Stuttgart school before the summer holidays. He taught the so-called "Bible Class" up to the time the school had to close in 1938.

This small class had around 12 children, whose first names were Magdalena, Johannes, Paul, Andreas, Thomas, Lukas—hence the name "Bibelklasse." But Manto, the son of the Chinese consul general Ho, was also part of this class, and a very beloved classmate at that.

676 Gerhard Volz: Besetzung Österreichs und Überlebenskampf der Rudolf Steiner Schule. In: Elisabeth Gergely and Tobias Richter (eds.): *Wiener Dialoge. Der österreichische Weg der Waldorfpädagogik.* 2011, p. 87.

677 http://biographien.kulturimpuls.org/detail.php?&id=1462 (site visited on March 5, 2016); Elisabeth Gergely: Bronja Zahlingen (January 8, 1912–January 24, 2000). N 26, 2000, p. 202.

School Leadership Challenges and Teacher Changes

AT THE END of the school year 1934/35, the school went through a major upheaval of the kind the schools experience time and again. As usual, this crisis had to do with questions around school leadership, working together, and mutual trust. Four teachers left the school: Helmuth Alscher-Bassenheim, Othmar Helf, Mr. Mlineritsch, and Franz Wunderer. The loss of Helmuth Alscher seemed to be particularly harmful for the school, because he had been in a position of leadership from the start and had gained the trust of many parents. He went on to become a state school teacher in the city.

The resulting gap was closed remarkably quickly, because strong personalities joined the school. There was Dr. Friedrich Hiebel (1903–1989), a German literature teacher who had gained teaching experience in the meantime, working at the Waldorf schools in Essen and Stuttgart. In 1934 he had been forced to leave the Stuttgart school because he was non-Aryan, and he took on a leading position in the school. He became a class teacher and also taught literature and art history in the high school. Heinz Frankfurt remembered him as one of the faculty members who set the tone. He remembered his tall, slender figure entering the classroom and giving captivating presentations.

But Friedrich Hiebel did more than that; for one thing, he managed to create a way of looking at the world not by talking about Goethe, but by bringing his spirit alive.[678] In 1938, Dr. Hiebel had to also leave the Vienna school, and he emigrated to the United States in 1939. He remained a Waldorf teacher and taught at the Rudolf Steiner school in New York for seven years before returning to Europe. A few years later, he was called to be on the Executive Council of the General Anthroposophical Society. Other teachers who joined the school were the young Wilhelm Mrazek and Dr. Hans Erhard Lauer (1899–1979), who had originally come to Vienna in 1922 in order to prepare the large West–East Conference. In this he worked together especially with Count Ludwig Polzer-Hoditz, the main initiator of the conference. His secretary, the pianist Marta von Stefanovic (1899–2002), became Hans Erhard Lauer's life's companion. He had written a dissertation that had been rejected by Karl Jaspers in Heidelberg; at the University of Vienna, it was accepted without problems. In 1938, he had to leave the Vienna school like all the others and ended up in Switzerland, where he taught in Basel from 1939 to 1952, and from 1952 until 1964 in Zürich. He taught German and history and was also a class teacher in Basel.[679]

Another teacher who worked in Vienna was Georg Unger (1909–1999). He taught at the Vienna school from 1935 until 1937, while trying to finish his PhD at

---

678 Heinz Frankfurt: Friedrich Hiebel als Lehrer an der Wiener Rudolf Steiner Schule. LR 6, 1972, p. 30.
679 Andreas Dollfuss: Hans Erhard Lauer. http://biographien.kulturimpuls.org/detail.php?&id=361 (site visited March 8, 2016).

the same time.[680] In 1937, Heinz Frankfurt (†2012) came as a student to the school in Vienna and was accepted into the ninth grade, where Georg Unger was class advisor.

Georg Unger was experienced by his students as someone whom you could ask the most profound questions, whereupon he would go on a "thinking walk" as it were, slowly turning the question into a direction that opened perspectives for an answer. He was 30 years old at the time, and when the situation seemed to demand it he could raise his voice one moment to a mighty roar, and then dampen it to go back to concentrated work the next moment.[681]

Trude Thetter (1907–1982) and Gritli Eckinger (1907–1993) stayed on as eurythmists, who took their subject really seriously. After World War II, they built up the Vienna Eurythmy School, which bore their distinctive signature for many decades. They were joined by Ilse Metaxa, née von Baravalle (1900–1987), who later emigrated to the United States.[682]

After the Waldorf School in Hannover had closed in 1938, Ferdinand Wantschura invited Werner Lamerdin and his wife Gretel to come to Vienna to teach at the small school. The students loved Werner Lamerdin. He and his wife gave special attention to the Jewish students, taking them under their wings despite the dangers. Werner Lamerdin awakened a sense of community in the high school students and tried to open up ways for each individual to find his or her specific path in life, thus building a strong bond with the students. On January 12, 1943, he died in Russia.

Other people who worked at the school were Annemarie Poch (1907–1946), the sister of Gretel Lamerdin-Poch, and Liselotte Zöppritz (†1996). Karl Ege was a frequent guest teacher and René Maikowski also came occasionally. Friedel Strasser was a class teacher and a mathematician, who was always ready to help. He was one of the teachers who had survived the big upheaval in the school, as had *Frau Schulrat* [school councilwoman] Leopoldine Weiss and Hermine Schmidt, a class teacher of great determination. She was the face of the elementary school to the outside world and held the position of faculty chair, while *Frau Schulrat* represented the high school.

Josef Dworschak, with his undying sense of humor, taught arts and crafts and Josefa Wiedler was the handwork teacher. Josef Dworschak had come to the school together with Franz Wunderer and they both contributed a strong artistic pedagogical impulse, which they had fostered during their apprenticeship with the painter Friedrich Thetter (1877–1955). Before coming to the school they had worked in state schools and at the Hyrtl orphanage, and with this experience they managed to bring out astonishing color work from the students, even from really challenging ones. The work was so striking that professionals outside the school took notice. In 1926 and

---

680 Renatus Ziegler: Georg Unger. http://biographien.kulturimpuls.org/detail.php?&id=725 (site visited March 8, 2016).

681 Heinz Frankfurt: Von der ersten Rudolf Steinerschule in Wien. LR 7, 1973, p. 65.

682 http://biographien.kulturimpuls.org/detail.php?&id=1540 (site visited March 10, 2016).

1929, they were invited to exhibit student work at two large exhibits of the Vienna Secession and the Museum for Art and Industry, the present-day Museum for Applied Art at the Stubenring. [683] Their work was highly innovative and they tried out working in many media with the students. Through their work with Friedrich Thetter, they had formed a strong connection to Rudolf Steiner and Goethe's color theory, but despite their intensity and enthusiasm, their work initially found little resonance with other Waldorf educators. They had come to the Vienna Waldorf School in the 1930s.

In the summer of 1935, after the school crisis, the remaining teachers spent a few weeks together with the new ones on the large agricultural estate Autal, in the southeastern part of Steiermark. This estate belonged to Heinz Tomsche, an engineer who was part of a circle of supporters of the school. He was aware that the teachers were not able to afford holiday outings, and therefore he invited them to stay on the estate. For the teachers, the stay on the Autal estate presented a great opportunity to study Rudolf Steiner's education courses together and prepare for the new school year.

As long as the school did not yet have the so-called *Öffentlichkeitsrecht* [official recognition] required for private schools, the teachers were free to shape the curriculum in theory. In practice, however, they were not free, because the teachers had to prepare the children every year for state exams. After the school had acquired the *Öffentlichkeitsrecht*, they were obliged to apply the curriculum as they had stated they would, i.e., a curriculum that complied with official examination requirements. By hook or by crook, the teachers were obliged to put up with this split between their own intentions and official requirements up to the time the school was closed. Three years of good and intensive collaboration followed, during which they were supported by enthusiastic helpers on the board of the School Association, by parents, and by the school secretary, Ms. Petz. Financially, the school was supported during these three years by the board, especially by rich donors such as Else Weisheit, née Pollak (1901–1979), as well as parents like Mr. and Mrs. Rawitz, for there was no state support.

On March 15, 1938, right after the Anschluss on March 12, 1938, when Austria was annexed by the National Socialists, an edict came.[684] It contained regulations for civil servants in Austria, requiring an oath of allegiance to Adolf Hitler and excluding Jews from holding public office. The day after, the Rudolf Steiner School Association called an extraordinary meeting, in which the entire sitting board stepped back. They talked about the consequences of the edict and Ferdinand Wantschura became the head of the association. On March 26, 1938, the remaining teachers all became members of the National Socialist Teachers Union (NSLB). From now on, the association's balance sheets had to be reported to the authorities overseeing the finances of all organizations and institutions.[685] Ferdinand Wantschura, Friedrich Hiebel, and

683 Doris Rosenstingl: Friedrich Thetter. EK 9, 1976, p. 399ff.
684 Registerblatt I, 1938, p. 245; http://alex.onb.ac.at/cgi-contentalex?apm=0&aid=dra&datum=19380004 &seite=00000245&zoom=2 (site visited March 10, 2016).

The College of Teachers of the Rudolf Steiner School of Vienna, 1937/38 (from left to right): back row: J. Kral, W. Lamerdin, E. Blümel, F. Strasser, F. Hiebel, Dworschak, E. Zawischa, W. Mrazek; middle row: handwork teacher, school inspector Leopoldine Weiss, I. Metaxa, G. Eckinger, H. Schmidt, T. Thetter; front row: handwork teacher, school secretary, and L. Zöpritz.

Werner Lamerdin expected that all private schools would have to be closed. They tried to avoid this for the Waldorf school by making the Vienna school a member of the German Federation of Waldorf Schools. As early as March 14, 1938, Werner Lamerdin wrote a letter to that effect, addressed to René Maikowski, who wrote back: "I'm expecting to receive a positive answer soon to my request to continue a number of Waldorf schools in the Reich as recognized experimental schools, and am hopeful that the Vienna Rudolf Steiner School can be part of that new arrangement."

On April 4, 1938, Ferdinand Wantschura wrote to the school inspector in Vienna, asking that the Waldorf school could continue as it had been under the former state regulations. The request was accompanied by a letter from René Maikowski, in which he asked, in the name of the German Federation of Waldorf Schools, for permission to continue operating as a Waldorf school with Werner Lamerdin as his deputy. Werner Lamerdin proceeded to negotiate on behalf of the Vienna Waldorf School with the city's school inspector, supplying further documentation. On April 13, 1938, the Vienna school inspector directed his request to the Austrian ministry of education, which was technically subordinate now to the ministry of education

685 Gerhard Volz: Besetzung Österreichs und der Überlebenskampf der Rudolf-Steiner-Schule. In: Elisabeth Gergely and Tobias Richter (eds.): *Wiener Dialoge. Der österreichische Weg der Waldorfpädagogik.* 2011, p. 92.

of the German Reich. The request was read, whereupon department head Hansel signed a ministerial decree on May 4, 1938, stipulating that the curriculum would have to conform to state school requirements. However, no official permission could be granted because of discrepancies between the Waldorf curriculum and that of state schools.

René Maikowski spent a few days in Vienna and gave his impressions to Ernst Bindel in a letter of May 5, 1938. He does not speak very highly about the school, writing, "I was able to get an impression of how the school was running and to give a talk to the parents. A lot needs to be done and the school is a long way from being a Waldorf school. As it continues to build itself up, a lot of energy will have to be expended first and foremost on finding good teachers, but it seems that they are hard to find, especially considering the low salaries."[686] On May 12, René Maikowski had a conversation with department head Hansel, to clear up remaining sticking points. In spite of that, the Austrian ministry of education turned to its German counterpart to ask for a determination in this matter.

On July 12, 1938, an unexpected missive from the appointed second president of the city's Bureau of School Inspection came to the ministry in Vienna with a determination advising officials to reject the request of the Rudolf Steiner School Association, on the grounds that "they were dealing with anthroposophists and Rosicrucians, both belonging to the Masonic order." This position was worded even more sharply a few days later: "Dr. Rudolf Steiner is the founder of the teaching of anthroposophy. An association supporting a school that bears his name is therefore clearly an anthroposophical institution. It is well-known that anthroposophists and Rosicrucians are closely connected. In addition, I have to note that the Rudolf Steiner school was a gathering place for Jewish children who exceeded the degeneration of this race to a more than usual extent. The school shows that wild lack of discipline we associate with all Masonic educational systems."[687] This position was reported to Berlin by department head Hansel with a recommendation to withhold permission for the school's continued operation. On September 12, 1938, the answer came from Berlin, recommending they "take measures to dissolve the Rudolf Steiner schools (Waldorf schools)."

At the time the school was closed in 1938, it had just been built up to ninth grade and had about 160 students, some of whom came from Holland, India, or the United States. The school's inventory was donated to Dresden. The School Association was dissolved on December 30, 1938.[688]

---

686 René Maikowski in a letter to Ernst Bindel dated May 5, 1938. Archiv CB.

687 Gerhard Volz: Besetzung Österreichs und der Überlebenskampf der Rudolf-Steiner-Schule. In: Elisabeth Gergely and Tobias Richter (eds.): *Wiener Dialoge. Der österreichische Weg der Waldorfpädagogik.* 2011, p. 96f.

688 Facsimile in Gerhard Volz: Besetzung Österreichs und der Überlebenskampf der Rudolf-Steiner-Schule. In: Elisabeth Gergely and Tobias Richter (eds.): *Wiener Dialoge. Der österreichische Weg der Waldorfpädagogik.* 2011, p. 99f.

1928: Waldorf Education in Nürnberg

THE FOUNDING of a Waldorf school in Nürnberg in 1927–1928 came from the initiative of Andreas Körner (1875–1949), a state school teacher. He had been one of the very few guests who had attended Rudolf Steiner's lectures, published as *The Foundations of Human Experience,* and Rudolf Steiner had actually wanted to engage him as one of the teachers at the Stuttgart school. A small Waldorf playgroup started up in Nürnberg as early as 1927, and Klara Hattermann, who was highly interested but had no training yet, moved to Franconia and began working in this first kindergarten initiative.

Apart from the playgroup, the initiative group organized lectures by the Stuttgart Waldorf teachers and attempted to introduce Waldorf education to the public. The local authorities had a positive attitude toward the initiative and even promised the use of school rooms. An association for an independent school was founded, and Dr. Ludwig Rüll (†1942) took on the responsibility of chairing it. On January 21, 1928, he wrote that teachers were available and that as many as 35 children had enrolled.

Eduard Riegel and Anton Treiber, both in possession of state school certificates, were the two prospective teachers who were to found the school. The plan was to open the school at Easter 1928 in order to enable the children to attend the Nürnberg Waldorf school for the new school year. However, the city authorities withheld permission. The Nürnberg school department and the Bavarian state chancellorship in Munich were arguing back and forth, and could not reach agreement on the question of which paragraphs to base permission for founding the school on. The end of the story was that the Bavarian education ministry declined the application on December 29, 1928. The reasons they gave were that perusal of the curriculum and other documents had given rise to considerable doubts about the educational and scientific underpinnings.[689] Apparently the tried methods of the Bavarian school system saw no need for reform ideas of an independent school system, especially one that was free of any religious affiliations.[690]

1928: The Rudolf Steiner School in Berlin

BEFORE THE OFFICIAL Rudolf Steiner school in Berlin actually opened its doors there was a "back room school" in the living room of Dr. Bastiner on the Günzelstrasse, which they called the *Circle*. It started up at Easter of 1923 with six children and their teacher, Else Krause. After a few months the little group moved to the house of the Schublink family close to the Prager Platz, but their eurythmy periods were given in the eurythmy school at Potsdamer Strasse 39A. During the second school

---

689 Missive from the Bavarian ministry dated December 29, 1928. LS 3.21.025.
690 Wenzel M. Götte: *Erfahrungen mit Schulautonomie.* 2006, p. 301ff.

year, the little group of children was taught by Kurt Schreiber in the house of the Gall family on the Niebuhrstrasse. In the third and fourth years, 1925–1927, the school was located at Pragerstrasse 27, in the house of Mrs. Krüger, privy counselor and grandmother of one of the six children, Götz von Helmolt. Mr. Seidel took the third grade and Dr. Helmut Knauer the fourth, and both teachers also had lodgings in the large house. This little private school was in existence until the Rudolf Steiner school was founded in 1928.[691] This *Circle* was actually only one of the initiatives that prepared the founding of the school. Another one was a local group of the Stuttgart Association for Independent Schools.

During the preparatory years, Dr. Paul Oldendorff (1880–1950) was the one who formed the work of the local group. He was a professor in Berlin, one of the coworkers in the state advisory board on education, and had made a name through his dissertation on the work of the philosophy of Rudolf Eucken. He was the principal organizer of the great Waldorf conference sponsored by the Central Institute for Education, held May 31–June 2, 1926, featuring many of the Stuttgart Waldorf teachers.[692] Another prominent figure among the founders was the famous Assyria scholar Walter Andrae (1875–1956), who was on the board of the school and a parent representative.

The Stuttgart teachers had of course been informed about the preparatory steps that were taken in Berlin. It goes without saying that they would have preferred to wait with the founding of a new school until the existing schools had been consolidated and had enough teachers, but this did not get through to the Berliners. In any case, they did want to at least reserve the right to have the final say in the appointment of teachers.[693]

Meanwhile, Paul Oldendorff was pursuing a totally different approach, and withdrew from the endeavor when Waldorf teachers, primarily those from Stuttgart, rejected his attempts to develop experimental classes inside state schools. With regard to experimentation with Waldorf education within state institutions, there was the fear that too many compromises would have to be made, and teachers were determined to establish Waldorf schools without state interference. So in the uncompromising conflict between proponents of completely independent schools versus those who wanted to work within the system, Stuttgart threw its weight behind those who were proponents of freedom from state interference, and that ended up being the side that won out, so to speak.[694]

---

691 Götz von Helmolt: *70 Jahre Waldorfpädagogik in Berlin*. 1998, p. 55.
692 Wenzel M. Götte: *Erfahrungen mit Schulautonomie*. 2006, p. 304.
693 E. A. Karl Stockmeyer in a letter dated December 5, 1926, to Paul Oldendorff. In: W.M. Götte: *Erfahrungen mit Schulautonomie*. 2006, p. 305, note 825.
694 Curt Englert-Faye comments in *Versuchsschule oder Freie Schule*, saying something like, "When people start talking in terms of an antithesis such as 'state school versus free school,' you'll soon see them getting lost in abstractions like the banal either/or thinking of an 'only' world." Archiv LS 3.18.37. This controversy continued into the 2010s, for example in the antithesis between charter Waldorf schools and private Waldorf schools in the United States.

Students of the Rudolf Steiner School Berlin in the early 1930s with their teachers, Mr. Ferber and Miss Düberg

At Easter time 1928, the Freie Schule Berlin Association opened up the first three grades of a private elementary school based on Rudolf Steiner's pedagogical ideas. The chairman of the association was Mr. Rödenbeck, who had an office in Berlin-Lichterfelde, Mittelstrasse 1a. He was the one to go to for information or to enroll children in the new school. They presented themselves as follows: "The first [Waldorf] school in Berlin … sprang from the initiative of members of the Anthroposophical Society and interested parents, not from the wish of teachers. Fifty-six children started in the Genthiner Strasse at the festive opening on May 1. Dr. Herbert Hahn, representing the original Stuttgart faculty, opened the assembly."[695]

The 56 children, divided among a first grade and a combined grade 2/3/4, were taught by Herbert Schiele (1889–1940) and Magdalene-Ithwari Kiefel (1898–1988). Herbert Schiele had long experience as a teacher and therefore took on the combined class. On August 3, 1928, they received official permission from the authorities. Herbert Schiele had been a vice principal in a state school for many years, and as such he had gained a lot of experience in dealing with the officials. Besides, he was an arch Berliner, an indispensable asset for establishing the school. Therefore he became the contact person for dealing with the authorities. His class was soon divided into two when Anni Heuser (1896–1962) became the third teacher to join the school in December 1928.

Magdalene-Ithwari Kiefel was born in East India as the daughter of a missionary, and that was where she spent the first seven years of her life. After the death of her father the family returned to Pomerania. She went to school in Stettin and Köslin, and she completed her teacher training in Stargard, which qualified her to teach K–12. She began teaching as a private teacher and in those years she came into contact with anthroposophy and Waldorf education. At the same time, she also pursued

695 M.-I. Kiefel: 1927/28 Rudolf-Steiner-Schule Berlin. Festschrift. Other sources say May 7, 1928.

Lotte Ahr

an advanced course of study, resulting in a second state certificate, with a dissertation titled "My Attempts to Bring Art and Life into My Lessons, Inspired by Goethe." She sent this dissertation to Caroline von Heydebrand, with the request to be accepted into the Stuttgart teacher training seminar. Instead, the dissertation was printed in the magazine *Erziehungskunst*[696] and she was invited to take the first class of the new school in Berlin, starting in October 1928. That's what she ended up doing, and she remained in that position until 1938.[697]

In 1929, a former girls' school building became available, and the school moved from the Genthiner Strasse to the Kreuzberger Grossbeerenstrasse. In the same year, Clara Düberg (1876–1943) joined the faculty. She was born in the Baltic Sea region and had completed her studies at the Waldorf teacher training center in Stuttgart. In these years, the economic situation in Germany became ever more difficult, but, Berlin being the vibrant, open, and innovative city it has always been, the school thrived and with it arose the need for more teachers. In 1931 the school counted 322 children in seven grades—strong growth for a school that was only three years old.

Many children lived far away and many of them had a 1½-hour commute to school by train. This presented a considerable problem because of the growing economic troubles, and with mounting inflation many parents could no longer afford paying for transportation.

Gustav Spiegel had studied German in Jena after he completed the Christian Community priest training in 1922. He was a very young man at the time and did not pursue the priesthood, but finished his studies in Jena with a double major in German literature and theology. For a while he worked for the state of Thuringia, and in 1933 he took a first grade at the Waldorf school in Berlin. He got along very well with his colleagues there, something that did not always work as well later on in his life.

Ernst Weissert (1905–1981) taught in the school from 1930 until 1938, the same years as Maria Schröfel (1896–1978), who had taught in the school in Essen before that. In Berlin, she taught handwork. She developed a strong and close

---

696 EK 1, Oktober 1927, p. 45ff.
697 Dietrich Chrometzka: Gedenken an Magdalene-Ithwari Kiefel. LR 36, 1988, p. 102ff. M.-I. Kiefel gave private lessons in the home of the Hellmers family in Bremen from 1938 until 1946, looking after Marianne Hellmers especially. At the end of the war, the group of children she taught in the Stuckenborstel summer home of the family had grown to 12. After the war, M.-I. Kiefel founded the independent Rudolf Steiner School of Ottersberg (called Freie Schule Stuckenborstel when it was founded on May 9, 1946, and then renamed Freie Rudolf Steiner Schule Ottersberg after a move in November of that year). She taught religion lessons there until she was 80.

friendship with Anni Heuser (1896–1962), Inez Arnold (1900–1989), and Lotte Ahr (1904–1981). These four women devoted their whole lives to the building up of Waldorf schools, working in Germany, Finland, Scotland, and Switzerland. All of them played leading roles in building up the movement after the Second World War. Ella Rothe (1903–1982) also taught at the school in Essen first and then moved to Berlin early in the summer of 1931, in order to take over a seventh grade midstream. She taught there until the school had to close in 1938. Further teachers who came were, amongst others, Helmut Hundhausen, Werner Rosenthal (1898–1961), and Robert Schiller (†1945).

Maria Schröfel

The Rudolf Steiner School in Berlin during the Time of National Socialism

THE EURYTHMIST Lola Jaerschky (1902–1991) was half Jewish and left the faculty in 1933 in order to save the school from getting into trouble. As in all private schools, Waldorf schools were subject to employment regulations for civil servants, passed on April 7, 1933, which forced them to no longer employ anybody with questionable political affiliations or of non-Aryan origin.

As mentioned above, Herbert Schiele was in charge of dealing with the authorities, and he was also in charge of any written correspondence. As such, he was the one who negotiated in July 1933 with Hans Schemm, the official head of the National Socialist Teachers Union, when the question came up whether teachers would have to be members of that body. Herbert Schiele argued that the Waldorf schools were not teaching a worldview, explaining, in response to a question from Hans Schemm, that the independent Waldorf schools had "nothing in common" with Judaism or Marxism. Apart from that, he stressed the willingness of the Waldorf schools to cooperate with the National Socialist authorities. Hans Schemm accepted his reasoning, and Herbert Schiele's tactics worked for the time being.

But then, in August 1933, the school in Berlin, with Herbert Schiele and Ernst Weissert in the vanguard, suddenly announced a change of course, saying they did not trust the National Socialists' intentions and distancing themselves at the same time from the relative pliability of the German Federation of Waldorf Schools. Herbert Schiele wrote to the Waldorf school in Dresden, for example, that they should not invest too much effort in complying with the conformation measures, arguing that this would not guarantee acceptance by the authorities; it was much more important to defend what Rudolf Steiner stood for.[698]

698 Letter from the Berlin school to the Dresden school, dated August 24, 1933. Archiv LS 4.2.115.

Students of the Rudolf Steiner School Berlin with their teacher, Magdalene-Ithwari Kiefel, 1932

In February 1934, the school moved to a larger building in the Berliner Strasse (the present-day Otto-Suhr-Allee in Charlottenburg), because many more children wanted to enroll and the Grossbeerenstrasse could no longer house the student population, which had grown to 367 at that point. That same year, Erich Weismann (1905–1984), who built up the Waldorf School in Reutlingen after the war, joined the faculty. Starting at Easter 1936, the Berlin Rudolf Steiner School also fell under the edict that no students could be accepted anymore into first grades. Herbert Schiele, Ella Rothe, and Ernst Weissert became more vocal in questioning the political strategy in the negotiations their colleagues from the German Federation of Waldorf Schools were pursuing. They no longer trusted the Nazi regime's intentions, and began to distance themselves from the attempts to find ways and means to guarantee the Waldorf schools' continued operation.

In looking back on those years, Ernst Weissert signaled that the growing political threats were matched by a growth in awareness. He later called Ella Rothe "a guardian of the spirit of education." The decision taken in the summer of 1937 was characteristic of the faculty. At that point, the authorities demanded that the teachers, like all private school teachers, had to swear allegiance to Adolf Hitler and put that in writing as well. This led to their decision to focus on preparing the students to make the transition to state schools. They freely decided to close the school, because they did not want to go too far in compromising and becoming untrue to themselves. On August 26, 1937, the faculty in Berlin notified the Stuttgart school as follows: "We would like to inform you that our school will stop functioning as a Rudolf Steiner school as of today. There is no financial need to do so, but we felt inwardly obligated to take this step and have informed both parents and the authorities that we feel we have to close the school in order to remain true to Rudolf Steiner's work. In a well-attended meeting, the parent body was informed and has accepted this step in full seriousness. We are preparing the children to make the transition into other schools. We foresee that this process of preparation will be completed by Easter 1939."[699] On March 14, 1938, school inspector Fielitz informed the ministry of education that the Berlin Steiner school was being dissolved and was only continuing to prepare the third and fourth grades for transition into state schools. As was to be expected, he could not resist adding some deprecatory remarks about the feminine character of the Waldorf school system.[700]

During the year that followed, Maria Schröfel, Ernst Pönisch, Lotte Ahr, Erich Weismann, and Ernst Weissert taught the transition course, which was completed on April 1, 1939. Next to that there was instruction for remaining children, which included many Jewish children who immigrated or did not want to be prepared for a National Socialist school.[701]

Ernst Weissert during the retraining course in Berlin, 1939

Together with her colleagues Lotte Ahr, Ernst Weissert, and Erich Weismann, Maria Schröfel still gave private lessons until 1941 to so-called *Attestkinder*, that is to say, children whose parents could attest that they could only be in a classroom with up to five other children. When the Gestapo put a halt to this, Ernst Weissert, Lotte Ahr, and Erich Weismann were locked up for a few months because they had continued this forbidden education. Erich Weismann was taken to Hiddensee, where he spent the summer of 1941 with 12 students, teaching in the summer residence of Martha and Konrad Delius in Vitte.

Anna-Sophie Bäuerle gave a picture of this time through children's eyes: "A few teachers and children, whose parents were not afraid of the government, continued to be taught in small groups 'in order to prepare for a transition.' First we occupied apartments which were destined for the wrecking ball: Charlottenburger Ufer, then a place close to the Ernst Reuter Platz, and finally in a house opposite the Charlottenburg town hall. Small classes were taught by Lotte Ahr, Ernst Weissert, and Erich Weismann—the 'indestructible' teachers from the old guard. The only classes allowed were little groups of a maximum of six children. Of course, the 12 of us were always together. Until the day came that the school inspector appeared, but we were prepared for that. Fortunately he first went to look for the little ones, so what we had practiced would have a chance. Pictures on the walls were turned around or hidden; all of a sudden the silly 'History Book for German Youth' was lying on the benches. There was a quick countdown, and six of us, our satchels on our backs, snuck down the back stairs in our socks, shoes in hand. Nobody noticed us. Then, at the time we

699 Detlef Hardorp: *70 Jahre Waldorfpädagogik in Berlin.* 1998, p. 62f.
700 BArch Ella 0697-38 / 276-277.
701 Anna-Sophia Bäuerle: *70 Jahre Waldorfpädagogik in Berlin.* 1998, p. 58.

Communication of the
Rudolf Steiner School
Berlin to the parents on
March 28, 1938, to close
the school

UMSCHULUNG
Berlin-Charlottenburg
Berlinerstr. 39

An die Eltern und Freunde der Rudolf Steiner Schule!

Der Schulschluss wurde, wie Sie ja schon von den Kindern erfahren haben, auf Dienstag, den 29. März 38, festgesetzt, da wir das Schulhaus räumen müssen. An diesem Tage werden die Kinder von uns entlassen werden.

Die von uns im August 1937 übernommene Umschulungsarbeit ist mit dem gewünschten Ergebnis abgeschlossen. Die zur Umschulung erforderlichen Prüfungen sind allgemein bestanden worden, soweit das von uns jetzt schon überschaut werden kann.

Am 14.3.38 erhielten wir die Nachricht, dass der Freien Waldorfschule in Stuttgart die Weiterführung der Schule ab Ostern untersagt worden ist. Alle Schüler müssen zum neuen Schuljahr in andren Schulen angemeldet werden.

Uns Lehrern der Rudolf Steiner Schule Berlin obliegt heute nur noch, Ihnen als den Eltern und Freunden der Schule aufs herzlichste zu danken für all Ihre Hilfe bei dem Aufbau und der Erhaltung der Schule. Dass solche fruchtbare Arbeit, wie sie durch die Pädagogik Rudolf Steiners möglich ist, nicht weiter fortgesetzt werden kann, ist eine Tatsache geworden, die uns mit tiefstem Schmerz aber auch mit tiefer Sorge erfüllt. Jeder, der mit der Schule verbunden war, kann die wirkliche Tragweite des jetzigen Geschehens ermessen. Wir stellen noch einmal fest, dass die Verantwortung für die Schliessung der Schule nicht auf denen ruht, die für die Schule gearbeitet haben.

Jetzt ist eines notwendig, dass wir alle die Ideen wahrhafter Menschenbildung in uns lebendig halten und pflegen, und dass

wir uns immer stärker besinnen auf die Quellen, aus denen allein diese Ideen geholt werden können. In diesem Streben fühlen wir uns weiter verbunden allen, welche diese Schule liebten.

Das Lehrerkollegium
der Rudolf Steiner Schule Berlin.

had made out, we returned just as punctually and innocently to take our turn...." At the instigation of the Delius family, a remaining group of just a handful of children continued to be taught by Frau Wieth until 1942.

After the war, Maria Schröfel, together with her former colleagues, Lotte Ahr and Ernst Weissert, worked in the Stuttgart Waldorf School.[702] From 1948, Ella Rothe helped with the rebuilding of the Berlin Rudolf Steiner School—a strict authority, who also, as Sigrid Gräfe recalls, set "an example of deep inward, religious devotion to education."[703]

1928: The Rudolf Steiner School in New York

THE SMALL, private Rudolf Steiner school in New York City celebrated its opening on October 1, 1928. The founders wrote a telegram to the Stuttgart Waldorf School, together with a circle of anthroposophical friends in New York: Virginia Field Birdsall, Irene Brown, Rupert Carr, Irene S. Foltz, Alice Heckel, Arvia MacKaye, Leopold Neuscheller, Lucy van der Pals-Neuscheller, Margret Peckham, Louise Tuxbury, Mrs. Deterpitz, Miriam Loder Wallace, Ione Taylor, and Christoph Linder. It ran: "At the opening of Rudolf Steiner School in New York in October, first we send you all our hearting [sic] greetings asking you to unite with us in thoughts and hopes for a fruitful and strong development of this first American school in the spirit of Rudolf Steiner." So, when the very first Waldorf school outside Europe started up, it was the wish of the founders to seek common ground in building up the Waldorf school movement and to be united in spirit.

Twelve children, Maria and Mechthild Neuscheller and Sabina Zay among them, met with the two class teachers Virginia Field Birdsall and Irene Foltz in Irene Brown's three-story house at 111 East 39th Street in Murray Hill, Manhattan. The property had been acquired especially for that purpose, but served as teacher accommodation as well, so the house had to be rearranged for teaching every day.[704] The school began with these few children and five teachers. Starting in 1926, the initial steps were taken by a group of people, first among them Virginia Field Birdsall and Irene Brown. In order to prepare the ground, they founded an American sister-branch of the British Educational Union for the Realization of Spiritual Values. In issue 5/6 of their members newsletter, it was reported that the American branch of the educational union had been founded with the hope to invite Rudolf Steiner to the United States, but that this intention had been prevented by his early death.[705]

702 Ernst Weissert: Maria Schröfel. LR 9, 1979, p. 98f.
703 Sigrid Gräfe: Ella Rothe (January 16, 1903–December 31, 1982). LR 26, 1983, p. 96.
704 Virginia Birdsall, for example lived on the third floor, and rearranged her room every morning to serve as a classroom.
705 American Branch of The Educational Union for the Realization of Spiritual Values Vol I, Nos. 5 and 6, February and May 1927, p. 1.

Soon people came to the realization that a school in America could only be built up by an independent association, whereupon this American branch was made independent, named Rudolf Steiner Educational Union. Professor Olin D. Wannamaker (1875–1974) was asked to be chairman. At the wish of his wife, his daughter Margaret had been enrolled in the Stuttgart Waldorf School, where he visited her several times. So in a sense he had much more practical experience with Waldorf education than the women interested in founding a school, with whom he had been in conversation for a number of years. Virginia Field Birdsall (1878–1963) had been on a quest to find new paths in the field of education. She had founded a Montessori kindergarten in her house, for example, and was teaching at the progressive Unkowah School in Bridgeport, Connecticut. When Irene Brown told her about Rudolf Steiner, she was heading the elementary school department of a well-known girls' school, the Baird School in Orange, New Jersey. During the time that she was directing this school, she had invited Lucy Neuscheller, who had newly arrived in the US, to teach eurythmy to the children and had asked Arvia MacKaye and Irene Brown to teach painting. At the suggestion of Irene Brown, Virginia attended Rudolf Steiner's lectures in Ilkley, Yorkshire, in August 1923, after which she did a few weeks' practicum at the school in Stuttgart.

Both experiences, the lectures in Ilkley and the children at the Stuttgart school, made a big impression on her and marked a new beginning in her work. She felt confirmed in her quest to find new ways in education. It followed naturally that she would take an active part in the founding of the new Waldorf school, in which she became a teacher and took on a position of leadership by representing the school to the outside world, especially because private school parents were used to dealing with a head of school. Irene Foltz was one of the first students at the Stuttgart teacher seminar and returned to the US, just in time for the beginning of the new school year 1927/28.

Irene Brown (†1934)[706] was a painter and cousin of the painter, William Scott Pyle. Her acquaintance with Rudolf Steiner dated back to the time before World War I. During the war, when she needed assistance with the education of two adopted boys, her friend, Hazel MacKaye, recommended her niece, Arvia, to help her. This niece was the daughter of the writer Percy Wallace MacKaye. From childhood on, it was apparent that Arvia was a very special young woman. A verse written by Edwin Arlington Robinson, a friend of her father's, speaks volumes.[707] When spending the summer of 1920 together in Putney, Vermont, Arvia MacKaye (1902–1989) was introduced to Rudolf Steiner and anthroposophy by Irene Brown. The two of them

---

706 Henry Barnes: *Into the Heart's Land*. 2005, p. 86ff.

707 The poem is printed in Henry Barnes: *Into the Heart's Land*. 2005, p. 89. Henry Barnes was married to Arvia's sister, Christy MacKaye. Christy MacKaye-Barnes published a biography of her sister, *Arvia MacKaye-Ege: A Pioneer for Anthroposophy*. 1995.

Math lesson at the Rudolf Steiner School, New York, in the 1930s

participated in the Christmas meeting of 1923 in Dornach, a decisive meeting for the Anthroposophical Society. This meeting made an enormous impression and heralded a new chapter for Irene Brown, who from then on felt she had to do everything she could to bring anthroposophy to North America. She played a decisive role in building up anthroposophical life in the United States. As early as 1923, Marie Steiner put her in touch with Lucy van der Pals-Neuscheller (1888–1962), and she ended up inviting her and her husband Leopold Neuscheller to come to New York in order to anchor eurythmy in North America. Ita Wegman introduced her to Christoph Linder, whereupon Irene Brown asked the young Swiss physician to come to New York in 1926 to open an anthroposophical doctor's practice there. She was a member of the Spalding family, which enabled her to contribute a lot to the first steps toward an expansion of art, medicine, and education through anthroposophy.

In the autumn of 1929, the school, which counted eight grades by now and 28 students, moved into a suitable five-story building at 20 West 73rd Street, which had previously been occupied by the New York Dalton School of Mrs. Packhurst, who, by the way, was herself a participant in Rudolf Steiner's lectures on education in England. It is not known whether what she heard there had any influence on her own pedagogical work. So, next to the two class teachers Virginia Field Birdsall and Irene Foltz, three more teachers were working at the school from the beginning: Arvia MacKaye taught painting, sculpture, and handwork; Lucy Neuscheller, eurythmy; and Leopold Neuscheller, German and music.

The rent for the school amounted to $8000 per year. Then came Black Friday and with it the onset of the Great Depression. Even though Mrs. Packhurst had opened the prospect that her students would enroll in the new school, this did not happen, and with the few Waldorf students they had, the large building became much too expensive. They could not afford the rent anymore. So there was nothing for it but to let out the top half of the building in order to cover the costs by collecting rent.[708] This worked for a while.

From April 1–15, 1929, the school put on its first official presentation. The plan was to exhibit children's drawings and student work from the Waldorf School in Stuttgart. The event was sponsored by Baron von Pechmann of the German Museum in Munich and organized by the American Federation of Arts. The exhibition was to be held at the Art Center, 65 East 56th Street, but there was just one problem: The pictures did not arrive on time for the opening.

With the onset of the worldwide economic crisis in the early 1930s, the school's continued existence was constantly in danger. The situation became acute, and the board members of the school association decided to close the school, fully intending to open it again at a later date. This met with adamant resistance on the part of the teachers. They wanted to keep the school going no matter what and to continue to work with the children no matter how.

In order to enable the work to go on, they offered to take cuts in their salaries, low as they were. Through these saving measures, they got through the crisis. In the school year 1932/33 Virginia Birdsall and Irene Foltz did a practicum at the Waldorf School on the Uhlandshöhe in Stuttgart and gratefully took in suggestions, learning as much as they could in the span of time they had. From the middle of the 1930s onward, enrollment went up remarkably, mainly because of the increasing number of immigrants finding their way to New York.

Among them was William Harrer (1905–1978), who laid important groundwork for teaching science in the upper grades and made sure the quality of teaching was on a solid footing. John (1912–1999) and Carol Gardner, as well as Marjorie Spock (1904–2008) were teachers at the school for a few years, but left in 1937. One of the teachers who had emigrated from Vienna was Friedrich Hiebel, who published the magazine *Education as an Art*, which became the official publication of the Rudolf Steiner Educational Union in 1940 and continued to be published until 1978. Other immigrants who supported the school one way or another were Hermann Poppelbaum (1891–1971), the composer Egon Lustgarten (1887–1961), Arnold Wadler (1882–1951), a lawyer and linguist who found political asylum in the US, and Sigurd Rascher (1907–2001), a former student at the Stuttgart Waldorf School and a renowned classical saxophone player.

Another immigrant who made an essential contribution was Hermann von Baravalle, who used to be a mathematics teacher at the Stuttgart school and had been the leader of the section for mathematics and astronomy at the Goetheanum in Dornach. Just like Leopold Neuscheller, he challenged people to shape their lessons

708 Henry Barnes: *Into the Heart's Land.* 2005, p. 177ff.

in accordance with North American circumstances rather than copying the Stuttgart model. At the occasion of one of his many visits to the small school on January 20, 1938, he emphasized this very clearly.

In 1940, Henry Barnes (1912–2008) started as a class teacher at the New York School. He had studied at Harvard, completed his Waldorf teacher training in Stuttgart, and taught at the New School in London from 1935–1939. Apart from a short interruption between 1943 and 1945, when he served in the American army, Henry Barnes taught at the New York Steiner School until 1977, first as a class teacher and later as a history teacher in the high school. During these many years he put his stamp not only on the New York Steiner School, but on the whole Waldorf school movement of North America as well. His wife, Christy MacKaye-Barnes, was just as interested in the school as her husband and also started teaching at the school. Henry

Children of the Rudolf Steiner School, New York, on the way to the park, 1940s.

Barnes held the office of General Secretary of the Anthroposophical Society in the United States from 1974–1991, thus helping to shape anthroposophical work in America for nearly three quarters of a century. Between his 90th and his 93rd years, he wrote a monumental work called *Into the Heart's Land, A Century of Rudolf Steiner's Work in North America*. In it, he gave an extensive picture of how anthroposophical initiatives and institutions were built up during the 20th century in America, with many a story from personal experience.

During the 1930s, the school was a member of the Progressive Schools Association, and the teachers were able to contribute to conferences in a variety of ways, sometimes assisted by Hermann von Baravalle, as for example in the conference held November 29–30, 1939. The Waldorf school was viewed as an example of the way American education could possibly be reformed, at least by those on the inside.

In 1941, the lease was canceled and the school had to leave the building at 20 West 73rd Street. The school found another location on East 91st Street. After only three years, this house was suddenly and unexpectedly sold as well, and they had to search all over again. In the meantime, however, the school had gained the support of a strong group of parents, who were solidly behind the school. Real estate prices had shot up at the end of the 1930s, due to the influx of immigrants. At last they found an empty house at 15 East 79th Street. It almost seemed impossible that they could afford the asking price of $50,000. This situation inspired the idea to create shares and get individuals to invest. The plan succeeded and the school occupies the building until this very day. The number of students increased in the course of World War II, partly because many parents were forced to stay in New York due to the war. This changed radically after 1945. Many parents moved away, causing the school to lose so many children that they were facing a serious financial problem. The board of the School Association wanted to give up a second time, but consulted with the teachers before carrying out such a decision. They asked each teacher individually, and their unanimous willingness to take on the financial risk was so convincing that all board members except one stepped back and turned the responsibility for the future of the school over to the teachers. It took three years before all hurdles were cleared.

In 1948, Karl Ege, one of the last persons to be asked to join the Stuttgart faculty by Rudolf Steiner, was invited to come to the Waldorf school in New York City and help build up the high school. This was a life-changing move for him, because in 1950 he married Arvia MacKaye. It took until 1955 until the teachers took the step of going beyond the elementary school to start a ninth grade, which graduated four years later, thus becoming the first graduating class of a kindergarten through grade 12 Waldorf school in America. Karl Ege led this first twelfth grade, which graduated from the school in 1959. He worked for over 20 years in the United States and also helped in the building up of other schools.

1928: Waldorf Education in Prague

In 1928, Zdená Topicová and Marianne Eisner tried to organize a Waldorf kindergarten in Prague, but their attempts were thwarted at first because of bureaucratic obstacles.[709] In spite of that, they somehow managed to start teaching a little group that year, which was subsequently led by a kindergarten teacher from Halle an der Saale from 1931 onward. In 1931, Marianne Eisner began preparing to open a first grade, intended as a private school to begin with. At this time, Dr. Hans Eiselt (1895–1936), who represented the German-speaking branch of the Anthroposophical Society in Prague, headed the Anthroposophical Society in the Czech Republic together with Otakar Krkavec. Rudolf Peissig (1907–1988)[710] worked with them to prepare a Waldorf school in Prague. He had been an elementary school teacher in Aussig, Grosstschochau, and Karwitz, spoke Czech, and had met anthroposophy early in his life, when he was 21 years old. He visited pedagogical conferences in Dornach again and again, coinciding with the time that this planning process was going on. As they were searching for a suitable teacher, they asked Caroline von Heydebrand whether she could recommend somebody who could come to Prague as early as September.[711]

The initiators called a meeting on June 5, 1931, to present their plans to all who might be interested. At this point in time, Ms. Stankova was ready to start teaching,

---

709 Zdenek Vana: Rudolf Steiner in Prag. In: Beiträge aus der Rudolf Steiner Gesamtausgabe Nr. 109, 1992, p. 36.
710 Lotte Hopp: Rudolf Peissig. LR 36, 1988, p. 107f. Starting in 1948, Rudolf Peissig was a class teacher at the Freie Waldorfschule Ulm for 24 years.
711 Card written by M. Eisner, dated May 9, 1931. Archiv LS 3.15.01.

and perhaps G. E. Mayer from Dresden. Erich Schwebsch also recommended Heinrich Wollborn and René Maikowski from the school in Essen. But the initiators in Prague were not able to come up with the money that could support an entire family, so they did not ask either of the two gentlemen, but decided to opt for Mrs G. E. Mayer instead. When they notified Erich Schwebsch of their decision, he answered that they had to decide this at their own risk, because Mrs. Mayer was unknown in Stuttgart. In order to prepare for her work, Marianne Eisner wanted Mrs. Mayer to do two practicums beforehand, three weeks in Dresden and another two weeks in Stuttgart starting September 8, 1931. But the Stuttgart faculty thought these practicums would be too short, and that the timing was not right.[712] Nothing came of this attempt to found a school because of the political developments.

1929: The Rudolf Steiner School in Bergen

In January 1926, Maren Marstrander (1882–1967) started teaching a few children in her home in Fjøsanger, close to the city of Bergen on the coast of Norway. She started this private school venture in spite of the fact that her husband was middle school director of a state school. She had done her teacher training in Munich and had no experience or specific knowledge of Waldorf education at the time, even though she was very interested in it. Children kept coming to her school, and her house soon became too small to harbor them all. So she started looking for a teacher who would be able to build up a Waldorf school together with her.

At this point of her life, she suffered a frightful blow of destiny. Her husband died in a traffic accident in 1927. She now had to go on alone, without his help, and had to face many tasks she never had to deal with before. In need of much more support, she now turned to Ellen Krebs, a eurythmist in Dornach who had been recommended to her by Signe Roll. As was customary at the time, one needed to ask the executive council at the Goetheanum for permission to found a Waldorf school, so the Bergen school was under the same obligation. In a letter dated April 22, 1926, Günther Wachsmuth gave permission on behalf of the Goetheanum. At that time, he was the one in the executive council who was responsible for the entire correspondence of the General Anthroposophical Society in Dornach.[713]

With the Goetheanum's backing, the first thing Ellen Krebs did was to go to Norway, and once there she started teaching the combined 1/2 grade. In addition, she taught the 25 other children in the school eurythmy and painting. This homeschool in the house of the Marstrander family was the forerunner of the Waldorf school in Bergen.

---

712 Marianne Eisner wrote this on August 12, 1931. Archiv LS 3.15.06. Erich Schwebsch answered on August 17, 1931. Archiv LS 3.15.07.
713 Letter by Günther Wachsmuth, dated April 22, 1926. Archiv LS 3.16.02.

The Founding of the Rudolf Steiner School

IN 1929, the actual Rudolf Steiner school in Bergen was founded by Mimi Grieg-Bing (†1941),[714] in close collaboration with Johanne Jebsen. At the time, Mimi Grieg-Bing led an anthroposophical group in Bergen, and it was she who was the driving force behind the founding, working in tandem with Johanne Jebsen. In the position of head of school, she took financial responsibility and formed a board of trustees to sponsor the venture. The school started with a small first grade of five boys and six girls, housed in a villa in the section of town called Kalvedalen. The authorities took no notice of the little school, so for the next years it could operate completely undisturbed. Berghild Thunold (1900–1981), one of the first two teachers, prepared for her task by studying at the teachers seminar in Stuttgart and did a practicum at the schools in Stuttgart and Zürich.

She was committed, heart and soul, to putting Rudolf Steiner's pedagogy into practice; so, she proved to be the right person at the right time when the school started up. Hilde Jung (1902–1958), a eurythmist from Tübingen, was by her side. The following year, the new first grade was taken by Edith Mohn-Gundersen, who also studied at the teacher seminar in Stuttgart. Lessons were held in the very beautiful house at Kalfarveien 88B, which had been rented for three years to begin with. In order to cover rent, salaries, and all the other costs, they charged each child 20 kroner per year. Many parents had a hard time coming up with this amount, and therefore the income had to be supplemented by donations to the association. The school owed

714 Mimi Grieg-Bing gives a detailed description of the founding in a letter to E. A. Karl Stockmeyer, dated November 10, 1929. Archiv LS 3.09.01.

its economic foundation largely to generous contributions from Wilhelm Jebsen, a ship owner who had no specific relationship to anthroposophy or Waldorf education. He simply supported the activities of his wife and put a total of 50,000 kroner at the disposal of the school.

Two years later, Dan Lindholm (1908–1998) joined the faculty and stayed as a class teacher for seven years. In the years after that, the new teachers who came to the school were Ernst Sørensen (1903–1972), Jörgen Smit (1916–1991), Nils Gustav Hertzberg (1913–1995), Gustava Hertzberg, and Sissi Tynæs (1905–1979). The faculty of the Stuttgart Waldorf School still felt responsible for the quality of the teaching and the development of Waldorf pedagogy. The Stuttgart teachers therefore tried to help the young fledgling schools as much as possible, and supplement the teacher training by visiting the schools and sitting in on lessons. Thus Herbert Hahn visited the Bergen school in 1927 and 1928 to do mentoring. The above-mentioned Ernst Sørensen began as a class teacher in 1935 and soon became a leading figure in the school. "To a large extent, we owe it to him that a large circle of people came to respect the school and that the parents then began to develop more of an understanding of what the school tries to achieve. Without respect and understanding, a Steiner school cannot exist after all. In his capacity as a lecturer and writer, and as the editor of the news bulletin of the school, he managed to build bridges from the school to the surrounding cultural life."[715]

In 1939, Bjarne Eliassen (1901–1986) joined the faculty and also took on the business administration of the school. He made it possible for the teachers to work without constant financial worries. In 1938, Signe Roll-Wikberg moved back to Norway together with her husband and her two sons, and settled in Bergen this time. She started off as a class teacher in the Rudolf Steiner school, then continued to work as a eurythmist until 1951.

With the increasing number of creative personalities in the faculty during the 1930s and 1940s, the school's quality of teaching reached a high level, both in terms of subject matter and pedagogical caliber, in spite of—or perhaps due to—meager resources, which only increased when Norway was occupied by the Nazis in April 1940. And they constantly had to move from one rental location to another.

In the autumn of 1940, Jörgen Smit moved back to his hometown of Bergen, after studying philology in Oslo and Basel and becoming an active member of the Anthroposophical Society. In January 1941 he took a first grade, unperturbed by the fact that he had to sleep on a folding bed in his classroom, for he had no choice but to use the classroom as his house, since the meager income did not suffice to cover any rent. Dan Lindholm recounted afterward: "It was delightful to see Jörgen

---

715 Report about the Rudolf Steiner School in Bergen, written by Signe Roll-Wikberg in 1946. Archiv BFWS.

Jörgen Smit, a teacher at the Bergen Waldorf School, summer of 1941

Smit among the school children. He was over six feet tall, and the children were not much higher than his knees! And then there was his strikingly conscientious care and steady patience in helping the children!"[716] "The effort he took with his students must have been enormous. He was a doer, who lived for and with his students. He combined deeply spiritual human insight with a practicality. One girl among the Bergen Waldorf school students, who had him as a gymnastics teacher, a subject she was weak in, told me how he managed to spur her on to practice, practice, and practice. That was his motto for everything in life. He worked a total of 24 years at the Waldorf school in Bergen.

In the school year 1955/56 Jörgen Smit had a sabbatical. He traveled through his beloved Greece and visited the different anthroposophical initiatives in Europe one by one, 33 schools in all, as he told me with a twinkle in his eye [...]. They were not flash visits; he took his time, was highly interested in the way other people worked, and he had a keen eye for the essence of things. It was not always easy to be with him, because he had zero aptitude for small talk. He rejected empty chatter, and was known to dismiss difficult circumstances with one, at most two words."[717] He stayed in Bergen until 1965, having taken three classes through from grades one through seven.

Both Jörgen Smit and Nils G. Hertzberg, who had joined the school in the autumn of 1941, took on a hefty public lecture schedule next to their teaching, each tackling different subjects. During the German occupation, the school was temporarily closed, but they kept it going, underground so to speak, from 1940 until 1945.[718] Because of the bombing raids during the winter of 1944/45, classes were evacuated to several places outside the city and could go on functioning relatively undisturbed.

716 Dan Lindholm: Jörgen Smit (June 21, 1916–May 10, 1991). LR 43, 1991, p. 71.
717 Rembert Biemond: http://joergensmit.org/de/html/biografie/biografie_biemond.html (site visited October 14, 2016.)
718 The history of Waldorf education in Norway: Erik Marstrander: *Menneske først! Steinerpedagogikk i Oslo 1926-1996.* 1996.

1929: The Rudolf Steiner School Dresden

In 1924, the newly founded Christian Community started building up a congregation in Dresden, and Reverend Gerhard Klein (1902–1980) was sent to lead it. His wife Elizabeth von Staudt (1901–1983), who had grown up in an anthroposophical household in Munich and had studied natural sciences, came with him. She kept remembering what Michael Bauer had said to her: "Many people can marry. The first line of order for you, however, is to found a Waldorf school. That's your main task."[719]

She first became a private teacher in the household of a government official, Walter Chrambach (1887–1944). He and his wife Bertha became highly interested in the type of education she practiced, which led to an invitation to speak about Waldorf education in their *salon*. She went on to give more lectures in different settings, such as a talk for the *Freidenker* [freethinkers] and one for a workers' group.

So Elisabeth Klein used every opportunity to give introductory courses on Waldorf pedagogy in Dresden and to draw attention to what it had to offer. She managed to get a few teachers interested in the new education, among them Frida Funk and Thea Achtnich (1893–1969). To augment her own efforts, she invited teachers from the Stuttgart school to give lectures, among them Caroline von Heydebrand, Herbert Hahn, Eugen Kolisko, Walter Johannes Stein, and Hermann von Baravalle. Teachers and parents worked for three years, studying all of Rudolf Steiner's pedagogical lectures in a study group specifically dedicated to this work.

The preparatory work for founding an independent school needed more support, of course, requiring a joint effort of a larger circle of people. One of those people working in the initiative group was Monica von Miltitz (1885–1972), who would prove to be one of the absolutely vital people who carried things through in difficult situations. She knew many people and was therefore able to help Elisabeth Klein in many ways, one of which was to open the channels to the local authorities. Wilhelm Hartnacke (1878–1952), minister of culture in Saxony, gave his permission and predicted that the school would have to close soon because of lack of funds. Permission to operate would only be granted when proof of accommodation was given, so, since a school building was the prerequisite for official recognition, Gerhard and Elisabeth Klein moved out of their living quarters. Once they had done that, all local obstacles were cleared.

Some people at the Goetheanum felt that all available energy was now going into the work of building up anthroposophical institutions and that nobody was available anymore to work for the Goetheanum. This led Hermann von Baravalle to the decision that he would advise against the founding of the school, even though he had supported it enthusiastically before and had been ready to bring greetings

---

719 Elisabeth Klein: Vorbereitung, Gründung und Leben der Schule. In: *Gedenken an die Rudolf Steiner Schule Dresden*. 1980, p. 14.

The building of the Rudolf Steiner School Dresden, Jägerstrasse, 1930

from the Stuttgart faculty. Elisabeth Klein acted immediately. Together with Monica von Miltitz, she traveled to Berlin, met with Marie Steiner, talked with her for many hours, and explained the founding initiative in Dresden. Marie Steiner also invited Hermann von Baravalle for the conversation and heard his side. She ended up giving her permission to go ahead with the founding in Dresden. With her consent, the two women subsequently went to Stuttgart and gave a report to the Waldorf School faculty about their school initiative. The Stuttgart teachers gave their consent as well.[720]

On April 8, 1929, the Dresden Waldorf school was opened, bearing the name *Freie Schule Dresden–Einheitliche Volks- und höhere Schule nach dem Vorbild der Freien Waldorfschule Stuttgart* [Independent School of Dresden–a K-12 school modeled on the Waldorf School of Stuttgart]. Its first location was Franklinstrasse 23, but after a short time the school moved into a property the School Association had acquired at Jägerstrasse 3. In spite of their classroom workload, the teachers went on giving public lectures and arranging monthly assemblies in addition, and there were many parent evenings. The school became known more widely and grew apace. After one year they already had 180 students, so they had to look for a new place to stay. At first it was not clear that the solution would be so close by, but it all turned out for the best. A chocolate factory had just gone bankrupt. It was located on the Jägerstrasse, and the factory building it occupied had been used by the Pestalozzi Foundation of the Teacher Association in Dresden. One half of the premises was used by the city for boarding students, the other half was now offered to the Waldorf school by the local authorities, so they moved to Jägerstrasse 34 on April 1, 1930, where the school is still located today.

A larger hall, the *Waldschlösschensaal*, had been rented for this day so that a festive assembly could be arranged for the 90 new first graders and a new fifth grade. It was a bright and sunny day, and the festival featured recitations and musical contributions by the students. After that, the whole student body of over 200 children moved into the newly renovated building, which was painted in glorious colors. Of course the

---

720 Elisabeth Klein: *Begegnungen. Mitteilenswertes aus meinem Leben.* 1978, p. 67.

children were happy to discover the leftover chocolate in the factory, and they made short shrift of it. The school was renamed Rudolf Steiner School Dresden on January 1, 1932, which some of the founding members had intended right from the start. Dr. Albin Preuss, a lawyer at AEG in Dresden, became president of the school board. He and his wife felt very connected to the school and made financial contributions whenever they could. They entertained many guests in their large house, and their gigantic garden was the scene of numerous celebrations.

Elisabeth Klein

Albin Preuss died the night of February 13, 1945, when Dresden was bombed by the Allies. Dr. W. Chrambach had been instrumental in getting the school started, and it was he who became vice president of the board. In 1944 he was murdered in Buchenwald because of his anti-National Socialist convictions. Karl Eymann (1889–1943), owner of Emil Weise's bookstore and publishing house, was secretary and treasurer. There were many more parents who supported the school, among them Martin Büttner (*1890), and Alfred (1896–1992) and Wera Bockemühl (1903–1988), who were all active on the school board.

In preparation for the founding of the school, Elisabeth Klein was on the lookout for teachers. She knew Dr. Gerbert Grohmann (1897–1957) from the Jena Zwätzen Circle. He was employed at the curative institution in Gerswalde, but she convinced him to take the second grade. Fritz Jacquet took the third grade, and Elisabeth Klein herself took the first grade. All three of them had studied natural science, biology, and chemistry. Gerbert Grohmann's basic Goethean work, *Die Pflanze* [The Plant], was published the year the school was founded.

Thea Achtnich taught English and French and took on mentoring tasks in the high school after a few years. Suse König (1900–1977) taught eurythmy and Käthe Fischer (later Grohmann; 1898–1976), who had studied music and expressive dancing with Mary Wigman, taught music. All of them were avant-garde personalities. After a few years they were joined by Erich Schneider, and later by Fritz Steglich (1903–1976), who both taught music. The latter inspired everybody with his elaborate performances of pieces such as G.F. Handel's *Messiah* and Joseph Haydn's *Seasons*.

In the second school year they welcomed a new colleague from the Baltic region, Meta Roller (1882–1968), who soon became beloved by most students and teachers because of her humor. In her wake came Paul and Helene Fritzsche, school janitors, who remained at Jägerstrasse 34 for as long as the Waldorf school was housed there. In 1933, Meta Roller took the first grade, which would grow from 14 to 48 children by seventh grade. Johannes Grube, one of her students, recounted later: "She did not miss a single day of school. I would certainly have turned around and gone home again if

Dr. Gerbert Grohmann with his class at the Rudolf Steiner School Dresden, 1931

Miss Roller had been absent. Her very presence was able to lift children's sorrows. She had our full confidence. […] Her love was there for all in equal measure."[721] Other teachers who joined the school were Hans Jacobi, a linguist and philosopher, Theo Leupold (1896–1945), killed in a bombing raid on Greifswald), Martha Fritsche, and Oskar Salzmann (1902–1945).

Dr. Hornemann taught Greek and Latin. Dr. Kurt Magerstädt (1899–1964) became the school doctor, and Milly Körner (†1969) taught therapeutic eurythmy. In 1932, Luise Stadler (1896–1987)[722] began her work as a handwork teacher after studying at the Arts and Crafts Academy in Munich. She was much admired for her ability to make the most enchanting costumes using a minimum of materials, serving all manner of performances, big or small. She stayed until 1941 and bridged the time between the closing and the reopening of the school by teaching at a public high school in Dresden. When the Dresden Waldorf school was closed by the new regime in 1949, Luise Stadler went to West Germany and became a teacher at the Waldorf school of Rendsburg. Her colleague Anna Schlick, who taught gardening, likewise taught both in the first and the second Waldorf school in Dresden. In 1932, the faculty was joined by another avant-garde artist, the expressionist painter Siegfried Berndt (1880–1946), who came to the school to teach both art and vocational subjects. He had studied at the Art Academy of Dresden and was a master at colored printing and various other printing techniques. He based his lessons on his rich work experience in arts and crafts, and his motto was: "It does not matter at all if a picture succeeds. What is important is the work itself. My creative work is a search for myself."[723]

721 Johannes Grube: Erinnerungen an Meta Roller. In: *Gedenken an die Rudolf Steiner Schule Dresden*. 1980, p. 26.
722 Walter Blume: Luise Stadler. LR 35, 1988, p. 95.
723 Andreas Albert: Vom Ergreifen zum Ergriffensein. G 29, 2010, p. 13.

The Rudolf Steiner School Dresden during the National Socialist Regime

WHEN THE NATIONAL SOCIALISTS came to power, representatives of the Waldorf schools came together to consider a unified approach to the new regime. There's a letter to the Stuttgart faculty, dated March 31, 1933, written jointly by Elisabeth Klein and Theodor Leupold on behalf of the Rudolf Steiner School Dresden. They anticipated the National Socialists would centralize education and suggested that the Stuttgart faculty initiate sending representatives to the ministry of education in Berlin and inform them about Waldorf pedagogy, hoping to find officials who might be open to it and building up relationships with them to have a basis for future negotiations.[724] With this approach, which was outwardly compromising but inwardly totally uncompromising, Elisabeth Klein managed to keep the Dresden Waldorf school open for a long time, longer than any other Waldorf school in Germany. Despite losses and illusions, she fought like a lioness for her children.[725]

In 1933, Saxony carried out National Socialist measures against blacklisted employees in the school system much more harshly than other German states. The ministry of culture of Saxony demanded, for example, that only teachers who had a state-recognized diploma were allowed to teach at the school. This harshness was in conformance with the regime's Gleichschaltung, rigorous measures to impose conformity involving intense scrutiny of teacher qualifications.[726] As a result, Hanna Helene Merian had to leave the Rudolf Steiner School Dresden at the behest of the *Kommission für die höheren Privatlehranstalten,* a committee checking on private high schools that found she didn't have the required qualifications for high school teachers in Saxony.[727] Thus the Dresden school was subjected to various forms of harassment: Teaching religion was no longer allowed; there were to be no double breadwinners, so the ministry objected to Thea Achtnich earning a teacher's salary, because she was

724 Uwe Werner: *Anthroposophen in der Zeit des Nationalsozialismus (1933–1945).* 1999, p. 98f.; Wenzel M. Götte: *Erfahrungen mit Schulautonomie.* 2006, p. 275f.

725 It is hard to evaluate matters long after they took place, and I have never had to face any existential challenges like these. For that reason I think it would be presumptuous to want to pronounce judgment on whether these actions were good or bad. I am cognizant of all objections toward Dr. Klein's actions, and I also hold Dr. Ernst Weissert in high esteem, who was one of those who initiated the closing of the Berlin school, and I therefore try merely to describe and do justice to all parties. I do agree with the assessment given by Wenzel M. Götte in his book *Erfahrungen mit Schulautonomie.* 2006, p. 536, where he says that Elisabeth Klein was acting with a clean conscience at the time, but was suffering from an illusory assessment of the totalitarian powers in that she believed that human connections could change the circumstances for more than a second. It seems that a case could also be made for proving that her efforts sometimes got her onto a slippery slope, that she came dangerously close to the ideology of those in power, and also that her choleric temperament led her to overestimate herself, thereby neglecting the necessary collaboration with her Waldorf colleagues.

726 Dr. Woelker of the Dresden school department wrote to the committee for private high schools on May 6, 1933. Archiv LS 4.2.144.

727 Karen Priestman: *Illusion of Coexistence.* 2009, p. 190.

supposed to stay home to take care of her children; the school was required to be either an elementary or a high school, not both.

A certain Mr. Dörffel brought a suit against the school, which he lost, whereupon 24 National Socialist parents of the Dresden Waldorf School wrote a letter to Prime Minister Manfred Freiherr von Killinger (1886–1944), arguing that Mr. Dörffel's accusations were groundless. In their letter of May 29, 1933, they emphasized that many parents sought out the Waldorf schools because they were concerned about the national and religious orientation of their children. They also emphasized that the school was a *Volksschule* [people's school] in the true sense of the word because it accepted children regardless of parental status or ability to pay.[728] That same day, a much larger group of parents, which did not identify as National Socialist, informed the minister of culture of Saxony, Dr. Wilhelm Hartnacke, that of the 304 students of the school, three were 100 percent Jewish and seven legally Jewish. They also wrote that there were no Marxist teachers, that the school did not even come close to a pacifist attitude, that the spirit of the school was Christian and that they could not imagine a better place for fostering German spirit and heroism. In addition, teachers were highly enthusiastic in their profession. Even though students did not excel in testable knowledge, they exhibited intellectual versatility, great freshness, and a lofty fitness for life.[729] In addition, the National Socialist parents group wrote to Christoph Boy in Stuttgart, head of the German Federation of Waldorf Schools at the time, reporting that 11 to 12 percent of the parents of the Dresden Waldorf School were members of the NSDAP.

The so-called *Berufsbeamtengesetz* [civil servants ordinance] of April 7, 1933, signaled the first wave of the conformity measures, and the National Socialist Teachers Union (NSLB) was ordered to incorporate all existing teachers unions, so the Waldorf teachers were required to comply. The NSLB in Saxony, however, refused to accept teachers who were not members of the National Socialist party, and rejected the faculty members of the Waldorf School of Dresden.

In addition, Minister of Culture Wilhelm Hartnacke did not condone the independent Christian religion teaching at the school, a measure that was initially blocked by the Reich's head of the NSLB, Hans Schemm, who at that time seemed to have a friendly attitude toward the schools. In September 1933, Christoph Boy had brokered relations between the Dresden Rudolf Steiner School and Hans Schemm, whereupon the latter had actually helped to settle the school's conflicts with the NSLB Dresden, allowing them to join the Nazi Teachers Union. In October 1933, Hans Schemm (who was both head of the NSLB and minister of culture of Bavaria) spoke

728 Letter from parent representatives dated May 29, 1953, addressed to Prime Minister von Killinger. Archiv LS 4.2.027.
729 Letter from parent representatives to Minister Dr. Wilhelm Hartnacke, dated May 29, 1933. Archiv LS 4.2.026.

up for the Waldorf School Association. Since he had helped the school in Dresden, the Waldorf schools trusted that he knew what Waldorf education was about. He himself only saw this as an opportunity to strengthen his sphere of influence within the Nazi hierarchy.[730]

When Gerbert Grohmann of the school in Dresden learned in October 1933 that a new committee to inspect private schools was being formed within the Department of the Interior, which was to be headed by Minister Rudolf Buttmann (1885–1947), he immediately informed Christoph Boy.[731] The representatives of the Waldorf schools changed their strategy in time, and wanted to meet with Rudolf Buttmann before the committee had officially met.[732] In November 1933, Gerbert Grohmann tried different ways to avert the repressive measures to which the school was increasingly subjected, without much success. Once Elisabeth Klein took the bull by the horns, there was a change. Instead of writing letters or making telephone calls, she personally went to meet the National Socialist officials in charge. On one occasion, she only managed to get through to them by posting herself in front of their doors for hours.[733] She was helped in her efforts by Mrs. Von Lingelsheim, a parent in the school and cousin of Ilse Hess (1900–1995), who established the contact and enabled Elisabeth Klein to do what she did. Elsa Meineke-Pröhl, the mother of Ilse Hess, lived in Bremen and was an opponent of National Socialism. She did not hide her opinion in the Hess household. Elisabeth Klein and René Maikowski sought her out for support.[734]

In spite of all these worries about the continued existence of the school, there was growth, new colleagues were worked in, and the lessons carried on without being influenced overmuch by the circumstances of the time. Berthold Walter Meyer (1906–1978)[735] first studied German, history, and physical education, after which he attended the Stuttgart teachers seminar in 1933/34. He went on to teach at the Waldorf School in Dresden, where he was able to work for six years, teaching art history and German until his conscription order came. After the war (and a period of captivity), he taught in Nürnberg and subsequently in Hannover.

Elisabeth Klein continued her efforts to stay in touch with the authorities. Because of her acquaintance with Ilse Hess, she first focused on building a relationship with the office of Rudolf Hess, which had a branch in Berlin, where her main contact person was Hess's deputy Alfred Leitgen (1902–1977), a great admirer of Dr. Paul Oldendorff from the grammar school Berlin-Neukölln who went on to become one

730 Letter by Christoph Boy to all German Waldorf schools, dated October 3, 1933. Karen Priestman: *Illusion of Coexistence*. 2009, p. 116.
731 Letter by Gerbert Grohmann to Christoph Boy, dated October 25, 1933. Archiv LS 4.2.195.
732 Circular letter by Christoph Boy to the Waldorf schools, dated November 2, 1933. Archiv LS 4.2.205.
733 Karen Priestman: *Illusion of Coexistence*. 2009, p. 192.
734 René Maikowski to Stefan Leber in a letter dated June 28, 1983. Archiv CB.
735 Rüdiger Voigt: Berthold Walther Meyer (June 29, 1906–February 15, 1978). LR 17, 1978, p. 90f.

of the most important founding members of the Berlin Rudolf Steiner School. Paul Oldendorff had been very enthusiastic about anthroposophy and Waldorf education, so because of this Alfred Leitgen was open and ready to support the school. It only took Alfred Leitgen one week to reverse the official order to vacate the school premises, and in the time after that he was one of the most consistent advocates for the Waldorf school in Dresden. Elisabeth Klein reported about the state of affairs to Christoph Boy, who was the faculty chair of the Waldorf School in Stuttgart at the time. But she reserved the right to maintain the relationship she had made herself, and to act independently.[736] Because of her contacts with Director Rudolf Buttmann of the ministry of the interior, she was able to get through to the minister of culture of Saxony, Wilhelm Hartnacke, who, for the time being, did not put further obstacles in the way of the school. Of all the anthroposophists involved, Elisabeth Klein was most actively in touch with the authorities and maintained the contacts she had established independently.[737]

On April 30, 1934, Bernhard Rust became imperial minister for science and education. In early May 1934, Elisabeth Klein contacted Reichsleiter Philipp Bouhler on the staff of Rudolf Hess (1899–1945), inducing him to write a request to Bernhard Rust in which he asked him to clarify his position vis-à-vis the Waldorf schools. Philipp Bouhler informed Elisabeth Klein about the content of his letter to the minister of education and wrote to her on May 16, 1934, that "there were no objections to the continued operation of the Waldorf school in Dresden as far as the NSDAP was concerned."[738]

This was especially important for the Dresden Waldorf School, because the premises it occupied belonged to the National Socialist Teachers Union and were rented from them. Philipp Bouhler gave Elisabeth Klein permission to use his written request in her dealings with the NSLB. Philipp Bouhler was succeeded in his position on the staff of Rudolf Hess by Ernst Schulte-Strathaus (1881–1968), whom Elisabeth Klein visited together with René Maikowski. As René Maikowski was speaking with Ernst Schulte-Strathaus, Elisabeth Klein was waiting for Alfred Leitgen, when Martin Bormann came by and told her: "I'm warning you, we will do you in."[739] She continued her fight. Ernst Schulte-Strathaus, who read lectures by Rudolf Steiner and was in the habit of discussing his questions with anthroposophical visitors,[740] wrote a report on the Waldorf schools that was sent to the ministry of culture with the intent to convince the ministers of Württemberg and Saxony to withdraw the enrollment

---

736 Uwe Werner: *Anthroposophen in der Zeit des Nationalsozialismus (1933–1945)*. 1999, p. 111f. In reference to a letter dated April 3, 1934. Archiv LS 4.2.318.

737 Ibid., p. 112.

738 Ibid.

739 René Maikowski to Stefan Leber in a letter dated June 28, 1983. Archiv CB.

740 René Maikowski in a mimeographed account of the Hitler years, written January 1988. Archiv CB.

ban for new first grades. On June 5, 1934, Elisabeth Klein and René Maikowski spoke with Reinhard Sunkel (1900–1945), personal counselor to the minister of culture, who drew up a letter directed to the relevant ministers of the German states, asking them to "make sure these schools would be able to continue their work without obstacles" until a uniform policy had been established for Waldorf schools.[741]

Margarete Neuloh was a class teacher at the school from 1935 until 1938, and subsequently from 1947 until 1949. She also taught Greek and Latin. After she had joined the faculty, hardly any new faculty members were hired.

On March 12, 1936, Minister Bernhard Rust sent a decree to all official education institutions in Germany, which ran like this: "I request that ordinances are put in place to no longer accept students into the Waldorf or Rudolf Steiner schools (based on the anthroposophical worldview)."[742] The Waldorf School of Dresden was the only school that still kept on growing after this year. René Maikowski and Elisabeth Klein still cherished the hope to continue to operate the schools and considered this to be a temporary decree. They kept negotiating and developed the idea to continue operating their schools as experimental institutions. They thought there would be a realistic chance of survival for the schools once they had that status, and prepared requests to that effect, which gave rise to considerable discussions within the school in Dresden and within the German Waldorf school movement.

The question was whether they would be understood as experimental schools run by the state or independently. Elisabeth Klein approached Albert Steffen to ask for his advice. He argued that they should go for the experimental school idea, because there was a chance that it could provoke the authorities to close the schools, which would be preferable to the schools giving up of their own account. Elisabeth Klein gave weight to this advice, coming as it did from Rudolf Steiner's successor in his function as head of the General Anthroposophical Society in Dornach, Switzerland. Within the German Federation of Waldorf Schools there were opposing views. The way the negotiations were conducted by René Maikowski and especially Elisabeth Klein, was rejected by the Rudolf Steiner School of Berlin,[743] because they showed too much willingness to compromise with the regime. A few months later, the Stuttgart school declared itself to be of the same conviction and likewise rejected being represented by René Maikowski and Elisabeth Klein. This unanimous stance taken by both the Berlin and Stuttgart colleagues clearly did not impress Elisabeth Klein and did not cause her to change her position. She kept on fighting for her school.

In October 1936, the Waldorf schools of Hannover, Dresden, Kassel, and Hamburg-Wandsbek appealed to the authorities to renew their licenses to continue

---

741 Uwe Werner: *Anthroposophen in der Zeit des Nationalsozialismus (1933–1945)*. 1999, p. 114.
742 Ibid., p. 136, note 370.
743 Letter from the Rudolf Steiner School of Berlin to the Waldorf School of Stuttgart, dated June 20, 1936. Archiv LS 4.3.166.

operating, with the request to be officially recognized as experimental schools. The other schools did not go along with this step. These requests led to further inspections by various officials from the Reich, especially Superintendent Thies, as well as representatives of the NSLB. The resulting reports[744] were unanimously negative and provided no basis for approval of the requests to continue as experimental schools.

The inspectors consistently criticized a "feminine educational style" and complained about the lack of National Socialist educational content. In the reports on Hannover, Wandsbek, and Kassel, mention was made that there were pictures in classrooms of Rudolf Steiner and Madonnas, but none of Adolf Hitler, the Führer. In Dresden and Hannover, the report mentioned that a global spiritual ideal was being held up instead of a view based on *Blut und Boden* [blood and soil]. The inspectors did recognize exemplary community building with a great deal of camaraderie and connectedness, as well as great engagement on the part of both students and teachers. In January 1937, the Rudolf Steiner School Dresden was inspected by Annemarie Pahl, who was especially shocked by elements of mysticism, by coeducation, and the fact that boys were knitting and girls were doing woodwork. She also noted there was no trace of National Socialism.

The contacts with Rudolf Hess that Elisabeth Klein had fostered prompted him to gather information about Waldorf schools, both from the ministry of education and from the NSLB. In October 1937, Rudolf Hess requested that representatives from the authorities who concerned themselves with this complex of questions should inspect the Rudolf Steiner School Dresden together with him. They chose November 26, 1937, as the date of their visit. Councillor Thies did not get permission from his minister, but six others ended up visiting the Dresden school: Lothar Eickhoff, councillor to the minister of the interior (but not as an official representative); Alfred Leitgen on behalf of the staff of Hitler's deputy, Rudolf Hess; Alfred Bäumler, officially appointed by Hitler to lead the department that supervised educational questions regarding spiritual and church matters of the NSDAP (i.e., the Rosenberg office); Otto Ohlendorf of the Security Department; a representative of the NSLB; and a local educational official.[745] Despite vehement clashes of opinions among the inspecting personages, Alfred Bäumler put his impressions about Waldorf schools on paper after this visit, and his report was completed as early as December 8.[746] Alfred Bäumler's evaluation of Waldorf pedagogy and of Rudolf Steiner was much more serious and encompassing than any other. At the end of it, he drew the conclusion that in Waldorf education humanity had come to the position that the people occupies in National Socialist philosophy, whereby community is understood to mean spiritual community. "As far as methodology is concerned, we have to recognize that Steiner's curriculum is

744 Uwe Werner: *Anthroposophen in der Zeit des Nationalsozialismus (1933–1945).* 1999, p. 218, note 95.
745 Ibid., p. 218.
746 Ibid., p. 220f.

the first of its kind that is fully penetrated throughout without being an intellectual construct."[747]

Alfred Bäumler had many more interesting observations, which led him to conclude that, in the final analysis, Waldorf pedagogy was incompatible with National Socialism. There was an addendum to the reports concerning the situation of the Dresden Rudolf Steiner School, in which he focused especially on the economic consequences of the ban on further enrollment. Alfred Bäumler's report formed the basis for the suggestion that Rudolf Hess wrote to Bernhard Rust on January 14, 1938, which was that the ministry of culture should allow two or three Waldorf schools to continue functioning as experimental schools.[748] Whereas the Stuttgart school was closed on April 1, 1938, Bernhard Rust lifted the enrollment ban for Dresden and Hamburg-Wandsbek.

Now Elisabeth Klein started negotiating with the school authorities of Saxony. Her subsequent reports on the negotiations reveal points of contention. According to her report, the authorities demanded that an older member of the NSDAP should take on the directorship of the school. Elisabeth Klein countered that this was unthinkable and that she would take over the leadership role herself. The other point of contention was that the authorities demanded that coeducation should cease, which Elisabeth Klein rejected, arguing that this was the hallmark of an experimental school. In addition, the school was to decide to opt for being either a *Volksschule* (grades 1–10) or a *Höhere Schule* (grades 5–12), which she also rejected as being inconceivable because one of the basic premises of an experimental school was that it should comprise all ages. She had no objections against the wish to place the school more strongly within the context of the state.[749]

After the Stuttgart school closed, eight teachers from Stuttgart came to join the school in Dresden: Erich Schwebsch, Martin Tittmann, Konrad Sandkühler, Max Wolffhügel, Margarete Boerner, Erika Zoeppritz, Emil Kimmich, and Peter Prömm. They formed the "Stuttgart contingent." Teachers also came from other schools that had closed. Mathilde Hoyer, Gerhard Ott, and Robert Zimmer came from Hannover, Harald Dähnhard and Hermann Schüler from Hamburg, and Wilhelm Beck moved to Dresden from Breslau.[750] Parents who wanted their children to continue at a Waldorf school came as well, among them the Karutz family from Stuttgart. Students also came from Hamburg and Breslau.

The three years from 1938 until 1941 made a deep impression, as can be gleaned from the reports from former students. Especially in high school there were highly

---

747 Printed in its entirety in Uwe Werner: *Anthroposophen in der Zeit des Nationalsozialismus (1933–1945)*. 1999, p. 390f, as appendix 11.

748 Large sections of this letter are printed in Uwe Werner: *Anthroposophen in der Zeit des National-sozialismus (1933–1945)*. 1999, p. 222.

749 Uwe Werner: *Anthroposophen in der Zeit des Nationalsozialismus (1933–1945)*. 1999, p. 232.

750 List of teachers in: *Gedenken an die Rudolf Steiner Schule Dresden*. 1980, p. 45.

original, erudite, and open-minded teachers, preeminently Erich Schwebsch, even though he kept his students at a distance and taught more in the style of a university professor. His art history presentations made an indelible impression on the students. In a parent evening, he is reported to have coined the wonderful sentence: "One should love the children away from oneself,"[751] which made sense to them apparently. The number of children rose to 450, which necessitated teaching in morning and afternoon shifts.

On March 12, 1939, Elisabeth Klein took the initiative to send a draft of a constitution of the Rudolf Steiner School Dresden to Alfred Bäumler, which stated in its introduction that the school would stand "on the ground of the National Socialist state."[752] She promised to only hire politically dependable persons, but maintained that the school leadership would find the personnel and would subsequently ask the authorities for confirmation. As far as the curriculum was concerned, she maintained that Rudolf Steiner's works would serve as the guideline for the work.[753]

The Stuttgart contingent did not accept this draft. Martin Tittmann wrote a counterproposal that stressed the autonomy of the school. A third proposal, dated March 23, 1939, tried to find middle ground and presumably stemmed from E. A. Karl Stockmeyer. The fourth draft was formulated by Erich Schwebsch. In his preface to the essential characteristics, Erich Schwebsch wrote: "The Rudolf Steiner School Dresden would like to note down once more the fundamental concepts needed for a healthy development of this type of school, by means of which this institution will be able to contribute to solutions for educational questions within the National Socialist state."[754]

At the members meeting of the Association for Independent Schools in Stuttgart on July 16, 1939, the decision was made to give financial support to the schools that were still operating, the ones in Dresden and Hamburg-Wandsbek. The school in Dresden received RM 36,000, payable in monthly installments of RM 3000, which, of course, was a highly welcome support and was acknowledged as such.

Shortly after Elisabeth Klein had sent in her draft of the constitution, there came a decree that guaranteed the continued existence of the school in Dresden, which was elaborated further in a document issued by the ministry of the Reich on September 23, 1939.[755] Elisabeth Klein kept working and arranged school visits from representatives of the ministry of Saxony, which led to an outcome that was different from what she had expected.

---

751 Eva-Ursula Melzer: Eine Schülerin erzählt aus der Zeit von 1939 bis 1941. *Gedenken an die Rudolf Steiner Schule Dresden.* 1980, p. 31.

752 Norbert Deuchert: Zur Geschichte der Waldorfschule 1933–1940. BhB Advent 1984, p. 80.

753 Uwe Werner: *Anthroposophen in der Zeit des Nationalsozialismus (1933–1945).* 1999, p. 233.

754 A facsimile of the draft is printed in Norbert Deuchert: Zur Geschichte der Waldorfschule 1933–1940. BhB Advent 1984, p. 81f.

755 Uwe Werner: *Anthroposophen in der Zeit des Nationalsozialismus (1933–1945).* 1999, p. 233.

The College of Teachers,
the Rudolf Steiner School
Dresden, 1940/41

In March 1941, 15 students took their final exams, in which the questions were being asked by their own teachers for the first time in the history of the school. Another 15 students took the middle school exams. On March 31, 1941, the graduation of the students was celebrated, and in the assembly for that occasion, Martin Tittmann's *Kantate zur Schulentlassung*, set to music by Fritz Steglich, was performed. After Rudolf Hess's flight to Britain on May 10, 1941, the school lost the protection of his office, as a result of which the school was closed within the framework of a special action against secret doctrines and so-called occult sciences. The closing assembly took place on July 4, 1941. Hans Jacobi said in his report: "The address at the occasion of the closing of the school in the assembly hall ended with the words "The school is closed." Oskar Salzmann rushed to the playground and pulled down the flag. The children of his class were crying as they thronged out of the door, whereupon he said to them, "Do not be sad, we will soon open the school again."[756]

Before the final closing of the school, Elisabeth Klein was arrested by the Gestapo, not long after they had come for her husband and had left her in the dark as to his whereabouts. She remained in prison for nine months. Her own four children were between three and 14 years old at the time, and it is not known to me who took care of them during that time. After her release she was not allowed to publish or work and she lived with her family in a village in the Black Forest until 1945. After the war she wanted to become a teacher again, but was rejected by the Waldorf schools to which she applied. Emil Bock and Ernst Weissert[757] interceded for her, whereupon she was employed as a teacher at the school in Hannover, but she was never allowed to occupy a leading position again.[758]

756 Uwe Werner: *Anthroposophen in der Zeit des Nationalsozialismus (1933–1945)*. 1999, p. 236.
757 Letter by Elisabeth Klein to Ernst Weissert, dated May 10, 1970. Archiv BFWS.
758 Theodor Spitta, amongst others at the Waldorf school in Hannover, reports on her later activity, in LR 28, 1984, p. 73ff.

Klara Hattermann came from Hannover and led a little kindergarten in Dresden in the late 1930s and early 1940s

In spite of everything, she was a teacher with a great talent for teaching pictorially and her personality left a great impression. The children in Hannover called her *die liebe Sonne* [dear sun].[759] She promised Emil Bock, the *Oberlenker* [leader] of the Christian Community, that she would not defend herself against allegations of fraternization with the National Socialists. However, she did ask Lothar Eickhoff—spokesman of the Prussian ministry of the interior from 1933–1937, later head of the government of Ostfriesland—for a sworn affidavit. In this document he wrote: "Dr. Elisabeth Klein was a smart, fiery, and highly energetic personality; she stood her ground in tenacious negotiations with the authorities, fighting with great perseverance and admirable courage to preserve the Waldorf schools. During these extensive discussions, Dr. Klein did not in any way grant concessions and stuck to the basic principles of anthroposophy. She did, however, to the extent she thought responsible, entertain suggestions and wishes, mostly about unimportant externalities. As far as basic principles were concerned, especially in her attitude toward Dr. Rudolf Steiner, she did not give an inch. I was highly impressed at the time by her stance, her courage, and her indefatigable effort. After all, she personally went all the way to 'the lion's den,' that is to say to the leader of the party chancellery in Munich, Martin Bormann."[760] In a letter to Ernst Weissert of October 17, 1975, Dr. Elisabeth Klein asked at the end: "When you meet me after death on the other side, dear Ernst, you will be able to let go of your reservations. Then you will recognize that I was always motivated by good will. (My heart is in the right place, and I've got a pretty good head on my shoulders)." Thus we can see that the whole tragic entanglement happened with the best of motives; looking back, we can describe what happened and understand the steps she took, even if we do not approve.

759 Peter Lampasiak: Dr. Elisabeth Klein (May 5, 1901–December 30, 1983). N 22.7.1984, p. 134.
760 Affidavit by Lotar Eickhoff of December 6, 1965. Archiv BFWS.

After the school had closed, the children and parents were still there of course, and their love for the school was undiminished. Underground schooling of one kind or another did continue. Between 1941 and 1945, a number of children turned up on a regular basis to do eurythmy with Milly Körner, despite adverse circumstances. When asked, they just said they were going to gymnastics lessons. There were practices and performances at the home of the Jacobi family, and St. Christopher plays were rehearsed in the house of the Ott family.

So during the last four years of the war, when the school was officially forbidden to operate, some form of Waldorf schooling continued for a number of children.[761] A Waldorf teacher from Dresden, Oskar Salzmann, was shot as late as May 8, 1945, because he had described the war as lost.[762]

The Rudolf Steiner School Dresden between 1945 and 1949

THE RUDOLF STEINER SCHOOL Dresden was opened again on October 15, 1945 by Hans Jacobi and Gerhard Ott, two former teachers of the school. There were 450 students and 20 teachers in 12 grades. The Teacher Association of Dresden put the relatively undamaged building at their disposal once again. The school inspector, a Social Democrat, signed off on it as a city supported school, because a privately operated school would not have been officially allowed. A preparatory conversation was held in Schloss Siebeneichen, in which Monica von Miltitz, Fritz Jacquet, and Hans Jacobi took part, among other people. They decided to press ahead with the reopening and keep going for as long as possible, because nobody was sure what to expect under Russian occupation. During the first four years, the school was free to determine matters of enrollment and teacher employment, and they could determine the curriculum according to the principles of Waldorf pedagogy. The school was being conducted as an experimental school with an approved special curriculum.[763]

A school director was needed to keep its license to operate, and in order to fulfill that obligation Gerhard Ott became a member of the Socialist Party (SPD) on February 1, 1946. He could not know at the time that this party and the Communist Party would form a coalition soon and that he would end up as a member of the SED [Socialist Union Party of Germany]. Students, parents, relatives: they all took part in rebuilding the school during the summer months of 1945. Gerda Koch and Wilhelm Schwarz (1921–1988)[764] had both been students of the first school. Wilhelm Schwarz

---

761 Konrad Schulze: Erinnerungen an die Jahre nach der Schliessung und an die Zweite Schule. *Gedenken an die Rudolf Steiner Schule Dresden.* 1980, p. 55ff.

762 Johannes Lenz: Im Gedenken an die Dresdner Schulzeit und an Oskar Salzmann. *Gedenken an die Rudolf Steiner Schule Dresden.* Gerlingen 1980, p. 26.

763 Hilde Hennig: Über die Rudolf Steiner Schule in Dresden. N 6. April 1947, p. 54.

764 Rudolf Stibill: Wilhelm Schwarz. LR 38, 1989, p. 116.

Lore Blume, class teacher at the Rudolf Steiner School Dresden, 1945 to 1949

had joined the Dresden school from November 1939 onward, after his school in Hamburg-Wandsbek had been closed. In the meantime, Gerda Koch had begun studying music in Dresden and told Gerhard Ott about Wilhelm Schwarz one day. When Gerhard Ott heard about him, he immediately sent a telegram and asked him to come to Dresden in order to take the fourth grade, which was without a teacher. Wilhelm Schwarz came, taught the class while completing his teacher training at the same time, and Gerda Koch, who had become his wife in the meantime, took the new first grade, which counted 50 students.

The school grew and in October 1946 there were already 760 students. In the years thereafter the number of students rose to more than 1000, who came from all over town because the school had a good reputation.[765]

Roland Schultze-Florey, for example, attended the school from 1936 until 1941 and from 1945 until 1948. He later became a Waldorf teacher in Hannover and gave lectures on anthroposophy.[766] Lore Blume likewise was a student first and then taught at the school after the war. Just like Irene Schultze, she ended up teaching in Rendsburg. Interesting teacher personalities came to join the school and all subjects were well taken care of. High school teachers also had to teach elementary school classes, so that upper school classes could only start at 10:00 a.m. Fritz Jacquet, for example, first taught main lesson in his fifth grade, and then went on to teach his beloved botany blocks in the upper school.

By all accounts, there were four years of remarkably free and vibrant teaching, years in which pedagogical life was able to blossom despite increasing repression and the increase of restrictive measures all around. The students loved their school and in order not to disappoint them, their eurythmy teacher came to the Jägerstrasse every single day, even though she had to go to great lengths to regain mobility in her legs, damaged by hunger swelling during the war. They did have to work under lamentable circumstances. Gerhard Ott's letters to Erich Schwebsch frequently mention how strenuous everyday life was. He lived in a one-room apartment together with his wife, four little children, a grandmother, and a helper. On top of everything, he had to prepare his lectures there as well. There was no coal and no butane gas, rooms could not be heated, there were no hot meals for the children, and the light was switched off every other day. The teachers were unable to attend Waldorf school

765 Hans Jacobi: Vom Übergang der ersten zur zweiten Schule. *Gedenken an die Rudolf-Steiner-Schule Dresden.* 1980, p. 47ff.
766 Rüdiger Voigt: Roland Schultze-Florey (June 26, 1929–April 28, 1979). LR 19, 1979, p. 115.

Rudolf Steiner School Dresden
between 1945-1949

conferences such as the one from October 18–20, 1946, in Stuttgart, because of the travel restrictions imposed by the Soviet occupation. Cohesion among the faculty grew extremely strong and so did the relationships with the parents. Parents flocked to parent evenings in great numbers and were overjoyed to join in conversations about the essence of Waldorf education, which provided short periods of respite from the countless everyday worries and the struggle for survival. One of them said, "That was one evening where we could be truly human for a change."

At first the inspections by the Russian occupation authorities went so smoothly that the school was left alone. During the school year of 1948/49, however, conflicts began with the school department, and Soviet educational methods gained momentum, as a result of which students were required to focus on a specific area of study and the faculty had to submit to restrictions in hiring other teachers. Gerhard Ott wrote on March 8, 1948, that the faculty had decided to no longer call the school a Rudolf Steiner school, even though they kept on practicing Waldorf pedagogy to the extent that that was possible.[767] During the summer holidays of 1949, Gerhard Ott was ordered to appear before the party authorities in the city's education department, where he was told that the school could no longer teach according to the principles of Rudolf Steiner's pedagogy. He was told he was deposed as the school director, and that the school would have to continue as a state school on the basis of the teachings of Marx and Lenin, as interpreted by the Soviets.[768] That's how the second closure of the Dresden Waldorf School came about under the SED government of the German Democratic Republic. Wilhelm Schwarz and Gerhard Ott faced arrest and trial. They

---

767 Archiv LS 3.30.018.
768 Gerhard Ott: Die Neuerrichtung der Dresdener Waldorfschule nach dem zweiten Weltkrieg. *Gedenken an die Rudolf-Steiner-Schule Dresden.* 1980, p. 51ff.; Letter from Gerhard Ott to Erich Schwebsch, dated August 26, 1949. Archiv LS 3.30.019.

fled to West Berlin that very night, August 28, 1949.[769] More and more teachers and students fled to the West from that moment onward. Many of them became teachers, especially in the Waldorf schools of Rendsburg and Hannover.

On June 14, 1979, former teachers and members of the German Federation of Waldorf Schools organized a celebration of the school's 50-year anniversary at the Stuttgart Waldorf School, to which more than 200 former students and teachers of the Rudolf Steiner School Dresden came. In 1990, Gerhard Ott was invited to the reopening ceremony of the school, the third Waldorf school in Dresden. At age 85, he was still able to attend and join in the celebration.

1930: The Waldorf School in Kassel

THE IMPORTANT German anthroposophical physician Dr. Ludwig Noll (1872–1930) was head of the branch of the Anthroposophical Society in Kassel. He cultivated a growing interest in Waldorf education and supported the founding of a local group of the Association for Independent Schools as well as a study group on Waldorf pedagogy. He invited Herbert Hahn and Caroline von Heydebrand to give lectures in Kassel, and enthusiasm for the founding of a Waldorf school began to grow. Finally, in April 1929, an association for an independent school in Kassel was founded with Dr. Wolfgang Gessner (1881–1974) as president; Martin Schmidt (1892–1964), a mechanical engineer and agriculturalist, supplied the starting capital. At Easter time of 1929, lessons began with a first grade, which had only six children to begin with but later grew to 12.

Since it was not easy to find the needed space in Kassel, lessons were first held in the house of the Breda family, then in the house of the Schindlers. From these home surroundings, the school moved into its own space as soon as the opportunity presented itself to rent an entire floor. Leonie von Mirbach had taken a class in the Stuttgart school in September 1919, so she belonged to the original circle of 12 founding teachers. She and Anton Treiber, who was to have been a founding teacher in Nürnberg, became the first teachers in Kassel. Since there was no official permission yet, students were first admitted as students of a private school when they had a doctor's certificate. This situation could not last of course, so they gathered signatures, and once they had 2000, they succeeded. With an official document issued on May 10, 1930,

---

769 Lotte Hopp: Gerhard Ott (October 29, 1906–February 11, 1991). LR 48, 1993, p. 67f.; From April 1950, Wilhelm and Gerda Schwarz were founding teachers of the Waldorf School in Rendsburg. They had been recommended by his former high school teacher from Hamburg-Wandsbek, Dr. Fröbe-Meyer. Wilhelm Schwarz first took two classes through from grades 1–8, after which he worked in the high school. He became an advisor for newly founded schools, was a member of the executive council of the German Federation of Waldorf Schools, and taught at the teacher seminars of Witten-Annen and Kiel.

their efforts were rewarded, so they now had official permission to build up a private elementary school. Not counting the initial housing with the two families, they were the eighth Waldorf school that opened in Germany. At Easter 1930, they had their official start with 150 students in five grades,[770] in a residence at Ulmenstrasse 24 which had been put at their disposal.[771] Apart from the two aforementioned teachers, Ilse Staedtke (1902–1981), Elsa Niemann (†1965), Heiner Garff (1896–1967), Marianne Garff (1903–1995),[772] Dr. Ernst Kühner (1906–1972), Käte Albrecht, and Marie Kruse (1883–1977) taught at the school. Marie Kruse had a lot of experience as a teacher and had been head of school in Landeshut, Silesia. Ernst Weissert described her as "ein kerniges, tüchtiges pädagogisches Wesen" [a solid and hard-working pedagogue].[773]

The school building of the Waldorf School in Kassel at Ulmenstrasse 24, circa 1930

Internal conflicts started in the very first year. People accused each other of being power-hungry, and it was hard to reach unanimity in the hiring process of new teachers. For this reason the board appealed to the Stuttgart faculty for help, hoping to stake out their position vis-à-vis the teachers. The Stuttgart faculty had to help many schools and managed to deal with many requests of this nature, which they felt obliged to honor. That meant extra work next to their teaching responsibilities, but of course their ability to help had its limits. For that reason they suggested to the board that the faculty should try to solve the problems in house, and since it was only their first year, 1930, board president Wolfgang Gessner went along with that suggestion. In the conversations that followed, it was possible to assuage the differences between the board and teachers, but not among the members of the faculty itself. This struggle ended with the dismissal of one controversial person.[774]

Soon, a second building was added, which had a large garden, located at Kölnischen Allee 58. The children were overjoyed that the pears Heiner Garff harvested in October were divided among all children and teachers. The Garff family lived in the school building just as the Rudolph family did later, and the Bässler families did after them. At Easter of 1933, Karin von Falck (1900–1987) took over the eighth

770 In the letter mentioned below, dated June 27, 1938 (Archiv LS 4.3.441) it says that there were 160 students when the school was founded.
771 Marianne Garff: Die erste Freie Waldorfschule in Kassel 1930–1939. LR 7, 1973, p. 67.
772 Gertraud Flegler: Marianne Garff (April 18, 1903–July 25, 1995). LR 55, 1995, p. 74f.; Gertraud Flegler: Marianne Garff. N December 3, 1995, p. 208f.
773 Ernst Weissert: Marie Kruse (August 10, 1883–July 22, 1977). LR 16, 1977, p. 72; Ernst Weissert: Marie Kruse zum 90. Geburtstag. LR 7, 1973, p. 70.
774 Wenzel M. Götte: Erfahrungen mit Schulautonomie. 2006, p. 319f.

grade. She had grown up as a daughter of a Protestant minister in Livland, had gone to school in what was then Dorpat (present-day Tartu) and had gone to the teacher seminar in Königsberg, after which she studied biology and geography in Munich, Berlin, and Heidelberg. In 1945, right after World War II, she became the founding teacher of the Waldorf School in Marburg.[775]

Chief government building surveyor Wolfgang Gessner, who presided over the School Association and also was a member of the Anthroposophical Society council of Kassel, started thinking about the consequences of the Nazi takeover as early as February 1933. He considered how they would have to deal with National Socialists within their own ranks, because it was clear to him "that we cannot be trapped in the narrow confines of National Socialist officialdom."[776] After the Anthroposophical Society had been officially forbidden in Kassel, one SD office in the city was becoming particularly overzealous. Wolfgang Gessner and Frau Claussen-Pelk were arrested and held for a short time (on allegations of having had contacts with the German Communist Party). After the local Anthroposophical Society had been forbidden on November 1, district president Konrad von Monbart (1881–1945) was also planning to close the Waldorf School as soon as possible, because to him the two seemed to be connected. That is why school inspections were done December 17–19, 1935, carried out by inspectors Kellner, Betting, and Dr. Heilig.[777] They commented on a number of methodological particulars, such as the teaching of foreign languages in the lower grades instead of having practice periods in reading, writing, and arithmetic. They also complained that there were still no schoolbooks, German readers and history books in particular, and that the teachers were hired without having been approved by state officials.

Early in 1936, the state Department of Education wanted to close grades 9 and 10 as a first step toward reducing the school to an elementary school. This called forth a vehement protest from René Maikowski of the German Federation of Waldorf Schools, who approached the Reich's minister of education directly. René Maikowski let the education officials know that he had involved the authorities in Berlin, and this caused some uncertainty in the regional counsel of Kassel; if nothing else, it bought time, because now they had to check in with Berlin. René Maikowski did what he could by informing various officials, knowing all the while that all he could do was pass on what various people had said and were hoping in various conversations and that the outcome was uncertain.[778] In 1936, it was decreed that the school could no

<hr>

775 Ursula Dittrich: Karin von Falck. LR 35, 1988, p. 108.
776 Uwe Werner: *Anthroposophen in der Zeit des Nationalsozialismus (1933–1945)*. 1999, p. 28.
777 Letter from the district president to the minister of education, dated January 7, 1936, BArch Ella 0159-36 / 299, 300.
778 Letter by René Maikowski on behalf of the German Federation of Waldorf Schools, dated March 18, 1936, to the district president of Hessen-Nassau, BArch Ella 0851-36 / 326, or the letter of March 23, 1936, to the district president in Kassel, BArch Ella 0851-36 / 325.

longer accept new students, a decree that affected all private schools; in 1938 it was no longer allowed to have an eleventh grade, and the faculty made the decision to close at Michaelmas. At the closing assembly, the eighth grade performed Friedrich Schiller's play, *Wallensteins Lager* [Wallenstein's Camp]. In the letter the school sent to the minister for science and education on June 27, 1938, Marie Kruse wrote on behalf of the faculty of the Waldorf School of Kassel: "We have come to the point where we think it is necessary to no longer connect the name of Rudolf Steiner with what remains of the Waldorf School in Kassel, but to close the school as a Waldorf school by October 1938 and only continue to teach classes until Easter 1938 for those who wish to go on. We conclude that the sole responsibility for the closing of this growing and blossoming school, which should have fulfilled a precious task in German spiritual life, rests with the departments in charge."[779]

At the occasion of the parent meeting preceding the closing, Dr. Rudolph said, "There is a law that everything that dies will also resurrect."[780] And that is how it went. The transition courses went until Easter 1939. On July 5, 1938, René Maikowski sent in an application to the education minister, requesting employment in state schools for seven teachers of the Waldorf School in Kassel, and pension payments for Marie Kruse.[781] District president Konrad von Monbart and his school inspector Wischnack, who had openly attempted to bring about the school's closing for a number of years, complied only reluctantly.[782]

As early as the autumn of 1945, Elsa Niemann called together the remaining colleagues and brought about the reopening of the school on February 27, 1946. The former teachers that were there were Heiner and Marianne Garff, Dr. Ernst Kühner, and Käte Albrecht. Some of the new teachers were Dr. Hans Koch, Irmentraud Salzmann, and Heidi Geertz.

1930: The Waldorf School in Breslau (present-day Wrocław)

Anthroposophical Life in Breslau and Silesia

IT TOOK THREE YEARS of preparatory work before the first Waldorf school in Silesia could be founded. Principal Moritz Bartsch (1869–1944), president of the Teacher Association of Breslau and spokesperson for elementary school teachers, played an active role in that. He combined uprightness, idealism, and a fiery temperament with an endearing personality and professional competence, which made him a respected

---

779 Uwe Werner: *Anthroposophen in der Zeit des Nationalsozialismus (1933–1945).* 1999, p. 226.
780 Marianne Garff: Die erste Freie Waldorfschule in Kassel 1930–1939. LR 7, 1973, p. 68.
781 Letter dated July 5, 1938. BArch Ella 1730-38 / 51.
782 Letter from the district president to the minister of education, October 15, 1938, BArch Ella 2467-38 / 56–57.

figure who attracted a large circle of people.[783] "In the pivotal time after World War I, when people were open for new initiatives, Rudolf Steiner asked him to help. He worked tirelessly for Waldorf education and the threefold social order movement, giving lectures as far away as East Prussia."[784]

Late in the summer of 1920, Herbert Hahn and Walter Johannes Stein, prompted by Rudolf Steiner, went on a lecture tour to make people acquainted with the social ideas behind the Waldorf school. "Of the far-away places we traveled to, Breslau was the most memorable. Everything seemed to fall into place by itself there, and we ended up speaking in a space that was filled to overflowing, the hall of the Friebeberg. Without having done anything for it, we harvested something of the fruit of years of preparatory work done by friends of our movement, especially the beloved principal Bartsch."[785] From 1908 onward, Rudolf Steiner himself had regularly given lectures in Breslau, and the first time he came again after World War I was in 1922. His lecture, "Das Wesen der Anthroposophie" [The Essence of Anthroposophy],[786] took place in the large hall of the Konzerthaus on January 31, 1922, and it was followed by a eurythmy performance the next evening in the Lobe Theater, which had almost 1100 seats. Karin Ruths-Hoffmann was present at this lecture and described her experience as follows: "I can only describe the way he lectured as a mixture of holy and sober. There was nothing suggestive, fanatical, or mystical about it even though one would be inclined to expect such qualities from him. [...] But what spoke to me that evening was not primarily the personality of the speaker or the content of his lecture. It was the way he spoke, his methodology, how he approached the material. This completely selfless devotion to his theme seemed exemplary to me, he was the archetype of a real teacher.[787]

This lecture was followed in 1924 by a cycle of nine lectures, "Karma als Schicksalsgestaltung des menschlichen Lebens" [Karma as the Shaper of Our Destiny],[788] held every evening while he was lecturing during the course held at the estate of the Countess Johanna and Count Adalbert von Keyserlingk in Koberwitz.

783 Johannes Kiersch: Moritz Bartsch. In: Bodo von Plato (ed.): *Anthroposophie im 20. Jahrhundert.* 2003, p. 55f.

784 Gertraud Bessert: *Ein Quell wird zum Strom.* Anthroposophisches Leben und heilpädagogische Impulse aus der Breslauer Zeit 1924–1948, undated, p. 9; Johannes Kiersch: Moritz Bartsch. In: Bodo von Plato (ed.): *Anthroposophie im 20. Jahrhundert.* 2003, p. 56. This book reports that Bartsch held 366 lectures in 22 months of the years 1921/22, followed by lectures from mid-January until July of 1925, titled "Das gegenwärtige Bildungsideal und die Freie Waldorfschule" [Present Day Educational Ideals and the Independent Waldorf School], which he held at the request of Rudolf Steiner.

785 Rosa Lüdicke and Heinrich Wollborn: Aus dem geistigen Umfeld vor der Gründung. EK 5, 1980, p. 296.

786 This lecture by Rudolf Steiner was not preserved because there were no stenographers. The lecture given the evening after, February 1, 1922, is printed in CW 210.

787 Karin Ruths-Hoffmann: Aus der Waldorfschülerschaft. In: M. J. Krück von Poturzyn (ed.): *Wir erlebten Rudolf Steiner.* 1980, p. 200f.

788 Rudolf Steiner: *Esoterische Betrachtungen karmischer Zusammenhänge.* Lectures of June 7–15, 1924, CW 239, 1975.

This was the so-called Agricultural Course,[789] in which about 130 people participated. This cycle formed the basis of biodynamic agriculture. This course was structured in such a way that there was a discussion at eleven o'clock, after the morning lecture. In the break between the lecture and the discussion, a delicious breakfast was served for the guests, who had come from far and wide. This was made possible by the fact that all employees of the estate were actively engaged in the preparation and running of this course on agriculture. After the discussion, the lecture hall was cleared to serve as a dining hall, and the food they served was delicious, which was pretty unusual for that time. Every day in the afternoon, Rudolf Steiner and his entourage were taken by car from Koberwitz to Breslau for his lecture there and at night, he was driven back again to Koberwitz,[790] where he was the guest of the count. This marathon work schedule also included addresses to young people.

Moritz Bartsch

Some of the young people attending the lectures wanted to get to work and engage in tasks that were waiting to be taken up. Two of these people, Hermann Kirchner (1899–1978) and Albrecht Strohschein (1899–1962), founded a curative home in Schloss Pilgramshain in Lower Silesia, which they were able to acquire in 1929. Next to these two, Dr. Karl König (1902–1966) worked there until he went to Vienna in 1936 and emigrated to Great Britain in 1938, where he founded the Camphill movement. In 1922, during Advent time, three priests, Rudolf von Koschützki (1866–1954), Rudolf Meyer (1896–1985), and Kurt von Wistinghausen (1901–1986), founded a branch of the Christian Community in Breslau. Anthroposophists worked together in three different branches at the same time: the Rudolf Steiner branch, led by principal Moritz Bartsch, the Angelus Silesius branch, led by Maria Dedo-Brie (1877–1960), and the Christian-Morgenstern branch, which had been built up by Rudolf Meyer.

Next to the practical work in agriculture and curative education and the study in the various branches, lively artistic work was also being done, especially in eurythmy, a totally new art of movement at the time. Clara Alwes had started giving eurythmy courses in Breslau as far back as 1921. In 1922/23, Marie Steiner sent Nina Bogojawlenskaja (†1945) to Silesia to give courses, which made it possible for a number of young women to do a eurythmy training, among them Erna Grund (1904–1991), Hanni Engel, Luitgard Leo, and Magdalena Stephan (1895–1980). In

---

789 Rudolf Steiner: *Landwirtschaftlicher Kursus June 7–16, 1924*. CW 327.
790 Christoph Lindenberg: *Rudolf Steiner. Eine Chronik. 1861–1925*. 1988, p. 581f.

1926, Elisabeth Hensel (1887–1954) founded the Goetheanum Eurythmy School in Breslau, which Marie Steiner supported and visited on several occasions. Elisabeth Hensel remained in Silesia for a few years before moving on. Obituaries describe her as a modest, unassuming person, someone who had heavy burdens to bear but achieved goodness and maturity by acceptance and hard work.[791]

Around 1930, Hilde Britz took over the leadership of the eurythmy school and she and her pupils put on many performances in the city.[792]

Preparing for a Waldorf School

EARLY IN THE 1920S, there was a general impulse for renewal in schools, and in Breslau there were teachers who individually experimented with pedagogical reform. There was a widespread feeling that moved people to search for new ideas both in education and in the social realm, and this impulse led some of them to try to work with Waldorf pedagogy. One of them was Richard Dürich (1890–1983).[793] He knew about anthroposophy through Moritz Bartsch, had been to Stuttgart, and was familiar with the threefold social order and Waldorf education. At Easter of 1921, he took a first grade in an elementary school and taught this class for eight years, incorporating Waldorf principles as much as possible. Clara Alwes taught eurythmy. His achievements gained the approval of the school authorities, and he had a growing wish to found an urban school with principles of reform and an anthroposophical faculty. It soon became clear, however, that state certified teachers who espoused anthroposophy were hard to find, and there were not enough around to risk the actual founding of a school. It also was not clear how many parents were willing to send their children to such a school.[794]

As soon as the teachers in Stuttgart got wind of what was going on, Herbert Hahn wrote with the urgent request that Richard Dürich and Moritz Bartsch should get in touch with the Stuttgart faculty to get the necessary approval.[795] Moritz Bartsch immediately assured him of their willingness to work together, but had to report also that plans were already in the making and could not be altered.

In 1926, a few teachers from the Stuttgart school were invited to come to a conference of the teachers union of Silesia, arranged by Moritz Bartsch. The conference took place from January 3–6, and Walter Johannes Stein, Caroline von Heydebrand and Alexander Strakosch[796] were among those who were invited. They gave lectures

791 Martina Maria Sam: *Eurythmie. Entstehungsgeschichte und Porträts ihrer Pioniere.* 2014, p. 180.
792 Rosa Lüdicke and Heinrich Wollborn: Im Gedenken an die Freie Waldorfschule Breslau. EK 5, 1980, p. 296ff.
793 http://biographien.kulturimpuls.org/detail.php?&id=1498 (site visited November 23, 2016).
794 Report of Moritz Bartsch. Archiv LS 3.19.012.
795 Letter from Herbert Hahn to Georg Klingberg and Moritz Bartsch, dated August 4, 1925. Archiv LS 3.19.006 and 3.19.007.
796 Program printed in G 12.12.1926, p. 400.

with examples from their school practice and there were more than 1000 teachers in attendance. At one point one of the teachers from Silesia asked, "And what about salaries and pensions?" First there was silence, then Caroline von Heydebrand climbed onto the podium and answered with her delicate voice: "This is where one needs to have faith in God." She did report that teachers had managed financially so far, partly because they had been willing to sacrifice.[797] Because of remarks of this kind, the good mood and the willingness to risk a new pedagogical venture evaporated.

Soon after the founding of the Stuttgart Waldorf School, people in Breslau had organized a local group of the Association for Independent Schools. So teachers from Stuttgart regularly came to lecture to the individual local groups in order to keep the warm stream of goodwill flowing and possibly spark interest in the new education. The next Waldorf school conference was held January 3–6, 1927, with Eugen Kolisko, E. A. Karl Stockmeyer, Alexander Strakosch, Karl Schubert, and Ernst Uehli in attendance. It took place in the Guildhall in Breslau, and Maria Dedo-Brie reported that the warmhearted enthusiasm and spiritual nature of Karl Schubert moved the audience especially, regardless of whether people had heard of Waldorf pedagogy or something like the "powers of destiny."[798]

The idea to found a school was pursued further. In 1927, a group of parents turned to the school in Stuttgart to ask permission to found an independent Waldorf school. They reported there were around 500 parents who were interested and that there were around 130 applicants for the early grades. Richard Dürich wanted to do a practicum at the Stuttgart school in order to prepare, and sent a request to E. A. Karl Stockmeyer.[799] The plan was to start at Easter of 1927 with four grades at once, if the Stuttgart teachers would give the go-ahead. Permission was basically given in a letter Herbert Hahn sent on March 18, 1927, the only condition being that the individual teachers would have to be screened by the Stuttgart faculty.

The next hurdle was obtaining permission from the educational authorities of Breslau. A request was sent on April 20, 1927, on receipt of which school inspector Dr. Lauterbach decided he should first visit the Waldorf school in Stuttgart before he could say anything. The education department then made the proposal that they would take on the founding of an urban school, using principles for reform, allowing teachers the freedom to determine the curriculum and methods. Some of those in the preparatory group thought this was a favorable option that had potential, because a completely independent school, such as the Stuttgart faculty envisioned, gave no guarantee of financial security. In the autumn of 1927, the preparatory committee was divided about the two options, an urban school in the style of reform or an

797 Gertraud Bessert: *Ein Quell wird zum Strom*. Anthroposophisches Leben und heilpädagogische Impulse aus der Breslauer Zeit 1924–1948. Undated, p. 14.
798 Maria Dedo-Brie: Waldorf School Conference at Breslau, January 3–6, 1927. AM 30.1.1927, p. 37f.
799 Letter of February 5, 1927. Archiv LS 3.19.017.

independent Waldorf school. Moritz Bartsch had wanted to stay out of it, but now he had to broker compromises and calm the waves. The upshot of it all was that those who had lobbied for Waldorf education within a state school ended up leaving the Association for Independent Education of Breslau and stopped coming to the meetings. Marie Kruse took over the pedagogical preparation at this point. Since there was no adequate financial basis, the founding date was postponed until October 1929, and they were also thinking about starting up with a few children beforehand in a private setting.[800]

On October 10, 1928, the Rudolf Steiner School Association of Breslau was founded, which continued the highly energetic parent work done before by the Association for Independent Schools, organizing many lectures and parent discussions. A number of prominent board members were elected to this new association: Lutz Engel, MD (1895–1977); two parent representatives, the vocational school teacher Arthur Knoff and Georg Hahn, who in years to come would become a highly sought-after mediator, trusted by both parents and teachers, and a pillar of the school; and Johannes Perthel (1888–1944), a priest of the Christian Community.

Before the school was officially founded, Hildegard Richter (1896–1945) had started up at Easter 1928, as planned. Lutz Engel helped to organize this and Hildegard Richter taught a small class of children in a private home.[801] She was married to Gottfried Richter (1901–1980), a priest of the Christian Community, who understood what she was doing and could support it. His own family had turned its back on him after he had interrupted his art history studies in order to pursue anthroposophy. After his ordination as a priest in the Christian Community, he had been sent to the Breslau congregation in 1927,[802] where he stayed until he was conscripted in 1939. He worked together with Rudolf Meyer and Johannes Perthel.[803] Gottfried Richter had met Hildegard Stahnke while he was a private tutor on the Isle of Rügen, and she went along to Breslau when he was sent there. She made it her task to help with the preparations to found a Waldorf school and took on teaching the first group of children. It was sad that she lost her life near the end of the war. After the war, Gottfried Richter took over the Christian Community congregation in Ulm.

800 Letter from A. Knoff to the Waldorf School in Stuttgart, dated January 22, 1928. Archiv LS 3.19.029.

801 Letter from A. Knoff to E. A. Karl Stockmeyer, dated October 18, 1928. Archiv LS 3.19.036.

802 Tobias Richter: Gottfried Richter. In: Bodo von Plato (ed.): *Anthroposophie im 20. Jahrhundert.* 2003, p. 653.

803 Johannes Perthel married the sister of Gerbert Grohmann in 1915. As a young student–before the Christian Community was founded–he belonged to an anthroposophical study group in Tübingen.

The Waldorf School of Breslau Begins

THE WALDORF SCHOOL of Breslau celebrated its opening on Thursday, April 24, 1930, a radiant spring day. There were 54 students in three classes: a first grade, a second grade, and a combined grade 3/4. The first teachers were Hildegard Richter, who took the second grade with the children she had already taught; Magdalena Stephan (1895–1980), who was from Breslau, had studied eurythmy, and took the first grade; and Fritz Weiss from Pilgramshain, who taught the combined third and fourth grades until he moved to Yugoslavia in 1932.

The Breslau Pavillion from the Centennial Exhibition of 1913 at the entrance to the Snowy Park served as the school building for the Waldorf School of Breslau.

Walter Johannes Stein came to the opening ceremony, bringing greetings from the Stuttgart colleagues. In his address, he also turned to the children and said "You cannot learn anything unless you love what you learn, and you can only learn from somebody you love. Therefore I would like to tell you that we, who want to be your teachers, have been able to learn something because we were able to look up to our teacher Dr. Rudolf Steiner, whom we love […]. The purpose of learning is that we want to be good and want to take our place in life in the right way. As you are going to this school, there also will be hard work

to be done. And you can expect to hear many stories that will take you to enchanted castles. I can reveal that your school journey will take you through 12 such enchanted castles. You will be exploring all of them and every single one will be different from the one before. And then, you will find a key with which you will be able to open a hidden room. This hidden room is life itself. […]"[804]

Municipal school inspector Wilhelm Schremmer, a well-known school reformer in Silesia at the time, spoke to them and wished them well on behalf of the authorities of Breslau. Principal Moritz Bartsch spoke heartfelt words about the love that should reign in the school. That evening, Walter Johannes Stein gave a public lecture about the foundations of Waldorf education.

Obtaining an official permit for the school was made substantially easier because of the reputation of Pilgrimshain, an institution where anthroposophical curative

804 Newsletter of the Waldorf School in Breslau, Nr. 1, May 1930, p. 5. Archiv LS 3.19.001.

work and education were being practiced. One of the government officials thought so highly of the curative education work at Pilgrimshain that he became a staunch advocate for a Waldorf school and made sure it was being recognized in spite of considerable resistance in the city's education department.

Soon after the school started, the faculty was joined by Herbert Weiss (1903–1986), who came from a teacher family in Silesia. He had completed his teacher training when he was only 19, and had subsequently abandoned the idea of becoming a teacher in favor of a music training. He received a full scholarship with all expenses paid to pursue this dream, studied with Bronislav von Poczniak for seven years, and became a pianist. Herbert Weiss came to the school to teach music and became a universally beloved teacher, while his wife Hilde (1903–1986)[805] taught eurythmy until the government put a stop to it. After the war, both of them helped to build up the Waldorf School of Schloss Hamborn, where they worked for 40 years. One of the students of the Breslau school was Hannah Heim (1923–1990). She escaped to West Germany in 1946, did the teacher training in Stuttgart, and after teaching at the Waldorf school in Hannover, she ended up working at the Waldorf School Stuttgart-Uhlandshöhe.

In the second school year, 1932, the kindergarten was started at Easter time, led by Ms. Folgner. Wilhelm Beck (1904–1984) and Hans-Eberhard Schiller (1899–1965) joined the faculty in the years after that. Handwork was taught by Hildegard Steinke, who later married Lutz Engel, the school doctor; in 1936, the couple emigrated to England to escape persecution.[806] After they left, Traute Roesler took over the handwork lessons, teaching gymnastics as well.[807] Another anthroposophical doctor in Breslau, Dr. Herbert Zellner, whose son Johannes was in the class together with Gertraud Bessert, also had to emigrate because of his Jewish heritage. He sent his two older children to England and two years later he fled himself, together with his wife and his youngest daughter. They went to Chile and stayed there for the rest of their lives. It is likely that he brought the anthroposophical medical impulse to Chile. His two older children remained in England.

The freestanding kindergarten pavilion at the entrance of the Scheitniger Park, built back in 1913 for the Centennial Exhibition, soon became too small, and around Easter 1933 they moved from the northern part of town to the south, where a private lyceum had become available on the Kleiststrasse.[808] Hildegard Richter, who was gifted with a deep resonating voice that drew all to her, formed the heart of the school. In the summer of 1932 they were joined by Heinrich Wollborn and Hans Eberhard Kimmich from the school in Essen. Ernst Lehrs, on loan from the Stuttgart school,

805 Linde de Ris: Herbert Weiss (August 27, 1903–August 18, 1986). LR 33, 1987, p. 73.
806 Before he emigrated, Dr. Lutz Engel taught the children of the extra-help class. The children liked to go to his practice on the Hobrechtufer because they could watch white mice in a terrarium there.
807 Sabine Steglich: Traute Roesler (January 24, 1905–December 31, 1979). LR 23, 1981, p. 98.
808 Heinrich Wollborn: Vom Schicksalsweg der Breslauer Waldorfschule. LR 5, 1972, p. 79ff.

took the new first grade, and was succeeded after a short time by Herbert Fischer, who had to finish his teacher training at the Stuttgart seminar before he could take over. Heinrich Wollborn took the fifth grade and worked at the school until it closed, after which he taught for a short stint at a private school for handicapped children until 1940, when he was called up to serve as an antiaircraft helper. His first wife died that same year and he had to take care of his four-year-old daughter.[809]

After a short preparation at the Stuttgart teacher seminar, Karin Ruths-Hoffmann (1904–1986) took the new first grade in 1933. She had grown up in Breslau and had become acquainted with Waldorf education when she was part of the circle of anthroposophical youth work in Breslau. She became so enthusiastic–becoming enthusiastic was a capacity she had until the end of her days—that she went to Stuttgart, where she lived with the family of Dr. Friedrich Rittelmeyer and attended the twelfth grade of the Stuttgart Waldorf School. She was a classmate of Rudolf Grosse; they both were part of that senior grade which was still able to have an in-depth discussion with Rudolf Steiner about their future plans before leaving the school. When Karin Ruths-Hoffmann told him she wanted to become a Waldorf teacher, Rudolf Steiner recommended she should first study physics and chemistry along with philosophy and psychology, which turned out to be just the right advice for her.

The same year, 1933, Margarete Bessert-Weinhold started teaching English and French at the school in Breslau. She was a born pedagogue and was an experienced curative teacher; from 1934 she built up a so-called extra-help class. Her husband died in World War I, and before she joined the Waldorf school, she had led her own small school using principles of reform in which the children of the upper crust were educated, including those of Count Keyserlingk. She ended up marrying the Keyserlingk's estate manager Bessert, moved to Jannowitz, and taught in a home for children of parents on welfare. She only started teaching at the Waldorf school when the family moved back to Breslau in 1933.[810] Her great pedagogical qualities were known among parents as well as education officials in Breslau.

There were a few Jewish children among the students, among them Anita and Renate Lasker,[811] as well as the daughter of the Cohn-Dobers family. They had to endure anti-Semitic slurs from fellow students.

In 1933, a mother who was a member of the National Socialist Party, Dr. Oberstein, lodged a complaint with the local party head about Ernst Lehrs being of Jewish heritage, lamenting that the school leadership was not behind National Socialism. She took her daughter out of the school. The local party head took the

809 Rüdiger Voigt: Heinrich Wollborn. LR 34, 1987, p. 90.
810 According to an interview of February 23, 2017, with Gertraud Bessert and a letter of hers dated March 19, 2017. Archiv NG.
811 See also Anita Lasker-Wallfisch: *Ihr sollt die Wahrheit erben–Die Cellistin von Auschwitz.* 2000.

complaints seriously and reported to the district administration of the NSDAP, accusing the school of being in league with the Jewish conspiracy. Heinrich Wollborn defended Ernst Lehrs, stressing the fact that anthroposophy puts the individual above race.[812] However, in October 1933 the faculty distanced itself from the letter written by Heinrich Wollborn, emphasizing that the school was based in the National Socialist state and that no more Jewish students would be accepted. The Breslau school authorities confirmed this with the National Socialist Teachers Union after a school inspection.[813] The obligatory Hitler portrait, painted by a father who could not afford the tuition, was hung on the wall as well, in the eurythmy room of all places, much to the displeasure of Magdalena Stephan. She declared, "I will not do eurythmy here as long as that trashy painting is not covered up."[814]

The school developed splendidly in the beautiful building on the Kleiststrasse, where it had its glory years. A strong inner community was established. Heinrich Wollborn gives a picture of an extraordinary number of active, talented, and motivated boys and girls among the students; "The student body was an exceptional support for the teachers in building up and expanding the school."[815] But this phase was short-lived. The last two new class teachers joined in 1935: Rose Lüdicke and Dr. Bruno Galsterer, who was hired to teach fifth grade, because their teacher, Hans-Eberhard Schiller, switched to the Hamburg school.[816]

Rose Lüdicke (1906–1990) was born in Trebnitz, Silesia, and had to be apprenticed early in life, so she was not able to get her high school diploma until she was 24, after many highways and byways. She studied history and theology in Rostock and Tübingen, but academic studies did not answer her questions. One day she discovered a purple brochure about the Christian Community in the library, which pointed her in the right direction. In 1933/34 she studied at the teacher seminar in Stuttgart where she was especially fond of Caroline von Heydebrand, whom she respected a great deal and felt connected with inwardly. She first started teaching three children on an estate in Pomerania, until the call from Silesia reached her. She then moved to Breslau and took the first grade. After the end of the war and her flight to West Germany, she settled in Nürnberg, where she took a fifth grade in 1946. After that she taught two more classes from grades one through eight.[817]

Dr. Bruno Galsterer (1908–2000) originally came from Nürnberg and ended up in Breslau after studying chemistry, biology, and geology at the University of Erlangen (he did his PhD in geology). His parents, an anthroposophical teacher's

812 Uwe Werner: *Anthroposophen in der Zeit des Nationalsozialismus (1933–1945)*. 1999, p. 100.
813 Ansgar Martins: *Waldorfschule 1933–1945*. 2015, p. 7.
814 According to a letter from Gertraud Bessert dated March 19, 2017. Archiv NG.
815 Heinrich Wollborn: Vom Schicksalsweg der Breslauer Waldorfschule. LR 5, 1972, p. 80.
816 In an interview with Gertraud Bessert on February 23, 2017, she says the students didn't like this teacher and made life pretty hard for him.
817 Alma Schmidt: Rose Lüdicke (June 3, 1906–October 3, 1919). LR 41, 1991, p. 88f.

family, had made it possible for him to attend the upper three grades of the Waldorf School in Stuttgart. Even though he was guided by his interest in natural science at the university, he always made time to study works of Rudolf Steiner next to his regular studies. Soon after completing his degree, he went to Breslau, took the fifth grade, and went up to grade eight with that class.

In May 1935, the school was notified that it could not accept any more new students and was not allowed to have a ninth grade. This was catastrophic, because the plan had been to build up a high school, and this was to have been the first ninth grade. The official grounds given for this *Verbot* were "poor teaching results." One of the students who was affected by this measure was Carl-Heinz Schiel (1922–2019), who passed the entrance exam and was accepted into the Protestant Reform-Realgymnasium. After military service and American captivity, he landed in Bonn, where he spent the rest of his life working as the general secretary of the *Deutsche Forschungsgemeinschaft* [German research funding organization].[818]

As a result of the ordinance the school could not expand and one of the teachers had to go. Karin Ruths-Hoffmann, who was pregnant, volunteered to step back. In October of that year she moved with her family to Sweden, where she was active as a social worker. Much later she was a cofounder of the Waldorf education work in Järna.

The remaining teachers decided to provide lessons after school for those children they were no longer allowed to accept, mainly younger siblings of students in the school, teaching them eurythmy, painting, and fairytales in the afternoon. Some of these courses were kept going after the school was closed. The school building on the Kleiststrasse was appropriated by the *Luftgaukommando* [district air command], so the school was without a home at the beginning of 1936. It became more and more difficult to escape the dark specter of the regime. At Easter 1936, the Waldorf school found refuge in a former printing company building situated just off the Neue Graupenstrasse. Around this time, teaching eurythmy was prohibited by the Secret State Police.[819] Parents and teachers were united by the impulse to keep going for as long as possible, which asked for great sacrifices. Since housing could no longer be paid for with the low salaries, teachers moved in with one another and families took turns feeding them lunch. There was an assembly every month, however, and the Christmas plays from Oberufer were put on every year with the help of parents.

When the request to be recognized as an experimental school was turned down, the school, which by now had shrunk to four grades, closed definitely on March 24, 1939.[820] The closing was voluntary and was sealed by an assembly that all those present experienced as painful. Up to then, teachers had basically done without much of a salary and survived by accepting donations from a circle of friends of the school.

818 Letter written by C.H. Schiel, dated June 14, 2016. Archiv NG.
819 Written by H. Richter to the Waldorf School in Stuttgart on March 23, 1936. Archiv LS 3.19.071.
820 Uwe Werner: *Anthroposophen in der Zeit des Nationalsozialismus (1933–1945)*. 1999, p. 227.

Now they had to find new ways to fend for themselves. After the school had closed, a curative "family school" continued on, led by Margarete Bessert-Weinhold. It had about 100 children, and its existence was largely made possible because the city's education officials looked the other way.[821]

The school was composed of both children of the former Waldorf school and many others, whose parents were able to rustle up a physician's consent form needed for enrollment. To her great delight, Hildegard Fuhlendorf[822] was one of the children who was able to go to Margarete Bessert-Weinhold's school; she was in the same class as Bringfried Schubert[823] and Christian Klingenberg. She had been evacuated from Hamburg to Breslau, where she lived with the local anthroposophical physician Hans Joachim Pohl (1909–1963) and his wife Kyra Pohl-Zirkenbach (1914–1968).[824] Kyra Pohl taught English and mathematics at the so-called family school; Magdalena Stephan gave eurythmy lessons. The lessons took place in a gigantic house that was standing empty, the second floor of a patrician house at Charlottenstrasse 24. It still had furniture of the Jewish owners, who had probably been driven out. A few children also found a home in this grand dwelling. Above them on the third floor there was an SA [storm trooper] office, below them on the ground floor was an SS officer. Gertraud Bessert, the daughter of Margarete Bessert, remembers that the children of this officer, whose name was Schneider, also went to this so-called Bessert School.[825] Of course the school inspector knew what kind of school it was, and when he came for an inspection, his office announced the visit ahead of time so that the necessary preparations could be made.

After the closing of the Waldorf school, people with an anthroposophical orientation also used this building to meet in. The SS never inspected the dwelling, so many friends brought their anthroposophical books, which would otherwise have been confiscated from their homes. Here people worked intensively with the anthroposophical physician Dr. Waltraud Hoffmann-Starke, who, together with her

---

821 Magdalena Stephan quotes the official of the education department as saying, "We understand each other but won't tell anybody." In: EK 5, 1980, p. 304.

822 Interview with Hildegard Fuhlendorf on November 11, 2016, in Rendsburg. Hildegard Fuhlendorf, born Hildegard Glüder in Hamburg in 1932, was evacuated to Breslau from 1943 until January 1945. Together with her husband, she shaped the Waldorf school in Rendsburg for decades.

823 In that same interview, she mentions that Bringfried Schubert was the daughter of the owner of a Reformhaus [health food store] in Breslau. Before the war, her father was very ill with diphtheria and was healed by Dr. Lutz Engel, the predecessor of Hans Joachim Pohl in the anthroposophical doctor's practice in Breslau. Lutz Engel was at least half Jewish and left Breslau as early as 1936 together with his wife. It may be that the Pohl family lived in their house.

824 Kyra and Hans Joachim Pohl went to Fellbach near Stuttgart after the war, and, according to a report of Karl Kaltenbach, dated August 9, 2001 (Archiv NG), they emigrated to Australia in 1951 at the invitation of the Anthroposophical Society of Australia. He founded the first anthroposophical curative institute, Inala, in Sydney. Karl Kaltenbach also reports that Kyra Pohl was "a charismatic personality who had an extraordinary knowledge of the anthroposophical picture of the human being."

825 Stated in an interview with Gertraud Bessert on February 21, 2017, and in a letter she wrote, dated March 19, 2017. Archiv NG.

husband Gotthard Starke, founded the curative home Schloss Bingenheim after the war. At Christmas of 1944, the Christmas play from Oberufer was performed for all the children, which marked the last celebration they were able to have together in the school. When Breslau was declared a fortress, the family school closed in January 1945 and the children were evacuated.[826] Most of the surviving parents and teachers who remained in Breslau left Silesia after the war and fled from the new occupying powers.

An attempt was made after the war to reopen the Waldorf school, but it was short-lived. The Soviet authorities allowed it for a few months, but the experiment had to be stopped when the Polish government was instated. In May 1946 Magdalena Stephan and Margarete Bessert-Weinhold were able to leave Breslau by joining a Jewish community transport. The two women helped build up the Waldorf school in Heidenheim for a few years before turning to curative work again. Irmgard von Esebeck, who had taught handwork in Breslau for a few years (until 1939), also came to Heidenheim. When her husband, the Christian community priest Constantin von Esebeck, was declared missing in Russia, she first returned to Breslau, but when the Russians marched in in 1945, she and her little son fled to Heidenheim.[827]

On June 15, 1980, the 50-year anniversary was celebrated by students and teachers of the Breslau school at the Waldorf school in Stuttgart. In preparation, Ruth Seiss, working alongside Herbert Greif in the office of the German Federation of Waldorf Schools, efficiently put together lists of all grades and their teachers. As a result of her efforts, many former people from Breslau pitched in to create a comprehensive picture, making it possible for all those who had survived to be invited. Of the former teachers from Breslau, Wilhelm Beck, Dr. Bruno Galsterer, Rose Lüdicke, Karin Ruths-Hoffmann, Magdalena Stephan, Heinrich Wollborn, Traute Rössler, and Herbert Weiss were present.

1930: The Waldorf School in Pressburg (Bratislava)

THERE WAS AN INDEPENDENT, German-speaking Waldorf kindergarten in the Holuby Strasse in Pressburg, which the eurythmist Erika Mursalle (1908–1990) built up and worked in from 1930 until 1944.[828] Svatava Klenovská[829] remembers how, in 1930, about 15 children came to the kindergarten, where Erika Mursalle created a joyful, open atmosphere in which children immediately felt at ease. The children were of three or four nationalities, and none of them had heard a word of German before, but because of the atmosphere she created, they lost any inhibitions they might have had. Ms. Mursalle, or Aunt Rika, as they called her, had a boundless imagination,

---

826 Uwe Werner: *Anthroposophen in der Zeit des Nationalsozialismus (1933–1945)*. 1999, p. 228.
827 Emma Pommerenig: Irmgard von Esebeck (January 1, 1913–September 11, 1979). LR 20, 1979, p. 80f.
828 Ingeborg Schröder: Erika Mursalle. LR 40, 1990, p. 112.
829 Svatava Klenovská: Erinnerungen aus Bratislava (Slowakei). LR 68, 2000, p. 75.

Hannah Krämer-Steiner and her husband, Paul Steiner, in Bratislava, 1941

and they loved her. There were many artistic activities: painting, modeling, sculpting, and making music. Irene Ramharter, a pianist, was by her side, and the children loved singing and doing eurythmy. One of these children was Theodora Krausová (1927–2013), who became a biodynamic farmer later in life. Her father was murdered in Theresienstadt, and during the Prague Spring, she left Czechoslovakia together with her sister and her mother.

Hannah Krämer-Steiner, named Aunt Hannah, would come to the kindergarten and sing English songs with the children. It was a special treat when Hannah Krämer-Steiner put on a puppet play, which she did two or three times a year. These were celebrations the children looked forward to for a long time. During the war, Erika Mursalle led a kindergarten in the Penenská Gasse. After 1945, she moved to Frankfurt am Main.

In 1930, Hannah Krämer-Steiner (1895–1984) opened a small Waldorf school not far from the kindergarten, at Moysesgasse 7, which was carried by the local Rudolf Steiner School Association.[830] It was like a one-room schoolhouse with about ten children, spanning grades one through five. There were Slavic children; others were of Hungarian or Jewish origin. Two or three children had special needs. Hannah Krämer-Steiner was friends with Walter Johannes Stein, Eugen Kolisko, and Otto Fränkl from the time when she studied in Vienna. She also had friendly relations with some of the preeminent Stuttgart teachers of the first hour.[831] Back in 1922, she had received permission from Rudolf Steiner to study his pedagogical lectures and take part in the courses given to teachers. When she had finished her teacher training, she first stayed in Vienna, then worked for a short time in the new Waldorf school in Budapest, until she was ready to be a founding teacher at the new Waldorf school in Vienna. She gave up her work in Budapest with a heavy heart, but she followed the call and went back to Vienna. Only after she had arrived there did they tell her that she had been rejected in the meantime because of her Jewish origin. Bitterly disappointed, she moved to Pressburg and helped prepare the founding of the new Waldorf school.

Hannah Krämer-Steiner was a truly outstanding teacher who worked individually with every single child entrusted to her care. She did not only teach the children, but taught them to be attentive to other children's needs, even root for one another. Practicing empathy with the children was just as important to her as the teaching per

830 Andreas Worel: Hannah Krämer-Steiner (October 29, 1895–March 20, 1984). N of October 28, 1984, p. 182f.
831 Jakob Streit: Drei Todesfälle in der Wiener Arbeit. Mitteilungen aus der anthroposophischen Bewegung Nr. 77, 1984, p. 34.

se. Erika Mursalle came regularly and taught eurythmy, bringing Irene Ramharter along to accompany the eurythmy lessons on piano.

Thanks to the support of the Czech minister of education, the school was able to work undisturbed for a number of years. He would actually send teachers of other Pressburg schools to the introductory pedagogical lectures that Hannah Steiner gave. But when his successor took office, he immediately withdrew the school's license;[832] the little Waldorf school was the last German-speaking school in Slovakia. As a result, the school closed in 1939.

Hannah Krämer-Steiner survived the concentration camp in Theresienstadt, and after the war she and her husband ended up in Brno. In the 1950s, she managed to get permission to return to Vienna.

1931: The Waldorf School in Hamburg-Altona

THE CONFLICTS WITHIN the faculty of the Goethe School in Hamburg-Wandsbek caused a number of faculty members to leave. In 1931, Paula Dieterich (1892–1974), Dr. Franz Brumberg (1896–1973), Gertrud Jasper, Henni Lemcke, and the school physician, Dr. Julius Solti (1899–1983), founded the Waldorf school at Flottbeker Chaussee 101 (called Elbchaussee today) in Hamburg-Altona.[833] In a social sense, an exciting time of living and working together was in store for this school. At the time, Altona was situated outside the city limit of Hamburg and was Prussian territory. Therefore the new school needed a license from Berlin. The school had its official opening at Easter of 1931, starting with five grades: a first and second grade, two third grades, and a sixth grade. There were about 100 children and the above-mentioned five teachers.[834]

In an account he wrote in 1933, Franz Brumberg paints the following picture: "The school is located on the Flottbeker Chaussee in Altona. From the classrooms and the school yard one has a broad view of the river Elbe and the harbor of Hamburg. Its location is on the periphery of a metropolis. The special way it is situated is a reminder for the students that they have special tasks. Because of its surroundings, the school feels it is imperative to educate the children truthfully, in a way that prepares them for practical life and is moral to the core. Wakefulness and courage have played their part in making Hamburg a world harbor. A child growing up in Hamburg is embedded in these forces of consciousness and will. Children can only meet the tasks of the future when these forces are not weakened by a one-sided intellectual education, so that they

832 Elisabeth Gergely and Tobias Richter (eds.): *Wiener Dialoge. Der österreichische Weg der Waldorfpädagogik.* 2011, p. 79.
833 Ernst Weissert: Dr. Paula Dieterich (February 19, 1892–January 5, 1974). LR 8, 1973, p. 68.
834 Report of the Rudolf Steiner Schule Altona of May 9, 1933. Archiv LS 4.2.129.

will be able to help transcend materialistic habits of thought in all areas of culture, politics, and economics [...].”[835]

Conflicts arose within the faculty in the very first year of school. Henni Lemcke married a colleague who had recently joined, Dr. Ernst Emmert, and they both worked as class teachers at the school in Altona until they were summarily dismissed on February 5, 1933. The parents of their two classes, however, valued their pedagogical work and did not want their children to have to deal with a change in teachers. So with a few exceptions, they followed the teachers and found shelter in the Milbergrealschule, the headmistress and owner of which, Berta Schmalfeldt, was interested in Waldorf education and welcomed this new opportunity. In conversations with the Goethe School, there was hope the new venture could be made a branch of that school.[836]

By 1936, 360 students and more than 12 teachers passed through the doors of the Waldorf School Hamburg-Altona [now called the Rudolf Steiner School of Altona] every day of the week. At the end of March 1936, the teachers were informed that the government had put a ban on further enrollment of new students, and also that everyone in school would be obliged to swear allegiance to Adolf Hitler, just like in public schools. In a meeting that went far into the night, the faculty decided to refuse to take the oath. As a consequence of this decision, the faculty chose to close the school voluntarily. This decision was carried out ten days after the parents had been informed, on April 6, 1936. In his speech to the assembly at the end of the school, Franz Brumberg said he had first looked for a way to cooperate, but after the Anthroposophical Society had been prohibited, it had become clear to him that Waldorf education and National Socialism would never be able to find common ground. These were the reasons that had made the closing of the school inevitable. Courses to prepare students for the transition into state schools were put in place, and they continued until March 1938.[837]

On July 3, 1936, Franz Brumberg, the official head of the school in Altona, wrote on behalf of the school to all the other Waldorf schools in Germany, saying they did not want to make any further compromises until Rudolf Steiner’s name had been rehabilitated and anthroposophical work and free education would be possible again. He told them that his school had divested itself of its name and was in the process of shutting down its operation, apart from courses given to students in order to facilitate their transition into state schools with their different curricula.[838]

From then on, Paula Dieterich gave courses for parents of the school and former students in her apartment, especially courses in philosophy and history of art. In the

---

835 Report of the Rudolf Steiner Schule Altona of May 9, 1933. Archiv LS 4.2.129.
836 Letter written by Dr. Ernst Emmert, dated March 29, 1933, addressed to the faculty of the Waldorf School in Stuttgart. Archiv LS 3.2.305.
837 Uwe Werner: *Anthroposophen in der Zeit des Nationalsozialismus (1933–1945)*. 1999, p. 137f.
838 Ibid., p. 138, note 378.

afternoon, Dagmar Funcke (1910–2005) painted with the schoolchildren, and Alice Schürer (1902–1991) gave eurythmy. For some reason the Gestapo did not disturb these activities. This work and many little groups continued after May 1945, and Paula Dieterich gradually expanded and opened up the work step-by-step. In October, she received permission from the English occupying forces to start up anthroposophical work in Hamburg again. After the war, she became a major force in the rebuilding of the Anthroposophical Society in Germany. Her public lectures, her activities in the advisory circle of the Waldorf schools in Hamburg, of which she formed an indispensable part, and her cosmopolitan engagement in Hamburg made her one of the most prominent personalities in the anthroposophical movement in Germany.

1931: A Waldorf Class in Stockholm

WHEN SIGNE ROLL-WIKBERG was working as a teacher in the Waldorf school of Oslo, she organized courses and conferences for years and also gave lectures, both on Waldorf education and on the mission of Norway. From July 27–August 11, 1931, a course was held at the initiative of Anna Wager-Gunnarsson (1873–1957) and Lisa Svanberg in Viggbyholm, close to Stockholm, which several Norwegian teachers took part in. The indefatigable Curt Englert-Faye was the main speaker, and he gave 20 lectures. At his request, Signe Roll-Wikberg came to Sweden together with him and contributed to the course by giving six lectures. Both the lectures and the ensuing discussions were so stimulating that the participants often did not pay attention to the lunch bell. The afternoons were for painting and practicing eurythmy.[839]

This course formed the seed for a Waldorf school in Sweden, which a small group had been thinking about for quite some time. Ruth Nilsson (1894–1981) had publications of the Stuttgart Waldorf School from the 1920s, and she definitely was part of this group. On September 15, 1931, a few weeks after the course, a start was made with a first grade in Stockholm, which could be seen as a practical outcome of the course. The teacher of this class was the speech artist and self-proclaimed guardian of the anthroposophical movement, Margaret Langen-Riedel (1908–1993).[840] She grew up in London and Stockholm, attended the Waldorf teacher seminar in Stuttgart and taught first at the New School in England. Together with the eurythmist Karin Flack-Selling (1880–1958)[841] and Karin Axelsdotter Larsson, she opened the little Stockholm Waldorf school at Rådmansgatan 14. The school had six children, and the building housed the anthroposophical library as well. A little later, the school moved to an apartment in Stockholm Östermalm.

839 Ingeborg Sjögre: Aus Schweden, N 46, 15.11.1931, p. 182f.
840 http://biographien.kulturimpuls.org/detail.php?&id=1071 (site visited August 2, 2016).
841 Ibid.

Herbert Hahn cultivated very warm relationships with the teachers in Sweden and was a source of inspiration for them, especially Karin Larsson and Margaret Langen-Riedel, who hitchhiked to Dornach twice in the 1930s in order to participate in further training.[842] In the middle of the 1930s, Margaret Langen-Riedel left Sweden. The little Waldorf school existed until 1939, when it had to close, mainly due to dwindling interest, which resulted in a weak economic basis.

1932: A Waldorf Kindergarten in Smestad, Oslo

Gulle Brun-Landau

In 1932, the eurythmist Gulle Brun (1891–1988)[843] taught a private class at home for the eight or ten youngest children in her neighborhood, for whom the way to the nearest school was too long. Her husband, the German musician Vult Simon (1902–1988), substituted for her in school in the meantime. This was the first step in the pedagogical activities of the couple. Apart from the Waldorf schools in Bergen and Oslo, these two founded a third anthroposophical institution in 1934, which had a highly artistic orientation. It was located at Bernhard Herres Vei 43 in the section of Oslo called Smestad,[844] where they had already built a house. Gulle Brun and Vult Simon led this home kindergarten together, and it became a pioneering Waldorf kindergarten for Norway, serving as a training center as well because it was there that some of the later kindergarten teachers became acquainted with Waldorf early childhood education. The parents of the children were invited for individual conversations, which Gulle Brun used to show them how each individual child was developing, using drawings, paintings, and other work so that parents could closely follow the steps of their child. Many parents welcomed being involved this way, and the reputation of the school grew by word-of-mouth, resulting in increased enrollment. The kindergarten was able to continue operating during and after the war.

Next to this, Gulle Brun-Simon kept up her work as a eurythmy teacher at the Rudolf Steiner school in Oslo for some time and maintained the connection. All the while, she kept teaching the little group of students in her house, as mentioned above. When the Rudolf Steiner school was closed in 1936, Gulle Brun and Vult Simon kept working artistically with a few of the students. In 1937, *Det Nye Teater* showed eurythmy pieces she had practiced with the children. In the same year, she gave public

---

842 Interview with Göran Fant in Järna on July 22, 2016; På Väg 1, 2007.
843 Terje Christensen: http://biographien.kulturimpuls.org/detail.php?&id=835 (site visited August 2, 2016).
844 Terje Christensen: Steinerskolens impuls føres videre i privat regi. In: Erik Marstrander (ed.): *Menneske først*. 1996, p. 83ff.

performances with older students of the Rudolf Steiner school in Oslo and later in Lillehammer. She showed opera pieces such as W.A. Mozart's *Bastien und Bastienne*; Carl Maria von Weber's *Abu Hassan* was performed in a number of places, among them Kongsberg; and Claudio Monteverdi's *Orfeo* received positive praise in an article by the important music critic and composer Pauline Hall.

Edith Roger (born 1922), a former student of the Rudolf Steiner school, who participated in this work, later became one of the best-known dancers and choreographers of Norway. Numerous people who later became teachers in the Rudolf Steiner school and in the Waldorf kindergarten received their first theoretical and practical training from Gulle Brun and Vult Simon. The two of them continued their pedagogical work after the German occupation in 1940.

Neither the Rudolf Steiner schools nor the Anthroposophical Society were forbidden in Norway. The little school kept growing during the war because parents anxiously witnessed the attempts the authorities made to integrate National Socialist ideology into Norwegian schools. Hallvard Blekastad (born 1883) taught English in the school. In 1943, the little private school in Smestad-Oslo managed to attract Dan Lindholm (1908–1998). Between 1938 and 1943 he had studied botany and chemistry in Oslo and had been a class teacher in the Bergen Waldorf School for seven years.

But the war did cause problems. The Germans took action against the Oslo university and arrested 600 students and teachers, among them Dan Lindholm. Most of them were transported to concentration camps in Germany, but Dan Lindholm was let go after a few weeks in an internment camp. The Germans also made several attempts to conscript Vult Simon. In 1944, he finally fled to Sweden together with Gulle Brun and their son, in order to escape military service. At the request of parents, Dan Lindholm kept the school going on his own at first, and he soon was able to continue the education of all the children with two new teachers by his side, Christian Faye Smit and Helene Cecilie Vogt. After the war, Gulle Brun and Vult Simon came back to Norway, and at first they worked together again.[845] A little later, they parted ways.[846] Dan Lindholm remained a teacher at the school until 1986. He was part of a younger generation of teachers who took the helm and, in the autumn of 1945, founded the school anew and changed the name to Rudolf Steiner School, which it still has today. At the end of the war, the school was housed in army barracks in Frogner Park. Again it was Curt Englert who inspired the new teachers in Oslo, as he had done in Bergen. He left Zürich in 1936 and remained in Oslo until his death on December 1, 1945. Next to his work as an author, he unfolded a rich activity as a lecturer. In 1949, the school moved to Hovseter, where it still is today.

845 Undated report by Signe Roll-Wikberg. Archiv BFWS.
846 Terje Christensen: http://biographien.kulturimpuls.org/detail.php?&id=835 (site visited August 2, 2016).

1933: The Selter School in Marburg

IN 1933, Herta Schlegtendal (1898–1981) was invited to come teach at the Selter School in Marburg on the recommendation of the Stuttgart Waldorf School. It was a private school that had been founded by Anna and Johanna Selter in 1898, and it had a high reputation in Marburg, hence the name Selter School. It was a lyceum for girls, based on the methods and aims of Walter Diltheys, which Johanna Selter (1865–1942) adhered to. She had been a student of Prof. Walter Dilthey and was a devotee of his educational philosophy. Anna Selter (1872–1945), however, became acquainted with anthroposophy through Friedrich Rittelmeyer in 1925 and did everything she could to convince her sister to adopt Waldorf education. She did not let up in her efforts to convince her sister. It took years, but in the end Johanna agreed. So they appointed Herta Schlegtendal and gave her the assignment to introduce Waldorf pedagogy in Marburg. The teachers in Stuttgart knew her well, because she had studied at the teacher seminar there and had done a practicum with Caroline von Heydebrand. During one of her visits in the Stuttgart school she sat in on a watercolor painting class. She was especially struck by one little girl and watched her intently as she painted, which the little girl found quite annoying. This was Anna Sophia Bäuerle,[847] who later became a class teacher in Marburg. Herta Schlegtendal worked at the Selter School until the National Socialists closed it down at Easter of 1939.

In order to create better conditions for the Waldorf school, the two sisters refurbished their house and created four classrooms and a teachers room on the ground floor. The authorities required recognition as a middle school as a legal prerequisite for coeducation, which of course was not allowed in a lyceum for girls. Furthermore, the Selter School was also subject to the enrollment-stop ordinance the authorities laid down in 1933. The number of students was around 50 at that point.

The Selter School was a member of the Association for Independent Schools in Stuttgart, and as such formed part of the German Waldorf school movement before World War II. A number of faculty members had been dismissed from their former schools because they were deemed "politically unreliable" by the Nazis. One of them was Dr. Friedrich Bunnemann (1881–1953), up until then the faculty chair of the Elizabeth School in Marburg. Two other teachers in this category were Dr. Schüler and Dr. Vonnoh. They were all given positions as teachers in the Selter School. Ida Marche taught English and French, Elsbeth Lippert singing and music, and Irene Ochsenius taught Loheland gymnastics.

The circumstances of that time affected everybody's lives. Everything became tighter, financially as well. At Christmas of 1938, teachers received one last quarter-

---

847 Friederun C. Karsch: 50. Schuljubiläum in Marburg. LR 56, 1996, p. 42ff.; Anna Sophia Bäuerle became a class teacher at the Waldorf school in Marburg in 1949, where she stayed until she retired.

year salary payment, but after that the financial perspectives dried up. On January 31, 1938, the Selter School received a missive ordering the school closed by March 31. The students and teachers had their closing assembly on March 23, 1939. After the school closed, the Christian Community used their rooms for two years.

Johanna Selter died in 1942, when she was 77 years old. The school building at Liebigstrasse 16 (called Wörthstrasse at the time) was completely destroyed during an air raid on March 5, 1945, burying both Anna Selter and Irene Ochsenius beneath it.

The Selter School was licensed as a "reopened school" soon after the war. On October 8, 1945, the Marburg Waldorf School opened its doors to 91 students.[848]

1933: The Waldorf School in Zeist

In September 1932, the young physician Bernard Lievegoed (1905–1992) and a few of his coworkers at the Zonnehuis gave the impulse to found the Waldorf school in Zeist, Holland for their own children and children who lived close by. The Zonnehuis had been founded in 1931 and was the first anthroposophical curative-education institute in Holland. The little Waldorf school began in the living room of a home on the Tavernalaan in Bosch en Duin. Soon, in January 1933, it moved into a garden pavilion of the Veldheim estate on the Utrechtseweg in Zeist. That's why it was known as the *Nieuwe Veldheimschool* for a while. Daan van Bemmelen (1899–1982), who lived in Zeist with his family between 1934 and 1938, helped to build up the little school, especially by starting a teachers training specifically geared to Holland.

Another big help was Maria Uhland (1893–1978), who taught a small group, first of three, later four children, at the request of the parents. One girl was the daughter of Countess Anna van Solms Loudon (1890–1970), another was the daughter of the conductor and composer, Henri Daniel van Goudoever (1898–1977), and there was the son of a Dutch lawyer. Maria Uhland had come from Stuttgart to The Hague together with Herbert Hahn, and the two of them frequently traveled to Zeist from there. Daan van Bemmelen also lived in Zeist during the war. When three or more children were enrolled, Marie Pouderoyen became the second teacher for the younger children. After the war she was the head kindergarten teacher of the Vrije School in Zeist for many decades. Daan van Bemmelen had a house built on the grounds of the estate, earmarked for the teacher training he was planning. His children were also enrolled in the school, which moved into this *van Bemmelenhouse*. In January 1934, Jan Baggerman (†1988) became the third teacher to join the school, but he later accepted a position at the Geert Groote School in Amsterdam.

---

848 Paul Johannes Höll: Herta Schlegtendal (October 8, 1898–July 3, 1981). LR 24, 1982, p. 70f.; Herta Schlegtendal: *Vom Werden und Wachsen der Marburger Waldorfschule*. Published in the 1950s. There is a copy in Archiv NG.

Teachers of the Free Waldorf School in Zeist, 1936

It seems that the school was consolidated in 1934, and a little boarding school was part of it. The latter had been set up in such a way that the students could really feel as if they were living at home there. The school also had a little kindergarten right from the start, so it was possible for very young children to be enrolled. On September 12, 1935, the school was officially incorporated in an association called *Vereniging Zeister Vrije School*. Among the small number of students in Daan van Bemmelen's teacher training was Daniel Udo de Haes (1899–1986), a sculptor who also had a degree in mathematics and physics. After one year of teacher training, he took the next class. Another student in the course was Jetty van Leeuwen, who had grown up in Indonesia and was a widow. She came with her two-year-old son and lived in the boarding school with him. In 1935, when Marie Pouderoyen left Zeist, she took her class and remained as a teacher at the school for the rest of her working life.

In September of 1935, the Nieuwe Veldheimschool moved into a somewhat dilapidated villa on the Kroostweg. Johan Hendrik Theissen (1908–1994), a chemistry student, was appointed head of school because he possessed the necessary qualifications. The teachers studied together, helped each other out, and received medical advice from Bernard Lievegoed. The task was not easy; the curriculum had to be implemented, habits formed, and new ways of learning established—pioneering work from the ground up. Even though the number of children was small, classes could be quite disorderly, especially in foreign languages lessons, because the subject was being taught quite unconventionally for the time. There also were problems with the neighbors, because there was a lot of mistrust against the school. It was getting a bad reputation, fed by rumors that had been disseminated by a Protestant minister. He spread allegations that the school was heathen in character, because myths and stories from the most diverse cultural epochs were being taught.

When Holland was occupied by the Nazis, the small school managed to escape notice because the number of students was so small and because any signs or marks were removed in the nick of time. The school managed to continue operating on the second floor of the villa, and the teachers lived right above it. They were even able to absorb students from the Vrije School in the Hague during the war. And all this time German soldiers had their quarters on the ground floor of the same building. That was also the reason why the male colleagues had to hide in the loft when there were house searches.[849]

After the war, the school grew rapidly despite financial restrictions. As early as 1945, the school could resume operating openly, with seven classes. It was especially due to the efforts of Frans Everbag that the school was able to receive subsidies from the government in 1955. A new school building was erected on the Burgemeester van Tuyllaan. In the early 60s, when new high school legislation called the *Mammoetwet* [mammoth law][850] was about to be implemented, the teachers acted swiftly and opened a high school while it was still possible to obtain a permit.

1933: Geert Groote School in Amsterdam

THE WALDORF SCHOOL in Amsterdam[851] had a forerunner at Euterpestraat (later Gerrit van der Veenstraat) 177, in a building of which there is no trace left today. In 1933, the school started with seven students, who mainly came from two small independent kindergartens that had been housed in homes, one of them on the Parnassusweg bordering on meadows surrounding the city, the other on the Deltastraat in the New South section of the city, amid what were then called skyscrapers (12 floors!). These groups had grown after Max Stibbe, a teacher at the Vrije School in The Hague, had held a few lectures in Amsterdam in 1929 for parents who were interested in Waldorf education. During the first two years, Mieneke Rosenwald (1909–1982) was the only teacher. In the second year, she had the responsibility for a combined grade 1/2 with 12 students. She is remembered as a lovable woman with a warm heart, and she taught in the children's room of the van Royen family, situated at Euterpestraat 177. With the arrival of more children for a new first grade, it became necessary to find more space.

In 1935, the school moved into a mansion at De Lairessestraat 153, which had a little garden in the back, as is customary in Holland. The garden was used as a playground, and the house also had a large kitchen in which the teachers ate lunch. In the meantime, Mieneke Rosenwald had married and moved away. Mies Wils, later Mies Boeke (†1979), took over her class and Joly Schmidt became the teacher for the new first grade. The two teachers lived on the second floor of this house, and the concierge, a former sailor, lived in the basement flat. One room had been transformed

---

849 Marianne de Jong: *De eerste jaren*. Unpublished report. Archiv NG; H. van Leeuwen: Wat er in de Zeister Vrije School gedurende en na de oorlogsjaren is voorgevallen. VOK Oktober 1946, p. 47.

850 Wet op het voortgezet onderwijs (WVO) [high school legislation], February 14, 1963, see also: https://nl.wikipedia.org/wiki/Wet_op_het_voortgezet_onderwijs (site visited September 14, 2016).

851 Mark Mastenbroek: http://www.ggca.nl/index.cfm?PAGE=Geschiedenis (site visited September 16, 2016).

into a eurythmy room, which even had a harmonium. So everything was pretty much improvised and family-like.

Caroline von Heydebrand took on the mentorship of the school during the winter months of 1935/36. Twice a week, she came from The Hague by train, and she also stayed on the upper floor for a short span of time. But health problems prevented her from keeping up this mentorship for long, and she had to go to Arlesheim to recuperate. After she had left, Max Stibbe took over the mentoring.

To begin with, the school was named New School of the Association for *Vrije Opvoedkunst* [independent education]. It was Max Stibbe who suggested the name Geert Groote School, because he was strongly interested in the 14th-century Dutch theologian, Geert Groote, and the Brethren of the Common Life. The reason he had started reading about Geert Groote was because Rudolf Steiner had stressed this theologian's importance for the history of pedagogy in the lectures on education he gave in Holland. The suggestion to name the school after him was enthusiastically accepted and turned out to be a saving grace for the school.

With each new grade, another teacher was added, and the faculty grew. The early teachers were Mrs. Talsma, Carel van der Willigen (†1984), Jan Baggerman, who moved from Zeist, Ans Hezemans (†1989), and Kees van der Linden (1908–1992). The little group of pioneers learned about Waldorf education as they went along; they lived out of strong ideals and were willing to make sacrifices. There was little support or recognition from society at large, and there was no state support either. Teacher salaries amounted to 75 Gulden (about $35), 15 of which went to pay for the lunches they had together. This was too much for most of the teachers, so they stopped the practice. With the disappearance of the communal meal, it also was not as easy for them to resolve quibbles about who should carry the coal scuttle up from the cellar or keep the stove going in winter. Many teachers also went on parent visits regularly, with the added incentive of a free meal. Students mostly came from well-to-do homes and could afford the tuition, but there also were a number of students from Social Democrat families of the northern section of Amsterdam whose tuitions were paid by parents who wished to remain anonymous.

On Tuesday mornings, Max Stibbe came from The Hague to sit in on classes and work on fundamental aspects of Waldorf pedagogy with the teachers. He was usually invited to have supper with Marie Thérèse Bienfait and her family, who belonged to the circle of founders and supporters of the school. After that he would take part in the teachers meeting, which were held on Tuesdays in Amsterdam, because Max Stibbe had to be present for the teachers meeting in The Hague on Thursdays. Max Stibbe was known among the teachers for his choleric outbursts; words of praise were rare.

The school soon outgrew the mansion at De Lairessestraat 153. The Hagedoorn-school in the Quinten Massijsstraat, behind the Euterpestraat, had a building it no longer used. That's where the Geert Groote School moved to in 1940. It was built out of yellow brick in the "New Objectivity" style of the time, featuring large windows.

The school stayed in this building for seven years, and was housed there for most of the wartime.

The fact that it was not closed during that time, like all the other independent schools, was due to a number of factors. Nobody wanted to give up even though its existence was somewhat illegal. The first strategic move Mr. Heintz, the business manager, took was to liquidate all business accounts of the school. After that, Kees van der Linden bought old school desks for very little money and handed them over to the German occupation forces, as was required. Through this action they could keep their own. Also, the school's credit of 112 Gulden (about $60) was transferred to the new authorities, increased to a more respectable sum by a few of the parents. As a result, the school no longer existed on paper, but in reality it kept on going, as a guest in another school. It was a lucky thing that all those involved did not reveal anything, and the school inspectors did exactly the same for the entire duration of the war. So the school operated next to the headquarters of the SS in the Euterpestraat, where nobody suspected subversive activities in any way. The name of the school was a help as well, because it evoked Catholic rather than anthroposophical connotations. Official papers mentioned a school based on artistic principles and no mention was made of Waldorf pedagogy or Rudolf Steiner. At the beginning of the war, there still was leeway for some outings, such as a trip to a pancake restaurant for a child's birthday, or even a sailing trip on one occasion.

However, in this school as well as in Germany, Jewish children no longer attended, either because they were in hiding, or because they were deported. On September 1, 1941, a decree was issued that obliged Jewish children to only attend Jewish schools.

In order to avoid being apprehended on his way to school and deported for the so-called *Arbeitseinsatz* [forced labor], Carel van der Willigen lived in the teachers room during the last years of the war, stowing his bed away when the teachers gathered in the morning to say a verse together. Jan Baggerman, a teacher who was known for his exceptional moral integrity, was one of the first to tell Mark Mastenbroek (to whom we owe this chronicle of the Geert Groote School) about the fate of the Jewish students. Years later, Wilhelmina Woldijk (1918–2000) pointed Mark Mastenbroek in the direction of Michael Ogilvie, who could give him the names of some of the Jewish students and what happened to them. Ruth Lisser (1928–1944), Robert Kahn (1931–1944) and Harry Kahn (1935–1944) were murdered in Auschwitz.

The last years of the war, getting something to eat and finding fuel became a major preoccupation. Nel Klinkenberg, the eurythmist, went twice behind the *Ijssellinie* [The IJssel Line, the Dutch portion of the NATO Cold War line of defense for Western Europe during the 1940s, 1950s, and 1960s] by bicycle to forage for potatoes and flour. Some students could no longer attend class because walking to school became too much for them. In 1940 there had been as many as 100 students. Because of the proximity of the SS headquarters, bombs dropped by the Allies also hit school buildings, and the damage done to their building made it necessary to continue in private homes. Except for one single time, the Sunday services for children were continued regularly during the entirety of the war.[852] But life was difficult. When the eurythmist had set off on her bicycle to find some nourishment, knocking on farmers' doors on the other side of the river Ijssel, she found her way back across the river barred. Not only was there no food now, but also no eurythmy. One teacher had gone into hiding and stayed within the confines of the school, another led a double life because he had joined the Dutch resistance. He was teaching in the teacher training seminar, which continued throughout the war, and didn't miss a single lesson. Nobody knew anything about the double life he led.

At the end of the war, only a tiny group of freezing students was left who had made it through the winter. When the liberation was celebrated, all the students who were left of both the Geert Groote School and the Hagedoornschool walked to the nearest square and sang the national anthem. In 1947, the school moved to its own building on the Hygiëaplein. New teachers joined, and the faculty consisted of a group of such diverse figures as Dick van Romunde, Walter Soesman, Hermien Cox, Erna Landweer, Henk Sweers, and Kees van der Linden. The school grew, and in 1948 the momentous decision was made to accept state support, with the inevitable loss of a certain amount of freedom.

1934: Waldorf Education in Bandung

In 1932 the General Secretary of the Dutch Anthroposophical Society, Willem Zeylmans van Emmichoven, visited the scattered anthroposophists who lived on Sumatra and Java and gave lectures in about 14 different places. One of these places was Bandung, which had cooler temperatures due to its altitude, an important reason why Europeans liked to spend time there, and why it had developed into the administrative center of the Dutch colony. Zeylmans's lectures in Bandung fell on fertile ground, and gave the impulse for a new school founding.

The Jansen family was keenly interested in anthroposophy and they started looking for a teacher for their two daughters, Digma and Carolientje, by advertising in Holland. Fred Poeppig (1900–1974) was seeking a meaningful task for his life and was attracted to the position. Instead of returning to Argentina, where his father wanted him to succeed him as director of his factory, he decided to go to Java, Dutch Indonesia, at that time. Part of his motivation was also that he wanted to move away from the bourgeois milieu he had grown up in. He had completed a practicum at the Stuttgart Waldorf School and saw himself as perfectly qualified for that reason. He arrived in Batavia in October 1933 and began to teach six children.

---

852 M.C.S. Poldermans: Iets uit het leven van de Geert Grooteschool te Amsterdam tijdens de oorlogsjaaren. VOK Oktober 1946, p. 44ff.

At about that same time, Thea Gischler was teaching the children living on a sugar plantation in Kladden and was toying with the idea to open a Waldorf school in Bandung. However, she wanted to avoid working with Fred Poeppig and let people know it. In the face of this, Fred Poeppig did not want to stay and left Indonesia early in May 1934.[853]

The newspaper *De Indische Courant* [the Indonesian Journal] carried the following notice on November 26, 1934: "By decree of the government, permission is given for the establishment of the *Vereniging de Vrije School in Nederlandsch-Indië* [Independent School Association for Dutch Indonesia] in Bandung in Western Java (West-Java). With this announcement, the association was a licensed legal entity."[854]

Thea Gischler had been teaching for six years at the Vrije School in The Hague and had done a practicum in Stuttgart before setting sail from the port of Genoa. She arrived in Bandung in March 1934 and became the founding teacher of the first grade of the Waldorf school. She made sure the legal announcement was duly published in *De Indische Courant*. The small school unfolded a rich cultural life that influenced local culture, primarily restricted to the Dutch population, as is to be expected for that time. At Christmas, they prepared the Christmas plays from Oberufer, and performed them for the local population. The space at their disposal was not big enough for everybody who wanted to see the plays, and therefore there were four performances in 1938. More than 300 people were able to see them and take in all they have to offer.[855]

At the time of the Japanese invasion in March 1942, the school consisted of eight small classes. When Bandung fell, education of any kind was forbidden and Dutch life ceased to exist in Indonesia. Most of the surviving Dutch were interned in camps, and many of the captured Allied soldiers perished in work camps. These camps were there until the bitter end of World War II. After the war, the Indonesians fought a war of independence and after establishing their own state, most traces of European culture in Indonesia vanished.[856]

1934: Michael House School in Ilkeston

IN 1934 the Michael House School was founded in Ilkeston, Derbyshire, a coal district in the industrial Midlands of England. The school owes its existence to the owner of the Meridian hosiery factory and philanthropist Edith Brenda Lewis (1862–1933).[857] Edith Lewis met anthroposophy around 1910, and she became one of the pioneers

---

853 Fred Poeppig: *Abenteuer meines Lebens*. 1975, p. 242.
854 Copy in Archiv FdE.
855 Karla Heidt: Das Oberuferer Christ-Geburtsspiel in Indien. N 4, January 22, 1939, p. 16.
856 Arie Boogert in an email of May 9, 2012, to the FdE.
857 http://biographien.kulturimpuls.org/detail.php?&id=1077 (site visited October 8, 2016); Marie Steiner: Edith Brenda Lewis. H. Collison, Miss E. Lewis. N 50, 12/10/1933, p. 199; Marie Groddeck: Edith Brenda Lewis. N 48, December 2, 1934, p. 192.

Edith Lewis

of the anthroposophical movement in England. She founded the Ilkeston group, the oldest anthroposophical branch in Great Britain. Edith Lewis found inspiration in the ideas and impulses of Rudolf Steiner, and worked not only for anthroposophy in general, but especially for eurythmy and Waldorf education. Because of her intense connection with the anthroposophical movement, she moved to Dornach in 1917, where she lived in one of the three so-called eurythmy houses that she built in close proximity to the Goetheanum. She was a beloved philanthropist, both in Dornach and in her home country.

As early as 1926, she had a hall built on a hill, which she called Michael Hall. "This space has a special mission. It is to serve as a school as soon as the experimental school, for which preparatory steps are being taken, has received official permission to operate. This will bring into being a new variant of our Waldorf schools!"[858] It is not known what became of this specific endeavor. The name, however, was transferred to Michael Hall School in Forest Row.

She had heard a lot about the Stuttgart Waldorf School and probably read a number of Rudolf Steiner's education lectures. Thus she came to understand what Waldorf education was about and to realize the potential it had, so much so that she made this impulse her own. She was especially impressed by the social motives of Emil Molt and by what he had done for the children of his Waldorf Astoria workers. She became more and more convinced that a Waldorf school should also be founded for the factory her family owned in Ilkeston. She wanted to make such a founding possible for the workers' children in the first place, but also took great pains to make the school accessible for all children, regardless of their parents' income or employment in the factory. After her death, her legacy was used for the establishment of the Michael House School, thereby carrying out her wishes, including her wish for free tuition for children who needed it. The school owned shares of the Meridian factory and was thus able to finance scholarships.

In 1939, a new school building was erected, designed by George Neames. The school was able to inhabit this building for many, many years, until it became too small and was sold in 1977. The school moved into a building that had formally housed the administrative offices of a coal mine. Even though it was now situated outside the city on a big estate, this did not affect its principles of social engagement.

858 E. Vreede: Eine anthroposophische Wirkungsstätte in Ilkeston. N 25, June 20, 1926, p. 105.

1934: Elmfield Steiner School

IN SELLY OAK near Birmingham was a house called Elmfield, the property of Henry Lloyd Wilson and his wife Theodora. They were open-minded and used the house for many cultural and social occasions. Both Wilsons were active Quakers. Theodora Wilson was an active member of the Labour Party and was on the city council of Birmingham. Henry Lloyd Wilson (1862–1941) became the owner of the chemical factory J. & E. Sturge in Birmingham, which specialized in the production of citric acid. In 1934, the Elmfield Steiner School started in their house.

During a Quaker meeting in Holland in 1919, Theodora Wilson had discovered a book by Rudolf Steiner about social threefolding. With her intense social interests, she was impressed by the thoughts expressed in this book, and after she had returned to England she read all she could find about Rudolf Steiner. She also managed to hear one of Rudolf Steiner's lectures in Stratford-upon-Avon. She started organizing anthroposophical lectures in her house. When she invited Fried Geuter (1894–1960) one day in 1929, she asked her son, Michael Wilson (1901–1985), to pick him up at the train station. It was a last minute request so Michael had to rush to be on time since he wanted to go to the opera; as a result he ended up being too late for the performance. Because of this, Fried Geuter and Michael Wilson, who otherwise had little in common, discovered that they both loved music. This discovery led to a lifelong friendship; they studied together in Berlin and ended up founding a curative education institute in November 1930, called Sunfield.

Thus Michael Wilson and Fried Geuter, a curative education worker, came to work together in order to build up Sunfield Children's Home, the first anthroposophical curative-education institution in England. They shared a great love for music, and many performances, often of their own compositions,[859] were part of the life of the home. Originally they both had the intention to create a school for the children of coworkers, in Clent. The two friends therefore invited Eileen Hutchins (1902–1987), whose sister Shirley already worked at Sunfield. They asked her to start a small school, where she taught the children of Fried Geuter, who were soon joined by the daughter of Rudolf and Margarethe Hauschka in 1931. In time, however, the school was intended to be open to other children as well, and so it was disconnected from the Sunfield Children's Home.

Theodora and Henry Lloyd Wilson opened the doors of their own house in Selly Oak to make room for a larger school and put it at the disposal of this new school impulse. At the outbreak of the war in 1939, the school was evacuated. Two grades found a temporary home with Sir Hugh and Lady Chance in their house in Bromsgrove, and the other grades went back to Sunfield Children's Home in Clent.

---

859 Michael Wilson composed the song *In the Quest of the Holy Grail* in Sunfield, a song which was a favorite in many schools, especially in the English-speaking world.

But after one trimester, all the children were back together again in Sunfield, where space was made for lessons in the workshops. Two years later, the school needed to be closed and Eileen Hutchins led only a small remaining group of preschoolers during the war years.

After 1945, Eileen Hutchins's father bought a mansion near Stourbridge called Park Hill, still in use today as the main building of the school. American soldiers had been stationed in this building during the war and had left the house in shambles. Both home and garden needed to be restored and major repairs and a large-scale cleanup needed to be done before the school could be reopened October 16, 1946. Thornhill, the neighboring house, was acquired in 1962 under the condition that the peacocks living on the grounds would be well taken care of.

Even though her eyesight and hearing deteriorated as she was getting older, Eileen Hutchins was able to lead the school until 1984 and continued to play a leading role in the Waldorf school movement of Great Britain. She was the editor of the British Waldorf movement's magazine *Child and Man* from 1964 until 1979, in addition to which she taught in the teacher training centers. She was a born storyteller, wrote poetry, plays, and crystal-clear commentaries and articles in teacher periodicals. She also translated Novalis, and when she lectured she spoke completely freely, without using any notes.[860]

1937: Wynstones Steiner School, Gloucester

THE WYNSTONES STEINER SCHOOL owes its existence to the initiative of Margaret Bennell (1893–1966)[861] and Cora Nokes. Around 1935, the two women started looking for teachers and a suitable piece of land for the Waldorf school they wanted to found. Both of them were educated by Charlotte Cowdroy (1864–1932), who was a pioneer in education in the early 1900s and an independent feminist, and they were teaching at the Crouch End High School in North London. Moreover, Margaret Bennell had been adopted by Charlotte Cowdroy after the premature death of her mother, who had asked Charlotte to take care of her child. When Charlotte Cowdroy died in 1932, Margaret Bennell became co-owner of the Crouch End School.[862]

As she was teaching at Crouch End, she was longing all the while to find a deeper source for her pedagogical tasks, which Magda Maier elucidated as follows: "When she was working at Crouch End, she was always inwardly searching for sources that can feed pedagogical work. No one who has heard her speak about T.S. Eliot's *Waste Land* or his "Hollow Men" will forget the extent to which Margaret Bennell was able

860 Jan Pohl: http://biographien.kulturimpuls.org/detail.php?&id=331 (site visited May 4, 2016).
861 Magda Maier: http://biographien.kulturimpuls.org/detail.php?&id=58 (site visited May 4, 2016).
862 Magda Maier: Margaret Bennell (December 24, 1890–July 24, 1966). EK 11, 1966, p. 364.

to portray the spiritual desolation of modern people. She knew what it means to live in thought clichés and vividly experienced the decline of spiritual forces. But the demands of daily life had always fired her–she lived with humor, grace, and zest, cultivating the gifts she had been born with and which she had been able to develop under the guidance of Charlotte Cowdroy."[863] Always on the lookout for new pedagogical impulses, Cora Nokes and Margaret Bennell discovered Rudolf Steiner's lectures, after the death of Charlotte Cowdroy. Without knowing that there were already schools in England based on his insights, they decided to transform their school in accordance with the picture of education that arose for them in reading his lectures.

One day they were at a performance at the New School in Streatham, London, later called Michael Hall School, which had been founded on January 20, 1925. What they saw there took them by surprise, and their first experience of Waldorf education left them deeply moved. From then on they were contemplating how to transform their own school into a Waldorf school. Magda Maier reports what happened during a pedagogical conference in the summer of 1935 in Harrogate, a scene that was highly characteristic of Margaret Bennell: "Right in the middle of a eurythmy lesson, she left the room together with her colleague Cora Nokes: 'Cora–we've got to found a school.' 'Have we really?' 'Yes, indeed.'"[864]

A simple solution would not do for Margaret Bennell. So instead of trying to change the existing Crouch End High School with all its existing customs, a new school was to be founded. Initial conversations were held with Cecil Harwood, who introduced them to H.E. Wood, who became a partner in the founding of the new school. He became a class teacher and took a class through three times. Some of the teachers did the recently started teacher training at Michael Hall School in London and were thus able to learn from the experiences of people like Caroline von Heydebrand or Karl Schubert. Others went for short internships to Stuttgart and Dornach. The two women were supported in their search by Herbert and Mabel Askew, two enthusiastic parents, and after a considerable search they found a place that could house the school—an old mansion in Brooksthorpe, Gloucestershire, situated in the picture-perfect hills of the Cotswolds in central England. As soon as they saw the Wynstones mansion, they were convinced that this was the right place. Before they had even spoken with the owners, they bought seeds for vegetables and gave them to Mr. Critchley, who was to become the beloved gardening teacher at the school.[865]

That summer they got the house ready with the help of other future teachers like Isobel Bruce Smith and John Benians. The starting group consisted of 14 children, joined by students from Crouch End in North London who were following their teachers to Gloucestershire. After the school had been founded on September 23,

863 Magda Maier: Margaret Bennell (December 24, 1890–July 24, 1966). EK 11, 1966, p. 364.
864 Magda Maier: http://biographien.kulturimpuls.org/detail.php?&id=58 (site visited May 6, 2016).
865 21 Years Wynstones School, undated, p. 2. Archiv RSHL o. Nr.

1937, more students from London followed. When the mother school in Stuttgart was forced to close its doors, one of their faculty members, Bettina Mellinger (1885–1953), joined them for a year as a consultant, but was prevented from returning from a holiday in Germany when the war broke out. John Benians and his wife Violet joined the faculty. He became one of the three founding class teachers and was there for the long run; she became a dearly beloved kindergarten teacher. A girl once said of her: "Mrs. Benians never does any work, she plays with us all the time." A little while after that, Elizabeth Loader and Renate Talmon-Gros, a eurythmist, started teaching at the school, as did Isobel Bruce Smith. Introduced by Bettina Mellinger, the two physicians, Norbert Glas (1897–1986)[866] and Maria Glas-Deutsch (1897–1983),[867] who had fled Nazi Germany and settled not far from Stroud, joined the small faculty in 1940.

Norbert Glas became the school doctor of Wynstones. He did this work in addition to his work in the medical practice he had started together with his wife, which he led until the end of his life. Others came on the scene as well, people who had been forced to emigrate from central Europe, including several students. Walter Johannes Stein (1891–1957) and Violetta Plincke (1883–1968)[868] were regular visitors to the growing school community. After the death of Eugen Kolisko, Lili Kolisko moved to live close by in November 1939, and that way anthroposophical work that had begun in Stuttgart could be continued. Rudi Lissau (1911–2004)[869] was in the starting group of committed pioneers, teaching Greek and Latin. His wife Hedda Lissau (1909–2002) had successfully secured this position for him, which was the only way she found that he could be released from his internment as an enemy alien on the Isle of Man. On the day the National Socialists marched into Austria in 1938, the couple had emigrated and they first settled in London. Until he started teaching at Wynstones, Lissau had only worked with blind children and knew nothing about Waldorf pedagogy. Now he successfully resolved to change that. A few years later, it was Rudi Lissau who pioneered the high school where he taught history, geography, Latin, Greek, German, and music. He remained at the school for 40 years, until his retirement.

Because of the war, the number of students grew rapidly, either in spite or because of its remote country location. No bombs were dropped outside of the major cities. There were many children of German immigrants among the students, which gave the school a reputation of being a *German school*, not quite to its advantage during the war. Magda Maier and her brother Georg were among the immigrant children who had come to England. They had come together with their mother due to the foresight

866 Susanne Hofmeister: http://biographien.kulturimpuls.org/detail.php?&id=227 (site visited May 6, 2016).
867 http://biographien.kulturimpuls.org/detail.php?&id=226 (site visited May 6, 2016).
868 Martin Sandkühler: http://biographien.kulturimpuls.org/detail.php?&id=1379 (site visited May 7, 2016).
869 Marjatta van Boeschoten: http://biographien.kulturimpuls.org/detail.php?&id=390 (site visited May 7, 2016).

of their father, who thus managed to protect his Jewish wife and children successfully. After the Second World War, Reinhold Maier became the first prime minister of Baden-Württemberg. Magda Maier, his daughter, became a highly influential English teacher at the Stuttgart Waldorf School, a position she held for decades. In the late 1980s, she helped with the building up of the Waldorf school movement in Israel. At Wynstones, she had been the classmate of Peter Bridgemont, who later became a well-known speech artist and theater director.

Many children found a new home in the school's boarding house, and the children of coworkers of the Camphill establishment in Scotland were able to live there as well. Many people flocked there and their number increased continually during the war. It took a lot of ingenuity to figure out new ways to accommodate them all. In 1941, the school acquired a mansion in Whaddon, situated a mile away from where they had been up to then. It had been occupied by a single elderly lady with her maid. The children of the elementary school were given a week off, and during that time all the high school students worked to clean and refurbish the newly acquired house before they could move in.

The opening celebration took place on June 24, and the former school was now transformed into a boarding house for the students. More fugitives came to Wynstones, among them Agathe Lippusch (†2008), later Agathe Glas, and Ms. Brühl, a eurythmist, as well as Tilde von Eiff. She said of herself that she did not have a clue about teaching, but that she had the necessary enthusiasm, and because of that the children were attracted to her, so much so that they practiced avidly for eurythmy performances in the evenings or on weekends. Introductory courses and conferences were held regularly in Wynstones at Whitsun, in which teachers of Michael Hall School were frequent lecturers.

After the war, the Wynstones Steiner School was expanded further. It has gone through many transformations and operates today with vibrant financial support of former students.

1938: A Waldorf School in Vanceboro, Maine

AFTER THE WALDORF SCHOOL in Stuttgart closed, Sophie Porzelt (1897–1975) first worked at the small Mainewoods school in Maine, which was founded by Roger and Marion Hale in 1938 and had only a short lifespan. Roger and Marion Hale discovered anthroposophy when they were looking for a curative education for one of their sons, who was handicapped. As they were surveying possibilities, they came upon the Sonnenhof in Arlesheim. Highly enthusiastic about what they found, they soon became interested in anthroposophy, to such a degree that they used a large part of their assets to establish anthroposophical work in the United States.[870] Roger

870 Henry Barnes: *Into the Heart's Land*. 2005, p. 119, note 116.

Roger and Marion Hale, the founders of the Mainewoods School in Vanceboro, ME

Hale (†1963) from Boston, was heir to an industrial fortune, and he bought 12,000 acres of woodland on the Canadian border. Here he practiced forestry, established a biodynamic farm, and built a laboratory for Ehrenfried Pfeiffer. A small school was planned as well.

In November 1938, the Mainewoods School in Vanceboro opened. The small school was to function according to the principles of Waldorf pedagogy, and the venture began with 15 children of kindergarten age up to sixth grade. Even though the Hales had invited all children of Vanceboro to attend the school free of charge, the majority of the local parents did not send their children, so that the school had to start only with their own children and those of coworkers. The school was situated about half a mile from where the Hales lived, and was housed in a building with two wings, painted dark red and surrounded by pine trees. The little ones were on one side, the older ones on the other side, with an assembly hall in between for performances, Christmas plays, concerts, and meetings. The locals were highly skeptical about this avant-garde school with its musical and artistic aspirations, and continued to prefer sending their children to the school in the village.

Sophie Porzelt directed the little school until the outbreak of the war, which made it impossible for her to stay on in the United States. In December 1938, she directed the Christmas plays in the translation by Arvia MacKaye, performed by children and teachers. The local population came in great numbers, even though people had to walk two miles through the snowy woods in order to get to Sunrise Farm, where the performance was held.[871] Because of the danger of the impending war, Sophie Porzelt had no choice but to move, because as a German citizen there was a real risk she would be interned in the United States.[872] She planned to go to England in order to work together with Erich Gabert there.

Hermann von Baravalle was also involved in building up this little school in the solitary woods close to the Canadian border. During the first year of the school, he taught the children mathematics for a month. The prejudices of the neighbors became stronger because of the perceived influence of the Germans in the school. At this point, Roger Hale invited Marjorie Spock (1904–2008), who was working in a progressive school in New York, to work in the Mainewoods school. She said yes and took on the leadership in 1939, joined a few months later by Agnes MacBeth

871 Hermann von Baravalle: Weihnachtsspiele der neuen Schule von Vanceboro. G4, January 22, 1939, p. 30.
872 Arnold Krammer: Feinde ohne Uniform. Deutsche Zivilinternierte in den USA während des Zweiten Weltkrieges. Vierteljahreshefte für Zeitgeschichte 44, 1996, p. 581ff.

(1903–1990). Now there were two teachers and the children could be divided into two groups according to their ages. However, both teachers stayed only for one year; they were succeeded by Edward Barnes and his wife.

In this remote region near the Canadian border, the German-speaking coworkers were very unpopular and had to endure several highly unpleasant meetings with the local population. It was soon rumored that people with a German accent would do well to stay away from Vanceboro. Everybody ended up leaving, and one day the school no longer had any teachers. At this point, Marion Hale thought of Hermann von Baravalle and wanted to ask him to lead the school, but he was already committed to working in Greenwich. Marion Hale, with the help of her husband, ended up taking on the teaching responsibilities for the remainder of the school year 1940/41.[873] With this, the school experiment in Vanceboro came to an end.

1938: The Edgewood School in Greenwich, Connecticut

DURING THE FALL and winter of 1936, Dr. Günther Wachsmuth, Dr. Ehrenfried Pfeiffer, and Dr. Hermann von Baravalle visited the United States and gave lectures in many cities. During this time, a connection was established with the Edgewood School in Greenwich. A year later, Hermann von Baravalle emigrated to the United States after a short stay in England, because he had been asked to teach at the Edgewood School. In a report of the English pedagogical conference at the Goetheanum, von Baravalle told about recent developments in the United States: "The Edgewood School in Greenwich, Connecticut, one of the best-known progressive schools of the country, decided to introduce an organic daily schedule by unanimous acclamation of the faculty on January 3, 1938, modeled on indications by Rudolf Steiner for Waldorf schools.

"In the months after it had been introduced, both individual visitors and delegations from other schools came to study how this was working out in practice. Lectures about it were organized, for example at the faculty meeting of one of the big New York schools, the Brearley school [...]. At Yale University in New Haven, which houses the largest collection of books on Goethe in America, it has become a regular practice to constantly add literature from the Goetheanum, seen as the natural continuation of Goethean culture, and at New York University, Rudolf Steiner's pedagogy is being introduced in university lectures and workshops."[874]

At a faculty meeting of December 15, 1937, the head of the high school at Edgewood School, Dr. Maud Thompson, proposed to adopt Waldorf pedagogy as the basis for the school's education. The headmistress, Euphrosyne Langley, immediately gave her consent, as did the president of the board, Beulah Emmet. The decision was

---

873 Judson D. Hale: *The Education of a Yankee. An American Memoir.* 2014, pp. 100–122.
874 Hermann von Baravalle. Probably a newsletter, 1938.

made there and then to make an immediate start. Changes were announced during the Christmas holidays, and Waldorf pedagogy was introduced in January, to the acclaim of both students and teachers.[875] In 1938, Erich Schwebsch visited the United States and on the fourth day after he had arrived he already taught history of art to the seniors of the Edgewood School. Attendance was not limited to the students. Every single day, colleagues, guests, friends of the school, and parents came to hear the classes given by Erich Schwebsch. The lessons had to be continued in increasingly large spaces, reaching maximum size in the school's auditorium.[876] In the course of the first years of the war, conflicts and division in the Edgewood School faculty resulted in Beulah Emmet's departure; she left in 1942 in order to found the High Mowing School in Wilton, New Hampshire. With this, the Edgewood School ceased to exist as a Waldorf school.

1938: Through the Winter in Bremen and Stuckenborstel

HERMANN HELLMERS (1889–1975), a cotton merchant in Bremen, and his wife Minnie Schomaker learned about the Christian Community in the early 1920s. Hermann Hellmers had long occupied himself with deeper questions of how to lead a meaningful life as an active citizen, both during the time he was in training and when he was interned in Southeast Asia, where he had spent about eight years up to 1920. He had found no real answers until he met people who were actively "living Christianity," such as Friedrich Rittelmeyer, Emil Bock, Rudolf von Koschützki and Johannes Hemleben, all of them founders or priests working in the Christian Community. In the winter of 1924/25, the Hellmers helped to build up a local group of the Association for Independent Schools in Bremen and invited several teachers from the Stuttgart Waldorf School to lecture in Bremen. Among the lecturers were Caroline von Heydebrand, Max Wolffhügel, Erich Schwebsch, and Hans Rutz. The group wanted to found a Waldorf school in 1928, but their application for official permission in Bremen was voted down by a narrow margin of one single vote. Both the Social Democrats and the National Socialists voted against it.[877]

A daughter was born to the Hellmers in this year, who later, at age five, became so ill that she had to live separately from the family for years to receive special treatment. She recovered, and was able to return to Bremen in 1938. Even though she was healthy now, the family secured medical dispensation for her to be educated by a private tutor. Most Waldorf schools had been closed by now and therefore Hermann and Minnie Hellmers were confident that they could easily find an unemployed

---

875 Hermann von Baravalle: *The International Waldorf School Movement*. 1976, p. 18.
876 Hermann von Baravalle: Dr. Erich Schwebsch an der Edgewood School in Greenwich-Conn. N 52, December 25, 1938, p. 203.
877 M.-I. Kiefel: Hermann Hellmers (June 6, 1889–August 2, 1975). LR 12, 1976, p. 78.

Waldorf teacher for this task. They succeeded in hiring Magdalene-Ithwari Kiefel, a teacher at the Berlin Waldorf school, who began teaching their daughter privately that winter in Bremen and in the summer in their vacation home in Stuckenborstel. Other children joined the little group during the course of the war, resulting in a little family school. When the bombing raids increased in Bremen, the family decided to stay in the country house in Stuckenborstel during the winter as well. In these difficult times they thus managed to create an island of freedom and protection. Hermann Hellmers belonged to the leadership circle of the cotton merchant exchange and together with his colleagues he was able to extend a protective hand over this little school.

When the war came to an end, it did not take long for the English authorities to give permission for the founding of the long hoped-for Waldorf school. It opened on May 9, 1946, and went by the name of Independent School of Stuckenborstel, which started off with 56 children. Magdalena-Ithwari Kiefel became the founding teacher. A year later, this school became the Ottersberg Waldorf School. In 1949, the Waldorf school started up in Bremen as well, and this one was likewise supported and protected by Hermann Hellmers.[878]

1939: The Edinburgh Rudolf Steiner School

AFTER THREE YEARS of preparation, during which lectures about Waldorf education were held regularly during the winter and a booklet titled, "What a School Should Do for Your Child," was distributed to thousands of households, the Edinburgh Rudolf Steiner School started with a kindergarten group on May 2, 1939. Two people worked especially hard to prepare the ground in Edinburgh, a city with a strong university life and a long academic tradition. First of all there was Pelham S. Moffat, PhD (1898–1978), whose doctoral thesis was on the theme of child development. He lost his arm when he was wounded in World War I and decided to dedicate his life to education. In order to prepare himself, he attended the Waldorf teacher training in Stuttgart and did a practicum at the Waldorf School which lasted several months. He also visited Dornach.

Another founder was Inez Arnold (1900–1989),[879] a eurythmist with practical experience at Kings Langley and in Berlin. She was born in Switzerland and had taken part in the first eurythmy training in Stuttgart. Her fellow student Elena Zuccoli described her as "ein stummes und sehr eigenwilliges Wesen mit krausigen, roten Haaren,"[880] [a stubborn, frizzy redhead, who very much did her own thing]. After the Berlin Rudolf Steiner School had closed, she first accompanied Anni Heuser to

878 M.-I. Kiefel: Hermann Hellmers (June 6, 1889–August 2, 1975). LR 12, 1976, p. 77f.
879 Irene L. Binhammer: Inez Arnold (November 23, 1900–August 26, 1989) N 12.12.1989, p. 231f.
880 Elena Zuccoli: *Eine Autobiographie*. 1999, p. 56.

Dr. Pelham S. Moffat, affectionately called Dockie, with his students at the Edinburgh Rudolf Steiner School

Stockholm, where they arrived on May 3, 1938. The very next day, Inez Arnold traveled on to Scotland, where she was engaged in the school from then on. When Pelham S. Moffat gave a lecture, she added demonstrations in eurythmy.

Of course, another very important prerequisite for founding a school was a house. Luckily there was a woman who left her house to be used by the initiative, a house with a central location on Rothesay Square, and it was there that they first furnished a kindergarten room. A few more children applied, so Pelham Moffat counted on two preschool groups in October 1939. Since an extra seven children had applied who were of school age, they considered starting with a first grade as well. But then war broke out. Inez Arnold and Helen St. John, a kindergarten teacher, had traveled to Switzerland that summer and since she was a Swiss citizen, Inez Arnold was not allowed to return to Edinburgh. Helen St. John had no reason to return anymore because the parents and children had left the city and moved to the country. Only the seven school-age children were still there, and Pelham Moffat was the only remaining teacher. He was convinced that he would find more teachers, and, because all other schools in Edinburgh had evacuated to the country, he looked for an opportunity to do the same. A house was found close to Kelso—and new teachers emerged. In Kelso they were joined by a few more children from the little hamlet, so the school could start with 11 children now. A second house they were using in Kelso was sold, and in June 1940, the little group moved into the hunting lodge of the Duke of Roxburgh, situated in the region of the Cheviot Hills.

They spent two years among hills, woods, and streams, living a paradisiacal life in nature with intense summers and winters. In the meantime the two kindergarten teachers who were left stranded in Switzerland had been able to return due to the intervention of a member of Parliament. The small faculty now consisted of these two ladies together with the founding teacher, Pelham Moffat, whom the children affectionately called Dockie, together with Mollie Mackintosh and Helen Grant, who had found their way to this circle of colleagues. Early in the summer of 1942, the parents suggested that the children return to the city. Of course this was not all that easy, because the school had outgrown the old schoolhouse. Nevertheless, they succeeded because a close-knit group of parents worked together in acquiring a large Victorian villa surrounded by spacious grounds, situated at 38 Colinton Road. Thirty children and their teachers returned to Edinburgh in July 1942, and by the fall of the same year the school had grown to 60 children.[881]

881 Andrew Farquharson and Neil Mackay (eds.): *Seventy Years Young. The Edinburgh Rudolf Steiner School.* 2009.

In 1944, the school organized an exhibition in the city that attracted many visitors. A public lecture about Rudolf Steiner education was held as well. More than 300 people flocked to it, and the hall was filled to overflowing.[882] In 1945 the school counted nine teachers and 140 children in two kindergartens and six grades. Except for Pelham S. Moffat, only female teachers were employed at the school during the war.

Lawrence Edwards, who taught in the school from 1948 on and made a major contribution in building up the high school, wrote such a vivid article on the founder in a booklet published at the occasion of the school's seventieth birthday that we should quote from it here: "Dear, choleric, one-armed Dockie, renowned for his dramatic powers, for the plays he wrote and produced, and for his exciting story-telling! To hear Dockie recounting the story of some old-time battle was enough to stir the blood and quicken the pulse of the most apathetic child. When suitably stirred, which was not infrequently, his lion's roar would reverberate through the building, the while his children would look to one another with mingled awe, affection and admiration—'Just hark to what our Dockie can do!' But the warm heart of the man ensured the affection and trust of every child in the school. He was an incisive and keen thinker, with impeccable logic, but not, maybe, very subtle. I think that in his classroom the world seemed a fairly simple place; black was black and white was white, and you knew where you were."[883]

The school's success, however, was not only due to these human qualities, because there was Inez Arnold. Her contributions, in the words of Lawrence Edwards, were of an entirely different nature: "Inward-looking, quiet and shy, every word and act were imbued with an artistic quality. It was due to her that the walls of our classrooms became a blaze of color which through the years formed an exhibition of child art which was unique in the city. She was the object of envy on the part of her colleagues; how does one become such a person that one's very presence in the classroom, with little or nothing said, is enough to ensure that every child present immediately, and quietly, starts, and continues. To do his or her very best, right through to the end of the lesson? They do not teach such things in the training courses for teachers!"

The school organized a second kindergarten in a different part of town in order to keep the children's walk to school as short as possible. Most of the first graders came from the two kindergartens. During the bitter years of the war and after it, both the kindergarten and the elementary school grew steadily. Soon after World War II ended, they were able to celebrate the first seven years of the Edinburgh Rudolf Steiner School on May 2, 1946. Dr. Alfred Heidenreich gave a festive lecture, "Citizenship

882 I. Mackenzie: The Edinburgh Rudolf Steiner School. N 26, July 1, 1945, p. 103.
883 Lawrence Edwards: Our school – early years. In: Andrew Farquharson and Neil Mackay (eds.): *Seventy Years Young. The Edinburgh Rudolf Steiner School.* 2009, p. 44f.

and Social Service in Rudolf Steiner Education." At the same occasion, an exhibition of student work in the classrooms brought the school to the public eye.[884]

The Scottish education ministry as well as the Edinburgh school inspector had looked kindly on the school ever since it returned to the capital in 1942. After a successful school inspection in the spring of 1951, the school was entered into the National Register of Independent Schools.[885] The school remained located at 38 Colinton Road until 1994.

1939: The Waldorf School in Hampstead, London

ON JANUARY 14, 1939, about 100 people gathered for the opening of the Waldorf school in Hampstead, which was housed in a newly acquired and renovated home at 104 Fitzjohn Avenue, London NW3, a large, central street running from Swiss Cottage to Hampstead. The avenue is lined with beautiful houses, and, to this day, the well-heeled occupants of this neighborhood have a reputation of being upper class, intellectual, and liberal.

After the split in the Anthroposophical Society in England of 1935, the two groups continued to develop independently from one another. The group that maintained its connection to the Goetheanum in Dornach was headed by Harry Collison (1868–1945).[886] At the occasion of the opening ceremony, he spoke "warmhearted and supportive"[887] opening words that expressed the hope that something larger would be able to grow from this seed. The little school started with only a first grade and a handful of children. A kindergarten and eurythmy courses for elementary school children were added soon after. Nora von Havas (1915–1941), who died young, started these eurythmy courses, which attracted more and more children.[888] One of the children whose mother had found out about this kindergarten was Andrew Wolpert, who later taught at Waldorf teacher seminars both in Germany and England. One of his playmates in the kindergarten was Peter Rauter (1948–2006). He became a photographer later in life and was the son of a well-known pianist and composer, Ferdinand Rauter (1902–1987), whose wife Claire was actively involved in building up the little school. Another friend of the young Andrew Wolpert was Susan Masters. The children felt extremely well in this loving environment with such dedicated teachers. For a short period of time, the school was led by Erich Gabert (1890–1968) from the Waldorf School in Stuttgart, to whom the new school felt

---

884 M.V. Mackintosh: Mitteilung aus Schottland. N 25, June 23, 1946, p. 100.
885 Pelham Moffat: *25 Years Rudolf Steiner School of Edinburgh.* 1964, p. 1ff.
886 Philip Martyn: http://biographien.kulturimpuls.org/detail.php?&id=120 (site visited May 12, 2016).
887 Waldorf School Hampstead. N 7, February 12, 1939, p. 28.
888 Friedrich von Havas: In Memoriam: Nora von Havas. N 7, February 12, 1943, p. 27.

a close connection. He was planning to build up the school together with Sophie Porzelt, who wanted to come to England from Vanceboro, Maine. This was prevented by the outbreak of World War II, which necessitated their return to Germany in 1939.

Dorothy Pethick (1881–1970) worked in the office and carried the administration. Both she and her sister Emmeline Pethick-Lawrence (1867–1954) were famous suffragettes in England. As fighters for women's rights, they supported this new education that fostered social integration, because schools that admitted children of all classes were a new thing in Britain at the time. Another important friend and supporter of the school was Freda Budgett (1902–1988), who made an important contribution to the financing of the small venture. Jean Lynch and Eileen Wreford worked in the kindergarten, as well as Walburga Hauschka, the daughter of Rudolf Hauschka, the founder of the Wala health and hygiene products company. Betty Parker taught eurythmy and gave courses for elementary school children. Masie Bowron, Stanley Messenger, Molly von Heider, and Sheilaugh Ryan were class teachers at the Hampstead school. Francis Edmunds, who later founded Emerson College, gave complementary courses at the school for teachers who wanted to pursue Waldorf education.

The school existed until about 1953 and was not continued after that year, for unknown reasons.

1939: A Waldorf Kindergarten in Milan

THE FIRST ANTHROPOSOPHICAL study group in Milan was organized as early as 1911, and Dr. Giovanni Colazza (1877–1953) was the center of this activity. Through him, his wife's sister, Lidia Baratto Gentilli (1903–1996) came in contact with anthroposophy, which led her to study eurythmy in Stuttgart. After working in Dornach and Berlin, she returned to Italy in 1939, where she opened a private kindergarten in her house in Milan on the Via Maurizio Gonzaga.

Eurythmy, singing, and sculpting fairytale figures became the favorite occupation of both the kindergarten teacher and the children, who were with her from 9:00 to noon every morning. Noticing the effect of this pedagogy on their children, a number of mothers asked after a few years about starting an elementary school class. Their request was answered, and in 1942 Emma Minoja started a first grade with six children in the same building that housed the kindergarten. After severe bombing raids on Milan, everybody who was able to do so moved to the countryside, and the class could no longer be continued, because the children were no longer living in the city.

Lidia Baratto Gentilli

After the war, Dr. Fanny Podreider wanted to reestablish a school as quickly as possible, but this did not succeed. The Socialist Party made an offer that they could take over the Matteotti kindergarten, but Lidia Baratto declined, because she insisted on pedagogical independence. The party could not guarantee this. The next opportunity came when Emma Reciputti wanted to introduce Waldorf pedagogy into her community school, which was damaged by the bombs. She wanted the city of Milan to finance the rebuilding. Helped by Lavinia Mondolfo, this plan succeeded and the city contributed a small amount to the cost of restoration. Finding teachers was the next hurdle. They were to be the noblest people and committed to self-improvement, while living on 25 Swiss francs a month. Emma Minoja and Elisabeth Unger said "yes," as well as Marisa Albertario and Giannina Noseda. Thus the Waldorf school of Milan began in the autumn of 1946 with about 80 children in three grades.

1939/40: The Rudolf Steiner School in Buenos Aires

THE NUCLEUS of the faculty of the first Waldorf school in Latin America was formed by Ingeborg Knäpper (1910–1973), Eli Lunde (1903–1996), and Herbert Schulte-Kersmecke (1899–1979). Ingeborg Knäpper came originally from Dortmund and Herbert Schulte-Kersmecke grew up close to Arolsen in the Sauerland. Eli Lunde was the oldest of the ten children of the Lunde family from Lillehammer in Norway, whose parents, Einar Lunde and his wife, were anthroposophists who had frequently hosted Rudolf Steiner when he came to Norway. They sent some of their children to the Friedwart School in Dornach, where they spent their younger years under the wings of Marie Groddeck. Eli Lunde, the oldest, traveled to Dornach in 1918 and studied painting, handwork, music, speech formation, and eurythmy. The three founding teachers had each emigrated for a different reason.

Herbert Schulte-Kersmecke had a successful career as an architect in Hagen, but he could not and would not conform to National Socialist ideology. His efforts on behalf of Jewish friends attracted the attention of the Gestapo. In 1938, he managed to flee in the nick of time and escaped imprisonment. Lucky circumstances made it possible for him to go to Buenos Aires. His wife, who had helped him escape, barely managed to reach Switzerland. She did the speech and drama training in Dornach, where she lived until 1950. Early that year, she traveled to rejoin her husband in Buenos Aires. Everyone who knew her described her as a positive personality, radiating harmony. In spite of that, she was not able to smooth the waters when her husband had social difficulties, nor was that her task. After a severe illness, she died in the autumn of 1951.[889]

---

889 Walter and Gerdraute Schulte-Kersmecke: http://biographien.kulturimpuls.org/detail.php?&id=1444 (site visited November 6, 2016).

Ingeborg Knäpper, who knew Herbert Schulte-Kersmecke as a child, left Nazi Germany and reached Buenos Aires in April of 1938. Eli Lunde's story was quite different. She studied eurythmy in Dornach and started working as a eurythmist at the Friedwart School, and subsequently in Oslo, Dresden, and Zagreb. A family of Norwegian and Uruguayan origin asked her if she could teach and educate their children. This she did, and in 1938 she moved to Uruguay with this family.[890]

The three of them met for the first time in December 1938, when they had all been invited by Annelotte Lahusen to participate in a shepherds' play in Buenos Aires. This marked the birth of Waldorf education in Argentina. There had been an anthroposophical working group for quite a while, because Fred Poeppig and Francisco Schneider had started a study group together early in the 1920s.[891] Annelotte and Hanno Lahusen ran a few large farms in the province of Buenos Aires and in Patagonia and I assume they supplied wool to their former family firm Nordwolle near Bremen. After they had met Eli Lunde, they engaged her to take care of their two daughters.

Work in the kindergarten started in March 1939. A group of children gathered in the little garden house of the two teachers. For furniture, they used apple crates covered with colorful cloth, and so they started performing German plays, singing, and listening to stories. On Saturday afternoons, Ingeborg Knäpper performed *Kasperletheater*, puppet plays that soon became famous, and Eli Lunde gathered children on Sunday mornings for short religious ceremonies. When Ingeborg Knäpper, who worked at the German school, heard before the winter holidays that her contract would not be renewed after the first six months in 1939, she decided to build up a school on her own. Later that year, Eli Lunde and Ingeborg Knäpper rented a house at 1546 Warnes, where they started organizing play mornings for several children, amongst them the children of the Wölcken family, before officially opening the kindergarten. Ingeborg Knäpper, or "Aunt Ingeborg," was the kindergarten teacher and Eli Lunde assisted her in handwork. Else Offergeld Wölcken taught singing, Gertrude Graetzer eurythmy, and Frida Vollmar painting.

Gertrude Graetzer (1893–1953) was a eurythmist from Berlin of Jewish heritage. While still in Germany she had worked in Kiel and Lübeck but had left the country as early as 1934, spent four years in Trieste, Italy, working with eurythmy until the Nazi persecutions reached that town as well. Just in time, she managed to get a visa for Argentina in 1938, and was able to go to Buenos Aires.

890 Rosa Körte: http://biographien.kulturimpuls.org/detail.php?&id=1447 (site visited November 6, 2016).
891 Fred Poeppig (1900–1974) grew up in Neustadt an der Orla (Thuringia) and as a student in Weimar, he discovered a book by Rudolf Steiner. That's how he discovered anthroposophy. His father, Alfred Poeppig, had emigrated to Argentina before World War I and he ran a soap factory there. Fred Poeppig followed him in 1920, together with his mother and his sister. In Buenos Aires, he befriended Francisco Schneider, who arrived in Argentina a little later to work for the overseas branch of Deutsche Bank. Francisco Schneider (1896–1994) already knew about anthroposophy because he had heard Rudolf Steiner lecture in Stuttgart. He later translated many of Rudolf Steiner's works into Spanish. In 1924 he married Ilse, the sister of Fred Poeppig.

One day she found a small advertisement in a German newspaper, asking if there was somebody who could say something about eurythmy. That's how she discovered the circle of people around the three founders working with Waldorf pedagogy.[892] "What Trude Graetzer has achieved with and for her students, next to a life full of friendships with the most diverse group of people, is spiritual substance that will forever remain connected with the work of our movement in Argentina. She had the wonderful gift to be fully there for others, to such a degree that all around her felt a special connection with her."[893] She taught eurythmy in Buenos Aires all her life.

This is how the work started, and when the seven-year-old son of Else Wölcken needed a school, the wish grew to found an independent Waldorf school in Buenos Aires, a wish that became reality in March 1941.[894] Eli Lunde took a combined class 1/2/3 with six children. By the middle of the 1940s the number of children had grown to 12, and Ursula Arndt had joined to be the second teacher in the combined class. In the meantime, 20 children were enrolled in the kindergarten. The students came primarily from German-speaking families, and for that reason the parents wanted German spoken in the school. Some main-lesson blocks were given in Spanish, and English was taught as a foreign language. Due to the small number of children, it was not possible to cover the operating costs of the institution during the years it was being built up, but the school was able to keep its head above water because the deficits were always covered by the generous contributions of Hanno and Annelotte Lahusen.[895]

In 1944, a house was acquired at 1322 Warnes, financed once again by the Lahusens. Due to this move, both kindergarten and school had more room, so Ingeborg Knäpper could expand the kindergarten. The school had never been officially registered, and for that reason it was not affected when all German schools in Argentina had to be closed in 1945. But in 1953 a neighbor, who felt disturbed by the noise the children made, lodged an official complaint about the little school, which led to conflicts among faculty members on how to proceed. In the end, the private school was officially recognized under the name Paula Albarracín de Sarmiento. A year later they started the process of gaining official permission to work according to Rudolf Steiner's pedagogical indications, which was granted in 1963 when the school was recognized by the educational system of Argentina.

On the grounds of 1322 Warnes, a larger school building in organic style was built in 1958. It included the existing smaller house and was designed by Herbert Schulte-Kersmecke, who thereby combined the work of architect, builder, and carpenter, in addition to being janitor, substitute teacher, and kindergarten assistant.

892 Maria Cassini: Gertrude Graetzer †. N 35, August 30, 1953, p. 139.
893 Annelotte Lahusen: Trude Gretzer. N 34, August 23, 1953, p. 135.
894 Eli Lunde: Bericht über die pädagogische Arbeit in Buenos Aires. Msch 6, 1950, p. 163.
895 Origenes del Colegio Rudolf Steiner de Florida. 70. Aniversario Colegio Rudolf Steiner 1940–2010. El Puente.

1941: Kimberton Farms Waldorf School in Phoenixville, PA

ALARIK MYRIN WAS a rich industrialist from Sweden, where he had worked in the oil company of the Nobel brothers. He emigrated to America, where he joined the Sun Oil Company of his father-in-law. Together with his wife, Mabel Pew, who came from an influential philanthropic family, he took the initiative to found a Waldorf school on his farm west of Philadelphia in Pennsylvania.

One day, on a return trip from Latin America in his airplane, he read *God Is My Adventure* by Rom Landau. The author describes various cultural streams of the beginning years of the 20th century. Revisiting them 15 years later, he reports enthusiastically about anthroposophical institutions. This awakened Alarik Myrin's wish to get to know Rudolf Steiner's work, which in turn led to his wish to found a Waldorf school himself on the grounds of his farm.

In 1939, in northern Chester County west of Philadelphia, Alarik Myrin and his wife, Mabel Pew Myrin, acquired a thousand acres of farmland, to which they gave the name Kimberton Farms. In order to realize the school he envisaged, he contacted Hermann von Baravalle, known to be a Waldorf expert. The latter recommended asking the help of Elisabeth von Grunelius, who had recently come to the US. And thus it came about that the founder of the first Waldorf kindergarten in Stuttgart built up a kindergarten with 18 children in Phoenixville, Pennsylvania, and became headmistress of the school.[896] At the same time, a first grade started up with about 20 children from close by, with Virginia Field Birdsall as their class teacher.[897] She had been one of the founders of the Waldorf school in New York and was one of the most experienced Waldorf teachers in the United States.

The Myrins were also interested in finding out how Rudolf Steiner's biodynamic farm method functioned in reality. By 1941 they had convinced Dr. Ehrenfried Pfeiffer that he should lead the farm and a biodynamic training center. Even though he stayed there for only a short time, he did lay the groundwork for this form of agriculture in America. After his Edgewood adventure, Hermann von Baravalle traveled a lot and visited Pennsylvania regularly. He and Alarik Myrin were both convinced that Rudolf Steiner's course, *The Foundations of Human Experience*, always had to be embedded in a local context, and with that in mind he began preparing a few local teachers for Waldorf education.

Hermann von Baravalle

896 Hermann von Baravalle: *The International Waldorf School Movement.* 1976, p. 19f.
897 Hermann von Baravalle: Der Fortschritt der pädagogischen Arbeit in Amerika. N 49, December 7, 1941, p. 195.

Alarik Myrin visits the students of Kimberton Farms Waldorf School on horseback.

Alarik Myrin cherished the wish to found more Waldorf schools in the United States and realized he had to somehow find a solution for the enormous task of training teachers. During one of his visits to Kimberton Farm, he spoke about this with Hermann von Baravalle. He hoped to find an American college that would train Waldorf teachers, and he asked Hermann von Baravalle to take this on. At that time, Hermann von Baravalle was teaching mathematics at Adelphi College in Garden City, New York, and knew that its director was open to supporting his efforts to promote Waldorf education. No sooner said than done! He introduced Alarik Myrin to the principal of Adelphi College, Paul Dawson Eddy, and the two of them arranged to work closely together. With this in place, Hermann von Baravalle was able to institute a Waldorf teacher training as part of the general education program at Adelphi starting in 1946.

Paul Dawson Eddy was convinced that teacher training at a college made sense only when it included a large classroom practice component. To fulfill his wish, Hermann von Baravalle founded the Waldorf Demonstration School of Adelphi in 1947, which later became the Waldorf School of Garden City. Alarik and Mabel Myrin financed both a new school building, completed within a year, and the operating expenses of the school. It started with a kindergarten, for which Elisabeth von Grunelius was fetched to come to Garden City—only the highest quality would do. A new grade was added each subsequent year. In addition, the Myrins helped to steer the economically endangered college back toward financial stability. Alarik Myrin and Mabel Pew maintained the connection with Adelphi College [now Adelphi University], and the other way round.

1942: High Mowing School in Wilton, New Hampshire

DURING THE FIRST YEARS of the war, the conflicts among faculty members of the Edgewood School in Greenwich, Connecticut, resulted in a split that caused the departure of Beulah Emmet. In April 1942, she moved to her farm in New Hampshire. A number of colleagues soon followed her, among them Dr. Maud Thompson, who had chaired the high school in Greenwich. They came to Wilton, New Hampshire, and in April 1942 the transformation of the High Mowing Farm into High Mowing School began.

Beulah Emmet had bought the farm in 1929 as a summer residence for her family. Now, starting in April, she faced the task of rebuilding it in such a way that a high school with boarding facilities could start on the old farm by October. The New Hampshire State Board of Education gave its stamp of approval; Beulah Emmet was not quite sure whether that was because her husband's father was a famous Navy officer or because she had money. In any case, she had permission to operate a school. There were several more obstacles, but none of them proved unsurmountable. Beulah Emmet called herself and Hermann von Baravalle, who supported her, "the world's most complete optimists."

A few students from the Rudolf Steiner school in New York came that very summer to be enrolled, and other students also found their way to Wilton. The school started in September 1942, with 53 students in four high school classes. Hermann von Baravalle stayed for only one year; in 1943 he became professor of mathematics and chair of the mathematics department at Adelphi College. High Mowing School has been in continuous operation since it was started during the war.

Appendix

The Collected Works of Rudolf Steiner

CW Available in English, in print, CW
GA Unavailable in English (never translated or out of print)

Writings 1884–1925

Written Works

CW 1 Goethe: Natural-Scientific Writings, Introduction, with Footnotes and Explanations in the text by Rudolf Steiner
CW 2 Outlines of an Epistemology of the Goethean World View, with Special Consideration of Schiller
CW 3 Truth and Science
CW 4 The Philosophy of Freedom
GA 4a Documents to "The Philosophy of Freedom"
CW 5 Friedrich Nietzsche, A Fighter against His Own Time
CW 6 Goethe's Worldview
CW 6a *[Now in CW 30]*
CW 7 Mysticism at the Dawn of Modern Spiritual Life and Its Relationship with Modern Worldviews
CW 8 Christianity as Mystical Fact and the Mysteries of Antiquity
CW 9 Theosophy: An Introduction into Supersensible World Knowledge and Human Purpose
CW 10 How Does One Attain Knowledge of Higher Worlds?
CW 11 From the Akasha-Chronicle
CW 12 Levels of Higher Knowledge
CW 13 Occult Science in Outline
CW 14 Four Mystery Dramas
CW 15 The Spiritual Guidance of the Individual and Humanity
CW 16 A Way to Human Self-Knowledge: Eight Meditations
CW 17 The Threshold of the Spiritual World. Aphoristic Comments
CW 18 The Riddles of Philosophy in Their History, Presented as an Outline
CW 19 [Contained in CW 24]
CW 20 The Riddles of the Human Being: Articulated and Unarticulated in the Thinking, Views and Opinions of a Series of German and Austrian Personalities

* This is based on the list found at the back of the CW volumes in English. The titles are rough literal translations of the German and do not neccessarily correspond to the titles of volume numbers available in English.

CW 21   The Riddles of the Soul
GA 22   Goethe's Spiritual Nature and Its Revelation in "Faust" and through the "Fairy Tale of the Snake and the Lily"
CW 23   The Central Points of the Social Question in the Necessities of Life in the Present and the Future
CW 24   Essays Concerning the Threefold Division of the Social Organism and the Period 1915-1921
GA 25   Cosmology, Religion and Philosophy
CW 26   Anthroposophical Leading Thoughts
CW 27   Fundamentals for Expansion of the Art of Healing according to Spiritual-Scientific Insights
CW 28   The Course of My Life

Collected Essays

GA 29   Collected Essays on Dramaturgy, 1889-1900
GA 30   Methodical Foundations of Anthroposophy: Collected Essays on Philosophy, Natural Science, Aesthetics and Psychology, 1884-1901
GA 31   Collected Essays on Culture and Current Events, 1887-1901
GA 32   Collected Essays on Literature, 1884-1902
GA 33   Biographies and Biographical Sketches, 1894-1905
GA 34   Lucifer-Gnosis: Foundational Essays on Anthroposophy and Reports from the Periodicals "Lucifer" and "Lucifer-Gnosis," 1903-1908
GA 35   Philosophy and Anthroposophy: Collected Essays, 1904-1923
GA 36   The Goetheanum-Idea in the Middle of the Cultural Crisis of the Present: Collected Essays from the Periodical "Das Goetheanum," 1921-1925
CW 37   *[Now in CWs 251 and 260a]*

Publications from the Literary Estate

GA 38   Letters, Vol. 1: 1881-1890
GA 39   Letters, Vol. 2: 1890-1925
CW 40   Truth-Wrought Words
GA 40a   Sayings, Poems and Mantras; Supplementary Volume
CW 42   *[Now in CWs 264-266]*
GA 43   Stage Adaptations
GA 44   On the Four Mystery Dramas. Sketches, Fragments and Paralipomena on the Four Mystery Dramas
CW 45   Anthroposophy: A Fragment from the Year 1910

Lectures

Public Lectures

GA 83 Western and Eastern World-Contrast. Paths to Understanding It through Anthroposophy

GA 84 What Did the Goetheanum Intend and What Should Anthroposophy Do?

Lectures to the Members of the Anthroposophical Society

CW 88 Concerning the Astral World and Devachan

GA 89 Consciousness–Life–Form. Fundamental Principles of a Spiritual-Scientific Cosmology

GA 90 Participant Notes from the Lectures during the Years 1903-1905

GA 91 Participant Notes from the Lectures during the Years 1903-1905

GA 92 The Occult Truths of Ancient Myths and Sagas

CW 93 The Temple Legend and the Golden Legend

GA 93a Fundamentals of Esotericism

CW 94 Cosmogony. Popular Occultism. The Gospel of John. The Theosophy in the Gospel of John

CW 95 At the Gates of Theosophy

GA 96 Origin-Impulses of Spiritual Science. Christian Esotericism in the Light of New Spirit-Knowledge

CW 97 The Christian Mystery

GA 98 Nature Beings and Spirit Beings – Their Effects in Our Visible World

CW 99 The Theosophy of the Rosicrucians

CW 100 Human Development and Christ-Knowledge

CW 101 Myths and Legends. Occult Signs and Symbols

CW 102 The Working into Human Beings by Spiritual Beings

CW 103 The Gospel of John

CW 104 The Apocalypse of John

CW 104a From the Picture-Script of the Apocalypse of John

CW 105 Universe, Earth, the Human Being: Their Being and Development, as Well as Their Reflection in the Connection between Egyptian Mythology and Modern Culture

CW 106 Egyptian Myths and Mysteries in Relation to the Active Spiritual Forces of the Present

CW 107 Spiritual-Scientific Knowledge of the Human Being

GA 108 Answering the Questions of Life and the World through Anthroposophy

CW 109 The Principle of Spiritual Economy in Connection with the Question of Reincarnation. An Aspect of the Spiritual Guidance of Humanity

CW 110 The Spiritual Hierarchies and Their Reflection in the Physical World. Zodiac, Planets and Cosmos

CW 111 [Contained in CW 109]

Lectures and Courses on Specific Realms of Life

Lectures on Art

GA 271   Art and Knowledge of Art. Foundations of a New Aesthetic

CW 272   Spiritual-Scientific Commentary on Goethe's "Faust" in Two Volumes. Vol. 1: Faust, the Striving Human Being

CW 273   Spiritual-Scientific Commentary on Goethe's "Faust" in Two Volumes. Vol. 2: The Faust-Problem

GA 274   Addresses for the Christmas Plays from the Old Folk Traditions

CW 275   Art in the Light of Mystery Wisdom

CW 276   The Artistic in Its Mission in the World. The Genius of Language. The World of Self-Revealing Radiant Appearances – Anthroposophy and Art. Anthroposophy and Poetry

CW 277   Eurythmy. The Revelation of the Speaking Soul

CW 277a   The Origin and Development of Eurythmy

GA 278   Eurythmy as Visible Song

GA 279   Eurythmy as Visible Speech

CW 280   The Method and Nature of Speech Formation

GA 281   The Art of Recitation and Declamation

CW 282   Speech Formation and Dramatic Art

CW 283   The Nature of Things Musical and the Experience of Tone in the Human Being

CW 284/285   Images of Occult Seals and Pillars. The Munich Congress of Whitsun 1907 and Its Consequences

GA 286   Paths to a New Style of Architecture. "And the Building Becomes Human"

CW 287   The Building at Dornach as a Symbol of Historical Becoming and an Artistic Transformation Impulse

CW 288   Style Forms in the Living Organic

CW 289   The Building Idea of the Goetheanum: Lectures with Slides from the Years 1920-1921

CW 290   The Building Idea of the Goetheanum: Lectures with Slides from the Years 1920-1921

CW 291   The Nature of Colors

GA 291a   Knowledge of Colors. Supplementary Volume to "The Nature of Colors"

CW 292   Art History as Image of Inner Spiritual Impulses

Lectures on Education

CW 293 General Knowledge of the Human Being as the Foundation of Pedagogy

CW 294 The Art of Education, Methodology and Didactics

CW 295 The Art of Education: Seminar Discussions and Lectures on Lesson Planning

CW 296 The Question of Education as a Social Question

CW 297 The Idea and Practice of the Waldorf School

GA 297a Education for Life: Self-Education and the Practice of Pedagogy

CW 298 Rudolf Steiner in the Waldorf School

CW 299 Spiritual-Scientific Observations on Speech

CW 300a Conferences with the Teachers of the Free Waldorf School in Stuttgart, 1919 to 1924, in 3 Volumes, Vol. 1

CW 300b Conferences with the Teachers of the Free Waldorf School in Stuttgart, 1919 to 1924, in 3 Volumes, Vol. 2

GA 300c Conferences with the Teachers of the Free Waldorf School in Stuttgart, 1919 to 1924, in 3 Volumes, Vol. 3

CW 301 The Renewal of Pedagogical-Didactical Art through Spiritual Science

CW 302 Knowledge of the Human Being and the Forming of Class Lessons

CW 302a Education and Teaching from a Knowledge of the Human Being

CW 303 The Healthy Development of the Human Being

CW 304 Methods of Education and Teaching Based on Anthroposophy

CW 304a Anthroposophical Knowledge of the Human Being and Pedagogy

CW 305 The Soul-Spiritual Foundational Forces of the Art of Education. Spiritual Values in Education and Social Life

CW 306 Pedagogical Praxis from the Viewpoint of a Spiritual-Scientific Knowledge of the Human Being. The Education of the Child and Young Human Beings

CW 307 The Spiritual Life of the Present and Education

CW 308 The Method of Teaching and the Life Requirements for Teaching

CW 309 Anthroposophical Pedagogy and Its Prerequisites

CW 310 The Pedagogical Value of a Knowledge of the Human Being and the Cultural Value of Pedagogy

CW 311 The Art of Education from an Understanding of the Being of Humanity. Lectures on Medicine

CW 312 Spiritual Science and Medicine

CW 313 Spiritual-Scientific Viewpoints on Therapy

CW 314 Physiology and Therapy Based on Spiritual Science

CW 315 Curative Eurythmy

CW 316 Meditative Observations and Instructions for a Deepening of the Art of Healing

CW 317 The Curative Education Course

CW 318 The Working Together of Doctors and Pastors

CW 319 Anthroposophical Knowledge of the Human Being and Medicine

Lectures on Natural Science

CW 320 Spiritual-Scientific Impulses for the Development of Physics 1:
The First Natural-Scientific Course: Light, Color, Tone, Mass, Electricity,
Magnetism

GA 321 Spiritual-Scientific Impulses for the Development of Physics 2:
The Second Natural-Scientific Course: Warmth at the Border of Positive
and Negative Materiality

CW 322 The Borders of the Knowledge of Nature

GA 323 The Relationship of the Various Natural-Scientific Fields to Astronomy

CW 324 Nature Observation, Mathematics, and Scientific Experimentation and
Results from the Viewpoint of Anthroposophy

CW 324a The Fourth Dimension in Mathematics and Reality

GA 325 Natural Science and the World-Historical Development of Humanity
Since Ancient Times

CW 326 The Moment of the Coming Into Being of Natural Science in World
History and Its Development Since Then

CW 327 Spiritual-Scientific Foundations for Success in Farming. The Agricultural
Course

Lectures on Social Life and the Threefold Arrangement of the Social Organism

GA 328 The Social Question

GA 329 The Liberation of the Human Being as the Foundation for a New Social
Form

GA 330 The Renewal of the Social Organism

GA 331 Work Council and Socialization

GA 332 The Alliance for Threefolding and the Total Reform of Society.
The Council on Culture and the Liberation of the Spiritual Life

CW 332a The Social Future

CW 333 Freedom of Thought and Social Forces

CW 334 From the Unified State to the Threefold Social Organism

GA 335 The Crisis of the Present and the Path to Healthy Thinking

GA 336 The Great Questions of the Times and Anthroposophical Spiritual
Knowledge

GA 337a Social Ideas, Social Reality, Social Practice, Vol. 1: Question-and-Answer
Evenings and Study Evenings of the Alliance for the Threefold Social
Organism in Stuttgart, 1919-1920

GA 337b Social Ideas, Social Realities, Social Practice, Vol. 2: Discussion Evenings
of the Swiss Alliance for the Threefold Social Organism

CW 338 How Does One Work on Behalf of the Impulse for the Threefold Social
Organism?

GA 339 Anthroposophy, Threefold Social Organism, and the Art of Public
Speaking

CW 340 The National Economics Course. The Tasks of a New Science of Economics, Volume 1

CW 341 The National Economics Seminar. The Tasks of a New Science of Economics, Volume 2

Lectures and Courses on Christian Religious Work

CW 342 Lectures and Courses on Christian Religious Work, Vol. 1: Anthroposophical Foundations for a Renewed Christian Religious Working

GA 343 Lectures and Courses on Christian Religious Work, Vol. 2: Spiritual Knowledge – Religious Feeling – Cultic Doing

GA 344 Lectures and Courses on Christian Religious Work, Vol. 3: Lectures at the Founding of the Christian Community

GA 345 Lectures and Courses on Christian Religious Work, Vol. 4: Concerning the Nature of the Working Word

CW 346 Lectures and Courses on Christian Religious Work, Vol. 5: The Apocalypse and the Work of the Priest. Lectures for Workers at the Goetheanum

GA 347 The Knowledge of the Nature of the Human Being According to Body, Soul and Spirit. On Earlier Conditions of the Earth

CW 348 On Health and Illness. Foundations of a Spiritual-Scientific Doctrine of the Senses

CW 349 On the Life of the Human Being and of the Earth. On the Nature of Christianity

CW 350 Rhythms in the Cosmos and in the Human Being. How Does One Come to See the Spiritual World?

CW 351 The Human Being and the World. The Influence of the Spirit in Nature. On the Nature of Bees

CW 352 Nature and the Human Being Observed Spiritual-Scientifically

CW 353 The History of Humanity and the World Views of the Folk Cultures

CW 354 The Creation of the World and the Human Being. Life on Earth and the Influence of the Stars

References and Resources

Literature Cited

Archives

Archiv BFWS	Archiv im Bund der Freien Waldorfschulen Stuttgart, Wagenburgstrasse 6
Archiv CB	Privatarchiv Christiane Brosamer
Archiv FdE	Archiv der Freunde der Erziehungskunst in Berlin, Weinmeisterstr. 16
Archiv LS	Archiv im Lehrerseminar Stuttgart, Haussmannstrasse 44
Archiv NG	Privatarchiv Nana Göbel
Archiv RSHL	Archiv im Rudolf Steiner House, London, Park Road
BArch	Bundesarchiv

Journals and Magazines

A	Anthroposophie. Wochenschrift für freies Geistesleben
AM	Anthroposophical Movement. Weekly News for English-speaking Members of the Anthroposophical Society
Aww	Anthroposophie weltweit. Beilage zum Nachrichtenblatt "Was in der Anthroposophischen Gesellschaft vorgeht"
BhB	Berichtsheft des Bundes der Freien Waldorfschulen
Biedronka	Anthroposophische Aktivitäten und Initiativen in Polen. Mitteilungsblatt für Freunde, Förderer und Mitgestalter
CaM	Child and Man
DD	Die Drei
EJES	European Journal of Educational Studies
EK	Zeitschrift Erziehungskunst, hrsg. vom Bund der Freien Waldorfschulen
FoKi	Forschungsstelle Kulturimpuls, Dornach
G	Das Goetheanum. Wochenschrift für Anthroposophie
Gateways	Newsletter of the Waldorf Early Childhood Association of North America
LR	Lehrerrundbrief, hrsg. vom Bund der Freien Waldorfschulen
MaD	Mitteilungen aus der anthroposophischen Arbeit in Deutschland
MPK	Medizinisch-Pädagogische Konferenz
Msch	Die Menschenschule, Allgemeine Monatsschrift für Erziehung und Lehrerbildung im Sinne Rudolf Steiners
MVfS	Mitteilungsblatt für die Mitglieder des Vereins für ein freies Schulwesen
N	Was in der Anthroposophischen Gesellschaft vorgeht. Nachrichten für deren Mitglieder
på väg	Tidskrift för waldorfpedagogik
RoSE	Research on Steiner Education
VOK	Vrije Opvoedkunst
ZPRSt	Zur Pädagogik Rudolf Steiners (ab 1932 fortgeführt als Zeitschrift Erziehungskunst)

Photographs Credits

Archiv Helga Beeck
Archiv Rembert Biemond
Archiv Christiane Brosamer
Archiv Margret Constantini
Archiv Nana Göbel
Archiv Stefan Grosse
Archiv Christine Murphy
Archiv Shirley Noakes
Archiv Jeremy Smith
Archiv Ruth Stiglechner
Archiv Robert Thomas
Archiv Christof Wiechert
Archiv der Rudolf Steiner Schule Berlin
Archiv des Regionalis Gymnazium, Budapest
Archiv der Vrije School in Den Haag (Lot Hoghiemstra)
Archiv der Waldorfschule Dresden
Archiv des Research Institute for Waldorf Education, Hudson, NY
Archiv in der Freien Hochschule Stuttgart (inkl. Sammlung von Dietrich Esterl)
Archiv der Rudolf Steiner Schule Zürich
Archiv der Forschungsstelle Kulturimpuls, Dornach

E. Brenda Biermann-Binnie, Agnes Linde, Anna Cerri
Erinnerungen an Rudolf Steiner und die Fortbildungsschule am Goetheanum (1921–1928).
Elisabeth Gergely, Tobias Richter (eds.): Wiener Dialoge. 2011
Maria Göllner in Budapest
Judson D. Hale: The Education of a Yankee. 2014
Eugen Kolisko (ed.): Bilder von der Freien Waldorfschule. 1926
Helga Lauten (ed.): Waldorfpädagogik in Essen. 2008
Joy Mansfield: A Good School. 2014
Anne-Mette Stabel: Steinerskolens Historie i Norge 1926–2016. 2016
Schwarzwälder-Bote vom 9.8.2013
Verlag am Goetheanum
Wikipedia

Interviews

All interviews were carried out in the course of my visits to schools and conferences. Names of persons interviewed and dates of the interviews are given in the notes.

Bibliography

Altehage, Günter. *Religion, Weltanschauung, Waldorfschule*, edition Waldorf. Stuttgart 2007.
Altemüller, Frithjof. *Erinnerungen an meinen Vater Otto Altemüller. Skizze eines Waldorflebens.* Elmshorn 2013.

Barnes, Henry. *Into Heart's Land. A Century of Rudolf Steiner's Work in North America.* Great Barrington 2005.
Barnes, John Michael (ed.). *Henry Barnes – A Constellation of Human Destinies.* Hillsdale 2008.
Beltle, Erika and Kurt Vierl (eds.). *Erinnerungen an Rudolf Steiner.* Gesammelte Beiträge aus den "Mitteilungen aus der anthroposophischen Arbeit in Deutschland" 1947– 1978. Stuttgart 1979.
Berger, Manfred. *Frauen in der Geschichte des Kindergartens: Ein Handbuch.* 1995.
Bessert, Gertraud. *Ein Quell wird zum Strom.* Anthroposophisches Leben und heilpädagogische Impulse aus der Breslauer Zeit 1924–1948. Laufenburg-Ost o.J.
Biermann-Binnie, E. Brenda with Agnes Linde and Anna Cerri. *Erinnerungen an Rudolf Steiner und die Fortbildungsschule am Goetheanum (1921–1928).* Basel 1982.

Deimann, Götz (ed.). *Die anthroposophischen Zeitschriften von 1903 bis 1985.* Bibliographie und Lebensbilder. Stuttgart 1987.

Edmunds, Francis. *Rudolf Steiner Education – The Waldorf Impulse.* London 1962.
Ege, Karl. *An Evident Need of Our Times. Goals of Education at the Close of the Century.* Hillsdale 1979.
Esterl, Dietrich. *Emil Molt 1876–1936. Tun, was gefordert ist.* Stuttgart 2012.
_____. *Die erste Waldorfschule Stuttgart-Uhlandshöhe 1919–2004.* Daten - Dokumente - Bilder. Stuttgart 2006.
Eymann, Friedrich. *Kulturerneuerung und Erziehung.* Bern 1946.

Fried, Anne. *Farben des Lebens. Erinnerungen.* Leipzig 1991.

Gabert, Erich. *Lehrerbildung im Sinne der Pädagogik Rudolf Steiners.* Stuttgart 1961.
Gerbert, Hildegard. "Heb auf, was Gott Dir vor die Türe legt." *Erinnerungen.* Arlesheim 1973.
Gergely, Elisabeth and Tobias Richter (eds.). *Wiener Dialoge. Der österreichische Weg der Waldorfpädagogik.* Wien 2011.
Göbel, Nana and Silke Heuser (ed.). *Waldorfpädagogik weltweit.* Edited by Freunde der Erziehungskunst Rudolf Steiners eV. Berlin 2001.
Götte, Wenzel M. *Erfahrungen mit Schulautonomie.* Das Beispiel der Freien Waldorfschulen. Stuttgart 2006.
Grosse, Rudolf. *Erlebte Pädagogik. Schicksal und Geistesweg.* Dornach 4th Edition, 1998.

Hahn, Herbert. *Begegnungen mit Rudolf Steiner. Eindrücke – Rat – Lebenshilfen*. Stuttgart 1991.

_____. *Der Weg, der mich führte. Lebenserinnerungen*. Stuttgart 1969.

Haid, Christiane. *Auf der Suche nach dem Menschen. Die anthroposophische Jugend- und Studentenarbeit in den Jahren 1920–1931*. Dornach 2001.

Hardorp, Detlef. *70 Jahre Waldorfpädagogik in Berlin. 1928–1998*. Berlin 1998.

Heydebrand, Caroline von (ed.). *Rudolf Steiner in der Waldorfschule*. Stuttgart 1927.

Hiebel, Friedrich. *Entscheidungszeit mit Rudolf Steiner. Erlebnis und Begegnung*. Dornach 1986.

Husemann, Armin J. *Der Musikalische Bau des Menschen. Entwurf einer Plastischen Menschenkunde*. Stuttgart 3. Aufl. 1993.

Husemann, Gisbert and Johannes Tautz (eds.). *Der Lehrerkreis um Rudolf Steiner in der ersten Waldorfschule 1919–1925*. Stuttgart 1979.

Jünemann, Margrit. *Der Winter weicht. Caroline von Heydebrand. Pionierin der Waldorfpädagogik*. Stuttgart 2003.

Klein, Elisabeth. *Begegnungen. Mitteilenswertes aus meinem Leben*. Freiburg 1978.

Kolisko, Eugen. *Auf der Suche nach neuen Wahrheiten. Goetheanistische Studien*. Dornach 1989.

_____. *Vom Therapeutischen Charakter der Waldorfschule*. 2002.

Kolisko, Eugen (ed.). *Bilder von der Freien Waldorfschule mit Berücksichtigung der sämtlichen Schwesteranstalten*. Stuttgart 1926.

Krück von Poturzyn, M.J. (ed.). *Wir erlebten Rudolf Steiner*. Stuttgart 1980.

Langen, Gerda. *Kindheit und Jugend im Umkreis Rudolf Steiners. Erinnerungen einer Waldorfpädagogin*. Dornach 1996.

Lauten, Helga (ed.). *Waldorfpädagogik in Essen. Die erste Essener Waldorfschule 1922–1936*. Eine Dokumentation. Essen 2008.

Lehrerkollegium der Rudolf Steiner Schule Zürich (ed.). *Zur Menschenbildung*. Aus der Arbeit der Rudolf Steiner Schule Zürich 1927–1977. Basel 1977.

Leinhas, Emil. *Aus der Arbeit mit Rudolf Steiner*. Basel 1950.

Leist, Manfred. *Entwicklungen einer Schulgemeinschaft. Die Waldorfschulen in Deutschland*. Stuttgart 1998.

Leroi, May Vera and Willem Frederik Veltman. *Alexandre Leroi. Ein Menschenschicksal im Umbruch der Zeiten*. Hemrik (NL) 1998.

Lindenberg, Christoph. *Rudolf Steiner. Eine Biographie* (2 Bände). Stuttgart 1997.

_____. *Rudolf Steiner. Eine Chronik 1861–1925*. Stuttgart 1988.

Maikowski, René. *Schicksalswege auf der Suche nach dem lebendigen Geist*. Freiburg 1980.

Mansfield, Joy. *A Good School. A History of Michael Hall. A Steiner Waldorf School*. With additions and editing by Brien Masters and Stephen Sheen. Bexley 2014.

Marstrander, Erik (ed.). *Menneske Først! Steinerpedagogikk i Oslo 1926–1996*. Oslo 1996.

Molt, Emil. *Entwurf meiner Lebensbeschreibung*. Stuttgart 1972.

Müller, Heinz. *Spuren auf dem Weg – Erinnerungen*. Stuttgart, 4. Aufl. 1983.

Murphy, Sophia Christine. *The Multifaceted Life of Emil Molt. Entrepreneur, Political Visionary and Seeker for the Spirit*. Chatham, NY 2012.

Nagy, Maria von. *Dialog der Hemisphären. Eine kulturbiographische Skizze. 1212–1952.* Heidenheim 1963.

_____. *Rudolf Steiner über seine letzte Ansprache, über Ungarn und über die Schweiz,* Memoiren I. Brugg 1974.

Oberman, Ida. "Waldorf History: Case Study of Institutional Memory." Paper presented at the Annual Meeting of the American Education Research Association, Chicago, 24. - 28. 3. 1997. ED 409 108, http://files.eric.ed.gov/fulltext/ED409108.pdf.

Osterrieder, Markus. *Welt im Umbruch: Nationalitätenfrage, Ordnungspläne und Rudolf Steiners Haltung im Ersten Weltkrieg.* Stuttgart 2014.

Paull, John. "Rudolf Steiner and the Oxford Conference, The Birth of Waldorf Education in Britain," *European Journal of Educational Studies* 3 (1), 2011.

Plato, Bodo von (ed.). *Anthroposophie im 20. Jahrhundert. Ein Kulturimpuls.* Dornach 2003.

Priestman, Karen. *Illusion of Coexistence: The Waldorf Schools in the Third Reich, 1933–1941.* 2009. http://scholars.wlu.ca/etd/1080.

Ravagli, Lorenzo. *Unter Hammer und Hakenkreuz: Der völkisch-nationalsozialistische Kampf gegen die Anthroposophie.* Stuttgart 2004.

Röhrs, Hermann and Volker Lenhart (eds.). *Die Reformpädagogik auf den Kontinenten. Ein Handbuch,* 19th edition. Heidelberger Studien zur Erziehungswissenschaft Bd. 43. Frankfurt am Main 1994.

Rutz, Hans. *Bilder und Gestalten aus einer unteren Klasse der Freien Waldorfschule.* Stuttgart 1928.

Sagarin, Stephen Keith. *The Story of Waldorf Education in the United States.* Great Barrington, MA 2011.

Sam, Martina Maria. *Eurythmie. Entstehungsgeschichte und Porträts ihrer Pioniere.* Dornach 2014.

Saurer, Rudolf. *Schule, Kirche und Staat.* Bern 1945.

Schenk, Douwe and Lot Hooghiemstra. *De Vrije School Den Haag in de 20e eeuw.* no date.

Schmelzer, Albert. *Die Dreigliederungsbewegung 1919.* Stuttgart 1991.

Schöffler, Heinz Herbert. *Das Wirken Rudolf Steiners 1917–1925.* Dornach 1987.

Schwebsch, Erich. *Der Lehrerkurs Dr. Rudolf Steiners im Goetheanum 1921.* Stuttgart 1922.

Sheen, A. Renwick. *Geometry and the Imagination. The Imaginative Treatment of Geometry in Waldorf Education.* Fair Oaks, CA 2002.

Skiera, Ehrenhard. *Reformpädagogik in Geschichte und Gegenwart. Eine kritische Einführung.* München 2003.

_____. Reformpädagogik und Schule in Europe. In *Handbuch der reformpädagogischen und alternativen Schulen in Europa,* Theodor F. Klassen, Ehrenhard Skiera, and Bernd Wächter (eds.). Baltmannsweiler 1990.

Stabel, Anne-Mette. *Hva skal vi med skole? Steinerskolens Historie i Norge 1926–2016.* Oslo 2016.

Staudenmaier, Peter. *Between Occultism and Nazism: Anthroposophy and the Politics of Race in the Fascist Era.* Leiden 2014.

Steiner, Rudolf. *Balance in Teaching.* CW 302a.

_____. *Conferences with the Teachers of the Free Waldorf School in Stuttgart, 1919 to 1924,* Vol. 1. CW 300a.

_____. *Conferences with the Teachers of the Free Waldorf School in Stuttgart, 1919 to 1924*, Vol. 2. CW 300b.

_____. *Conferences with the Teachers of the Free Waldorf School in Stuttgart, 1919 to 1924*, Vol. 3. CW 300c.

_____. *Discussions with Teachers*. CW 295.

_____. *Education for Life: Self-Education and the Practice of Pedagogy*. GA 297a, Dornach 1998.

_____. *The Foundations of Human Experience*. CW 293.

_____. *The Kingdom of Childhood*. CW 311.

_____. *A Modern Art of Education*. CW 307.

_____. *The New Spirituality and the Christ-Experience of the 20th Century*. CW 200.

_____. *Practical Advice to Teachers*. CW 294.

_____. *Rudolf Steiner in the Waldorf School. Lectures and Addresses to Children, Parents and Teachers 1919–1924*. CW 298.

_____. *Soul Economy*. CW 303.

_____. *Soziale Ideen, Soziale Wirklichkeit, Soziale Praxis* [Social Ideas, Social Reality, Social Practice]. GA 337b.

_____. *Waldorf Education and Anthroposophy*. CW 304.

Strakosch, Alexander. *Lebenswege mit Rudolf Steiner. Erinnerungen*. Dornach 1994.

Tautz, Johannes. *Die Freie Waldorfschule. Ursprung und Zielsetzungen*. Stuttgart 1972.

_____. *W. J. Stein. Eine Biographie*. Dornach 1989.

Tedesco, Juan Carlos (ed.). *Thinkers on Education*. Vols. 1–4, UNESCO, Paris 1997.

Treichler d.Ä., Rudolf. *Wege und Umwege zu Rudolf Steiner*. Printed manuscript 1974.

Vámosi Nagy, Istvan. *A kissvábhegyi Waldorf-iskola 1926–1933*. Printed manuscript 1989.

Visser, Rinke. *Zwaarte van stofgoud en licht in diamant. Een biografie van Arnold Cornelis Henny en Paula Henny-van Suchtelen*. Rotterdam 2014.

Wember, Valentin. *Die fünf Dimensionen der Waldorfpädagogik im Werk Rudolf Steiners. Übersichten. Kommentare. Geschichte. Perspektiven*. Tübingen 2016.

Wennerschou, Lasse. *Vom Werden der Heileurythmie. Aus den Lebensläufen von Ilse Rolofs und Trude Thetter*. Undated.

Werner, Uwe. *Anthroposophen in der Zeit des Nationalsozialismus (1933–1945)*. München 1999.

Widmer, Max. *Friedrich Eymann 1887–1954*. Liebefeld 1992.

Zdražil. Tomas. *Gesundheitsförderung und Waldorfpädagogik*. 2000.

Zeylmans, Emanuel. *Willem Zeylmans van Emmichoven. Ein Pionier der Anthroposophie*. Arlesheim 1979.

Zimmermann, Heinz and Robert Thomas. *Die Rudolf Steinerschulen in der Schweiz. Eine Dokumentation*. Zürich 2007

Zuccoli, Elena. *Eine Autobiographie*. Edited and expanded by Ingrid Braunschmidt. Dornach 1999.

Additional Resources

Adick, Christel (ed.). *Bildungsentwicklungen und Schulsysteme in Afrika, Asien, Lateinamerika und der Karibik*. Münster 2013.

Angress, Judith. *Einblick in die Waldorfschule. Erfahrungen einer Israelischen Pädagogin*. Stuttgart 1994.

Anweiler, Oskar with Hans-Jürgen Fuchs, Martina Dorner and Eberhard Petermann (eds.). *Bildungspolitik in Deutschland 1945–1990*. Ein historisch-vergleichender Quellenband. Opladen 1992.

Anweiler, Oskar with Ursula Boos-Nünning, Günter Brinkmann, Friedrich Kuebart and Hans-Peter Schäfer. *Bildungssysteme in Europa*, Weinheim 1996.

Bana, Aban. *Anthroposophische Initiativen in Indien*. Private Vervielfältigung. Dornach 1995.

Baravalle, Hermann von. *The International Waldorf School Movement*. Spring Valley, NY 1976.

Baumann, Ansbert (ed.). *Die Protokolle der Regierung des Volksstaates Württemberg*. Erster Band: Die provisorische Regierung und das Kabinett Blos, November 1918–Juni 1920. Kabinettsprotokolle von Baden und Württemberg 1918–1933, Stuttgart 2013.

Beresford-Hill, Paul (ed.). "Education and Privatisation in Eastern Europe and the Baltic Republics." *Oxford Studies in Comparative Education* Vol. 7 (2), UK 1998.

Blom, Philipp. *Die zerrissenen Jahre 1918–1938*. München 2014.

Borchert, Manfred and Robert Bell (eds.). *Atlas zum Menschenrecht auf Bildung und zur Freiheit der Erziehung (Schulfreiheit) in Europa*. Witten 2003.

Brachmann, Jens. *Reformpädagogik zwischen Re-Education, Bildungsexpansion und Missbrauchsskandal. Die Geschichte der Vereinigung Deutscher Landerziehungsheime 1947–2012*. Bad Heilbrunn 2015.

Brodbeck, Heinz. *Rudolf Steiner Schule im Elterntest. Lob – Kritik – Zukunftsideen. Ergebnisse einer empirischen Elternstudie an schweizerischen und liechtensteinischen Waldorfschulen*. Aesch 2018.

Bruijn, Michiel A. de. *Spiegelend Perspectief. De Vrije School Den Haag 70 jaar. Levenservaringen en reacties van oud-lerlingen op hun vroegere school*. Den Haag 1993.

Bühler, Ernst. *Mosaik des Lebens – Erinnerungen eines Lehrers*. Stuttgart 1996.

Bungenstab, Karl Ernst. *Umerziehung zur Demokratie? Re-education Politik im Bildungswesen der US Zone 1945–1949*. Düsseldorf 1970.

Carlgren, Frans. *Den antroposofiska rörelsen*. Verksamheter, bakgrunder, framtidsperspektiv. Täby 1985.

Carlgren, Frans (ed.). *Erziehung zur Freiheit. Die Pädagogik Rudolf Steiners*. Bilder und Berichte aus der internationalen Waldorfschulbewegung, 6th edition. Stuttgart 1990.

Carnie, Fiona with Martin Lange and Mary Tasker (eds.). *Freeing Education. Steps Towards Real Choice and Diversity in Schools*. Stroud 1996.

Cherry, Thanh and Benjamin. *Of Pandas and Wandering Geese*. London 1999.

Chistolini, Sandra. *Nella Libertà Educare alla Libertà*. Documenti dalla manifestazione internazionale di Bologna 17 gennaio–3 febbraio 2000. Lecce 2001.

Dahlin, Bo. "The Waldorf School – Cultivating Humanity?" A report from an evaluation of Waldorf schools in Sweden. Karlstad University Studies 2007:29. Karlstad 2007.

Dahlin, Bo with E. Langmann and C. Andersson. Waldorfskolor och medborgerligt-moralisk kompetens. En jämförelse mellan waldorfelever och elever i den kommunala skolan. Karlstad 2004, in: www.waldorfanswers.org/Dahlin3-October2004.pdf [25th November 2012].

Dam, Imke Jelle van. *100 jaar euritmie in Nederland.* 2013.

Detjen, Joachim. *Politische Bildung: Geschichte und Gegenwart in Deutschland.* München 2007.

Döbert, Hans with Wolfgang Hörner, Botho von Kopp and Lutz R. Reuter. *Die Bildungssysteme Europas.* Baltmannsweiler 42017

Edusei, Kofi. *Für uns ist Religion die Erde, auf der wir leben. Ein Afrikaner erzählt von der Kultur der Akan*, 2nd edition. Stuttgart 1995.

Egorova, Ekaterina. *Das Bildungswesen in Russland unter dem Gesichtspunkt der Individualisierung.* Hildesheim 2016.

El Puente. 70° aniversario Colegio Rudolf Steiner 1940–2010. Buenos Aires 2010.

Fedjuschin, Victor B. *Russlands Sehnsucht nach Spiritualität. Theosophie, Anthroposophie und die Russen.* Schaffhausen 1988.

Freie Pädagogische Vereinigung Bern (eds.). *Waldorfpädagogik in öffentlichen Schulen.* Versuche und Erfahrungen mit der Pädagogik Rudolf Steiners. Freiburg 1976.

Frielingsdorf, Volker with Rüdiger Grimm and Brigitte Kaldenberg. *Geschichte der anthroposophischen Heilpädagogik und Sozialtherapie.* Entwicklungslinien und Aufgabenfelder 1920–1980. Dornach 2013.

Fucke, Erhard. *Siebzehn Begegnungen.* Stuttgart 1996.

Führ, Christoph. *Deutsches Bildungswesen seit 1945. Grundzüge und Probleme.* Bonn 1996.

Gädeke, Rudolf F. *Die Gründer der Christengemeinschaft. Ein Schicksalsnetz.* Dornach 1992.

Gedenken an die Rudolf Steinerschule Dresden. Gerlingen 1980.

Gevers, Emile and Ernst Lehrs. *Een verreikende sociale daad. De opening van de Vrije School in Antwerpen op 11 September 1954.* Antwerpen 2018.

Giloy, Birgit (ed.). *Bildung und Wissenschaft in Litauen.* Ministerium für Bildung und Wissenschaft. Vilnius 1998.

Granly, Oddvar and Oskar Borgman Hansen (eds.). *Antroposofien i Norden – Fem landen i samarbejde.* Oslo 2008.

Green, Doug. *Rudolf Steiner School Hastings. 50th Anniversary 1950–2000.* Hastings 2000.

Gronemeyer, Marianne. *Lernen mit beschränkter Haftung. Über das Scheitern der Schule.* Berlin 1996.

Grunelius, Elisabeth M. *Erziehung im frühen Kindesalter. Der Waldorfschul-Kindergarten.* Freiburg 1964.

Hahn, Herbert. *Kursus über Religionsunterricht.* Manuskriptdruck, Stuttgart 1948.

Hansen-Schaberg, Inge (ed.). *Waldorfpädagogik.* Reformpädagogische Schulkonzepte Band 6, Baltmannsweiler 2012.

Haris, Susan. *Stumbling Blocks into Stepping Stones. A Memoir.* Castle Hill 2007.

Herrlitz, Hans-Georg with Dieter Weiland and Klaus Winkel (eds.). *Die Gesamtschule. Geschichte, internationale Vergleiche, pädagogische Konzepte und politische Perspektiven.* Weinheim/München 2003.

Herskovits, Béla and Annie S. Miley Clarke. *Mr. Béla. A Jewish Musician's Odyssey through the 20th Century and Four Continents.* Sydney 2010.

Heuser, Annie. *Betrachtungen eines Erziehers.* Dornach 1958.

Höfer, Nikolai. "Waldorfschulen in Russland." Studienarbeit 2001 (private publication).

Hofmann, Ulrike with Christine von Prümmer, Dieter Weidner and Bernhard Vier. *Forschungsbericht über Bildungslebensläufe ehemaliger Waldorfschüler.* Eine Untersuchung der Geburtsjahrgänge 1946 und 1947. Stuttgart 1981.

Howard, Susan. "The First Waldorf Kindergarten: The Beginnings of Our Waldorf Early Childhood Movement." *Gateways*, 49, 2005.

Hurner, Eric. *Janine Hürner. Ein Geist in fremdem Lande.* o.O. 2015.

_____. *Kultureller Rassismus, Anthroposophie und die Integration der südafrikanischen Waldorfschulen.* Tetenhusen 2016.

Jach, Frank-Rüdiger. *Schulverfassung und Bürgergesellschaft in Europa.* Berlin 1999.

Kallaway, Peter (ed.). *The History of Education under Apartheid 1948–1994.* New York 2002.

Kerr, Ruth. *Waters of Double Reflections: The Story of Michael Park School.* Auckland 2006.

Keyserlingk, Adalbert Graf von. *Koberwitz 1924. Geburtsstunde einer neuen Landwirtschaft.* Stuttgart 1974.

Klassen, Theodor F. with Ehrenhard Skiera and Bernd Wächter (eds.). *Handbuch der reformpädagogischen und alternativen Schulen in Europa.* Baltmannsweiler 1990.

Klein, Agnes. "Waldorfpädagogik in Ungarn," in: *Mensch – Raum – Mathematik. Historische, reformpädagogische und empirische Zugänge zur Mathematik und ihrer Didaktik.* Festschrift für Michael Toepell, editors von Simone Reinhold and Katrin Liebers. Münster 2017.

Kloss, Heinz. *Waldorfschule und Staatsschulwesen.* Stuttgart 1955.

Koelmans, Laura. *Freie Schule. Menschenbildung in Freiheit - Waldorfschule in den Niederlanden. Masterarbeit an der Freien Hochschule.* Stuttgart 2016.

Koester, Hans. *Indien zwischen Gandhi und Nehru.* Mannheim 1957.

Kolligs, Ludolf. Beiträge zur Geschichte der Rudolf Steiner Schule Hamburg-Wandsbek. http://www.schulewandsbek.createweb.de/. 2011.

Koslowski, Steffi. *Die New Era der New Education Fellowship.* Ihr Beitrag zur Internationalität der Reformpädagogik im 20. Jahrhundert. Bad Heilbrunn 2013.

Krause, Daniela. "Waldorfschule in Japan. Vom Ideenkonstrukt bis zur Umsetzung. Magisterarbeit an der LMU." Abschlussarbeiten am Japan-Zentrum der Ludwig-Maximilians-Universität München. Edited by Steffen Döll, Martin Lehnert, Peter Pörtner, Evelyn Schulz, Klaus Vollmer, Franz Waldenberger. Band 2. Japan-Zentrum der LMU. München 2013.

Krull, Edgar and Karmen Trasberg. *Changes in Estonian General Education from the Collapse of the Soviet Union to EU Entry.* 2006, http://files.eric.ed.gov/fulltext/ED495353.pdf.

Kugler, Walter (ed.). "Rudolf Steiner und die Gründung der Weleda. Beiträge zur Rudolf Steiner Gesamtausgabe." Veröffentlichungen aus dem Archiv der Rudolf Steiner-Nachlassverwaltung Dornach. Heft Nr. 118/119, Sommer 1997.

Lambrechts, Wilbert (ed.). *Een verreikend sociaal daad. De opening van de Vrije School Antwerpen in 1954.* Antwerpen 2018.

Leber, Stefan. *Die Pädagogik der Waldorfschule und ihre Grundlagen.* Darmstadt 1992.

_____. "Die Waldorfschulen in der Bildungslandschaft der Bundesrepublik. 1945–1989," in: *EK* 8/9, 1989.

_____. *Weltanschauung, Ideologie und Schulwesen. Ist die Waldorfschule eine Weltanschauungsschule?* Stuttgart 1989.

Leber, Stefan (ed.). *Anthroposophie und Waldorfpädagogik in den Kulturen der Welt.* Stuttgart 1997.

Lindenberg, Christoph. *Waldorfschulen: angstfrei lernen, selbstbewusst handeln. Praxis eines verkannten Schulmodells.* Hamburg 1975.

Loebell, Helmut von. *Der Stehaufmann. Berlin, Bogotá, Salzburg – im Unterwegs zu Hause.* Salzburg 2016.

Loubser, Trinity (ed.). *Michael Oak Waldorf School. The First 50 Years. 1962–2012.* Kapstadt 2012.

Lutters, Frans. *Daniel Johan van Bemmelen. Wiedergeboren am Beginn des lichten Zeitalters.* Sammatz 2012.

Mason, Peter. *Independent Education in Western Europe.* London 1992.

Masters, Brien. *con.gusto @ three score years and twenty.* Forest Row 2011.

Mattke, Hans-Joachim (ed.). *Waldorfschule weltweit – 75 Jahre Freie Waldorfschule Uhlandshöhe Stuttgart.* Stuttgart 1994.

Maydell, Renata von. "Anthroposophy in Russia," in: Glatzer Rosenthal, Bernice (ed.). *The Occult in Russian and Soviet Culture.* New York 1997.

Mazzone, Alduino Bartolo. *Islands of Culture. Waldorf (Rudolf Steiner) Schools in Australia: Their Origin and Development.* Adelaide 1995.

_____. Waldorf (Rudolf Steiner) Schools as schools in the progressive education tradition. 1999, http://www.passionateschooling.com/resources/publications_progressive.pdf.

_____. Waldorf teacher education: the implications for teacher education of Rudolf Steiner's educational philosophy and its practice in Waldorf schools. Adelaide 1999. https://digital.library.adelaide.edu.au/dspace/handle/2440/37875.

McGregor, Robin and Anne. *McGregor's Education Alternatives.* Juta 1992.

Meyer, Thomas. *D.N. Dunlop. Ein Zeit- und Lebensbild.* Basel 1996.

_____. *Ludwig Polzer-Hoditz. Ein Europäer.* Basel 1994.

Michael, Berthold and Heinz-Hermann Schepp (eds.). *Die Schule in Staat und Gesellschaft. Dokumente zur deutschen Schulgeschichte im 19. und 20. Jahrhundert.* Göttingen/Zürich 1973.

Mitchell, David. *AWSNA Timeline 1965–2010.* Wilton 2010. https://waldorfeducation. org/Customized/Uploads/ByDate/2015/August_2015/August_26th_2015/ AWSNA-8-29-10_(2)79640.pdf.

Mowday, Glennis A. *Steiner Education in Australia: Maintaining an Educational Theory Given the Necessity of Practice. Glenaeon Rudolf Steiner School. Sydney 1957–2000.* Sydney 2004.

Müller, Eberhard and Franz Josef Klehr (eds.). *Russische Religiöse Philosophie. Das wiedergewonnene Erbe: Aneignung und Distanz.* Akademie der Diözese Rottenburg-Stuttgart (Hohenheimer Protokolle Bd. 41). Stuttgart 1992.

Müller-Rolli, Sebastian and Reiner Anselm. *Evangelische Schulpolitik in Deutschland 1918–1958.* Göttingen 1999.

Müller-Wiedemann, Hans. *Karl König: eine mitteleuropäische Biographie.* Stuttgart 2016.

Nobel, Agnes. *Education through Art. The Steiner School Approach.* Edinburgh 1996.

Oelsner, Verónica and Claudia Richter (eds.). *Bildung in Lateinamerika. Strukturen, Entwicklungen, Herausforderungen. Historisch-Vergleichende Sozialisations- und Bildungsforschung Bd. 15.* Münster 2015.

Paalasmaa, Jarno. *Steinerkoulun tulo Suomeen. Vaihtoehtopedagogiikan juurtuminen osaksi suomalaista koulua.* Helsinki 2011.
Pädagogische Forschungsstelle beim Bund der Freien Waldorfschulen (ed.). *Zur religiösen Erziehung.* Stuttgart 2013.
Pohl, Hans Joachim. *Des Menschen Heilung.* Edited by Michael Schnur. Dresden 2008.

Randoll, Dirk and Heiner Barz (eds.). *Bildung und Lebensgestaltung ehemaliger Schüler von Rudolf Steiner Schulen in der Schweiz.* Eine Absolventenbefragung. Frankfurt 2007.
Rawson, Martyn and Tobias Richter (eds.). *The Educational Tasks and Content of the Steiner Waldorf Curriculum.* Forest Row 2000.
Rexheuser, Rex. *Kulturen und Gedächtnis. Studien und Reflexionen zur Geschichte des östlichen Europas.* Wiesbaden 2008.
Rinke, Stefan. *Lateinamerika.* Darmstadt 2015.
Roldán Vera Eugenia. "Das Bildungssystem Mexikos," in: Richter, Claudia and Verónica Oelsner (eds.), *Bildungsentwicklungen in Lateinamerika.* Münster 2014.
Rose, Robert. Transforming Criticisms of Anthroposophy and Waldorf Education - Evolution, Race and the Quest for Global Ethics. 2013. http://www.anthroweb.info/fileadmin/pdfs/RR_Transforming_Criticisms.pdf.
Roth, Maren. *Erziehung zur Demokratie? Amerikanische Demokratisierungshilfe im postsozialistischen Bulgarien.* Münster 2005.

Schiller, Hartwig. *Physiognomie der Lehrerbildung: Menschen, Ideen und Praxis an der Freien Hochschule Stuttgart.* Stuttgart 2008.
Schleicher, Klaus (ed.). *Zukunft der Bildung in Europa. Nationale Vielfalt und europäische Einheit.* Darmstadt 1993.
Schleicher, Klaus and Wilfried Bos (eds.). *Realisierung der Bildung in Europa. Europäisches Bewusstsein trotz kultureller Identität?* Darmstadt 1994.
Schlögel, Karl. *Der grosse Exodus. Die russische Emigration und ihre Zentren 1917 bis 1941.* München 1994.
Schmidt, Pedro. *Zwischen Ideal und Realität.* Dornach 2005.
Schoepp, Sebastian. *Das Ende der Einsamkeit. Was die Welt von Lateinamerika lernen kann.* Frankfurt/Main 2011.
Seyfarth-Stubenrauch, Michael and Ehrenhard Skiera (eds.). *Reformpädagogik und Schulreform in Europa.* Hohengehren 1996.
Shapumba, Shapumba. "Wie ist Namibia? Eine Einführung für Waldorf Lehrer/innen aus Deutschland." Diplomarbeit am Seminar für Waldorfpädagogik der Freien Hochschule Stuttgart, Stuttgart 2011.
Smit, Jörgen (ed.). *Erziehung und Meditation. Wie entsteht erzieherisches Wirken aus meditativ erübter Menschenerkenntnis?* Dornach 1983.
Spence, Michael. *The Story of Emerson College. Its Founding Impulse, Work and Form.* Forest Row 2013.

St. Clair, Linda (ed.). *Fruits of a Life's Work. Sylvia Brose and Rudolf Steiner Education.*
Brookvale 2007.

Steiner, Rudolf. Anthroposophische Pädagogik und ihre Voraussetzungen. GA 309, Dornach
1972.

_____. Gegensätze in der Menschheitsentwicklung. GA 197, Dornach 1996.

_____. Mein Lebensgang. GA 28, Dornach 2000.

Stossun, Harry. "Die Deutsche Oberrealschule bzw. das Deutsche Gymnasium in Kaunas."
Annaberger Annalen 11, 2003.

Tautz, Johannes. Lehrerbewusstsein im 20. Jahrhundert. Erlebtes und Erkanntes. Dornach
1995.

Tippett, Eileen. *Act of Faith: A History of Michael Mount Waldorf School, 1960–2010.*
Johannesburg 2010.

Toncheva, Svetoslava. *Out of the New Spirituality of the Twentieth Century. The Dawn of
Anthroposophy, the White Brotherhood and the Unified Teaching.* Berlin 2015.

Townsend, Geoffrey. *Outline of the History of the Anthroposophical Society/Movement in New
Zealand.* Manuskriptdruck 2001.

Turbott, Garth John. *Anthroposophy in the Antipodes. A Lived Spirituality in New Zealand
1902–1960s.* Manawatu 2013.

Vekerdy, Tamás. *És most belülről … Álmok és lidércek.* Budapest 2011.

Veltman, Willem Frederik. *De Vrije School. Ondergang en nieuwe geboorte?* Den Haag
undated.

Weissert, Matthias. *Wir waren dreizehn. Geschichte und Geschichten einer grossen Familie.* Köln
2012.

Woods, Donald. *Steve Biko. Der Schrei nach Freiheit.* 1988.

Yoshida, Atsuhiko. "Interface of Holistic Changes in Japanese Schools and Waldorf
Education," in: John P. Miller, et al. (eds.). *Holistic Learning and Spirituality in
Education. Breaking New Ground.* New York, 2005.

Young, John. *The School on the Flat. Collingwood College. 1882–2007.* Collingwood 2007.

Index of Persons

Morgenstierne von Munthe, Otto af 67
Mothes, Hans 228
Mousson, Heinrich 285
Mrazek, Wilhelm 294, 297
Mulder, Elisabeth (see Mulder-Seelig, Elisabeth)
Mulder-Seelig, Elisabeth 238, 240, 242
Müller, Beatrice 213
Müller, Heinz 52, 208, 209, 213, 218-220
Müller-Fürer, Hildegard 206
Müller-Fürer, Konrad 24, 203-205, 242
Mundt, Erika 224
Mursalle, Erika 349, 350, 351
Myrin, Alarik 43, 381, 382
Myrin, Mabel 43, 381, 382

Naef, Emilie 104, 105, 106
Nägelin, Friedel 242
Nagy, Emil von 272, 273, 277, 278
Nagy, István von 274, 277
Nagy, Maria von 272-275, 277, 278, 290
Nelessen, A. 233
Neuloh, Margarete 325
Neuscheller, Leopold 307, 309, 310
Neuscheller, Lucy 237, 307-309
Neuscheller, Maria 307
Neuscheller, Mechthild 307
Ney, Elli 234
Nicking, Wilhelm 55
Niederhäuser de Jaager, Isabella 89
Niederhäuser, Hans Rudolf 104-106, 288
Niemann, Elsa 335, 337
Nieuwkerken 240
Nilsson, Rut 84, 353
Noakes, Shirley 48
Noeth, Othmar von 84
Nokes, Cora 41, 366, 367
Noll, Ludwig 122, 334
Noseda, Giannina 378
Nunhöfer, Karl 152, 153

Oberstein 345
Obstner, Hildegard 277
Ochsenius, Irene 356, 357
Oehlschlegel, Friedrich 49, 50, 51, 119, 121, 122, 127, 129
Offergeld Wölcken, Else (see Wölcken, Else)
Ogilvie, Michael 361
Ohlendorf, Otto 95, 102, 326
Oldendorff, Paul 79, 300, 323, 324
Olivier, Daphne (see Harwood, Daphne)
Ott, Gerhard 131, 258, 327, 331-334
Overhage, Wilfried 104

Packhurst 309
Pahl, Annemarie 326
Pallat, Ludwig 79, 86
Papkovách, Elvira 277
Parker, Betty 377
Pater, Otto (Carl Alexander Herzog von Württemberg) 174, 175
Pechmann, Baron von 310
Peckham, Margret 307
Peissig, Rudolf 312
Pelikan, Wilhelm 239, 257
Perthel, Johannes 342
Pethick, Dorothy 377
Pethick-Lawrence, Emmeline 377
Petz 296
Pew, Mabel (see Myrin, Mabel)
Pfeiffer, Ehrenfried 95, 96, 370, 371, 381
Pfister, Robert 104
Pickert, Siegfried 80
Pippich, Josef 84
Plincke, Violetta 25, 79, 236, 368
Poch, Annemarie 295
Poch, Gretel (see Lamerdin, Gretel)
Poczniak, Bronislav von 344
Podreider, Fanny 378
Poeppig, Fred 69, 362, 363, 379
Pohl, Hans Joachim 348
Pohlmann, Emilie 29, 208, 210, 211, 219, 220
Pohlmann, Hans Mathias 29, 207-213, 219, 220
Pohl-Zirkenbach, Kyra 348
Politzer, Anny (see Fried-Politzer, Anne)
Polzer-Hoditz, Graf Ludwig 294
Pönisch, Ernst 305
Pönitz, Annemarie 220
Poppelbaum, Hermann 310
Porger, Gustav 256
Porzelt, Sophie 165, 166, 189, 369, 370, 377
Potondy, János 277
Pouderoyen, Marie 357, 358
Preuss, Albin 319
Priess, H. 213
Priess-Kändler, Ilse (see Kändler, Ilse)
Prömm, Peter 182, 183, 327
Pütz, Siegfried 147
Pyle, William Scott 308

Raab 163, 249
Rabinowitsch 58
Raether, Hans 172
Raetz, Marie 269
Raetz, Rosa 269
Ramharter, Irene 350, 351

Made in the USA
Middletown, DE
29 August 2020